Advances in
Clinical Child
Psychology

Volume 17

ADVANCES IN CLINICAL CHILD PSYCHOLOGY

A Continuation Order Plan is available for this series. A continuation order will bring delivery of each new volume immediately upon publication. Volumes are billed only upon actual shipment. For further information please contact the publisher.

Advances in

Clinical Child Psychology

Volume 17

Edited by

THOMAS H. OLLENDICK

Virginia Polytechnic Institute and State University
Blacksburg, Virginia

and

RONALD J. PRINZ

University of South Carolina
Columbia, South Carolina

1977

Plenum Press • *New York and London*

The Library of Congress cataloged the first volume of this title as follows:

Advances in clinical child psychology, v. 1–

New York, Plenum Press, ©1977–

v. ill. 24 cm.
Key title: Advances in clinical child psychology. ISSN 0149-4732

1. Clinical psychology—Collected works. 2. Child psychology—Collected works.
3. Child psychotherapy—Collected works.
RJ503.3.A37 618.9'28'9   77-643411

ISBN 0-306-44799-1

©1995 Plenum Press, New York
A Division of Plenum Publishing Corporation
233 Spring Street, New York, N.Y. 10013

Printed in the United States of America

Contributors

Jo-Ann Birt — Department of Psychology, Children's Hospital of Western Ontario, London, Ontario, Canada N6A 2L2

Diane L. Christian — Department of Pediatrics, Child Development Center, University of California at Irvine, Irvine, California 92715

Dante Cichetti — Mt. Hope Family Center, University of Rochester, Rochester, New York, 14608

Robert J. Coplan — Department of Psychology, University of Waterloo, Ontario, Canada N2L 3G1

Alan Hudson — Department of Psychology and Intellectual Disability Studies, Royal Melbourne Institute of Technology, Bundoora, Victoria 3083, Australia

Peter S. Jensen — National Institute of Mental Health, Rockville, Maryland 20857

Benjamin B. Lahey — Department of Psychiatry, University of Chicago Medical School, Chicago, Illinois 60628

Scott O. Lilienfield — Department of Psychology, State University of New York at Albany, Albany, New York 12203

Michael Lynch — Mt. Hope Family Center, University of Rochester, Rochester, New York 14608

Keith McBurnett — Department of Pediatrics, Child Development Center, University of California at Irvine, Irvine, California 92715

Editha D. Nottelmann *National Institute of Mental Health, Rockville, Maryland 20857*

John E. Richards *Department of Psychology, University of South Carolina, Columbia, South Carolina 29208*

Kenneth H. Rubin *Department of Psychology, University of Waterloo, Ontario, Canada N2L 3G1*

Sandra W. Russ *Department of Psychology, Case Western Reserve University, Cleveland, Ohio 44106*

Shawn L. Stewart *Department of Psychology, University of Waterloo, Ontario, Canada N2L 3G1*

James M. Swanson *Department of Pediatrics, Child Development Center, University of California at Irvine, Irvine, California 92715.*

Sheree L. Toth *Mt. Hope Family Center, University of Rochester, Rochester, New York 14608*

Irwin D. Waldman *Department of Psychology, Emory University, Atlanta, Georgia 30322*

Tim Wigal *Department of Pediatrics, Child Development Center, University of California at Irvine, Irvine, California 92715*

Vicky Veitch Wolfe *Department of Psychology, Children's Hospital of Western Ontario, London, Ontario, Canada N6A 2L2*

Preface

This volume of *Advances in Clinical Child Psychology* is the third under our editorship and the seventeenth of the series. It continues the tradition of examining a broad range of topics and issues related to the study and treatment of child and adolescent behavior problems. Over the years, the series has served to identify important and exciting new developments in the field and provide scholarly review of current thought and practices.

In the opening chapter, Cichetti, Toth, and Lynch examine attachment theory and its implications for psychopathology. They provide exacting commentary on the status of the construct of attachment and its potential role in the development of diverse psychopathologies. Similarly, Richards explores the impact of infant cognitive psychophysiology and its role in normal and abnormal development in the second chapter. Both of these chapters address issues of risk for subsequent psychopathology and are deeply embedded in developmental theory.

In Chapter 3, Nottelmann and Jensen tackle the important issue of comorbidity in psychiatric diagnosis from a developmental perspective. As they aptly note, comorbidity is more the rule than the exception. They explore important developmental processes which may account for this state of affairs. Rubin, Stewart, and Coplan address social withdrawal in children from conceptual and empirical perspectives. They also explore developmental issues, giving the chapter a context in which to interpret current findings and project future developments. The next two chapters are a critique of facilitated communication by Hudson and an examination of the psychological sequelae of child sexual abuse by Veitch-Wolfe and Birt. They review extremely important, timely, and controversial topics. We hope that they will serve as benchmark treatises on these topics for the years ahead.

Waldman, Lilienfeld, and Lahey highlight issues related to the construct validity of the disruptive behavior disorders in DSM-IV. Swanson, McBurnett, Christian, and Wigal review the use of stimulant medications in the treatment of children with ADHD. Finally, Russ examines state of the science (or art) for play psychotherapy. These chapters address important clinical issues and should be of direct and immediate interest to practicing clinicians.

Throughout this volume we have tried to highlight exciting developments and future directions for the discipline of clinical child psychology. The field is extremely varied and defies narrow boundaries.

In no small way, the success of each volume is directly related to the caliber of the contributors. We have been fortunate to recruit some of the best in the field today. We thank them for their timely and scholarly contributions. Finally, we wish to extend our warm thanks to the editorial and production staffs of Plenum Press. They have been a tremendous asset in bringing this project to fruition.

THOMAS H. OLLENDICK
RONALD J. PRINZ

Contents

Chapter 3. Comorbidity of Disorders in Children and Adolescents: Developmental Perspectives 109

Editha D. Nottelmann and Peter S. Jensen

Chapter 4. Social Withdrawal in Childhood: Conceptual and Empirical Perspectives 157

Kenneth H. Rubin, Shannon L. Stewart, and Robert J. Caplan

Chapter 5. Disability and Facilitated Communication: A Critique

Alan Hudson

Chapter 6. The Psychological Sequelae of Child
Sexual Abuse   233

Vicky Veitch Wolfe and Jo-Ann Birt

Chapter 7. Stimulant Medications and the Treatment of
Children with ADHD   265

*James M. Swanson, Keith McBurnett, Diane L. Christian,
and Tim Wigal*

Chapter 8. Toward Construct Validity in the Childhood
Disruptive Behavior Disorders: Classification and Diagnosis
in DSM-IV and Beyond   323

Irwin D. Waldman, Scott O. Lilienfeld and Benjamin B. Lahey

Chapter 9. Play Psychotherapy Research: State of the Science   365

Sandra W. Russ

1

Bowlby's Dream Comes Full Circle

The Application of Attachment Theory to Risk and Psychopathology

DANTE CICCHETTI, SHEREE L. TOTH,
AND MICHAEL LYNCH

1. Introduction

In formulating his theoretical perspective on the development of human attachment relationships, Bowlby incorporated knowledge from a variety of disciplines, viewpoints, and research paradigms (Ainsworth & Bowlby, 1991; Bretherton, 1992). Psychoanalysis, object relations theory, Sullivanian interpersonal psychiatry, social, experimental and developmental psychology, evolutionary theory, and ethology all exerted major impacts on Bowlby's hypotheses regarding the origins, course, and sequelae of secure and insecure attachment relationships (Ainsworth, 1967, 1969; Ainsworth, Blehar, Waters, & Wall, 1978; Bowlby, 1969/1982, 1973, 1980; Bretherton, 1987, 1991).

As depicted in his article, "The Making and Breaking of Affectional Bonds," Bowlby (1977a) described attachment theory as a "way of conceptualizing the propensity of human beings to make strong affectional bonds to particular others and of explaining the many forms of emotional distress and personality disturbance . . . to which unwilling separation and loss give rise" (p. 201). Throughout his career, Bowlby articulated how attachment theory could inform our understanding of the different path-

DANTE CICCHETTI, SHEREE L. TOTH, AND MICHAEL LYNCH • Mt. Hope Family Center, University of Rochester, Rochester, New York 14608.

Advances in Clinical Child Psychology, Volume 17, edited by Thomas H. Ollendick and Ronald J. Prinz. Plenum Press, New York, 1995.

ways leading to mental health and psychopathology, as well as provide a framework for implementing therapeutic interventions with a variety of clinical conditions (Bowlby, 1977a, 1977b, 1988).

In the preface to his book *A Secure Base* (1988), Bowlby stated that he found it somewhat "unexpected that, whereas attachment theory was formulated by a clinician for use in the diagnosis and treatment of emotionally disturbed patients and families, its usage . . . has been mainly to promote research in developmental psychology" (p. ix). Fortunately, during the past decade, a growing concern for investigating attachment relationships in high-risk and disordered populations across the life span has emerged (Cicchetti & Greenberg, 1991). Through these explorations into pathological processes, attachment theory has returned to the roots of Bowlby's ideas. In fact, we believe that these investigations of attachment relationships in child and adult clinical populations, in tandem with the implementation of prevention and intervention programs based on the principles of attachment theory, will result in the fulfillment of Bowlby's original vision.

2. Basic Elements of Attachment Theory and Research

As Bowlby (1988) noted, attachment researchers primarily have focused their efforts on elucidating attachment processes in infancy and on the developmental sequelae of secure and insecure infant-caregiver[1] attachments (Ainsworth, et al., 1978; Sroufe, 1983, 1988). The predominant measure used to assess quality of attachment in infancy has been the Strange Situation (Ainsworth & Wittig, 1969), a 21-minute structured laboratory procedure designed to produce low-level infant stress of sufficient magnitude to activate the infant's attachment behavioral system (cf. Bischof, 1975; Bretherton, 1980). Three particular stressors (introduction to an unfamiliar place, interaction with a new person, and brief separations from mother) were selected for inclusion in the Strange Situation because they are common occurrences and relatively nontraumatic; yet they provide gradations of stress that ensure activation of the attachment systems of most infants.

Utilizing a system developed by Ainsworth and her colleagues (1978), coders classify records of the videotaped Strange Situation into three major attachment categories. Studies conducted with normative samples reveal

---

[1]Because the majority of work on attachment has been directed toward the mother–child relationship, mother and caregiver are used throughout the text to refer to this dyadic relationship.

that approximately 70% of infants are coded as securely attached (Type B) to their primary caregiver. These babies respond unambivalently toward their mothers in reunions following brief separations; they greet or approach their caregivers, are readily comforted if they have been upset, then move back to exploration and play.

Twenty percent of infants are classified as having insecure-avoidant (Type A) attachment relationships with their caregivers. These babies respond to maternal reunions with a lack of either proximity seeking or positive affect, even ignoring the caregiver in some cases. The remaining 10% of infants form insecure-ambivalent (Type C) attachment relationships with their mothers. Infants in this group are distressed by separation and seek proximity to their mothers upon reunion; however, they are unable to be comforted by the contact they receive from their mothers, remaining fussy or angry and unable to return with ease to play.

The attachment categories established through these investigations are best thought of as assessments of coherent, organized strategies for relating to the caregiver in times of stress, weariness, or illness (Sroufe & Waters, 1977). The quality of an infant's attachment relationship to his/her caregiver is believed to be a function of the history of the infant's interactions with that particular caregiver over the course of the first year of life, especially during those situations in which the infant's needs are expressed (Ainsworth et al., 1978).

Secure attachments (Type B) have been linked with a history of maternal warmth and sensitive responsivity. In contrast, insecure-avoidant attachments (Type A) have been associated with parental rejection and emotionally unavailable or harsh caregiving. Moreover, insecure-ambivalent (Type C) attachments are related to histories of inconsistent caregiving (Ainsworth et al., 1978; Isabella, 1993; Sroufe & Waters, 1977). All three attachment patterns represent organized strategies on the part of the infant to negotiate separation anxiety and reunion with the caregiver. More recently, atypical patterns of attachment characterized by behavioral disorganization and disorientation have been identified (Main & Hesse, 1990; Main & Solomon, 1986). We discuss these atypical attachment patterns in more detail later. Table 1 contains a description of the major classifications of infant attachment.

A large number of investigations conducted on normative samples of mother–infant dyads have discovered that securely attached infants are more likely to resolve the subsequent stage-salient developmental issues in an adaptive fashion (Sroufe, 1983, 1988). Specifically, because development is conceptualized as an organized and hierarchically integrated process (Kaplan, 1966; Werner, 1957), successful resolution of an early developmental issue (e.g., attachment security) forebodes later competent

TABLE 1

Patterns of Children's Interactive Behavior with the Caregiver in the Strange Situation Associated with the Four Major Attachment Classifications[a]

Patterns of attachment	Description of interactive behaviors
Type A: Insecure-avoidant	Independent exploration (e.g., readily separates to explore during preseparation; little affective sharing; affiliative to stranger) Active avoidance upon reunion (e.g., turning away, looking away, moving away, ignoring; no avoidance of stranger)
Type B: Secure	Caregiver is a secure base for exploration (e.g., readily separates to explore toys; affective sharing of play; affiliative to stranger in mother's presence; readily comforted when distressed) Active in seeking contact or interaction upon reunion (e.g., if distressed, immediately seek and maintain contact, and contact is effective in terminating distress; if not distressed, active greeting behavior and strong initiation of interaction).
Type C: Insecure-ambivalent	Poverty of exploration (e.g., difficulty separating to explore; may need contact even prior to separation; wary of novel situations and people). Difficulty settling upon reunion (e.g., may mix contact seeking with contact resistance such as hitting and kicking; may continue to cry and fuss; may show noticeable passivity).
Type D: Disorganized-disoriented	Sequential and/or simultaneous displays of contradictory behavior patterns; undirected and incomplete movements and expressions; stereotypes; asymmetrical movements; anomalous postures; freezing, stilling and dazing; apprehension toward the caregiver.

[a]Adapted from Ainsworth et al. (1978) and Main and Solomon (1990).

adaptation (e.g., continued secure attachment; the development of an autonomous and positive sense of self; effective peer relations; etc.). Conversely, early maladaptive resolutions forecast subsequent maladaptive outcomes (Elicker, Englund, & Sroufe, 1992; Sroufe, 1983; Sroufe, Carlson & Shulman, 1993; Urban, Carlson, Egeland, & Sroufe, 1991).

For example, Urban and her colleagues (1991) assessed a group of 47 low socioeconomic status (SES) preadolescent children followed longitudinally since infancy in a study on the consequences of attachment security (cf. Sroufe, 1983). These children were intensively observed for 4 weeks at a summer daycamp when they were 10–11 years of age. Children with histories of insecure attachment were rated as more dependent, less socially competent, less ego resilient, and more likely to interact with camp counselors than were children who were securely attached in infancy. Additionally, children with insecure-ambivalent (Type C) attachment histories were more often the recipient of adult-initiated supportive and nurturant interactions than were those with insecure-avoidant histories.

Elicker and his colleagues (1992) also examined the friendship patterns of these same preadolescents and found that children with histories of secure attachment were more likely to form a friendship during the camp. Moreover, the friendships that developed during camp were likely to form along the lines of children's attachment histories, with secure-secure pairs the most common pattern.

In a recent assessment of a subsample of these 47 preadolescents at a reunion camp held when the attendees were between 14 and 15 years of age, Sroufe and his colleagues (1993) likewise discovered that adolescents with histories of secure attachments were rated emotionally healthier, higher in self-esteem and ego resilience, and more competent with peers.

By focusing on stage-salient developmental issues in the preadolescent and adolescent periods (e.g., peer relations), targeting key social relationships, and aggregating their data in a way that emphasized patterning among variables and the organization of behavior in context, Urban et al. (1991), Elicker et al. (1992), and Sroufe et al. (1993) were able to uncover a remarkable coherence in individual adaptation over time. In agreement with our own theoretical viewpoint, these researchers do not view coherence of individual adaptation as a static trait residing within the child. Instead, individual adaptation is conceived as a transactional process in which children's developmental histories and their expectations of attachment figures and self-representations that arise from those histories, bring about styles of engaging the environment and relating socially that encourage perpetuating feedback from the environment.

Research that has investigated the links between attachment quality and the development of later behavior problems in these nonclinical samples has yielded equivocal results. While some studies have revealed that insecurely attached youngsters are more likely to develop behavior problems (e.g., Erickson, Egeland, & Sroufe, 1985; Lewis, Feiring, McGuffog, & Jaskir, 1984; Sroufe, 1983), others have failed to discover any such association (e.g., Bates, Maslin, & Frankel, 1985). Moreover, even the investigations that have documented relations between quality of attachment and behavior problems have shown that not all insecurely attached youngsters develop subsequent behavioral difficulties. However, because the prospective longitudinal studies that examined attachment-behavior problem links were generally short-term in nature, and because the investigators relied on maternal reports of the child difficulties due to the paucity of child self-report measures before age 6–7 years, more questions remain unanswered than resolved.

3. Goals of the Chapter

In this chapter, we examine the theoretical and empirical advances in attachment theory and the field of psychopathology that have stimulated research on attachment organization in high-risk and psychiatrically disordered populations. Because a number of reviews have considered the various patterns of attachment organization and their developmental sequelae in normative populations (e.g., Sroufe, 1983, 1988), we chose attachment in high-risk and psychopathological populations as our focus.

Specifically, we address the research that has been conducted with populations at risk for maladaptation due to the presence of experienced trauma and/or maladaptive caregiving related to parental psychopathology. We also present findings that link attachment dysfunction to psychopathological conditions. To achieve this goal, we review attachment organization in maltreated children, children with a depressed or substance-abusing caregiver, and children with oppositional defiant or conduct disorders. These populations represent the conditions in which the most work has been directed specifically toward the examination of attachment organization and risk of psychopathology.

Although most of the empirical work in this area has focused on the early years of life, we provide a life-span perspective on attachment organization in these populations as data permit. By piecing together the results of cross-sectional and short-term longitudinal studies, we can identify possible developmental trajectories from insecure attachment in infancy and childhood to the presence of attachment dysfunction and/or psychopathology in later life.

After reviewing the relevant research, we explore the implications of these findings for intervention. Although the existing data necessitate an emphasis on childhood, the central role that caregivers play in exacerbating or alleviating child distress requires attention to adult-attachment organization and its impact on parents' representational models of their children as well as on parents' subsequent caregiving.

We conclude by providing suggestions for future theory and research that are essential for continued progress in our knowledge of attachment theory and its application to the understanding of psychopathology and the promotion of mental health.

4. Recent Advances in Attachment Theory

In this section, we focus on recent advances in the study of attachment as it pertains to conditions of risk and psychopathology.

4.1. Attachment as a Life-Span Developmental Issue

A growing number of theoreticians and researchers, influenced by Bowlby's viewpoint, have conceptualized attachment as remaining critical to the ongoing adaptational strivings of the person, even though attachment changes in organization throughout the course of ontogenesis (Ainsworth, 1989; Greenberg, Cicchetti, & Cummings, 1990). While attachment is conceived as one of the stage-salient developmental issues of the infancy period, we believe that attachment, as is the case with other major developmental tasks, continues to differentiate beyond its period of developmental ascendance. Moreover, once an attachment develops, it continues to undergo transformations and integrations with subsequent accomplishments such as emerging autonomy, entrance into the peer world, adaptation to school, and identity throughout the life course (cf. Cicchetti & Schneider-Rosen, 1986; Erikson, 1950; Sroufe, 1979). Thus, persons are continuously renegotiating the balance between being connected to others and being autonomous as they encounter each new developmental phase.

Furthermore, we contend that, at these periods of reorganization or transition, persons have the opportunity not only to acquire new strengths, but also to develop new vulnerabilities. Thus, we believe that not all problems in attachment necessarily have their roots in infancy. In essence, we hold that individuals are neither completely inoculated against future problems by having experienced positive early caregiving nor are they doomed to develop maladaptively by having received negative early caregiving experiences. We view attachment as a transactional process and not as an unchanging trait within the person (Cummings & Cicchetti, 1990). It is these theoretical assumptions that guide us as we explore the role of attachment in the emergence of psychopathology.

In the first volume of his trilogy on attachment, Bowlby (1969/1982) presented a description of a developmental theory of attachment beyond infancy. In essence, Bowlby's theory posits that a major developmental task of young children is to form a "goal-corrected" partnership with their attachment figures. While this partnership is enacted across the wide range of interactions that constitute the parent–child relationship, it is highly likely that it first develops in the context of attachment–caregiving interactions. Subsequently, a goal-corrected partnership can be seen evolving in relationships with others beyond the attachment figures (Marvin & Stewart, 1990).

Bowlby (1969/1982) suggested that when children become cognitively able to represent their mothers' goals and plans to themselves, to distinguish their mothers' plans from their own, and to bring mothers' goals and plans more into alignment with their own, they have then achieved a "goal-corrected partnership." Typically, children achieve this phase of attachment during the preschool years (Marvin, 1977).

Although our brief discussion of the goal-corrected partnership has necessarily omitted several important issues, one point that should be mentioned is particularly relevant to some of the material covered later in this chapter. Whenever two goal-corrected systems are closely coupled, conflict between opposing goals and plans is inevitable. Marvin and Greenberg (1982) have demonstrated that resolving conflict concerning an upcoming separation and constructing an agreed-upon, shared plan for separation and reunion is associated with low levels of conflict during reunions between mothers and their 4-year-old children. In dyads where this shared plan is not constructed, reunion is much more likely to be characterized by anger and overly controlling behavior on the part of the child. We contend that conflict and conflict resolution concerning attachment interactions is a core issue in the development and maintenance of the goal-corrected partnership throughout the life course.

4.2. The Move to the Level of Representation

Attachment undergoing differentiation throughout the life span integrates and coordinates not only with other emergent developmental issues, but also with all domains of the mind (e.g., cognition, emotion, language, social cognition, etc.). Consequently, as research on attachment has become more life-span in nature, theoreticians and researchers necessarily have had to place greater emphasis on identifying the attitudes, feelings, thoughts, goals, and plans of children and adults concerning their own behavior and internal events. Representational or working models of the self, others, and relationships have been put forth as a psychological construct that helps to organize the individuals' thoughts, plans, and internal states.

Bowlby describes working models as an individual's conscious and unconscious mental representations, "of the world and of himself in it, with the aid of which he perceives events, forecasts the future, and constructs his plans" (Bowlby, 1973, p. 203). According to Bowlby, early experiences with the caregiver are central in the formation of working models of the self, others, and self–other relationships. These models allow children to form expectations about the availability and probable actions of others with complementary models of how worthy and competent the self is. Bretherton (1990) has suggested that representational models of the self and attachment figures may be hierarchically organized in terms of event schemas. Such a hierarchy would include low-level interactional schemas (e.g., "When I get hurt, my mother comes to comfort and help me") and more general schemas (e.g., "My mother is usually there for me when I need her"). At the top of the hierarchy would be overarching schemas such as "My mother is a loving person" and "I am loved and worthy of love." Attachment theory proposes that these organized mental representations are carried forward by the individual and used in subsequent interpersonal contexts.

Internal representational models may act as a mechanism of continuity in the transactions between self-organization and relationships with others. Observed continuities in the quality and pattern of interaction with different relationship figures can result from the increasingly internal organization of affects and beliefs that the individual possesses. Representational models of individual relationships contain information that is specific to those relationships. Expectations about the availability of the other person, how effective the self is likely to be in eliciting desired responses from the person, attitudes and commitment toward the relationship, and the affective tone of the relationship all may be incorporated into models of specific relationships. However, these specific models also may contribute information to more generalized models of relationships, the self, and others (Crittenden, 1990; Lynch & Cicchetti, 1991). It is possible that internal representational models of early attachment relationships begin to provide the individual with general information and expectations about how new social partners will act and react and how successful the self is likely to be in relation to those partners and the broader social context.

Because psychoanalysts in the British object relations school (e.g., Winnicott, 1965) and in the American school of interpersonal psychiatry (e.g., Sullivan, 1953) have paid great attention to the impact that different relationship histories have on different selves, as well as the course of individual differences in healthy and pathological self development, the recent emphasis on representational processes within attachment theory has a built-in conceptual bridge to psychopathologists from a variety of disciplinary persuasions.

4.3. The Emergence of Developmental Psychopathology

Over the past decade, developmental psychopathology has made major advances toward becoming a mature scientific discipline (Cicchetti, 1984, 1989, 1993; Cicchetti & Toth, 1991a, b; Hay & Angold, 1993; Lewis & Miller, 1990; Rutter & Garmezy, 1983). Developmental psychopathology has enhanced empirical work on attachment and risk/psychopathology and facilitated clinical applications of attachment theory to prevention and intervention efforts (Belsky & Nezworski, 1988; Cicchetti & Greenberg, 1991; Cicchetti & Toth, 1992; Guidano & Liotti, 1983; Lieberman, 1993; Sameroff & Emde, 1989, Toth & Cicchetti, 1993; Zeanah, 1993).

Sroufe and Rutter (1984) originally defined developmental psychopathology as "... the study of the origins and course of individual patterns of behavioral maladaptation, whatever the age of onset, whatever the causes, whatever the transformations in behavioral manifestation and however complex the course of the developmental pattern may be" (p. 18; italics theirs). As such, rather than focusing only on conditions of psychopathology, developmental psychopathologists also appreciate that knowledge of normal development is necessary to understand deviations or distortions from normality. Similarly, information obtained from studying pathology can enhance the understanding of normal development. For this reason, developmental psychopathologists are as interested in high-risk individuals who, over time, do not manifest pathology as they are in individuals who develop an actual disorder (Sroufe & Rutter, 1984). A related component of the developmental-psychopathology perspective involves an interest in the mechanisms and processes that affect the ultimate outcome of risk factors (Cicchetti & Aber, 1986; Cicchetti & Lynch, 1993; Kopp & Recchia, 1990; Rutter, 1988). Developmental psychopathologists dedicate themselves to uncovering pathways to competent adaptation despite exposure to conditions of adversity (Masten, 1989; Masten, Best, & Garmezy, 1990; Rutter, 1990). Finally, because a developmental-psychopathology perspective advocates a life-span approach to understanding ontogenetic processes, the only way in which developmental continuities and discontinuities can be elucidated fully is through prospective longitudinal investigations of various high-risk conditions and pathological populations from infancy through adulthood (cf. Sroufe et al., 1993).

Researchers examining the developmental consequences of secure and insecure infant–caregiver attachment relationships have discovered that linear main-effect models do not account for links between insecurity and later child behavior problems (Cummings & Cicchetti, 1990; Sroufe, 1983). Rather, they have found it necessary to take into account the developmental transformations and reorganizations that occur over time, to analyze the risk and protective factors and processes operating in individuals and their environments, to investigate how emergent functions, competencies, and developmental tasks contribute to the appearance of new symptoms and difficulties, and to recognize that a particular underlying mechanism may result in different behavioral difficulties, at different times in the developmental process and in different contexts.

Since not all children who have an insecure attachment relationship with their primary caregiver will develop behavior problems or psychiatric disorders, attachment researchers had to turn their attention to learning more about individual differences in how attachment relationships were represented, as well as how these internalizations affected later relationship development and other realms of personality functioning. Developmental psychopathologists must be informed about the pathways of normal or healthy development, discover deviations from these pathways, articulate the developmental transformations that occur as individuals progress through these deviant ontogenetic courses, and identify the factors and mechanisms that may deflect an individual out of a particular pathway and onto a more or less adaptive course (Cicchetti & Schneider-Rosen, 1986). Therefore, it is not surprising that research and theoretical work in the fields of attachment and developmental psychopathology have become more mutually enriching.

4.4. Measurement Advances

As researchers have attempted to delineate the processes involved in linking quality of attachment with risk for psychopathology, advances in measurement have been needed to allow cross-sectional and longitudinal studies to be conducted beyond the period of infancy with a variety of populations. Extending attachment research to older children and adults and to atypical populations has necessitated the development of some new assessment procedures and scoring criteria.

An important prerequisite for conducting research on attachment beyond the period of infancy is the development and validation of measurement schemes to assess the nature and quality of attachment relationships. One goal of the research is to examine stability and change in parent–child attachment relationships. Further, children also may form attachments to siblings, friends, grandparents, day-care personnel, teachers, and others as their network of social relationships expands. Thus, another goal is to develop methods to assess attachments other than parent–child attachments.

We have chosen to describe the most commonly employed new measures and coding systems being utilized in studies of attachment from infancy through adulthood. Moreover, we are discussing only those paradigms that possess reasonably sound psychometric properties and that have been used in research on conditions of risk and psychopathology.

4.4.1. The Discovery of the Disorganized-Disoriented (Type D) Attachment Relationship

In 1981, Main and Weston reported that a small but significant minority of infants, approximately 12.5%, who participated in their Berkeley Social Development Project and were assessed at 12 or 18 months in the Strange Situation (Ainsworth & Wittig, 1969), could not be classified using Ainsworth's conventional criteria (Ainsworth et al., 1978). Originally labeled "U" or unclassifiable, Main and Solomon (1986, 1990) subsequently relabeled them "D" or disorganized-disoriented to describe the essential nature of their behavior during separation/reunion episodes in the Strange Situation. In contrast to infants with insecure-avoidant (Type A), secure (Type B), and insecure-ambivalent (Type C) attachment classifications who possess coherent strategies to deal with the stress of separation/reunion from their caregivers, infants with Type D attachments appeared to possess no such organized coping mechanism. Rather, upon reunions with their caregivers following brief separations, these infants either blended contradictory features of several strategies (e.g., strong proximity seeking followed by strong avoidance) or appeared dazed and disoriented upon reunion with the caretaker. Disorganization clearly was evident in the infants left unclassified in the following ways: disordering of expected temporal sequences; incomplete or undirected movements; some direct indices of confusion, apprehension, or depression; and simultaneous displays of contradictory behavior patterns. Main and her colleagues have speculated that children who display this insecure-disorganized pattern of attachment with their caregivers are basing their attachment behaviors with their caretakers on an internal working model of self-in-relation to the attachment figure that is qualitatively distinct from the internal working models that guide the behavior of Type B, A, and C infants (Main, Kaplan, & Cassidy, 1985).

In order to evaluate the continuity in children's internal working models of attachment relationships, Main and her colleagues (1985) followed a sample of 39 children from 12- or 18-months-old to their sixth birthdays. The children's attachment classifications to their mothers during infancy had been B (N = 14), A or C (N = 13), or D (N = 12). As part of the battery of measures they administered at age 6, children were then videotaped in reunion episodes with their parents after a 1-hour separation. During this separation, parents were interviewed about their attachment relations with their own parents.

Among the most striking results that emerged from this important longitudinal investigation were that:

1. Children classified as "insecure-disorganized" in infancy displayed a unique form of reunion behavior at 6 years of age labeled by Main and her collaborators as "insecure-controlling." These children did not flexibly reunite with their parents (as did the B's) or avoid their parents (A's) upon reunion. Rather, they took charge of the interaction in a controlling fashion, either punitively or in a pseudocaretaking manner. These investigators interpret their findings as evidence for an impressive continuity in the quality of the child's internal working model of the attachment relationship to the parent.

2. Upon their review of the life histories of the parents of insecure-disorganized versus other children, these researchers discovered that the parents of children classified as D's were much more likely to have experienced the loss of a parent prior to maturity, or the loss of a sibling or another major attachment figure other than the parent with whom they had been reared.

The ability to identify disorganized-disoriented attachments results in an improvement both in the ability to assess individual differences in the mental representations of attachment relationships and to trace the longitudinal consequences of secure and insecure attachments more precisely. In order to increase our knowledge about the Type D category, Main and Solomon (1986) recommend that whenever a disorganized-disoriented classification is assigned to a case, the coder also should identify the A, B, or C category that would have been the "forced classification" had the D category not been available.

4.4.2. System for Classifying the Quality of Attachment in Preschool-Aged Children

Cassidy and Marvin (1992) in collaboration with the MacArthur Working Group on Attachment proposed a system to classify quality of attachment organization in 3- and 4-year-olds assessed in the Strange Situation (Ainsworth & Wittig, 1969) or similar separation–reunion pro-

tocols in laboratory contexts. Secure, insecure-avoidant, insecure-ambivalent, insecure controlling-disorganized, and insecure-other groups are
specified within this system.[2] The system includes 6 subtypes of security,
2 of avoidance, 2 of ambivalence, and 4 of controlling-disorganized. No
subtype of the insecure-other group has been identified as yet.

Because of their recent development and discovery, as well as their
importance for research on risk and psychopathology, the controlling subtypes merit elaboration. Children with controlling-caregiving attachment
relationships deal with maternal-reunion episodes by displaying overly
"bright" and "cheerful" greeting behavior or showing of toys that is not
followed up with positive affect and synchronous interactions (cf. Crittenden & DiLalla, 1988). Those children who develop controlling-punitive
attachments display punitive and hostile behavior toward their caregivers
that is manifested by telling their parents what to do in a derogatory,
angry, or annoyed manner. Children who are classified as controlling-
general attachments either exhibit both caretaking and punitive behaviors
toward their caregivers or else clearly control their interactions with parents in some other manner.

In addition, ratings of avoidance (7-point scale) and security (9-point
scale) are given to each child. This system has been used by the MacArthur
Working Group on Attachment in collaborative assessments of diverse
and difficult-to-classify Strange Situations sessions involving 3- and 4-
year-olds. Validation of this new system is ongoing in many laboratories
across the country and includes samples ranging across a variety of socioeconomic strata and diagnostic conditions (e.g., maltreated preschoolers,
offspring of parents with a mood disorder, "high-risk" offspring of adolescent mothers drawn from the lower SES, etc.). Later in this chapter, we
review representative findings from investigators who have employed this
classification system in their research on attachment in the postinfancy
period.

4.4.3. Five- to Seven-Year System for Classifying Parent–Child Reunion Behavior

Main and Cassidy (1988; see also Cassidy, 1990) developed a procedure to code parent–child reunion behavior in a laboratory situation.
Growing evidence suggests that reunion behavior of children between 5

---

[2]Although the terminology employed by theorists to describe attachment organization in the
preschool years has varied, for purposes of clarity and consistency we use the terminology
of the 1992 Cassidy and Marvin system throughout.

.and 7 years of age is reflective of the quality of the parent–child attachment relationship (Cassidy, 1990; Main, et al., 1985).

In this procedure, child and parent are together in a toy-filled play-room with an experimenter. After 20 minutes, the parent departs while the child and experimenter remain together in the playroom for approximately an hour doing a variety of tasks. For 15 minutes prior to the parent's return, the child engages in free play. When the parent reenters the room, the child's behavior during the first 5 minutes of reunion is rated and classified.

Security versus insecurity of attachment is rated on a 9-point scale. A 9-point scale of avoidance reflects the intensity and persistence of the child's avoidance of physical or emotional interaction, proximity, or contact. Additionally, child-reunion behavior is classified according to one of five patterns of child–parent attachment: secure, insecure-avoidant, insecure-ambivalent, insecure-controlling, or insecure-other. Because Main and Cassidy (1988) consider it more difficult to classify attachment organization in the 5- to 7-year reunion procedure than in the Strange Situation, they recommend utilizing a second reunion classification or a concurrent measure that would tap the child's representational model of attachment (e.g., the child's family drawing; see Main et al., 1985 for additional illustrations).

4.4.4. Feelings and Patterns of Relatedness

Wellborn and Connell (1987) devised a method for assessing the quality of children's feelings of relatedness with a variety of relationship figures (e.g., mother, father, best friend, teacher, etc.) through a self-report questionnaire that can be used with children between 7 and 13 years of age. According to Connell's (1990) model of self-system processes, the need for relatedness is one of three fundamental psychological needs. The other two needs are the need for competence and the need for autonomy. Connell views the self-system as a set of appraisal processes through which the self evaluates the degree to which these psychological needs are being met. The need for relatedness, which has its conceptual roots in attachment and self-system theory, reflects the need to feel securely connected to the social surround and the need to experience oneself as worthy and capable of love (Connell, 1990). Appraisals of the degree to which these needs are being met involve activation of the relevant representational model. Prior normative research conducted by Lynch (1990) and by Connell and Wellborn (1991) indicates that children's responses to the relatedness scales form patterns that are consistent with attachment and self-system theory. In general, the more positive affect a person reports feeling when with a relationship partner, the less he or she reported needing to feel psychologically closer to that individual (Lynch & Cicchetti, 1991). This pattern parallels the relationship between felt security and the need for physical proximity among infants and toddlers in attachment theory.

The relatedness scales are read aloud to the children individually by an interviewer and require responses on a 4-point scale. The scales, which include 17 items, are completed separately for each relationship. Most of the items are adopted from the Rochester Assessment Package for Schools (RAPS) (Wellborn & Connell, 1987), a 261-item questionnaire that measures children's perceived autonomy, competence, and relatedness as they connect to engagement and disaffection in school. The RAPS assesses children's feelings of relatedness with their mother, teacher, and classmates.

The Relatedness Scales have two subscales that measure children's feelings of relatedness to specific others. These subscales have been labeled (1) emotional quality seeking, and (2) psychological proximity seeking. The emotional quality dimension consists of items that assess specific positive and negative emotions that children feel when they are with a specified relationship partner. Children are asked to rate on a 4-point scale items such as: "When I'm with _____, I feel happy." The psychological proximity-seeking dimension consists of items that assess the degree to which children wish they were psychologically closer to their relationship partner. In this case, children rate on a 4-point scale items such as: "I wish _____ paid more attention to me," and "I wish _____ understood me better."

Individual patterns of relatedness are obtained by examining children's scores on both the emotional quality-seeking and psychological proximity-seeking dimensions of relatedness for a particular relationship. Patterns based on the configuration of both scores are intended to capture the dynamic interaction between the two dimensions of relatedness.

Children are classified as having a particular pattern of relatedness based on their scores on both the emotional quality- and psychological proximity-seeking dimensions of relatedness. Children who cannot be assigned to one of the designated patterns of relatedness are labeled "unclassifiable." The structure of these patterns and cutoff scores are described in Lynch and Cicchetti (1991). Qualitatively, children with *optimal* patterns of relatedness report high levels of positive emotion and low levels of psychological proximity seeking. They feel positive and secure in their relationships, and they are satisfied with existing degrees of closeness. Children with *deprived* patterns of relatedness report low levels of emotional quality, but high amounts of psychological proximity seeking.

These children want to feel closer to others, but their relationships are characterized by feelings of negativity and insecurity. Children with *disengaged* patterns of relatedness report low levels of emotional quality and low amounts of psychological-proximity seeking. They have predominantly negative feelings about others and do not want to be closer with them. Children with *confused* patterns of relatedness report high levels of emotional quality as well as extremely high amounts of psychological proximity seeking. Despite feeling emotionally positive and secure in their relationships, they feel that they need much more psychological proximity than they have. In other words, they report feeling positive affect and security despite feeling very unsatisfied with how close they are to others. Children with *average* patterns of relatedness are nondescript in their relationships, reporting average levels of emotional quality- and psychological proximity seeking.

4.4.5. Adult Attachment Interview

George, Kaplan, and Main (1985) developed the Adult Attachment Interview as a method for identifying different types of adult-attachment organization. The Adult Attachment Interview is comprised of 15 questions that require the individual to describe and evaluate significant attachment-related experiences and their impact upon the person's development. Interview questions probe for adults' verbal descriptions of early attachment relationships and experiences, supportive and contradictory memories, and current evaluations of early attachment relationships and experiences.

Coders score the interview by working with the verbatim transcript in its entirety. They review the transcript and make inferences about the individual's probable childhood experiences on three primary domains— love, rejection, and neglect—for each caregiver, if possible. The coder examines the entire transcript with regard to the individual's current state of mind with regard to attachment. The primary state-of-mind scale deals with the coherence of the individual's attachment-related speech. To rate coherence of mind, the rater considers the speakers's linguistic form, whether the speech flowed easily, whether questions by the interviewer were answered directly, and whether the relationship characteristics described by the speaker were supported by specific memories. Some examples of attachment material that would yield low coherency scores include: (a) idealization of the parent, in which generally positive statements about parents are not corroborated by specific memories; (b) instances in which individuals cannot recall their childhood; or (c) anger at the parent that is so salient that the individual attempts to enlist the interviewer's agreement. Another type of incoherency can arise if the individual is unresolved about the loss of a parent. In addition to vague or poor linguistic form, unresolved individuals make bizarre or inadvertent slips of the tongue, such as talking about the dead parent as if he or she were alive, or confusing the dead person and the self.

Based on the adult's childhood experiences and current state of mind with respect to attachment, four different patterns of attachment organization that are consistent with the infant patterns of Ainsworth et al. (1978) and Main and Solomon (1990), have been delineated (Main & Goldwyn, in press). The three primary patterns include a *Free/Autonomous* pattern analogous to the secure-infant pattern, and two insecure patterns: *Dismissing*, related to the infant anxious-avoidant patterns, and *Preoccupied-Entangled*, related to the infant anxious-ambivalent pattern.

These patterns of adult attachment organization offer a means of identifying potential continuity between early relational experiences and current state of mind regarding attachment relationships in terms of internal representational models. The internal representational models inherent in the three different adult attachment patterns involve both the organization of memories of differential early parent–child relational experiences as well as the individual's current state of mind regarding attachment relationships. As such, these models will likely have a strong influence on the character of parenting behavior and the parent's experience of attachment phenomena with the parent's own children.

The Free/Autonomous or secure adult attachment pattern has been linked to loving and supportive parenting experienced in childhood. Individuals with this pattern are clear and coherent about their experiences, having ready access to attachment-related information and the ability to integrate cognition and affect regarding attachment experiences. They have a respect for the importance of their early relationships and have a balanced and empathic view of themselves and others. In contrast, the Dismissing pattern is associated with childhood experiences of parental rejection. Internal representational models have developed that defend against the pain of early experience. The effects of early relationships with parents are minimized, and one's parents may be defensively idealized. Attachment-related information is excluded from awareness and attachment-related phenomena are processed without integrating affect. These individuals tend to be distant, terse, and incoherent in discussing attachment. The Preoccupied-Entangled pattern is associated with experiences in childhood of parent–child role reversal, guilt, and inconsistency. These individuals tend to be consumed by memories of their childhood experiences and have much unresolved affect regarding their parents. As such they have ready access to attachment-related information and associated affects. However, affects are not effectively integrated with cognitions. The appropriate affects poorly coordinate with cognitions. Ambivalence is prominent in processing attachment-related experiences and phenomena.

Individuals with one of the three primary patterns of adult attachment organization may also be classified as Unresolved/Disoriented-Disorganized. This pattern is characterized by the display of lapses in the monitoring of discourse or reasoning while discussing loss or abuse experiences. Main and Hesse (1990) have linked infant disorganized-disoriented (Type D) attachments to frightened or frightening behavior in parents, and these parental behaviors have been shown to relate to parental history of having been maltreated as well as to unresolved loss.

Finally, if an interview cannot be classified as Free/Autonomous, Dismissing, or Preoccupied-Entangled, and it cannot be assigned to the Unresolved/Disoriented-Disorganized category, then the interview is rated as "cannot classify."

The Adult Attachment Interview has been used to examine the correspondence between parental attachment and infant attachment (e.g., Fonagy, H. Steele, & M. Steele, 1991; Main & Goldwyn, in press). Additionally, researchers have utilized the Adult Attachment Interview in investigations of high-risk and clinical populations to determine whether risk conditions or psychiatric disturbances in adults and/or children relate to mental representations of past attachment experiences.

In an effort to capture more variability in the measurement of adult attachment, Kobak (see, e.g., Kobak, Sudler, & Gamble, 1991) translated the descriptive features of Main and Goldwyn's (in press) adult-classification system into Q-sort items. Criteria Q-sets have been developed for security/anxiety and deactivation/hyperactivation, thereby permitting attachment strategies to be indexed as continuous variables. Kobak and Cole (1994) have obtained validity for the Q-sorts by demonstrating that the continuous variables can differentiate between the classifications from the Main and Goldwyn system. The Q-sort methodology offers several psychometric advantages over rating scales because it is less subject to halo effects and artificially inflated interrater reliability scores, and it allows for the identification of unreliable items. Moreover, as Block (1971) and Waters and Deane (1985) have noted, Q-sorts enable researchers to decrease measurement error by developing composites based on ratings of multiple individuals. Researchers have begun to employ the Q-sort items that Kobak has developed with clinical samples.

The results of studies that have administered the Adult Attachment Interview to risk and clinical populations, using either the Main and Goldwyn (in press) or Kobak and Cole (1994) methodologies, are discussed throughout the next section. See Table 2 for a summary of the attachment classifications yielded by the different assessment techniques across ages ranging from infancy to adulthood.

5. Attachment and Psychopathology

The theoretical and methodological advances in the conceptualization of attachment have made new studies possible. A recent meta-analysis conducted by van IJzendoorn, Goldberg, Kronenberg, and Frenkel (1992) revealed that maternal problems that fall along the continuum of caretaking casualty (Sameroff & Chandler, 1975), such as psychiatric illnesses or child maltreatment, produce more deviant distributions of attachment classifications than do more biologically based, child-oriented problems of reproductive casualty, such as Down syndrome, prematurity, or deafness. Specifically, van IJzendoorn and colleagues (1992) discovered that groups with a primary identification of maternal problems exhibited distributions of A, B, and C attachment patterns that were highly discrepant from distributions found in normal, low-risk samples. Conversely, van IJzendoorn et al., (1992) found that groups whose primary defining characteristics were biologically child-based problems displayed distributions of attachment classifications that were very similar to those obtained in normal samples. The introduction of the D or A/C category in the attachment classifications of the child problem groups resulted in an overrepresentation of these atypical attachment patterns compared to groups of normal distributions. Nonetheless, the D or A/C distribution of the child problem groups were far closer to those of normal samples than those of the distributions of samples with maternal problems, which were highly discrepant from the norm. Van IJzendoorn and colleagues concluded that mothers play more critical roles than do child factors in shaping the quality of mother–child attachment relationships in risk and clinical populations.

Now that a general framework has been provided for conceptualizing findings derived from attachment theory, we review research and theory that is relevant to risk and psychopathology. We begin by discussing attachment and maltreatment, an area that has received considerable attention due to the extensive caregiving dysfunction that is present in maltreating families. We then examine depression, both with respect to the effects of having a depressed caregiver on attachment insecurity and depression and with regard to attachment organization in individuals who have been diagnosed as having a depressive disorder. Work that has examined the effects of parental substance abuse on the quality of attachment is then presented. Our discussion of attachment and psychopathol-

TABLE 2

Putative Mapping of Attachment Classification Systems Across Age Periods and Methods

Infancy[a]	Preschool[b]	Developmental Period		Adolescence and adulthood[e]
		5–7 years[c]	School-age[d]	
Secure	Secure	Secure	Optimal and average	Free/autonomous
Insecure-avoidant	Insecure-avoidant	Insecure-avoidant	Disengaged	Dismissing
Insecure-ambivalent	Insecure-ambivalent	Insecure-ambivalent	Deprived	Preoccupied/entangled
Insecure-disorganized-disoriented	Insecure controlling-disorganized/disoriented and insecure-other	Insecure-controlling	Confused	Unresolved loss/disorganized disoriented

[a]Ainsworth et al. (1978) coding scheme for Strange Situation Procedure
[b]Cassidy and Marvin (1992) coding scheme for Strange Situation, or Separation-Reunion Procedures
[c]Main and Cassidy (1988) coding scheme for Reunion Procedure
[d]Lynch and Cicchetti (1991) Patterns of Relatedness
[e]Main and Goldwyn (in press) Coding scheme for Adult Attachment Interview

ogy concludes with an examination of studies that have posited a link between attachment dysfunction and the emergence of externalizing disorders in childhood.

5.1. Attachment and Child Maltreatment

Studies of the consequences of child maltreatment constitute a well-established area of research that can shed light on the links between attachment processes and risk for behavior problems and psychopathology. Maltreatment is a complex and heterogeneous phenomenon that includes a range of negative caretaking experiences (Cicchetti & Rizley, 1981). Many subtypes of maltreatment have been represented in the literature, including physical abuse, sexual abuse, physical neglect, and emotional neglect. It is important to note that many of the subtypes of child maltreatment are often comorbid.

In the early to mid-1980s, a number of studies using the Strange Situation (Ainsworth & Wittig, 1969) demonstrated that maltreated children do form attachments to their caregivers, and that these attachments are more likely to be insecure than those of nonmaltreated children (Crittenden, 1985; Egeland & Sroufe, 1981; Lamb, Gaensbauer, Malkin, & Schultz, 1985; Schneider-Rosen & Cicchetti, 1984; Schneider-Rosen, Braunwald, Carlson, & Cicchetti, 1985). In studies that employed the traditional Ainsworth et al. (1978) classification scheme, approximately two-thirds of the maltreated infants had insecure attachments to their mothers, while one-third of these children were securely attached. The reverse pattern was found for the nonmaltreated comparisons in these investigations (see, e.g., Schneider-Rosen et al., 1985). In addition, both cross-sectional and longitudinal studies revealed that with increasing age, maltreated infants' attachments were more likely to be manifested as insecure-avoidant (Type A).

During the coding of these videotapes of mothers and children in the Strange Situation, a number of investigators of maltreated children became increasingly dissatisfied with the traditional A-B-C attachment-coding scheme because they observed patterns of behavior in their assessment of attachments in the Strange Situation that did not fit smoothly into the original attachment-rating system (e.g., Egeland & Sroufe, 1981). Earlier, we described how one outgrowth of this situation led to the discovery of a new type of attachment, the disorganized-disoriented, or Type D pattern. In 1988, Crittenden identified another atypical attachment pattern through her observations of children who had experienced various forms of maltreatment. Crittenden found that approximately 90% of the maltreated children that she observed in the Strange Situation were insecurely attached. This percentage is very congruent with the 90% insecurity rate reported by Lyons-Ruth, Connell, and Zoll (1989; Lyons-Ruth, Connell, Zoll, & Stahl, 1987). Interestingly, however, when Crittenden examined the relationship between quality of attachment and type of maltreatment, she found that children who were abused, or abused and neglected, were far more likely to be classified as A-C (50% and 58%, respectively). Crittenden noticed that these maltreated children displayed unusual patterns of mod- erate-to-high levels of avoidance in combination with moderate-to-high levels of resistance (hence the label "A-C" or avoidant-ambivalent).

While there are theoretical distinctions between Main and Solomon's (1990) and Crittenden's (1992) theories of disorganization, most investiga- tors have chosen to view the A-C category as a subtype of the disorga- nized-disoriented (Type D) category. Moreover, all researchers consider the A-C and D classifications as atypical patterns of attachment. Fully aware of the differing viewpoints of Main and Solomon (1990) and Crit- tenden (1992), we nonetheless have chosen to view the A-C pattern as a variant of the disorganized-disoriented category (Carlson, Cicchetti, Bar- nett, & Braunwald, 1988b).

The discovery of the disorganized-disoriented pattern has proven to be very useful to maltreatment researchers. When samples of maltreated children that had been coded using the traditional A-B-C system were reexamined by coders unaware of maltreatment status or prior attachment classifications, and raters considered the new Type D category along with the avoidant, secure, and ambivalent subtypes, the findings changed dra- matically. For example, Carlson et al. (1989a) reported the reanalysis of 12-month-old babies in the Strange Situation (Schneider-Rosen, et al., 1985). In comparison to the earlier finding that one-third of the maltreated infants were securely attached, the reanalysis revealed that only 14% of the maltreated sample were securely attached, while 82% of the infants had Type D attachments with their primary caregiver and 4% had Type A attachments. In contrast, 52% of the nonmaltreated infants had secure attachments, while 19% were classified as Type D. The remaining 29% were either insecure-avoidant (Type A) or insecure-ambivalent (Type C).

In addition to improving the reliability of the attachment-coding sys- tem, the disorganized/disoriented category enhances the validity of the classification system. Six maltreated infants who were insecure Type D would have been classified as secure Type B had the new category not been available. This finding parallels Crittenden's (1988) and Spieker and Booth's (1988) A-C results with other high-risk samples. Infants given the avoidant/ambivalent classification in their studies were frequently rated as secure prior to the development of the new category, and they were often among the most severely maltreated in the sample, or from families who had the most difficulties. By indicating limitations in the traditional tripartite scheme, these findings underscore the importance and validity of the current expanded system, as well as the influence of atypical populations in informing theory and research.

Moreover, the D category has great potential for increasing the predictive validity of the attachment system. As discussed earlier, Main et al. (1985) have already demonstrated differential sequelae at 6 years for children who were rated as insecure A and D and secure B at 12 months. Unfortunately their sample size of C's was not large enough to be included in their analyses. Still, these findings are in contrast to other studies that have not been able to distinguish sequelae of different insecure groupings. A significant criticism of the attachment paradigm has focused on the absence of specific hypotheses regarding the outcomes of the different attachment categories (Connell and Goldsmith, 1982; Lamb, 1987). The D category may help to resolve this issue. By eliminating false B's and by identifying infants who would have been force-classified as A's or C's, the D category may greatly increase the predictive power of the attachment system.

Recently, there have been findings of substantial stability in the Type D attachment pattern across the ages of 12, 18, and 24 months. Barnett, Ganiban, and Cicchetti (1992) found that approximately 60% of the maltreated infants who were classified as Type D at 12 months received the same classification at 24 months, while over 90% of the infants classified as Type D at 24 months had been classified as Type D at either 12 or 18 months.

As maltreated children grow older, though, it appears less certain that they will have disorganized-disoriented patterns of attachment and that these atypical patterns will be stable over time. In an investigation of the attachments of 125 maltreated and nonmaltreated preschool children. Cicchetti and Barnett (1991) found that maltreated children were more likely to develop insecure attachments than were nonmaltreated children. Interestingly, they found that 30-month-old children who had been maltreated were significantly more likely to have disorganized patterns of attachment (i.e., Types D and A-C). However, even though approximately one-third of the 36-month-old and 48-month-old maltreated children were classified as having this atypical attachment pattern, this was not significantly greater than the proportion of nonmaltreated comparison children who had such disorganized attachment patterns.

Concerning the stability of these disorganized attachments, Cicchetti and Barnett (1991) found that 13 out of 28 (46.4% stability) maltreated children received a disorganized-attachment classification both on their initial attachment assessment and at follow-up 6 months later. In contrast, only 2 out of 12 nonmaltreated children exhibited stability of their atypical attachment pattern over time (16.6% stability). Thus, it appears that the stability of these disorganized-atypical attachments may be less stable during the preschool years than they are in infancy, especially for non-maltreated children.

An inspection of the total number of atypical-attachment classifications (e.g., D's and A-C's) for the entire Cicchetti and Barnett (1991) sample of preschoolers revealed that 10 of the 14 Type D classifications in the maltreatment group were force-classified as secure, while 9 of the 11 Type D classifications in the nonmaltreated group were force-classified as insecure (5 A's, 4 C's). Furthermore, in the maltreatment group, 23 of the 28 Type A-C classifications were force-classified as insecure (15 A's, 8 C's) as were 9 of the 10 Type A-C attachments of nonmaltreated children (7 A's, 2 C's). Thus, in the nonmaltreated sample, both D and A-C attachments were largely force-classified as insecure, while in the maltreatment group, Type D attachments were predominantly force-classified as secure and Type A-C attachments were primarily insecure.

As was the case in the work of Carlson et al. (1989a) with maltreated infants, a fairly large number (15.4%; $N = 10$) of maltreated children would have been classified incorrectly as secure had the Type D pattern not been discovered. In contrast, most of the Type D attachments in the comparison group would have been correctly classified as insecure. Of note here is the finding that 53.5% (15 of 28) of maltreated A-C's and 70% (7 of 10) of nonmaltreated A-C's were force-classified as Type A. Given the findings of Lyons-Ruth, Repacholi, McLeod, and Silva (1991) regarding differential-development sequelae for children with atypical attachment patterns of varying etiologies, it will be important to ascertain whether the maltreated children with anomalous attachment patterns who were force-classified as secure have a better prognosis that those who were force-classified as insecure. Despite the fact that a greater percentage of maltreated children were insecurely attached to their mothers at each of the ages studied, 29.6%, 20.5%, and 30.6% of the 30-, 36-, and 48-month-old maltreated children, respectively, exhibited secure relationships with their mothers. Rather than assuming that these children represent a resilient group who are less vulnerable to the negative impact of early maltreatment, an examination of our longitudinal results reveals instability of security in the maltreated children, with the majority shifting to insecure classifications in subsequent assessments. Unlike the instability found in security among maltreated children, the high stability of secure attachments in the non-maltreatment group is consistent with the conclusions reached by Lamb, Thompson, Gardner, Charnov, and Estes (1985). After reviewing the lit-erature on the longitudinal stability of attachment, Lamb and his colleagues found that secure attachments were characterized by greater stability than were insecure attachments. In contrast, in the Cicchetti and Barnett (1991) sample as well as in other samples (Schneider-Rosen et al., 1985), the maltreated children are characterized by less stability of secure attachments, and a greater stability of insecure attachments, while comparison children in these studies mirror the findings reported by Lamb et al. (1985).

While the low percentage of stable-secure attachments found in maltreated children is illuminating, the occurrence of secure attachments in maltreated children also must be addressed. While one might again question the accuracy of the coding system, this interpretation seems unlikely. Rather, these data are consistent with models which posit that transactions among parent, child, and environmental factors determine quality of attachment (see Cicchetti & Schneider-Rosen, 1986; Cummings & Cicchetti, 1990). According to such conceptualizations, a maltreated child could manifest a secure attachment relationship with the caregiver because of other factors that have protected the child, such as the provision of intervention services to the family. In these instances, it is possible that the child will evidence resiliency over time. This outcome is most likely in those cases where maltreatment has been more transient. In cases of severe, chronic maltreatment perpetrated by the caregiver, secure attachment relationships are highly unlikely.

In a study of school-age children, Lynch and Cicchetti (1991) found that approximately 30% of maltreated children between the ages of 7 and 13 years reported having "confused" patterns of relatedness to their mothers. As described earlier, children with this confused pattern report high levels of emotional quality as well as extremely high amounts of psychological-proximity seeking. Despite feeling emotionally positive and secure in their relationships, children with confused patterns of relatedness feel that they need much more psychological proximity than they are receiving. In other words, they report feeling positive affect and security despite feeling very unsatisfied with how close they are to the other person. The identification of a confused pattern of relatedness may be consistent with reports that some maltreated children manifest a basic confusion, disorganization or disorientation in how they mentally represent their relationships with their mothers. This finding of significantly more confused patterns of relatedness in maltreated than in nonmaltreated school age children suggests that distortions in maltreated children's relationships with, and mental representations of, their caregivers may persist up through the preadolescent years, though at a lower rate than found in early infancy but comparable to that found during the preschool years.

There are several possible explanations for the apparent decline in disorganized/atypical attachment patterns at older ages. It is conceivable that the attachment coding system for preschool children (Cassidy and Marvin, 1992) may utilize overly conservative criteria for detecting disorganization in the attachments of older children. It also is possible that older children represent their maltreating attachment relationship in ways that are organized differently than the representations of younger children. Cognitive maturity may play a role in how children are able to represent maltreating relationships and themselves in such relationships, and how they are able to organize their attachment-behavior strategies. Disorganization may be a characteristic feature of less-differentiated and less-integrated mental relationships and strategies (cf. Kaplan, 1966). Severity, chronicity, and type of maltreatment, as well as specific abuse history, most likely also interact with cognitive maturity in determining the nature of mental representation. It is clear that many important questions remain to be answered regarding the manner in which relationship experiences and cognitive maturity interact as determinants of mental representation.

Regardless of these issues, the findings on the prevalence and stability of disorganized attachments in maltreated children point to the extreme risk that these children face in achieving adaptive outcomes in other domains of interpersonal relationships. Working models of these insecure and often atypical attachments, in concert with complementary models of self and other, may generalize to new relationships, leading to negative expectations of how others will behave and how successful the self will be in relation to others (Bowlby, 1973, 1980; Bretherton, 1991; Cicchetti, 1991; Lynch & Cicchetti, 1991).

Supporting evidence that points to the potentially deleterious effect of maltreated children's early representational models on their subsequent relationships with others can be seen in reports of their feelings of relatedness with others. When children respond to relatedness items dealing with the emotional quality of, and the desire for greater psychological proximity in relationships with different social partners, they presumably are accessing the relevant representational models of these partners and of themselves in relation to those partners. Moreover, information from both models that are specific to a given relationship and models of relationships that reflect an aggregation of general experience with many individuals may be evaluated (Crittenden, 1990; Lynch & Cicchetti, 1991). Factual knowledge about the relationship as well as affects connected to the relationship are recalled. This is possible because similar relationship events are encoded into episodic memory when they are organized into prototypical memories (Stern, 1985). These prototypes are representatives of general emotions and cognitions, events, and behavioral patterns located in the semantic, episodic, and procedural memory systems, respectively (Crittenden, 1990; Tulving, 1985).

School-age children's reports of their feelings of relatedness to others indicate the potentially damaging ways in which maltreated children's representational models may be interlinked. First, maltreated children report feeling significantly less close to their mothers, as well as to their best friends and their peers in school and in camp, than do nonmaltreated children (Lynch & Cicchetti, 1991). Moreover, maltreated children's patterns of relatedness with their mother have a significant effect on their feelings of relatedness with others. Maltreated children are less likely to have optimal patterns of relatedness with their mothers than nonmaltreated children and more likely to have confused patterns (Lynch & Cicchetti, 1991). Along these lines, maltreated children have been found to be more likely to report confused patterns of relatedness with their best friends than nonmaltreated children. The prevalence of confused and other nonoptimal patterns of relatedness in maltreated children's relationships with others may suggest a more general problem in these children's ability to form goal-corrected partnerships. By examining maltreated children's feelings of relatedness with multiple relationship partners, it may be possible to identify the separate and joint contributions of generalized and specific representational models in children's relationships.

Attachment theory suggests that organizing effects of earlier representational models are brought forward through later childhood and into adulthood (Sroufe, 1989). For individuals who have had abusive or neglectful experiences of being parented in childhood, insecure patterns of adult-attachment organization are likely to predominate. Among mothers with early maltreatment experiences and consequent dismissing or preoccupied adult-attachment organizations, repetition of maladaptive parenting practices and maltreatment has been demonstrated (Main & Goldwyn, 1984), whereas mothers who have been able to work through and resolve early aversive experiences were shown to be unlikely to engage in maltreatment (see also Egeland, Jacobvitz, & Sroufe, 1988; Hunter & Kilstrom, 1979). The insecure adult-attachment organizations, as a result of difficulties in processing and integrating cognition and affect, allow for internal representational models to guide interpersonal relations in ways consistent with prior experiences. Because aspects of both the attachment figure and the self are incorporated into the internal representational model (Sroufe & Fleeson, 1986), the maltreatment aspects of early relationships may be replayed as internal representational models guide and direct current parenting behavior with one's child. Thus, attachment theory, through its characterization of internal representational models, has offered a valuable organizing framework for understanding why maltreatment may be transmitted across generations as well as offering an integrative system for understanding cognitive and affective components of a parent's processing of attachment relationships that may eventuate in maltreatment.

Crittenden (1988; Crittenden & Ainsworth, 1989) discusses aspects of abusing and neglecting parents in conjunction with their insecure internal-representational models of attachment and consequences for family relationships. Abusing mothers, more frequently characterized by a dismissing attachment organization, are seen as having internal representational models based on power, conflict, control, and rejection. Interpersonal relations are guided by the expectations that others are out to dominate and subjugate them coercively, and that the self will be rejected if fulfillment of one's own needs is sought. Needed psychological resources from others are expected to be withheld. Coercion and victimization are prominent interpersonal strategies, with anger being the predominant affect. Guided by power and coercion, one either asserts a powerful position or responds submissively, depending on the evaluation of power differentials in relationships. When harshness and punitiveness are prevalent in their own upbringing, parents believe that harshness is essential to direct children to meet high parental standards, and so they rely on harsh physical discipline to structure the children's behavior. Because these parents defend against the recognition of the resentment and anger they experienced in childhood, they do not recognize the relationship between their harsh parenting behaviors and affective reactions of their children.

In contrast, neglecting mothers have internal representation models organized around helplessness (Crittenden, 1988). They typically do not see others or themselves as being able to provide needed support and resources. Emptiness and depression are prominent associated affective experiences. Having likely experienced pervasive neglect in their own childhoods, these parents have difficulty asserting themselves or taking responsibility for their children; they are usually dependent and have limited coping skills to take charge of their lives. They also generally have few expectations for their children or themselves and tend to be unresponsive and withdrawn. Due to their ambivalence, they tend to be inconsistent in responding to their children; they may yell when upset, but following through with parenting directives is difficult. Through their passivity, they tend to deprive their children of needed social and environmental stimulation.

Crittenden (1998) also discusses maltreating families in which both abuse and neglect are involved. The co-occurrence of abuse and neglect may evolve as punitive disciplinary strategies or detached styles of relating increasingly are ineffective in managing family life. As family disorganization increases as a result of disturbances in relating and consequent behavioral difficulties in the children, parents tend to lash out more frequently in anger, frustration, and exasperation. Punishment is not employed to modify child behavior; rather it occurs randomly and erratically when parental frustration and helplessness are high. The demands of the family increasingly become overwhelming, and disorganization and rigid or limited coping skills and parenting skills contribute to greater difficulty in meeting the growing physical and emotional needs of the children. The erratic nature of parental behavior results in children having greater difficulty in predicting parental behavior, leading to chronic anxiety and uncertainty.

Not only do the internal representational models of maltreating parents guide their behavior with their children, but they also have a powerful influence on the selection of and relational quality between spouses or parenting partners (Crittenden, Partridge, & Claussen, 1991). In examining the Adult Attachment Interviews of a sample of maltreating mothers and their spouses or partners, Crittenden and her colleagues found rates of Dismissing or Preoccupied-Entangled adult-attachment organizations in both the females and males exceeding 90%. Comparison of the attachment organizations of the women and men demonstrated two patterns. There was either a match between the adults' attachment organizations, both Dismissing or both Preoccupied, or there was a complementary "mesh" between them with one partner Dismissing and the other Preoccupied. In contrast, in low-income families parenting their children adequately, secure adult-attachment organizations were common, as were matches between spouses, with both partners being secure. In the maltreating families, secure adult-attachment organization, a match of secure organization between partners, and a union between secure and insecure partners were all nearly nonexistent.

The melding of insecure attachment organizations in the spousal subsystem in maltreating families poses further risks for the quality of parenting these parents are likely to implement based on dysfunctional relational patterns that are extended across relationships to interactions with children. In matched couples, either Dismissing or Preoccuppied-Entangled, the individuals have sought partners who deal with affect and relational experience in similar ways and consistently with the history of relationships the individuals have internalized. Historical relational conflicts are likely to be replayed in these partnerships. In meshed couples, partners may be seeking mates who fulfill incomplete aspects of their personalities. The Dismissing partner, defended against affect, relies on the Preoccupied partner, focused on affect, to maintain the relationship, and the Preoccu-pied-Entangled partner desperately clings dependently to the Dismissing partner for fulfillment of needs and fear of abandonment. These patterns in couples are likely to result in considerable disharmony and frequent conflicts. A pattern of coerciveness and victim–victimizer relational inter-actions is frequent in maltreating families (Howes & Cicchetti, 1993). Spou-sal violence and abuse is also common. The conflictual nature of these partner relationships is likely to detract from attention paid to the chil-dren's needs as well as increase the volatility of the emotional climate in the family, intensifying the risk for violence being extended to the children.

Although some marital or partner relationships may be enduring, it is more likely that instability in the partner relationships predominates. Ei-ther partner goes through frequent and erratic separations and reunions, or mothers may have a series of idealized relationships that quickly de-teriorate and impulsively are terminated (Howes & Cicchetti, 1993). Howes and Cicchetti note a customary peripheral role of men in maltreat-ing families. These patterns of couple instability are likely to relate to the inability of the individuals to integrate their experiences of the relationship and the associated aspects into their internal representational models. As such, the likelihood of repetition of these problems is increased (Critten-den & Ainsworth, 1989), and the chaotic, disorganized character of family life in which parenting is conducted is perpetuated.

5.2. Depression

Throughout his writings on separation and loss, Bowlby (1969/1982, 1973, 1980) argues that, when faced with separation from their primary caregiver, children experience anxiety. In cases of prolonged or sustained loss, an intense mourning process ensues, and if continued beyond the normally expected period of grieving, is viewed as a reflection of an unresolved loss. Without the presence of a secure, internal working model of the primary caregiver, Bowlby believed that any loss would be ex-perienced as paramount. Conversely, the development of a good-quality working model of the major attachment figure was thought to serve as a buffer for minimizing the extent and duration of devastation experienced in the face of loss.

In terms of the development of internal working models, the psycho-logical unavailability of parents for long periods can be viewed as a power-ful influence in shaping expectations that attachment figures are unavail-able and the self is unlovable. The implicit communication to the child is that he or she is unworthy of love, that is, worthless and rejected, and that the parent is "lost" to the child. The recurrent loss of the parent as a function of major depressive episodes that some children experience may be equivalent in impact on the child's self-concept to the effects of recurrent major separations. This "loss" can also be seen as parallel to the perceptions of loss that precipitate depressive patterns (Beck, 1967). Early experiences of "loss" may be particularly powerful because they mold fundamental cognitive, emotional, and social-response patterns. The psychological unavailability of parents, the development of insecure attachments and representational models of attachment figures and of the self in relation to others in children, and children's developing precursors of depression or clinical depression thus may be conceptualized as interrelated processes.

Children of depressed parents are particularly likely to be faced with the psychological unavailability of parents for long periods, especially during, but not necessarily restricted to, episodes of depression (Field, 1989). Such children are exposed to sad and dysphoric affect, helplessness and hopelessness, irritability, confusions, and, in bipolar depression, to these episodes sometimes alternating with periods of euphoria and grandiosity. Thus, there are compelling reasons for considering psychological unavailability of the parent to be a risk factor for the development of insecure attachment in children of depressed parents.

On the other hand, not all children of depressed parents will develop insecure attachments. A secure relationship with a nondepressed parent may act as a protective factor against attachment insecurity. This psychological protection might be especially salient if the nondepressed parent is able to be emotionally available to the child at times when the spouse is experiencing more acute episodes of depression (Cummings & Cicchetti, 1990; Downey & Coyne, 1990). Additionally, it is the nature of the caregiving provided, not depression *per se* that will contribute to the child's insecurity (Hammen, 1992).

Several studies have been conducted that have assessed the quality of parent–child attachment relations in the offspring of parents with unipolar and bipolar mood disorders. In a pioneering study, Egeland and Sroufe (1981) compared the effects of (a) psychological unavailability and depression, (b) physical abuse and hostility, and (c) neglect. One focus of their study addressed changes in attachment patterns between the ages of 12 and 18 months. The greatest increase in insecure attachment between the ages of 12 and 18 months was in the group characterized by maternal depression and psychological unavailability. At 18 months, 100% of the children of psychologically unavailable mothers were insecurely attached, with over three-fourths of these children classified as avoidant and the rest classified as ambivalent.

Radke-Yarrow, Cummings, Kuczynski, and Chapman (1985) compared patterns of attachment in children of mothers with major unipolar and bipolar depression, minor depression, and no affective disorder. The children ranged in age from 15 to 52 months when they were observed in the Strange Situation and all sessions were coded using Ainsworth's original classification system, with adaptations made to the coding system to accommodate the developmental changes in the older children of their sample.

When these investigators examined the patterns of attachment in their four groups, they found a higher proportion of insecure attachments in children of parents with major unipolar and bipolar depressive disease than in children from the other two groups. For children with a caregiver having major unipolar depression, 47% had insecure attachments with their primary caregiver (27% A, 3% C, 17% A-C) and 53% were classified as securely attached. In contrast, 25% of the offspring of parents with a minor depression (17% A, 75% B, 8% C, 0% A-C) and 29% of the no-depression control group (29% A, 71% B, 0% C, 0% A-C) were classified as securely attached. Additionally, children of bipolar-depressed parents were most likely to develop insecure attachments (43% A, 21% B, 7% C, 29% A-C).

Recently, DeMulder and Radke-Yarrow (1991) recoded the Strange Situations of the children described in the earlier Radke-Yarrow et al. (1985) study. DeMulder and Radke-Yarrow (1991) utilized the Ainsworth et al. (1978) coding system for children under 30 months of age and employed the Cassidy and Marvin (1992) classification system when categorizing the attachments of children 30 months of age and older. Not surprising given the use of the more age-sensitive coding schemes that were employed by DeMulder and Radke-Yarrow (1991), the results of their attachment recoding differed somewhat from the initial report. Across ages studied, 42% of the offspring of the unipolar and no-affective-disorder groups were insecurely attached to their caregiver. In contrast, 67% of bipolar offspring had developed insecure attachments. Because the investigators combined the major unipolar depressive and minor depression groups from the earlier study into one unipolar group and apparently added some additional new subjects ($N = 112$ vs. 98) to this recoding of the data, it is difficult to comment about the lack of differences found between the unipolar and well groups. However, the rate of insecurity in the bipolar groups was comparable to that reported in the prior paper (67% vs. 79%, respectively). Approximately 50% of the offspring of bipolar mothers were found to have disorganized-disoriented attachments, a rate consistent with findings for other high-risk samples (Carlson et al., 1989a; Lyons-Ruth, Connell & Zoll, 1989).

Lyons-Ruth, Connell, Grunebaum, and Botein (1990; see also Lyons-

Ruth et al., 1987) found that infants of depressed mothers who had been receiving a 1-hour weekly home-visiting service for 9 or more months were twice as likely to develop a secure attachment (40% vs. 20%) and only one-sixth as likely to develop an insecure attachment (9% vs. 54%) than infants whose mothers were depressed and untreated. Interestingly, unserved infants of depressed mothers displayed particularly high rates of disorganized-disoriented attachments compared to infants of depressed mothers who received the family-support treatment (54% vs. 22%, respectively).

As is apparent, the rates of insecurity are far higher in the Lyons-Ruth et al. sample than in the DeMulder and Radke-Yarrow sample. However, there are important differences in social class background, and other demographic factors between the two groups of depressed women. The sample of Lyons-Ruth and her colleagues is a multirisk, low-SES one, while the DeMulder and Radke-Yarrow sample is comprised primarily of volunteer middle- and upper-middle-SES families (see also Cohn & Campbell, 1992, for similar results to DeMulder & Radke-Yarrow, 1991, from a large community-based screening of middle-SES women for depression during the postpartum period).

When these children were between 4 and 6 years of age (mean age = 59 months), approximately 80% (N = 62) of the original sample participated in a subsequent investigation (Lyons-Ruth, Alpern, & Repacholi, 1993). During the follow-up assessment period, teachers completed the Preschool Behavior Questionnaire (PBQ) (Behar & Stringfield, 1974a) for the children in the study, as well as for three same-sex classmates nearest in age. Factor analyses of the PBQ have yielded three factors: *anxious, hostile,* and *hyperactive* (Behar & Stringfield, 1974b).

The most powerful single predictor of deviant levels of hostile behavior being exhibited toward peers was disorganized-disoriented attachment status. Looking backward from the teacher assessment to earlier assessments, it was found that 71% of hostile preschoolers were classified as having a disorganized attachment at their 18-month Strange Situation assessment. In contrast, only 12% of children manifesting deviant hostile behavior were securely attached during infancy. It is likely that for some infants, disorganized attachment may prove to be a potential precursor of later maladaptation, long before actual childhood disorders develop and become manifest.

In the most recent longitudinal assessment of the Lyons-Ruth et al. (1987, 1990) sample, Easterbrooks, Davidson, and Chazan (1993) located 45 of the 62 children seen at 5 years of age. When the children were age 7, security of attachment to their mothers was assessed in an hour-long separation-reunion procedure in the laboratory. In addition, the mothers and teachers of these children provided reports of the children's behavior problems using the Child Behavior Checklist (CBCL; Achenbach & Edelbrock, 1981, 1986).

The Main and Cassidy (1988) separation-reunion codings revealed that 45% of the sample were insecurely attached to their caregivers (19% A, 12% C, 14% D-controlling). Quality of attachment also was related to children's reported behavior problems. Specifically, both mothers and teachers rated children who were securely attached to manifest fewer internalizing and externalizing symptoms and to evidence fewer total behavior problems than children who were classified as insecurely attached.

In a further exploration of the behavior-problems data, classifications were made as to whether the children's behavior-problem scores fell into the "clinical range" using the standard Achenbach and Edelbrock (1981, 1986) cutoff scores. The results of these analyses revealed that maternal reports placed 42% of the children in the clinical range, while teachers' ratings resulted in a 24% placement above the clinical cutoff. Examinations of the relationship between attachment status and the presence of behavior problems in the clinical range revealed that securely attached children were significantly less likely to be placed in the clinical range by either mother- or teacher-CBCL ratings. Finally, 45% of the children with a secure attachment relationship to their mother received scores above the clinical cutoff from either their mothers or teachers, compared to 83% of those with insecure attachment relationships (88% of A's; 60% of C's; and 100% of the D-controlling groups).

Utilizing a developmental pathways model (Bowlby, 1988; Cicchetti, 1993; Sroufe, 1986), Kobak et al. (1991) examined the relations between adolescents' quality of attachment on the Adult Attachment Interview and their self-reported depressive symptoms. The Adult Attachment Interviews were scored using the Q-Set developed by Kobak. Adolescents who were characterized by insecure attachment strategies had elevated levels of depressive symptomatology, both concurrently and 10–11 months prior to receiving the Adult Attachment Interview. In contrast, teenagers with secure strategies had significantly lower levels of depressed symptomatology. Thus, an adolescent's ability to generate coherent discourse about him- or herself in relation to attachment figures appeared to act as a protective factor against depressive symptoms. The findings reported by Kobak and his colleagues (1991) dovetail nicely with an earlier study by Kobak and Sceery (1988), which found an association between adolescent secure-attachment strategies and positive outcomes during the transition to college. Furthermore, the reported association between insecure-attachment strategies and depressive symptoms provides important evidence that attachment remains as an important developmental task in adolescence.

Pearson, Cohn, P. Cowan, and C. Cowan (1994) also have investigated the association between quality of attachment and depressed symptomatology. These investigators administered the Adult Attachment Interview in conjunction with an assessment of depressive symptoms to adults predominantly in their mid-thirties. Using the Main and Goldwyn (in press) classification system for rating the nature of early relationships and coherency of discourse, Pearson and her colleagues identified three types of adult attachment: *earned-security, continuous security,* and *insecurity.* Earned-secure classifications were assigned to individuals who were classified as securely attached despite their discussion of difficult or adverse early relationships during the Attachment interview, while those designated as continuous-secures were characterized by both early and current secure models of attachment. Those classified as insecure had adverse early attachment-relationship experiences as well as a current insecure state of mind with respect to attachment issues.

When Pearson et al. (1994) examined the relation between attachment-security and depressive symptomatology, interesting findings emerged. Adults who received earned-secure classifications had comparable depressive symptoms to adults who were rated as insecurely attached. Thirty percent of the insecures and 40% of the earned-secures had depression scores that exceeded the clinical cutoff on the self-report measure employed in this investigation (i.e., the Center for Epidemiological Studies Depression (CES-D) Scale; Radloff, 1977). In contrast, only 10% of the adults classified as having continuous-secure attachments exceeded the clinical cutoff on the CES-D. The increased amount of depressive symptomatology in the earned-secure than in the continuous-secure group provides suggestive evidence that adult reconstructions of past relationship difficulties may remain as emotional vulnerabilities despite the presence of a currently secure working model of attachment relationships.

Additionally, ratings of the parenting style of these adults were made based on observations of a series of structured and unstructured parent–child interactional tasks conducted in the laboratory. Interestingly, consistent with the predictions of attachment theory, the parenting styles of the earned-secure adults were remarkably similar to those of the continuously secure adults.

Because developmental psychopathologists are interested in alternate pathways to competence and in how adverse experiences and adaptational failures in early development place children at risk for subsequent difficulties (Cicchetti, 1993), we believe that attachment research will profit greatly from future examinations of the similarities and differences between individuals with earned-secure and those with continuous-secure attachments. As is apparent, secure attachment does not ensure absence of psychopathology, nor is insecure attachment a sufficient cause for clinical difficulties. It is conceivable that certain insecure strategies (in particular, the deactivation of attachment or dismissing strategy observed in the Pearson et al. study) may prevent the adult from confronting his or her emotional difficulties, while a secure strategy against the backdrop of early adversity may be associated with a greater openness to dealing directly with emotional pain (i.e., becoming depressed; cf. Zigler & Glick, 1986). While individuals with insecure and secure working models are trying to cope with their histories in an adaptive fashion, longitudinal investigations of individuals with earned-secure working models reveal that these individuals develop more competently than insecures, even if at some points they experience periods of emotional difficulty.

In an investigation of adult-attachment organization, Patrick, Hobson, Castle, Howard, and Maughan (1994) administered the Adult Attachment Interview to 12 adults on the psychotherapy waiting list at a major hospital who were diagnosed as dysthymic. Patrick et al. (1994) found that 10 of the 12 dysthymic persons they interviewed (83%) were classified as insecurely attached. Utilizing the Main and Goldwyn (in press) system of considering the entire transcript of the interview, Patrick et al. (1994) discovered that 6 of the dysthymic adults (50%) had Dismissing attachment organizations, 4 received Preoccupied-Entangled classifications (33%), and 2 were considered to be Free or Autonomous (17%). In addition, 2 of the 12 dysthymic individuals received the Unresolved/disorganized-disoriented classification. Interestingly, while 5 of the persons with dysthymia had experienced physical beatings and other major trauma in childhood, none were classified as Unresolved/disorganized-disoriented.

Clearly, a wealth of data has accumulated from research conducted with groups of infants, toddlers, preschoolers, and school-aged children who have depressed caregivers. Additionally, studies examining links between attachment organization and the development of depression in normal, nonrisk individuals, as well as in individuals with dysthymia, have begun to emerge. However, direct evidence of a relationship between insecure attachment and later depression has not yet been obtained. Insecure attachment can only be regarded as a risk factor for deviant outcomes, including depression, within the context of a complex developmental model (see Cummings & Cicchetti, 1990). It is important to remember that there are diverse familial mechanisms through which depression might be linked with insecure attachment and risk for depression. These include maternal attributions toward the child, childrearing practices associated with the socialization of affect, and facial expressions and body posture as aspects of the caregiver's emotion language (Cicchetti & Schneider-Rosen, 1986; Cohn, Matias, Tronick, Connell, & Lyons-Ruth, 1986). Identification of the links between parental depression and insecure attachment is only an initial step toward delimiting the bases for such relations. If depression in parents is linked to insecure attachment, the insecurity may be attributable to the effect that depression has in influencing aspects of parent–child interaction, as well as to its role in determining broader aspects of the childrearing environment. An important aspect of this caregiving environment is likely to be the psychological unavailability of the parent during periods of depression.

Early insecure-attachment relationships may lead children to be more vulnerable to depression by causing them to have very low internalized feelings of felt security. When faced with stress, such children are likely to have few resources for coping and may easily be prone to developing lower self-esteem, intensified feelings of insecurity, and sad affect. In addition, the cognitions that the insecurely attached individual develops in the context of attachment relationships may contribute to the emergence of thought processes and affect that are associated with depression. As noted by Cummings and Cicchetti (1990), these cognitions centering around loss and the unacceptability of the self are likely to resemble patterns of cognitive processes that have been linked with depression in adults (Beck, 1976).

Even though an early secure-attachment relationship with the primary attachment figure increases the probability of maintaining a positive working model of the self and of attachment relations, an insecure attachment can manifest itself at any point across the life span. Accordingly, a life-span perspective suggests that the specifics of the relationship between attachment and depression may change greatly over time. For example, an insecure attachment at one period of development may have very different consequences for the emergence of depression than that of insecurity at another developmental period. The resulting causal network will be very complex. A depressive episode, when it occurs, may lead to insecure attachment and in turn result in a variety of effects, some perhaps maintaining the depression, others predisposing for future maladaptation, and still others leading to adaptation that may buffer against the experience of subsequent depressive episodes. Of course, insecure attachment and its role in the etiology of depression will vary as a consequence of the neurophysiological and biochemical systems that constitute the biological bases of depression.

5.3. Alcohol and Drug Abuse

The past several decades have witnessed an increasing number of investigations that have examined the detrimental sequelae of maternal substance abuse prenatally. Until recently, however, there was strikingly little information about the quality of the attachment relationship that develops between these children and their caregivers.

In the first study that investigated quality of attachment in such families, O'Connor, Sigman, and Brill (1987) examined 144 infants of women who had consumed varying amounts of alcohol before, during, and after delivery. The sample comprised a select group of predominantly highly educated, middle-SES, married, Caucasian women over 35 years of age. When the traditional Ainsworth et al. (1978) forced-classification system was applied, O'Connor and her colleagues found 65% of the sample to be securely attached, 24% to be insecure-avoidant, and 11% to be insecure-ambivalent. Their distribution of A, B, C percentages does not differ significantly from the 20%, 70%, and 10% proportions, respectively, found in other white, middle-SES samples (Ainsworth et al., 1978). However, the addition of the four-category A, B, C, D system resulted in different findings. Forty-eight percent of the babies were classified as secure, 13% as insecure-avoidant, 4% as insecure-ambivalent, and 35% as insecure-disorganized-disoriented (Type D). Although the authors did not provide the forced-classifications of the infants with disorganized-attachments, it is apparent that a number of infants who would have been classified as securely attached using the Ainsworth et al. (1978) system were more accurately placed in the D category. Infants of mothers who had consumed greater amounts of alcohol were significantly more likely to develop an insecure attachment than were those babies whose mothers had either abstained or had been light drinkers over a comparable temporal duration. Disorganized-disoriented attachments were especially common in the moderate-to-heavy drinking group of women, with a number infants who had been force-classified as securely attached found to be more appropriately categorized as Type D.

Rodning, Beckwith, and Howard (1991) studied quality of attachment in a group of 18 to 20-month-old toddlers from the low-SES who had been exposed to a variety of drugs before birth (N = 18) and compared them to toddlers from similar SES backgrounds who were born prematurely (N = 39). All toddlers born prematurely, including the drug-exposed, were assessed at corrected gestational age. The mothers of the drug-exposed group had used a variety of drugs prenatally, including cocaine (N = 14), heroine (N = 8), methadone (N = 6), and phencyclidine (PCP)(N = 4).

Of the toddlers who were drug-exposed, 61% had formed insecure attachments with their caregivers (50% A, 11% C), while only 23% of the toddlers who had been born prematurely were insecurely attached (5% A, 18% C). Only 39% of the drug-exposed toddlers, compared with 77% for the premature group, were securely attached.

Finally, while the toddlers whose mothers had abused drugs prenatally were no more likely to develop disorganized-disoriented attachments than the toddlers who had been born prematurely (39% vs. 29%, respectively), an examination of the forced-classifications of these two groups yielded interesting information. Of the toddlers whose mothers had abused drugs prenatally, 7 were classified as Type D. Six of the 7 were force-classified as insecure-avoidant, while one was force-classified as insecure-ambivalent. In contrast, 10 of the premature toddlers were given a disorganized-disoriented attachment classification. However, forced-classification categorized 6 of the premature toddlers as secure and 4 as insecure-ambivalent. Longitudinal follow-up will clarify whether the toddlers with disorganized-disoriented classifications who were force-classified as secure have a better prognosis than those force-classified as insecure (cf. Lyons-Ruth et al., 1991).

Rodning, Beckwith, and Howard (1991) compared the attachment organization of a group of 15-month-old infants who had been prenatally exposed to the drugs PCP and cocaine with a group of infants with non-substance-abusing mothers of comparable ethnicity and SES who also were living in the same inner-city environment. Postnatally, the substance-abusing biological mothers continued to use hard drugs (e.g., 74% used cocaine). In addition, more of these mothers drank alcohol (80%) than those in the comparison group (17%).

Because Rodning and her colleagues (1991) conducted a prospective longitudinal study from early infancy, it is not surprising that a number of the drug-exposed infants had been placed in alternate forms of care. Thus, Rodning et al. (1991) wisely chose to study these infants with their primary caregiving figure and not exclusively focus on the biological mother in their assessments of quality-of-attachment organization. Thus, 20 of these infants were observed with their biological mother as the primary caregiver, 11 were seen with their primary caregiver from the extended family with whom they were residing, and 7 were observed with their primary caregiver in the foster family in which they lived.

The vast majority of drug-exposed babies were found to have developed insecure attachments to their primary caregivers. Of the 38 infants who were seen in the Strange Situation, 31 (82%) were insecurely attached (15 A's, 16 C's). Only 18% of the drug-exposed infants had developed a secure attachment, compared to 64% of the comparison infants. In addition, the drug-exposed infants did not differ in their percentage of secure attachments across the three caregiving environments in which they were growing up. Only 20% of the infants living with their biological mothers ($N = 4$), 10% of the infants living with an extended family ($N = 1$), and 30% of those being reared in foster care ($N = 2$) developed secure attachments. Furthermore, change in caregivers during the infant's first year of life was not related to the rate of attachment insecurity in any of the childrearing environments.

The majority of the drug-exposed children had developed disorganized-disoriented (Type D) attachments. Twenty-six of the group of 38 drug-exposed babies were classified as Type D (69%), compared with 3 of the 25 comparisons (12%). An analysis of the forced-classifications reveals that of the 15 D's in the biological-mother group, 5 were force-classified as A's, 9 as C's, and 1 as B. Of the 7 D's in the extended-family group, 4 were force-classified as A, and 3 as C. Lastly, of the 4 D's in the foster-care group, 2 were force-classified as A, 1 as C, and 1 as B. In contrast, in the comparison group, 1 of the infants with disorganized-disoriented attachments was force-classified as A, whereas the other 2 were force-classified as C.

We find it noteworthy, yet logical, that there were so few securely attached babies in the substance-abuse group. In fact, their rates of insecurity are comparable to what has been found in most samples of maltreated infants (e.g., Carlson et al., 1989a; Cicchetti & Barnett, 1991; Crittenden, 1988). A number of investigators view mothers who ingest drugs prenatally or who administer drugs or illicit substances to their children as perpetrators of maltreatment (Barnett, Manly, & Cicchetti, 1993; Giovannoni & Bercerra, 1979).

5.4. Oppositional Defiant and Conduct Disorders

In examining the roots of externalizing symptomatology in childhood, the role of attachment and dysfunctional parent–child relationships has been implicated (Greenberg, Speltz, & DeKlyen, 1993). Insecure-attachment relationships may be a risk factor for the emergence of oppositional defiant and conduct disorder, either via mechanisms of parental representations of attachment relationships or through alternate routes that may operate independent of attachment. Specifically, in cases of externalizing behavior problems, caregiver expectations for the child may be either negative or unrealistic or based on a history of negative attachment representations. Greenberg and his colleagues (1993) specified three ways in which attachment may contribute to the emergence of these disorders:

1. The crystallization of working models in which relationships are viewed as characterized by anger, mistrust, chaos, and insecurity

2. Child behavior that serves as a strategy to gain the attention of and proximity to the caregiver when other strategies have failed
3. Insecure attachments that provide a motivational basis for developing a non-prosocial/resistant orientation to relationships

Speltz, Greenberg, and DeKlyen (1990) observed the responses of 50 preschool children, aged 3 to 6 years, to their mothers in a clinic laboratory using a modified separation-reunion procedure. Speltz and his colleagues employed a shorter procedure than that devised by Main and Cassidy (1988), opting for a briefer 3-minute maternal separation followed by a 3-minute reunion. The clinical group (n = 25) included children at a psychiatric clinic who had a primary diagnosis of oppositional defiant disorder. The comparison group (n = 25) were case-matched to the clinic children on the basis of age, sex, and a variety of demographic characteristics. All of the children in the comparison group had neither a history of a developmental delay or disability, nor of behavior problems.

Children who were under the age of 5 were classified according to the Cassidy and Marvin (1992) coding system, while those older than 5 were assessed by the Main and Cassidy (1988) reunion-coding procedure.

Speltz et al. (1990) found that 84% of the children with oppositional defiant disorder (ODD) were insecurely attached to their mothers compared with only 28% of the comparisons. Sixteen percent of the children with ODD and 72% of the comparison youngsters had developed secure attachments with their mothers. In addition, children with ODD were significantly more likely to protest their mother's departure and to search for her during the separation. Moreover, within the ODD groups, 95% of boys with ODD were insecurely attached, compared with 23% of males in the comparison group. Furthermore, 57% of the girls with ODD were insecurely attached, a percentage that was not significantly different from that of the girls in the comparison group. While the very small number of girls (7) precludes a definitive statement on gender differences in attachment in children with ODD from being made, the results underscore the need for future research with larger samples of girls with disruptive disorders.

Finally, a greater percentage of atypical attachments were present in the group with ODD. Fifty-six percent of the clinic-referred group had atypical attachments (i.e., 40% insecure-controlling and 16% insecure-other), while only 12% of the comparison groups received an atypical-attachment classification (i.e., 12% insecure-controlling and 0% insecure-other).

In a subsequent study, Greenberg, Speltz, DeKlyen, and Endriga (1991) recruited another cohort of children with ODD. These children, boys between the ages of 3.5 and 5.5 years, all had ODD as their primary disorder; in addition, the mothers of each of these boys rated them at the

98th percentile or above on at least one of the externalizing narrow-band scales of the CBCL (Achenbach & Edelbrock, 1981). Twenty-five boys served as case-matched comparisons. None of these boys had ODD or any other psychiatric disorder or developmental disability.

All children were observed with their mothers in a modified Strange Situation procedure conducted in a clinic laboratory. In the modified Strange Situation, each boy played together with his mother for 4 minutes; next, mothers were instructed to depart the room for 3 minutes, followed by a 3-minute mother-child reunion; finally, the 3-minute separation and 3-minute reunion sequence was repeated. Quality of attachment in boys less than 5 years of age was classified using the Cassidy and Marvin (1992) system, while the Main and Cassidy (1988) scheme was utilized with boys older than 5 years.

Twenty percent of the children with ODD were securely attached, compared with 72% of the comparisons. Of the 80% insecure attachments in the ODD group, 48% were atypical (i.e., 32% insecure-controlling and 16% insecure-other). In contrast, only 12% of the 28% insecurely attached comparison boys were classified as having an atypical attachment (i.e., 4% insecure-controlling and 8% insecure-other). Interestingly, of the insecure-controlling attachments, none were of the controlling-caretaking subtype.

Additionally, parents of the children in this investigation were administered the Adult Attachment Interview. Greenberg and his collaborators found a high degree of correspondence between adult-attachment organization and the child's security of attachment. Specifically, there was an 82% concordance for secure versus insecure attachment between parental state of mind with respect to attachment and child quality of attachment as indexed by children's patterns of behavioral organization in the separation-reunion procedure. Mothers of the children with ODD were more likely to have dismissing or Unresolved/disorganized-disoriented attachment organizations and less likely to be Free-Autonomous than were the mothers of the nonclinic children.

Now that research on attachment organization in a number of clinical populations has been discussed, we direct our attention toward the impact of this work on the provision of clinical services.

6. Intervention

6.1. Historical Considerations

Despite its historical links with psychoanalytic and object-relations perspectives, attachment theory has been slow to emerge as a mainstream force with respect to treatment. Discussions of the therapeutic implications of attachment theory have been primarily speculative, with few actual guidelines and even fewer efforts to evaluate the effectiveness of attachment-based interventions. In fact, Lieberman's (1991) observation that the senior author on the first book devoted to the clinical implications of attachment theory is a developmental researcher and not a clinical psychologist underscores the reluctance of clinicians to view attachment theory as relevant to the provision of intervention. Research guided by attachment theory has burgeoned, while clinical applications of this work have been much less visible. The reasons for this state of affairs are most likely multidetermined but may stem, in part, from the reluctance of Bowlby's colleagues in the field of psychoanalysis to embrace his departure from a more traditional theoretical stance (cf. Bretherton, 1992). Additionally, the preponderance of developmental psychologists who have integrated attachment theory into their research may have contributed to attachment theory falling victim to the all-too-frequent schism that exists between researchers and clinicians (Cicchetti & Toth, 1991b). Because research in developmental psychology often is conducted with little investment in seeing that resultant findings are disseminated and applied to problems of clinical import, difficulties in incorporating attachment theory into clinical interventions most likely have been exacerbated. In view of these obstacles, the emergence of interventions based in attachment theory speaks to the power of this theoretical paradigm not only for understanding the emergence of psychopathology, but also for guiding treatment.

6.2. Specific versus General Attachment Dysfunction

In order to integrate an attachment-theory perspective into clinical work, it is first necessary for the clinician to ascertain whether a psychopathological condition is the result of attachment dysfunction or whether the psychopathological condition has contributed to a disruption in attachment relationships. For example, it cannot be assumed that attachment difficulties have contributed to the symptomatology of every child who presents with oppositional defiant disorder, even if current difficulties are present in the parent–child relationship. Rather, parent–child conflict may have arisen in tandem with or subsequent to the emergence of the disorder. Additionally, although attachment dysfunction has been implicated in a number of psychiatric disorders, the ways in which insecure attachments promote the emergence of psychopathology are likely to vary (Cummings & Cicchetti, 1990). Moreover, insecure attachment may contribute to disorder in a number of ways (Cicchetti & Schneider-Rosen, 1986; Zeanah & Emde, 1994). In some disorders, insecure attachment may be a necessary but not a sufficient cause of dysfunction. In other cases, an individual may evidence a wide array of maladaptations, with insecurely organized attachment being one among many symptoms and not contributing any specific etiological role to the disorder. Finally, individuals with an actual attachment disorder also may have other disorders, resulting in comorbidity of diagnoses. In order for clinicians to organize an intervention strategy, they must ascertain the specific and independent or more general contributions that insecure attachment is making to dysfunction (Zeanah & Emde, 1994). Moreover, an exploration of insecure attachment as a *cause* or *correlate* of disorder must be made (cf. Cicchetti & Schneider-Rosen, 1986).

6.3. Assessment

As this discussion begins to elucidate, before intervention is initiated an assessment of the role of attachment dysfunction in presenting symptomatology must be conducted. Toward this end, observations of the parent–child relationship are necessary. Because a child may respond differently to different relationship figures (Crittenden, 1990; Main, 1991), interactions should be observed with both parents. This approach will provide a more comprehensive evaluation of the child's stance with respect to various relationship figures. If the child responds similarly to both caregivers even if they act differently toward him/her, the child may have developed a "crystallized" model of relationships that may be more difficult to modify than would a more "open" model of relationships (Crittenden, 1990). Additionally, if a child has generalized an insecure-attachment organization to new relationship opportunities, the child might be less likely to trust the therapist and attention would need to be directed toward issues related to the formation of a therapeutic alliance. Information on relationships with nonparental attachment figures (e.g., teachers, peers) also will be helpful in evaluating the pervasiveness of possible attachment difficulties, as well as in suggesting methods of intervention. With infants, the capacity to use the caregiver as a secure base from which to explore should be assessed, while in toddlerhood issues related to the negotiation of disparate goals of the child and caregiver (e.g., the goal-corrected partnership; see Bowlby 1969/1982; Marvin, 1977) reach ascendance. Naturalistic observations are especially critical and, whenever possible, the clinician should visit the child at home and/or day care and school. Interviews and history gathering, while always important, become more integral to the assessment process as children move from toddlerhood into early and later childhood. With adults, retrospective recall must be relied upon in reconstructing early attachment relationships and in ascertaining the role of resulting representational models on current functioning.

Although paradigms and interviews developed for use in research studies have not been validated for use in clinical settings, a number of the research measures previously described could be helpful in elucidating attachment organization. However, generalizations from group norms to the individual level would not be appropriate for clinical diagnosis or decision making. The problems associated with the use of research measures in clinical contexts have been emphasized by Greenspan and Lieberman (1988), who discussed the limitations of trying to apply the Strange Situation paradigm to clinical settings. Rather than drawing conclusions based on the use of assessments developed for research purposes, attachment paradigms could be helpful in information gathering that would then need to be evaluated clinically and integrated with collaborative information. As the use of research measures with clinical populations becomes more prevalent in studies developed specifically to evaluate treatment effectiveness, it may become possible to integrate these measures into clinical settings. However, in order to avoid any misuse of these measures, it is strongly recommended that this not occur until extensive work has been done regarding the necessary training and interpretive skills required to use these instruments appropriately.

6.4. Approaches to Intervention

In recent years, a number of attachment-based approaches to treatment have been developed and, increasingly, efforts to evaluate the effectiveness of these approaches have been initiated. Although attachment is an organizational construct that exerts influence on functioning across the life span, the preponderance of interventions derived from attachment theory have been directed toward the periods of infancy and toddlerhood. Nonetheless, we view attachment as being applicable to work with older children and adults and, therefore, will structure our discussion of intervention within a life-span perspective. Additionally, because research has implicated insecure attachment in a number of populations, including individuals with a history of maltreatment, children with a depressed caregiver or a substance-abusing parent, and children with oppositional defiant disorders, when possible we present intervention approaches that have been developed for use with these populations. However, because attachment-based intervention has not advanced as rapidly as has research, our ability to address all populations is limited. In fact, much of current intervention has been directed toward preventive interventions with populations at risk for the development of behavioral difficulties or a clinical disorder. As research findings on the role of attachment in psychopathology become more widely disseminated, it is likely that treatment strategies developed for use with specific disorders will become more visible. Rather than attempting to review all attachment-based intervention efforts, we focus on those that have been evaluated or have been especially integral to guiding work in this area.

6.4.1. Infancy and Toddlerhood

Infant–parent psychotherapy, perhaps the most widely utilized and evaluated approach to the treatment of attachment disorders in infancy and toddlerhood, is being applied to a range of populations (Fraiberg, 1980; Lieberman, 1992; Lieberman & Pawl, 1993). Based on the view that disorders of attachment emerge as a result of the baby's engulfment in the unresolved psychological conflicts of their mothers, Fraiberg, Adelson, and Shapiro (1975) eloquently portrayed an approach toward relationship therapy in their seminal article, "Ghosts in the Nursery." In this view, the baby was seen primarily as the recipient of parental projections of emotions, and as such, considered to have little contributory role in the relationship dysfunction.

Building on Fraiberg's work, Lieberman and her colleagues (Lieberman, 1991; Lieberman & Pawl, 1988, 1993) have placed increased emphasis on the contributions to interactional difficulties made by a young child's individual characteristics. Currently, infant–parent psychotherapy reflects an integration of object relations, psychoanalytic theory, and attachment theory that is geared toward the amelioration of attachment disorders by focusing on the role that early parental history exerts on the caregiving context. The physical presence of the infant or toddler in the therapeutic sessions also provides the therapist with the opportunity to assess the cause of interactional difficulties and to intervene directly with parent, child, or the dyad. In infant–parent psychotherapy, traditional individual, analytically based psychotherapy is used to explore the caregiver's past in order to understand current functioning. Although most commonly employed with mothers and their infants, infant–parent psychotherapy also can be utilized with fathers, couples, and single parents (Lieberman, 1991). However, the overarching goal of the intervention is not the alleviation of individual distress, but rather the reduction of parent–child conflict and the promotion of more affectively positive and developmentally appropriate interactions between young children and their caregivers.

In describing the influences of attachment theory on infant–parent psychotherapy, Lieberman (1991) summarizes a number of points. These include:

1. Clinical intervention with real-life events
2. The use of observable behavior as a reflection of inner experience
3. The employment of therapeutic terminology that incorporates experiences of protection, felt security, and felt insecurity
4. The therapeutic relationship as a "corrective attachment experience."

In the application of infant–parent psychotherapy, the primary goal is the preservation or restoration of the infant's mental health (Lieberman, 1991). Although the therapeutic relationship with the caregiver is a necessary component of treatment, it serves not as an end in itself, but as a means of facilitating the infant's attachment security. Basically, as the caregiver's models of self and self-in-relation-to-others become modified through a corrective attachment experience with the therapist, it is hypothesized that the caregiver's perception of and interaction with her child improves. In turn, an increasingly secure attachment relationship is thought to have a beneficial impact on the infants' evolving sense of self and on current and future relationships (Lieberman, 1991).

The utilization of infant–parent psychotherapy is especially exciting, as its effectiveness has been demonstrated with a group of low-SES Spanish-speaking immigrant mothers and their offspring (Lieberman, Weston, & Pawl, 1991). These mothers were considered to be at risk for disorders of attachment due to the presence of high rates of depression and anxiety, poverty, unemployment, and cultural issues related to their recent immigrant status. At 12 months of age, the attachment organization of infants was assessed in the Strange Situation and anxiously attached dyads were randomly assigned to an intervention or to a control group. Securely attached dyads comprised a second control group.

The infant–parent psychotherapy intervention consisted of weekly sessions with mother and infant that were primarily home based and that continued until the infant reached 2 years of age. At that time, mother and child were observed in a videotaped laboratory session designed to assess maternal empathy, dyadic interaction, and child socioemotional functioning. The findings revealed that the intervention was successful in enhancing maternal empathy and interaction with the child, increasing the goal-corrected partnership between mother and child, and decreasing child avoidance, resistance, and anger. In addition to demonstrating the effectiveness of a preventive intervention in infancy, the incorporation of attachment theory into the measurement strategy, the conceptualization and provision of the intervention, and the evaluation of outcome eloquently demonstrated the contributions to effective clinical practice that can be made by an attachment-based therapeutic approach.

Another example of an intervention derived from attachment theory that has been applied to work with infants and their caregivers was initiated in 1987 at the University of Minnesota by Egeland and Erickson (1990; Erickson, Korfmacher, & Egeland, 1992). Similar to the previously described intervention, the program was developed to promote healthy relationships and to prevent socioemotional difficulties in infants. The target of intervention was a group of mothers at risk for parenting difficulties due to the presence of a number of stressors, including poverty, limited education, social isolation, and stressful life circumstances. The intervention was governed by the belief that in order to modify a maladaptive attachment relationship, the goal must be to alter the working model of the relationship for both parent and child. The intervention involved an array of services, including the initiation of home visits during the mother's second trimester of pregnancy that continued through the child's first birthday, as well as biweekly support groups for mothers in which parent–infant activities and social interaction were followed by a discussion group that addressed emotional concerns and needs as well as life-management skills (Erickson et al., 1992). The breadth of this intervention precludes attributing therapeutic change to a single program component, and the program developers believe that the intervention in its entirety contributed to success.

The influence of attachment theory in this intervention is evident in a number of ways. The outreach prior to the birth of the child allowed the intervenor to begin to address maternal representations of her unborn child, previously shown to be a powerful predictor of postbirth attachment relationships (Fonagy, H. Steele & M. Steele, 1991). Because the investigators viewed the birth of a first child as a "special window of opportunity to have an impact on the prospective mother's view of herself, her child, and their relationship" (Erickson et al., 1992, p. 502), this was a critical time to address attachment-related issues. The relationship between the mother and the individual who provided the intervention (referred to as the facilitator) is considered critical in helping the mother to develop new models of relationships. Toward this end, a number of principles are incorporated in the intervention, including consistency with the mother, the identification and affirmation of strengths in mother and baby, maternal empowerment, communication directed at the alteration of working models, and elucidation of interactional patterns between the facilitator and mother with the goal of linking these styles with maternal-relationship history (Erickson et al., 1992).

Preliminary data analysis from early phases suggests that this program promoted a number of positive changes, including improved maternal understanding of infant needs, more appropriate home environments, and fewer maternal depressive symptoms and anxiety. Differences in security of attachment were not found between the intervention and control groups, but follow-up assessments revealed a trend for those dyads who received intervention to move toward a more secure relationship during the infant's second year, while the opposite was true of non-intervention infants.

In another intervention designed to promote positive parent–child relationships in low-income families that evidenced caregiving difficulties, an intervention consistent with attachment theory was provided and evaluated (Lyons-Ruth, 1992). In addition to the presence of poverty, 63% of mothers identified as having caregiving difficulties also reported high levels of depressive symptomatology. Thirty-two percent of mothers in the intervention group also were identified as maltreating. Thus, maternal depression and child maltreatment, two variables demonstrated to be linked with insecure attachment and future child psychopathology (Cummings & Cicchetti, 1990; Downey & Coyne, 1990), were present in this sample.

Of note from an attachment-theory perspective were findings on the relation between maternal-childhood history and current caregiving. In exploring these relations, two clusters emerged (Lyons-Ruth, 1992). Mothers who had experienced more stable environments during childhood provided more attentive, involved care to their own infants than did mothers from less-cohesive household environments. Additionally, hostile-intrusive maternal behavior was related to a childhood history characterized by family conflict, severe punishment, lack of warmth, maternal psychopathology, and poor peer relationships. Thus, the childrearing difficulties evidenced by these mothers could be hypothesized to originate in their childhood, when their representational models of self and other were formed.

The intervention for these families was initiated when infants were less than 9 months of age and involved a weekly home-based visit designated to support adequate parenting and to address an array of general daily living skills. Four primary goals were identified for the intervention, including:

1. Provision of an accepting and trustworthy relationship
2. Facilitation of the family's ability to meet their basic needs
3. Modeling of more interactive, positive, and developmentally appropriate interchanges between mother–infant dyads
4. A decrease in maternal social isolation.

Although the array of services associated with these goals could result in multiple routes of influence on the mother–infant relationship, Lyons-Ruth (1992) attributed the success of the intervention as most likely due to the provision of new maternal models of relationships. This interpretation is consistent with the finding that maternal depression and social isolation continued to be present, even though increasingly positive interactions between mothers and their infants were assessed at 12 months of age. Because mother–infant dyads were enrolled in the intervention at different infant ages, the 12-month assessment included an evaluation of dyads who had received the intervention for various lengths of time. Mothers who had received a longer course of intervention were significantly more in-volved with their 12-month-old infants, as evidenced by greater warmth, more verbal communication, more physical comforting, and less with-drawal. At 18 months of age, when all dyads had received at least 9 months of intervention, variations in maternal behavior as a result of time in intervention were no longer evident.

Significant differences in security of attachment also emerged as a result of intervention, with insecure-disorganized attachment more pre-valent in nontreated risk dyads. When maltreating mothers were elim-inated from the analyses, infants with depressed caregivers who received the intervention displayed twice the rate of secure attachments and only one-sixth the rate of least-secure attachment (Lyons-Ruth, 1992). Thus, a theoretically guided and evaluated approach to treatment with an impov-erished group of mothers experiencing depression and their infants was again demonstrated to be effective. However, a lack of randomization to intervention and nonintervention groups and the multifaceted nature of service delivery tempers conclusions that can be drawn regarding the specificity of modifications of maternal representational models as being responsible for the observed outcome.

A final and compelling theoretical approach to the treatment of inse-cure attachment in infancy stems from the work of Crittenden (1992). Crit-tenden integrates attachment theory with perspectives drawn from etho-logical, psychodynamic, evolutionary, learning, and cognitive theories. According to her conceptualization, procedural models of the self and of attachment figures are thought to develop in infancy, to be maintained across the life span and to be accessed preconsciously to regulate daily be-havior. Considerable emphasis is given to memory systems (Tulving, 1985), each of which is considered to store a different type of information, and to the associated internal representational models that summarize the information held in the memory system (Bowlby, 1980). Specifically, pro-cedural, semantic, and episodic memory systems contain information on behavior sequences, verbal generalizations, and events, respectively (Tulving, 1972, 1985). Crittenden (1992) hypothesizes that each memory system and associated model regulates behavior under different circumstances. Moreover, inconsistency among models is thought to be related both to anxious attachment and to risk for emotional disturbance. Crittenden draws parallels between methods of processing information and patterns of attachment, with anxiously attached infants possessing procedural models that represent their sensorimotor understanding of relationships in ways that will skew their management of new information. Avoidant infants are expected to evidence tendencies to ignore perceptions, to interpret information idiosyncratically, and to inhibit the expression of feelings and needs. Both types of insecurely attached infants are posited to encounter experiences that are too complex to process and that lead to coping difficulties and disorganization. These patterns of processing information, if applied to potentially supportive relationships, could impede the infant's development of more adaptive relationships (Crittenden, 1992).

For Crittenden, insecure attachment reflects not only current relationship dysfunction but also, more importantly, the acquisition, integration, and evaluation of incoming information in ways that result in skewed developmental trajectories. Thus, a central goal of intervention conceptualized within this framework is to help children perceive and respond to their actual environments rather than engaging in mental processing that obfuscates reality. Crittenden links proposed treatment strategies for each of the three memory systems to different theoretical approaches. She considers procedural memory and models to be amenable to family-systems interventions, semantic memory and models to be receptive to cognitive modes of treatment, and episodic memory and models to require psychodynamically based treatment (Crittenden, 1992). Rather than suggesting a direct correspondence between memory system and treatment, however, Crittenden proposes an integration of various theoretical perspectives.

In treating insecurely attached infants, Crittenden stresses that the role of intervention needs to be directed at changing the infants' procedural internal-representational model with the objective of keeping models open rather than closed. To achieve this, Crittenden states that the intervenor can strive to (a) change the behavior of the primary attachment figure; (b) help infants perceive their attachment figures accurately and experience their true feelings; and (c) provide infants' with alternate and positive relationship opportunities. Although Crittenden's approach to intervention with insecure attachment remains to be evaluated, the sophisticated integration of attachment theory with a concrete approach to treatment holds great promise for facilitating both research into and the clinical application of this theory.

6.4.2. Preschool and School-Age Children

Crittenden's (1992) theoretical approach to treating insecure attachments in infancy also has been applied to preschool-age children. In addition to the options of modifying parental behavior, intervening directly with the child and/or providing alternate attachment figures in efforts to change procedural models, Crittenden views the preschool period as providing additional opportunities for intervention due to the emerging preoperational capacities of the young child. Thus, treatment can be directed toward the content of memory systems and models, the integration of various types of information, and the translation of processing into behavior. As was true in infancy, Crittenden believes that intervention efforts can be targeted either toward attachment figures or toward the children.

In work with attachment figures of preschoolers Crittenden stresses the importance of encouraging the accuracy of the child's semantic and episodic representations, as well as the role of these representations in fostering children's motivations for competence. The facilitation of positive statements and the reduction of negative statements by attachment figures may be helpful, but more importantly, Crittenden emphasizes the need for caregivers to accept and encourage the child to *accurately* express feelings.

Intervention with preschool-age children can focus on helping them to deal with confusing situations by exploring mixed feelings, discrepancies between felt and expressed emotions, and the occurrence of different attitudes toward the same situation. The overarching goal of the intervention is to help insecurely attached children develop a mental approach for integrating content across memory systems and for being able to cope adaptively with disparate feelings and discordances between memory systems, between others' perspectives, and between feelings and behaviors (Crittenden, 1992). As in infancy, the goal of treatment with preschool-age children is to facilitate the processing of information about relationships in ways that are likely to increase the probability that the child will develop a secure relationship with their caregiver or, if not possible, that the child's representational model will remain open to potentially more positive interactions.

In an interesting extension of attachment-based theory into the arena of manifest clinical disorder, Greenberg, Kusche, and Speltz (1991) explore externalizing behavior problems in preschool-age children. According to their ABCD (Affective-Behavioral-Cognitive-Dynamic) model, primary emphasis is placed on the dynamic developmental integration of affect and emotion language, overt behavior, cognitive understanding and expectancies, and linguistic and communicative skill for understanding social competence and psychopathology. The model posits that child coping is a result of emotional awareness, affective-cognitive control, and social-cognitive understanding. Moreover, coping ability is seen as a function of constitutional factors, the sensitivity and nurturance present in the environment, the degree of experienced child trauma, and the quality of cognitive and linguistic stimulation that is provided (Greenberg et al., 1991).

In the previously discussed research on children with oppositional defiant or conduct disorders, Greenberg and his colleagues (1991, Speltz et al., 1990) found that a significantly higher percentage of children with externalizing symptomatology evidenced insecure-attachment relationships. Based on these findings, Greenberg and his colleagues (1991) conclude that treatment models for children with conduct disorders need to consider the functioning of age-appropriate developmental tasks (e.g., self-control and affect regulation) that emerge from the context of the formation of working models of self and of others. Specifically, the ability of caregivers to provide their child with secure relations is hypothesized to result in optimal integration among components specified in the ABCD model. Difficulties with respect to the absence of appropriate sharing of joint goals and plans as well as in sharing and tolerating affective states in both self and other (e.g., the goal-corrected partnership) are believed to be present in the parents of children with conduct disorders (Greenberg & Speltz, 1988). Insensitive, nonresponsive caregiving is viewed as leading the child to engage in behaviors labeled as "conduct problems" in efforts to gain the attention or proximity of caregivers who ignore more subtle child requests. To prevent behavior problems and the deficits in emotional regulation and social cognition associated with oppositional and conduct disorders, Greenberg proposes that parents provide a warm, supportive presence, help their child to recognize and symbolically mediate affective states, and involve their child in interactions that support planning and anticipation of future events. The provision of a caregiving context that is characterized by these interactional styles will help the child to develop confidence in the caregiver and in the self, thereby preventing the emergence of externalizing symptomatology.

One approach that incorporates these goals in the treatment of preschoolers' conduct problems has been described by Speltz (1990), who modified a behavioral parent-training model to incorporate aspects of attachment theory. While retaining components of operant parenting skills such as praise and limit setting, consideration is given to the encouragement of negotiation and joint planning between parent and child, the discussion of parental affects and the facilitation of child identification of internal states, and a focus on parent and child attributions for behaviors (Speltz, 1990). In accord with the views of other attachment interventionists, the importance of exploring parental models of relationships and the effect of these representations on caregiving also are afforded attention in this model.

6.4.3. Adulthood

Although this chapter is focused on the relationship between attachment dysfunction and child psychopathology, we would be remiss to omit adult treatment from our discussion for two primary reasons. First, because dysfunctional attachment relationships in infancy have been hypothesized to be linked with psychopathology in adulthood (Bemporad & Romano, 1992; Toth, Manly, & Cicchetti, 1992), attention to this possible developmental trajectory is important. Second, issues related to the intergenerational (i.e., parent to child) transmission of insecure attachment are paramount to treatment considerations with risk and disordered mother–child relationships.

While less attention has been directed toward attachment-guided intervention with adults, theoreticians and clinicians are beginning to apply principles of attachment theory to the consideration of intervention approaches with adult populations (Guidano & Liotti, 1983). Cummings and Cicchetti (1990) suggest that an insecure-attachment organization places an individual at risk for psychopathology for a number of reasons, including manifested lower levels of felt security, an increased tendency to perceive one's environment and relationships negatively, and interactions with others that are counterproductive to the establishment of positive relationships. These characteristics also are likely to impede intervention efforts unless they are recognized and addressed. In fact, different patterns of responsiveness to therapists have been noted among adults with psychopathological disorders, with variability in the degree to which help is rejected or overdependence emerges (Sheets, Prevost, & Reihman, 1981).

In a study of adults with serious psychopathology, including affective and psychotic disorders, Dozier (1990) found relations between attachment organization and treatment usage. Specifically, patients with greater security were found to be more compliant with treatment, while avoidant tendencies were associated with less self-disclosure, more rejection of treatment providers, and poorer use of treatment. Diagnosis also was found to be related to security, with individuals with mood disorder (e.g., unipolar and bipolar patients) evidencing greater security than patients with schizophrenia (Dozier, 1990). Findings such as these possess implications for therapeutic strategies that are likely to be effective with individuals suffering from diverse forms of psychopathology. Specifically, patients who are more avoidant of relationships may be more likely to respond to concrete and relatively directive forms of intervention than to treatment that needs to be built gradually on a foundation of trust. Of course, if the overarching treatment goal is to improve functioning in the interpersonal arena, a significant period of intervention is likely to be necessary in order to impact upon representational models.

In working with parent–child dyads in which an insecure-attachment relationship is present, research has demonstrated that the probability is high that the parent had an insecure attachment with his/her own parent during childhood (Main et al., 1985). Therefore, in order to break the intergenerational transmission of insecure attachment, both parent and child must be considered in the development of an intervention strategy (Cicchetti, Toth, & Bush, 1988). Unless the level of caregiving dysfunction is so great that the child will be removed from the home, we believe that attention must be directed toward the representations that the parent has carried forward into the caregiving context. In many cases, efforts to establish a therapeutic relationship with the parent may reflect the first opportunity that the parent has had to feel accepted. Although it may be difficult for the therapist to observe harsh or intrusive parental acts, or to be faced with an emotionally unresponsible caregiver, it is only through empathy with the parent that a possible bridge can be established between parent and child (Toth & Cicchetti, 1993). Depending on the magnitude of parental distrust and insecurity, early work may need to focus exclusively on the caregiver. This is likely to be especially true of parents struggling with a multitude of stressors such as poverty, domestic violence, and social isolation, as well as in instances of severe parental psychopathology. In these cases, only gradually will the positive effects of the caregivers' modified representations be evident in their interactions with their children. If individual therapy for the parent is the chosen mode of intervention, the child may need the opportunity to experience other potentially positive relationships through involvement in day care and/or peer groups (Cicchetti & Toth, 1987). While an array of therapeutic strategies may be provided, we believe that the effects of any program of intervention directed toward the promotion of mental health in young children are likely to be more enduring if the parents' stance with respect to relationships is improved.

7. Conclusion and Future Perspectives

A confluence of factors, most notably the changing foci that have arisen within attachment theory and research and the emergence of the discipline of developmental psychopathology, with its emphasis on the interplay between normal and abnormal development, have contributed to the increased number of investigations on attachment in high-risk and psychiatrically disordered populations. This renascence reflects the beginning phases in the culmination of Bowlby's dream. As is the case with research that has been conducted on the etiology and sequelae of secure and insecure attachments, work that extends the investigation of attachment across the life course, through examinations of attachment organization and explorations of representational processes, holds great promise for elucidating the organization of development in normal and abnormal populations. Clearly, knowledge of the normal development of the attachment system has informed much of the research on attachment in high-risk and psychopathological persons. Conversely, research on atypical populations has enhanced our understanding of attachment in normal populations, predominantly by challenging, affirming, and expanding theoretical notions derived from research with nondisordered individuals. In order to sustain the momentum generated by investigations of attachment organization in high-risk and clinical populations, theoreticians, researchers, and clinicians must address a number of critical issues. We close this chapter by proposing a series of recommendations that we think will insure that the important progress that has been made continues and reaps fruition.

1. There must be ongoing construct validation of the new measures that have been developed to assess attachment organization in preschool and school-aged children, adolescents, and adults. We advocate strongly that this validation process be carried out in multiple contexts (e.g., home, school, laboratory, playground, and summer camp settings; cf. Lynch & Cicchetti, 1991; Urban et al., 1991), utilizing multiple measures (e.g., observations, interviews, drawings, projectives, etc.), assessing relationships with multiple attachment figures (e.g., mothers, fathers, grandparents, siblings, teachers, best friends, and peers; cf. Howes & Segal, 1993; Lynch & Cicchetti, 1991, 1992; Marvin & Stewart, 1990), and with a variety of typical and atypical populations.

2. It is essential that additional prospective longitudinal research on attachment and its correlates and consequences be conducted. To date, most of the research on the sequelae of attachment has involved cross-

sectional or short-term longitudinal investigations (see Urban et al., 1991; Elicker et al., 1992; and Sroufe, et al., 1993 for important exceptions).

We believe that longitudinal studies should strive to meet the following recommendations:

a. Sample sizes should be large enough to permit investigators to assess the differential sequelae of all insecure groups. Typically, much of the research on attachment in normative populations has utilized approximately 40 subjects. Thus, given the low base rate of 10% for Type C attachments, most studies cannot discriminate between avoidant and ambivalent groups (Lamb, 1987). Because we believe that we are at a point in time where longitudinal studies can make many of the major contributions to expanding our knowledge, we suggest that sample sizes minimally should be large enough to ensure adequate numbers of subjects with secure and insecure attachments in long-term assessments of adaptation.

b. Because attachment organization can change over time, work on the temporal stability of attachment is critical. Thus, we suggest that attachment should be assessed at each longitudinal point. Age-appropriate measures of attachment must be collected, thereby also enabling concurrent as well as predictive links to be made between attachment organization and quality of adaptation on other salient developmental tasks. Following from the organizational and hierarchical model that we described earlier, assessments of each stage-salient issue must also occur over time.

c. Little attention has been paid to gender differences in attachment quality for children or adults. This is unfortunate, given the much noted observation that men and women behave in consistent and distinctly different ways in intimate relationships. Furthermore, while many questions remain unanswered, it can be said that issues of gender appear to become more salient as the level of stress and dysfunction increases for a family (Howes & Cicchetti, 1993). Consequently, we urge researchers to accord the investigation of gender a higher priority in their research and to examine differential longitudinal pathways to outcome for each gender.

d. Most studies that have examined the link between quality of attachment and childhood behavior problems have relied on maternal and teacher assessments of the child's behavior problems or disorders. While many of these studies have had to rely on such external informants because of the relatively young age of the children studied, it is critical to expand this focus to include both interviews and self-reports with the child.

e. It is clear that insecure attachment is not synonymous with psycho-pathology and that secure attachment does not guarantee immunity to disorder (e.g., Cicchetti, et al., 1990; Pearson, et al., 1994). Thus, in prospective longitudinal investigations of attachments, it is critical that theoretically derived measures of moderators and mediators of attachment and its outcomes be included in the research protocol (cf. Cummings & Cicchetti, 1990).

3. Concurrently, prospective longitudinal studies of attachment organization in the offspring of parents with diagnosed psychiatric disorders, and of children receiving extremely poor-quality care, must be conducted. These investigations should adopt the principles we suggested for similar studies of normal populations to the degree feasible (e.g., it may not be possible to enroll as large a sample of parents in certain low base-rate psychiatric disorders). Given the knowledge that we possess about developmental processes in maltreated children, conduct-disordered children, and the children of depressed parents, we believe that longitudinal studies of attachment and its correlates and sequelae in these populations are likely to yield important information about differential pathways to adaptation.

4. Cross-sectional and prospective longitudinal investigations of attachment organization in adults with psychiatric disorders must be carried out. In addition, studies linking such adult's attachment organization to their child's attachment organization and psychiatric status are essential to implement.

5. Research on the attachment organization of children with a diagnosed mental disorder is greatly needed. Currently, there is a paucity of research addressing this topic. Now that diagnostic interviews for childhood disorders possess more robust psychometric properties and are more sensitive to developmental considerations, investigators are in a better position to obtain accurate measurements of psychopathological conditions in childhood. In tandem with the growing number of age-appropriate measures of attachment beyond infancy, we believe that the time is ripe to initiate these studies.

6. The results of the proposed investigations on normal, high-risk, and disordered children and adults should be used to test competing models of the nature of the relation between attachment and psychopathology. Because insecure attachment is not a necessary and/or sufficient cause for the development of psychopathology, assessments of attachment and other potential etiological factors should occur (Cummings & Cicchet-

ti, 1990). As such, attachment may make an independent contribution to the development of pathological outcomes in combination with additional independent risk- and protective factors. Alternatively, attachment may not contribute independently to the development of disordered outcomes; it is conceivable that some children may function deviantly on an array of measures of adaptation, including attachment security (Cicchetti & Schneider-Rosen, 1986). Finally, regardless of their ultimate outcome with respect to the presence of psychopathology, some insecurely attached children may have an actual attachment disorder or relational psychopathology (cf. Cicchetti, 1987; Sameroff & Emde, 1989; Sroufe, 1989).

7. Investigations of high-risk and psychiatrically ill children and adults should be used not only to further our understanding of attachment and developmental psychopathology, but also to address questions posed by normal theoreticians and researchers that are perhaps best answered by work with nontypical populations. For example, questions such as "How do children form an integrative working model of relationships when several models exist with different caregivers?" or "Can a discordant working model (e.g., a secure representational model with a grandparent or teacher and an insecure working model with both parents) serve as a buffer or protective mechanism for a child?" may be more readily approached in high-risk samples where concordance rates among working models of attachment figures are lower than in normal or low-risk groups (see, e.g., Lynch & Cicchetti, 1991).

Along these lines, Crittenden (1990) has described representational models as operating on a working continuum ranging from open to closed. Demonstrations, for example, that maltreated children can form secure relationships with other persons and/or that parent–toddler therapy can change an early insecure attachment can provide inroads into how to investigate major theoretical constructs in attachment that have thus far received little empirical investigation. Whether models are open or closed to new experiences may also be related to development in other domains such as language (especially connected to internal states) and to self-introspection. High-risk populations with deficits in these areas may reveal linkages between other domains and the metastructuring of attachment representations.

8. Ongoing validation of the "Disorganized-Disoriented" Type D attachment category is critical. Given their documented high base-rate of occurrence in certain very high-risk and pathological populations, investigations of such samples should prove promising for elucidating our understanding of the antecedents, correlates, and consequences of disorganized-disoriented attachments. One of the most significant demon-

strations will be that response in laboratory contexts or other settings is predicted by attachment behavior in the home. As we illustrated in this chapter, the identification of the disorganized-disoriented attachment category has led to improvements in the accuracy of attachment classifications. While children with avoidant and ambivalent attachments have been found to be more properly classified as disorganized, most striking to us are the high percentages of children from high-risk backgrounds who were classified as secure before the advent of the D category. Furthermore, the discovery of the D category should increase investigators' abilities to differentiate among subtypes of insecurely attached persons, especially if sufficiently large samples of high-risk and disordered populations are enrolled in these studies.

In addition, empirical work on the precursors and sequelae of Type D attachments in non-normative samples can shed light on existing theoretical claims concerning the nature of the etiology and sequelae of disorganized attachment relationships. For example, in their middle-SES Berkeley sample, Main and her colleagues (1985) discovered that children with disorganized-disoriented attachments in infancy developed insecure-controlling relationships with their primary caregiver at age 6. Prospective studies tracking the later attachment patterns of Type D infants drawn from non-normative populations should provide a further test of the Main et al. hypothesis. Similarly, Main and Hesse (1990) found that parents' unresolved traumatic experiences were related to the development of infant's disorganized attachment. They further proposed that frightened and/or frightening parental behavior was the linking mechanism. While Carlson and her colleagues (1989b) provide evidence compatible with Main and Hesse's hypothesis, prospective longitudinal research with a variety of populations that offer tests of this assertion are in order. Maltreated children, offspring of parents who experience "loss" depressions, children exposed to community and intrafamilial violence, and offspring of parents with post-traumatic stress disorder (PTSD), offspring of parents with multiple personality disorder or with a dissociative disorder are several populations that we believe would offer good tests of Main and Hesse's hypothesis.

Finally, work must be conducted that follows up on Lyons-Ruth et al's. (1991) findings that the disorganized-disoriented attachments that are force-classified as securely attached differ from Type D attachments that are forced-insecure-alternate classifications. Lyons-Ruth and her colleagues (1991) report that these two subtypes of disorganized infant attachment differ in their age of emergence, developmental history with their mother, severity of associated risk factors in the family, and the degree to which their mothers manifested lack of involvement with the infant in the home. Investigations of large samples of extremely high-risk and disordered populations across the life span should provide a compelling test of the hypothesis that there are differential etiologies and sequelae for disorganized attachments force-classified as secure or insecure.

9. Researchers should routinely examine children's attachments to multiple caregivers. In particular, for all children, but especially for those reared in adverse caretaking environments, secure attachments with nonparental adults (e.g., grandparents, teachers), siblings, and best friends may serve as a palliative factor or a protective mechanism for optimizing positive outcomes (i.e., resilience) in high-risk children (Freud & Dann, 1951; Masten, Best, & Garmezy, 1990; Werner & Smith, 1992). Positive and secure relationships with other familiar adults may begin to compensate for the negative relationship histories that children from disrupted and chaotic families have with their parents by providing new information for these children's representational models of themselves and others. As a protective mechanism, these relationships can influence children's beliefs about themselves and others.

Two recent investigations of maltreated children's relationships with nonparental adults reveal that these children often form attachments similar in quality to those they develop with their caregivers (Howes & Segal, 1993; Lynch & Cicchetti, 1992). These results underscore the importance of intervening with families from an attachment-theory perspective (Toth & Cicchetti, 1993). If maltreated children are less able to engage in secure relationships with significant adults such as teachers or alternate caregivers, then they may be cutting themselves off from possible sources of corrective emotional experiences (cf. Fraiberg et al., 1975; Lieberman, 1991) that could alter their working models of self and others. For example, in an important study, Egeland et al. (1988) discovered that the ability to form an emotionally supportive relationship with a nonabusive adult served as a protective factor in breaking the cycle of maltreatment in mothers who had been abused as children.

Similarly, the results of Pearson and her colleagues (1994) underscore the need to examine the protective processes that enable individuals with poor relationship histories in their childhoods to develop a secure, coherent attachment organization as adults. Furthermore, congruent with several recent reports in the literature on resiliency (see Cicchetti & Garmezy, 1993), these adults with "earned-secure" attachments had higher levels of depressive symptomatology, suggesting that their resilient adaptations did not occur without emotional difficulties. Future work on adults with earned-secure relationships is clearly warranted. We believe that if such research focuses on the protective processes and mechanisms of security despite a childhood history of insecurity and turmoil, major insights into the nature of working (i.e., open vs. closed) models will be achieved.

10. Along similar lines, attachment theorists should direct their attention increasingly to the role of father–child relationships in the emergence of childhood psychopathology or in the promotion of childrens' mental health. Historically, mothers typically functioned as the primary or sole caregiver to young children. However, with increased out-of-home work involvement for mothers, as well as changing societal views of male-versus-female roles, fathers have assumed a more central position in the caregiving environment. As such, emphasis on mother–child attachment may be missing a critical component of the quality of the caregiving environment. While a number of investigators have explored father–child attachment in normative populations (see, e.g., Fox, Kimmerly, & Schafer, 1991; Lamb, 1976/1982; Main & Weston, 1981), it is important that efforts such as these be extended into the arena of risk and psychopathology.

11. Studies investigating the link between quality of attachment and brain organization in high risk and disordered children, as well as in psychiatrically ill adults, should be conducted. As recently demonstrated by Dawson, Klinger, Panagiotides, Spieker, and Frey (1992), the intertwined development of neurobiological functioning and attachment can be altered by compromised caregiving. Dawson and her colleagues (1992) found that securely attached infants of depressed mothers displayed reduced left-frontal brain activity (EEG), both during positive emotional situations (e.g., interactions with their mothers) and during baseline compared with securely attached infants whose mothers were not depressed. Because the left hemisphere has been shown to be associated with approach behavior and emotions, and because decreased left-hemispheric activation often results in, or accompanies depressive symptomatology (Davidson, 1991), the findings of Dawson and her colleagues are especially important to developmentalists.

Evidence on the emergence of discrete affects in maltreated infants likewise provides suggestive links between quality of caregiving and brain organization. Specifically, Gaensbauer (1980, 1982) discovered that fear expressions were present as early as 2–3 months of age in physically abused babies. In contrast, in normal ontogenesis this affect does not usually appear before age 6–9 months. Thus, it may be that early maltreatment experiences speed up the emergence of fear in infancy. Conceivably, maltreatment may accelerate the "hard wiring" of negative affect in the brain. Because 2- to 3-month-old babies lack the cognitive capacity to process fear-inducing stimuli, these physically abused infants may be vulnerable to developing disorganized-disoriented attachments. An important related line of inquiry would be to ascertain whether the aberrant brain organizations of children experiencing extremes of caregiving casualty could become normalized as a result of attachment-oriented interventions (Cicchetti, 1993).

12. With respect to the application of attachment theory to intervention, much work remains to be done. Although efforts to provide and evaluate intervention guided by attachment theory have begun, a number of difficulties need to be addressed as research in this area continues.

a. Because many interventions have focused on the provision of treatment to multiproblem populations, an array of services have been provided. Although conceptualized within an attachment framework, these multifaceted approaches make it extremely difficult to evaluate outcomes that may be due to modified representational models versus results that can be attributed to any number of other factors, including the provision of support. In order to build upon prior evaluation efforts, it is critical that more specific and targeted interventions be provided. To achieve this, it will be necessary to intervene with populations that may not be confronted with stressors requiring a multiplicity of intervention services, such as nondisadvantaged children with a depressed caregiver.

b. As is true of most efforts to evaluate treatment effectiveness, a host of difficulties confront investigators who are invested in developing and assessing attachment-based treatment strategies. Limitations regarding random assignment to treatment or no-treatment groups become especially problematic when a young child is experiencing distress. However, the failure to deal with issues of randomization compromises investigators' abilities to determine whether their interventions have been effective. Therefore, we strongly recommend that various strategies for addressing this issue be explored. The comparison of alternative forms of treatment or of varying levels of intervention are two approaches that can be utilized effectively. Moreover, because *preventive* interventions are not constrained by the realistic ethical considerations that exist when actual psychopathology is present, it is more possible to employ random assignment in the provision of prevention programs. Finally, the application of quasi-experimental designs to the evaluation of services should be considered when randomized treatment is not possible (see, e.g., Hauser-Cram, 1990).

c. To date, most interventions for infants and children have focused on the modification of insecure attachment with the goal of preventing the emergence of psychopathology. Unfortunately, thus far, served populations have not been followed-up longitudinally in order to evaluate the long-term effectiveness of the preventive interventions. Ideally, studies should be developed with the intent of following young children into later childhood and even adulthood, when the emergence of actual psychopathological conditions are more likely. Only through work such as this can attachment-based interventions truly demonstrate effectiveness in preventing psychiatric disorder.

d. Efforts should be directed toward continuing to develop assessment methods that can be utilized in intervention evaluations and that eventually might be appropriately incorporated into clinical settings. In order to achieve a true nexus between research efforts and clinical applications of attachment theory, the development of shared methods of evaluation and a common language will be necessary. Toward this end, both researchers and therapists will need to be committed to the facilitation of communication and the interchange of knowledge.

ACKNOWLEDGMENTS: The writing of this chapter was supported by grants from the Prevention Research Branch of the National Institute of Mental Health (MH45027) and the Spunk Fund, Inc. We thank Jennifer Boehles for typing this manuscript.

8. References

Achenbach, T. M., & Edelbrock, C. S. (1981). Behavioral problems and competencies reported by parents of normal and disturbed children aged four through sixteen. *Monographs of the Society for Research in Child Development, 46* (Serial No. 188).

Achenbach, T. M., & Edelbrock, C. S. (1986). *Manual for the teacher's form and teacher version of the child behavior profile.* Burlington, VT: Child Psychiatry, University of Vermont.

Ainsworth, M. D. S. (1967). *Infancy in Uganda: Infant care and the growth of love.* Balitmore, MD: Johns Hopkins University Press.

Ainsworth, M. D. S. (1969). Object relations, dependency and attachment: A theoretical review of the infant–mother relationship. *Child Development, 40,* 969–1025.

Ainsworth, M. D. S. (1989). Attachments beyond infancy. *American Psychologist, 44,* 709–716.

Ainsworth, M. D. S., Blehar, M. C., Waters, E., & Wall, S. (1978). *Patterns of attachment; A psychological study of the Strange Situation.* Hillsdale, NJ: Erlbaum.

Ainsworth, M. D. S., & Bowlby, J. (1991). An ethological approach to personality development. *American Psychologist, 46,* 331–341.

Ainsworth, M. D. S. & Wittig, B. A. (1969). Attachment and the exploratory behavior of one-year-olds in a strange situation. In B. M. Foss (Ed.), *Determinants of infant behavior,* (Vol. 4, pp. 113–136). London: Methuen.

Barnett, D., Ganiban, J., & Cicchetti, D. (April, 1992). *Temperament and behavior of youngsters with disorganized attachments: A longitudinal study.* Paper presented at the International Conference on Infant Studies, Miami, FL.

Barnett, D., Manly, J. T., & Cicchetti, D. (1993). Defining child maltreatment: The interface between policy and research. In D. Cicchetti & S. L. Toth (Eds.), *Child abuse, child development, and social policy* (pp. 7–74). Norwood, NJ: Ablex.

66 DANTE CICCHETTI et al.

Bates, J., Maslin, C., & Frankel, K. (1985). Attachment security, mother–child interaction, and temperament as predictors of behavior problem ratings at age three years. In I. Bretheron & E. Waters (Eds.), *Growing points in attachment theory. Monographs of the Society for Research in Child Development, 50,* (1–2, Serial No. 209), 167–193.

Beck, A. T. (1967). *Depression: Causes and treatment.* Philadelphia: University of Pennyslvania Press.

Beck, A. T. (1976). *Cognitive therapy and the emotional disorders.* New York: International Universities Press.

Behar, L. B., & Stringfield, S. (1974a). *Manual for the Preschool Behavior Questionnaire.* (Available from Dr. Lenore Behar, 1821 Woodburn Road, Durham, NC 27705).

Behar, L. B., & Stringfield, S. (1974b). A behavior rating scale for the preschool child. *Developmental Psychology, 19,* 601–610.

Belsky, J., & Nezworski, T. (1988) (Eds.). *Clinical implications of attachment theory.* Hillsdale, NJ: Erlbaum.

Bemporad, J. R., & Romano, S. J. (1992). Childhood maltreatment and adult depression: A review of research. In D. Cicchetti & S. L. Toth (Eds.), *Rochester Symposium on Developmental Psychopathology, Vol. 4: Developmental perspectives on depression* (pp. 351–376). Rochester, NY: University of Rochester Press.

Bischof, N. (1975). A systems approach toward the functional connections of attachment and fear. *Child Development, 46,* 801–817.

Block, J. (1971). *Lives through time.* Berkeley, CA: Bancroft Books.

Bowlby, J. (1969/1982). *Attachment and loss, Vol. 1: Attachment.* New York: Basic Books.

Bowlby, J. (1973). *Attachment and loss, Vol. 2: Separation.* New York: Basic Books.

Bowlby, J. (1977a). The making and breaking of affectional bonds. *British Journal of Psychiatry, 130,* 201–210.

Bowlby, J. (1977b). The making and breaking of affectional bonds. *British Journal of Psychiatry, 130,* 421–431.

Bowlby, J. (1980). *Attachment and loss: Loss, sadness, and depression.* New York: Basic Books.

Bowlby, J. (1988) Developmental psychiatry comes to age. *American Journal of Psychiatry, 145,* 1–10.

Bretherton, I. (1980). Young children in stressful situations: The supporting role of attachment figures and unfamiliar caregivers. In G. V. Coelho & P. Ahmed (Eds.), *Uprooting and development* (pp. 179–210). New York: Plenum Press.

Bretherton, I. (1987). New perspectives on attachment relations: Security, communication, and internal working models. In J. Osofsky (Ed.), *Handbook of infant development* (2nd ed.) (pp. 1061–1100). New York: Wiley.

Bretherton, I. (1990). Open communication and internal working models: Their role in the development of attachment relationships. In R. Thompson (Ed.), *Nebraska Symposium on Motivation, Vol. 36: Socioecnomic development* (pp. 57–113). Lincoln, NE: University of Nebraska Press.

Bretherton, I. (1991). Pouring new wine into old bottles: The social self as internal working model. In M. Gunnar & L. A. Sroufe (Eds.), *The Minnesota Symposia on child development: Vol. 23. Self processes and development* (pp. 1–41). Hillsdale, NJ: Erlbaum.

Bretherton, I. (1992). The origins of attachment theory: John Bowlby and Mary Ainsworth. *Developmental Psychology, 28,* 759–775.

Carlson, V., Cicchetti, D., Barnett, D., & Braunwald, K. (1989a). Disorganized/disoriented attachment relationships in maltreated infants. *Developmental Psychology, 25,* 525–531.

Carlson, V., Cicchetti, D., Barnett, D., & Braunwald, K. (1989b). Finding order in disorganization: Lessons from research in maltreated infants' attachments to their caregivers. In D. Cicchetti & V. Carlson (Eds.), *Child maltreatment: Theory and research on the causes and consequences of child abuse and neglect* (pp. 494–528). New York: Cambridge University Press.

Cassidy, J. (1990). Theoretical and methodological considerations in the study of attachment and self in young children. In M. Greenberg, D. Cicchetti, & E. M. Cummings (Eds.), *Attachment in the preschool years* (pp. 87–119). Chicago: University of Chicago Press.

Cassidy, J., & Marvin, R. (1992). *Attachment organization in preschool children: Procedures and coding manual.* Unpublished manuscript: Pennsylvania State University and University of Virginia.

Cicchetti, D. (1984). The emergence of developmental psychopathology. *Child Development, 55,* 1–7.

Cicchetti, D. (1987). Developmental psychopathology in infancy: Illustration from the study of maltreated youngsters. *Journal of Consulting and Clinical Psychology, 55,* 837–845.

Cicchetti, D. (Ed.). (1989). *Rochester Symposium on Developmental Psychopathology: Vol. 1. The emergence of a discipline.* Hillsdale, NJ: Erlbaum.

Cicchetti, D. (1991). Fractures in the crystal: Developmental psychopathology and the emergence of self. *Developmental Review, 11,* 271–287.

Cicchetti, D. (1993). Developmental psychopathology: Reactions, reflections, projections. *Developmental Review, 13,* 471–502.

Cicchetti, D., & Aber, J. L. (1986). Early precursors to later depression: An organizational perspective. In L. Lipsitt & C. Rovee-Collier (Eds.). *Advances in infancy, Vol. 4,* (pp. 87–137). Norwood, NJ: Ablex.

Cicchetti, D., & Barnett, D. (1991). Attachment organization in preschool-aged maltreated children. *Development and Psychopathology, 3,* 397–411.

Cicchetti, D., Beeghly, M., Carlson, V., & Toth, S. (1990). The emergence of the self in atypical populations. In D. Cicchetti and M. Beeghly (Eds.), *The self in transition: Infancy to childhood* (pp. 309–344). Chicago: University of Chicago Press.

Cicchetti, D., & Garmezy, N. (Eds.). (1993) Special issue: Milestones in the development of resilience. *Development and Psychopathology, 5*(4), 497–783.

Cicchetti, D., & Greenberg, M. T. (Eds.). (1991). Special Issue: Attachment and developmental psychopathology. *Development and Psychopathology, 3*(4), 347–531.

Cicchetti, D., & Lynch, M. (1993). Toward an ecological/transactional model of community violence and child maltreatment. Consequences for children's development. *Psychiatry, 56,* 96–118.

Cicchetti, D., & Rizley, R. (1981). Developmental perspectives on the etiology, intergenerational transmission, and sequelae of child maltreatment. *New Directions for Child Development, 11,* 31–55.

Cicchetti, D., & Schneider-Rosen, K. (1984). Theoretical and empirical considerations in the investigation of the relationship between affect and cognition in atypical populations of infants: Contributions to the formulation of an integrative theory of development. In C. Izard, J. Kagan & R. Zajonc (Eds.), *Emotions, cognition and behavior* (pp. 366–406). New York: Cambridge University Press.

Cicchetti, D., & Schneider-Rosen, K. (1986). An organizational approach to childhood depression. In M. Rutter, C. Izard, & P. Read (Eds.), *Depression in young people, clinical and developmental perspectives* (pp. 71–134). New York: Guilford.

Cicchetti, D., & Toth, S. L. (1987). The application of a transactional risk model to intervention with multi-risk maltreating families. *Zero to Three, 7,* 1–8.

Cicchetti, D., & Toth, S. L. (Eds.). (1991a). *Rochester Symposium on developmental psychopathology, Vol. 2: Internalizing and externalizing expressions of dysfunction.* Hillsdale, NJ: Erlbaum.

Cicchetti, D., & Toth, S. L. (1991b). The making of a developmental psychopathologist. In J.

68   Dante Cicchetti et al.

Cantor, C. Spiker, & L. Lipsitt (Eds.), *Child behavior and development: Training for diversity* (pp. 34–72). Norwood, NJ: Ablex.

Cicchetti, D., & Toth, S. L. (Eds.). (1992). Special Issue: Developmental approaches to prevention and intervention. *Development and Psychopathology, 4*(4), 489–728.

Cicchetti, D., Toth, S. L., & Bush, M. (1988). Developmental psychopathology and incompetence in childhood: Suggestions for intervention. In B. Lahey & A. Kazdin (Eds.), *Advances in clinical child psychology, Vol. 11* (pp. 1–71). New York: Plenum Press.

Cohn, J. F., & Campbell, S. B. (1992). Influence of maternal depression on infant affect regulation. In D. Cicchetti & S. L. Toth (Eds.), *Rochester Symposium on Developmental Psychopathology, Vol. 4: Developmental perspectives on depression* (pp. 103–130). Rochester, NY: University of Rochester Press.

Cohn, J. F., Matias, R., Tronick, E. Z., Connell, D., & Lyons-Ruth, K., (1986). Face-to-face interactions of depressed mothers and their infants. *New Directions for Child Development, 34,* 31–46.

Connell, J. P. (1990). Context, self, and action: A motivational analysis of self-system processes across the life-span. In D. Cicchetti & M. Beeghly (Eds.), *The self in transition: Infancy to childhood* (pp. 61–97). Chicago: University of Chicago Press.

Connell, J. P., & Goldsmith, H. H. (1982). A structural modeling approach to the study of attachment and strange situation behaviors. In R. Emde & R. Harmon (Eds.), *The development of attachment and affiliative systems* (pp. 213–243). New York: Plenum Press.

Connell, J. P., & Wellborn, J. G. (1991). Competence, autonomy and relatedness: A motivational analysis of self-system processes. In M. Gunnar & L. A. Sroufe (Eds.), *Minnesota Symposia on Child Psychology, Vol. 23: Self processes and development* (pp. 43–78). Hillsdale, NJ: Erlbaum.

Crittenden, P. M. (1985). Maltreated infants: Vulnerability and resilience. *Journal of Child Psychology and Psychiatry and Allied Disciplines, 26,* 85–96.

Crittenden, P. M. (1988). Relationships at risk. In J. Belsky & T. Nezworski (Eds.), *Clinical implications of attachment theory* (pp. 136–174). Hillsdale, NJ: Erlbaum.

Crittenden, P. M. (1990). Internal representational models of attachment relationships. *Infant Mental Health Journal, 11,* 259–277.

Crittenden, P. M. (1992). Treatment of anxious attachment in infancy and early childhood. *Development and Psychopathology, 4*(4), 575–602.

Crittenden, P. M., & Ainsworth, M. (1989). Attachment and child abuse. In D. Cicchetti & V. Carlson (Ed.), *Child maltreatment: Theory and research on the causes and consequences of child abuse and neglect* (pp. 432–463). New York: Cambridge University Press.

Crittenden, P. M., & DiLalla, D. (1988). Compulsive compliance: The development of an inhibitory coping strategy in infancy. *Journal of Abnormal Child Psychology, 16,* 585–599.

Crittenden, P. M., Partridge, M. F., & Claussen, A. H. (1991). Family patterns of relationship in normative and dysfunctional families. *Development and Psychopathology, 3,* 491–512.

Cummings, E. M., & Cicchetti, D. (1990). Attachment, depression, and the transmission of depression. In M. T. Greenberg, D. Cicchetti, & E. M. Cummings (Eds.), *Attachment in the preschool years,* (pp. 339–372). Chicago: University of Chicago Press.

Davidson, R. (1991). Cerebral asymmetry and affective disorders: A developmental perspective. In D. Cicchetti & S. L. Toth (Eds.), *Rochester Symposium on Developmental Psychopathology: Vol. 2. Internalizing and externalizing expressions of dysfunction* (pp. 123–154). Hillsdale, NJ: Erlbaum.

Dawson, G., Klinger, L. G., Panagiotides, H., Spieker, S., & Grey, K. (1992). Infants of mothers with depressive symptoms: Electroencephalographic and behavioral findings related to attachment status. *Development and Psychopathology, 4*(1), 67–80.

DeMulder, E. K., & Radke-Yarrow, M. (1991). Attachment with affectively ill and well mothers: Concurrent behavioral correlates. *Development and Psychopathology, 3*, 227–242.

Downey, G., & Coyne, J. C. (1990). Children of depressed parents: An integrative review. *Psychological Bulletin, 108*, 50–76.

Dozier, M. (1990). Attachment organization and treatment use for adults and serious psychopathological disorders. *Development and Psychopathology, 2*, 47–60.

Easterbrooks, A. M., Davidson, C. E., & Chazan, R. (1993). Psychosocial risk, attachment, and behavior problems among school-aged children. *Development and Psychopathology, 5*, 387–400.

Egeland, B., & Erikson, M. F. (December, 1990). Rising above the past: Strategies for helping new mothers break the cycle of abuse and neglect. *Zero to Three, 11*(3), 29–35.

Egeland, B., Jacobvitz, D., & Sroufe, L. A. (1988). Breaking the cycle of abuse. *Child Development, 59*, 1080–1088.

Egeland, B., & Sroufe, L. A. (1981). Developmental sequelae of maltreatment in infancy. *New Directions for Child Development, 11*, 77–92.

Elicker, J., Englund, B., & Sroufe, L. A. (1992). Predicting peer competence and peer relationships in childhood from early parent–child relationships. In R. D. Parke & G. Ladd (Eds.), *Family-peer relationships: Modes of linkage* (pp. 77–106). Hillsdale, N.J.: Erlbaum.

Erickson, M. F., Egeland, B., & Sroufe, L. A. (1985). The relationship between quality of attachment and behavior problems in preschool in a high-risk sample, In I. Bretherton & E. Waters (Eds.), *Growing points in attachment theory and research. Monographs of the Society for Research in Child Development, 50*, (1–2, Serial No. 209), 147–167.

Erickson, M. F., Korfmacher, J, & Egeland, B. (1992). Attachments past and present: Implications for therapeutic intervention with mother–infant dyads. *Development and Psychopathology, 4*, 495–407.

Erikson, E. H. (1950). *Childhood and society.* New York: Norton.

Field, T. (1989). Maternal depression effects on infant interaction and attachment behavior. In D. Cicchetti (Ed.), *Rochester Symposium on Developmental Psychopathology: Vol. 1. The emergence of a discipline* (pp. 139–163). Hillsdale, NJ: Erlbaum.

Fonagy, P., Steele, H., & Steele, M. (1991). Maternal representations of attachment during pregnancy predict the organization of infant–mother attachment at one year of age. *Child Development, 62*, 891–905.

Fox, N. A., Kimmerly, N. L., & Schafer, W. D. (1991). Attachment to mother/attachment to father: A meta-analysis. *Child Development, 62*, 210–225.

Fraiberg, S. (Ed.). (1980). *Clinical studies in infant mental health.* New York; Basic Books.

Fraiberg, S., Adelson, E., & Shapiro, V. (1975). Ghosts in the nursery A psychoanalytic approach to impaired infant–mother relationships. *Journal of the American Academy of Child Psychiatry, 14*, 387–421.

Freud, A., & Dann, S. (1951). An experiment in group upbringing. *The Psychoanalytic Study of the Child, 6*, 127–168.

Gaensbauer, T. J. (1980). Anaclitic depression in a three-and-one-half-month-old child. *American Journal of Psychiatry, 137*, 841–842.

Gaensbauer, T. J. (1982). Regulation of emotional expression in infants from two contrasting caretaker environments. *Journal of Pediatric Psychology, 9*, 241–256.

George, C., Kaplan, N., & Main, M. (1985). *Attachment interview for adults.* Unpublished manuscript, University of California, Berkeley.

Giovannoni, J., & Becerra, R. M. (1979). *Defining child abuse.* New York: Free Press.

Greenberg, M. T., Cicchetti, D., & Cummings, E. M. (Eds.). (1990). *Attachment in the preschool years.* Chicago: University of Chicago Press.

Greenberg, M. T., Kusche, C. A., & Speltz, M. (1991). Emotional regulation, self-control, and psychopathology: The role of relationships in early childhood. In D. Cicchetti & S. L. Toth (Eds.), *Rochester Symposium on Development Psychopathology: Vol. 2. Internalizing and externalizing expressions of dysfunction* (pp. 21–55). Hillsdale, NJ: Erlbaum.

Greenberg, M. T., & Speltz, M. (1988). Attachment and the ontogeny of conduct problems. In J. Belsky & T. Nezworksi (Eds.), *Clinical implications of attachment theory* (pp. 177–218). Hillsdale, NJ: Erlbaum.

Greenberg, M. T., Speltz, M., & DeKlyen, M. (1993). The role of attachment in the early development of disruptive behavior problems. *Development and Psychopathology, 5,* 191–214.

Greenberg, M. T., Speltz, M. L., DeKlyen, M., & Endriga, M. (1991). Attachment security in preschoolers with and without externalizing behavior problems: A replication.*Development and Psychopathology, 3,* 413–430.

Greenspan, S., & Lieberman, A. (1988). A clinical approach to attachment. In J. Belsky and T. Nezworski (Eds.), *Clinical implications of attachment* (pp. 387–424). Hillsdale, NJ: Erlbaum.

Guidano, V. F., & Liotti, G. (1983). *Cognitive processes and emotional disorders: A structural approach to psychotherapy.* New York: Guilford.

Hammen, C. (1992). The family-environmental content of depression: A perspective on children's risk. In D. Cicchetti and S. L. Toth (Eds.), *Rochester Symposium on Psychopathology, Vol. 4: Development perspectives on depression* (pp. 25–281). Hillsdale, NJ: Erlbaum.

Hauser-Cram, P. (1990). Designing meaningful evaluations of early intervention services. In S. J. Meisels & J. P. Shonkoff (Eds.), *Handbook of early intervention* (pp. 538–602). New York: Cambridge University Press.

Hay, D., & Angold, A. (Eds.). (1993). *Precursors and causes in development and psychopathology.* New York: Wiley.

Howes, C., & Segal, J. (1993). Children's relationships with alternate caregivers: Special case of maltreated children removed from their homes. *Journal of Applied Developmental Psychology, 14,* 71–81.

Howes, P., & Cicchetti, D. (1993). A family/relational perspective on maltreating families: Parallel processes across systems and social policy implications. In D. Cicchetti & S. L. Toth (Eds.), *Child abuse, child development, and social policy* (pp. 249–299). Norwood, NJ: Ablex.

Hunter, R. S. & Kilstrom, N. (1979). Breaking the cycle in abusive families. *American Journal of Psychiatry, 136,* 1320–1322.

Isabella, R. (1993). Origins of attachment: Maternal interactive behavior across the first year. *Child Development, 64,* 605–621.

Kaplan, B. (1966). The study of language in psychiatry: The comparative developmental approach and its application to symbolization and language in psychopathology. In S. Arieti (Ed.), *American handbook of psychiatry* (pp. 659–688). New York: Basic Books.

Kobak, R., & Cole, H. (1994). Attachment and meta-monitoring: Implications for adolescent autonomy and psychopathology. In D. Cicchetti & S. L. Toth (Eds.), *Rochester Symposium on Developmental Psychopathology: Vol. 5. Disorders and Dysfunctions of the Self* (pp. 267–297). Rochester, NY: University of Rochester Press.

Kobak, R., & Sceery, A. (1988). Attachment in late adolescence: Working models, affect regulation and representations of self and others. *Child Development, 59,* 135–146.

Kobak, R., Sudler, N., & Gamble, W. (1991). Attachment and depressive symptoms during adolescence: A developmental pathways analysis. *Development and Psychopathology, 3,* 461–474.

Kopp, C., & Recchia, S. (1990). The issues of multiple pathways in the development of handicapped children. In R. Hodapp, J. Burack, & E. Zigler (Eds.) *Issues in the develop-*

mental approach to mental retardation (pp. 272–293). New York: Cambridge University Press.

Lamb, M. E. (Ed.). (1976/1982). *The role of the father in child development.* New York: Wiley.

Lamb, M. E. (1987). Predictive implications of individual differences in attachment. *Journal of Consulting and Clinical Psychology, 55,* 817–824.

Lamb, M., Gaensbauer, T. J., Malkin, C. M., & Schulz, L. A. (1985). The effects of child maltreatment on security of infant–adult attachment. *Infant Behavior and Development, 8,* 35–45.

Lamb, M., Thompson, R, Gardner, W., Charnov, E., & Estes, D. (1985). Security of infantile attachment as assessed in the strange situation: Its study and biological interpretation. *Behavioral and Brain Sciences, 7,* 124–147.

Lewis, M., Feiring, C. McGuffog, C., & Jaskir, J. (1984). Predicting psychopathology in six-year-olds from early social relations. *Child Development, 55,* 123–136.

Lewis, M., & Miller S. (Eds.). (1990). *Handbook of developmental psychopathology.* New York: Plenum Press.

Lieberman, A. F. (1991). Attachment theory and infant–parent psychotherapy: Some conceptual, clinical, and research considerations. In D. Cicchetti & S. L. Toth (Eds.), *Rochester Symposium on Developmental Psychopathology: Vol. 3. Models and Integrations* (pp. 261–287). Rochester, NJ: University of Rochester Press.

Lieberman, A. F. (1992). Infant–parent psychotherapy with toddlers. *Development and Psychopathology, 4,* 559–574.

Lieberman, A. F. (1993). *The emotional life of the toddler.* New York: The Free Press.

Lieberman, A. F., & Pawl, J. H. (1988). Clinical applications of attachment theory. In J. Belsky & T. Nezworski (Ed.), *Clinical implications of attachment* (pp. 325–351). Hillsdale, NJ: Erlbaum.

Lieberman, A. F., & Pawl, J. H. (1993). Infant–parent psychotherapy. In C. Zeanah (Ed.), *Handbook of infant health* (p. 427–442). New York: Guilford.

Lieberman, A. F., Weston, D., & Pawl, J. H. (1991). Preventive intervention and outcome with anxiously attached dyads. *Child Development, 62,* 199–209.

Lynch, M. (1990). *Children's relatedness to peers: Attachment beyond infancy and its organization across relationships.* Unpublished master's thesis. University of Rochester, Rochester, NY.

Lynch, M., & Cicchetti, D. (1991). Patterns of relatedness in maltreated and nonmaltreated children: Connections among multiple representational models. *Development and Psychopathology, 3,* 207–226.

Lynch, M., & Cicchetti, D. (1992). Maltreated children's reports of relatedness to their teachers. *New Directions for Child Development, 57,* 81–107.

Lyons-Ruth, K. (1992). Maternal depressive symptoms, disorganized infant–mother attachment relationships and hostile-aggressive behavior in the preschool classroom: A prospective longitudinal view from infancy to age five. In D. Cicchetti & S. L. Toth (Eds.), *Rochester Symposium on Developmental Psychopathology: Vol. 4. Developmental perspectives on depression* (pp. 131–171). Rochester, NY: University of Rochester Press.

Lyons-Ruth, K., Alpern, L., & Repacholi, B. (1993). Disorganized infant attachment classification and maternal psychosocial problems as predictors of hostile-aggressive behavior in the preschool classroom. *Child Development, 64,* 572–585.

Lyons-Ruth, K., Connell, D., Grunebaum H., & Botein, S. (1990). Infants at social risk: Maternal depression and family support services as mediators of infant development and security of attachment. *Child Development, 61,* 85–98.

Lyons-Ruth, K., Connell, D., & Zoll, D. (1989). Patterns of maternal behavior among infants at risk for abuse: relations with infant attachment behavior and infant development at 12 months of age. In D. Cicchetti & V. Carlson (Eds.), *Child Maltreatment: Theory and research on the causes and consequences of child abuse and neglect* (pp. 464–493). New York: Cambridge University Press.

Lyons-Ruth, K., Connell, D., Zoll, D., & Stahl, J. (1987). Infants at social risk: Relations among infant maltreatment, maternal behavior, and infant attachment behavior. *Developmental Psychology, 23,* 223–232.

Lyons-Ruth, K., Repacholi, B., McLeod, S., & Silva, E. (1991). Disorganized attachment behavior in infancy: Short-term stability, maternal and infant correlates. *Development and Psychopathology, 3,* 207–226.

Main, M. (1991). Metacognitive knowledge, metacognitive monitoring, and singular (coherent) vs. multiple (incoherent) models of attachment: Findings and directions for future research. In P. Marris, J. Stevenson-Hinde, & C. Parkes (Eds.), *Attachment across the life cycle* (pp. 127–159). New York: Routledge.

Main, M., & Cassidy, J. (1988). Categories of response to reunion with a parent at age 6: Predictable from infant attachment classifications and stable over a one-month period. *Developmental Psychology, 24,* 415–426.

Main, M., & Goldwyn, R. (1984). Predicting rejecting of her infant from mother's representation of her own experience. Implications for the abused-abusing intergenerational cycle. *Child Abuse and Neglect, 8,* 203–217.

Main, M., & Goldwyn, R. (in press). Interview-based adult attachment classifications: Related to infant–mother and infant–father attachment. *Developmental Psychology.*

Main, M., & Hesse, P. (1990). Parents' unresolved traumatic experiences are related to infant disorganized attachment status: Is frightened and/or frightening parent behavior the linking mechanism? In M. Greenberg, D. Cicchetti, & E. M. Cummings (Eds.), *Attachment in the preschool years* (pp. 161–182). Chicago: University of Chicago Press.

Main, M., Kaplan, N., & Cassidy, J. C. (1985). Security in infancy, childhood and adulthood: A move to the level of representation. *Monographs of the Society for Research in Child Development, 50* (1–2. Serial No. 209), 66–104.

Main, M., & Solomon, J. (1986). Discovery of a disorganized/disoriented attachment pattern. In T. B. Brazelton and M. W. Yogman (Eds.), *Affective development in infancy* (pp. 95–124). Norwood, NJ: Ablex.

Main, M., & Solomon, J. (1990). Procedures for identifying infants as disorganized/disoriented during the Ainsworth Strange Situation. In M. Greenberg, D. Cicchetti & E. M. Cummings (Eds.), *Attachment in the preschool years* (pp. 121–160). Chicago: University of Chicago Press.

Main, M., & Weston, D. (1981). The quality of the toddler's relationship to mother and father. *Child Development, 53,* 932–940.

Marvin, R. (1977). An ethological-cognitive model for the attenuation of mother-child attachment behavior. In T. M. Alloway, L. Krames, & P. Pirer (Eds.), *Advances in the study of communication and effects, Vol. 3* (pp. 25–60). New York: Plenum.

Marvin, R. S., & Stewart, R. B. (1990). A family systems framework for the study of attachment. In M. T. Greenberg, D. Cicchetti, & E. M. Cummings (Eds), *Attachment in the preschool years* (pp. 51–86). Chicago: University of Chicago Press.

Masten, A. (1989). Resilience in development: Implications of the study of successful adaptation for developmental psychopathology. In D. Cicchetti (Ed.), *Rochester Symposium on Developmental Psychopathology: Vol. 1. The emergence of a discipline* (p. 261–294). Hillsdale, NJ: Erlbaum.

Masten, A., Best, K., & Garmezy, N. (1990). Resilience and development: Contributions from the study of children who overcome adversity. *Development and Psychopathology, 2,* 425–444.

O'Connor, M. J., Sigman, M., & Brill, N. (1987). Disorganization of attachment in relation to maternal alcohol consumption. *Journal of Consulting and Clinical Psychology, 55*, 831–836.

Patrick, M., Hobson, R. P., Castle, D., Howard, R., & Maughan, B. (1994). Personality disorder and the mental representation of early social experience. *Development and Psychopathology, 6*, 375–388.

Pearson, J. L. Cohn, D. A., Cowan, P. A., & Cowan, C. P. (1994). Earned- and continuous-security in adult attachment. Relation to depression and parenting style. *Development and Psychopathology, 6*, 359–373.

Radke-Yarrow, M., Cummings, E. M., Kuczynski, L., & Chapman, M. (1985). Patterns of attachment in two- and three-year-olds in normal families and families with parental depression. *Child Development, 56*, 884–893.

Radloff, L. (1977). The CES-D scale: A self-report depression scale for research in the general population. *Applied Psychological Measurement, 1*, 385–401.

Rodning, C., Beckwith, L., & Howard, J. (1991). Quality of attachment and home environments in children prenatally exposed to PCP and cocaine. *Development and Psychopathology, 3*, 351–366.

Rutter, M. (1988). Epidemiological approaches to developmental psychopathology. *Archives of General Psychiatry, 45*, 486–495.

Rutter, M. (1990). Psychosocial resilience and protective mechanisms. In J. Rolf, A. S. Masten, D. Cicchetti, K. H. Nuechterlein, & S. Weintraub (Eds.) *Risk and protective factors in the development of psychopathology* (pp. 181–214). New York: Cambridge University Press.

Rutter, M., & Garmezy, N. (1983). Developmental psychopathology. In E. M. Hetherington (Ed.), *Socialization, personality and social development* (pp. 775–911). New York: Wiley.

Sameroff, A. J., & Chandler, M. J. (1975). Reproductive risk and the continuum of caretaking casualty. In F. D. Horowitz (Ed.), *Review of child development research, Vol. 4* (pp. 187–244). Chicago, IL: University of Chicago Press.

Sameroff, A., & Emde, R. N. (Eds.). (1989). *Relationship disturbances in early childhood.* New York: Basic Books.

Schneider-Rosen, K., Braunwald, K., Carlson, V., & Cicchetti, D. (1985). Current perspectives in attachment theory: Illustration from the study of maltreated infants. In I. Bretherton and E. Waters (Eds.), *Growing points in attachment theory and research. Monographs of the Society for Research in Child Development, 50* (1–2.Serial No. 209), 194–210.

Schneider-Rosen, K., & Cicchetti, D. (1984). The relationship between affect and cognition in maltreated infants: Quality of attachment and the development of visual self-recognition. *Child Development, 55*, 648–658.

Sheets, J. L., Prevost, J. A., & Reihman, J. (1981). Young adult chronic patients: Three hypothesized subgroups. *Hospital and Community Psychiatry, 33*, 197–203.

Speltz, M. L. (1990). The treatment of preschool conduct problems: An integration of behavioral and attachment concepts. In M. T. Greenberg, D. Cicchetti, & E. M. Cummings (Eds.), *Attachment in the preschool years* (pp. 399–426). Chicago: University of Chicago Press.

Speltz, M. L., Greenberg, M. T., & DeKlyen, M. (1990). Attachment in preschoolers with disruptive behavior: A comparison of clinic-referred and nonproblem children. *Development and Psychopathology, 2*, 31–46.

Spieker, S. J., & Booth, C. L. (1988). Maternal antecedents of attachment quality. In J. Belsky & T. Nezworski (Eds.), *Clinical implications of attachment quality. In J. Belsky & T. Nezworski (Eds.), Clinical implications of attachment* (pp. 95–135). Hillsdale, NJ: Erlbaum.

Sroufe, L. A. (1979). Socioemotional development. In J. Osofsky (Ed.), *Handbook of infant development,* (1st ed.) (pp. 462–516). New York: Wiley.

Sroufe, L. A. (1983). Infant-caregiver attachment and patterns of adaptation in preschool: The roots of maladaptation and competence. In M. Perlmutter (Ed.), *Minnesota Symposium in Child Psychology* (pp. 41–83). Hillsdale, NJ: Erlbaum.

Sroufe, L. A. (1986). Bowlby's contribution to psychoanalytic theory and developmental psychopathology. *Journal of Child Psychology and Psychiatry, 27,* 841–849.

Sroufe, L. A. (1988). The role of infant–caregiver attachment in development. In J. Belsky & T. Nezworski (Eds.), *Clinical implications of attachment* (pp. 18–38). Hillsdale, NJ: Erlbaum.

Sroufe, L. A. (1989). Relationships and relationship disturbance. In A. Sameroff and R. Emde (Eds.), *Relationship disturbance in early childhood* (pp. 97–124). New York: Basic Books.

Sroufe, L. A., Carlson, E., & Schulman, S. (1993). Individuals in relationships: Development from infancy through adolescence. In D. Funder, R. Parke, C. Tomlinson-Keasey, & K. Widaman (Eds.), *Studying lives through time* (pp. 315–342). Washington, DC: American Psychological Association.

Sroufe, L. A., & Fleeson, J. (1986). Attachment and the construction of relationships. In W. Hartup & Z. Rubin (Eds.), *Relationships and development* (pp. 51–76). Hillsdale, NJ: Erlbaum.

Sroufe, L. A., & Rutter, M. (1984). The domain of developmental psychopathology. *Child Development, 55,* 17–29.

Sroufe, L. A., & Waters, E. (1977). Attachment as an organizational construct. *Child Development, 48,* 1184–1199.

Stern, D. (1985). *The interpersonal world of the infant: A view from psychoanalysis and developmental psychology.* New York: Basic Books.

Sullivan, H. (1953). *Interpersonal theory of psychiatry.* New York: Norton.

Toth, S. L., Manly, J. T., & Cicchetti, D. (1992). Child maltreatment and vulnerability to depression. *Development and Psychopathology, 4,* 97–112.

Toth, S. L. & Cicchetti, D. (1993). Child Maltreatment: Where do we go from here in our treatment of victims? In D. Cicchetti & S. L. Toth (Eds.) *Child abuse, child development and social policy,* (pp. 399–438). Norwood, NJ: Ablex.

Tulving, E. (1972). Episodic and semantic memory. In E. Tulving & W. Donaldson (Eds.), *Organization of Memory* (pp. 382–402). New York: Academic Press.

Tulving, E. (1985). How many memory systems are there? *American Psychologist, 40,* 385–398.

Urban, J., Carlson, E., Egeland, B., & Sroufe, L. A. (1991). Patterns of individual adaptation across childhood. *Development and Psychopathology, 3,* 445–460.

Van IJzendoorn, M. H., Goldberg, S., Kroonenberg, P. H., & Frenkel, O. J. (1992). The relative effects of maternal and child problems on the quality of attachment: A meta-analysis of attachment in clinical samples, *Child Development, 63,* 840–858.

Waters, E., & Deane, K. E. (1985). Defining and assessing individual differences in attachment relationships: Q-methodology and the organization of behavior in infancy and early childhood. In I. Bretherton & E. Waters (Eds.), *Growing points of attachment theory and research. Monographs of the Society for Research in Child Development, 50* (1–2, Serial No. 209), 41–65.

Wellborn, J. G., & Connell, J. P. (1987). *Manual for the Rochester Assessment Package for Schools.* Unpublished manuscript, University of Rochester, Rochester, NY.

Werner, H. (1957). The concept of development from a comparative and organismic point of view. In D. B. Harris (Ed.), *The concept of development* (pp. 125–148). Minneapolis: University of Minnesota Press.

Werner, E. E., & Smith, R. S. (1992). *Overcoming the odds: High-risk children from birth to adulthood.* Ithaca, NY: Cornell University Press.

Winnicott, D. (1965). *The family and individual development.* London: Tavistock.

Zeanah, C. (Ed.). (1993). *Handbook of infant mental health.* New York: Guilford.

Zeanah, C., & Emde, R. (1994). Attachment disorders in infants and young children. In M. Rutter, L. Hervov, & E. Taylor (Eds.), *Child and adolescent psychiatry* (3rd ed.) (pp. 490–504). Oxford: Blackwell.

Zigler, E., & Glick, M. (1986). *A developmental approach to adult psychopathology.* New York: Wiley.

2

Infant Cognitive Psychophysiology

Normal Development and Implications for Abnormal Developmental Outcomes

JOHN E. RICHARDS

1. Introduction

Psychophysiology may be defined as "the study of relations between psychological manipulations and resulting physiological responses, measured in the living organism, to promote understanding of the relation between mental and bodily processes" (Andreassi, 1989). The main impetus of psychophysiology is to relate psychological behavior to underlying physiological systems. Psychophysiology is also the study of parallel relations between psychological behavior and physiological systems. Psychophysiological research typically uses noninvasive recording methods and human subjects. Other scientific areas, such as physiological psychology, psychobiology, and behavioral neuroscience study physiological–psychological relations. These fields use more invasive physiological measures and, as a result, use animal models rather than human subjects in the study of behavior.

Cognitive psychology is the study of behavior such as attention, memory, information processing, thinking, and language. Cognitive psychophysiology uses physiological functions to study these functions. Cognitive psychophysiology sometimes merely uses physiological systems in

JOHN E. RICHARDS • Department of Psychology, University of South Carolina, Columbia, South Carolina 29208.

Advances in Clinical Child Psychology, Volume 17, edited by Thomas H. Ollendick and Ronald J. Prinz. Plenum Press, New York, 1995.

the study of cognitive psychology. Many cognitive psychophysiologists are interested in how physiological systems (e.g., brain, central nervous system, autonomic nervous system) affect cognitive behavior.

Researchers interested in infant cognitive development have turned to psychophysiological theories and methods to aid their study. This chapter reviews some studies of infant cognitive development that have used psychophysiological models. The focus will be on those research models in which the infant's cognitive development is thought to be inextricably related to the development of the physiological system.

It is not possible to review the entire field of infant cognitive psychophysiology in this chapter. The reader may consult other sources for reviews of infant developmental psychophysiology (e.g., W. Berg & K. Berg, 1987; Porges & Fox, 1986), as well as reviews of the development in infancy of specific systems (e.g., EEG/ERP: Courchesne, 1990; Kurtzberg et al., 1984; Nelson, 1993; Salapatek & Nelson, 1985; Vaughan & Kurtzberg, 1992; Heart Rate: Finlay & Ivinkis, 1987; Fox & Fitzgerald, 1990; Von Bargen, 1983). Two foci guide the presentation. First, the emphasis is on those research paradigms and models in which complex infant cognitive behaviors are studied. The use of simple stimuli with underlying simple cognitive behavior will not be emphasized. Second, the chapter emphasizes research conducted within the past 10 years, even though infant cognitive psychophysiology has a long history (30 to 40 years). This chapter emphasizes research reflecting recent attempts to integrate theories of infant cognitive development with theoretical models of psychophysiological development. Finally, a brief presentation is given of some research looking at abnormal and high-risk infant development from a cognitive psychophysiological perspective.

2. Evoked Scalp Potentials

The study of electrical potentials measured with surface electrodes on the scalp in infants has a long history. There have been two main trends of research. One trend has studied spontaneous electrical activity measured on the scalp, the *electroencephalogram* (EEG). Perhaps the most frequent use of spontaneous EEG has been the patterns of potentials that occur in different sleep states. EEG in sleep states has been studied extensively in newborn and infants. The characteristics of EEG in sleep and waking states are an essential component of the definition of sleep states in infants.

A second trend of research is the study of scalp electrical activity that occurs in response to stimulus challenge, called *evoked scalp potentials*. The evoked scalp potentials have an important advantage over EEG in the study of infant cognitive behavior. Stimuli and experimental manipulations known to have significant psychological consequences may be studied with the evoked EEG at the same time the psychological process is occurring. The evoked scalp potentials and their relation to infant cognitive activity are reviewed in this section.

2.1. Definition and Methodology

Scalp potentials are measured with small electrodes placed on the scalp at specified locations. The electrode placement is typically done according to an accepted system, for example, the 10–20 System, in which electrode placement occurs over the frontal, central, temporal, parietal, and occipital portions of the scalp (Jasper, 1958). The electrical potential measured at each location is measured in reference to a common electrode placed on the body near the scalp that does not have electrical activity occurring as a result of brain activity (e.g., ear or ear mastoid). The electrical activity measured on the scalp is generated by the electrical activity of groups of neurons in the brain, summed over large numbers of neurons and synapses. The amplitude of the electrical potential measured at the scalp in infants ranges from 0.1 microvolts to 20–30 microvolts.

Spontaneous EEG consists of constantly varying electrical potentials that occur under a variety of stimulus conditions. However, psychophysiologists are interested in brain activity occurring as a result of psychological processes. Thus, EEG activity synchronous with externally observable events, and thought to be occurring simultaneously with psychological activity, is of most interest. These scalp potential changes are labeled *event-related potential* (ERP).

The ERP is extracted from spontaneous EEG activity with averaging procedures. The spontaneous EEG activity is semirandom with respect to the events manipulated by the experimenter. The ERP activity is time-locked to those events. Spontaneous EEG activity is generated at several sources in the brain, whereas the ERP activity synchronous with the psychological activity is generated by only a few sources. Thus, spontaneous EEG activity is much larger than ERP activity. Therefore, averaging from a few (20) to many (100–200) EEG changes following an event will lead to a gradual diminution of the semirandom EEG and an enhancement of the electrical activity specifically linked to the event, and to the concomitant psychological process.

Figure 1 shows two types of ERP. Figure 1a is an example of the *brainstem auditory evoked response*, BAER (or brainstem auditory evoked

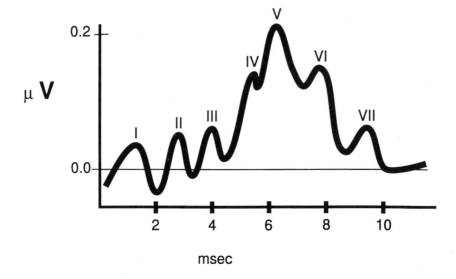

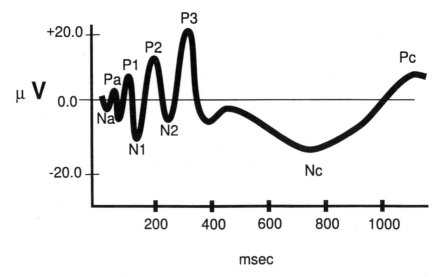

FIGURE 1. A schematic illustration of the evoked response potentials. The top figure shows a brainstem auditory evoked response (BAER) with the seven positive peaks labeled with Roman numerals I to VII. The bottom figure shows an evoked response potential (ERP) with the negative (N) and positive (P) waves, each occurring approximately at specific msec intervals (e.g., N2 is negative wave occurring approximately 200 msec following stimulus onset). The BAER and ERP components Na, Pa, P1, N1 and P2 are exogenous, and the ERP components N2, P3, Nc, and Pc are endogenous.

potential, BAEP). The BAER has a very short latency, occurring during the first 10 msec following auditory stimuli, and has the smallest amplitude of the evoked potentials. The BAER occurs as a result of electrical activity occurring in the auditory primary sensory pathway. The BAER waves I through IV are known to occur in specific neural groups in this pathway. Figure 1b is an example of later-occurring electrical activity in the ERP. The later ERP activity has components that occur in response to visual, auditory, and somesthetic stimuli. The earliest components (e.g., Pa, Na, P1, N1, and P2), along with the BAER, are labeled *exogenous* potentials. They represent neural activity in the sensory pathways that is closely related to the physical properties of the stimulus.

Most of the ERP research with infants has been with exogenous ERP components. These studies have used simple stimuli and experimental conditions to elicit the evoked potentials. This methodology is useful for the study of sensory processing and for understanding how the developing infant processes the psychophysical properties of sensory stimuli. This approach may also be extremely useful in the understanding of how cortical maturation is reflected in the ERP components in the early phases of information processing (Courchesne, 1990; Vaughan & Kurtzberg, 1992). Reviews of such work can be found in Courchesne (1990), Kurtzberg et al. (1984), Nelson (1993), Salapatek and Nelson (1985), Vaughan & Kurtzberg (1989, 1992), among others.

The later-occurring potentials in Figure 1b (N2, P3, Nc, Pc, and N400) are labeled *endogenous* potentials. These potentials are affected by psychological processes, such as discrimination difficulty, attention, expectancy, and intention. They are unrelated to physical changes in the stimulus, and may occur in the absence of external stimulation. The endogenous potentials are of more interest to cognitive psychophysiology because they are related to complex psychological processes that occur during cognitive activity.

2.2. Infant Recognition Memory

The study of endogenous potentials in infant cognitive psychophysiology has had two influences. First, the P3 (P300; P3a; P3b) is an ERP component that is known to be related in adults to several psychological processes. It is generally evoked in the "oddball" paradigm, which consists of one stimulus set being presented frequently (e.g., 80%) and another infrequently (20%). The P3 is an ERP component of positive electrical potential, which occurs at around 300 msec after the stimulus presentation, primarily over the parietal scalp region, and occurs with greater magnitude to the infrequently presented stimulus. Second, investigations by

Courchesne (1977, 1978) with young children older than 2 years has identified two ERP components occurring primarily in children. The Nc is a negative ERP component, has a latency between 400 to 1000 msec is distributed over the frontal and central scalp regions, and is thought to be a sign of enhanced attention to surprising, interesting, or psychologically significant visual or auditory stimuli. The Pc is a positive ERP component, has a latency longer than 1000 msec, has a similar scalp distribution as Nc, and occurs in response to interesting visual or auditory stimuli.

The first publications studying endogenous ERP components in young infants in experimental settings came in 1981. One of those was a study of ERP during the oddball paradigm by Courchesne, Ganz, and Norcia (1981). Courchesne et al. reported data from 10 infants who ranged in age from 4 to 7 months. The infants were presented with slides of two women for 100 msec. One slide was presented on 88% of the trials, and the other on 12%. The frequently presented face should become familiar to the infant over the course of stimulus presentation, whereas the one presented infrequently should be a discrepant or novel stimulus (e.g., the "oddball" stimulus). Research with older children and adults showed that the endogenous component P3 occurs over the parietal region, whereas the Nc and Pc components occur over the frontal region (Courchesne, 1977, 1978). In the Courchesne et al. (1981) study, EEG was recorded over the frontal and parietal regions. By recording at these sites, they could determine if these endogenous potentials existed in young infants, and distinguish them by scalp location and relation to the frequent/infrequent events.

The Courchesne et al. (1981) study had two main findings. First, a significant negativity occurred in the ERP in all 10 infants over the frontal region, with a latency of about 500–700 msec. Because of its latency and scalp distribution, it was concluded this was a Nc component (cf. Courchesne, 1977, 1978). This negative ERP occurred for both the familiar and the novel face, but was largest for the infrequently presented face. Figure 2 (bottom tracing) shows the tracing from the ERP to the frequent and infrequent faces. The difference between the two types of stimuli is highlighted by the crosshatching on the recordings occurring at the Fz (frontal) site. Second, a late positive component in the ERP occurred, primarily over the frontal electrode sites (Fig. 2). This component had a latency and distribution like that found with older children for a Pc component. This infant Pc component was not different in amplitude for the familiar and the novel faces. No evidence was found for a positive ERP component near 300 msec over the parietal region (i.e., the P3 component found in research with older children and adults).

The finding of late ERP components in 4- to 7-month-olds that were

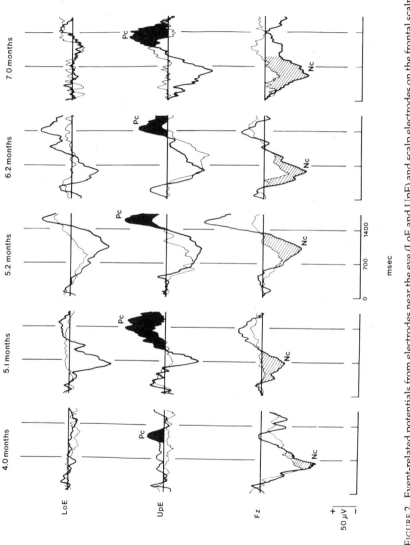

FIGURE 2. Event-related potentials from electrodes near the eye (LoE and UpE) and scalp electrodes on the frontal scalp location (Fz) to frequent (thin lines) and infrequent (thick lines) faces from five infants ranging in age from 4 to 7 months. The crosshatching represents the difference between the two stimuli types. Reprinted by permission from Courchesne et al., 1981. Copyright 1981 Society for Research in Child Development.

related to the frequent/infrequent manipulation was extended to younger and older infants by Karrer and Ackles (1987). Karrer and Ackles used infants at ages 6 weeks, 6 months, 12 months, and 18 months. They used a frequent/infrequent presentation of stimuli similar to Courchesne et al. (1981), with checks and random stimuli for the youngest group, faces for the 6-month-olds, and pictures of stuffed animals and toys for the older infants. They recorded the ERP from frontal, central, parietal, and occipital sites. Their results were similar to those of Courchesne et al. (1981). There was a large negative ERP component around 600 msec following stimulus presentation. For the three oldest groups, at the central scalp region, the amplitude of this component was larger for the infrequent than for the frequent stimulus. There was a significant Nc response at the frontal recording location that was not differentially affected by the oddball presentation. No large negativity was found at the parietal or occipital sites. The Nc component at both the frontal and central scalp locations increased in magnitude over the age range of 6 to 18 months. Studies by Kurtzberg and associates (e.g., Kurtzberg, Vaughan, & Novak, 1986) with speech sounds ("da" and "ta") presented frequently/infrequently extended the finding of a Nc component to auditory stimuli.

These studies have two findings. First, significant ERP changes are found in conjunction with the frequent/infrequent presentation of stimuli. This indicates recognition by the infant of the relative novelty/familiarity, or probability of the stimuli. As such, it shows a recognition memory for the stimulus, and an increased attention level to the novel stimulus. This parallels what has been found in adults with the P3 ERP component. It complements the finding that infants at this age in visual preference paradigms spend more time looking at a novel stimulus than at a familiar one. The possibility that there are developmental changes in these components (Karrer & Ackles, 1987, 1988) indicates the possibility of assessing developmental changes in recognition memory.

The second finding in these studies is the absence of a ERP component that could be related to the P3 found in adults. The components that were found in these studies with infants were at different scalp sites (frontal, central, rather than parietal) and at different latencies (700 msec, 1300 msec, rather than 300 msec than the P3 component. The frequent/infrequent presentation style was an analog to the oddball paradigm used with adults, and had similar effects in all of the cited studies on the Nc component, but no P3 component was found. It has been argued that the exogenous ERP's in infants, reflecting sensory processing, occur at 200 to 300 msec so that a P3 sensitive to psychological variables might be physically impossible (Vaughan & Kurtzberg, 1992). It has been concluded by Courchesne (1990; Courchesne & Yeung-Courchesne, 1988) that the P3 does not exist in infants, and emerges as a distinct ERP component late in the second year of life.

A different set of research findings has reported a probability effect with positive waves in the ERP around 300–600 msec. The first of these, published in the same year as the Courchesne et al. (1981) study, was done by Hoffman, Salapatek, and Kuskowski (1981). They presented 3-month-old infants with high-contrast square wave gratings for 500 msec for several trials. Their procedure differed from the studies cited earlier in that they had a *familiarization phase* that consisted of a single stimulus presented for 40 trials. Then, in a *test phase*, the familiar stimulus was presented for 80% of the time (frequent-familiar) and a new stimulus was presented for 20% of the time (infrequent-novel). They recorded scalp potentials at occipital and parietal (Study 1), and frontal (Study 2) locations, during the stimulus. A positive ERP component in the occipital scalp leads was found around 300–400 msec following stimulus presentation. This ERP component was larger to the infrequent-novel stimulus ERP in the test phase compared to the ERP during the familiarization phase. They did not find a difference between the frequent-familiar and infrequent-novel stimuli presented in the test phase. Nelson and Salapatek (1986), using a similar test protocol but employing longer recording intervals, found a negative ERP component at the central leads between 500 to 700 msec distinguishing the familiar phase ERP from the test phase infrequent-novel stimulus. A positive component was found at central and frontal leads at longer intervals (900 msec) that distinguished between the frequent-familiar and infrequent-novel stimuli on the test trials.

The studies of Courchesne et al. (1981) and Karrer and Ackles (1987) reported the later components (Nc and Pc), whereas the Hoffman et al. (1981) and the Nelson and Salapatek (1986) studies reported earlier positive ERP components. There were several differences between these studies that might account for the different results. A major difference is the use of a familiarization phase in the latter studies, and the lack of such a phase in the former ones. The use of a familiarization phase is probably important in this research. In the studies without the familiarization phase, it is likely that a memory for the frequently presented stimulus is gradually building up over the course of the presentations, whereas the infrequently presented stimulus retains its relative novelty. A possible confound with each of these studies is that the "infrequent" stimulus is also the "novel" stimulus. Thus, it may not be the "novelty" of the stimulus that elicits the ERP differences, but the mere "frequency."

A study by Nelson and Collins (1991) addressed these problems. They recorded EEG over several scalp locations in 6-month-old infants, with long enough recording intervals to detect the Nc and Pc components. A familiarization phase consisted of presenting two facial stimuli with equal probability to the infants on multiple trials. The test phase had three types of presentations: (1) a familiar stimulus presented frequently (60%; frequent-familiar); (2) a stimulus from the familiarization period but presented infrequently in the test phase (20%; infrequent-familiar); and (3) a stimulus never presented, and presented infrequently (20%; infrequent-novel). This study was unique in that the infrequent-novel stimulus was a different face on each trial, thus prohibiting any familiarization to the novelty of the face. This study could compare the relative probability of the stimulus separate from its novelty (frequent-familiar compared with infrequent-familiar), and the novelty of the stimulus separate from its relative probability (infrequent-familiar compared with infrequent-novel).

The most important results from this study were ERP differences found in the central scalp locations (Fig. 3). First, there were no differences before 750 msec or after 1400 msec in the three conditions. Second, at the central lead between 750 and 1400 msec, there was an increased positivity in the test-phase ERP to the infrequent-familiar stimulus relative to the frequent-familiar (or to the familiar stimuli during the familiarization phase). Thus, though the infrequent-familiar should be recognizable to the infant, its relative probability alone (a frequency effect) was sufficient for infants to distinguish it from the frequently presented familiar stimulus. There was also a "novelty" effect. The ERP to the frequent-familiar stimulus was positive at this latency, whereas the ERP to the infrequent-novel stimulus was negative. The ERP to the infrequent-novel stimulus was similar to the Nc component found in the previous studies. Thus, in the oddball paradigms, modified from adult versions, infants are responsive both to stimulus novelty and to the frequency of stimulus occurrence. Nelson and his colleagues have used this technique in several recent studies to examine recognition memory and frequency effects in infants (e.g., Nelson & Collins, 1992; Nelson & deRegnier, 1992; Nelson, Ellis, Collins, & Lang, 1990; Nelson, Henschel, & Collins, 1993; see review by Nelson, 1993). An important developmental finding from some of those studies is that at 4 months of age there is no difference between the ERP's to the three conditions, whereas by 6 months (Nelson & Collins, 1991) or 8 or 12 months (Nelson & Collins, 1992; Nelson & deRegnier, 1992) the ERP components differ.

The studies cited thus far indicated that very late components (e.g., greater than 700 msec) of the ERP distinguish the oddball stimulus from the familiar stimulus, whereas earlier components (e.g., around 300 msec) do not. One relatively recent study with 5- to 10-month-old infants reported an ERP component that was very similar in duration and topography to the adult P3 (McIssac & Polich, 1992). That study used the pres-

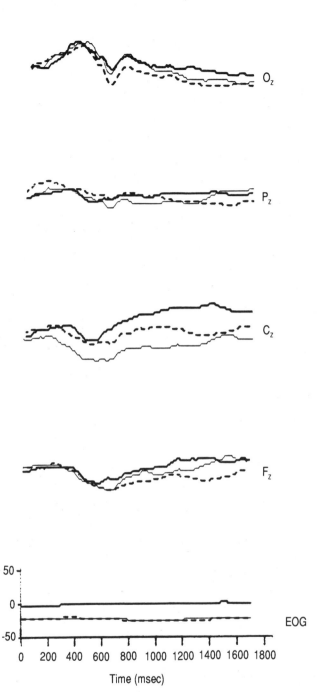

FIGURE 3. Event-related potentials for the test phase in a recognition memory study. These come from the occipital, parietal, central, and frontal scalp recording locations (Oz, Pz, Cz, Fz). The data are from the frequent-familiar (dashed line), infrequent-familiar (thick solid line) and infrequent-novel (thin solid line). Significant differences between conditions occurred at Cz. Reprinted by permission from Nelson & Collins, 1991. Copyright 1981 American Psychological Association.

entation of tones (1000 or 2000 Hz), with a fixed presentation of 10 auditory stimuli, with the oddball or "target" stimulus occurring in the 7th, 8th, 9th, or 10th position in each 10-tone sequence. They found an enhanced positive component of the ERP around 600 msec in the infants to the target (infrequent-novel) tone. Adults tested in the same study showed positive ERP component that was much larger, had a larger frequent/infrequent difference, and had latencies around 300 msec. The largest ERP differences for both infants and adults were in the central and parietal recording locations. This finding of a P3-like component in the infant ERP is different from that found with infant subjects for visual stimuli or for previous studies with auditory stimuli (e.g., Kurtzberg et al., 1986). This finding needs to be replicated with testing protocols similar to those used in past research (e.g., Courchesne et al., 1981; Nelson & Collins, 1991) in order to compare it with the previous studies. It is promising in the selection of a test protocol that elicits a significant ERP component with scalp topography similar to that found with adults.

2.3. Implications for Abnormal Development

There is a long history of using EEG and ERP in the study of abnormal infant development. Almost all of the work in this area with infants has been with spontaneous EEG or with the exogenous ERP components. The work with exogenous ERP components of abnormal infants has focused on Down's syndrome infants, infants and children with autism, preterm infants, infants with respiratory difficulties at birth, infants with developmental delays, and infants with hearing and visual problems (Courchesne & Yeung-Courchesne, 1988; Kurtzberg, 1982; Salapatek & Nelson, 1985; Vaughan & Kurtzberg, 1989). The endogenous ERP components and ERP components during complex cognitive processes have not been extensively investigated in abnormal infant development. The studies with the endogenous ERP components of interest to infant cognitive psychophysiology for the assessment or diagnosis of abnormal children have evaluated older children (Courchesne & Yeung-Courchesne, 1988).

The study of abnormal development with endogenous ERP's would be useful. It is usually assumed that prenatal and perinatal risk factors, particularly medical risk factors, have their effects on cognitive or intellectual functioning carried through childhood by changing CNS systems responsible for information processing. These structures may prohibit appropriate interaction with the environment in infancy, retarding appropriate developmental changes throughout early childhood, leading to poor cognitive performance in the early school years. Although with exogenous or sensory ERP's some of these affected areas can be identified in infants, it is not basic sensory processes for which the risk exists—it is higher cognitive functioning. Thus, the psychophysiological tasks that evaluate cognitive activity related to physiological systems would be inherently more useful in identifying abnormal cognitive behavior in infants that should be related to abnormal cognitive outcome in childhood. The ERP/recognition–memory relation might be useful for identifying infants at risk for later poor intellectual function. Some behavioral tests of infant recognition memory are the best predictors in young infants of normal intellectual outcome at 5 years of age (Fagan, 1992; Thompson, Fagan, & Fulkner, 1991). This prediction may be aided by examining indicators of the underlying physiological abnormality, if any, with ERP recording.

There is at least one example of the use of endogenous ERP with infants having developmental abnormalities. Karrer and Ackles (1988) recorded Nc in infants with Down's syndrome at ages 6 months through 2 years and found the physical characteristics (latency, amplitude, duration) of this endogenous ERP component to be similar in the infants with Down's syndrome and normal infants. The normal infants showed larger Nc amplitudes to the oddball stimuli than to repeated stimuli, whereas the infants with Down's syndrome showed the same Nc amplitude to both novel and repeated stimuli (Figure 4). The infant with Down's syndrome was thus responding to the stimulus, but did not discriminate the novel properties or show recognition memory. Older children with Down's syndrome show abnormal endogenous potentials associated with cognitive processing (Courchesne, 1988; Courchesne & Yeung-Courchesne, 1988).

3. Evoked Heart Rate Changes

The most common measure used by psychophysiologists studying infants is heart rate. Heart rate (HR) is obtained from surface electrodes on the chest, arms, or legs, derived from the electrocardiogram (ECG). As with EEG, there have been studies of spontaneous HR and evoked HR in infant cognitive-psychophysiological research. Unlike the EEG/ERP research, there have been numerous studies of evoked HR changes during complex cognitive activity in infants. The ECG is much easier to measure in behavioral situations, can be used in single-trial analyses, requires less signal processing, and uses inexpensive and easily used recording equipment.

At one level, HR might appear to be not as closely related as EEG/ERP to "cognitive" activity because of its relative "physiological distance" from the brain. However, HR has been found to be functionally related to many cognitive activities. Recent understanding of the brain systems involved in HR control have led to a sophisticated understanding of the relation of HR

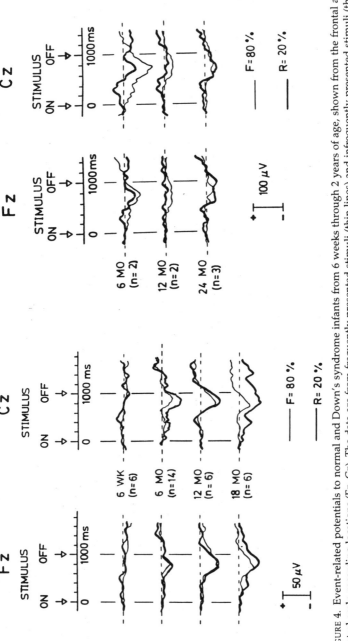

FIGURE 4. Event-related potentials to normal and Down's syndrome infants from 6 weeks through 2 years of age, shown from the frontal and central scalp recording locations (Fz, Cz). The data are from frequently presented stimuli (thin lines) and infrequently presented stimuli (thick lines). The Fz/Cz recordings on the left are from normal infants, and show larger Nc responses to the infrequent stimuli in the Cz lead beginning at 6 months of age. The recordings on the right are from the Down's syndrome infants, and show slightly larger Nc responses to the *frequent* rather than the *infrequent* stimuli, or show no difference between the frequent and infrequent stimuli. Reprinted by permission from Karrer & Ackles, 1988. Copyright 1988 Prentice-Hall, Inc.

to the brain. Spontaneous and evoked HR are both indices of arousal and attention systems, index brainstem, vagal and frontal lobe functioning, and are closely related to many psychological behaviors. The HR changes occurring in response to cognitive challenges, evoked HR, will be emphasized in this section.

3.1. Definition and Methodology

The electrocardiogram (ECG) is a strong electrical signal that may be recorded over the entire body. Electrode placement is not critical in measuring heart rate (HR). For convenience, the ECG is typically recorded by surface electrodes placed on the chest. The ECG is generated by electrical activity in the divisions of the heart as it pumps blood through the lungs and body. The amplitude of the ECG is in several millivolts rather than the microvolt range found with EEG. The ECG consists of several *waves* generated by different parts of the heart, and are labeled *P, Q, R, S,* and *T.* The interval between two R-waves is defined as the *interbeat interval* (IBI, R–R interval). The inverse of the IBI, or the number of beats in a specific time period, defines HR (beats-per-minute, BPM).

The original use of the R-wave for defining a beat was based on convenience rather than physiological rationale. The R-wave is very large relative to the other ECG waves. Psychophysiologists could use a *level-detector* that timed the occurrence of electrical potentials above a certain level, and could set the level such that the R-wave was the only ECG wave reaching that amplitude. The R-wave represents the depolarization of the atrium after the initiation of the heartbeat, and is not really the beginning of the beat. Recently, researchers have begun to use continuous analog-to-digital sampling to identify the peak of the R-wave, or the onset of the P, Q, S, or T waves, to identify different chronometric components of the ECG signal.

Like EEG, spontaneous HR changes occur under a variety of conditions. The HR changes occurring in synchrony with psychological processes or observable psychological activity are of greatest interest. These event-related HR changes are functionally related to several cognitive activities. Unlike EEG, the evoked HR changes are in magnitude several times larger than the spontaneous changes. Thus, the HR changes that are synchronous with psychological activity can be measured without averaging procedures. This has the advantage of allowing single-trial HR changes, manipulations involving several factors in repeated-subjects designs, and the recording of longer experimental sessions than is possible with ERP. Alternatively, HR changes contain less information than do EEG/ERP changes (e.g., Fig. 1).

There have been three or four trends in infant psychophysiological HR research. The first research studies were of the *cardiac orienting response*. There is a sudden deceleration of HR of 8 to 10 bpm in infants 3 months of age and older in response to almost any stimulus. Graham and Clifton (1966) proposed that this HR response was part of the orienting reflex studied by Sokolov (1963). There were a number of studies in the late 1960s and throughout the 1970s that investigated the characteristics of this HR response in infants, the age of its onset and characteristics at different ages, and its relation to infant characteristics (e.g., prematurity, race, sex). This work (like exogenous ERP components in infants) has used simple stimuli and experimental conditions to elicit the HR changes. These studies have been useful for understanding basic infant sensory and perceptual processing, but not very useful for understanding infant cognitive development or infant cognitive behavior. There have been many reviews of this work (e.g., W. Berg & K. Berg, 1987; Finlay & Ivinskis, 1987; Fox & Fitzgerald, 1990).

A second trend in the use of heart rate has been as an index of infant attention. Two characteristics of HR noted by Graham and Clifton, which characterize orienting responses in general, are the magnitude of the response to initial stimulus presentation, and the habituation of the response with repeated stimulus presentation. The first presentation of a novel stimulus evokes large HR changes. With repeated presentations, the HR gradually diminishes so that little or no HR change occurs, (i.e., habituation). When large HR changes are found, it is assumed that the infant is "attending" or "orienting" to a novel stimulus. The lack of HR changes indicates inattention, habituation, or disinterest. These two characteristics of the infant HR response, along with the habituation paradigm, led to the extensive use of HR in studies of infant attention and memory, and other aspects of cognitive development. A third trend in infant HR research has been the study of many other psychological dimensions of infant behavior (emotion, temperament, social interactions, risk status). Reviews of HR in infant attention, cognition, and other behavior, can be found in W. Berg and K. Berg (1987), Fox (1989), Fox and Fitzgerald (1990), and Von Bargen (1983), among others.

3.2. Infant Sustained Attention

The study of HR as a manifestation of the *cardiac orienting response*, or as a measure of nonspecific infant attention, is of limited use in understanding infant cognitive behavior. These studies have been unsophisticated in their model of the HR changes and the physiological systems controlling such changes. The HR changes were merely an alternative index of attention, a convenient response if the infant who could not respond with another type of behavioral response (e.g., verbal answers, press a button indicating a choice or reaction time).

The HR changes that occur during stimulus presentation may be broken down into components. Several researchers have hypothesized that the HR changes occurring during stimulus presentation can be broken down into several attention phases (Graham, 1979; Graham, Anthony, & Ziegler, 1983; Porges, 1976; Richards, 1988; Richards & Casey, 1991, 1992). Figure 5 shows the HR changes that occur while 3- to 6-month-old infants view an interesting visual stimulus. This figure illustrates the HR changes that occur during stimulus orienting, sustained attention, and attention termination. Stimulus orienting represents the initial processing of the novelty of the stimulus. Sustained attention amplifies and maintains the stimulus-orienting phase, and detailed stimulus information is processed during this phase. The attention-termination phase is hypothesized to be when the infant fixates on the stimulus following sustained attention, but is not processing information in the stimulus, and is resistant to responding to stimulus change. The phases of sustained attention and attention termination are of more importance to infant cognitive psychophysiology

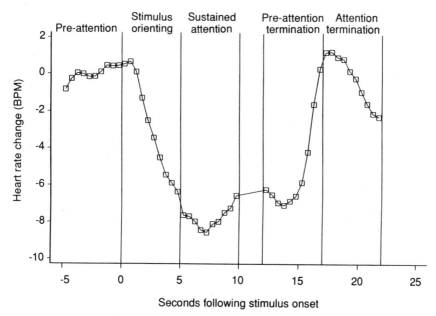

FIGURE 5. Heart-rate changes and hypothesized associated attention phases during fixation of infants to visual stimuli. Reprinted by permission from Richards & Casey, 1991. Copyright 1991 Society for Psychophysiological Research.

than are those of stimulus orienting because the former are thought to be related to complex cognitive activity. In addition, they parse the HR changes so that specific cognitive activity may be indexed during HR changes.

The study of the HR-defined attention phases has been enhanced by the on-line evaluation of HR changes occurring during visual attention. On-line evaluation allows the identification of HR changes as they occur during psychological behavior, and the modification of experimental events based on those changes. The evaluation of HR is done with micro-computer-controlled analog-to-digital conversion of the ECG at high speeds (1 msec, the identification of the R-wave in the ECG, and the software evaluation of HR changes. For example, Richards (1987) defined a significant HR deceleration as a sequence of 5 heartbeats with IBI's greater than the median of the IBI's occurring in a prestimulus interval. This was evaluated immediately after each beat occurred. Once the criterion for HR deceleration was met, then modification of the experimental situation was done to examine the characteristics of the attention phases.

The use of on-line evaluation of HR in the study of sustained attention and attention termination can be found in several studies by Richards and colleagues (e.g., Casey & Richards, 1988; Richards, 1985, 1987, 1989a, 1989b, 1991, 1994; Richards & Casey, 1991; see reviews by Richards, 1988, and Richards & Casey, 1992). These studies presented interesting visual stimuli on a TV monitor to elicit the HR changes. Active processing of the information in the stimulus should occur during sustained attention. During active stimulus processing, the infant should not be distractible by other events. During inattention (e.g., prestimulus or attention termination), the infant should be easily distracted from fixated stimuli by other events.

Distractibility during the HR-defined attention phases has been tested in several studies with infants from 2 to 6 months of age. An interesting stimulus was presented on a centrally located TV monitor. After some delay, a stimulus was presented in the periphery in order to interrupt the fixation on the central stimulus. Figure 6 is a schematic illustration of this procedure. The peripheral stimulus was presented with no central stimulus present (preattention); with the central stimulus fixated, accompanied by a significant HR deceleration (sustained attention); and with the central stimulus fixated, accompanied by a return of HR to its prestimulus level (attention termination). As expected by an understanding of the attention phases, the infants took longer to be distracted by the peripheral stimulus during the lowered, sustained HR deceleration (approximately 7 seconds; Fig. 6), than when HR had returned to its prestimulus level (approximately 3 seconds; Fig. 6) (e.g., Casey & Richards, 1988; Richards, 1987). If the

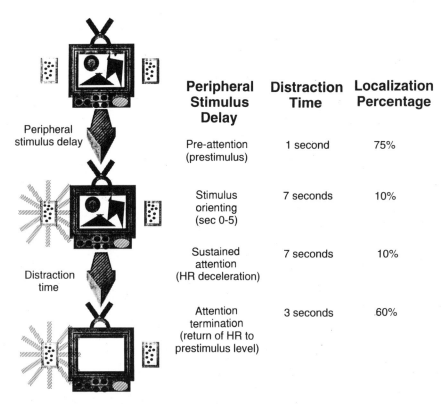

	Peripheral Stimulus Delay	Distraction Time	Localization Percentage
	Pre-attention (prestimulus)	1 second	75%
	Stimulus orienting (sec 0-5)	7 seconds	10%
	Sustained attention (HR deceleration)	7 seconds	10%
	Attention termination (return of HR to prestimulus level)	3 seconds	60%

FIGURE 6. Schematic illustration and typical results using on–line evaluation of heart rate to measure attention phases with the "interrupted stimulus paradigm." The peripheral stimulus delay is defined by time (preattention, stimulus orienting) or by on-line evaluation of heart–rate changes (sustained attention, attention termination).

peripheral stimulus was presented for a limited duration (e.g., 2 seconds), the infant did not localize the peripheral stimulus during stimulus orienting or sustained attention, but localized it very quickly during preattention and attention termination (Richards, 1991). The lack of distractibility by the peripheral stimulus during stimulus orienting and sustained attention indicates that attention was actively directed toward the centrally located stimulus. The ease with which distraction by the peripheral stimulus occurred during preattention and attention termination indicates that attention was no longer engaged by the central stimulus.

The findings from these studies show both developmental changes and individual differences in sustained attention. First, there were developmental changes in this age range in sustained attention but not in the other phases. For example, the level of the initial HR change during stimulus orienting was approximately 8 to 10 bpm across the age range from 8 weeks to 6 months of age (Richards, 1985, 1989b). The HR change during sustained attention increased across this age range, with the older infants (6-month-olds) showing sustained HR responding as long as they viewed the central stimulus (especially, Richards, 1985, Fig. 1; also see Table 1a). Second, HR changes and behavior in sustained attention showed reliable individual differences. On one level, this may be seen by correlations of around 0.4 or 0.5 between HR or fixation responses during sustained attention, between the ages of 3 and 4.5 months, and 4.5 and 6 months (Richards, 1989a, 1994). The individual differences are also shown by the strong relation between HR changes in sustained attention and HR variability due to respiration (RSA; respiratory sinus arrhythmia) in these age ranges. Across the age ranges from 3 to 6 months, the HR response during sustained attention is larger for infants with high levels of RSA than those with low RSA (Table 1b). RSA itself has a strong stability over this age range (Izard et al., 1991; Richards, 1989a, 1994). The relation between RSA and sustained attention appears to be due to fluctuations in RSA that occur as a result of development (Table 1c), and the corresponding close association of RSA and sustained attention at each age (Richards, 1989a, 1994; Richards & Casey, 1992). The individual differences and developmental changes are also paralleled by patterns of attention found in abnormally developing infants (see section 3.3).

A model of the attention-linked HR changes has been proposed by Richards and Casey (1992). It is supposed in this model that the HR changes are controlled by a widespread arousal system involving the mesencephalic reticular formation, limbic system, and frontal lobes. HR is an index of this system's activity, and HR changes during attention reflect this system's dual influence on cortical systems involved in attention and midbrain and brainstem systems involved in HR control. Developmental changes occur from birth through age six months in this system itself, as well as in this system's influence over the rapidly developing cortical areas involved in cognitively controlled attention. The increasing HR changes found in sustained attention from 2 to 6 months of age are a result of the development of this system, the development of this system's role in invigorating neural systems involved in attention, and the increasing level of integration between this nonspecific arousal system and attention systems that act specifically on cognitive operations. The developmental changes in the attention system parallel development in the neural systems controlling attention, fixation, and eye movement (e.g., Johnson, 1990). The integration between the arousal system and the systems controlling eye movement results in increasingly integrated brain-fixation-HR responses on the part of the developing infant.

TABLE 1
Table 1a: *Heart rate changes in attention phases from 2 to 6 months*

	8 weeks	14 weeks	20 weeks	26 weeks
Stimulus orienting	−3.7	−4.2	−5.2	−4.7
Sustained attention	−6.9	−6.9	−8.5	−11.0
Attention termination	−1.7	−2.8	0.3	0.3

Table 1b: *Heart rate changes in attention phases for high and low RSA infants*

	Low RSA	High RSA
Stimulus orienting	−4.8	−5.2
Sustained attention	−7.9	−11.5
Attention termination	−1.3	−0.5

Table 1c: *Baseline HR and RSA in full–term infants from 3 to 6 months of age*

	14 weeks	20 weeks	26 weeks
Baseline HR	152	148	142
Baseline RSA	0.78	0.86	0.92

Table 1d: *HR during sustained attention, and baseline RSA,
low risk preterm infants from 3 to 6 months of age*

	14 weeks	20 weeks	26 weeks
Baseline RSA	0.14	0.17	0.49
HR during sustained attention	−2.22	−3.90	−4.22

Table 1e: *HR during sustained attention, and baseline RSA, in preterm infants
with Respiratory Distress Syndrome from 3 to 6 months of age*

	14 weeks	20 weeks	26 weeks
Baseline	−0.14	−0.20	−0.67
HR during sustained attention	−2.80	−2.49	−1.89

Source: Richards, 1985; 1987; 1989a,b; 1994.

3.3. Implications for Abnormal Development

There have been many studies using HR of infant cognitive-psycho-physiological development with abnormal children. And, unlike that with EEG/ERP, this work has been with research paradigms of interest to infant cognitive psychophysiology. This work has been reviewed in places such as W. Berg and K. Berg (1987), Fox and Fitzgerald (1990) and Von Bargen (1983).

An example of a study of sustained attention in high-risk preterm infants was done by Richards (1994). HR variability (such as RSA) is lower in preterm infants with severe respiratory difficulty than in low-risk pre-term infants, or full-term infants (Kero, 1973; Fox, 1983; Rother et al., 1987). The HR responses of preterm infants are smaller or abnormal in response to psychological stimuli and situations (e.g., Fox & Lewis, 1983). A recent study by Richards (1994) found that HR responses of preterm infants during sustained attention were markedly different from low-risk preterm infants, or full-term infants. The infants were tested at 3, 4.5, and 6 months "conceptional" age, (e.g., gestational age + postnatal age). They were presented with an interesting visual stimulus on a TV monitor. As in previous studies with full-term infants (Richards, 1987, 1989a), the infant's HR was evaluated on-line for changes indicating stimulus orienting, sustained attention, and attention termination. The attention phases defined by HR were related to the distractibility of the infants to a peripheral visual stimulus.

There were two findings in this study of relevance to abnormal attention development. First, as in previous studies, level of RSA (HR variability) in a baseline recording was related to level of HR responding in the attention task. Figure 7 shows the HR changes in sustained attention for infants with high RSA relative to full-term infants, low RSA relative to full-term infants, and very-low-RSA infants found only in preterm groups. It can be seen that there was an increasing responsiveness of HR during sustained attention as the level of RSA increased. The very-low-RSA infants had HR responses that returned to prestimulus levels by about 5 or 6 seconds, whereas the other two groups had a sustained HR response during this time. The second finding was that low-risk preterm infants showed smaller HR responses in sustained attention, but had the same pattern of RSA increases and sustained attention increases found in full-term infants (Table 1d). High-risk preterm infants, those with respiratory distress syndrome at birth, had diminished HR responses in sustained attention, diminished levels of RSA, and no change in the diminished HR response or RSA levels over this age range (Table 1e). The attention deficit that was found in low-risk infants began to change as the infants became older, similar to full-term infants. The "deficit" found in the high-risk infants continued to exist over the entire age range.

The study of abnormal infant development with HR and cognitive tasks would serve a purpose similar to that outlined earlier with ERP. Damage to a CNS system caused by prenatal or perinatal events might be detected by psychophysiological tasks using HR or ERP measures. In some cases one measure might be specifically related to the perinatal event. For example, it is known that respiratory distress syndrome results in diminished HR variability, so one might expect abnormal cognitive behavior in infants in psychophysiological tasks using HR, but maybe not ERP's. This may be especially true in tasks designed to measure sustained attention, which is closely related to HR changes and HR variability in normal infants. On the other hand, if the CNS areas controlling attention were not affected, but those controlling visual association were, then one might expect the ERP measures taken during recognition memory to show abnormal patterns in infants, rather than HR measures. In both cases, or in cases where both HR and ERP were abnormal, the psychophysiological tasks that evaluate cognitive activity would be inherently more useful in identifying abnormal cognitive behavior in infants than psychophysiological tasks that evaluate simple sensory system.

4. Summary and Conclusions

This chapter reviewed two areas of infant cognitive psychophysiology. Both were chosen because they measured psychologically relevant physiological responses that occurred synchronously with psychological processes. Both of these areas showed developmental changes in the relation between the physiological measure and the psychological response.

There were several areas of infant cognitive psychophysiology that were not mentioned. Two in particular may be of interest. One area that has received a lot of attention is the relation between "spontaneous" or baseline physiological recordings, and psychological processing. The most relevant of these show parallel developmental changes in the physiology and the psychology, leading to the inference that the physiological changes underlie the psychological development. An example of a study of this type was reported by Bell and Fox (1992). They measured spontaneous EEG power in the frontal scalp regions, as well as coherence between the frontal brain region and other scalp regions. The EEG power and coherence, and its development, was presumed to show the maturity of the frontal brain area. They reported that infants at 12 months of age who

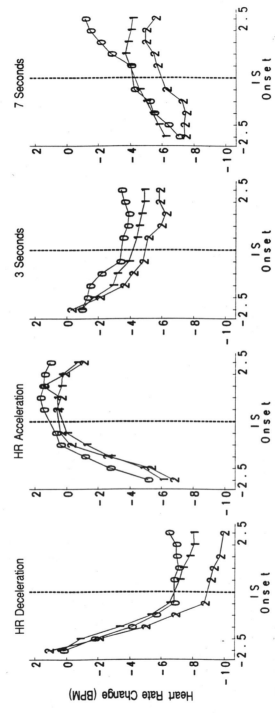

FIGURE 7. Mean heart-rate change preceding and following the interrupting stimulus onset for four interrupted-stimulus procedures, separately for pre- and full-term infants with high RSA (symbol: 2), pre- and full-term infants with low RSA relative to the full-term group (symbol: 1), and for preterm infants with very low RSA (symbol: 0). Reprinted by permission from Richards, 1994. Copyright 1994 Society for Psychophysiological Research.

successfully performed Piaget's object concept task with long levels of delay between exposure and test showed significant increases in frontal EEG power, and had larger coherence between the frontal and occipital brain regions. They proposed that the frontal region integrates representational memory with behavior control of response inhibition during the object concept task. Those with mature developmental patterns in EEG activity and interhemispheric coherence perform best on this task requiring frontal brain activity. In the Bell and Fox (1992) study, EEG/ERP was not measured at the same time as the cognitive behavior. Thus, the inferences about the brain–behavior relations exposed by the EEG measurements must be indirect. Such studies might be reasonably linked with ERP studies to show that concurrent brain activity, synchronous with the cognitive systems underlying the behavior, might be done in scalp areas recorded by these investigators.

There also have been many HR studies of developmental changes in baseline or spontaneous HR, and the relation of those changes to psychological development in the infant. One area that has received a lot of recent study is respiratory sinus arrhythmia (RSA) in HR. RSA is variability in HR that occurs at the same frequency as respiration. It is controlled by the brainstem areas involved in respiratory control, is affected by coordination in higher CNS cardiovascular centers, and is directly controlled at the efferent connections to the heart by the vagus nerve. This chapter has described some studies showing how baseline RSA changes over various ages were related to infant sustained attention (e.g., Richards, 1987, 1989, 1994; see Table 1). RSA has also been shown to be related to infant recognition memory (Linnemeyer & Porges, 1986; Richards & Casey, 1990), and several aspects of personality, temperament, stress, and reactivity in infants (Fox, 1989; Fox & Fitzgerald, 1990; Porges, 1991). RSA is also related to general developmental level (e.g., Fox & Porges, 1985; Richards & Cameron, 1989; Izard et al., 1991), and RSA level predicts later developmental outcome (Fox & Porges, 1985). As with the spontaneous EEG/ERP measures, the inference of causal relations between RSA and psychological behavior is indirect and must be made based on their close developmental association. However, developmental studies of HR during sustained attention, and RSA during baseline, have an advantage because the HR changes during attention are known to be controlled by the vagus nerve (e.g., Richards & Casey, 1991), the same system that controls RSA. Thus the close RSA/sustained attention relation across ages has a more direct connection, allowing stronger causal inferences.

The developmental changes in HR response, the developmental changes in ERP during the oddball paradigm, and the changes in spontaneous HR (e.g., RSA) and EEG suggests that an integration of the HR and

EEG/ERP measures may be possible. Infant attention and recognition memory are closely linked from the ages of 3 to 12 months. Changes in the selective and information processing aspects of attention are at least partially responsible for the increases in recognition memory over this age range (Richards & Casey, 1990). The attention-HR and the recognition memory-ERP associations, along with the attention–recognition memory link, suggest that an integrative research strategy using evoked HR and ERP, and attention and recognition memory, would be fruitful in studying infant cognitive-psychophysiological development. The developmental changes in spontaneous EEG patterns and HR patterns (e.g., RSA) also may be multiple indicators of widespread cognitive changes in the infant in the first year. Such a research strategy might emphasize a common paradigm or behavior, while looking at the developmental manifestations of this in the various physiological domains. This research strategy also could be used to characterize patterns of abnormal recognition memory in young infants when the abnormality is caused by specific CNS deficits. Perinatal insults that affect recognition memory (e.g., Gunderson, Grant, Burbacher, Fagan, & Mottet, 1986; Jacobson, Fein, Jacobson, Schwartz, & Dowler, 1985) may operate via CNS damage that could be detected in psychophysiological studies of recognition memory.

A more sophisticated systems view of psychophysiological development is needed in the infant ERP work. Such questions as where is it generated, how those areas develop, and why is it related to significant psychological development, should be answered. Studies of the source generators of these ERP components (e.g., Scherg, 1990; Scherg & Picton, 1991) would be useful in identifying the locations in the brain of the endogenous ERP components studied in infant recognition memory. More sophisticated models of brain development and psychological development and their integration in psychophysiological recordings are necessary. The models of HR change and development, and psychophysiological relations of HR, RSA, and attention (Richards & Casey, 1992; Porges, 1992; Berg & Donahue, 1992) have more sophisticated models of brain-controlled, psychologically relevant HR change than do analogous review chapters dealing with EEG and ERP (e.g., Vaughan & Kurtzberg, 1992; Nelson, 1993).

This basic research in infant cognitive psychophysiology has enormous potential for the study of abnormal infant development. On one hand, the spontaneous-EEG and the exogenous-ERP work have already shown the contribution of measurable brain functioning on the assessment of concurrent infant psychopathology. The prediction of psychological developmental outcome with early measures of physiological functioning has been successful. One deficiency in this area is the evaluation of psychological processes concurrently with ERP activity in young infants. Whereas this work has been successful when dealing with abnormality or psychopathology in older children (e.g., Courchesne & Yeung-Courchesne, 1988), it has not been done with infant abnormal development. The evaluation of ERP with concurrent cognitive processes in young infants would aid the study of abnormal development by identifying the locus of the effects of early risk factors. It also should help in examining the disruption that occurs in higher order cognitive processes in high-risk infants (e.g., recognition memory, sustained attention, object concept), with a view to identification of children who are at risk for abnormal cognitive or intellectual functioning in the preschool and school years.

The work with HR, particularly evoked HR changes in psychological situations, has been more extensive than that with ERP. This work could be profitably expanded with more recent models of infant cognitive-psychophysiological development that has a reasonable theoretical model for the underlying brain systems that are developing (e.g., Johnson, 1990; Richards & Casey, 1992). These theoretical models hypothesize that normal infant psychological development results from changes in brain systems and the increasing integration/specialization of brain systems over the first year of life. Abnormal infant development could conceivably occur because of abnormal development in these brain systems. For example, the study with high-risk premature infants presented earlier (Richards, 1994) showed that the continuing deficit in the HR responses during sustained attention was a result of the continuing, abnormally low RSA level in the high-risk infants. This, in turn, must be related to the brain systems controlling RSA, and may have more wide-ranging implications for high-risk infant development because of the association of RSA with other psychological behaviors. With models like these, the conditions in infancy that lead to abnormal psychological development (e.g., prematurity with respiratory problems, genetic abnormalities, teratogens) could be characterized more precisely, and the nature of the effects better specified, with the more sophisticated models of brain-behavior development found in these infant cognitive-psychophysiological models.

ACKNOWLEDGMENTS: The preparation of this chapter was supported by a grant from the National Institute of Child Health and Human Development, #R01-HD18942, a Research Scientist Development Award from the National Institute of Mental Health, #K02-MH00958. Some of the research reported herein also was supported by a Social and Behavioral Sciences Research Grant from the March of Dimes Birth Defects Foundation.

5. References

Andreassi, J. L. (1989). *Psychophysiology*. Hillsdale, NJ: Erlbaum.

Bell, M.A., & Fox, N.A. (1992). The relations between frontal brain electrical activity and cognitive development during infancy. *Child Development, 63*, 1142–1163.

Berg, W. K., & Berg, K. M. (1987). Psychophysiological development in infancy: State, startle, and attention. In J. D. Osofsky (Ed.), *Handbook of infant development* (pp. 238–317). New York: Wiley.

Bert, W. K., & Donahue, R. L. (1992). Anticipatory processes in infants: Cardiac components. In B. A. Campbell, H. Hayne, & R. Richardson (Eds.), Attention and information processing in infants and adults (pp. 61–80). Hillsdale, N. J.: Erlbaum.

Casey, B. J., & Richards, J. E. (1988). Sustained visual attention in young infants measured with an adapted version of the visual preference paradigm. *Child Development, 59*, 1514–1521.

Courchesne, E. (1977). Event-related brain potentials: Comparison between children and adults. *Science, 197*, 589–592.

Courchesne, E. (1978). Neurophysiological correlates of cognitive development: Changes in long-latency event-related potentials from childhood to adulthood. *Electroencephalography and Clinical Neurophysiology, 45*, 468–482.

Courchesne, E. (1988). Physioanatomical considerations in Down's syndrome. In L. Nadel (Eds.), *The psychobiology of Down's syndrome. Issues in the biology of language and cognition.* (pp. 291–313). Cambridge, MA: MIT Press.

Courchesne, E. (1990). Chronology of postnatal human brain development: Event-related potential, positron emission tomography, myelinogenesis, and synaptogenesis studies. In J. W. Rohrbaugh, R. Parasuraman, (Eds.), *Event-related brain potentials: Basic issues and applications.* (pp. 210–241). New York: Oxford University Press.

Courchesne, E., Ganz, L., & Norcia, A. M. (1981). Event-related brain potentials to human faces in infants. *Child Development, 52*, 804–811.

Courchesne, E., & Yeung-Courchesne, R. (1988). Event-related brain potentials. In M. Rutter, A. H. Tuma, I. S. Lann (Eds.), *Assessment and diagnosis in child psychopathology.* (pp. 264–299). New York: Guilford Press.

Fagan, J. (1992). Intelligence: A theoretical viewpoint. *Current Directions in Psychological Science, 1*, 82–86.

Finlay, D., & Ivinkis, A. (1987). Cardiac change responses and attentional mechanisms in infants. In B. E. McKenzie & R. H. Day (Eds.), *Perceptual development in early infancy* (pp. 45–63). Hillsdale, NJ: Erlbaum.

Fox, N. A. (1983). Maturation of autonomic control in preterm infants. *Developmental Psychobiology, 16*, 495–504.

Fox, N. A. (1989). Heart-rate variability and behavioral reactivity: Individual differences in autonomic patterning and their relation to infant and child temperament. In J. S. Reznick (Ed.), *Perspectives on behavioral inhibition.* (pp. 177–195). Chicago: University of Chicago Press.

Fox, N.A., & Fitzgerald, H. E. (1990). Autonomic function in infancy. *Merrill Palmer Quarterly, 36*, 27–51.

Fox, N.A., & Lewis, M. (1983). Cardiac response to speech sounds in preterm infants: Effects of postnatal illness at three months. *Psychophysiology, 20*, 481–488.

Fox, N. A., & Porges, S. W. (1985). The relation between neonatal heart period patterns and developmental outcome. *Child Development, 56*, 28–37.

Graham, F. K. (1979). Distinguishing among orienting, defense, and startle reflexes. In H. D.

Kimmel, E. H. van Olst & J. F. Orlebeke (Eds.), *The orienting reflex in humans* (pp. 137–167), Hillsdale, N. J.: Erlbaum.

Graham, F. K., Anthony, B. J., & Ziegler, B. L. (1983). The orienting response and developmental processes. In D. Siddle (Ed.), *Orienting and habituation: Perspectives in human research* (pp. 371–430), Sussex, England: Wiley.

Graham, F. K., & Clifton, R. K. (1966). Heart-rate change as a component of the orienting response. *Psychological Bulletin, 65,* 305–320.

Gunderson, V. M., Grant, K. S., Burbacher, T. M., Fagan, J. F., & Mottet, N. K. (1986). The effect of low-level prenatal methylmercury exposure on visual recognition memory in infant crab-eating macaques. *Child Development, 57,* 1076–1083.

Hoffman, M. J., Salapatek, P., & Kuskowski, M. (1981). Evidence for visual memory in the averaged and single trial evoked potentials in human infants. *Infant Behavior and Development, 4,* 401–421.

Izard, C. E., Porges, S. W., Simons, R. F., Haynes, O. M., Hyde, C., Pavisi, M., & Cohen, B. (1991). Infant cardiac activity: Developmental changes and relations with attachment. *Developmental Psychology, 27,* 432–439.

Jacobson, S. W., Fein, G. G., Jacobson, J. L., Schwartz, P. M., & Dowler, J. K. (1985). The effect of intrauterine PCB exposure on visual recognition memory. *Child Development, 56,* 853–860.

Jasper, H. H. (1958). The 10–20 electrode system of the International Federation. *Electroencephalography and Clinical Neurophysiology, 10,* 371–375.

Johnson, M. H. (1990). Cortical maturation and the development of visual attention in early infancy. *Journal of Cognitive Neuroscience, 2,* 81–95.

Karrer, R., & Ackles, P. K. (1987). Visual event-related potentials of infants during a modified oddball procedure. In R. Johnson, J. W. Rohrbaugh, & R. Parasuraman (Eds.), *Current trends in event-related potential research* (pp. 603–608). Amsterdam: Elsevier.

Karrer, R., & Ackles, P. K. (1988). Brain organization and perceptual/cognitive development in normal and Down's syndrome infants: A research program. In P. Vietze & H. G. Vaughan, Jr. (Eds.), *The early identification of infants with developmental disabilities* (pp. 210–234). Philadelphia: Grune & Stratton.

Kero, P. (1973). Heart rate variation in infants with the respiratory distress syndrome. *Acta Paediatrica Scandanavica,* Supplement No. 250.

Kurtzberg, D. (1982). Event-related potentials in the evaluation of high-risk infants. *Annals of the New York Academy of Sciences, 388,* 557–571.

Kurtzberg, D., Vaughan, H. G., Courchesne, E., Friedman, D., Harter, M. R., & Putnam, L. E. (1984). Developmental aspects of event-related potentials. *Annals of the New York Academy of Sciences, 425,* 300–318.

Kurtzberg, D., Vaughan, H. G., & Novak, G. P. (1986). Discriminative brain responses to speech sounds in the newborn high-risk infant. In V. Gallai (Ed.), *Maturation of the CNS and evoked potentials* (pp. 253–259). Amsterdam: Elsevier.

Linnemeyer, S. A., & Porges, S. W. (1986). Recognition memory and cardiac vagal tone in 6-month-old infants. *Infant Behavior and Development, 9,* 43–56.

McIsaac, H., & Polich, J. (1992). Comparison of infant and adult P300 from auditory stimuli. *Journal of Experimental Child Psychology, 53,* 115–128.

Nelson, C. A. (1993). Neural correlates of recognition memory in the first postnatal year of life. In G. Dawson & K. Fischer (Eds.), *Human behavior and the developing brain.* (pp. 269–313). New York: Guilford.

Nelson, C. A., & Collins, P. F. (1991). Event-related potential and looking-time analysis of infants' responses to familiar and novel events: Implications for visual recognition memory. *Developmental Psychology, 27,* 50–58.

Nelson, C. A., & Collins, P. F. (1992). Neural and behavioral correlates of visual recognition memory in 4- and 8-month-old infants. *Brain and Cognition, 19,* 105–121.

Nelson, C. A., & deRegnier, R. A. (1992). Neural correlates of attention and memory in the first year of life. *Developmental Neuropsychology, 8,* 119–134.

Nelson, C. A., Ellis, A. E., Collins, P. F., & Lang, S. F. (1990). Infants' neuroelectric responses to missing stimuli: Can missing stimuli be novel stimuli? *Developmental Neuropsychology, 6,* 339–349.

Nelson, C. A., Henschel, M., & Collins, P. F. (1993). Neural correlates of cross-modal recognition memory by 8-month-old human infants. *Developmental Psychology, 29,* 411–420.

Nelson, C. A., & Salapatek, P. (1986). Electrophysiological correlates of infant recognition memory. *Child Development, 57,* 1483–1497.

Porges, S. W. (1976). Peripheral and neurochemical parallels of psychopathology: A psychophysiological model relating autonomic imbalance in hyperactivity, psychopathology, and autism. In H. Reese (Ed.), *Advances in child development and behavior* (Vol. 11, pp. 35–65). New York: Academic Press.

Porges, S. W. (1991). Vagal tone: An autonomic mediator of affect. In J. Garber, K. A. Dodge (Eds.), *The development of emotion regulation and dysregulation.* (pp. 111–128). New York: Cambridge University Press.

Porges, S. W. (1992). Autonomic regulation and attention. In B. A. Campbell, H. Hayne, & R. Richardson (Eds.), *Attention and information processing in infants and adults: Perspectives from human and animal research.* (pp. 201–223). Hillsdale, NJ: Erlbaum.

Porges, S. W., & Fox, N. A. (1986). Developmental psychophysiology. In M. G. H. Coles, E. Donchin, & S. W. Porges (Eds.), *Psychophysiology: Systems, processes, and applications* (pp. 611–625). New York: Guilford.

Richards, J. E. (1985). The development of sustained visual attention in infants from 14 to 26 weeks of age. *Psychophysiology, 22,* 409–416.

Richards, J. E. (1987). Infant visual sustained attention and respiratory sinus arrhythmia. *Child Development, 58,* 488–496.

Richards, J. E. (1988). Heart rate changes and heart rate rhythms, and infant visual sustained attention. In P. K. Ackles, J. R. Jennings & M. G. H. Coles (Eds.), *Advances in psychophysiology* (Vol. 3. pp. 189–221). Greenwich, CT: JAI Press.

Richards, J. E. (1989a). Development and stability in visual sustained attention in 14-, 20-, and 26-week old infants. *Psychophysiology, 26,* 422–430.

Richards, J. E. (1989b). Sustained visual attention in 8-week-old infants. *Infant Behavior and Development, 12,* 425–436.

Richards, J. E. (1991). Infant eye movements during peripheral visual stimulus localization as a function of central stimulus attention status. *Psychophysiology, 28,* S4. (abstract)

Richards, J. E. (1994). Baseline respiratory sinus arrhythmia and heart-rate responses during sustained visual attention in preterm infants from 3 to 6 months of age. *Psychophysiology, 30,* 235–243.

Richards, J. E., & Cameron, D. (1989). Infant Heart-rate variability and behavioral developmental status. *Infant Behavior and Development, 12,* 45–58.

Richards, J. E., & Casey, B. J. (1990). Infant visual recognition memory performance as a function of heart-rate defined phases of attention. *Psychophysiology, 27,* S58. (abstract)

Richards, J. E., & Casey, B. J. (1991). Heart-rate variability during attention phases in young infants. *Psychophysiology, 28,* 43–53.

Richards, J. E., & Casey, B. J. (1992). Development of sustained visual attention in the human infant. In B. A. Campbell, H. Hayne, & R. Richardson (Eds.), *Attention and information processing in infants and adults: Perspectives from human and animal research.* (pp. 30–60). Hillsdale, NJ: Erlbaum.

Rother, M., Zwiener, U., Eiselt, M., Witte, H., Zwacka, G., & Frenzel, T. (1987). Differentiation of healthy newborns and newborns-at-risk by spectral analysis of heart rate fluctuations and respiratory movements. *Early Human Development, 15,* 349–363.

Salapatek, P., & Nelson, C. A. (1985). Event-related potentials and visual development. In. G. Gottlieb & N. A. Krasnegor (Eds.), *The measurement of audition and vision in the first year of postnatal life: a methodological overview.* (pp. 419–453). Norwood, NJ: Ablex.

Scherg, M. (1990). Fundamentals of dipole source potential analysis. In F. Grandori, M. Hoke, & G. L. Romani (Eds.), *Auditory evoked magnetic fields and potentials* (pp. 40–69). Karger, Basel.

Scherg, M., & Picton, T. W. (1991). Separation and identification of event-related potential components by brain electrical source analysis. In C. H. M. Brunia, G. Mulder, & M. N. Verbaten (Eds.), *Event-related brain research* (pp. 24–37). Amsterdam: Elsevier.

Sokolov, E. N. (1963). *Perception and the conditioned reflex.* New York: Macmillan.

Thompson, L. A., Fagan, J. F., & Fulkner, D. W. (1991). Longitudinal prediction of specific cognitive abilities from infant novelty preference. *Child Development, 62,* 530–538.

Vaughan, H. G., & Kurtzberg, D. (1989). Electrophysiological indices of normal and aberrant cortical maturation. In P. Kellaway & J. L. Noebels (Eds.), *Problems and concepts in developmental neurophysiology* (pp. 263–287). Baltimore, MD: Johns Hopkins University Press.

Vaughan, H. G., & Kurtzberg, D. (1992). Electrophysiologic indices of human brain maturation and cognitive development. In M. R. Gunnar, C. A. Nelson (Eds.), *Developmental behavioral neuroscience. The Minnesota Symposia on Child Psychology* (Vol. 24, pp. 1–36). Hillsdale, NJ: Erlbaum.

Von Bargen, D. M. Infant heart rate: A review of research and methodology. *Merrill-Palmer Quarterly, 29,* 115–149.

3   Comorbidity of Disorders in Children and Adolescents

Developmental Perspectives

Editha D. Nottelmann and Peter S. Jensen

1. Introduction

Since the advent of the *Diagnostic and Statistical Manual of Mental Disorders*, Third Edition and Third Edition, Revised (DSM-III and DSM-III-R), clinicians and investigators have shown increasing interest in the significance of comorbid disorders in children and adolescents. Coincident with a sharpened focus on comorbidity, some investigators have developed detailed data on child and adolescent comorbid diagnoses in clinical and epidemiological studies (e.g., Bird, Gould, & Staghezza, 1993; Cohen, 1993; Pfeffer & Plutchik, 1989); and comorbidity has been the subject of recent reviews of child and adolescent disorders research (e.g., Biederman, Newcorn, & Sprich, 1991; Zoccolillo, 1992). Accumulating evidence suggests that comorbidity is pervasive. Concerns about weaknesses of the nosological system are being advanced to account for the high rates of comorbidity in general (Achenbach, 1990/1991; Caron & Rutter, 1991; Pfeffer & Plutchik, 1989; Rutter, 1989), as well as for the co-occurrence of specific disorders (e.g., Biederman et al., 1991; Carlson, 1990). With respect to children and adolescents, these concerns intersect with developmental and methodological issues. For the advancement of knowledge about child and adolescent disorders, it is essential that comorbidity patterns be identified

EDITHA D. NOTTELMANN AND PETER S. JENSEN • National Institute of Mental Health, Rockville, Maryland 20857.

Advances in Clinical Child Psychology, Volume 17, edited by Thomas H. Ollendick and Ronald J. Prinz. Plenum Press, New York, 1995.

and examined, not only for their implications for prognosis and treatment, but also for evaluation of the classification system on which they are based.

2. Background

In this chapter, we begin with current questions about the meaning and significance of comorbid psychiatric disorders in children and adolescents, examine data on the prevalence of disorders in the general population, survey available data concerning age- and sex-related differences and changes in noncomorbid and comorbid disorders for developmental trends, explore the patterns of comorbidity of the most prevalent disorders, examine the correlates and longitudinal predictors of comorbidity, and conclude with implications of comorbidity findings for child- and adolescent-disorders research and practice.

2.1. Current Issues for Comorbidity in Child and Adolescent Disorders

2.1.1. Developmental Considerations

Childhood and adolescence span periods of significant changes in cognitive capacity, social status, and social functioning. Stability/continuity is an especially critical factor in child and adolescent psychopathology, raising questions about disorders that are developmentally specific and the short- versus long-term significance of various disorders. Such questions can best be addressed in longitudinal studies that span developmental stages and, at the same time, consider familial and extrafamilial contexts, examining adaptive as well as maladaptive behavior and functioning. However, from what is known about developmental processes in childhood and adolescence, not only age- but also sex-related differences are likely to influence the expression of psychopathology and the prevalence and course of specific disorders.

From a developmental perspective, comorbid disorders may reflect amorphous, nonspecific expressions of psychopathology in younger children, in contrast to more clearly articulated clinical presentations by older children or adolescents. Boundary problems between disorders, for example, may be due to many nonspecific early responses to family psychopathology (Carlson, 1990). However, comorbidity also could be a developmentally influenced, transient phenomenon. That is, the expression of a disorder may change with age or developmental stage, and the earlier and later manifestations of an underlying condition may co-occur during transition, while symptomatology changes from the earlier to its later form. Thus, one disorder may be the early manifestation of another (Caron & Rutter, 1991). Finally, psychopathology may interfere with the developmentally appropriate acquisition of social and academic skills, which become increasingly important for daily functioning in later childhood and adolescence. As a result, a comorbid second or third disorder may develop when early problems remain unresolved.

Questions of etiology as well as concerns with the course of disorders (whether co-occurring disorders arise simultaneously or whether one disorder leads to the other) are closely related to developmental considerations, especially when the developmental status of children and adolescents is taken into account. These include questions of vulnerabilities, risk factors, and familial (genetic as well as environmental) transmission that involve both child/adolescent characteristics and the familial and extra-familial contexts in which development takes place. Specifically, with regard to comorbidity, it has been suggested that co-occurring disorders in children and adolescents may result from shared risk factors, such as temperamental adversity or family discord, or overlap between risk factors; for example, in comorbid depression and conduct disorder, depressed parents for the former and family disorder for the latter (Rutter, 1989).

2.1.2. Questions of Classification

A major question regarding classification is whether problems with boundaries between co-occurring disorders may be inflating the rate of comorbid diagnoses. On the one hand, diagnostic criteria for frequently co-occurring disorders may not discriminate sufficiently between separate disorders (Achenbach 1990/1991; Caron & Rutter, 1991). General social impairment could result in a high rate of nonspecific symptoms included in psychopathology criteria for different disorders (Caron & Rutter, 1991). Critical features for drawing clear boundaries between distinct disorders may be missing. On the other hand, higher order patterns of co-occurring problems, in fact, may represent single diagnostic entities (Achenbach, 1990/1991); and artificial subdivision of syndromes may contribute to high levels of comorbidity (Caron and Rutter, 1991). A closely related issue concerns the point at which boundaries are drawn between the normal and pathological range of functioning. Inappropriately low boundaries may be contributing to comorbidity (Achenbach, 1990/1991; Caron & Rutter, 1991); likewise, the stipulation of severity and/or impairment criteria may result not only in lower disorder prevalence, but also in lower comorbidity rates. While inappropriately low boundaries may inflate apparent comorbidity, it is important that elevated subclinical levels are considered in investigations of comorbidity, especially when children and adolescents are followed across time, so that the significance of incipient stages of comorbidity can be examined.

Although our current nosologic system (DSM III-R) serves an important organizing function in research and has facilitated communication, it is largely atheoretical and descriptive. As the database generated under the DSM system expands and reveals limitations, it must necessarily accommodate further revisions. The findings on comorbid disorders are likely to contribute to this process. The relative prognostic significance of disorders in their comorbid and noncomorbid forms, for instance, should help to define a hierarchy among co-occurring disorders and establish entities that cross current classification boundaries.

2.1.3. Methodological Issues

One methodological issue in the assessment of children and adolescents concerns the best method of combining data from multiple informants. For both research and clinical purposes, it is considered necessary to rely on information about children's functioning from parents and teachers, in addition to—depending on the child's age—children's self reports. The way in which information from different informants is integrated for diagnosis influences comorbidity as well as prevalence rates. For example, whereas prevalence rates of internalizing disorders based on parent report tend to be lower than those based on child or adolescent report, prevalence rates of externalizing disorders based on child or adolescent report may be lower than those based on parent report (e.g., Bird et al., 1992). If parent–child concordance is sought, the rates of most disorders are likely to be lower than single-informant reports (Jensen, Shervette, Xenakis, & Richters, 1993), because parent- and child-based diagnoses rarely overlap. Similarly, because of evidence of differences between parent and teacher reports (e.g., Offord, Boyle, Fleming, Blum, & Grant, 1989), if pervasiveness is included as a criterion for diagnosis (e.g., concordance between parents and teachers for psychopathology observed at home and at school), disorder rates are likely to be lower (e.g., Offord et al., 1989). It may be expected, therefore, that comorbidity rates also would be lower for child–parent concordant and parent–teacher concordant disorders.

An additional methodological issue concerns sampling. Questions continue to be raised about whether data on comorbid child and adolescent disorders may be artifactual (Caron & Rutter, 1991); that is, whether multiple disorders seen in clinic samples reflect the nature of psychopathology in the general population. Comorbidity seen in clinic settings may be merely a manifestation of severe psychopathology and/or substantial impairment in functioning, so that children and adolescents with co-morbid disorders are more likely to be referred for care than children and adolescents with less severe, noncomorbid conditions.

2.2. Overall Prevalence of Child and Adolescent Disorders

During the past decade, there has been a remarkable increase in data on child and adolescent disorders based on general population studies. Since Gould, Wunsch-Hitzig, and Dohrenwend (1981) reviewed 25 studies (published 1928 through 1974) and estimated the prevalence of childhood disorders to be 11.8%, recent reviews of epidemiologic studies by Offord et al. (1987), Costello (1990), Brandenburg, Friedman, and Silver (1990), and Fleming, Offord, and Boyle (1989) have indicated that the prevalence of child and adolescent mental disorders based on DSM-III criteria ranges from 5.0% to 26.0%. The larger, more methodologically rigorous general-population studies suggest prevalence rates in a narrower range (17.6% to 22.0%). Most of the studies show a higher prevalence rate of disorders for boys than girls in childhood, but a higher rate for girls than boys in adolescence. Many of these gender-related differences are disorder and age-specific. We examine several of these studies below.

2.2.1. Ontario Child Health Study (OCHS; Canada)

The Ontario Child Health Study six-month prevalence rate for 5- to 16-year-old children (N = 2674) was 18.1% (Offord et al., 1987). This study utilized the Survey Diagnostic Instrument (SDI), which consisted of items selected from the Child Behavior Checklist, augmented as needed, to operationalize DSM-III criteria for four disorders. The SDI was administered by interviewers to parents and teachers for children below age 12; and, for 12- to 16-year-olds, to parents and children. The study targeted four disorders: Conduct Disorder (CD), Hyperactivity (Attention Deficit Disorder with Hyperactivity), Emotional Disorder, and Somatization. Sixty-eight percent of the children with at least one of the four diagnoses had one or more additional disorders. Since some of these diagnoses represent aggregates, the comorbidity rate, although high, may be a conservative estimate.

Broken down by age, 4 to 11 and 12 to 16 years, as well as sex, the overall rate was higher for boys than girls in the younger age group and somewhat lower for boys than girls in the older group (see Table 1). In general, rates were higher for boys for externalizing disorders and, in the older age group, higher for girls for internalizing disorders.

TABLE 1.
Prevalence Rates by Disorder

		Age (in years)									
	N	2	4	6	8	10	12	14	16	18	20
Conduct Disorder											
Offord et al. (1987)	2674		←—	—	—	5.5%	—	—	—→		
Boys	1329		←—	—	6.5%	—	—	10.4%	—→		
Girls	1345		←—	—	1.8%	—	—	4.1%	—→		
Bird et al. (1988)	386		←—	—	—	1.5%	—	—	—→		
Anderson et al. (1987)	792					3.4%					
McGee et al. (1992)	750					2.0%	—	5.7%			
Feehan et al. (1993)	890							4.8%	—	3.5	
Velez et al. (1989)											
Time 2	776					←11.9%→		11.7%	←11.6%→		
Time 3	776						←10.9%→		←10.3%→	9.9%→	
Cohen et al. (1993)											
Boys	749						←16.0%→	←15.8%→		9.5%→	
Girls	746						←3.8%→	←9.2%→		7.1%→	
Kashani et al. (1987)	150								←8.7%→		
Boys	75							9.3%→			
Girls	75							←8.0%→			

Study	N	Prevalence
Kashani et al. (1989)	210	11.4% ← → 21.4%
Boys	105	5.7% ← 7.2% → 15.2%
Girls	105	15.2%
Costello et al. (1988)	300	2.6% ← → 7.6%

Oppositional Defiant Disorder

Study	N	Prevalence
Bird et al. (1988)	386	9.7%
Anderson et al. (1987)	792	5.7%
McGee et al. (1992)	750	1.3% ← → 2.0%
Feehan et al. (1993)	890	1.5%
Velez et al. (1989)		
Time 2	776	15.6% ← 17.4% → 18.6%
Time 3	776	22.5% ← 17.7% → 14.3%
Cohen et al. (1993)		
Boys	749	14.2% ← 15.4% → 12.2%
Girls	746	10.4% ← 15.6% → 12.5%
Kashani et al. (1987)	150	6.0%
Boys	75	4.0%
Girls	75	8.0%
Kashani et al. (1989)	210	6.7% ← → 5.7%
Boys	105	8.6%
Girls	105	8.6%
Costello et al. (1988)	300	2.6% ← → 4.8%

(continued)

TABLE 1. (Continued)

		Age (in years)									
	N	2	4	6	8	10	12	14	16	18	20
Attention Deficit Disorder[a]											
Offord et al. (1987)[b]	2674					6.2%					
Boys	1329				10.1%			7.3%			
Girls	1345				3.3%			3.4%			
Bird et al. (1988)	386					10.1%					
Anderson et al. (1987)	792						6.7%				
McGee et al. (1992)	750						1.7%		1.2%		
Velez et al. (1989)											
Time 2	776							12.6%			
Time 3	776						12.8%	9.3%		6.8%	
Cohen et al. (1993)											
Boys	749						17.1%	11.4%		5.8%	
Girls	746						8.5%	6.5%		6.2%	
Kashani et al. (1987)	150							2.0%			
Boys	75							1.3%			
Girls	75							2.7%			
Kash ani et al. (1989)	210				1.5%		1.4%		5.7%		
Boys	105						1.5%				
Girls	105						0%	2.9%			
Costello et al. (1988)	300					0.2%					

Separation Anxiety

Study	N	Prevalence
Bird et al. (1988)	386	4.8%
Anderson et al. (1987)	792	3.5%
McGee et al. (1992)	750	1.9%—1.7%
Velez et al. (1989)		
Time 2	776	25.6%—14.6%—6.8%
Time 3	776	15.3%—8.9%—4.4%
Cohen et al. (1993)		
Boys	749	11.4%—1.2%
Girls	746	13.1%—4.6%—1.8%
Costello et al. (1988)	300	4.1%

Overanxious Disorder

Study	N	Prevalence
Anderson et al. (1987)	792	2.9%
McGee et al. (1992)	750	2.5%—5.2%
Velez et al. (1989)		
Time 2	776	9.7%—9.0%—8.6%
Time 3	776	19.1%—15.3%—12.7%
Cohen et al. (1993)		
Boys	749	12.8%—5.3%—5.4%
Girls	746	15.4%—14.1%—13.8%
Costello et al. (1988)	300	4.6%

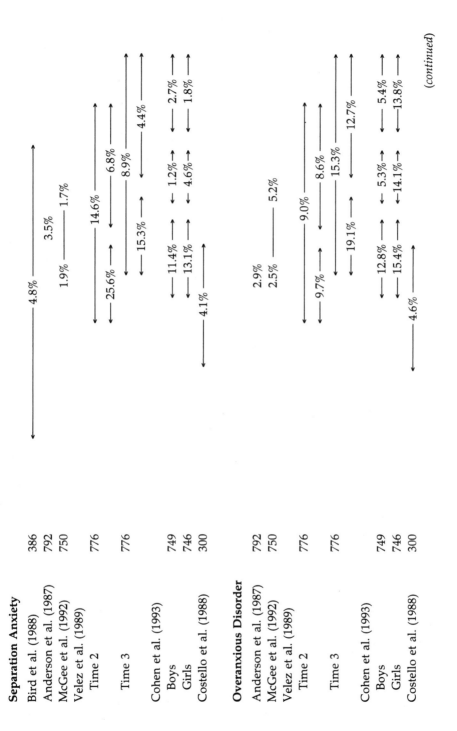

(continued)

Table 1. (Continued)

	N	||| Age (in years)									
		2	4	6	8	10	12	14	16	18	20
Simple Phobia											
Bird et al. (1988)	386		←————————			2.3%			————————→		
Anderson et al. (1987)	792					2.4%					
McGee et al. (1992)	750					2.5% ————		5.2%			
Costello et al. (1988)	300				←——— 9.2%		———→				
Anxiety Disorder											
Kashani et al. (1987)	150								← 8.7% →		
Boys	75								← 4.0% →		
Girls	75							← 13.3% →			
Kashani et al. (1989)	210				←——— 25.7%		21.0% ———→		21.4%		
Boys	105				←————		15.7% ———→				
Girls	105				←————		28.6% ———→				
Feehan et al. (1993)[c]	890							9.7% ————		14.9%	
Depressive Disorders											
Offord et al. (1987)[d]	2674		←————————			9.9%			————————→		
Boys	1329				←——— 10.2%		———→	4.9%			
Girls	1345				←——— 10.7%		———→	13.6%			
Bird et ai. (1988)[e]	386		←————————			5.9%			————————→		

Study	N	Prevalence
Anderson et al. (1987)	792	1.8%
McGee et al. (1992)[f]	750	1.4% —— 4.0%
Feehan et al. (in press)[g]	890	2.7% —— 13.0%
Velez et al. (1989)		
Time 2	776	2.5% ←→ 3.2% ←→ 3.7%
Time 3	776	2.5% ←→ 2.8% ←→ 3.1%
Cohen et al. (1993)		
Boys	749	1.8% ←→ 1.6% → 2.7%
Girls	746	2.3% ←→ 7.6% → 2.7%
Kashani et al. (1987)[h]	150	8.0% →
Boys	75	2.7% →
Girls	75	13.3% →
Kashani et al. (1989)[h]	210	1.5% ←→ 2.9% → 5.7%
Boys	105	1.9% ←→
Girls	105	3.8% ←→
Costello et al. (1988)	300	2.0% —— →

[a] ADD with and without hyperactivity

[b] Hyperactivity

[c] Age 15: Anxiety, Depression + Anxiety, Multiple Anxiety, and Simple Phobia. Age 18: Anxiety and Depression + Anxiety.

[d] Emotional Disorder

[e] Depression/Dysthymia

[f] Depression and Dysthymia

[g] Depression and Depression + Anxiety

[h] Depressive Disorder

2.2.2. Puerto Rico Child Psychiatry Epidemiologic Study

Based on the presence of DSM-III diagnoses and a functional impairment score greater than 61 on the Children's Global Assessment Scale (CGAS), Bird et al. (1988) reported a six-month prevalence rate of 17.9% for 6- to 16-year-old children. Using a two-stage design, first-stage parent and teacher reports (N = 777) screened for case identification. Clinical assessments in the second stage (N = 386) were based on parent and child interviews with the Diagnostic Interview Schedule for Children (DISC). The most frequently diagnosed conditions were Attention Deficit Disorder (ADD) and Oppositional Defiant Disorder (ODD), followed by Depression/Dysthymia, Separation Anxiety, and Enuresis. Least prevalent were Conduct Disorder (CD) and Simple Phobia (see Table 1). To examine comorbidity, diagnoses were collapsed into four "supraordinate domains": affective (Major Depressive Disorder [MDD] and Dysthymic Disorder [DD]), Anxiety Disorders, Attention Deficit Disorder (ADD) with and without hyperactivity, and Conduct/Oppositional (CD/ODD) disorders. Among the children who had diagnoses in these four domains, 46.1% were comorbid with diagnoses falling into more than one domain (Bird et al., 1993). Again, the high comorbidity rates are likely to be conservative estimates.

To examine developmental trends, these investigators compared the rates of mental disorders among three age groups in the Puerto Rico sample: 4- to 5-year-olds, 6- to 11-year-olds, and 12- to 16-year olds. Results indicated that the rate of ADD was lowest in the youngest group, compared to the two older groups. Also, the rate of Depression was higher in each successively older group. Separation Anxiety was seen at a higher rate in the 6- to 11-year-old group than in both the younger and older groups. In addition, there were significant sex differences, with more boys than girls having DSM-III diagnoses.

2.2.3. Dunedin Multidisciplinary Health and Development Study (New Zealand)

The 12-month prevalence rate in the Dunedin Multidisciplinary Health and Development Study among 11-year-old children (N = 792) was 17.6% based on DSM-III criteria for "definite" responses in nonclinician interviews of the children (DISC-C) and parent and teacher questionnaires (Anderson, Williams, McGee, & Silva, 1987). The most frequently diagnosed conditions in this sample were ADD and ODD, followed by Separation Anxiety, CD, Overanxious Disorder, and Simple Phobia. Least prevalent were Depression and Social Phobia. Fifty-five percent of diagnosed children had multiple disorders.

When the prevalence rate for the majority of these same 11-year-olds was adjusted to reflect parent and self report only, for comparability with the data that were available for follow-up four years later, the overall prevalence rate rose to 19.6% at age 15 (McGee, Feehan, Williams, & Anderson, 1992). The most frequently diagnosed conditions at age 15 were CD, Overanxious Disorder, and Simple Phobia. The rates were very low for MDD, ODD, Separation Anxiety, DD, Social Phobia, and ADD (see Table 1).

The Dunedin Multidisciplinary Health and Development Study male-female ratio for diagnoses in 11-year-olds was 1.3:1 overall; for specific disorders, males showed a preponderance of ADD, CD and ODD, and Depression/Dysthymia, while girls more commonly had anxiety disorders. Four years later, the male-female ratio had shifted to 0.7:1 overall, with higher rates for girls for all disorders except ADD (McGee et al., 1992).

Feehan, McGee, & Williams (1993) reported on a subsequent follow-up (ages 15 to 18) of this same sample, but it is difficult to compare the dramatically increased prevalence rate (36.3%) in 18-year-olds with data from the earlier ages, as these rates were derived from different informants and based on different diagnostic criteria.

2.2.4. Mannheim Study (Germany)

Esser, Schmidt, and Woerner (1990) screened a birth cohort of 1,444 eight-year-old school-age children in Mannheim, Germany, with a parent- and teacher-completed instrument adapted from the Conners scale. Using a two-stage design, parents of 216 children were randomly selected to receive a structured interview (adapted from Graham & Rutter, 1968) based on diagnostic criteria from the International Classification of Diseases (ICD). The six-month disorder prevalence rate in the randomly selected subsample was 16.2% at age 8. At age 13, five years later, 191 of the 216 children were reinterviewed, as were also 165 of the 183 children with the highest quartile scores on the parent and teacher screening instruments. Prevalence rates were remarkably similar at age 13: 16.2% without adolescent interview data and 17.8% with adolescent interview data. However, the distribution of disorders changed. For example, "conduct disorders associated with emotional problems" as well as "antisocial conduct disorders" (excluding those associated with emotional problems) increased, whereas "hyperkinetic syndromes" decreased. Across most of the disorder categories, boys were twice as likely as girls to have a diagnosable condition, both at initial interview and at follow-up.

2.2.5. New York Child Longitudinal Study

Cohen and colleagues (Cohen, Velez, Brook, & Smith, 1989; Velez, Johnson, & Cohen, 1989) conducted a longitudinal community study of 776 children and adolescents using child (DISC-C) and parent (DISC-P) interviews. Overall DSM-III prevalence estimates in this study for 9- to 18-year-olds was 17.7%. In order to conduct fine-grained analyses of sex and age differences, Cohen et al. (1993) pooled the data from two waves of the study, subdividing the sample into three age x sex groups: 10- to 13-year-olds (281 boys, 260 girls), 14- to 16-year-olds (246 boys, 262 girls), and 17- to 20-year-olds (222 boys, 224 girls); i.e., early, middle, and late adolescence. For both boys and girls, there was a significant decrease from early adolescence to middle adolescence in Separation Anxiety. For boys only, there was a significant decrease from early to middle adolescence in Overanxious Disorder, a steady, significant decrease with age in ADD, and a significant increase in CD and alcohol abuse from middle to late adolescence. For girls only, there was an increase in MDD from early to middle adolescence, followed by a decrease from middle to late adolescence.

Age-related sex differences were observed for Overanxious Disorder, ADD, CD, Alcohol Abuse, and MDD (see Table 1). Among the early and middle adolescents, prevalence rates were significantly higher for boys than girls for ADD and CD. Among middle and late adolescents, prevalence rates were significantly higher for girls than boys for Overanxious Disorder. Among middle adolescents, the prevalence rate for MDD was higher for girls than boys. Among late adolescents, boys had a higher prevalence rate for Alcohol Abuse than girls.

2.2.6. Midwestern U.S. Studies (Missouri)

Using the Diagnostic Interview for Children and Adolescents (DICA) to interview parents and children, Kashani et al. (1987) surveyed a small community age- and sex-stratified sample of 14- to 16-year-old adolescents ($N = 150$). They reported a prevalence rate of 41.3% for diagnoses meeting DSM-III criteria, and a lower rate of 18.7% with the imposition of additional criteria for impaired functioning and need for treatment. The most frequently diagnosed conditions were CD, ODD, Anxiety, MDD/DD, Alcohol Abuse and Dependence (AA/D), and Drug Abuse and Dependence (DA/D) (see Table 1). Seventy-five percent of these adolescents who also had impaired functioning and evidence of need for treatment had comorbid diagnoses.

In another study, Kashani, Orvaschel, Rosenberg, and Reid (1989) examined psychopathology in a community sample of 210 children and adolescents stratified by age and sex, one third (n = 70) each at ages 8, 12, and 17 years, with an equal number of boys and girls. Using child and parent versions of the Child Assessment Schedule (CAS and P-CAS) respectively, the overall prevalence rate (DSM-III criteria) was 34.3% and 24.8%. The most frequently diagnosed conditions were anxiety disorders (21.0%), followed at a much lower level by CD, ODD, and Substance Abuse. Diagnosed children had an average of 1.5 diagnoses. In this study Kashani and colleagues found no age or sex differences based on parent report. Based on child report, however, there were significant age differences in CD, substance abuse, MDD, and ADD. Also based upon child reports, sex differences were seen for most of the disorders, and the overall disorder rate was somewhat higher for girls than for boys (see Table 1).

2.2.7. Greater Pittsburgh Area Primary Care Study

Costello et al. (1988) reported a 12-month prevalence rate of 22.0% in a pediatric primary care sample of 7- to 12-year-old children (N = 789) in a two-stage study, based on child and parent DISC interviews (DSM III-R criteria) conducted in the second stage (N = 300). The most frequently diagnosed conditions were anxiety disorders, ODD, and CD (see Table 1). When all diagnoses except for elimination disorders were combined into five groups (i.e., ADD, ODD, CD, Anxiety, and affective disorders), 19.2% of the children with a diagnosed condition according to parent report and 17.6% according to child report had more than one disorder. Costello et al. (1988) reported that more boys than girls had ODD and CD and that more girls than boys had anxiety disorders.

3. Developmental Perspectives on Comorbidity

The above overview of the overall prevalence of disorders in children and adolescents sets the stage for the more specific forms of psychopathology (e.g., depression, anxiety, attention deficit hyperactivity disorder, etc.) that are seen in boys versus girls at various ages. In this next section we review these data for trends and differences by age and sex, examine the stability of given forms of psychopathology over the course of children's development, explore actual patterns of comorbidity, and review what is known/not known about the predictors and outcomes of various comorbid conditions.

3.1. Prevalence and Developmental Differences for Specific Disorders

The rates of the most prevalent child and adolescent disorders, CD, ODD, ADD, and affective disorders, and anxiety disorder are presented schematically by age and, as available, by sex, in Table 1.

3.1.1. Conduct Disorder

CD rates generally tend to be higher in adolescence than in childhood, peaking in mid-adolescence, and consistently are substantially higher for boys than for girls. Data from the New York Child Longitudinal Study (Cohen et al., 1993) suggest that the prevalence rate of CD decreases in late adolescence. Of note, the rates reported in the Dunedin sample (2.0% to 5.7%) (Anderson et al., 1987; Feehan et al., 1993; McGee et al., 1992) and the Puerto Rican sample (1.5%) (Bird et al., 1988) were considerably lower than those in the mainland United States and Canadian samples that spanned adolescence (3.8% to 16.0%) (Cohen et al., 1993; Offord et al., 1987; Velez et al., 1989).

3.1.2. Oppositional Defiant Disorder

ODD rates also tend to be higher in adolescence than in childhood, but, unlike CD rates, tend to be quite similar for boys and girls. In fact, in the Kashani et al. (1987) sample of 14- to 16-year-old adolescents, the rate was higher for girls (8.0%) than boys (4.0%). The rates were very high in the New York sample (10.4% to 22.5%), possibly related to threshold difficulties in previous versions of the DISC (Cohen et al., 1993; Velez et al., 1989). The ODD rate, like the CD rate, was notably low in the Dunedin sample (Anderson et al., 1987; Feehan et al., 1993; McGee et al., 1992). In the Puerto Rican sample (Bird et al., 1988), the ODD rate (9.7%) was substantially higher than the CD rate—and quite similar to the CD rate in the U.S. and Canadian samples that spanned adolescence.

3.1.3. Attention Deficit Disorder

ADD rates generally were higher for boys than for girls and tended to peak in late childhood and early adolescence. ADD rates were lowest among the children and adolescents in the U.S. samples studied by Kashani et al. (1987, 1989) and Costello et al. (1988) (0.2% to 5.7%) and highest among the children and adolescents in the U.S. sample studied by Cohen et al. (1993) and Velez et al. (1989) (5.8% to 17.1%).

3.1.4. Anxiety Disorders

The most frequently reported anxiety disorders were Separation Anxiety, Overanxious Disorder, and Simple Phobia, in addition to the overarching diagnostic category of Anxiety. In general, the rate for anxiety disorders was substantially higher than the rate for affective disorders. For Anxiety Disorder, which presumably subsumes several anxiety diagnoses, the rates were very high (8.7% to 28.6%) in the two Kashani et al. (1987, 1989) samples, especially for girls in the larger sample (Kashani et al., 1989). It also was high for 18-year-olds in the Dunedin sample (14.9%) (Feehan et al., 1993), in contrast to the low rates reported for Separation Anxiety, Overanxious Disorder, and Simple Phobia in samples of the 11- and 15-year-olds in the same study (Anderson et al., 1987; McGee et al., 1992). For Separation Anxiety, the rate was highest in late childhood (25.6%; Velez et al, 1989) and quite low in adolescence. The general pattern across studies suggests that Separation Anxiety is transient and most likely to be confined to late childhood or early adolescence. It is of interest whether Separation Anxiety may be a forerunner of other anxiety disorders (e.g., Overanxious Disorder, which is more prevalent in adolescence [see below]). For Overanxious Disorder, in contrast, there is some evidence that the rate is relatively low during childhood (4.6%; Costello et al., 1988), but quite high during early adolescence (19.1%; Velez et al., 1989). The data from the New York sample (Cohen et al., 1993), the only one to report rates separately for boys and girls, suggest that the high rates in adolescence are attributable primarily to girls, with those for boys lower in adolescence than in late childhood. For Simple Phobia, prevalence rates generally were low. The highest rate was reported by Costello et al. (1988) (9.2%) for their 7- to 12-year-old sample.

3.1.5. Depressive Disorders

Depressive disorder rates were quite variable across studies, ranging from a low of 1.4% in 11-year-olds in the New Zealand sample (Anderson et al., 1987) to the highest figures reported across all studies, again in the same sample seven years later (13.0%) (Feehan et al., 1993) and in the OCHS sample (13.6%) for 4- to 16-year-old girls. Rates tended to be more similar for boys and girls in childhood than in adolescence, when they generally were higher for girls than for boys (e.g., Cohen et al., 1993), but this was not a uniform finding across studies. Moreover, by late adolescence, the rates in the New York sample (Cohen et al., 1993) again were similar for boys and girls, suggesting that affective disorders among girls may peak during mid-adolescence.

3.1.6. Comment

From a developmental perspective, questions must be raised concerning the antecedents, correlates, and sequelae of these disorders, and the extent to which these factors are sex-related. For example, in the case of CD, the sex-related differences in rates pose questions about the defining features of CD. The pro's and con's of using different standards for assessment of CD for boys and girls (aggressive behavior is more likely to be in the repertoire of boys) have been discussed by Zoccolillo (1993) and Zahn-Waxler (1993). In contrast, the greater similarity in rates of ODD for boys and girls suggests that there are fewer sex-related behaviors among the ODD symptoms. For ADD, it is possible that sex-related predispositions and biological substrates of the disorder may account for higher rates in boys than girls—and possibly for both genders, once lower rates among boys are seen beginning in mid- to late adolescence. Similarly, for both affective and anxiety disorders, it is unclear to which extent various psychosocial and biological factors may contribute to the emergence of gender differences in early to mid-adolescence, with higher rates for girls than boys.

It may be asked whether the age- and sex-related patterns found in diagnostic prevalence studies are a function of the particular taxonomy embedded in the DSM approaches. However, similar patterns have been reported in studies using non-DSM dimensional approaches. For example, Achenbach, Howell, Quay, & Connors (1991) conducted a national survey of problems and competencies among 4- to 16-year-olds, collecting data on 2,600 referred and 2,600 matched nonreferred children with the ACQ (Achenbach, Connors, Quay) Behavior Checklist, administered in home interviews to parents. They found a decline with age for total behavior problems in the nonreferred sample (but an opposite tendency in the referred sample). They also found that externalizing problems decreased, whereas internalizing problems increased with age. In general, their findings supported the sex-difference findings from the general population studies described above, in that boys tended to score higher on externalizing problems and syndromes, while girls tended to score higher on internalizing problems and syndromes.

3.2. Continuities and Discontinuities

Because it is possible that comorbidity may simply reflect phenotypic change in the outward manifestations of an underlying condition, it is important to consider the stability/continuity of disorders diagnosed in childhood over time. Some data are available on continuities and discontinuities in child and adolescent disorders, not only in general population studies that focus on categorical classification of disorders (diagnoses based on DSM and ICD criteria), but also in studies concerned with behavior problems.

3.2.1. Dunedin Multidisciplinary Health and Development Study (New Zealand)

McGee et al. (1992) examined the longitudinal course of 750 children seen at age 11 and again, four years later, at age 15, as part of the Dunedin Study. They focused on the previous 12 months at each time of assessment. Of the 66 children who had a disorder at age 11, only 42% had a disorder at age 15. Of the 147 children with diagnoses at age 15, the majority (81%) had been diagnosis-free at age 11. Regardless of diagnoses at age 11, four years later, at age 15, boys were more likely to have externalizing disorders and girls were more likely to have internalizing disorders.

Feehan et al. (1993) examined the longitudinal course of 890 adolescents of the Dunedin sample seen at age 15 and again three years later, at age 18, focusing at both times on the previous twelve months. Of the adolescents with diagnosed conditions at age 15 ($n = 191$), 63% also had a disorder at age 18. Of the 323 adolescents with diagnoses at age 18, the majority (62.5%) were diagnosis-free at age 15. Whereas externalizing disorders at age 15 were associated with both internalizing and externalizing disorders at age 18, internalizing disorders at age 15 were more likely to be associated with internalizing than with externalizing disorders at age 18.

In further analyses, Feehan et al. (1993) used anxiety, depression, substance, and conduct disorder symptom scores to explore differences between adolescents with transient (age 15 only), recurrent (age 15 and 18), and new (age 18) disorders. At age 15, the combined scores for the four symptom scales were significantly higher in the recurrent than the transient group, and the new-disorder group had elevated symptom scores compared to the no-diagnosis group. At age 18, the recurrent-disorder group had significantly higher total symptom scores than the new-disorder group. Moreover, the adolescents in the recurrent group were more likely than adolescents in the new-disorder group to have an externalizing disorder as well as three or more disorders.

3.2.2. Mannheim Study (Germany)

In the Mannheim study described above, Esser et al. (1990) reported that of the 71 children with diagnoses at age 8, only 51% continued to have a disorder at age 13. In addition, of 78 children with diagnoses at age 13, 54% were disorder-free at age 8. The best predictors among several child and family attributes of psychiatric disorder at age 13 were psychiatric disorder, specific learning disabilities, and family adversity at age 8, and number of life events between age 8 and 13. Two significant indicators of remission (disorder at age 8, no disorder at age 13) were absence of conduct disorder at age 8 and improvement of adverse family conditions.

Although the ICD classification system differs from the DSM system, it is instructive to consider cross-age comparisons of disorders combined into three categories: neurotic (neurotic and emotional disorders + conduct disorders associated with emotional problems), conduct disorders, and developmentally related disorders (hyperkinetic syndromes + specific child-psychiatric syndromes). The children with neurotic disorders had the best prognosis and the children with conduct disorder had the worst prognosis. Of the children with neurotic diagnoses at age 8, about 75% were diagnosis-free at age 13. In contrast, of the children with conduct disorders at age 8, most still had conduct disorders at age 13. Of the children with developmentally related disorders at age 8, about half were diagnosis-free at age 13.

3.2.3. Zuid-Holland Study

Verhulst and Althaus (1988) reported on persistence and change in behavioral/emotional problems, based on parent report on the CBCL, in 4- to 11-year-old children over a two-year period ($N = 1412$). Of the children aged 4 to 5, 6 to 11, and 12 to 14 years, with problem scores in the deviant range (above the 90th percentile) at initial assessment, a large percentage (46%, 55%, and 56%, respectively) continued to score in the deviant range two years later. Only 2% of the children in these three age groups moved into the disturbed group, and a somewhat higher proportion moved from the deviant into the normal range (at or below the 50th percentile): 13%, 4%, and 9%, respectively, of the 4- to 5-, 6- to 11-, and 12- to 14-year-old children.

Verhulst and van der Ende (1993) examined predictive relations of syndromes in the same 4- to 11-year-old children across a six-year period. Based on quantitative scores, the highest correlations generally were between the same syndromes across time; i.e., for aggressive behavior ($r = .58$), attention problems ($r = .47$), withdrawn behavior ($r = .46$), anxious/depressed behavior ($r = .45$), delinquent behavior ($r = .37$), and social problems ($r = .36$). Based on categorical scores (deviant vs. nondeviant), odds ratios of the degree to which deviance on each of the syndromes predicted deviance on the same as well as the other syndromes six years later yielded similar results. In general, the highest odds ratios were found for deviance on the same syndrome and within each of the broadband syndromes (internalizing and externalizing problems).

3.2.4. Australian Temperament Project

Prior, Smart, Sanson, and Oberklaid (1993) explored the developmental course in psychological adjustment from infancy to 8 years of age in a random sample of 300 children from a representative cohort of 2,443 children enrolled in the Australian Temperament Project. Child variables included temperamental factors of inflexibility or cooperation/manageability and persistence, social maturity, intelligence, and reading achievement. Parent variables included mother's psychological and marital adjustment, social supports, and a stress factor. Interactional variables included two childrearing factors, "child centeredness" and "disciplinary techniques." Total behavior problems (CBCL) were the outcome variables. Using a sample with complete data ($N = 227$), the investigators compared several path models for predicting behavior problems from age 3 to 8 years. Different path models emerged for boys and girls. For boys, the child's persistence, temperamental inflexibility, social maturity, maternal adjustment, and maternal use of punishment were directly linked to behavior problems at ages 5 to 6 years. At 6 to 7 years, persistence, inflexibility, and maternal adjustment continued to be directly linked to behavior problems, but at age 7 to 8, only inflexibility was directly linked to behavior problems. For girls, temperamental inflexibility, punishment, maternal stress, and marital adjustment were directly linked to behavior problems at age 5 to 6 years. At ages 6 to 7 and 7 to 8 years, inflexibility, punishment, and marital adjustment continued to be directly linked to behavior problems; at age 6 to 7, persistence and maternal stress also were directly linked to behavior problems.

3.2.5. Berkeley Study of Ego and Development

Block and Gjerde (1990) examined personality antecedents of depressive symptoms (CES-D scores) in late adolescence (age 18) in a sample of 54 girls and 42 boys that had been followed for 15 years. Although it is not a probabilistic sample, we include this longitudinal study here for its heuristic value. Potential antecedents were sought in independent assessments of personality characteristics with the California Child Q-set at ages 3 to 4, age 7, and ages 11 and 14. At age 14, children also described themselves on a measure of self-esteem.

Relatively few characteristics of these children at ages 3 to 4, 7, and 11 correlated with depressive symptoms at age 18, but nevertheless were revealing. Among girls, the correlates represented affiliative behaviors, but also shyness and self-restrictive behavior. Among boys, they were representative of difficult temperament and a lack of affiliative and achievement-related behavior. A larger set of the children's age 14 characteristics was associated with depressive symptoms at age 18. For girls, the characteristics reflected self-absorption, social awkwardness, anxiety, somatization, and lack of purpose; for boys, they reflected self-indulgent, antisocial, and unproductive behavior, as well as lack of moral sensibility. Moreover, whereas girls' self-esteem at age 14 correlated negatively with depressive symptoms four years later, boys' self-esteem at age 14 was not related to depressive symptoms at age 18.

3.2.6. Summary

From general population studies, there is evidence of less continuity in psychiatric disorders from childhood to early adolescence (e.g., Esser et al., 1990) or from early to mid-adolescence (e.g., McGee et al., 1992) than from mid- to late adolescence (e.g., Feehan et al., 1993). In general, a large number of children and adolescents had disorders at follow-up, but more than half previously had been diagnosis-free. More continuity was reported for behavior-problem syndromes (Verhulst & Althaus, 1988).

As far as specific disorders are concerned, children with externalizing disorders were more likely than children with internalizing disorders to have a diagnosable condition at follow-up. It is noteworthy that the majority of those who had internalizing disorders in early adolescence had been diagnosis-free when assessed in childhood (e.g., Esser et al., 1990). Adolescents with externalizing disorders were almost equally likely to have internalizing or externalizing disorders in later adolescence, whereas those with internalizing disorders were more likely to continue to have internalizing disorders than to develop externalizing disorders (Feehan et al., 1993). Those with recurrent disorders were more likely to have multiple disorders than those who previously had been diagnosis-free (e.g., Feehan et al., 1993). Among adolescents, there was some evidence of greater continuity for externalizing disorders for boys and for internalizing disorders for girls. Moreover, boys with either internalizing or externalizing disorders were more likely to have externalizing than internalizing disorders at follow-up (e.g., McGee et al., 1992).

The sex differences in the predictive paths found by Prior et al. (1993) suggest that the stability of boys' problem behaviors is linked quite strongly to child characteristics, but that, for girls, problem behavior is influenced and maintained by their social environment. The findings of Block and Gjerde (1990) suggest further that depressive symptoms or their precursors may not be identified in girls until early adolescence, which appears to be a particularly vulnerable period for them, whereas precursors in boys may be evident before adolescence (e.g., at about age 7, around the time of school entry). This sex difference may be related to their finding that precursors are likely to be internalizing problems among girls and to include antisocial, externalizing behaviors, and underachievement among boys.

3.3. Comorbidity Patterns

Because of the problems noted earlier with "artifactual comorbidity" (i.e., due to referral biases), comorbidity patterns ideally should be examined in general population and community-based studies. However, there have been relatively few general population studies of child and adolescent disorders (see Table 1); and of these, even fewer have reported data on comorbidity. Based on the Dunedin study (Anderson et al., 1987), the OCHS (Offord et al., 1989), the Puerto Rico study (Bird et al., 1993), the New York Child Longitudinal Study (Cohen, 1993), and the Midwestern U.S. studies (Kashani et al., 1987), comorbidity rates are high in children and adolescents, but these rates vary with specific disorder categories. Comorbidity among the disruptive disorders of CD, ODD, and ADD/ADHD and between the emotional disorders of depression and anxiety, have had the most scrutiny; in part, due to concern about their independence. However, the co-occurrence of disruptive and emotional disorders also is receiving attention. We describe these patterns below and, in specific instances, draw upon referred samples where general population data are inconclusive or unavailable.

3.3.1. Conduct Disorder/Oppositional Defiant Disorder

Many general population studies that have addressed comorbidity do not report separately on CD and ODD (e.g., Anderson et al., 1987; Bird et al., 1993). Cohen (1993), who did report separately on prevalence of CD and ODD, found that 60% of the children with CD diagnoses (n = 89) had comorbid ODD and that 47% of the children with ODD diagnoses (n = 112) had comorbid CD. Higher rates of comorbidity (e.g., 95% to 100%) between CD and ODD than reported by Cohen et al. have been found in referred samples, including recent studies by McBurnett et al. (1991), Walker et al.

(1991), and Schachar and Wachsmuth (1990), which focused exclusively on boys.

Important for addressing comorbidity between CD and ODD is a recent-meta-analysis of factor-analytic research based on 44 published studies of parent and teacher ratings of conduct problems in 28,401 children and adolescents, ages 5 to 18. This study revealed two bipolar dimensions underlying CD: an overt–covert dimension and a nondestructive–destructive dimension (Frick et al., 1993). Intersection of these dimensions resulted in four quadrants that grouped behavior into four categories: (a) oppositional behavior, (b) aggression, (c) property violation, and (d) status violation. Based on parent-reported median age at onset of ODD and CD symptoms, these four behavior categories were found to form a continuum, progressing from ODD to CD symptoms during the course of early development. Based on intensive examination of symptom overlap between ODD and CD (Russo, Loeber, Lahey, & Keenan, 1993; Loeber, Keenan, Lahey, Green, & Thomas, 1993), an alternative diagnostic system has been proposed for DSM-IV that collapses ODD and CD into a single disorder, with mutually exclusive assignment of symptoms to three "developmental" classification categories: "modified defiant disorder (MODD)," "intermediate conduct disorder (ICD)," and "advanced conduct disorder (ACD)." The longitudinal data collected by these investigators indicates that boys who develop advanced CD are likely to have had ODD at an earlier age and, based on the proposed three-category classification system, to have gone from MODD through ICD to ACD.

Based upon data available from general-population studies, comorbid ADD(H) ranges from 34.7% (Anderson et al., 1987) to 48% (Cohen, 1993) among children and adolescents with CD/ODD. The considerably higher rate seen in clinic-referred samples may be inflated by possible referral bias and should be regarded with caution.

Comorbid internalizing disorders are not as common among children and adolescents with CD/ODD. Estimates from general population studies range from 19% (Cohen, 1993) to 53.3% (Bird et al., 1993) for anxiety disorders and from 12% (Cohen, 1993) to 17.6% (Bird et al., 1993) for depressive disorders. Zoccolillo (1992) reviewed child and adult general population studies on the co-occurrence of CD with depressive and anxiety disorders. From data published from 1970 through 1990, he concluded that emotional disorders co-occur with CD at higher than expected rates, especially depression, but also, at a lower level, anxiety disorders. Moreover, he found some evidence of sex differences in the co-occurrence of depression with CD; namely, that it is most likely in boys in preadolescence, diminishing into adulthood, but most likely in girls from adolescence into adulthood.

3.3.2. Attention Deficit Disorder

A very large percentage of the children with ADD among the 9-to 16-year-olds in the Puerto Rico sample studied by Bird et al. (1993) were reported to have comorbid CD/ODD: 93.0%. The percentages were lower among the 4- to 16-year-olds in the OCHS sample studied by Offord et al. (1989), who reported on CD comorbid with Hyperactivity (42.7%), and the 11-year-olds in the Dunedin sample studied by Anderson et al. (1987) and 9- to 18-year-olds in the New York sample studied by Cohen (1993), who reported on CD comorbid with ADD (47.2% and 46%, respectively). Cohen also reported separately on comorbid ODD: 54% of ADD-diagnosed children and adolescents also had ODD.

In clinic-referred children, the rates of comorbid CD vary as widely among children and adolescents with ADHD, ranging in recent studies from 11.8% in preadolescent boys (Livingston, Dykman, & Ackerman, 1990) to 86% in 8- to 13-year-old boys (McBurnett et al., 1991). Biederman et al. (1991) reviewed 29 studies for data on comorbidity of ADHD with CD in referred as well as nonreferred samples and concluded that ADHD and CD co-occur in 30% to 50% of cases. They suggested that ADHD and CD are "at least partially independent disorders," noting that ADHD comorbid with CD may be a distinct subtype. Biederman and colleagues also examined comorbidity of ADHD with ODD and estimated that there is an overlap of at least 35%. They concluded that children with ADHD and ODD may constitute an "intermediate subgroup," in terms of clinical severity, between children with ADHD and children with ADHD and CD.

Compared to externalizing disorders, comorbidity with internalizing disorders is less marked among children and adolescents with ADD(H). In general population studies, comorbid anxiety disorders range from 23% (Cohen, 1993) to 58.8% (Bird et al., 1993) and comorbid depressive disorders from 13% (Cohen, 1993) to 26.8% (Bird et al., 1993). Interestingly, in their review, Biederman et al. (1991) found ADHD to co-occur with mood disorders in up to 75% of cases. However, the higher rates of comorbidity rates may be due to wide age ranges in many of the reviewed studies, as well as the effects of referral bias ("artifactual comorbidity") noted previously.

3.3.3. Anxiety Disorders

Among children and adolescents with anxiety disorders there is significant comorbidity with depressive disorders, ranging from 6% (Cohen, 1993) to 16.9% (Anderson et al., 1987). As one would expect, higher comorbidity estimates are seen in clinically referred subjects. In a recent review, Brady and Kendall (1992) provided comorbidity estimates up to 61.9% in studies focusing on either anxiety or depression published 1984 through 1989, based on DSM-III or DSM-III-R criteria. The highest rate (61.9%) was found in a sample of 17-year-old school refusers, followed by rates of 55.2% in a sample of inpatients, 36.4% in a sample of children of subjects with affective disorders and normal control children, 31.5% in a sample of 8- to 13-year-old outpatients, and 28.3% in a sample of 5- to 17-year-old outpatients.

Developmental factors may be related to the co-occurrence of anxiety and depression, since anxiety usually precedes depressive symptoms, and children with comorbid anxiety and depression tend to be older than children who are solely anxious or depressed. King, Ollendick, and Gullone (1991), who reviewed diagnostic, assessment, and treatment studies to examine implications of overlap between anxiety and depression, found that adolescents with an anxiety disorder were two times more likely than children with an anxiety disorder to also have a mood disorder. In addition, they concluded that co-occurrence of anxiety with depression is most likely in cases of severe anxiety symptomatology. Brady and Kendall (1992) suggest that longitudinal research is needed to generate data on onset, course, outcome, and correlates of anxiety and depression.

Among children and adolescents with anxiety disorders there is also considerable comorbidity with disruptive disorders like ADD(H); estimates range from 22.0% (Bird et al., 1993) to 33% (Cohen, 1993), according to general population studies. Biederman and colleagues' (1991) review of comorbidity studies of attention deficit disorder with anxiety, which included clinic samples, yielded a rate of approximately 25%. Comorbid CD/ODD shows wider variation, ranging from a relatively low 16% (Cohen, 1993) to 62.4% (Bird et al., 1993) among children and adolescents with anxiety disorders. In clinical studies, Walker et al. (1991) reported that 40% of clinically referred children with an anxiety disorder also met criteria for CD. Similarly, McBurnett et al. (1991) found that 34% of anxiety-disordered children also met criteria for CD. Perhaps the differences in comorbid disruptive disorders between referred and nonreferred samples reflect differences in ascertainment procedures.

3.3.4. Depressive Disorders

Not surprisingly, there is significant comorbidity of anxiety disorders with depression, ranging from 28% (Cohen, 1993) to 71.4% (Anderson et al., 1987). While seemingly counterintuitive, when these rates are compared with those cited above for comorbid depression in children with anxiety disorders (i.e., rates of 6% to 16.9% in the New York and Dunedin samples), these apparent discrepancies are due to differences between prevalence of depressive disorders (less common) and anxiety disorders (more common; many children with anxiety disorders do not suffer from depression).

Comorbid CD/ODD in population-based studies ranges from 44% (Cohen, 1993) to 82.2% (Bird et al., 1993) and 100% (Anderson et al., 1987) among children and adolescents with depressive disorders. Comorbidity with ADD is lower, ranging from 47.9% (Bird et al., 1993) to 57.1% (Anderson et al., 1987); Offord et al. (1989) reported a rate of 34.9% for comorbid Hyperactivity. The apparent discrepancy with the earlier figures of 13% to 26.8% for depression comorbid with ADDH in the New York and Puerto Rico samples also is due to differences between the prevalence of depressive disorders (less common) and ADD (more common; many children with ADD do not suffer from depression).

Lewinsohn, Rohde, Seeley, and Hops (1991), who examined comorbidity of depression in a community sample of 14- to 18-year-olds (N = 1,710), which included adolescents with pure MDD, pure DD, and comorbid MDD and DD, found that the probability of having a lifetime disorder other than depression in these three groups, respectively, was .42, .38, and .61.

3.3.5. Summary

Many children and adolescents with diagnosed conditions have more than one disorder. Not only in referred samples, but also in general population samples, there is considerable co-occurrence of disruptive or externalizing disorders with emotional or internalizing disorders, as well as comorbidity among disruptive (CD, ODD, ADD) and comorbidity among emotional disorders (depression and anxiety). The wide ranges in comorbidities across studies can be attributed to the wide age ranges covered, but undoubtedly also to differences in ascertainment, from instruments to criteria for diagnoses.

Even less is known about age- and sex-related differences in comorbidity patterns than about developmental differences and changes in the prevalence of disorders from childhood through adolescence. Moreover, the reported patterns of comorbidity between specific disorders are based on small numbers of children and adolescents. As subgroups of children and adolescents with any one disorder have additional comorbid disorders, there are practical limitations on further breakdown by age and sex. A report on comorbidity between ADDH and CD (DSM-III criteria) in the OCHS sample illustrates that very large samples are required (Szatmari, Boyle, & Offord, 1989). In this sample of 2,687 children, 4 to 16 years of age, 105 boys and 45 girls had ADHD and 105 boys and 43 girls had CD diagnoses, but only 45 boys and 19 girls had both diagnoses. Broken down into two age groups (4 to 11, 12 to 16 years) by gender, 27 of 46 (58.7%) 4- to 11-year-old boys with CD had comorbid ADDH, whereas only 18 of 59 (30.5%) 12- to 16-year-old boys with CD had comorbid ADDH. An opposite pattern of findings was observed among CD girls with comorbid ADDH (56.2% comorbid among 4- to 11-year-olds and 37.0% comorbid among 12- to 16-year-olds). Thus, more than half of the younger boys with CD also had an ADDH diagnosis, but only about one-third of the older boys with CD also had an ADDH diagnosis. In contrast, older girls with ADDH may be more likely to also have a CD diagnosis than younger girls. However, these comorbidity patterns by age and sex are based on very small numbers.

As far as our cursory review of comorbidity patterns is concerned, it is important to note that reports on comorbid disorders do not always tell the whole story. They tend to obscure the fact that quite a few children and adolescents have multiple (more than two) diagnoses. This complexity is revealed only when the focus is on individual profiles. Anderson et al. (1987), for example, reported that 29 (55%) of the 11-year-old children with ADD had comorbid disorders of CD/ODD, Anxiety, and Depression/Dysthymic Disorder (D/DD). Nineteen of these children had only one additional disorder (15 of CD/ODD, 4 of Anxiety), but 10 had multiple disorders (2 of CD/ODD + Anxiety and 8 of CD/ODD + Anxiety + D/DD). Again, practical limitations have a role in how many of these profiles can be examined separately for their implications for clinical practice and treatment.

3.4. Predictors, Course, and Outcome of Comorbid Disorders

Longitudinal studies that focus on the course and predictors of comorbid disorders in nonreferred samples are few. Therefore, we draw on community- and school-based studies that report on behavior problems as well as those that report on psychiatric disorders.

3.4.1. Ontario Child Health Study

Fleming, Boyle, and Offord (1993) studied the longitudinal course in the Ontario Child Health Study of CD and major depressive symptoms (MDS) in 652 adolescents (333 boys, 317 girls), age 13 to 16 years, who were followed up four years later, when they were 17 to 20 years old. They compared three diagnostic groups initially constituted as having (a) a major depressive syndrome (MDS), (b) conduct disorder (CD), and (c) both

MDS and CD (MDS + CD) with controls. At follow-up, they found that the comorbid group had a worse course than either the MDS or the CD group, which, in turn, fared worse than the controls. Although the MDS group had the highest rate of MDD (25.0% vs. 11.1%, 16.7%, and 6.9% in the MDS + CD, CD, and control groups), both the MDS and CD groups had higher rates of DD (16.0% and 16.7%, respectively) than the MDS + CD and control groups (7.7% and 4.1%, respectively); the MDS + CD group, like the MDS group, had high rates of generalized anxiety disorder (24.1% and 28.6%, respectively, vs. 14.8% and 15.1% in the CD and control groups) and, like the CD group, had high rates of drug abuse and dependence (28.6% and 23.1%, respectively, vs. 3.6% and 2.1% in the MDS and control groups). Distinctive about the MDS + CD group in particular was a very high rate of alcohol abuse and dependence (57.1% vs. 24.1%, 17.9%, and 14.8% in the MDS, CD, and control groups).

3.4.2. Dunedin Multidisciplinary Health and Development Study

Moffitt (1990) examined the developmental trajectories of 435 boys in the Dunedin (New Zealand) sample identified for study by their self-reported delinquent behavior and clinical diagnosis of ADD at age 13. Four groups were formed: ADD + delinquent, ADD only, delinquent only, and nondisordered controls. The boys in the ADD only group represented about 4% of the Dunedin birth cohort and 46% of the ADD cases; and the ADD + delinquent group similarly represented about 4% of the cohort and about half of all ADD cases. Non-ADD delinquents represented 12% of the cohort and 73% of all delinquents.

Available data at ages 3, 5, 7, 9, 11, and 13 on antisocial behavior, family adversity, verbal-cognitive ability, and reading achievement were compared in these four groups. At all ages, boys in the ADD + delinquent group consistently had higher levels of antisocial behavior, greater family adversity, poorer verbal ability, and less reading achievement than the boys in the three other groups. In relation to the other groups, the children in the ADD + delinquent group also showed motor skills deficits early in life and verbal IQ deficits by age 5. The greatest increase in antisocial behavior in the ADD + delinquent group occurred between the ages of 5 and 7 years, coinciding with relatively low reading achievement following school entry, reaching, at that early an age, a level of antisocial behavior that was not in evidence in the delinquent-only group until age 13. The delinquent group had trajectories similar to the ADD and nondisorder groups until age 13, when the level of their antisocial behavior, which defined them as delinquent, approached that of the ADD + delinquent group.

Anderson et al. (1989) compared age 5, 7, 9, and 11 cognitive and social correlates of the following DSM-III disorders diagnosed at age 11 in the Dunedin (New Zealand) sample (N = 792): anxious/depressed (n = 23), ADD (n = 36), CD/ODD (n = 21), multiple disorder (n = 16), vs. no-disorder controls (n = 702). On cognitive measures (verbal IQ, full-scale IQ, reading and spelling), children in the ADD and multiple diagnosis groups, at similar levels, had significantly lower scores than children in the other groups. These findings held across time when controlled for sex and cumulative family disadvantage differences. Only children in the multiple disorder group were increasingly more disliked and solitary across age, based on a peer-socialization measure. However, children in the ADD as well as the multiple diagnosis groups generally had self-esteem scores that were lower than the sample mean. Finally, with little change across time, family adversity was highest for the multiple disorder group, followed by CD/ODD, ADD, anxious/depressed, and nondisordered controls.

McGee et al. (1992) also examined the course of 45 children (40 boys, 5 girls) with ADD diagnoses at age 11 with onset at three different ages: 3 (n = 15), 5 to 6 (n = 15), and 7 years, compared to 369 children without diagnoses. The age 11 ADD diagnoses were based on parent-, teacher-, and self-identification in the two earliest onset groups (ages 3 and 5 to 6) and on teacher- and self-identification in the later onset group (age 7). At age 11, more children in the two early onset groups had comorbid disorders, 67% (at age 3) and 61% (at age 5 to 6), than those in the later onset group (27% at age 7). At age 15, the differences in comorbidity rates were similar: 67%, 77%, and 31%, respectively, in the age 3, 5 to 6, and 7 onset groups. Almost all of the disorders comorbid with ADD at age 11 were CD/ODD or CD/ODD + Anxiety/Depression.

Frost, Moffit, and McGee (1989) investigated neuropsychological deficits in a sample of 13-year-old children in the Dunedin (New Zealand) sample (N = 678), comparing children with diagnoses of ADD (n = 13), CD (n = 17), Anxiety (n = 14), Depression (n = 10), and multiple disorders (n = 19) vs. no disorders (n = 605), using "strict and multiple diagnostic criteria" (p. 309). They found generalized neuropsychological deficits to be more frequent among children with multiple disorders (26.3% vs. 15.4%, 7.1%, and 2.3% in the ADD, Anxiety, and no-disorder group, and 0% in both the CD and Depression groups).

3.4.3. Christchurch Health and Development Study

Fergusson and Horwood (1993), in their examination of the structure, stability, and correlations of the trait components of CD, ODD, ADD, and Anxiety/Withdrawal based on parent, teacher, and child behavior reports at ages 8, 10, and 12 years in 783 children in a Christchurch, New Zealand, birth cohort, found very high stability across time for CD/ODD behaviors (.88 to .96), ADD behaviors (.88 to .96), and anxiety/withdrawal (.82 to .91). They also found substantial relations across time between the disruptive CD/ODD and ADD behaviors (.73 to .82). The relations between CDD/ODD behaviors and anxiety/withdrawal (.18 to .35) and between ADD behaviors and anxiety/withdrawal (.18 to .45), although modest (with a median value of .29), suggest comorbidity also between these externalizing and internalizing disorders.

Fergusson, Horwood, and Lynskey (1993) tested models of relations between ADD and CD in middle childhood and academic achievement and offending in adolescence in children in the Christchurch birth cohort with complete data at ages 6, 8, 10, and 13 years ($N = 704$ to 761). Assessment of ADD and CD at ages 6, 8, and 10 was based on parent and teacher report obtained on instruments derived from questionnaires developed by Rutter and Connors. Cognitive development at age 13 was based on a measure of children's academic competencies (Test of Scholastic Abilities), and offending at ages 12 and 13 on the Self-Report Early Delinquency Scale, administered to both parents and children. Although conduct problems and attention deficit behaviors were strongly correlated, and there was strong continuity between conduct problems at ages 6, 8, and 10 and offending at age 13, conduct problems were related to later offending, but not to later academic achievement, and attention deficit behaviors were related to later academic achievement, but not to later offending.

3.4.4. Zuid-Holland Study

Verhulst and van der Ende (1993) examined the course of attention, conduct, and anxious/depressed problems in the deviant range (cross-informant syndromes on the CBCL, based on parent report), including comorbid problems, in 4- to 11-year-old children over a six-year period. Focusing on attention and conduct problems, they compared children who were deviant at initial assessment on both syndromes ($n = 76$) with children who were deviant only on attention problems ($n = 35$) or only on conduct problems ($n = 12$). They found children with "mixed" problems to have the worst outcome six years later. Similarly, focusing on anxious/depressed and conduct problems, they compared children who initially were deviant on both syndromes ($n = 62$) with children who were deviant only on anxious/depressed problems ($n = 40$) or only on conduct problems ($n = 14$). Again, those with "mixed" problems had the worst outcome six years later. Finally, focusing on attention and anxious/depressed problems, they compared children deviant on both syndromes ($n = 56$) with children deviant only on attention ($n = 13$) or only on anxious/depressed problems (n = 27). The "mixed" group had the worst outcome six years later. In addition, Verhulst and van der Ende (1993) compared children who initially were deviant on both internalizing and externalizing behaviors (n = 56) with children who were deviant on only one of these syndromes (internalizing, n = 15; externalizing, n = 27) and in the normal range on the other. At the broadband level, the children in the mixed category also had the worst outcome.

3.4.5. Montreal School Study

Ledingham and Schwartzman (1984) did a three-year follow-up study of children seen initially in Grades 1, 4, and 7 and identified, on the basis of peer ratings, as either aggressive (A), withdrawn (W), both aggressive and withdrawn (A + W) or neither (controls) (N = 753) in a sample of 4,107 children attending regular classes in Montreal. Children in the A group had scores above 95th percentile for same-sex classmates on aggression and below the 75th percentile on withdrawal. Children in the W group had scores above the 95th percentile on withdrawal and below the 75th percentile on aggression. Children in the A + W group had scores above the 75th percentile on both aggression and withdrawal. Controls had scores below the 75th percentile on both dimensions. At follow-up, three years later, the investigators looked into special class placement in these four groups. Only 52% and 59%, respectively, in the A + W and A groups were in regular classes, compared to 75% and 83%, respectively, in the W and control groups. In the A + W group, the proportion of children in regular classes decreased dramatically across grades, from 63% of the children identified Grade 1 to 45% of the children identified in Grade 4, and 35% of the children identified in Grade 7, compared to, respectively, 54%, 62%, and 59% in the A group, 81%, 72%, and 76% in the W group, and 92%, 83%, and 78% in the control group.

Moskowitz, Schwartzman, and Ledingham (1985) examined the stability of the aggression and withdrawal scores in this sample over the three-year time period. It was fairly substantial for both boys and girls in the three grade groups for aggression (.43 to .64) and for withdrawal in the two older grades (.42 to .65) but not the Grade 1 group (.26 for boys, −.05 for girls). However, group membership based on the categories of A, W, and A + W changed considerably. Only 27% remained in the same group, and 52% could not be classified as belonging to either the normal or the deviant group. Specifically, 18% in the A group, 34% in the W group, and 21% in the A + W group, compared to 34% of the control group, remained in the same category; and 60%, 49%, 42%, and 54%, respectively, could not be classified as belonging either in the normal or deviant groups. The greatest stability was found in the W group for both boys and girls (38% and 29%, respectively).

3.4.6. Oregon Youth Study

Another study of the course of comorbid behavior problems was conducted by Capaldi (1992), who examined elevated conduct problems (above the 70th percentile on the Teacher CBCL) (CP), elevated depression symptoms (above the 70th percentile on the Child Depression Rating Scale (CDRS) (DS), and the co-occurrence of elevated conduct problems and elevated depression symptoms (CP + DS) in a community sample of sixth-grade boys who attended schools in a high crime area. They were followed up after two years, when they were in Grade 8 (N = 201). Assessment of conduct problems was based on teacher ratings on the CBCL, and assessment of depressive symptoms was based on the boys' self report on the CDRS. Across the two-year period, CP stability was greater (r = .78) than DS stability (r = .40). Moreover, among boys in the early CP group, there was a significant increase in depressive symptoms, but there was no significant increase in conduct problems among boys in the early DS group.

Of the 35 boys initially in the CP group, 42% were in the same group two years later, 22% changed to the CP + DS group and 8% to the DS group, and 25% no longer had conduct problems. Of the 30 boys initially in the DS group, 36% did not change, 10% changed to the CP group and 3% to the CP + DS group, and almost half (48%) no longer had depressive symptoms. Of the 23 boys initially in the CP + DS group, 48% were in the same group two years later, 26% changed to the CP group and 17% to the DS group, and only 9% no longer had symptoms. The boys in the CD + DS group had the worst outcome.

3.4.7. Oregon Depression Study

Rohde, Lewinsohn, and Seeley (1991) reported on the temporal order of comorbid depression in their community sample of 14- to 18-year-old adolescents (N = 1,710). Based on current and lifetime comorbidity of depression, they found that, with the exception of eating disorders, there was a significantly greater likelihood for comorbid disorders to follow than to precede depression (79.1% vs. 20.9%). This was the case with Substance Abuse (64.5% vs. 35.5%), disruptive behavior (71.8% vs. 28.2%) and especially with Anxiety (85.1% vs. 14.9%). In the same sample, Lewinsohn et al. (1991) examined the temporal order of comorbid depressive disorders, MDD and DD, and found that of 292 adolescents with a lifetime diagnosis of MDD, 43 (14.7%) also had had two episodes (both MDD). None of the adolescents with a lifetime diagnosis of DD had had more than one episode. For 21 of the 23 adolescents who had a lifetime diagnosis of MDD and DD (91.3%), the episode of DD preceded the episode of MDD, a temporal sequence that did not differ for males and females. These findings suggest that it is highly likely that a dysthymic episode in adolescence will be followed by an episode of MDD.

3.4.8. Summary

In general, it appears that if children and adolescents have multiple disorders, they are more likely to have continuing problems than if they have a single diagnosis. There is evidence that children with comorbid disruptive disorders tend to have an early onset of problem behavior and persisting difficulties with social and academic functioning continuing into adolescence (e.g., Anderson et al., 1989; Fergusson et al., 1993; Frost et al., 1989; McGee et al., 1992; Moffitt, 1990). Children with emotional disorders or problems comorbid with disruptive disorders also appear to fare worse than children with disorders or problems in only one of these areas (e.g., Fleming et al., 1993; Verhulst & van der Ende, 1993). Among adolescents with diagnoses of Major Depressive Syndrome (MDS) comorbid with Conduct Disorder (CD) at ages 13 to 16 years, for instance, there was a higher rate at follow-up four years later of Alcohol and Drug Abuse and Dependence than among adolescent with MDS only and a higher rate of MDS, Dysthymic Disorder, Generalized Anxiety Disorder, and Alcohol Abuse and Dependence than among adolescents with CD only (Fleming et al., 1993). Similarly, among sixth-grade boys, those with both conduct problems and depressive symptoms were more likely to continue to have problems in eighth grade (91%) than boys with conduct problems only (75%) or boys with depressive symptoms only (52%) (Capaldi, 1992). Verhulst and van der Ende (1993) pointed out that they consistently found more children to score in the deviant range on two syndromes than on only one of the syndromes and that initial behavior problems predicted not only similar, but also different problem behavior six years later. Their findings led them to suggest that comorbidity may reflect "the actual complexities of child psychopathology" (p. 781).

3.4.9. Comment

Relatively little is known about the temporal order of comorbid conditions. In a general-population study, disorders comorbid with depression in adolescence have been found to be more likely to follow than precede depression; and, in the case of double depression, MDD and DD, DD episodes were found to be likely to precede MDD episodes (Rohde et al., 1991; Lewinsohn et al., 1991). Kovacs, who has conducted a long-term prospective study of childhood-onset depression, at ages 8 to 13, with follow-up at six-month intervals, also has reported comorbid internalizing and externalizing disorders (Kovacs, Paulauskas, Gatsonis, & Richards, 1988; Kovacs, Gatsonis, Paulauskas, & Richards, 1989), with clinical evaluations based on parent and child semistructured interviews with the Interview Schedule for Children (ISC). It is the only intensive study of the naturalistic course of early onset depression and is yielding detailed data on comorbid disorders.

Kovacs et al. (1989) reported on comorbid anxiety disorders in 104 of the 143 children in the depressed sample, who had come into the study during its first six years, when the mean follow-up interval was three years. Of those children, 43 (41%) were comorbid with anxiety disorders at the outset, 32 with Separation Anxiety, and 17 with Overanxious Disorder. Another three children developed anxiety disorders over the observation period. The age-corrected cumulative risk to age 18 for anxiety disorder in childhood onset depression was .47, with anxiety most likely to manifest itself before age 12 years. However, the presence of anxiety did not appear to influence the risk for subsequent depressive episodes. The children with comorbid anxiety disorders were younger than the other children in the sample. Among the children who had comorbid MDD and anxiety, anxiety preceded MDD two-thirds of the time; in one-third of these children the onset of anxiety was either at the same time as MDD or followed the onset of MDD. Comorbid anxiety was equally likely to persist and not persist after MDD had remitted. Temporal-order findings were different in the small number of children who had DD comorbid with anxiety ($n = 9$). In only two of the nine cases did anxiety precede the onset of DD. Thus, the temporal-order findings for DD comorbid with anxiety, but not for MDD comorbid with anxiety, are similar to the findings in lifetime diagnoses by Rohde et al. (1991) that comorbid disorders appear more likely to follow than to precede depressive disorders.

Kovacs et al. (1988) also reported on comorbid conduct disorder (CD) in these 104 children, when the mean follow-up interval was three years. They found that 17 of the children (16%) were comorbid with CD at the outset and that another 7 children developed CD after their index episode of depression remitted (23% total). Five of the 17 depressed children comorbid with CD had several episodes of CD, and 3 of these 5 children eventually developed Bipolar Disorder. Two of the 7 children who developed CD later also eventually developed Bipolar Disorder. There were no sex differences for depression with or without CD. However, the presence of ADD in depressed girls, but not in boys, appeared to shorten the time to onset of CD. Older age at onset of depression was associated with the presence of comorbid CD, and CD was most likely to manifest itself by ages 11 to 14 years. The age-corrected cumulative risk to age 19 for CD in childhood onset depression was .36. Among the children who had MDD or DD comorbid with CD, CD was most likely to follow the onset of depression. Comorbid CD was likely to persist after depression remitted. Thus, the findings for depressive disorders comorbid with CD were similar to those reported by Rohde et al. (1991).

In an 18-year follow-up of child and adolescent depression, Harrington, Fudge, Rutter, Pickles, and Hill (1991) found different outcomes between those with initial diagnoses of Depression (D) and those with initial diagnoses of Depression comorbid with Conduct Disorder (D + CD) $n = 63$) and raised the question whether depression comorbid with CD is different from D, and if D is secondary to CD. Identification and diagnosis of depression was based on intake data (RDC criteria). Of the 63 D cases, 46% had one CD symptom (DSM-III-R criteria) and 21% had three or more other symptoms. Of the psychiatric control cases ($n = 68$), 25% had three or more other symptoms. At the 18-year follow-up, the SADS-L was administered (RDC criteria). In the short term, the D + CD cases improved less and appeared more handicapped than the D cases; and, in adulthood, D + CD cases were more likely than D cases and controls to have an Antisocial Personality Disorder and more likely than D cases to be at risk for Alcohol Abuse and Dependence. In addition, there were trends indicating that D cases were at greater risk for MDD in adulthood than D + CD cases, but that D + CD cases were more impaired than D cases. It appears that D + CD has different implications than D, such that adolescents with D + CD have a course consistent with CD, whereas those with D only have a course relatively more consistent with "pure" depressive disorders in adulthood.

4. Implications

This overview of the prevalence of child and adolescent disorders, symptoms, and behavior problems, and their comorbidity, of course, is not exhaustive. Moreover, although only the bare essentials are presented, it should be clear that our general conclusions about prevalence and comorbidity rates rest on studies of samples of varying age ranges that have used different methods of assessment and procedures and, in some cases, employed different diagnostic criteria or cutpoints to establish clinical status. Some general-population studies used a two-stage procedure to screen for sample selection. Quite often investigators collapsed related diagnostic categories, especially for examination of comorbid disorders, to gain sufficient power for statistical analyses. Differences in findings across studies undoubtedly are influenced also by how investigators utilize data from multiple informants and by any imposition of additional criteria for diagnoses, such as pervasiveness, severity, or impairment. Nonetheless, this review of available information does provide a basis for recommendations for future studies. We summarize these issues below.

4.1. Developmental Considerations

Basic to developmental considerations of psychopathology in children and adolescents is the recognition that boys and girls tend to differ in the form in which it is expressed, and these differences tend to become more pronounced over the course of development. Thus, depression may be twice as common in girls than boys, especially after puberty. In contrast, ADHD may be more common in boys than girls, regardless of age. Although basic patterns of prevalence show these differences, it is less clear if patterns of comorbidity also differ in boys and girls. For example, beyond simple prevalence questions, once there is evidence of depression, is it more (or less) likely in boys or girls to be comorbid with other conditions (e.g., CD, ODD, ADD, or anxiety)? To our knowledge, only Bird et al. (1993) have begun to address such questions, by examining age and sex differences in observed versus expected comorbidity among more than two disorders (i.e., ADD, CD/ODD, Anxiety, and Depression). They found only one significant age difference for ADD + Depression (a higher observed than expected rate among 9- to 12-year-olds than 13- to 16-year-olds) and no significant sex differences. The general lack of such data, especially in longitudinal form, is not surprising. Very large samples would have to be followed over time, so that permutations in various comorbid subgroups can be examined by gender and age. In fact, such an effort may require aggregation across studies that use uniform methods of assessment and diagnosis.

Longitudinal research is needed to address many developmental questions. Children and adolescents must be studied repeatedly if we are to examine developmental pathways and temporal ordering of various forms of psychopathology and to explore the possibility that one condition may be the early manifestation of a later form of psychopathology. A good example of the type of research that is needed is the work that Loeber, Lahey, and colleagues (1993) have done on oppositional defiant disorder and conduct disorder, which suggests that oppositional defiant disorder is an early manifestation of conduct disorder. A closely related consideration is that one disorder may precede or lead to another. Other examples of this type of research is the work of Kovacs et al. (1988, 1989) on depression, and McGee et al. (1992) on attention deficit disorder.

It is extraordinarily difficult and expensive to do longitudinal studies. Although longitudinal research on childhood disorders has long been recognized as scientifically important, because so many questions regarding development (both normal and psychopathological) cannot be answered from cross-sectional studies, institutional support and funding has been lacking. A nationwide longitudinal epidemiological study of child and adolescent psychopathology in the United States could begin to address many of our current taxonomic and assessment problems.

4.2. Questions of Classification

Many of the difficulties inherent in the study of comorbidity are inextricably related to our diagnostic and nosologic systems. To some extent, comorbidity may be a problem of our own making, due to the complexity and nonhierarchical approach of our current classification systems. Dimensional approaches to the assessment of psychopathology may offer an advantage of parsimony when high levels of comorbidity are present and when available evidence does not support the merits and validity of separate diagnostic entities. Beyond posing taxonomic challenges, however, comorbidity may reflect the complex nature of the developing human organism, manifesting itself in the amorphous expression of psychopathology in young children that becomes more clearly defined as their personality begins to crystalize and the central nervous system reaches maturity, especially after puberty and mid-adolescence. The Rohde et al. (1991) study, for example, found comorbid disorders to be significantly lower in depressed adults than in 14- to 18-year-old depressed adolescents (42% in currently depressed adolescents and 43% in adolescents with lifetime diagnoses of depression, with comparable current and lifetime rates in adults of 7.7% and 25.4%), suggesting that comorbidity may indeed be developmental phenomenon.

There has been considerable debate concerning the validity of various taxonomic approaches. Edelbrock and Costello (1988) have suggested that a combination of dimensional and categorical approaches should be useful in the assessment of child psychopathology. Beyond problems with the validity of taxons, however, the various current descriptive approaches provide an opportunity to examine the phenomenology of emotional and behavioral problems. Given the complexity of the task, it would be prudent to make more attempts to systematically link the existing assessment approaches, in order to determine which methods of ascertainment work best under which conditions. Gould, Bird, and Jaramillo (1993), taking the same approach as Edelbrock and Costello (1988) did with a referred sample, examined the convergence between CBCL syndromes and DSM-III diagnoses in a general population sample and came to very similar conclusions; that is, that it is informative to use dimensional as well as categorical assessment strategies. Their finding of direct linear relations between corresponding CBCL-scale scores and the percentage of children with DSM-III diagnoses, for example, makes it clear that such a dual approach should be especially useful in the investigation of comorbid disorders. In their own words, referring to the Puerto Rico study, "Given the magnitude of comorbidity in the present community sample it would be daunting and tedious task to define a sufficient set of combination categories to represent the extensive co-occurrence of disorders (pp. 310–311)."

One area of research that may shed some light on questions of classification in the near future is the study of comorbidity and treatment response. To the extent that single and comorbid forms of psychopathology show different outcomes in response to treatment, there may be justification for considering the comorbid form as qualitatively different from the single, noncomorbid form. For example, Biederman et al. (1993) studied treatment response to desipramine (DMI) in clinic-referred children and adolescents with pure or comorbid ADHD diagnoses and found a tendency for "pure" ADHD children to show a lesser response to placebo and a greater difference between placebo and DMI response than comorbid ADHD children. Similarly, Hughes et al. (1990) studied the pharmacologic treatment response of "pure" MDD children with comorbid children (MDD and CD/OD) and found that MDD children were more likely to respond to medication (compared to MDD/CD/OD children), while MDD/CD/OD children were more likely to respond to placebo. In the coming years, response to treatment research will undoubtedly garner much more attention and, together with the ongoing search for biologic markers and other correlates, may help to distinguish various "pure" and comorbid disorder combinations.

4.3. Methodological Issues

How information from multiple sources is combined to arrive at diagnoses obviously influences the prevalence and comorbidity rates that are reported. Of particular importance for future research will be the determination of the contribution of different sources of information to comorbidity. Among 9- to 16-year-olds in the Puerto Rico sample, for instance, Bird et al. (1993) found the degree of comorbidity to be higher when based on parent report than when based on child report. Clearly, there is a need for parsimony in number of informants; all informants (e.g., parent, child, teacher) may not be equally valid or necessary for each and every form of psychopathology. While we agree with Achenbach, McConaughy, and Howell (1987) that information from more than one such source is necessary, since children's behavior may be influenced by particular relationships and the information on the child that is provided by any one source may be based on a child's behavior in the context of that particular relationship, there is a clear need for different informants for different situations, and we must determine which informants' data are most predictive and meaningful for which situations *over time*. Possibly, some of these issues may be addressed in the DSM-IV, where evidence of "pervasiveness" may be required (e.g., problems apparent across settings) as well as some degree of impairment in functioning.

Bird et al. (1992) compared two approaches to aggregating data from parents and 9- to 16-year-old children: simple aggregation versus optimal informant. The prevalence rates did not differ significantly with the two approaches except for overanxious disorder. However, they found that parents are the best informants for externalizing behavior problems— parental responses were most predictive of diagnoses of ADHD and OD— and that the children are the best informants for internalizing problems. Children's responses were similarly or more predictive of separation anxiety, overanxious disorder, and dysthymia. In addition, they noted that "employment of severity criteria for determining 'caseness' also appear to be essential for meaningful estimates of child psychiatric disorders" (p. 84) in community samples.

In the aggregation of information from multiple informants, methodological issues must be considered. For example, computer-based algorithms that combine information may work quite differently from approaches where information is assimilated/combined in the mind of a clinician. For example, Bird et al. (1993) examined rates of comorbidity for four disorder categories: ADD, depression, anxiety, and CD/ODD. They reported higher comorbidity rates based on algorithm-combined parent-child diagnoses than clinician-based diagnoses for ADD + conduct/oppositional disorder and for anxiety + conduct/oppositional disorder, and ADD + anxiety disorder.

Another methodological issue has to do with the need, especially in longitudinal research, to document and examine subthreshold conditions and their contributions to onset and offset of diagnosed conditions. To facilitate this work, instruments must be developed and data collected in such a way that patterns of symptoms can be examined empirically, permitting new configurations of symptoms to emerge.

4.4. Other Conceptual Problems

Other conceptual problems include questions of when comorbidity simply is a marker of "severity" or a quantitative index of increased levels of psychopathology (e.g., as in the Zuid-Holland Study [Verhulst & van der Ende, 1993]) and when it is indicative of qualitative differences (as in the Montreal School Study [Ledingham & Schwartzman, 1984], in which comorbid conditions A + W had a somewhat better outcome than the W-only group in terms of school performance and placement), in terms of course, treatment response, and outcome.

If comorbidity reflects severity of psychopathology, then children with comorbid disorders should be seen more frequently at mental health and social services facilities than children with noncomorbid disorders, and that is indeed what the data show. Bird et al. (1993) reported from the Puerto Rico Child Psychiatry Epidemiologic Study that among children and adolescents with one diagnosis, 23% were receiving services, whereas among those with two or more diagnoses, 77% were receiving services. The Dunedin Multidiscplinary Health and Development Study also showed that 13-year-old children with multiple diagnoses (25%) were significantly more impaired than children with a single diagnosis (Frost et al., 1989). As Cohen (1993) found comorbidity based on "severe" diagnoses to be somewhat lower rather than higher, perhaps impairment plays a larger role in service utilization than "severity." The Cohen findings also may indicate that less severe forms of psychopathology reflect generic or diffuse responses to environmental stressors, whereas more severe forms may be due to relatively specific etiologic factors, such as very high genetic loadings.

One might argue that the "severity" of a disorder and level of impairment should be related, but a recent study by Sanford, Offord, Boyle, Peace, & Racine (1992) suggests that this may not be the case. They examined social and school impairment in children with and without psychiatric disorders, using measures of impairment independent of symptoms, in order to avoid confounding impairment with symptom severity. Although significantly more children with impairments were more symptomatic than children without impairments, some children with a diagnosis were not identified as impaired; and many children who did not have a diagnosis were identified as impaired. Moreover, they found that there was low agreement on impairment between informants. Fewer children were identified as impaired by parents than by teachers or adolescents. The strongest relation was found between teacher-identified impairment and diagnosis.

Sanford et al. (1992) would like to see questions about impairments in children addressed in longitudinal studies. In particular, they call for the investigation of the clinical significance of psychiatric diagnoses in children without impairments, in order to clarify whether these children have a mild disorder, a newly emerging disorder, a resolving disorder, or a disorder with different risk factors. As far as children with impairments who have a disorder are concerned, they raise questions about what correlates, risk factors, and burden of suffering are reflected in these impairments, and what prognostic significance that they have for these children.

4.5. Future Research

It is clear that comorbidity must be considered in the design of research on disorders in children and adolescents—especially, in the selection of psychiatric control groups—as well as in clinical practice. Brown and Barlow (1992) laid out issues for treatment research in the form of the following three questions: (a) Does the presence of certain comorbid disorders or symptoms affect the short- and long-term response to treatment? (b) What type of adjustments should and can be made to extant treatments to enhance treatment efficacy when comorbidity is present? (c) What is the course of comorbid disorders and symptoms after successful treatment of the principal disorder? Comorbidity is likely to have implications for the evaluation of treatment efficacy.

We concur with Kendall & Clarkin (1992), who have defined the study of comorbidity as "the premier challenge facing mental health professionals in the 1990s" (p. 833). They call for studies of the frequency of comorbidity and related conditions, examination of symptom overlap and the potential role of symptoms in defining boundaries between related disorders, as well as to studies of differential effects of treatment of children with comorbid disorders and of children who, within the same disorder, differ on etiological factors.

Such studies may best be accomplished within the context of *longitudinal* epidemiological research with broad, developmentally appropriate measures of adaptation, strengths, and a range of risk and protective factors across domains, as well as measures of psychopathology. In such an effort, examination of how children move into and out of areas of risk, dysfunction, and comorbidity is critical. If such research is to be fully successful, it will of necessity have to draw on both categorical and dimensional approaches of assessment. For maximal benefit to the mental health field, such research must go beyond establishing base rates of child and adolescent disorders, address taxonomic problems that exist in current child psychopathology research, and determine how individual children change over their course of development.

While the research problems posed by comorbidity are daunting, we are persuaded that much of the research in child psychopathology over the last decade has not addressed this issue satisfactorily. To the extent that comorbid children have been excluded from studies, past results may not be generalizable to the majority of children (usually comorbid) seen in mental health settings. And to the extent that comorbid children have been included in studies, but their comorbidity characteristics have not been fully described, findings from studies may not be fully applicable to the presumed primary disorder. Such difficulties may explain discrepant or contradictory findings across studies.

But the issue of comorbidity is not just one of methodologic subtlety. It reaches to the heart of how we conceptualize child psychopathology. Only through vigorous attempts on the part of investigators from all relevant disciplines (clinical, epidemiologic, developmental) who study children can we hope to address these issues and see quantitative and qualitative improvements in our conceptual approaches to child psychopathology over the next decade. Only by avoiding the reification of any of our current taxonomic and assessment approaches, and by systematically building in "crosswalks" between the various alternatives in rigorous studies, may we avoid rediscovering that comorbidity is the premier challenge facing mental health professionals in the year 2000.

5. References

Achenbach, T. M. (1990/1991). "Comorbidity" in child and adolescent psychiatry: Categorical and quantitative perspectives. *Journal of Child and Adolescent Psychopharmacology, 1,* 1–8.

Achenbach, T. M., Howell, C. T., Quay, H. C., & Conners, K. (1991). National survey of problems and competencies among four- to sixteen-year-olds. *Monographs of the Society for Research in Child Development, 56* (Serial No. 225).

Achenbach, T. M., McConaughy, S. H., & Howell, C. T. (1987). Child/adolescent behavioral and emotional problems: Implications of cross-informant correlations for situational specificity. *Psychological Bulletin, 101,* 213–232.

Anderson, J. C., Williams, S., McGee, R., & Silva, A. (1987). DSM-III disorders in preadolescent children: Prevalence in a large sample from the general population. *Archives of General Psychiatry, 44,* 69–76.

Anderson, J., Williams, S., McGee, R., & Silva, P. (1989). Cognitive and social correlates of DSM-III disorders in preadolescent children. *Journal of the American Academy of Child and Adolescent Psychiatry, 28,* 842–846.

Biederman, J., Baldessarini, R. J., Wright, V., Keenan, K., & Faraone, S. (1993). A double-blind placebo controlled study of desipramine in the treatment of ADD: III. Lack of impact of comorbidity and family history factors on clinical response. *Journal of the American Academy of Child and Adolescent Psychiatry, 32,* 199–204.

Biederman, J., Newcorn, J., & Sprich, S. (1991). Comorbidity of attention deficit hyperactivity disorder with conduct, depressive, anxiety, and other disorders. *American Journal of Psychiatry, 148*, 564–577.

Bird, H. R., Canino, G., Rubio-Stipec, M., Gould, M. S., Ribera, J., Sesman, M., Woodbury, M., Huertas-Goldman, S., Pagan, A., Sanchez-Lacay, A., & Moscoso, M. (1988). Estimates of the prevalence of childhood maladjustment in a community survey in Puerto Rico. *Archives of General Psychiatry, 45*, 1120–1126.

Bird, H. R., Gould, M. S., & Staghezza, B. (1992). Aggregating data from multiple informants in child psychiatry epidemiological research. *Journal of the American Academy of Child and Adolescent Psychiatry, 31*, 78–85.

Bird, H. R., Gould, M. S., & Staghezza, B. M. (1993). Patterns of diagnostic comorbidity in a community sample of children aged 9 through 16 years. *Journal of the American Academy of Child and Adolescent Psychiatry, 32*, 361–368.

Block, J., & Gjerde, P. F. (1990). Depressive symptoms in late adolescence: A longitudinal perspective on personality antecedents. In A. S. Masten, D. Cicchetti, K. H. Nuechterlein, & S. Weintraub (Eds.), *Risk and protective factors in the development of psychopathology* (pp. 334–360). New York: Cambridge University Press.

Brady, E. U., & Kendall, P. C. (1992). Comorbidity of anxiety and depression in children and adolescents. *Psychological Bulletin, 111*, 244–255.

Brandenburg, N. A., Friedman, R. M., & Silver, S. E. (1990). The epidemiology of childhood psychiatric disorders: Prevalence findings from recent studies. *Journal of the American Academy of Child and Adolescent Psychiatry, 29*, 76–83.

Brown, T. A., & Barlow, D. H. (1992). Comorbidity among anxiety disorders: Implications for treatment and DSM-IV. *Journal of Clinical and Consulting Psychology, 60*, 835–844.

Capaldi, D. M. (1992). Co-occurrence of conduct problems and depressive symptoms in early adolescent boys: II. A 2-year follow-up at Grade 8. *Development and Psychopathology, 4*, 125–144.

Carlson, G. A. (1990). Annotation: Child and adolescent mania—diagnostic considerations. *Journal of Child Psychology and Psychiatry, 31*, 331–341.

Caron, C., & Rutter, M. (1991). Comorbidity in child psychopathology: Concepts, issues and research strategies. *Journal of Child Psychology & Psychiatry, 32*, 1063–1080.

Clarkin, J. F., & Kendall, P. C. (1992). Comorbidity and treatment planning: Summary and future directions. *Journal of Consulting and Clinical Psychology, 60*, 904–908.

Cohen, P. (1993). [Children in the Community Study: Comorbidity in 9- to 18-year-old children.] Unpublished data.

Cohen, P., Cohen, J., Kasen, S., Velez, C. N., Hartmark, C., Johnson, J., Rojas, M., Brook, J., & Streuning, E. L. (1993). An epidemiological study of disorders in late childhood and adolescence: I. Age and gender-specific prevalence. *Journal of Child Psychology and Psychiatry, 34*, 851–867.

Cohen, P., Velez, C. N., Brook, J., & Smith, J. (1989). Mechanisms of the relation between perinatal problems, early childhood illness, and psychopathology in late childhood and adolescence. *Child Development, 60*, 701–709.

Costello, E. J. (1990). Child psychiatric epidemiology: Implications for clinical research and practice. In B. B. Lahey & A. E. Kazdin (Eds.), *Advances in clinical child psychology* (Vol. 13, pp. 53–90). New York: Plenum Press.

Costello, E. J., Costello, A. J., Edelbrock, C., Burns, B. J., Dulcan, M. K., Brent, D., & Janiszewski, S. (1988). Psychiatric disorders in pediatric primary care. *Archives of General Psychiatry, 45*, 1107–1116.

Edelbrock, C., & Costello, A. J. (1988). Convergence between statistically derived behavior problem syndromes and child psychiatric disorders. *Journal of Abnormal Child Psychology, 16*, 219–231.

Esser, G., Schmidt, M. H., & Woerner, W. (1990). Epidemiology and course of psychiatric disorders in school-age children—Results of a longitudinal study. *Journal of Child Psychology & Psychiatry, 31,* 243–263.

Feehan, M., McGee, R., & Williams, S. M. (1993). Mental health disorders from age 15 to age 18 years. *Journal of the American Academy of Child and Adolescent Psychiatry, 32,* 1118–1126.

Fergusson, D. M., & Horwood, L. J. (1993). The structure, stability and correlations of the trait components of conduct disorder, attention deficit and anxiety/withdrawal reports. *Journal of Child Psychology and Psychiatry, 34,* 749–766.

Fergusson, D. M., Horwood, L. J., & Lynskey, M. T. (1993). The effects of conduct disorder and attention deficit in middle childhood on offending and scholastic ability at age 13. *Journal of Child Psychology and Psychiatry, 34,* 899–916.

Fleming, J. E., Boyle, M. H., & Offord, D. (1993). The outcome of adolescent depression in the Ontario Child Health Study follow-up. *Journal of the American Academy of Child and Adolescent Psychiatry, 32,* 28–33.

Fleming, J. E., Offord, D. R., & Boyle, M. H. (1989). Prevalence of childhood and adolescent depression in the community. *British Journal of Psychiatry, 155,* 647–654.

Frick, P. J., Lahey, B. B., Loeber, R., Tannenbaum, L., Van Horn, Y., Christ, M. A. G., Hart, E. A., & Hanson, K. (1993). Oppositional defiant disorder and conduct disorder: A meta-analytic review of factor analyses and cross-validation in a clinic sample. *Clinical Psychology Review, 13,* 319–340.

Frost, L. A., Moffitt, T. E., & McGee, R. (1989). Neuropsychological correlates of psychopathology in an unselected cohort of young adolescents. *Journal of Abnormal Psychology, 98,* 307–313.

Gould, M. S., Bird, H., & Jaramillo, B. S. (1993). Correspondence between statistically derived behavior problem syndromes and child psychiatric diagnoses in a community sample. *Journal of Abnormal Child Psychology, 21,* 287–313.

Gould, M. S., Wunsch-Hitzig, R., & Dohrenwend, B. (1981). Estimating the prevalence of childhood psychopathology. *Journal of the American Academy of Child and Adolescent Psychiatry, 20,* 462–476.

Graham, P., & Rutter, M. (1968). The reliability and validity of the psychiatric assessment of the child II: Interview with the parent. *British Journal of Psychiatry, 114,* 581–592.

Harrington, R., Fudge, H., Rutter, M., Pickles, A., & Hill, J. (1991). Adult outcomes of childhood and adolescent depression: II. Links with antisocial disorders. *Journal of the American Academy of Child and Adolescent Psychiatry, 30,* 434–439.

Hughes, C. W., Preskorn, S. H., Weller, E., Weller, R., Hassanein, R., & Tucker, S. (1990). The effect of concomitant disorders in childhood depression on predicting treatment response. *Psychopharmacology Bulletin, 26,* 235–238.

Jensen, P. S., Shervette, R. E., Xenakis, S. N., & Richters, J. (1993). Anxiety and depressive disorders in attention deficit disorder with hyperactivity: New findings. *American Journal of Psychiatry, 150,* 1203–1209.

Kashani, J. H., Beck, N. C., Hoeper, E. W., Fallahi, C., Corcoran, C. M., McAllister, J. A., Rosenberg, T. K., & Reid, J. C. (1987). Psychiatric disorders in a community sample of adolescents. *American Journal of Psychiatry, 144,* 584–589.

Kashani, J. H., Orvaschel, H., Rosenberg, T. K., & Reid, J. C. (1989). Psychopathology in a community sample of children and adolescents: A developmental perspective. *Journal of the American Academy of Child and Adolescent Psychiatry, 28,* 701–706.

Kendall, P. C., & Clarkin, J. F. (1992). Introduction to Special Section: Comorbidity and treatment implications. *Journal of Clinical and Consulting Psychology, 60,* 833–834.

King, N. J., Ollendick, T. H., & Gullone, E. (1991). Negative affectivity in children and adolescents: Relations between anxiety and depression. *Clinical Psychology Review, 11,* 441–459.

Kovacs, M., Gatsonis, C., Paulauskas, S. L., & Richards, C. (1989). Depressive disorders in childhood: IV. A longitudinal study of comorbidity with and risk for anxiety disorders. *Archives of General Psychiatry, 46,* 776–782.

Kovacs, M., Paulauskas, S., Gatsonis, C., & Richards, C. (1988). Depressive disorders in childhood: III. A longitudinal study of comorbidity with and [without] risk for conduct disorder. *Journal of Affective Disorders, 15,* 205–217.

Lahey, B. B., Loeber, R., Quay, H. C., Frick, P. J., & Grimm, J. (1992). Oppositional defiant and conduct disorders: Issues to be resolved for DSM-IV. *Journal of the American Academy of Child and Adolescent Psychiatry, 31,* 539–546.

Ledingham, J. E., & Schwartzman, A. E. (1984). A 3-year follow-up of aggressive and withdrawn behavior in childhood: Preliminary findings. *Journal of Abnormal Child Psychology, 12,* 157–168.

Lewinsohn, P. M., Rohde, P., Seeley, J. R., & Hops, H. (1991). Comorbidity of unipolar depression: I. Major depression with dysthymia. *Journal of Abnormal Psychology, 100,* 205–213.

Livingston, R. L., Dykman, R. A., & Ackerman, P. T. (1990). The frequency and significance of additional self-reported psychiatric diagnoses in children with attention deficit disorder. *Journal of Abnormal Child Psychology, 18,* 465–478.

Loeber, R., Keenan, K., Lahey, B. B., Green, S. M., & Thomas, C. (1993). Evidence for developmentally based diagnoses of oppositional defiant disorder and conduct disorder. *Journal of Abnormal Child Psychology, 21,* 377–410.

McBurnett, K., Lahey, B. B., Frick, P. J., Risch, C., Loeber, R., Hart, E. L., Christ, A. G., & Hanson, K. S. (1991). *Journal of the American Academy of Child and Adolescent Psychiatry, 30,* 192–196.

McGee, R., Feehan, M., Williams, S., & Anderson, J. (1992). DSM-III disorders from age 11 to age 15 years. *Journal of the American Academy of Child and Adolescent Psychiatry, 31,* 50–59.

McGee, R., Williams, S., & Feehan, M. (1992). Attention deficit disorder and age of onset of problem behaviors. *Journal of Abnormal Child Psychology, 20,* 487–502.

Moffitt, T. E. (1990). Juvenile delinquency and attention deficit disorder: Boys' developmental trajectories from age 3 to age 15. *Child Development, 61,* 893–910.

Moskowitz, D. S., Schwartzman, A. E., & Ledingham, J. E. (1985). Stability and change in aggression and withdrawal in middle childhood and early adolescence. *Journal of Abnormal Psychology, 94,* 30–41.

Offord, D. R., Boyle, M. H., Fleming, J. E., Blum, H. M., & Grant, N. I. R. (1989). Ontario Child Health Study: Summary of selected results. *Canadian Journal of Psychiatry, 34,* 483–491.

Offord, D. R., Boyle, M. H., & Racine, Y. (1989). Ontario Child Health Study: Correlates of disorder. *Journal of the American Academy of Child and Adolescent Psychiatry, 28,* 856–860.

Offord, D. R., Boyle, M. H., Szatmari, P., Rae-Grant, N. I., Links, P. S., Cadman, D. T., Byles, J. A., Crawford, J. W., Blum, H. M., Byrne, C., Thomas, H., & Woodward, C. A. (1987). Ontario Child Health Study: II. Six-month prevalence of disorder and rates of service utilization. *Archives of General Psychiatry, 44,* 832–836.

Pfeffer, C. E., & Plutchik, R. (1989). Co-occurrence of psychiatric disorders in child psychiatric patients and nonpatients: A circumplex model. *Contemporary Psychiatry, 30,* 275–282.

Prior, M., Smart, D., Sanson, A., & Oberklaid, F. (1993). Sex differences in psychological adjustment from infancy to 8 years. *Journal of the American Academy of Child and Adolescent Psychiatry, 32,* 291–304.

Rohde, P., Lewinsohn, P. M., & Seeley, J. R. (1991). Comorbidity of unipolar depression: II. Comorbidity with other mental health disorders in adolescents and adults. *Journal of Abnormal Psychology, 100,* 214–222.

Russo, M. F., Loeber, R., Lahey, B. B., & Keenan, K. (1994). Oppositional defiant and conduct disorders: Validation of the DSM-III-R and an alternative option. *Journal of Clinical Child Psychology, 23,* 56–68.

Rutter, M. (1989). Isle of Wight revisited: Twenty-five years of child psychiatric epidemiology. *Journal of the American Academy of Child and Adolescent Psychiatry, 28,* 633–653.

Sanford, M. N., Offord, D. R., Boyle, M. H., Peace, A., & Racine, Y. A. (1992). Ontario Child Health Study: Social and school impairments in children ages 6 to 16 years. *Journal of the American Academy of Child and Adolescent Psychiatry, 31,* 60–67.

Schachar, R., & Wachsmuth, R. (1990). Oppositional disorder in children: A validation study comparing conduct disorder, oppositional disorder and normal control children. *Journal of Child Psychology & Psychiatry, 31,* 1089–1102.

Szatmari, P., Boyle, M., & Offord, D. (1989). ADDH and conduct disorder: Degree of diagnostic overlap and differences among correlates. *Journal of the American Academy of Child and Adolescent Psychiatry, 28,* 865–872.

Velez, C. N., Johnson, J., & Cohen, P. (1989). A longitudinal analysis of selected risk factors for childhood psychopathology. *Journal of the American Academy of Child and Adolescent Psychiatry, 28,* 861–864.

Verhulst, F. C., & Althaus, M. (1988). Persistence and change in behavioral/emotional problems reported by parents of children aged 4-14: An epidemiological study. *Acta Psychiatrica Scandinavica, 77*(Suppl. 339), 1–28.

Verhulst, F. C., & van der Ende, J. (1993). "Comorbidity" in an epidemiological sample: A longitudinal perspective. *Journal of Child Psychology and Psychiatry, 34,* 767–783

Walker, J. L., Lahey, B. B., Russo, M. F., Frick, P. J., Christ, M. A. G., McBurnett, K., Loeber, R., Stouthamer-Loeber, M., & Green, S. M. (1991). Anxiety, inhibition, and conduct disorder in children: I. Relations to social impairment. *Journal of the American Academy of Child and Adolescent Psychiatry, 30,* 187–191.

Zahn-Waxler, C. (1993). Warriors and worriers: Gender and psychopathology. *Development and Psychopathology, 5,* 79–89.

Zoccolillo, M. (1992). Co-occurrence of conduct disorder and its adult outcomes with depressive and anxiety disorders: A review. *Journal of the American Academy of Child and Adolescent Psychiatry, 31,* 547–556.

Zoccolillo, M. (1993). Gender and the development of conduct disorder. *Development and Psychopathology, 5,* 65–78.

4

Social Withdrawal in Childhood

Conceptual and Empirical Perspectives

Kenneth H. Rubin, Shannon L. Stewart, and Robert J. Coplan

Dear Dr. Rubin,

I am a former elementary school teacher and I am very aware of the importance of a child's readiness in all areas—social as well as academic, physical, and emotional.

My daughter and I have never been close. She was one who as a baby would stop crying when I set her on the floor instead of cuddling her. I gave up my career to do special things with her and we oftentimes clash. She prefers doing things alone instead of playing cards with me or other game like involvement.

We had her repeat kindergarten for social reasons only. She would oftentimes say things like "Susie isn't nice to me." Last March on her own she told me she did not want to go to first grade. She is very passive at school, does not want group attention, prefers to play alone but likes to watch others play (she looks like she wants to be a part of the group but doesn't know how).

I feel Julie was born this way. This is not because I don't want to blame myself. But this all started when she was a toddler. She was very independent around both of us. My husband is a very close, participating member of the family. I know this is hard for you to give any suggestions without knowing our family but we are very close knit and happy. We have real need to help our daughter Julie because I feel it will get much worse for her when she's in school in the fall the whole day.

Thank you for your attention.

KENNETH H. RUBIN, SHANNON L. STEWART, AND ROBERT J. COPLAN. • Department of Psychology, University of Waterloo, Ontario, Canada N2L 3G1.

Advances in Clinical Child Psychology, Volume 17, edited by Thomas H. Ollendick and Ronald J. Prinz. Plenum Press, New York, 1995.

The letter reproduced above arrived in the office of the senior author shortly after an article appeared in newspapers across Canada concerning our research program at the University of Waterloo. It is this letter and countless others received in response to the wire service's publication of the article that lend a sense of urgency to a topic once relatively ignored by clinical child psychologists—social withdrawal, its meaning, its origins, its concomitants, and its consequences. In this chapter, we describe the conceptual basis that has driven, and the empirical findings that have supported our 15-year effort to provide a better understanding of this elusive construct. Our goal is to convince the reader that the study of social withdrawal in childhood merits far more attention than it has heretofore received by those who are interested in the development of psychopathology and the assessment of behavioral dysfunction.

1. Social Withdrawal and Developmental Psychopathology

In a highly influential special issue of the archival journal, *Child Development* Sroufe and Rutter (1984) provided readers with one of the first comprehensive definitions of developmental psychopathology. They refer to the discipline as " the study of the origins and course of individual patterns of behavioral maladaptation, whatever the transformations in behavioral manifestation, and however complex the course of the developmental pattern may be" (p.18). Generally, those who have focused on the development of psychopathology have attended to two *broad* forms of behavioral maladaptation, namely those involving difficulties of psychological *undercontrol* and those involving difficulties of psychological *overcontrol*. Problems of psychological undercontrol have also been referred to as *externalizing* difficulties and include attention deficit disorder with hyperactivity, conduct disorder, and aggression. Problems of psychological overcontrol, are often referred to as *internalizing* difficulties and include anxiety, fears, depression, and social withdrawal.

Clearly, the etiological study of externalizing difficulties in childhood has a broader, richer conceptual and empirical history than that of psychological overcontrol. Several factors account for these theoretical and empirical biases. First, from the very earliest years of childhood, externalizing problems are easier to identify than internalizing problems. The behavioral manifestations of undercontrol are highly salient and likely to evoke an immediate emotional and behavioral reaction from the perceiver (Mills & Rubin, 1990). On the other hand, behavioral manifestations of overcontrol are less salient and are less likely to evoke an immediate affective or behavioral response (Mills & Rubin, 1990; 1993; Younger, Gentile, & Burgess, 1993).

Second, children who are "out-of-control" are viewed as serious challenges to the delivery of appropriate group care and/or education. Thus, children who demonstrate aggressive, impulsive, or overactive symptomatology are targeted early and often for ameliorative attention. Quiet, sensitive, socially reticent young children, on the other hand, often represent veritable models of proper preschool and elementary school decorum. Given that they are not disruptive, their difficulties are more likely to go undetected or ignored by the typically harried caregiver/educator.

Third, aggressive behavior is not only salient, but also highly stable throughout the years of childhood (e.g., Olweus, 1979). Moreover, childhood aggression is predictive of antisocial behavior in adulthood (e.g., Parker & Asher, 1987) and it is contemporaneously associated with a plethora of other difficulties. For example, externalizers, as a group, have deficits in understanding the perspectives, feelings, and intentions of others (Dodge, 1986; Rubin, Bream, & Rose-Krasnor, 1991). They bully their classmates and quickly establish for themselves negative reputations amongst their peers (Coie & Kupersmidt, 1983; Dodge, 1983). Taken together, given the potential negative short- and long-term consequences of undercontrolled aggressive behavior for its producers and its victims, it is not surprising that the phenomenon has attracted voluminous and compelling conceptual and empirical treatments (see Pepler & Rubin, 1991 for recent reviews).

Social withdrawal, on the other hand, has had a relatively checkered research history. For example, social withdrawal has been described as relatively *unstable* and *non-significantly* predictive of psychological maladjustment during adolescence and adulthood (Kohlberg, LaCrosse, & Ricks, 1972; Parker & Asher, 1987; Robins, 1966). The data supportive of this "non risk" perspective on social withdrawal, when combined with the long-standing psychoanalytic position that childhood internalizing disorders (more specifically, depression) cannot be experienced until the superego has been fully developed in adolescence (Kashani, Husain, Shekim, Hodges, Cytryn, & McKnew, 1981), have failed to evoke the same kind of urgency to understand problems of an internalizing nature in childhood as has been the case for externalizing difficulties.

Nevertheless, the primary focus of our research program has been to understand, conceptually and empirically, the etiology of social withdrawal in childhood—the prime behavioral manifestation of psychological overcontrol. Our persistence in tracking what had been, heretofore, a problem of relatively insignificant proportions was spurred on by several factors. First, there has been a curious contradiction in views regarding the importance of psychological overcontrol. On the one hand, there has been the aforementioned reporting that behaviors reflecting internalizing difficulties (e.g., social withdrawal) are transient and unrelated to adult maladjustment (e.g., Ensminger, Kellam, & Rubin, 1983). Yet, on the other hand, the term "social withdrawal" can be found in almost every textbook on abnormal or clinical child psychology (e.g., Achenbach, 1982; Quay & Werry, 1986; Rosenberg, Wilson, Maheady, and Sindelar, 1991; Wicks-Nelson & Israel, 1989). It can also be found on most standardized assessments of abnormal socioemotional development (e.g., Achenbach & Edelbrock, 1981). Indeed, the lack of social interaction has been implicated in several DSM-III-R categories of psychopathology (e.g., adjustment disorder with withdrawal; avoidant personality disorder). Thus, our research program was inspired, in part, by a motivation to clarify the confusion in the clinical literature extant.

We have also been inspired by the seriousness with which clinicians and developmental psychopathologists have attended to the development of intervention and amelioration programs to deal with social withdrawal, its concomitants, and consequences (e.g., Furman, Rahe, & Hartup, 1979; Rubin, Hymel, Mills, & Rose-Krasnor, 1991; Strain & Kerr, 1981). It seemed to us rather ill-advised to ignore a phenomenon that (a) was taken seriously by front line, practicing psychologists and child-care workers, and (b) appeared relevant to the many different developmental theories (e.g., social learning theory, ethology) that appeared to underlie these intervention efforts.

Finally, our research program was inspired, in large part, by the conceptual impoverishment of the empirical extant literature concerning social withdrawal in childhood. For example, of the handful of prospective longitudinal studies in which the risk status of childhood social withdrawal has been examined (Janes & Hesselbrock, 1978; Janes, Hesselbrock, Myers, & Penniman, 1979; John, Mednick, & Schulsinger, 1982; Michael, Morris, & Soroker, 1957; Morris, Soroker, & Burruss, 1954; Robins, 1966), all have shared important methodological and conceptual flaws. First, in *all* cases, the samples comprised clinic or high-risk individuals; this procedure is known to result in an attenuated range of observed behavior and an underestimate of the association between the behavior of interest and later outcomes. Second, in all studies, the researchers used some form of teacher assessment, the validity of which was largely unknown, to measure social withdrawal (Hymel & Rubin, 1985). Third, the "outcome" measure typically assessed was some form of externalizing disorder. This latter procedure seems odd given that social withdrawal has long been regarded as behavioral reflection of internalizing difficulties.

Finally, in earlier research, investigators have viewed social withdrawal as some form of unitary construct; we now know, however, that different types of solitude carry with them very different meanings (Rubin & Asendorpf, 1993). Furthermore, the psychological "meanings" of these different forms of solitary behavior change with the age of the child (Asendorpf, 1991; 1993). In our work, for example, we have taken great pains to argue that social isolation can occur for a variety of different reasons, ranging from ostracism *by* the peer group to anxious withdrawal *from* the peer group (e.g., Rubin & Lollis, 1988; Rubin & Mills, 1988; Rubin, LeMare & Lollis, 1990). Thus, we contend that one reason for the lack of evidence that social withdrawal presages later maladjustment may be the failure by researchers to differentiate between subtypes of the phenomenon (see also Coplan, Rubin, Fox, Calkins, & Stewart, 1994; Rubin, 1982a).

Taken together, it seems obvious that the phenomenon of social withdrawal in childhood has been the victim of an identity crisis. It has been viewed as unworthy of consideration as a risk factor for later psychopathology, while at the same time being thought of as a reflection of internalizing problems. It has been viewed as a phenomenon that attracts little attention, to the point of peer neglect (e.g., Coie & Kupersmidt, 1983), while at the same time being very salient to caregivers and age-mates (e.g., Bacon & Ashmore, 1985; Bugental & Cortez, 1988; Bugental & Shennum, 1984; Younger & Boyko, 1987). It has not received much direct attention by theorists (e.g., there has not been an all-encompassing theory of social withdrawal), yet many developmentally and clinically relevant theories clearly identify the benefits of peer interactive experiences and the liabilities of the lack thereof. Thus, in writing this chapter we have several purposes.

First, we hope to convince the reader, following a brief review, that the study of social withdrawal does have a strong theoretical basis. Second, we describe the conceptual, working model that has guided our program of research on the etiology, concomitants, and consequences of social withdrawal in childhood. Third, we present recent findings, primarily from our laboratory, that lend credence to the aforementioned model. And finally, we pose several unanswered questions that merit attention in future research endeavors.

2. The Developmental Significance of Social Withdrawal

2.1. Theories Pertaining to Social Interaction

Much of the *developmental* research extant concerning social withdrawal has its origins not so much centered on the significance of behavioral solitude or a lack of social interaction in childhood, but rather on the importance of social exchange for normal growth and development. Thus, the conceptual basis for much current research on social withdrawal is drawn from the writings of Piaget, Mead, and Sullivan concerning the significance of social *interaction* in human development. More than half a century ago, Jean Piaget (1926, 1932) suggested that peer interaction provided a unique cognitive and social-cognitive growth context for children. He centered specifically on the relevance of peer conflict and the opportunities for negotiation that it creates; the experience of difference of opinion was assumed to create "cognitive conflict" that had to be resolved both intra- and interpersonally in order for positive peer exchanges and experiences to occur. Resolution of these conflicts through negotiation and cognitive accommodation was posited to result in the capacity for sensitive perspective taking in interpersonal relationships and for the understanding of cause–effect relations in social interaction.

These Piagetian beliefs found empirical support during the 1970s; during this decade, neo-Piagetian researchers forged an empirical link between peer interaction, perspective-taking skills, and the development of socially adaptive and maladaptive behavior. For example, evidence for the relation between peer interaction and the development of social cognition was derived from experimental demonstrations that peer exchange, conversations, and interactions produced *intrapersonal* cognitive conflict and a subsequent decline of egocentered thinking (e.g., Damon, 1977; Doise, Mugny, & Perret-Clermont, 1975).

At approximately the same time that Piaget was writing about the means by which childhood egocentrism might wane, George Herbert Mead (1934) proposed that the ability to self-reflect, to consider the self in relation to others, and to understand the perspectives of others was largely a function of participation in organized, rule-governed activities with peers. He suggested that exchanges among peers, whether experienced in the arenas of cooperation or competition, conflict or friendly discussion, allowed the child to gain an understanding of the self as both a subject and an object. Understanding that the self could be an object of others' perspectives gradually evolved into the conceptualization of a "generalized other" or an organized and coordinated perspective of the "social" group. In turn, recognition of the "generalized other" led to the emergence of an organized sense of self.

The classic personality theory of Harry Stack Sullivan (1953) also has served as a guide for much current research concerning children's peer relationships and social skills. Sullivan suggested that the foundations of mutual respect, cooperation, and interpersonal sensitivity derived initially from children's peer and friendship relationships. Sullivan specifically emphasized the importance of chumships, or special relationships, for the emergence of these concepts. Thus, once understanding the concepts of equality, mutuality, and reciprocity was acquired from chums, these concepts could be applied more generally to other less special peer relationships. And finally, theorists in the social-learning camp have long suggested (and found) that children learn social behaviors and social norms directly through peer tutelage, reinforcement and punishment, and indirectly by observing peers "in action" (Bandura & Walters, 1963).

Taken together, these early theories and the data supportive of them (see Hartup, 1992; Rubin & Coplan, 1992 for recent reviews) argue strongly and convincingly that peers are active, significant socializers of social-cognitive and social competence in childhood and that peer interaction is an important force in the development of normal social relationships. This being the case, we have asked the following questions in our program of research:

1. What happens to children who, for whatever reason, fail to take advantage of their opportunities to interact with peers?
2. Will such socially withdrawn children fail to develop acceptable social skills?
3. Will such children fail to develop qualitatively normal relationships with their peers?
4. Will socially withdrawn children fail to develop normal thoughts and feelings of self-regard?

Our hunch has been that the child who does not have adequate peer interactive experiences may indeed be at risk for later maladjustment.

2.2. Theories Pertaining to Social Reticence and Inhibition

The theories reviewed previously emphasize the significance of peer interaction for normal growth and development. From these theories, one can speculate about the developmental consequences for children who do not experience quantitatively or qualitatively normal peer interactions and exchanges. These theories fail to explain, however, who and how it is that children come to be socially withdrawn in the first place. Theoretically relevant explanations have been provided by several psychologists. For example, Kagan and colleagues (e.g., Kagan, 1989; Kagan, Snidman, & Arcus, 1993) have proposed that some infants are born with a physiology that biases them initially to be cautious, timid, and wary in unfamiliar social and nonsocial situations. These "inhibited" children differ from their uninhibited counterparts in ways that imply differences in the threshold of excitability of the amygdala and its projections to the cortex, hypothalamus, sympathetic nervous system, corpus striatum, and central grey (Kagan et al., 1993). Kagan and colleagues argue further that the physiological characteristics of children who demonstrate social wariness and withdrawal in the company of *unfamiliar* peers are largely inherited. Similar arguments for a *physiological* basis to social wariness, inhibition, and withdrawal stem from the writings of Fox and colleagues (e.g., Fox & Calkins, 1993). And Plomin and Daniels (1986) concur with Kagan and hold that social wariness is an *inherited* trait. For example, after an examination of eighteen twin studies, Plomin and Daniels reported that shyness was more highly associated in monozygotic than in dizygotic twins.

It is important to note that the models referred to pertain to the expression of *shyness*, or wary, timid, and withdrawn behavior in the face of *novel* social circumstances. Whether or not shyness is related to social withdrawal and the lack of peer interaction in *familiar* settings is relatively unknown. Recently, however, Asendorpf (1990) reported a significant association between the expression of shy, inhibited behavior with an unfamiliar peer and socially withdrawn behavior in preschool classrooms of familiar peers. With age, however, this association became statistically nonsignificant. Moreover, it was only the display of solitary behavior in the *familiar* peer group that was associated with observations of peer noncompliance to the withdrawn child's social overtures. Thus, Asendorpf argued that an uncomfortable dialectic develops between the expression of solitary behavior in the classroom and the experience of peer rejection; the latter leads the child to anticipate negative social evaluation and, thus, strengthens the child's motivation to avoid peer exchange. In related studies, others have argued that social wariness in the middle and late years of childhood is tied inextricably to the felt anxiety of being evaluated by peers and others (Buss, 1984, 1986).

Theorists who argue strongly for underlying biological and genetic components to the expression of social wariness and shyness have not generally suggested negative outcomes of a psychopathological nature for extremely shy or socially wary children. And, these theorists have not typically provided a strong account for how environmental circumstances may influence and modify these biologically based traits. Yet, in other relevant theories, causal connections have been made between experiential, familial factors and the development of socially wary and withdrawn behaviors.

For example, *attachment theorists* have posited that the parent–infant attachment relationship results in the child's developing an internal working model of the self in relation to others (Bowlby, 1973). This internal working model allows the child to feel secure, confident, and self-assured when introduced to novel settings; this sense of "felt security" fosters the child's active exploration of the social environment (Sroufe, 1983). In turn, exploration of the social milieu allows the child to address a number of significant "other-directed" questions such as "What are the properties of this other person?"; "What is she/he like?"; "What can and does she/he do?" (Rubin, 1993). Once these exploratory questions are answered, the child can begin to address "self-directed" questions such as "What can I do with this person?" Thus, felt security is viewed as a central construct in socioemotional development. It enhances social exploration, and exploration results in interactive peer play (Rubin, Fein & Vandenberg, 1983). Peer play, in turn, plays a significant role in the development of social competence (Rubin, Stewart, & Chen, in press).

Children who experience unresponsive, insensitive parenting, on the other hand, develop insecure internal working models of social relationships and come to view the world as unpredictable, comfortless, and unresponsive (Sroufe, 1983). This insecure internal representation may lead some children to "shrink from their social worlds . . ." (Bowlby, 1973, p. 208). Thus, there may be a group of insecurely attached young children who refrain from exploring their social environments; this lack of exploration is likely to impede social-peer play and, as attachment theorists posit, may interfere with the development of social competence. It is the behavioral response of insecurity/anxiety-induced withdrawal from the peer culture that best conveys, to us, the meaning of "social withdrawal."

The bottom line is that there is actually no shortage of theories relevant to the development, the concomitants, and the consequences of nonsocial behavior. It is essential to note, however, that theorists who discuss the etiology of shyness and wariness in the face of novelty may not be describing the same behavioral phenomenon as theorists who outline the forces leading to the day-to-day expression of wary, withdrawn behavior in familiar settings. It is on this latter phenomenon that we have focused our research program.

In the following section, we describe two conceptual models that have driven our own efforts in the study of social withdrawal in childhood. In the first model, we outline a developmental scenario of psychological adaptation. In the second, we suggest that a shy, inhibited temperament may set the stage for the development of socially wary and withdrawn behavior in familiar settings. In turn, social withdrawal may become associated with, and reflective and predictive of, markers of socioemotional maladaptation in childhood.

3. A "Fantasyland" Model of Behavioral Adjustment

In several reports, we have described a paradigm case for studying the optimal development of psychological adjustment (e.g., Rubin et al., 1990; Rubin et al., 1991). Essentially, we have attempted to provide ourselves with a model of how we think normalcy in socioemotional adjustment *might* develop; in so doing, we have come to terms with the distinct possibility that this model of development is probably beyond the reach of any "real" human child and her or his family.

We begin by suggesting that socioemotional adjustment derives from the interplay between intraindividual, interindividual, and macrosystemic forces. More specifically, we believe that psychological adjustment is influenced by the interactions between the child's dispositional and biologically based characteristics, her/his socialization experiences, the quality of her/his social relationships within and outside of the family, and the forces of culture, stress, and social support impinging on the child and the family.

Adopting a developmental and sequential approach, we posit that the combination of (a) an even-tempered, easy disposition, (b) the experience of sensitive and responsive parenting, and (c) the general lack of major stresses or crises during infancy and early childhood "conspire" to predict the development of secure parent–child attachment relationships (Rubin & Lollis, 1988; Rubin et al., 1990). And drawing from the early research on continuities of infant attachment, we hypothesize that these secure primary relationships influence the development of social and emotional adjustment (see Sroufe, 1983 for a review).

Thankfully, we know that most infants and toddlers have relatively easygoing dispositions (Thomas & Chess, 1977) and most do develop *secure* relationships with the parents (Ainsworth, Blehar, Waters, & Wall, 1978). These relationships appear to be caused and maintained, in part, by having parents who are in tune with the child's behaviors (Isabella & Belsky, 1991; Smith & Peterson, 1988; Spieker & Booth, 1988). These sensitive and responsive parents may, from time to time, be angered and off-put by their child's behavior; however, given such circumstances, they are accepting of the child and do not remain angry, hostile, or resentful. It is worth noting that parental responsivity and sensitivity is probably easier to deliver (a) when one's infant is relatively easygoing; and (b) when the family unit is relatively stress free.

As we noted above, a secure parent–child relationship provides the child with the felt-security and confidence to explore the peer milieu and to engage in healthy bouts of peer interaction. And also, as noted above, it is during play with peers that children experience the interpersonal exchange of ideas, perspectives, roles, and actions. From these social negotiations, discussions, and conflicts with peers, children learn to understand *others'* thoughts, emotions, motives and intentions (e.g., Doise & Mugny, 1981). And armed with these new social understandings, children are able to think about the consequences of their social behaviors, not only for themselves but also for others. In short, we posit that peer interaction helps children develop social competence.

Once socially competent behavior is demonstrated by the child and recognized by the parent, the secure parent–child relationship will be nutured and maintained by the dialectic between (a) the child who is willing and able to explore and play competently in a social milieu, and who is able to benefit social-cognitively and socially from peer interactive experiences; and (b) a competent parent who is emotionally available, sharply attuned to social situations, and to the thoughts and emotions of her or his child, able to anticipate the child's behaviors and the consequences of the child's actions, and able to predict the outcomes of her or his own actions for the child. This competent, secure family-relationship system serves both the parent and the child well, and barring any undue circumstances, a socioemotional outcome of positive intra- and interpersonal adjustment is predicted.

4. A "Temple of Doom" Scenario for Internalizing Difficulties

In our second model, we recognize that not all children and their parents live through a "Fantasyland" experience. For example, most families experience, from time to time, stress, crises, and day-to-day hassles. There is growing evidence that stressful environmental conditions can influence both the quality of the parent–child relationship and the social and emotional well-being of children. Stressors set the stage for positive and negative developmental "outcomes" by influencing (a) parental values, attitudes, and expectations concerning children and (b) the quality of parent–child interaction. Researchers have demonstrated, for example, that factors such as poverty, unemployment, and inadequate housing can produce a generalized maladaptive response set in parents that leads to the neglect or overdirection of the child (Crnic & Greenberg, 1990; Patterson, 1983; Wahler & Dumas, 1987).

Another potential stressor is the child her- or himself. Recently, we have described a developmental scenario that begins with the infant dispositional characteristic generally referred to as behavioral inhibition (Rubin et al., 1990; Rubin & Lollis, 1988). As we noted earlier, some newborns may be biologically predisposed to have a low threshold for arousal when confronted with social (or nonsocial) stimulation and novelty (e.g., Kagan, Snidman & Reznick, 1987; Miyake, Chen, & Campos, 1985)—a characteristic that may make them extremely difficult for their parents to soothe and comfort. Indeed, *some* parents find such infantile responses of hyperarousal aversive (Kagan, Reznick, Clarke, Snidman, & Garcia-Coll, 1984). Thus, we argue that parents who are experiencing stressful family conditions may react to their infant's wariness with hostility, insensitivity, and/or nonresponsivity (e.g., Engfer & Gavranidou, 1987).

Interestingly, each of these parental variables predicts the development of insecure parent–infant attachment relationships (e.g., Isabella, 1993). Thus, we posit that an interplay of endogenous-, socialization-, and early-relationships factors, as they coexist under an "umbrella" of negative-setting conditions, will lead to a sense of felt-insecurity. And we posit further that the internal working models of insecurely attached, temperamentally inhibited children may lead them onto a developmental pathway to social withdrawal.

Support for these conjectures derives from several recent sources. First, there is some evidence of an association between temperament and attachment. For example, Thompson, Connell, and Bridges (1988) reported that the temperamental characteristic of proneness to fear predicts infant distress to maternal separation. Such distress usually marks a child for "C" classification (anxious-resistant) in the traditional attachment paradigm. In addition, in their review of the literature concerning the relations between temperament and attachment, Belsky and Rovine (1987) argued that the temperamental characteristic, *proneness to distress*, is predictive of "B2" through "C2" attachment classifications. The strongest support for a wariness-attachment link emanates from the research of Fox and colleagues. Fox and Calkins, for example, have demonstrated that infants who are highly reactive to mildly stressful, novel social events are more likely to be classified as insecurely attached "C" babies than are their less reactive counterparts (Fox & Calkins, 1993; Calkins & Fox, 1992). Thus, they argue that behavioral and physiological assessments of *infant reactivity*, especially to situations involving mild stress or the introduction of novelty, predict attachment status of an anxious-resistant quality ("C" status) in infancy.

Following from these findings, the literature suggests also that insecure "C" status should predict the production of inhibited and passive–withdrawn behavior in toddlerhood and early childhood. The social behaviors of toddlers and preschoolers who have an insecure attachment, "C" type history are thought to be guided largely by fear of rejection. Conceptually, psychologists have predicted that when these insecurely attached children are placed in group settings with peers, they attempt to avoid rejection through the demonstration of passive, adult-dependent behavior and withdrawal from social interaction (Renken, Egeland, Marvinney, Sroufe, & Mangelsdorf, 1989).

Empirically, several researchers have provided support for these conjectures. For example, it has been reported that infants who experience an anxious-resistant ("C") attachment relationship are more whiny, easily frustrated, and socially inhibited at 2 years of age than their secure counterparts (Fox & Calkins, 1993; Matas, Arend, & Sroufe, 1978). Anxious-resistant babies also tend to be less skilled in peer interaction and to be rated by their teachers as more dependent, helpless, tense, and fearful (Pastor, 1981). At 4 years of age, "C" babies have been described as lacking in confidence and assertiveness (Erickson, Sroufe, & Egeland, 1985) and, at 7 years, as passively withdrawn (Renken et al., 1989). Thus, both conceptually and empirically, there is reason to believe that a relation exists between dispositionally based reactivity to novel stimulation, the quality of the parent–infant attachment relationship, and subsequent socially inhibited and withdrawn behavior.

As we noted earlier, children who refrain from interacting with peers may preclude themselves from (a) establishing normal social relationships; (b) the experience of normal social interactive play behaviors; and (c) the development of those social and cognitive skills that are supposedly encouraged by peer relationships and social play. Thus, one can predict a developmental sequence in which an inhibited, fearful, insecure child withdraws from the social world of peers, fails to develop those skills derived from peer interaction and, because of this, becomes increasingly anxious and isolated from the peer group.

Furthermore, it is now well-established that with increasing age, social reticence or withdrawal becomes increasingly salient to the peer group (Younger & Boyko, 1987; Younger et al., 1993). And, it is also known that perceived deviation from age-normative social behavior is associated with the establishment of negative peer reputations. Thus, in our model we predict that by the mid- to late years of childhood, social withdrawal and social anxiety will be strongly associated with peer rejection and unpopularity.

It seems natural to assume that, at some point in time, parents and teachers may come to recognize the insecurities and anxieties of socially withdrawn children and respond in some fashion. Given their reticence to explore their environments, these children may demonstrate difficulties in getting social "jobs" done or social problems ameliorated. Sensing the child's difficulties and perceived helplessness, some parents may try to provide instrumental aid directly by manipulating their child's social behaviors in a power-assertive, highly controlling, authoritarian manner (e.g., telling the child how to act or what to do). Others may respond by overprotecting and infantilizing their children; these parents may choose what appears to them to be the simplest and most humane course of action by "taking over " the solution of their child's social dilemmas (e.g., intervening during object disputes, inviting potential playmates to the home).

The choice of parenting styles is likely determined by the stresses facing the parent. Thus, the overstressed, overhassled parent may choose a "quick-fix" approach that reflects impatience and anger—an authoritarian, overcontrolling choice of action. The overprotective parent may actually be an oversensitive and extremely responsive parent who cannot bear to see her/his child in difficulty. Whatever the inspirations for parenting styles of overcontrol, overinvolvement, and overprotection, it is nevertheless the case that these socialization strategies have long been linked conceptually to social withdrawal in childhood; these associations, however, have rarely been investigated (e.g., Hetherington & Martin, 1986).

At any rate, parental overdirectiveness and overprotection are likely to maintain rather than to ameliorate the postulated problems associated with social inhibition. Either parenting style likely will not help the child deal firsthand with her or his social interchanges and dilemmas; they probably do little to aid in the development of a belief system of social self-efficacy, and they likely perpetuate feelings of insecurity within and outside of the family.

In summary, in our developmental model, we posit that an inhibited temperament, when responded to with insensitivity, overprotection, and/or overcontrol will predict the establishment of an insecure attachment relationship (see also, Mangelsdorf, Gunnar, Kestenbaum, Lang, & Andreas, 1990). Felt-insecurity may lead to an impoverished exploratory style that precludes the opportunity to experience those forms of peer exchanges hypothesized to promote the development of social competence. The relatively slow development of social competence, when combined with "wariness" and felt-insecurity may lead to the development of negative self-appraisals of competence, which in turn exacerbate withdrawal from peers. These factors, *taken together*, are hypothesized to predict difficulties of an internalizing nature, such as loneliness, negative self-esteem, poor perceptions of one's own social competencies and relationships, and depression.

Finally, we recognize that many, if not most, infants with a fearful, wary inhibited temperament may be "deflected" onto a pathway leading to the development of social and emotional well-being by responsive and sensitive caregiving and by a relatively stress-free environment. Thus, it is highly probable that dispositionally inhibited babies can develop secure relationships with their parents and will not experience the sort of parental overcontrol that we posit to be debilitating. Likewise, we contend that an inhibited temperament is *not* necessary for the development of internalizing problems. We hold that parental overcontrol, overprotection, and overinvolvement, especially when accompanied by familial stress and a lack of social support, may deflect the temperamentally easygoing infant to pathways of internalizing or externalizing difficulties (see also Rubin et al., 1990). Needless to say, these are testable hypotheses reaching out for empirical substantiation.

5. The Developmental Course of Social Withdrawal

In the developmental model offered above, we have suggested that children who preclude themselves from interacting with others may place themselves at risk of not developing, at a normal rate, those social and social-cognitive skills that are derived from peer interaction, and the opportunities it affords to develop skill in negotiation, persuasion, and conflict resolution (Doise & Mugny, 1981). Further, we have argued that when socially withdrawn children come to recognize their own difficulties, and when others behave toward them in a rejecting manner, they may begin to develop negative self-perceptions and emotions. Finally, we have suggested that the development of social withdrawal in childhood may be aided and abetted by the quality of childrearing received and the quality of parent–child relationships experienced in the family..

Empirical support for the speculations offered has been limited. Recenty, however, a relatively small group of researchers, many of them associated with projects and collaborations centered at the University of Waterloo, have begun to establish the veracity of many of the conceptual linkages described in the model. We turn now to an overview of the information gathered in these University of Waterloo studies, as well as in related projects in other research laboratories.

5.1 Defining and Measuring Social Withdrawal

We noted earlier that one reason for previous failures to link social withdrawal to any negative "outcome" of substance probably derived from weaknesses in defining the phenomenon of interest. We have taken the approach that the child who is observed or rated by peers as (a) a solitary player, (b) a child who is uncomfortable socially, and (c) one who spends more than a normal amount of time playing quietly alone, or watching others from afar qualifies as a candidate for being identified as "socially withdrawn." Thus, we have not been particularly interested in children who are inhibited or shy in *novel* social settings; rather, we have focused on the child whose social reticence can be observed, not only in novel settings, but also, and especially, in familiar peer milieus.

The means by which we have assessed social withdrawal have been described in a number of sources (e.g., Rubin, 1993; Rubin et al., 1991; Rubin et al., 1990). We now present an abbreviated description of these procedures.

In our research, we have relied mainly on the Play Observation Scale (POS, Rubin, 1986a,b) and the Revised Class Play (Masten, Morison, & Pelligrini, 1985) to assess social withdrawal in childhood. The POS is a time-sampling procedure that is used to observe children in their class-rooms (e.g., Rubin, 1982) or in structured groups (e.g., Coplan, Rubin, Fox, Calkins, Marshall & Stewart, 1994; Rubin & Mills, 1988). Generally, each child is observed for a specified number of 10-sec. time samples. All behaviors are typically coded on a checklist that includes the cognitive play categories of functional-sensorimotor, exploratory, constructive, dra-matic and games-with-rules behaviors nested within the social participa-tion categories of solitary, parallel, and group activities. Other categories include unoccupied and onlooker behaviors, aggression, and conversa-tions with peers. After recording play behavior, the observers note the names of the focal child's play partners and who it is that initiates the activity. Finally the affective quality of each interaction is coded as posi-tive, neutral or negative.

In early childhood (preschool and kindergarten), we identify three forms of solitude, each carrying with it different psychological meaning (Asendorpf, 1991; Coplan et al., 1994; Rubin, 1982a). *Reticence* (onlook-er+unoccupied behavior) is conceptualized as reflecting a social approach-avoidance motive (Asendorpf, 1991; 1993) and is associated empirically with independent assessments of social anxiety and wariness (Coplan et al., 1994). *Passive withdrawal* (solitary-constructive and -exploratory activ-ity) is conceptualized as reflecting a low approach low avoidance motiva-tion (Asendorpf, 1991; Rubin & Asendorpf, 1993) or social disinterest. Given that this behavior generally comprises instances of quiet, sedentary construction or exploration, it is not surprising that it is often reinforced and positively evaluated by preschool and kindergarten teachers (Rubin, 1982a). Unlike reticence, therefore, passive solitude in early childhood does not reflect social maladaptation; if anything, it reflects an object-focused rather than person-focused orientation (Coplan & Rubin, 1993).

Solitary active play (solitary-functional and -dramatic play) has been construed as reflecting immaturity and impulsivity (Coplan et al., 1994; Rubin, 1982a, Rubin & Mills, 1988). This type of solitude is very infrequent but highly salient when observed; thus, its significant empirical relation with maternal ratings of impulsivity (Coplan et al., in press) and with peer rejection (Rubin, 1982a; Rubin & Mills, 1988) is unsurprising.

Finally, it is important to note that all forms of solitude tend to de-crease with increasing age (Rubin, Maioni, & Hornung, 1976) and that some forms tend to merge both conceptually and empirically with other forms. Thus, although reticence and passive solitude reflect different subtypes of social withdrawal in *early* childhood, these behaviors become increasingly associated thereafter (Asendorpf, 1991). As such, by the mid-years of childhood (around 7 years of age), passive solitude takes on a new meaning, reflecting social uncertainty, wariness, and anxiety. The aggregate of passive solitude and reticence, although decreasing in the frequency with which it is demonstrated, ironically becomes increasingly salient and perceived of as deviant from peer norms (Younger & Daniels, 1992). It is this composite to which we refer when we discuss the *observed* assessment of the construct of social withdrawal.

We have also measured social withdrawal through the administration of a peer-assessment technique known as "The Revised Class Play" (Masten et al., 1985). This measure is used in our laboratory from the approximate age of 7 years. Children are typically requested to nominate up to three classmates who best fit each of 30 behavioral descriptors. Subsequently, nominations received from same-sex peers are used to compute each of three factor scores for each child following procedures outlined by Masten et al. (1985): Sociability-leadership, Aggression-disruption, and Sensitivity-isolation (CPISO).

A close inspection of the items that comprise the original CPISO factor reveals, however, that this factor actually consists of two subclusters of items (Rubin, Hymel, LeMare & Rowden, 1989; Rubin & Mills, 1988). Four of the items appear to describe passive-anxious withdrawal as we have construed it to be above ("someone who would rather play alone than with others," "someone whose feelings get hurt easily," "someone who is very shy," and "someone who is usually sad"). These items mirror our conceptualization of a child who is socially isolated *from* the peer group (CPISOW). The remaining three items appear indicative of peer rejection or isolation *by* the peer group (CPISOR, "a person who can't get others to listen," "someone who has trouble making friends," and "someone who is often left out"). In a recent factor-analytic study, we found that these conceptually distinct clusters of items *did* load on two orthogonal factors (Chen, Rubin, & Sun, 1992). As in Masten et al. (1985), the first two items on CPISOR actually loaded significantly on both the aggression-disruption and sensitivity-isolation factors. Given these findings, and given that peer rejection is associated with high frequencies of aggressive and disruptive behaviors (Coie & Kupersmidt, 1983; Dodge, 1983) as well as with social withdrawal (French, 1988; Rubin et al., 1989), it appeared to us important to examine separately the Revised Class Play items that reflect rejection *by* peers (CPISOR) and those that reflect passive, fearful withdrawal *from* peers (CPISOW). In this chapter, therefore, any results reported concerning the use of peer assessments to measure social withdrawal refer to only those items characterizing CPISOW.

Finally, it should be noted that our belief that the display of social solitude can carry with it a variety of "faces" (e.g., Rubin & Mills, 1988) and a variety of meanings has been supported empirically in several other research laboratories (e.g., Asendorpf, 1991, 1993; Hinde, Tamplin, & Barrett, 1993; Younger & Daniels, 1992; Zaia & Harrist, 1993). Thus, armed with replicable and reliable categories of social withdrawal, we turn now to a description of our findings concerning the childhood concomitants of this phenomenon.

5.2. The Correlates and Concomitants of Social Withdrawal

Much of the relevant research extant on this topic derives from the Waterloo Longitudinal Project (WLP), an ongoing 13-year study of an unselected sample of children attending public school. The primary focus of the WLP has been the contemporaneous and predictive correlates of social withdrawal in childhood and adolescence. The variables we have sought to correlate with our assessments of withdrawal stem from the developmental model described above; as such, the WLP, as well as our others programs of research described later, have been theory- rather than data-driven. Every measure taken was linked to the conceptual base described earlier. With this in mind, we turn now to a description of our findings.

5.2.1. The Stability of Social Withdrawal

From the outset, it is important to note that we have found social withdrawal, as we have defined it, to be a relatively stable construct (Rubin, 1993; Rubin & Both, 1989). Statistically significant intercorrelations were found between observations of social withdrawal at ages 5 and 7 years, and 7 and 9 years. Given that our observational settings differed considerably for the kindergarten and elementary school-age samples (i.e., regular free-play periods versus laboratory free play in quartets respectively), it is not surprising that the age 5 to 9 correlation was nonsignificant.

Interestingly, when peer assessments of withdrawal were considered, the correlations were somewhat higher than those found for the observational data. Thus, significant intercorrelations (all $p<.001$) were found between age 7-, 9-, and 10-year peer assessments of social withdrawal.

We have also developed extreme groups procedures for identifying socially withdrawn children (Rubin, 1993; Rubin, Chen & Hymel, 1993). Our analyses have shown that across any two-year period, from age 5 years to 11 years, approximately two-thirds of identified socially withdrawn children maintain their status.

Taken together, the data indicate that social withdrawal in childhood is a relatively stable phenomenon. When *extreme-group targeting procedures* are used, most children identified as extremely withdrawn in any given year appear to have been similarly identified in earlier years. This finding is in keeping with that of Kagan and colleagues (e.g., Kagan, 1989) who argue that the developmental continuity of *inhibition* is strongest when the longitudinal sample is composed of children who represent behavioral extremes. Year-to-year correlations of observed and peer-nominated withdrawal were consistently, albeit modestly, stable.

The relative stability reported herein bolsters the evidence extant documenting the longitudinal continuity of social withdrawal (Bronson, 1966; Kagan & Moss, 1962; Moskowitz, Schwartzman, & Ledingham, 1985). Although these studies vary considerably in time spans covered, developmental periods involved, and measures employed, they show quite consistently that social withdrawal tends to persist across time.

We have noted elsewhere that it is one thing to suggest that a phenomenon is stable; it is altogether different to argue that a given phenomenon is reflective of psychological maladaptation (Rubin, 1993). To examine the risk status of social withdrawal, we have examined the psychological concomitants of the construct throughout childhood.

5.2.2. Peer Rejection and Social Withdrawal

Given our argument that socially withdrawn children may have insecure and negative relationships with their parents, and that such relationships may conjure up for withdrawn children an "abnormal" internal working model of relationships, we have studied the quality of withdrawn children's peer relationships. As noted in our pathways model described earlier, it has been our contention that during the early years of childhood, the socially withdrawn child is generally less salient to peers than she/he is in the middle and later years of childhood. As such, we suggested that if social withdrawal were viewed as deviant from peer-group norms it would become associated with peer rejection.

To some extent, our thinking about the association between social withdrawal and peer acceptance/rejection has differed from those who have followed the sociometric tradition of equating peer-acceptance status groups with behavioral classifications of children. For example, in the early years of the neosociometric peer-relationships movement, it was fairly commonplace to suggest that socially withdrawn children were sociometrically *neglected* by the peer group (e.g., Coie & Kupersmidt, 1983). That is,

researchers suggested that when peers were asked to nominate three classmates with whom they would like to play or be friends, withdrawn children were those who received few, if any, peer nominations. This characterization of socially withdrawn children as sociometrically neglected led
initially to a number of unfortunate conclusions. Among them was the belief that since sociometrically neglected children did not appear to suffer
from contemporaneous difficulties with regard to anything other than their
sociometric neglect, they could hardly be viewed as a group at-risk for developing later difficulties. Thus, it appeared to follow, given that withdrawn children were sociometrically neglected, they could not be considered as a group at-risk for subsequent maladaption (Coie & Kupersmidt,
1983).

Although these initial conclusions have been altered somewhat in the
current literature (see Asher & Coie, 1990 for recent reviews), the original
perspective was challenged from its very outset by the conceptual basis for
and findings of the WLP. First, drawing from the original sociometric
reports, we argued that the suggestion that sociometrically neglected children are withdrawn appeared accurate only if the reference against which
neglected children were compared was the *popular* sociometric group.
Sociometrically neglected children appeared no more shy and withdrawn
than children identified as *average* in sociometric status (Rubin, et al., 1989;
Rubin et al., 1990). Thus, we concluded that the often-cited equation of
sociometric neglect and behavioral withdrawal was unwarranted.

Second, drawing from our pathways model, we found that extremely
withdrawn children, especially in the mid- to late years of childhood, were
more actively disliked by peers than their more sociable age-mates (Hymel
& Rubin, 1985; Rubin, Hymel & Chen, 1993; Rubin et al., 1989, 1990). We
also found that sociometrically *rejected* children were described as more
anxiously withdrawn than other sociometric groups (Rubin et al., 1990;
1993). These data corroborated findings reported in other research labs
(e.g., French, 1988, 1990). In keeping with our developmental perspective,
we did not find withdrawn *preschoolers* and *kindergarteners*, to be rejected
by their peers (Rubin, 1982b). These developmental differences in the peer
acceptance of socially withdrawn children supports our contention that as
solitary activity in group settings becomes increasingly rare, the frequent
demonstration of the behavior becomes increasingly less acceptable. These
conclusions are supported by the recent research of Younger and colleagues (e.g., Younger et al., 1993; Younger & Piccinin, 1989).

5.2.3. Interpersonal Problem Solving and Social Withdrawal

In addition to examining the peer relationships of socially withdrawn
children, we have also investigated how these children think about their

social worlds. We have done so in the belief that children behave as they do in social settings, in part, as a function of the means by which they interpret and process social information. An example of how social cognition may be implicated in the demonstration of social withdrawal is taken from a social information processing model described by Rubin and Krasnor (1986). These authors speculated that, when children face an interpersonal dilemma (e.g., making new friends or acquiring an object from someone else), their thinking follows a particular sequence. First, children may select a *social goal*. This entails the establishment of a representation of the desired *end state* of the problem-solving process. Second, they *examine the task environment*; this involves reading and interpreting all the relevant social cues. For example, boys and girls are likely to produce different solutions when faced with a social dilemma involving same-sex as opposed to opposite-sex peers (Rubin & Krasnor, 1983). As well, the social status, familiarity, and age of the participants in the task environment are likely to influence the child's goal and strategy selection (Rubin & Krasnor, 1983). Third, they *access and select strategies*; this process involves generating possible plans of action for achieving the perceived social goal, and choosing the most appropriate one for the specific situation. Fourth, they *implement the chosen strategy*. Finally, it is proposed that children *evaluate the outcome of the strategy*; this involves assessing the situation to determine the relative success of the chosen course of action in achieving the social goal. If the initial strategy is unsuccessful, the child may repeat it or she/he may select and enact a new strategy, or abandon the situation entirely.

In original analyses based on WLP data, we found that withdrawn preschoolers and kindergarteners were more likely than their nonwithdrawn counterparts to suggest that adults intervene to solve their interpersonal problems involving the acquisition of a desired object from a peer (Rubin, 1982b; Rubin, Daniels-Beirness, & Bream, 1984). We also found that in early childhood, withdrawn children were less able to take the social perspectives of others than nonwithdrawn age-mates (LeMare & Rubin, 1987). These data indicated clear social-cognitive deficits for socially withdrawn children and corroborated the Piagetian-based assumptions about the significance of peer interaction for the development of social cognition. Yet, interestingly, and in contrast, during mid- to late childhood, withdrawn children did not demonstrate difficulties in interpreting social cues and in generating competent solutions to interpersonal dilemmas when asked by an adult interviewer to do so (Rubin, 1985). Rather, they appeared to have difficulty in the production or enactment phase of the processing sequence.

We believe that social dilemmas may be affect laden and evocative of anxious-fearful responses in some children. Furthermore, we have proposed that the inability of these children to regulate and overcome their wariness results in an unassertive, submissive, social problem-solving style (Rubin & Rose-Krasnor, 1992). Although, there has been surprisingly little research in which the relations between emotion and affect regulation and social-information processing have been studied, we have found, in the WLP, that socially withdrawn children are less assertive than their nonwithdrawn counterparts (Rubin, 1985; Rubin & Borwick, 1984). When they do attempt to assert themselves and gain compliance from their peers, these children are more likely than their more sociable counterparts to be rebuffed (Rubin, 1985; Rubin & Borwick, 1984). They themselves, on the other hand, are extremely compliant in response to the social overtures of their peers. In short, these children are responsive to others but fail to gain normal levels of compliance from others; they are "easy marks." It is important to note that these findings have since been replicated in subsequent studies in our lab (e.g., Stewart & Rubin, 1993). Moreover, we have found that socially withdrawn children become increasingly less initiative of social interaction, and increasingly less assertive and successful in solving their interpersonal dilemmas with age (Stewart & Rubin, 1993).

The social problem-solving behavioral styles of withdrawn children may be a function, in part, of how they evaluate the consequences of their social exchanges with peers. In the case of a *failure* to meet their social goals (or *behavioral* rejection by the peer group), their interpretations are likely to evoke significant emotional and cognitive reactions that may have some bearing on their subsequent behaviors in the peer-group setting. Indirect support for this conjecture stems from the literature on children's causal attributions for their social failures (and successes). Relevant here are studies in which children are asked about the likely causes of their social successes and failures. Most children exhibit self-serving biases, taking credit for their successes (attributing them to internal and stable causes), and minimizing blame for their failures (attributing them to external causes). However, some children perceive their social successes as unstable and externally caused and they perceive their social failures as stable and internally caused (Goetz & Dweck, 1980; Hymel & Franke, 1985; Sobol & Earn, 1985). In our research, we have found that extremely withdrawn children interpret social failure as caused by internal, stable causes (Rubin & Krasnor, 1986). As noted earlier, we have also found that these children are less successful in gaining peer compliance, and they become increasing less initiative and successful with age. Thus, a feedback loop is suggested, whereby the initially fearful and withdrawn youngster comes to believe that her/his social failures are dispositionally based, and these beliefs are strengthened by the increasing failure of her/his social initiatives. Ultimately, the behavioral reaction of the child is to withdraw further from the peer milieu.

This scenario concerning the cognitions that may motivate social behavior must assuredly feed back into the child's evaluation of himself or herself relative to others. We now examine our findings that bear on this possibility.

5.2.4. Perceptions of the Self and Social Withdrawal.

We have noted that social failure, social rejection, and social anxiety are experiences characteristic of withdrawn children. It is not surprising, therefore, that by mid-childhood (ages 7 through 9 years), social withdrawal increasingly becomes associated with negative self-perceptions of social competence and self-esteem (Rubin, 1985; Rubin & Mills, 1988). By late childhood (ages 10 to 11 years), socially withdrawn children are not only more negative in their self-appraisals of social competence, but they also express greater loneliness and depression than their more sociable age-mates (Hymel, Rubin, Rowden, & LeMare, 1990; Rubin et al., 1993; Rubin, Hymel, & Mills, 1989; Rubin & Mills, 1988). These findings from the WLP provide strong initial evidence for our pathways perspective that social withdrawal becomes increasingly associated with internalizing difficulties from the mid- to late years of childhood.

Our findings have now been supported in a number of other research laboratories. For example, Hymel and colleagues (Hymel, Bowker, & Woody, 1993; Hymel, Woody, & Bowker, 1993) have reported that socially withdrawn 10- to 12-year-olds perceive themselves to lack social skills, social support, and a sense of belonging in the peer group. Similarly, several researchers have reported that withdrawn–rejected children feel more poorly about themselves and their social relationships than their nonwithdrawn counterparts; these results hold even when the comparison group is similarly disliked, but not withdrawn (e.g., aggressive–rejected children; Boivin, Thomassin, & Alain, 1989; Parkhurst & Asher, 1992). Finally, Asendorpf (1993) has found that socially withdrawn 7-year-old children reported more negative perceptions of social competence and greater loneliness than their more sociable age-mates.

5.2.5. Summary

In this section we have described the comtemporaneous correlates of social withdrawal from early to late childhood. Given the behavioral, social-cognitive, and affective characteristics of withdrawn children, it would appear reasonable to suggest that they may be at-risk for developing negative psychological "outcomes." We address this question in the following section.

5.3. Social Withdrawal as a Predictor of Maladaptation

The primary goal of the WLP has been to examine the hypothesis that social withdrawal in childhood suggests a prognosis of internalizing problems—anxiety, feelings of loneliness, and depression. Initial correlational analyses revealed that observed passive withdrawal in kindergarten predicted self-reported feelings of depression, and general self-worth, as well as teacher-rated anxiety *at age eleven.* Similar predictive correlations were found for observed passive withdrawal at age 7 years (Hymel et al., 1990; Rubin & Mills, 1988).

From the outset, however, it was never assumed that social withdrawal, in and of itself, is the sole potential cause of malevolent outcome. Rather, withdrawal has been viewed as a behavioral reflection of contemporaneous problems of an internalizing nature. The aforementioned characteristics associated concurrently with social withdrawal provide support for this conjecture. Accordingly, in a series of regression analyses, we have demonstrated that the *constellation* of early passive withdrawal, anxiety and negative self-perceptions of social competence at age 7 years is significantly associated with measures of depression, loneliness, and anxiety at age 11 years (Rubin & Mills, 1988). It appears, then, that anxiety and withdrawal, in concert with negative thoughts about the self, ultimately predict negative affect—most notably internalized feelings of loneliness and depression.

Finally, we have now collected data on approximately 70 high-school freshmen (ninth grade) who participated in earlier phases of the WLP. A composite of observed social withdrawal and peer- and teacher-assessed passive withdrawal at age 7 years was found to predict negative self-esteem, loneliness, and feelings of a *lack* of integration and involvement in the family and peer group. This latter measure was construed as an assessment of felt-security within the family and peer group in the teen years. In addition, a composite of peer- and teacher-assessed passive withdrawal at age 11 years was found to predict negative self-perceptions of social competence, loneliness, and feelings of a *lack* of integration and involvement in the family and peer group (Rubin, 1993). Thus, once again, the data supported the premises of the described developmental model.

Finally, in recent studies, researchers have provided additional support for the pathways model described. For example, Renshaw and Brown (1993) recently reported that indices of passive withdrawal at ages 9 to 12 years were predictive of loneliness assessed one year later. Also, in a recent report, Ollendick, Greene, Weist, and Oswald (1990) found that socially withdrawn fourth-grade children (approximately 10 years of age) were more likely to be perceived by peers as withdrawn and anxious, more disliked by peers, and interestingly, more likely to have dropped out of school than their well-adjusted counterparts five years later.

And finally, Morison and Masten (1991) found that children perceived by peers as withdrawn and isolated in middle childhood were more likely to think negatively of their social competencies and relationships in adolescence. Of further interest was the finding that withdrawn–isolated boys had more difficulties in adolescence than withdrawn–isolated girls. For example, boys reported less perceived athletic ability and lower self-esteem. These latter data were supported in a recent study by Caspi, Elder, and Bem (1988) in which boys rated by teachers as shy–withdrawn at ages 8 to 10 years were "off-time" in their transition to adult life. Withdrawn men were delayed, relative to the norm, in marrying, becoming a parent, and establishing stable careers. These delays were thought to have critical implications for adjustment in the life course. For example, Caspi et al. (1988) found that shyness–withdrawal in men predicted delayed entry into a career, which in turn, predicted occupational instability. Those men who were shy and withdrawn as children and who were off-time in establishing a stable career were also identified as at risk for divorce and separation in adulthood. On the other hand, Caspi et al. found that withdrawn women displayed no ill effects of their behavioral style. These latter findings were supported by the findings of Morison and Masten (1991), who likewise found limited evidence that withdrawn–isolated girls were at risk for subsequent difficulties. Finally, the results of both of these studies were supported recently in a study of the concurrent correlates of social withdrawal in 11-year-olds. Rubin et al. (1993) found that extremely withdrawn fifth-grade boys, but not girls, viewed themselves as more lonely and as having poorer social skills than a comparison group of average boys.

In light of these findings, future research would benefit from more careful consideration of the differential socialization of boys and girls and how these differences may impact on the outcomes associated with social withdrawal as a function of gender.

5.4. Summary and Conclusions

In our program of research, we have demonstrated that social withdrawal (a) is stable; (b) that it is associated concurrently, from early- through late childhood, with measures conceptually reflective of felt-insecurity, negative self-perceptions, dependency, and social deference; and (c) that in concert with indices of negative self-appraisal, social withdrawal is significantly predictive of internalizing difficulties in early adolescence and the early-teen period.

Given that our sample comprised unselected school-attending groups of children, however, the results described above support a predictive relation between withdrawal and *nonclinically assessed* problems. This leaves open the question of whether it will also prove possible to predict clinically assessed internalizing difficulties in early adolescence from earlier passive withdrawal and negative social self-perceptions. We attempted to address this issue by examining the data for the 11-year-olds in our sample. These children were administered the Child Depression Inventory (CDI; Kovacs, 1980/81). Those whose CDI scores were one standard deviation or more above the mean for their age group were identified. Eight children were so identified; they constituted the top 8% of children in terms of CDI scores. These children were then compared with their nondepressed schoolmates on indices of social and emotional well-being that had been assessed when they were 7 years of age. Follow-back discriminant-function analyses indicated that these children could *not* be distinguished from their normal counterparts on the basis of their popularity among peers at age 7 years. Furthermore, they were neither observed to be more aggressive in their free play, nor rated by their teachers as more hostile and aggressive. The depressed children could be distinguished from their normal counterparts, however, on the basis of observed social withdrawal, peer assessments of social withdrawal, and self-reported negative self-perceptions of social competence. Results of the discriminant analyses, then, serve to clarify and extend the previously reported correlational results concerning the predictive correlates of depression in early adolescence. Depressed 11-year-olds were those who expressed less positive perceptions of their own social competence three years earlier, were observed to play alone, and tended to be viewed by their second-grade peers as socially withdrawn. Taken together, these data support the premises of the developmental pathways model described earlier.

6. Contributing Factors to Social Withdrawal in Childhood

6.1. Temperament and Social Withdrawal

Thus far, we have examined the correlates and predictive outcomes of social withdrawal in childhood. Drawing from the pathways model, we have recently begun a series of studies to investigate potential contributors to the development and maintenance of social withdrawal in childhood. For example, in our developmental model we posited that endogenous, temperamental characteristics should be associated with and predictive of wariness and social withdrawal in early childhood. We cited several studies in support of this perspective (e.g., Kagan, Reznick, & Gibbons, 1989; Kagan et al., 1987). More recently, in collaborative work with investigators at the University of Maryland, we have discovered associations between physiological indices of temperament and the display of wariness and social reticence in the peer group (Fox, Rubin, Calkins, Marshall, Coplan, Porges, Long, & Stewart, in press).

This work draws its source from arguments that the pattern of electroencephalogram (EEG) activation recorded over the frontal region may reflect temperamental dispositions (Davidson, 1993; Fox, Bell, & Jones, 1992). It has been held further that infants exhibiting greater relative frontal EEG activation at four months of age are more likely to display "difficult" behavior contemporaneously and wary, fearful behavior at 14 months. Furthermore, such wariness predicts subsequent behavioral inhibition (Fox & Calkins, 1993), while, in turn, inhibition and wariness at 30 months predicts EEG right-frontal asymmetries at 38 months (Davidson, 1993). These results fit nicely with those of adult studies in which resting frontal asymmetry appears to be a stable characteristic related to the expression of negative affect (Tomarken, Davidson, Wheeler, & Doss, 1992).

Given these reports, we have recently initiated a longitudinal investigation of the relations between EEG asymmetries in early childhood and behavioral markers of psychological overcontrol (social withdrawal). A first cut of the data reveal that 4-year-olds who are observed to engage in high frequencies of reticent, fearful behavior in quartets of same-sex peers display greater relative right-frontal EEG activation. We are now following these children at 7 years of age to see whether those who were most socially withdrawn *and* who demonstrated EEG-activation asymmetries will appear not only more withdrawn, but also more revealing of negative self-regard. Additional studies are planned to examine the stability of EEG asymmetries from infancy through childhood. And still further studies are under-way in which temperament, as assessed physiologically during toddlerhood, is being examined as a predictor of *parental* behavior. In turn, it is expected that the dialectic between the dispositional characteristics of the child and parenting behavior will predict the development of social withdrawal, its concomitants, and its consequences in early-through late childhood.

6.2. Parenting and Social Withdrawal

6.2.1. Attachment and Social Withdrawal

In our model, we suggested that an insecure parent–infant attachment relationship may predict the development of anxious, withdrawn behavior and ultimately its posited sequelae. In collaborative work with Cathryn Booth and Linda Rose-Krasnor at the University of Washington, we have found that the parent–child attachment relationship is both predictive of and contemporaneously associated with the demonstration of reticent, withdrawn behavior at 4 years of age (Booth, Rose-Krasnor, Rubin, & Perman, 1990; Rose-Krasnor, Rubin, & Booth, 1993). And, in more recent analyses, we have found that insecure attachment at 4 years of age is predictive of social withdrawal and maternally rated internalizing problems at 8 years of age (Booth, Rose-Krasnor, McKinnon, & Rubin, 1994). These data are significant in that they support and extend earlier reported associations between the quality of the attachment relationship and the display of socially wary, reticent behavior (e.g., Renken et al., 1989). But they are also important because they demonstrate that the parent–child attachment relationship predicts not only subsequent child behavior, but also parental behavior. Thus, Booth, Rose-Krasner, & Rubin (1991) have demonstrated that an insecure parent–infant attachment relationship predicts adult-centered, power-assertive parenting practices.

6.2.2. Parenting Styles and Beliefs and Social Withdrawal

This latter finding is important because we had earlier suggested that overcontrolling parenting styles may be associated with the development and maintenance of social withdrawal in childhood. We argued, in our pathways model, that once an inhibited behavioral style is established, parents may sense the child's anxieties and insecurities, and seek to help in the child's mastery of the environment through authoritarian direction or by actually solving the child's interpersonal and intrapersonal problems for her or him. To address this possibility, we have investigated the associations between maternal reports of childrearing beliefs and preferences and social withdrawal in early childhood.

In a first study (Rubin, Mills, & Rose-Krasnor, 1989), mothers of preschoolers were asked to rate how important they felt it was for their children to develop a number of representative social skills (e.g., how to make friends), to what they attributed the development of these social skills (e.g., child-centered dispositional causes versus external direct and indirect causes), and what they might do to aid in the development of such skills. In addition, the children were observed during classroom free play. Those preschoolers whose mothers indicated that the attainment of social skills were relatively unimportant were observed to cry more often when attempting to meet their social goals and to experience less social problem-solving success; these latter results are much like those reported in our earlier studies of the social problem-solving behaviors of socially withdrawn children (Rubin & Krasnor, 1986). The children of those mothers who believed that social skills derived primarily from temperamental or dispositional factors were less socially assertive and successful during their peer exchanges. Furthermore, these children were rated by teachers as anxious, fearful, and withdrawn. Finally, mothers who indicated that they would use high-power assertive strategies to socialize social skills (e.g., overcontrolling behaviors such as using force, coercion, and strong commands) had children who were more likely to seek help from others, especially adults, and to use nonassertive social strategies to meet their social goals. These children were also rated by their teachers as fearful, withdrawn and anxious.

We gained additional insight into patterns of maternal cognition that may be associated with the development of internalizing difficulties in a subsequent study of mothers whose children were identified as being either extremely Withdrawn–Internalizing or Average in social competence (Rubin & Mills, 1990). We asked mothers about the most important influences on the development of social skills by giving them short descriptions of four social skills (getting acquainted with someone new, resolving peer conflicts, getting accepted into an ongoing play group of unfamiliar peers, and persuading other children to do what one wants) and asking them to rank, in order of importance, the most likely influences on the acquisition of these skills. For all four social skills, mothers of Withdrawn–Internalizing children placed significantly more importance on directive teaching than did the mothers of the Average children.

We also gathered information about mothers' *reactive cognitions* concerning the unskilled social behaviors of aggression and social withdrawal. We did this by presenting them with stories describing hypothetical incidents in which their own child behaved consistently in an aggressive or a socially withdrawn fashion. Following each story, mothers were asked how they would feel if their own child consistently acted this way, what *attributions* they would make about the causes of the behavior, and what they thought they would do to modify the behavior.

Mothers of Withdrawn–Internalizing children were more likely than mothers of Average children to report preferring the use of highly coercive strategies (e.g., directives) and less likely to report preferring low-power strategies (e.g., redirecting the child) and indirect–no response strategies (e.g., seeking information from others, arranging opportunities for peer interaction, not responding) in reaction to their children's demonstration of both socially withdrawn and aggressive behavior.

With respect to mothers' *attributions* about the causes of aggressive and socially withdrawn behavior, we found that mothers of Withdrawn–

Internalizing children were significantly more likely than mothers of Average children to attribute both of these types of behavior to a trait in the child. Finally, with regard to reported *emotional reactions* to socially withdrawn and aggressive behaviors, mothers of Withdrawn–Internalizing children were less puzzled and more angry, disappointed, embarrassed, and guilty about displays of withdrawal and aggression than were mothers of Average children.

Taken together, the findings of these two studies paint a remarkably consistent picture of mothers whose children are socially withdrawn and internalizing. The fact that these mothers placed greater importance on a directive approach to teaching social skills than did mothers of average children, and were more likely to choose controlling strategies for dealing with unskilled social behaviors, suggests that children with internalizing difficulties tend to have mothers who may be overinvolved. The causal attributions and emotional reactions of these mothers are also indicative of overinvolvement, and provide some tentative insights about why they may be overinvolved. These mothers were not only less tolerant of unskilled social behaviors than the other mothers, but they also felt more angry, disappointed, guilty, and embarrassed about these behaviors, and they were more inclined to blame them on a trait in their child. This constellation of emotions and attributions suggests that mothers of overcontrolled, withdrawn children may be highly prone to regard their child as an extension of themselves and therefore to consider their child's behavior as if it were their own. Moreover, the negative feelings reported by these mothers suggests that this overinvolvement has negative undercurrents. Interestingly, this dynamic is reminiscent of the pattern of anxious, overprotective parenting that has previously been linked to internalizing difficulties in children (Levy, 1943; Parker, 1983). While, in many ways, these data are consistent with the often-suggested but understudied belief that socially withdrawn children are overcontrolled by their parents (e.g., Hetherington & Martin, 1986), we believe that the relations between patterns of child behavior and patterns of parenting are extremely complex and that the parental beliefs and cognitions we examined reflect an intricate mix of causes and consequences of children's social behaviors. It may be that mothers of socially withdrawn children are anxious and internalizing themselves and transmit these problems to their children through an overinvolved pattern of parenting that creates a sense of felt-insecurity. It may also be that these mothers have an empathic response to their children's hyperreactivity and extreme wariness, which *causes* them to become overinvolved and produces a mixture of defensive reactions (e.g., downplaying the importance of social skills) and negative emotions. In keeping with the transactional nature of the parent–child relationship, we suggest that an interplay occurs between *both* these processes. Clearly, further *developmental* study of the relations between patterns of parenting and patterns of socioemotional adjustment is needed in order to gain a better understanding of this interplay (see for example, Mills & Rubin, 1993).

7. Summary and Conclusions

We began this chapter in a rather accusatory fashion. That is, we argued that the study of social withdrawal has been hampered by impoverished theoretical frameworks, flawed research methodologies, and the offering of premature conclusions. To help remedy the "state-of-the-art," we described a developmentally oriented model that has guided our research program for well over a decade. We also presented evidence in support of this pathways model which contends that socioemotional adjustment is a joint product of transactions between temperamental dispositions in the child, socialization experiences with parents, and certain setting conditions that affect the family (material resources, personal emotional and social-support resources of the parents, childrearing beliefs and values). For example, we have described the following findings:

1. A relation exists between dispositionally based reactivity to novel stimulation, the quality of the parent–infant attachment relationship, and subsequent socially inhibited behavior
2. Social withdrawal is stable from early-through late childhood and is associated concurrently with measures conceptually reflective of felt-insecurity, social unassertiveness, and internalizing difficulties (e.g., negative self-perceptions)
3. Passive withdrawal, in concert with indices of negative self-appraisal, is significantly predictive of internalizing difficulties in late childhood and early adolescence
4. Maternal overinvolvement is associated with social withdrawal and internalizing difficulties in early childhood.

Given what we believe to be a highly productive start to the study of social withdrawal in childhood, we are now setting our research agenda to take us through the remaining years of the century. For example, we recognize that parents may contribute to the development, maintenance, and amelioration of social withdrawal and its concomitants in childhood. However, much of the data extant have been taken from *maternal interviews*. To remedy this reliance on interview and questionnaire data, we have initiated observational studies of the parenting "styles" of mothers of extremely withdrawn and "average" children (e.g., Mills & Rubin, 1993). We have also begun to examine observed maternal behavior as it *predicts*, longitudinally, the frequent display of socially wary, withdrawn behavior (Booth, Rose-Krasnor, McKinnon, & Rubin, in press).

Since parenting does not occur in a vacuum, we are also examining relations between patterns of parenting and some of the socioecological and personal–social setting conditions that affect the amount of stress mothers are under as they carry out their parental role. For example, are mothers who lack support from others more likely to show evidence of overinvolvement? This is one indirect way in which *fathers* undoubtedly contribute to the development of internalizing difficulties. And following from this last note, it is clear that we must begin to pay attention to the *direct* roles that fathers may play in the development of social withdrawal in children. To this end, in our most recent research efforts we have begun to study the parenting styles of fathers as they relate to the development of socially wary behavior in their two-year-old sons and daughters.

Finally, it is important to note that most studies on the development of social withdrawal have been conducted in North American and Western European communities (see Rubin & Asendorpf, 1993 for reviews). Thus, little, if anything, is known about the developmental course of social withdrawal in other cultures. To this end, we are now in the process of investigating the veracity of our developmental models in The People's Republic of China (e.g., Chen & Rubin, 1992; Chen, Rubin, & Sun, 1992). One important initial finding has been that socially wary, withdrawn behavior is *not* associated with indices of maladjustment in 8- to 10-year-old Chinese children. We have attempted to explain this finding by contrasting the cultural values of Chinese and Western communities vis-à-vis the meaning and significance of sociability, social interaction, and compliance to adult norms and standards (Chen et al., 1992). The bottom line, nevertheless, is that the meanings of maladaption and psychopathology, and the developmental course of particular social behaviors may differ from culture to culture. Thus, it would seem in the best interests of the psychological community of scholars not to generalize to other cultures our own culture-specific theories of the developmment of psychopathology.

In summary, from our own egocentered (but certainly not isolated) perspective, we believe we have merely begun to touch the surface of some extremely interesting, vital, and important subject matter. And as we have concluded elsewhere (Rubin & Mills, 1991), we hope our work, and that of others, will put an end to what we believe has been the wrongful neglect of social withdrawal and internalizing difficulties in childhood.

8. References

Achenbach, T. M. (1982). *Developmental psychopathology*, New York: Wiley.

Achenbach, T. M., & Edelbrock, C. S. (1981). Behavioral problems and competencies reported by parents of normal and disturbed children aged four through sixteen. *Monographs of the Society for Research in Child Development, 46*, (1, Serial No. 188), 1–82.

Ainsworth, M. D. S., Blehar, M., Waters, E., & Wall, S. (1978). *Patterns of attachment.* Hillsdale, NJ: Erlbaum.

Asher, S. R. & Coie, J. D. (1990), *Peer rejection in childhood.* New York: Cambridge University Press.

Asendorpf, J. (1990). Beyond social withdrawal: Shyness, unsociability and peer avoidance. *Human Development, 33*, 250–259.

Asendorpf, J. (1991). Development of inhibited children's coping and unfamiliarity. *Child Development, 62*, 1460–1474.

Asendorpf, J. (1993). Beyond temperament: A two-factor coping model of the development of inhibition during childhood. In K. H. Rubin & J. Asendorpf (pp. 265–290), (Eds.), *Social withdrawal, inhibition, and shyness in childhood.* Hillsdale, NJ: Erlbaum.

Bacon, M. K., & Ashmore, R. D. (1985). How mothers and fathers categorize descriptions of social behavior attributed to daughters and sons. *Social Cognition, 3*, 193–217.

Bandura, A., & Walters, R. H. (1963). *Social learning and personality development*, New York: Holt, Rinehart & Winston.

Belsky, J., & Rovine, M. (1987). Temperament and attachment security in the Strange Situation: An empirical rapprochement. *Child Development, 58*, 787–795.

Boivin, M., Thomassin, L., & Alain, M. (1989). Peer rejection and self-perceptions among early elementary school children: Agressive rejectees. In B. H. Schneider, G. Attili, J. Nadel, & R. P. Weissberg (Eds.), *Social competence in developmental perspective.* (pp. 392–393). Boston, MA; Kluwer Academic Publishing.

Booth, C. L., Rose-Krasnor, L., & Rubin, K. H. (1991). Relating preschoolers' social competence and their mothers' parenting behaviors to early attachment security and high risk status. *Journal of Social and Personal Relationships, 8*, 363–382.

Booth, C. L., Rose-Krasnor, L., McKinnon, J., & Rubin, K. H. (1994). Predicting social adjustment in middle childhood: The role of preschool attachment security and maternal style. *Social Development.*

Booth, C. L., Rose-Krasnor, L., Rubin, K. H., & Perman, K. L. (1990, April). *Relating early insecure attachment to preschool indices of anxious withdrawal and insecurity.* Paper presented at the biennial meetings of the International Conference on Infant Studies, Montreal, Canada.

Bowlby, J. (1973). *Attachment and loss, Vol. 2; Separation.* New York: Basic Books.

Bronson, W. C., (1966). Central orientations: A study of behavioral organization from childhood to adolescence. *Child Development, 37*, 125–255.

Bugental, D. B., & Cortez, V. (1988). Physiological reactivity to responsive and unresponsive children— as modified by perceived control. *Child Development, 59*, 6886–693.

Bugental, D. B., & Shennum, W. A. (1984). "Difficult" children as elicitors and targets of adult communication patterns: An attributional-behavioral transactional analysis. *Monographs of the Society for Research in Child Develpment, 49*, (1, Serial No. 205).

Buss, A. H. (1984). A conception of shyness. In J.. Daly & J. C. McCroskey (Eds.), *Avoiding communication: Shyness, reticence, and communication apprehension*, Beverly Hills, CA: Sage.

Buss, A.H., (1986). A theory of shyness. In W. H. Jones, J. M. Cheek, & S. R. Briggs (Eds.). *Shyness: Perspectives on research and treatment.* New York: Plenum Press.

Calkins, S. D., & Fox, N. A. (1992). The relations among infant temperament, security of attachment, and behavioral inhibition at twenty-four months. *Child Development, 63,* 1456–1472.

Caspi, A., Elder, G., & Bem, D. (1988). Moving away from the world: Life course patterns of shy children. *Developmental Psychology, 24,* 824–831.

Chen, X. & Rubin, K. H. (1992). Correlates of peer acceptance in a Chinese sample of six-year-olds. *International Journal of Behavioral Developtment, l5,* (2), 259–273.

Chen, X., Rubin, K. H., & Sun, Y. (1992). Social reputation and peer relationships in Chinese and Canadian children: A cross-cultural study. *Child Development, 63,* 1336–1343.

Coie, J. D., & Dodge, K. A. (1983). Continuities and changes in children's social status: A five year longitudinal study. *Merrill-Palmer Quarterly, 29,* 261–282.

Coie, J. D., & Kupersmidt, J. (1983). A behavioral analysis of emerging social status in boys' groups. *Child Development, 54,* 1400–1416.

Coplan, R. J., & Rubin, K.. H. (1993). *Multiple forms of social withdrawal in young children: Reticence and solitary-passive behaviors.* Paper presented at the Bienniel Meetings of the International Society for the Study of Behavioral Development. Recife, Brazil.

Coplan, R. J., Rubin, K. H., Fox, N. A., Calkins, S. D., & Stewart, S. L. (1994). Being alone, playing alone, and acting alone: Distinguishing among reticence, and passive-, and active-solitude in young children. *Child Development.*

Crnic, K., & Greenberg, M. T. (1990). Minor parenting stresses with young children. *Child Development, 61,* 1628–1637.

Damon, W. (1977). *The social world of children.* San Francisco: Jossey-Bass.

Davidson, R. J. (1993). Childhood temperament and cerebral assymetry: A neurobiological substrate of behavior inhibition. In K. H. Rubin & J. Asendorpf (Eds.), *Social withdrawal, inhibition, and shyness in childhood.* Hillsdale, NJ: Erlbaum.

Dodge, K. A. (1983). Behavioral antecedents of peer social status. *Child Development, 54,* 1386–1399.

Dodge, K. A. (1986). A social information processing model of social competence in children. In M. Perlmutter (Ed.), *Cognitive perspectives on children's social and behavioral development. The Minnesota Symposia on Child Psychology.* (Vol. 18) (pp. 77–126). Hillsdale, NJ: Erlbaum.

Dodge, K. A., Murphy, R. R., & Buchsbaum, K. (1984). The assessment of intention-cue detection skills in children: Implications for developmental psychopathology. *Child Development, 55,* 163–173.

Doise, W., & Mugny, G. (1981). *Le développement social de l'intelligence.* Paris: Inter Editions.

Doise, W., Mugny, G., & Perret-Clermont, A. (1975). Social interaction and the development of cognitive operations. *European Journal of Social Psychology, 5,* 367–383.

Engfer, A., & Gavranidou, M. (1987). Antecedents and consequences of maternal sensitivity: A longitudinal study. In H. Rauh & H. Steinhausen (Eds.), *Psychobiology and early development* (pp. 71–99). North Holland: Elsevier.

Ensminger, M. C., Kellam, S. G., & Rubin, B. R. (1983). School and family origins of delinquency: Comparisons by sex. In K. T. Van Dusen & S. A. Mednick (Eds.), *Prospective studies of crime and delinquency* (pp. 73–97). Hingham, MA: Kluwer-Nijhoff.

Erikson, M., Sroufe, A., & Egeland, B. (1985). The relationship of the quality of attachment and behaviour problems in preschool schildren from a high risk sample. *Monographs of the Society for Research in Child Development, 50,* (1–2, Serial No. 209).

Fox, N. A., Bell, M. A., & Jones, N. A. (1992). Individual differences in response to stress and cerebral asymmetry. *Developmental Neuropsychology, 8,* 161–184.

Fox, N. A., & Calkins, S. D. (1993). Pathways to agression and social withdrawal: Interactions among temperament, attachment and regulation. In K. H. Rubin & J. Asendorpf (Eds.), *Social withdrawal, inhibition, and shyness in childhood,* (pp. 81–100). Hillsdale, NJ: Erlbaum.

Fox, N. A., Rubin, K. H., Calkins, S. D., Marshall, T. R., Coplan, R. J., Porges, S. W., Long,

J. M., & Stewart, S. (in press). Frontal Activation asymmetry and social competence at four years of age: Left frontal hyper- and hypoactivation as correlates of social behavior in preschool children. *Child Development*.

French, D. C. (1988). Heterogeneity of peer rejected boys: Aggressive and nonaggressive subtypes. *Child Development, 59*, 976–985.

French, D. C. (1990). Heterogeneity of peer rejected girls. *Child Development, 61*, 2028–2031.

Furman, W., Rahe, D. F., & Hartup, W. W. (1979). Rehabilitation of socially withdrawn preschool children through mixed-age and same-age socialization. *Child Development, 50*, 915–922.

Goetz, T. E., & Dweck, C. (1980). Learned helplessness in social situations. *Journal of Personality and Social Psychology, 39*, 246–255.

Hartup, W. W. (1983). Peer relations. In E. M. Hetherington (Ed.), *Handbook of child psychology: Vol. 4. Socialization, personality and social development* (4th edition, pp. 103–196). New York: Wiley.

Hartup, W. W. (1985). Relationships and their significance in cognitive development. In R. A. Hinde, A. Perret-Clermont, & J. Stevenson-Hinde (Eds.), *Social relationships and cognitive development* (pp. 66–82). Oxford, UK: Clarendon Press.

Hartup, W. W. (1992). Peer relations in early and middle childhood. In V. B. Van Hasset & M. Hersen (Eds.), *Handbook of social development*, (pp. 257–282). New York: Plenum Press.

Hetherington, E. M., & Martin, B. (1986). Family factors and psychopathology in children. In H. C. Quay & J. S. Werry (Eds.), *Psychopathological disorders of childhood*, 3rd ed. (pp. 332–390). New York: Wiley.

Hinde, R. A., Tamplin, A. & Barrett, J. (1993). Social isolation in 4 year olds. *British Journal of Developmental Psychology, 11*, 211–236.

Hymel, S., Bowker, A., & Woody, E. (1993). Aggressive versus withdrawn unpopular children: Variations in peer and self perceptions in multiple domains. *Child Development, 64*, 2004–2021.

Hymel, S., & Franke, S. (1985). Chiildren's peer relations: Assessing self-perceptions. In B. Schneider, K. H. Rubin, & J. E. Ledingham (Eds.), *Children's peer relationships: Issues in assessment and intervention*, (pp. 75–92). New York: Springer-Verlag.

Hymel, S., & Rubin, K. H. (1985). Children with peer relationship and social skills problems: Conceptual, methodological, and developmental issues. In G. J. Whitehurst (Ed.), *Annals of Child Development, Vol. 2*, (pp. 251–297). Greenwich, Connecticut: JAI Press.

Hymel, S., Rubin, K. H., Rowden, L., & LeMare, L. (1990). Children's peer relationships: Longitudinal prediction of internalizing and externalizing problems from middle to late childhood. *Child Developoment, 61*, 2004–2021.

Hymel, S., Woody, E., & Bowker, A. (1993). Social withdrawal in childhood: Considering the child's perspective. In K. H. Rubin & J. Asendorpf (Eds.), *Social withdrawal, inhibition, and shyness in childhood*, (pp. 237–264). Hillsdale, NJ: Erlbaum.

Isabella, R. A. (1993). Origins of attachment: Maternal interactive behavior across the first year. *Child Development, 64*, 605–621.

Isabella, R. A., & Belsky, J. (1991). Interaction synchrony and the origins of infant–mother attachment: A replication study. *Child Development, 62*, 373–384.

Janes, C. L., & Hesselbrock, V. M. (1978). Problem children's adult adjustment predicted from teachers' ratings. *American Journal of Orthopsychiatry, 48*, 300–309.

Janes, C. L., Hesselbrock, V. M., Myers, D. G., & Penniman, J. H. (1979). Problem boys in young adulthood: Teachers' ratings and twelve-year follow-up. *Journal of Youth and Adolescence, 8*, 453–472.

John, R. S., Mednick, S. A., & Schulsinger, F. (1982). Teacher reports as a predictor of schizophrenia and borderline schizophrenia: A Bayesian decision analysis. *Journal of Abnormal Psychology, 6,* 399–413.

Kagan, J. (1989). Tempermental contributions to social behavior. *American Psychologist, 44,* 668–674.

Kagan, J., Snidman, N., & Arcus, D. (1993). On the temperamental categories of inhibited and uninhibited children. In K. H. Rubin & J. Asendorpf (Eds.), *Social withdrawal, inhibition, and shyness in childhood,* (pp. 19–30). Hillsdale, NJ: Erlbaum.

Kagan, J. & Moss, H. A. (1962). *Birth to maturity: A study of psychological development,* New York: Wiley.

Kagan, J., Reznick, J. S., & Gibbons, J. (1989). Inhibited and uninhibited types of children. *Child Development, 60,* 838–845.

Kagan, J., Reznick, J. S., & Snidman, N. (1987). The physiology and psychology of behavioral inhibition in children. *Child Development, 58,* 1459–1473.

Kagan, J., Reznick, J. S., Clarke, C., Snidman, N., & Garcia-Coll, C. (1984). Behavioral inhibition to the unfamiliar. *Child Development, 55,* 2212–2225.

Kashani, J. H., Husain, A., Shekim, W. O., Hodges, K. K., Cytryn, L., & McKnew, D. H. (1981). Current perspectives on childhood depression: An overview. *American Journal of Psychiatry, 138,* 143–153.

Kohlberg, L., LaCrosse, J., & Ricks, D. (1972). The predictability of adult mental health from childhood behavior. In B. B. Wolman (Ed.), *Manual of child psychopathology* (pp. 1217–1284). New York: McGraw-Hill.

Kovacs, M. (1980/81). Rating scales to assess depression in school-aged children. *Acta Paedopsychiatra, 46,* 305–315.

LeMare, L. J., & Rubin, K. H. (1987). Perspective taking and peer interaction: Structural and developmental analyses. *Child Development, 58,* 306–315.

Levy, D. M. (1943). *Maternal overprotection,* New York: Columbia University Press.

Lewis, M. & Miller, S. M. (1990). *Handbook of developmental psychopathology.* New York: Plenum Press.

Mangelsdorf, S., Gunnar, M., Kestenbaum, R., Lang, S., & Andreas, D. (1990). Infant proneness-to-distress temperament, maternal personality and mother–infant attachment: Associations and goodness of fit. *Child Development, 61,* 820–831.

Masten, A. S., Morison, P., & Pellegrini, D. S. (1985). A Revised Class Play method of peer assessment. *Developmental Psychology, 3,* 523–533.

Matas, L., Arend, R. A., & Sroufe, R. L. (1978). Continuity of adaption in the second year: The relationship between the quality of attachment and later competence. *Child Development, 49,* 347–356.

Mead, G. H. (1934). *Mind, self, and society.* Chicago: University of Chicago Press.

Michael, C. M., Morris, D. P., & Soroker, E. (1957). Follow-up studies of shy, withdrawn children II: Relative incidence of schizophrenia. *American Journal of Orthopsychiatry, 27,* 331–337.

Mills, R. S. L., & Rubin, K. H. (1990). Parental beliefs about problematic social behaviors in early childhood. *Child Development, 61,* 138–151.

Mills, R. S. L., & Rubin, K. H. (1993). Patterns of socialization of mothers of socially withdrawn children. In K. H. Rubin & J. Asendorpf (Eds.), *Social withdrawal, inhibition, and shyness in children,* (pp. 117–150). Chicago: University of Chicago Press.

Miyake, K., Chen, C., & Campos, J. (1985). Infant temperament, mother's mode of interaction, and attachment in Japan: An interim report. In I. Bretherton & E. Waters (Eds.), Growing points of attachment theory and research. *Monographs of the Society for Research in Child Development, 50,* (Serial No. 209).

Morison, P., & Masten, A. S. (1991). Peer reputation in middle childhood as a predictor of adaptation in adolescence: A seven-year follow-up. *Child Development, 62,* 991–1007.

Morris, D. P., Soroker, E., & Burruss, G. (1954). Follow-up studies of shy, withdrawn, children I: Evaluation of later adjustment. *American Journal of Orthopsychiatry, 24*, 743–754.

Moskowitz, D. S., Schwartzman, A. E., & Ledingham, J. E. (1985). Stability and change in aggression and withdrawal in middle childhood and early adolescence. *Journal of Abnormal Psychology, 94*, 30–41.

Ollendick, T. H., Greene, R. W., Weist, M. D., & Oswald, D. P. (1990). The predictive validity of eacher nominations: A five-year follow-up of at risk youth. *Journal of Abnormal Child Psychology, 18*, 699–713.

Olweus, D. (1979). Stability of aggressive reaction patterns in males: A review. *Psychological Bulletin, 86*, 852–875.

Parker, G. (1983). *Parental overprotection: A risk factor in psychosocial development.* New York: Grune & Stratton.

Parker, J. G., & Asher, S. R. (1987). Peer relations and later personal adjustment: Are low-accepted children at risk? *Psychological Bulletin, 102*, 357–389.

Parkurst, J. T., & Asher, S. R. (1992). Peer rejection in middle childhood: Subgroup differences in behavior, loneliness, and concerns. *Developmental Psychology, 28*, 231–241.

Pastor, D. L. (1981). The quality of mother–infant attachment and its relationship to toddler's initial sociability with peers. *Developmental Psychology, 17*, 323–335.

Patterson, G. R. (1983). Stress: A change agent for family process. In N. Garmezy & M. Rutter (Eds.), *Stress, coping, and development in children* (pp. 235–264). New York: McGraw-Hill.

Pepler, D. J., & Rubin, K. H. (Eds.). (1991). *The development and treatment of childhood aggression.* Hillsdale, NJ: Erlbaum.

Piaget, J. (1926). *The language and thought of the child.* London: Routlege & Kegan Paul.

Piaget, J. (1932). *The moral judgment of the child.* Glencoe, IL: Free Press.

Plomin, R., & Daniels, D. (1986). Gentetics and shyness. In W. H. Jones, J. M. Cheek, & S. R. Briggs (Eds.), *Shyness: Perspectives on research and treatment,* New York: Plenum Press.

Quay, H., & Werry, J. (1986). *Psychopathological disorders in childhood.* New York: Wiley.

Renken, B., Egeland, B., Marvinney, D., Sroufe, L. A., & Mangelsdorf, S. (1989). Early childhood antecedents of aggression and passive-withdrawal in early elementary school. *Journal of Personality, 57*, 257–281.

Renshaw, P. D. & Brown, P. J. (1993). Loneliness in middle childhood: Concurrent and longitudinal predictors. *Child Development, 64*, 1271–1284.

Robins, L. N. (1966). *Deviant children grown up.* Baltimore, MD: Williams & Wilkins.

Rose-Krasnor, L., Rubin, K. H., & Booth, C. L. (1993, March). *Maternal control, mother-child attachment, and preschoolers' social play.* Paper presented at the biennial meetings of The Society for Research in Child Development, New Orleans, LA.

Roseberg, M. S., Wilson, R., Maheady, L., & Sindelar, P. (1991). *Educating students with behavior disorders.* Boston: Allyn & Bacon.

Rubin, K. H. (1982a). Nonsocial play in preschoolers: Necessary evil? *Child Development, 53*, 651–657.

Rubin, K. H. (1982b). Social and cognitive developmental characteristics of young isolate, normal, and sociable children. In K. H. Rubin & H. S. Ross (Eds.), *Peer relationships and social skills in childhood,* (pp. 353-374), New York: Springer-Verlag.

Rubin, K. H. (1985). Socially withdrawn children: An "at risk" population? In B. H. Schneider, K. H. Rubin, & J. E. Ledingham (Eds.), *Peer relationships and social skills in childhood: Issues in assessment and training,* (pp. 125–139). New York: Springer-Verlag.

Rubin, K. H. (1986). Play, peers, and social development. In A W. Gottfried & C. Caldwell Brown (Eds.), *Play interactions: The contribution of play materials and parental involvement to child development* (pp. 163–174). Lexington, MA: Heath.

Rubin, K. H. (1993). The Waterloo Longitudinal Project: The long-term predictive "outcomes"

194

KENNTH H. RUBIN et al.

of passive-withdrawal in childhood. In K. H. Rubin & J. Asendorpf (Eds), *Social withdrawal, inhibition, and shyness in childhood*, (pp. 291–314). Hillsdale, NJ: Erlbaum.
Rubin, K. H. & Asendorpf, J. (1993). *Social withdrawal, inhibition, and shyness in childhood.* Hillsdale, NJ: Erlbaum.
Rubin, K. H., & Borwick, D. (1984). The communication skills of children who vary with regard to sociability. In H. Sypher & J. Applegates (Eds.), *Social cognition and communication*, (pp. 152–170). Hillsdale, NJ: Erlbaum.
Rubin, K. H., & Both, L. (1989). Iris pigmentation and sociability in childhood: A re-examination. *Development Psychobiology, 22,* 717–726.
Rubin, K. H., Bream, L., & Rose-Krasnor, L. (1991). Social problem solving and aggression in childhood. In D. J. Pepler & K. H. Rubin (Eds.), *The development and treatment of childhood aggression*, (pp. 219–248). Hillsdale, NJ: Erlbaum.
Rubin, K. H., Chen, X., & Hymel, S. (1993). Socioemotional characteristics of withdrawn and aggressive children. *Merrill-Palmer Quarterly, 39,* 518–534.
Rubin, K. H. & Coplan, R. (1992). Peer relationships in childhood. In M. Bornstein & M. Lamb (Eds.), *Developmental psychology: An advanced textbook*, (pp. 519–578). Hillsdale, NJ: Erlbaum.
Rubin, K. H., Daniels-Beirness, T., & Bream, L. (1984). Social isolation and social problem solving: A longitudinal study. *Journal of Consulting and Clinical Psychology, 52,* 17–25.
Rubin, K. H., Fein, G., & Vanderberg, B. (1983). Play. In E. M. Hetherington (Ed.), *Handbook of child psychology: Socialization, personality and social development*, (pp. 693–774). New York: Wiley.
Rubin, K. H., Hymel, S., & Chen, X. (1993). Scioemotional characteristics of aggressive and withdrawn children. *Merrill-Palmer Quarterly, 49,* 518–534.
Rubin, K. H., Hymel, S., LeMare, L. J., & Rowden, L. (1989). Children experiencing social difficulties: Sociometric neglect reconsidered. *Canadian Journal of Behavioral Science, 21,* 94–111.
Rubin, K. H., Hymel, S., & Mills, R. S. L. (1989). Sociability and social withdrawal in childhood: Stability and outcomes. *Journal of Personality, 57,* 238–255.
Rubin, K. H., Hymel, S., Mills, R. S. L., & Rose-Krasnor, L. (1991). Conceptualizing different pathways to and from social isolation in childhood. In D. Cicchetti & S. Toth (Eds.), *The Rochester Symposium on Developmental Psychopathology, Vol. 2, Internalizing and externalizing expressions of dysfunction*, (pp. 91–122). New York: Cambridge University Press.
Rubin, K. H., & Krasnor, L. R. (1983). Age and gender differences in the development of a representative social problem solving skill. *Journal of Applied Developmental Psychology, 4.* 463–475.
Rubin, K. H., & Krasnor, L. R. (1986). Social-cognitive and social-behavioral perspectives on problem solving. In M. Perlmutter (Ed.), *Cognitive perspectives on children's social and behavioral development. The Minnesota Symposia on Child Psychology (vol. 18)*, (pp. 1-68). Hillsdale, NJ: Erlbaum.
Rubin, K. H., LeMare, L. J., & Lollis, S. (1990). Social withdrawal in childhood: Developmental pathways to rejection. In S. R. Asher & J. D. Coie (Eds.), *Peer rejection in childhood.* (pp. 217–249). New York: Cambridge University Press.
Rubin, K. H., & Lollis, S. (1988). Peer relationships, social skills and infant attachment: A continuity model. In J. Belsky & T. Nezworski (Eds.), *Clinical implications of attachment* (pp. 219–252). Hillsdale, NJ: Erlbaum.
Rubin, K. H., Maioni, T. L., & Hornung, M. (1976). Free-play behaviors in middle and lower class preschoolers: Parten and Piaget revisited. *Child Development, 47,* 414–419.
Rubin, K. H., & Mills, R. S. L., (1988). The many faces of social isolation in childhood. *Journal of Consulting and Clinical Psychology, 6,* 916–924.

Rubin, K. H., & Mills, R. S. L. (1990). Maternal beliefs about adaptive and maladaptive social behaviors in normal, aggressive, and withdrawn preschoolers. *Journal of Abnormal Child Psychology, 18*, 419–435.

Rubin, K. H., & Mills, R. S. L. (1991). Conceptualizing developmental pathways to internalizing disorders in childhood. *Canadian Journal of Behavioral Science, 23*, 300–317.

Rubin, K. H., Mills, R. S. L., & Krasnor, L. R. (1989). Parental beliefs and children's social competence. In B. Schneider, G. Atilli, J. Nadel, & R. Weissberg (Eds.), *Social competence in developmental perspective* (pp. 313–331). Dordrecht, Netherlands: Kluwer International.

Rubin, K. H., & Rose-Krasnor, L. (1992). Interpersonal problem-solving and social competence in children. In V. B. van Hasselt and M. Hersen (Eds.), *Handbook of social development: A life-span perspective.* New York: Plenum Press.

Rubin, K. H., Stewart, S. L., & Chen, X. (in press). The parents of aggressive and withdrawn children. In M. Bornstein (Ed.), *Handbook of Parenting.* New Jersey: Erlbaum.

Schneider, B., Rubin, K. H., & Ledingham, J. (Eds.), *Children's peer relations: Issues in assessment and intervention.* New York: Springer-Verlag.

Selman, R. L. (1980). *The growth of interpersonal understanding.* New York: Cambridge University Press.

Selman, R. L. (1985). The use of interpersonal negotiation strategies and communicative competences: A clinical-developmental exploration in a pair of troubled early adolescents. In R. A. Hinde, A. Perret-Clermont, & J. Stevenson-Hinde (Eds.), *Social relationships and cognitive development* (pp. 208–232). Oxford, UK: Clarendon.

Smith, P. B., & Peterson, D. R. (1988). Maternal sensitivity and patterns of infant–mother attachment. *Child Development, 59*, 1097–1101.

Sobol, M. P., & Earn, B. M. (1985). Assessment of children's attributions for social experiences: Implications for social skills training. In B. Schneider, K. H. Rubin, & J. E. Ledingham (Eds.), *Children's peer relationships: Issues in assessment and intervention,* (pp. 93–110). New York: Springer-Verlag.

Spieker, S. J., & Booth, C. L. (1988). Maternal antecedents of attachment quality. In J. Belsky & T. Nezworski (Eds.), *Clinical implications of attachment* (pp. 95–135). Hillsdale, NJ: Erlbaum.

Sroufe, L. A. (1983). Infant–caregiver attachment and patterns of adaptation in preschool: Roots of maladaptation and competence. In M. Perlmutter (Ed.), *Minnesota Symposia on Child Psychology, Vol. 16.* Hillsdale, NJ: Erlbaum.

Sroufe, L. A., & Rutter, M. (1984). The domain of developmental psychopathology. *Child Development, 55*, 17–29.

Strain, P., & Kerr, M. (1981). Modifying children's social withdrawal: Issues in assessment and clinical intervention. In M. Herson, R. Eisler, & P. Miller (Eds.), *Progress in behavior modification, Vol. 2,* (pp. 203-248). New York: Academic Press.

Stewart, S. L., & Rubin, K. H. (1993, March). *The social problem-solving skills of anxious-withdrawn children.* Poster presented at the biennial meetings of The Society for Research in Child Development, New Orleans, LA.

Sullivan, H. S. (1953). *The interpersonal theory of psychiatry.* New York: Norton.

Thomas, A., & Chess, S. (1977). *Temperament and development.* New York: Brunner/Mazel.

Thompson, R. A., Connell, J., & Bridges, L. J. (1988). Temperament, emotional, and social interactive behavior in the strange situation: An analysis of attachment functioning. *Child Development, 59*, 1102–1110.

Tomarken, A. J., Davidson, R. J., Wheeler, R. W., & Doss, R. (1992). Relations between individual differences in anterior brain asymmetry and fundamental dimensions of emotion. *Journal of Personality and Social Psychology, 62*, 676–687.

Wahler, R. G., & Dumas, J. E. (1987). Family factors in childhood psychology: Toward a coercion-neglect model. In T. Jacob (Ed.), *Family interaction and psychopathology: Theories, methods and findings* (pp. 581–627). New York: Plenum Press.

Wicks-Nelson, R., & Israel, A. (1989). *Behavioral disorders in childhood.* Englewood Cliffs, NJ: Prentice-Hall.

Younger, A. J., & Boyko, K. A. (1987). Aggression and withdrawal as social schemas underlying children's peer perceptions. *Child Development, 58,* 1094–1100.

Younger, A. J., & Daniels, T. M. (1992). Children's reasons for nominating their peers as withdrawn: Passive withdrawal versus active isolation? *Developmental Psychology, 28,* 955–960.

Younger, A. J., Gentile, C., & Burgess, K. (1993). Children's perceptions of withdrawal: Changes across age. In K. H. Rubin & J. Asendorpf (Eds.), *Social withdrawal, inhibition, and shyness in childhood* (pp. 215–236). Chicago: University of Chicago Press.

Younger, A. J., & Pinccinin, A. M. (1989). Children's recall of aggressive and withdrawn behaviors: Recognition memory and likeability judgements. *Child Development, 60,* 580–590.

Zaia, A. F., & Harrist, A. W., (1993). *Subtypes of social withdrawal in early childhood: Social-cognitive, behavioral, and sociometric correlates.* Pospter presented at the biennial meeting of the Society for Research in Child Development, New Orleans, LA.

5

Disability and Facilitated Communication

A Critique

Alan Hudson

1. Introduction

Extensive controversy has developed in relation to the use of what is termed facilitated communication, or more recently, facilitated communication training. The procedure can be considered to be part of the general field of augmentative and alternative communication (AAC). AAC is a global term used to refer to methods of communicating that replace or supplement ordinary methods such as speech and handwriting (Beukelman & Mirenda, 1992; College of Speech Therapists, 1989). AAC methods typically involve people with disabilities in the use of manual procedures such as signing, or in the use of communication boards, or finally in the use of electronic equipment. In general, AAC methods are used independently by the disabled person. Facilitated communication has been defined in various ways, but the most frequent definition is "a teaching strategy, used to help people with severe communication impairments develop the hand skills needed to use communication aids independently" (Crossley, 1992b, p. 43). The technique usually involves some form of physical assistance by another person, called a facilitator, to help the speech-impaired person accurately point at letters or push keys on a communication device of some sort. The letters then spell out the intended message. The communication device may be a high-technology device such as a computer, or a low-technology communication device such as an alphabet board. Very frequently the device used is a Canon Communicator, an instrument which

ALAN HUDSON • Department of Psychology and Intellectual Disability Studies, Royal Melbourne Institute of Technology, Bundoora, Victoria 3083, Australia.

Advances in Clinical Child Psychology, Volume 17, edited by Thomas H. Ollendick and Ronald J. Prinz. Plenum Press, New York, 1995.

is operated by a keyboard and generates a ticker-tape printout containing the message.

The controversy that has developed centers upon the fact that the facilitator, while providing physical assistance, may influence the communication generated by the person with the disability (Biklen, 1990, 1992a, 1992b; Calculator, 1992a, 1992b; Cummins & Prior, 1992; Prior & Cummins, 1992; Rimland, 1992).

2. History of Facilitated Communication

2.1. St. Nicholas Hospital

While the precise origins of facilitated communication are a little hard to trace, the contemporary controversy began in Melbourne in the 1970s at the St. Nicholas Hospital, a facility for children who were considered to be physically and intellectually disabled. Rosemary Crossley, a teacher at the hospital, introduced facilitated communication to the children and formed the view that a group of 12 of them were not intellectually disabled, but rather were of average or even superior intelligence. This view was strongly disputed by the hospital and, after a protracted legal battle, a judgement was handed down in the Supreme Court of Victoria in May 1979 to allow one of the children, Anne McDonald, to leave the hospital (Crossley & McDonald, 1980). From then until now, McDonald has lived with Crossley.

In late 1979, a Committee of Inquiry was established to investigate the situation regarding the remaining 11 children, whose ages then ranged from 9 to 19 years. The committee comprised a psychiatrist, a neurologist, an educational psychologist, and a special educator, all of whom were experienced in the disability field. After a nine-month inquiry the committee published their findings which included:

> Not one of the 11 children shows any evidence of a level of intellectual functioning beyond that expected of children of 2½ years of age. The 11 children function at a level indicative of severe or profound mental retardation. There is no valid evidence to support the claims that these children can communicate by the use of an alphabet board. Ms. Crossley's claims that these children are capable of understanding and communicating highly sophisticated concepts are false. No child shows evidence of even the most elementary level of literacy of numeracy (Eisen, 1980, p. 6).

The Committee of Inquiry was also asked to comment on the suitability of St. Nicholas Hospital as an accommodation option for the children. It concluded that the hospital was the best available option and all 11 children remained there.

About 18 months later, a supplementary report by two psychologists (Cummins & Bancroft, 1981) was critical of some of the methodology and conclusions of the Eisen Report. Cummins and Bancroft essentially argued that the methodology had not been sufficiently rigorous to warrant the conclusions drawn.

In 1983, an unsuccessful attempt was made to have one of the 11 children removed from the hospital. The disabled person, Ms. Angela Wallace, had cerebral palsy and was by now twenty-one years old. She made an application to the Health Commission of Victoria for release of her files by "signing" a typed letter with a felt pen attached to a head pointer (*Wallace v. Health Commission of Victoria*, December 1984). Ms. Wallace had been using facilitated communication with Crossley as the facilitator, and it was stated that she intended to take legal action to be allowed to leave the hospital (Pinto, 1984). The Commission refused release of the files to Ms. Wallace on the grounds that she did not have the intellectual capacity to make the application. Further, in regard to facilitated communication, the Commission indicated its belief that "she (Crossley) was manipulating the keyboard in order to spell out the messages and those messages were hers and not the appellant's" (Wallace v. *Health Commission of Victoria*, December 1984). Unsuccessful appeals against the Health Commission's decision were made to the County Court in the first instance, and then to the Supreme Court of Victoria.

2.2. The DEAL Communication Centre

One of the submissions to the St. Nicholas Hospital Committee of Inquiry (Eisen, 1980) was from an organization known as Dignity, Education, and Language (DEAL). This organization was favourably disposed toward facilitated communication and its submission strongly supported the position of Crossley. In 1986 the DEAL Communication Centre opened in a suburb of Melbourne with Crossley as the Program Coordinator. The Centre has been funded primarily by grants from the state and federal governments. It became very active in promoting the use of facilitated communication in services for people with an intellectual disability in the State of Victoria. The use of facilitated communication was quickly adopted in a variety of settings, particularly in day centers for adults with an intellectual disability.

2.3. Controversy Surrounding Facilitated Communication

The increased use of facilitated communication went without comment until 1988, when a group of professionals from the intellectual disability field made a submission to the State Government expressing concern about facilitated communication. The group comprised five psychologists, five speech pathologists, four special educators, one psychiatrist, one occupational therapist, and two managers of large services for the disabled. The working party presented evidence that in some instances the communications were being substantially influenced by the facilitators (Interdisciplinary Working Party on Issues in Severe Communication Impairment, 1988). As a consequence, the State Government asked the Intellectual Disability Review Panel (IDRP) to conduct an inquiry into the reliability and validity of facilitated communication (referred to by the IDRP as assisted communication). The IDRP had been established under the provisions of the Intellectually Disabled Persons' Services Act (1986) to protect the rights of disabled persons. The IDRP had difficulty in conducting its investigations, in part because of a lack of cooperation by DEAL, and eventually avoided making any global comments regarding the validity of facilitated communication. The report finally recommended that each case needed to be individually assessed (Intellectual Disability Review Panel, 1989).

Despite the concerns expressed by the Interdisciplinary Working Party and the IDRP, the growth of facilitated communication received little attention from government or other sources. That is, until the case of Carla (a pseudonym). Carla was a 29-year-old woman living with her family in suburban Melbourne and attending a local adult day center. She had contracted encephalitis as a young child and since then had been considered to be severely intellectually disabled. During 1990, while being facilitated by a staff member at the day center, Carla "alleged" that her father and her brother had repeatedly raped her. Furthermore, Carla "alleged" that her mother was complicit to the attacks by holding her down and muffling her objections.

Carla was removed from by her home by the government authorities in late 1990, but the family ultimately made an application to the Guardianship and Administration Board (GAB) to be appointed legal guardian of Carla. As part of the proceedings of the Board, Carla's ability to communicate using facilitated communication was assessed (Hudson, Melita, & Arnold, 1993). The GAB found that Carla had a severe intellectual disability and could not validly communicate using facilitated communication. Guardianship was jointly awarded to her mother and sister. Carla now lives at home again, does not attend the same day center, and does not use facilitated communication.

A second critical case that drew public attention was that of a worker in a community residential house for disabled people. The male staff member (Mr. W.) was sacked by the State Government after three women who lived at the house alleged, via facilitated communication, that he had drugged and raped them. Mr. W. was charged by the police but the magistrate dismissed the case because of the failure of a simple validation test conducted by the magistrate in court. The State Government, however, refused to reinstate Mr. W. This resulted in an investigation by the State Ombudsman, who supported the view that Mr. W. had been unjustly dismissed (Ombudsman Victoria, 1993). In his report the Ombudsman also raised general concerns about the use of facilitated communication, and recommended that a thorough review be conducted of its use in government and nongovernment agencies.

2.4. The Spread of Facilitated Communication Outside Victoria

Although the development of facilitated communication was rapid in the State of Victoria during the 1980s, curiously, it did not spread to other states of Australia. Apart from a small development in Queensland spearheaded by an ex-employee of the DEAL Communication Centre in Victoria, there is no evidence of it being used in other states of Australia.

Facilitated communication did, however, spread overseas quite rapidly. The major catalyst to this spread was a visit to Australia by Douglas Biklen of Syracuse University, who wrote of his experiences at the DEAL Centre in the Harvard Educational Review (Biklen, 1990). The comments by Biklen, perhaps combined with visits to North America by Crossley in the early 1990s, have led to a rapid spread in the use of facilitated communication in the United States and Canada. Sadly, disputes about the validity of facilitated communication, often enmeshed in allegations of sexual or physical assault, have also followed its use in these countries. In Syracuse, New York, a 10-year-old girl with Down's syndrome accused her father of sexual abuse. In Kingston, New York, a 13-year-old girl with autism accused her father of sexual abuse. In Marion, Indiana, a 10-year-old girl who was blind and severely intellectually disabled accused males from her home of sexual abuse. In Whittier, California, a 27-year-old male teacher was accused of sexually abusing four male students with autism. In Wichita, Kansas, a 17-year-old severely intellectually disabled girl accused her mother of sexual abuse. The Autism Research Institute (1992a, 1992b, & 1993) summarized these developments and commented that in the 20 or so cases they were aware of, all of the allegations had been judged false or not credible. They then went on to list lawsuits that the accused had subsequently initiated. These included a $6 million suit in New York, a $2.5 million suit in California, and a $700,000 suit in Indiana.

Facilitated communication is now also used in England and other parts of Europe. This use, however, appears to be less well-established than in Australia and North America.

3. Evaluation of the Ability of Individuals To Validly Communicate Using Facilitated Communication

Evaluations of the ability of individuals to validly communicate using facilitated communication have usually occurred in two contexts. The first of these is some form of dispute situation, in which the individual's ability to use the method to generate a legitimate communication is germane to the resolution of that dispute. Examples of these would be when the disabled person appears to be making an allegation of abuse or something similar, or when the disabled person appears to be making a statement regarding a major life decision. Under these circumstances some form of experimental testing will take place; however, the decision about the person's ability to validly communicate using facilitated communication will take into account many other sources of information. These sources may include the results of standardized tests administered by psychologists or speech pathologists, and also a range of qualitative data collected during interviews and periods of direct observation of the person. The decision about ability to validly communicate is made after a consideration of the convergence of all of this evidence (Hudson, 1992). Many of these evaluations occur in judicial or quasi-judicial settings, and hence are either not publicly recorded or are minimally recorded.

The second context in which evaluations occur is that in which the primary aim is to establish whether facilitated communication works. These evaluations usually involve a group of individuals and the results are published in the scientific literature. This review will include evaluations conducted in both of these contexts.

The validity evaluations themselves have been of several types. The majority of studies have been experimental, in that ability to communicate is assessed under controlled conditions. Other studies, however, have been essentially qualitative or ethnographic in nature, following the progress of individuals in naturalistic settings. Finally, some evaluations have involved alternative procedures such as linguistic analysis of language samples.

3.1. Experimental Methods of Evaluation

Experimental studies typically involve testing the ability of the individual to validly communicate using facilitated communication under conditions in which the facilitator is not aware of a specific piece of information that is intended to be communicated. Three particular methods have evolved in this regard. For the sake of clarity, the person with the disability is referred to as the *subject*, and the person providing the facilitation as the *facilitator*.

1. The first method involves asking the subject a question that requires a specific single-word or short-answer response. The facilitator is present at the time and may or may not know the correct answer. However, the facilitator is auditorily screened from hearing the question and cannot, except by guessing, assist the subject with the answer.

2. The second method involves showing the subject a stimulus object that requires a response. The facilitator is present but is visually screened from seeing the object. The stimulus object may be a picture about which a specific question is asked, for example, what the colour or shape of some element of the picture is. Alternatively, the stimulus object may be a written question requiring a single-word or short-answer response.

3. The third method involves having the facilitator leave the room, and then either showing some object to the subject, or discussing some topic with the subject. When the facilitator returns to the room, the facilitator asks the subject to indicate what happened during his or her absence. In this situation the facilitator can engage the subject in extended discourse, but must be able to accurately elicit the required event. This procedure is referred to as *message passing*.

The first formal testing of an individual's ability to communicate using facilitated communication was probably the testing of Anne McDonald, which took place in the Supreme Court of Victoria in 1979. This testing was not part of the proceedings of the landmark case in the Supreme Court in May 1979, in which Justice Jenkinson decided that she was not intellectually disabled and allowed her to leave St. Nicholas Hospital. However, it was part of a later case, heard in September 1979, in regard to her seeking release from the control of the Public Trustees to manager her own financial affairs. Crossley and McDonald (1980) reported that a variation of the message-passing methodology was used. The assessments were carried out by a Senior Master of the Court with only Anne and the facilitator (Rosemary Crossley) present. The facilitator was sent out of the courtroom and words were spoken to Anne. After several unsuccessful trials, Anne reproduced two words given to her; "string" and "quince" were reproduced as "string" and "quit." Crossley and McDonald reported that Justice Murphy accepted this as evidence that Anne could successfully communicate using facilitated communication and ruled in her favour.

The second formal assessment of any individual's ability to validly communicate using facilitated communication took place during the Inquiry to Investigate Claims about Children at St. Nicholas Hospital (Eisen, 1980). This investigation focused on claims that 11 children left at the hospital after the departure of Anne McDonald were of average or even superior intelligence, and could communicate using facilitated communication. The Eisen report stated that it "undertook a variety of testing sessions with all of the 11 children" (Eisen, 1980, p. 56). However, the final report only gave details of the assessments of 3 children. The assessment of these children used the message-passing methodology. The facilitators (Rosemary Crossley for 2 children and another facilitator for the third) were asked to leave the room while the tasks were presented. These tasks included passing-on short verbal messages and the provision of answers to short mathematical problems. Success on similar tasks had been easily achieved when they had been presented with the facilitators present. Under the experimental conditions of the facilitators not hearing the question, no meaningful response was achieved. The report states: "In summary, all these and other similar sessions with the 11 children provided no evidence of these children's claimed capacities for communication" (Eisen, 1980, p. 75).

The Interdisciplinary Working Party (1988) report was essentially a statement of concern to the government of the day, but it did contain some details of the assessment of 5 subjects conducted by members of the group in 1985. Each of the 5 subjects had severe cerebral palsy. There were only four facilitators involved as one facilitated 2 subjects. The subjects were asked to participate in visual matching tasks. First, the subjects were presented with a test pattern. This was then removed and the subjects were presented with a second pattern and they had to specify whether it was the same as or different from the first pattern. The first patterns were presented in three different conditions, namely a) presenting it so that both facilitator and subject saw it, b) presenting it only to the subject, and c) presenting different patterns to the subject and the facilitator (the facilitator was not aware of the difference).

The report pointed out that not all subjects were exposed to all three conditions, but indicated that certain trends appeared in the results. These were summarized as follows: a) When the same pattern was seen by both the facilitator and the subject, the responses were always correct. b) When the facilitator did not see the pattern presented, the responses were mostly wrong and those that were correct occurred at or below chance levels. c) When different patterns were presented to the facilitator and subject, the response given by the subject was the correct answer to the pattern presented to the facilitator in 28 out of 30 trials. On the basis of these data, the Working Party concluded that the use of facilitated communication had, on some occasions, led to communications being imposed on the subjects.

As was indicated earlier, the investigation carried out by the Intellectual Disability Review Panel (1989) was conducted in response to a request from the State Government of the day. This request was partially in response to the statement of concern expressed by the Interdisciplinary Working Party (1988). The IDRP intended to conduct a major experimental evaluation involving 25 subjects, but encountered a major obstacle. Almost all disabled people using facilitated communication were clients of the DEAL Communication Centre, and the Centre refused to cooperate with the study. The refusal was based on an objection to the experimental methodology proposed: DEAL preferred a qualitative methodology involving naturalistic observations of their clients' use of facilitated communication. However, the IDRP considered that experimental procedures were necessary if definitive answers were to be found. The search for subjects continued but only three were located.

The main experimental method used by the IDRP involved the subject being asked a set of 10 questions requiring single-word or short-answer responses under four different conditions. The 10 questions for each condition were randomly selected from a pool of 20 questions provided by the facilitator, and considered by the facilitator to be questions that the subject could answer.

In Condition A, the facilitator verbally asked the question of the subject and the subject was then facilitated to reply. The remaining three conditions involved both the facilitator and subject wearing headphones and listening to prerecorded questions played through the headphones. In Condition B, the facilitator and the subject heard the same questions. A comparison of performance under Condition B with that under Condition A gave information regarding the effect that the wearing of earphones had on performance. In Condition C, the facilitator and the subject heard different questions. Conditions B and C were conducted together, with the questions randomly mixed, so that the facilitator never knew to what condition the question belonged. In Condition D, the subject heard questions, but the facilitator heard only music. The results of the study are summarized in Table 1.

On the basis of these data the IDRP concluded that there was no evidence to support the proposition that subjects 1 and 3 could validly communicate using facilitated communication. However, for subject 2, the 2 out of 4 result in Condition C led the IDRP to the view that this subject could communicate. This conclusion has been contested by Cummins and Prior (1992), who describe it as an overly generous interpretation of the data. The Cummins and Prior view was supported by Jacobson et al. (1994).

Although the DEAL Communication Centre refused to participate in the major IDRP experimental study, it did agree to provide 3 subjects for

TABLE 1
Results of Intellectual Disability Review Panel (1989) Experimental Study

Condition	Subject 1 number of correct responses	Subject 2 number of correct responses	Subject 3 number of correct responses
A	10/10	3/3	8/8
B	2/10	3/6	3/4
C	0/10	2/4	1/6
D	0/10	0/5	0/2

participation in a message-passing exercise. Each subject was given a gift when the facilitator was out of the room and asked to identify the gift when the facilitator returned. The IDRP accepted the responses from all 3 of the subjects as being evidence that they could validly communicate using facilitated communication. Very little detail is provided about the subjects or the nature of the interactions that occurred when the facilitators returned. It was mentioned that 1 subject had demonstrated a clear ability to type complex words independently, and this would seem to invalidate the assessment for him, since facilitation was not required.

Hudson et al. (1993) reported on the assessment of a 29-year-old woman (known as Carla) as part of the proceedings of a quasi-judicial body. The woman had contracted encephalitis as an infant and throughout her life had been considered to be severely intellectually disabled. She was nonverbal, but it was purported that she had used facilitated communication to make accusations of sexual abuse against family members. The facilitation involved her being given physical assistance to operate a Canon Communicator. The assessment was to determine if she could validly communicate using facilitated communication. Hudson et al. (1989) used a variation of the four-condition experimental methodology developed by the Intellectual Disability Review Panel. The variation was that the facilitator provided an initial pool of 40 questions that were randomly allocated to four groups of 10. The questions were prerecorded and asked of the facilitator and subject via earphones. Two researchers also listened to the questions via earphones. One heard the questions to the subject; the other heard the questions to the facilitator. This was done to ensure that both the subject and the facilitator could hear what was intended for them to hear. The physical layout of the persons and equipment used in the assessment is shown in Figure 1.

In the assessment, the subject scored 8 out of 10 in Condition A, 4 out of 10 in Condition B, 0 out of 10 in Condition C, and 0 out of 6 in Condition

D (this condition was curtailed as the response pattern had been clearly established). The combined results of Conditions C and D (0 out of 16), together with a large quantity of information gathered from other sources, led Hudson et al. to conclude that the subject was, in fact, severely intellectually disabled and could not validly communicate using facilitated communication. It was interesting to note that in Condition C, the subject "typed out" correct answers to 4 of the 10 questions asked of the facilitator, providing clear evidence of facilitator influence. Such influence can, of course, be inferred from the fact that there was a high rate of correct responses in Condition A and B, but none in Conditions C and D.

Crossley (1993) made several criticisms of the assessment of Carla, arguing that the facilitator was new and untrained, that Carla had motor-

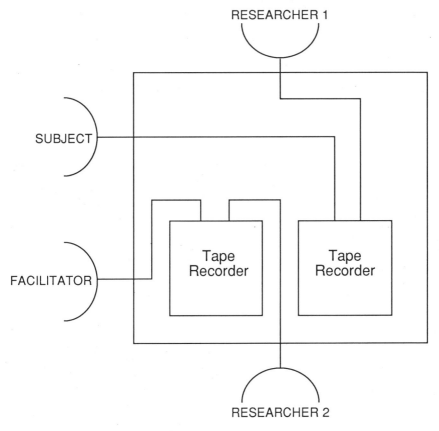

FIGURE 1. Physical layout of the persons and equipment used by Hudson, Melita, and Arnold (1993)

planning problems, and that she also had word-finding problems. Hudson (1993) rebutted the first point by indicating that the day center at which Carla was using facilitated communication was invited to provide the facilitator, and that given the seriousness of the allegations made at the center, it would be unthinkable that a new and untrained facilitator would be sent. With regard to the other points, Hudson argues that there was simply no evidence that Carla had either motor-planning or word-finding problems.

A very similar assessment of an individual subject is reported by Bligh and Kupperman (1993). The subject was a 10-year-old girl who had been diagnosed as being legally blind and severely mentally retarded. She attended a special education class for severely handicapped children. A few weeks after introduction to facilitated communication she was typing complex sentences. Eventually the subject typed out accusations of sexual abuse by two males at her home, and was immediately placed in foster care.

As part of the court proceedings, a series of questions were written on index cards and asked under different conditions with the following results. When the facilitator knew the question, and knew the answer, and was permitted to look at the keyboard, the answer was appropriate to the questions. When the facilitator knew the question but not the answer, and was permitted to look at the keyboard, the answer was language appropriate to the question, but not the right answer. When the facilitator did not know the question being asked but could look at the keyboard, the result was language but not appropriate to the question asked. Finally, whenever the facilitator could not look at the keyboard the answers consisted of random letters.

In light of these results, the lawyers involved in the case agreed that the source of the communications was the facilitator and not the subject. All charges were dismissed and the child was returned to her family.

The first large-scale validity evaluation reported in the literature is that conducted by Wheeler, Jacobson, Paglieri, and Schwartz (1993). The study involved 12 subjects living in a residential service for adolescents and adults with autism. All subjects met the DSM-III-R diagnostic criteria for autism and were aged between 16 and 30 years.

The subjects were shown pictures of familiar objects and asked to type the names of the objects on either a word processor or a printed representation of a QWERTY keyboard. The typing took place under three conditions. The first involved the subject being shown a picture and then asked to type the name with no facilitation. The second condition involved facilitation, but with the facilitator being visually screened from seeing the picture shown to the subject. The third condition was called the *distractor condition* and also involved facilitation. In this condition, however, the facilitator was shown a second picture at the same time as being screened from seeing the subject's picture. In half of the trials in this condition the picture shown to the facilitator was the same as that shown to the subject, but in the other half of the trials the picture was different. The facilitator was not aware of the picture being the same or different.

Each of the 12 subjects was given 10 trials in each condition, with the 10 trials in the distractor condition being equally divided between same and different distractors. Of the 120 trials in the facilitated condition, not one was judged as being correct, and only two were judged as being partially correct. For the 60 trials in the distractor condition in which the facilitator saw the same picture as the subject, there were 14 correct responses. Nothing could be concluded from these responses and Wheeler et al. (1993) referred to them as pseudocorrect responses. For the 60 trials in which the facilitator saw a different picture, there were no correct answers to the picture shown to the subject. There were, however, 12 answers that corresponded to the card shown to the facilitator. Wheeler et al. considered that these data "conclusively and incontrovertibly proves that, for this sample of facilitated communication participants, their communications were influenced (i.e., altered or determined) by their respective facilitators" (Wheeler et al., 1993, p. 56).

Moore, Donovan, Hudson, Dykstra, and Lawrence (1993) conducted a study at a day centre for people with intellectual disabilities in Victoria, Australia. The 8 subjects ranged in age from 22 to 41 years, and the etiology and severity of their intellectual disabilities varied considerably. The nature of the facilitation also varied in that 4 subjects were assisted to operate keyboards (mainly Canon Communicators), 2 were assisted to point with their hands to letters on alphabet boards, and the remaining 2 were assisted to use head pointers to point to letters on alphabet boards. The period of time that they had been using facilitated communication ranged from 17 to 33 months.

The general methodology used was similar to that developed by the Intellectual Disability Review Panel (1989). For each facilitator–subject pair, the facilitator was asked to provide 10 short-answer questions that the subject could answer. The questions were asked under three different conditions, referred to as Conditions A, B, and D. These correspond to Conditions A, B, and D as specified in the recommendations of the Intellectual Disability Review Panel (1989). Condition A contained 5 questions randomly selected from the original 10. Condition B contained the remaining 5 questions, and Condition D contained all 10 questions randomly ordered.

The responses to the questions were scored as being a) a *correct re-*

sponse, in that either the expected answer was given, or a response that was in the same semantic category was given; b) an *unscorable response*, in that the subject gave a correct verbal response audible to the facilitator; c) an *incorrect response*, in that the response contained one or more expected responses but they were responses to other questions; and d) *no response*, in that no response was given or the response was uninterpretable. The results of the study are summarized in Table 2. Although there were 8 subjects (referred to as S1 to S8) there were only 4 facilitators (referred to as F1 to F4).

Moore, Donovan, Hudson, Dykstra, and Lawrence (1993) considered that these data demonstrated that not one of the subjects could validly communicate using facilitated communication. Furthermore, they argued that the high rate of incorrect responses for subjects S1 to S4 demonstrated

TABLE 2
Results of the Moore, Donovan, Hudson, Dykstra, and Lawrence
(in press) Study

Subject	Facilitator	Condition	Q's asked	Correct R	Unscorable R	Incorrect R	No R
1	F1	A	5	5	—	—	—
		B	5	5	—	—	—
		D	10	1	—	9	—
2	F2	A	5	5	—	—	—
		B	5	3	—	—	2
		D	10	3	—	6	1
3	F3	A	5	5	—	—	—
		B	5	5	—	—	—
		D	10	1	2	6	1
4	F3	A	5	5	—	—	—
		B	5	5	—	—	—
		D	10	1	—	8	1
5	F4	A	No meaningful responses gained so assessment discontinued.				
6	F4	A	5	2	—	—	3
		B	5	1	—	—	4
		D	7	—	—	—	7
7	F4	A	5	4	—	—	1
		B	5	3	1	—	1
		D	10	—	4	—	6
8	F4	A	No meaningful responses gained so assessment discontinued.				

that facilitators F1 to F3 were all significantly influencing the communication of the subjects they were facilitating.

A follow up to the Moore, Donovan, Hudson, Dykstra, and Lawrence (1993) study is reported by Moore, Donovan, and Hudson (1993). Some of the facilitators in the Moore, Donovan, Hudson, Dykstra, and Lawrence study expressed concern about the experimental methodology used in that study. They argued that the subjects may have had "word-finding problems," and that they could therefore have been disadvantaged in any tasks that required single-word or short-answer responses. As a consequence, the facilitators were invited to develop an alternative methodology.

The invitation was accepted by two of the original four facilitators, who between them facilitated 5 subjects. The methodology they developed involved the message-passing procedure, conducted in two phases. In the first phase the facilitators left the room and the subjects were presented with a concrete object of some sort. The objects were things such as a flashlight, or a camera, or an umbrella. The subjects listened to a description of the object and it was given to the subject to touch. When the facilitators returned to the room they could ask the subjects whatever questions they liked, and could, if they wished, merely engage the subject in conversation. Their task was to elicit the name of the object from the subject, using whatever means they thought to be appropriate.

The second phase was similar to the first, but instead of being shown a concrete object, the subjects were engaged in a topic of conversation by their primary caregiver. Examples of the topics were the subject's favourite football team, or a trip to the supermarket. Upon returning to the room, the facilitator was required to identify that topic of conversation.

In each phase, 3 to 5 trials were run with each subject. There were a total of 18 trials in the first phase, and 17 trials in the second phase. In the first phase, the number of objects correctly identified was zero. Similarly, in the second phase, the number of conversation topics correctly identified was zero. Moore, Donovan, and Hudson concluded from these results that the presence of word-finding problems was not a plausible explanation of the results that the previous study, and that the results of the two studies were correctly explained in terms of the subjects not being able to validly communicate using facilitated communication.

The message-passing procedure was also used in a large-scale evaluation conducted by Szempruch & Jacobson (1992). Part of the rationale for using this methodology was that experimental procedures that used special apparatus, for example the earphones in Hudson et al. (1993), or the visual screens in Wheeler et al. (1993), created an environment that was not usual. In contrast, the message-passing procedure could be implemented in as natural a setting as possible.

The six facilitators and the 23 subjects involved in the Szempruch and Jacobson study were drawn from local service agencies that were using facilitated communication. The subjects were selected by the facilitators on the basis that they could, via facilitation, use an alphabet board to communicate. All were considered to have severe to profound intellectual disability, and their ages ranged from 21 to 75 years. The subject pool included people with cerebral palsy, Down's syndrome, Tourette syndrome, organic brain syndrome, autism, and schizophrenia.

The evaluation procedure involved the subjects being shown the picture of a common object when the facilitator was out of the room. The picture was presented for one minute and the object was identified verbally for the subject during this time. When the facilitator returned to the room, 10 minutes were allowed for the facilitator to elicit the name of the object from the subject. Each subject was given from 2 to 6 trials, with a total of 127 trials being conducted. Discernible responses were given in 121 of these trials, but the number of trials in which the object was correctly identified was zero.

A study by Eberlin, McConnachie, Ibel, and Volpe (1993) focused on the fact that many disabled people surprisingly demonstrate well-developed literacy skills when first introduced to facilitated communication. People who previously had demonstrated only minimal communication skills were suddenly able to produce sophisticated comments on a range of social issues. Eberlin et al. argued that the sudden emergence of literacy skills had only been studied using ethnographic methods, which they considered to be problematic methodologically for investigating this phenomenon. Their study was designed to use experimental methods to examine the emergence of literacy skills in people with autism when they were first introduced to facilitated communication.

Of the 21 subjects, 20 had a primary diagnosis of autism, and the other had a diagnosis of pervasive development disorder. Their ages ranged from 11 to 20 years and they attended an educational program for children and adults with autism and other developmental disorders. A number of instruments were used to assess speech and communication skills, the results suggesting that the maximum age-equivalent skills of any of the subjects was 5 or 6 years.

The facilitators were 10 volunteers who had experience in the field of autism, and an interest in facilitated communication. They were trained to be facilitators as part of the study. The training procedures used were those developed by Biklen and associates (Schubert, 1991). The facilitation involved the provision of physical assistance to the subjects to type out messages on a Canon Communicator.

Following the training of the facilitators, a number of experimental steps were followed. The first of these was a two-week period of rapport building between facilitator and subject. This was done because good rapport is seen as an essential ingredient for successful facilitation. The next step involved the baseline testing of the subjects' performance on the dependent measures. This was done without facilitation. Then, after an initial exposure to facilitated communication, a pretest involving the dependent measures was administered, but this time via facilitated communication. During the pretest the facilitator was screened from hearing the test questions and seeing the test stimuli. The subjects then received 40 one-half hour facilitated communication training sessions. These were conducted once or twice per day, 3 to 5 days per week. Following the last training session, a "warm up" for the posttest was conducted. Here, measures similar to the main dependent measures were used, and the facilitator was not screened in any way. Finally, a posttest of the dependent measures was administered with the facilitator being auditorily and visually screened.

The dependent measures used were the Vocabulary subtest of the Stanford–Binet Fourth Edition (Thorndike, Hagen, & Sattler, 1986), and a structured interview questionnaire developed by Eberlin et al. The questionnaire comprised both closed- and open-ended questions and was designed to assess literacy skills.

A comparison of the pretest performance with the baseline performance provided information about the appearance of unexpected literacy skills in the subjects when they first used facilitated communication. Taking the performance on the two dependent variables together, not one subject improved in the pretest. On the contrary, they all performed very significantly worse on the pretest, indicating that they communicated better without facilitation. A comparison of posttest with pretest performances provided information about the emergence of literacy skills during training. While 2 subjects did make some improvement, it needs to be noted that they both could type independently prior to the study commencing, and that their posttest scores differed only marginally from their baseline performances. The posttest performance of the other 19 subjects remained at the essentially zero level of pretest performance. A comparison of the posttest with posttest warm-up provided information about the facilitator influence. While 8 subjects had higher scores on the warm-up (1 subject had a lower score), care must be taken in interpreting this data, since the measures were only similar, not identical.

One criticism that has been made of this study is that the length of time spent training the subjects was inadequate (Crossley, in Eberlin et al., 1993). Eberlin et al. retorted that the primary aim of the study was to assess the sudden emergence of literacy skills when subjects are started on facilitation, and that such skills were not evident in this study. A second criticism is that the length of time spent training the facilitators was inadequate, and that facilitators must be closely supervised and trained for at least six months (Crossley, in Eberlin, 1993). It is clearly the case, however, that very few facilitators have had training which even approximates that stated by Crossley as being necessary. It is the author's experience that in Australia, few if any facilitators have had much by way of systematic training. In addition, the question as to whether further training improves performance is an empirical one that has not been tested yet.

In a smaller scale study, Smith and Belcher (1993) also investigated the apparent emergence of, or improvement in, literacy skills when subjects are introduced to facilitated communication. All subjects had been diagnosed as autistic according to DSM-III-R criteria. Five were verbal and 4 were known to have some literacy skills.

Canon Communicators were used and the facilitators were trained in formal workshops presented by either Biklen or consultants from the Adrianna Foundation, which specializes in facilitated communication. Training sessions were conducted from once to three times a week for 7 to 12 weeks. The tasks ranged from typing set letters, through answering specific questions like "What is your name?", to answering open-ended questions.

The subjects who had no verbal skills typed only random letters. Some verbal subjects did type short sentences, but in no instance did they type things that they could not say. Smith and Belcher concluded that they found no evidence of unexpected literacy skills when the subjects were first introduced to facilitated communication.

An experimental study with quite a different approach was conducted by Calculator and Singer (1992). The subjects were 5 children aged between 6 and 16 years, and all had been considered to be severely intellectually disabled. The study involved the administration of the Peabody Picture Vocabulary Test-Revised (Dunn & Dunn, 1981). The PPVT-R is a test of receptive language and involves the subject pointing to one of four displayed pictures to indicate the meaning of a particular word. The test was administered both with and without facilitation. During the facilitation administration the facilitator was auditorily screened from hearing the stimulus word by wearing earphones with white noise played through them. Both forms of the PPVT-R were used, one for each of the with- and without-facilitation conditions. The order of presentation of the forms, as well as the order in which the facilitated and nonfacilitated conditions were introduced, was counterbalanced to control for order effects.

For 2 of the subjects there was no difference between the facilitated and non-facilitated conditions. However, for 3 of the subjects there was a difference and for 2 of these the results were quite astonishing. The first subject (16.10-years-old) went from an age equivalent (AE) of 2.2 years to an AE of 9.3 years, placing him at the 30th percentile. The second subject (6.11-years-old) went from an AE of less than 1.9 years to one of 9.3 years, giving him a percentile ranking of 95. Similarly, the third subject (9.10-years-old) went from an AE of 2.6 years to one of 18.1 years, giving him a percentile ranking of 99.

The probabilities of these results are worthy of contemplation. The likelihood of taking an random sample of 5 children and having 2 of that sample at or above the 95th percentile would be quite low. The chances of finding the same thing with a sample of 5 children who have been considered to be severely intellectually disabled, and have probably had reduced opportunities for language development, must be infinitesimal, and must throw some doubt on the validity of the findings. Jacobson et al. (1994) have highlighted methodological concerns with the study in regard to the fact that the facilitators were not visually screened from the examiners and, despite being asked not to look at the examiner, may have taken cues from observing the same. As Jacobson et al. have indicated, this study could do with replication.

The progress of experimental evaluations of facilitated communications has been followed closely by Gina Green of the New England Center for Autism. The Autism Research Institute (1993) reproduced a chart compiled by Green which summarizes all of the evaluations she was aware of, both published and unpublished. Of a total of 187 individuals who had been tested, only 3 provided any evidence of being able to validly communicate using facilitated communication. These were the 3 involved in the study by Calculator and Singer (1992), a study which has attracted its fair share of methodological criticism. Four of the 6 subjects in the report of the Intellectual Disability Review Panel (1989) could perhaps be added to Calculator and Singer's 3, but that study has also been strongly criticized.

3.2. Qualitative Methods of Evaluation

Researchers who use qualitative methods for the study of facilitated communication are usually interested in studying the phenomenon itself, rather than focusing on the issue of the ability of individuals to validly communicate using facilitated communication. Indeed, it is claimed that the testing inherent in experimental evaluation is incompatible with the high expectations and emotional support necessary for the successful use of facilitated communication (Crossley, 1992b; Kurtz, 1992). Furthermore, it has also been argued that some subjects will deliberately "fail" a validity assessment because they object to being tested (Biklen, 1993).

Perhaps the best-known qualitative study of facilitated communication is that reported by Biklen (1990) in the Harvard Educational Review. The study was strongly criticized by Cummins and Prior (1992), and then their comments were rebutted by Biklen (1992a). Biklen (1990) reported on a study of 21 subjects who were attending the DEAL Communication Centre in Australia. The subjects were loosely described as having been labeled autistic or displaying autistic behaviours, and all were considered to be intellectually disabled before being introduced to facilitated communication. Interviews with the subjects were audio-recorded; the subjects' contributions were recorded by their typed words being read aloud by the facilitators. All subjects appeared to display advanced literacy skills. Little by way of precise detail is provided about the subjects' skill levels prior to being involved in the study, nor about the nature of the facilitation provided.

A second major qualitative study of facilitated communication is related to the introduction of the procedure by Biklen when he returned to Syracuse after his visit to Australia. The study is reported in several publications (Biklen, 1993; Biklen, Morton, Gold, Berrigan, & Swaminathan, 1992; Biklen et al., 1991; Biklen & Schubert, 1991). Although the numbers differ a little among the publications, the study involved a total of about 45 subjects studied over a period of 16 months. The focus in the reporting was on 21 subjects who were involved in facilitated communication for the full 16 months. All subjects were classified as autistic and their ages ranged from 3 years-10 months to 21 years. All publications describe the communications produced by the subjects during facilitated communication.

After six months all subjects except one (aged 4 years) displayed some literacy skills while using facilitated communication. None of the subjects had received much by way of formal training in literacy. It was hypothesized that they had developed these skills informally by watching television, and by reading newspapers, books, and magazines. Not only were the subjects literate, some were capable of producing elaborate prose, reflecting a high level of ability to deal with abstract concepts.

Attwood and Remington-Gurney (1992) provided details of a study conducted as part of a 12-month project conducted in Brisbane, Australia, and described as being designed to assess the viability of facilitated communication. The subject sample comprised 13 men and 7 women, all of whom had a severe communication impairment and had been assessed as being profoundly intellectually disabled. In regard to specific diagnosis, 11 had autism, 2 had cerebral palsy, 1 had Down's syndrome, and the remaining 6 had no specific diagnosis.

The subjects were all introduced to facilitated communication, and then their literacy skills were assessed via facilitated communication. The facilitator for all assessments was Remington-Gurney, who was trained at the DEAL Centre in Melbourne. The assessments involved examining the transcripts produced when the subjects conversed with the facilitator.

The assessments involved identifying four levels of conversation engaged in by the subjects. The scale used appears to have been developed by the authors. The levels ranged from copy typing (Level 1) through to open conversation (Level 4). Attwood and Remington-Gurney reported that on initial assessment, 17 of the 20 subjects produced responses at Level 4.

Attwood and Remington-Gurney went on to point out, however, that the communications of these subjects needed to be validated. To do this they used what they described as "content" validation. This involved examining the communication provided by the subject for material which was not known, or not expected, by the facilitator. By using this procedure, they identified 9 subjects whom they considered had validly communicated.

3.3. Other Methods of Evaluation

Alternative methods of evaluating the ability of individuals to validly communicate using facilitated communication were tried by a group of researchers in Denmark (Beck et al., 1992). In addition to the experimental methods described above, Beck et al., used two other approaches to validity assessment. First, they used electromyographical measurements of muscle activity, and electrogoniometric measurements of elbow movement to test whether the facilitator was initiating the movement of the subject toward the letters on an alphabet board. While the results of these methods of testing were not conclusive, they were consistent with the findings of the experimental testing which indicated that the subjects could not validly communicate using facilitated communication.

The second alternative approach used by Beck et al. was a procedure they called linguistic fingerprinting. They used this to compare and contrast the linguistic structure of communications produced during facilitation. If there are multiple subjects with one facilitator, and the facilitator does not influence any communication, the linguistic fingerprints should all be different. In contrast, however, the more similar the fingerprints, the more likely there is facilitator influence. The results of the Beck et al. testing using this approach were also consistent with their conclusions drawn from the experimental testing, that is, that the subjects could not validly communicate using facilitated communication.

Another validity assessment using linguistic structures is referred to in a report by the Ombudsman of Victoria regarding an investigation of a complaint about unjust dismissal because of allegations made via facilitated communication (Ombudsman Victoria, 1993). A male staff member of a community residential house for disable people was dismissed by the government after three women who lived at the house alleged, via facilitated communication, that he had drugged and raped them. All three women used the Canon Communicator when being facilitated. The man was charged by police but the case was not pursued after a simple validation test was carried out by the magistrate hearing the case. The magistrate asked the facilitator to turn away from the keyboard while one of the accusing women gave evidence. What emerged was not understood, and the staff member was discharged on the grounds that the evidence could not be heard.

Although discharged, the staff member was not reemployed by the government, so he took the case to the Ombudsman of Victoria. As part of his investigation, the Ombudsman commissioned a linguistic analysis of the three statements made by the women in their police interviews. The analysis was conducted at the University of Melbourne, and the conclusion was that there was a very high probability that all three statements were authored by the one person, the facilitator (Ombudsman Victoria, 1993).

A final study that used a form of linguistic analysis was that conducted by Wheeler et al. (1993). In addition to the use of experimental procedures, they analyzed the output from subjects who had the same facilitators. They found more-than-expected similarity in idiosyncratic word use, use of category responses rather than specific words, and occurrence of nonsense responses. These similarities were considered by Wheeler et al. to be indicative of facilitator influence.

4. A Theoretical Analysis of Facilitated Communication

The evaluations reviewed thus far have primarily focused on assessing the capacity of individuals to validly communicate using facilitated communication. Minimal research has been devoted to testing any of the theoretical elements of facilitated communication. A major stumbling block to such research is the total absence of a single comprehensive and coherent statement that articulates the basic theory of facilitated communication (Hudson, 1992; Jacobson et al., 1994; Minnes, 1992; Moore, Donovan, Hudson, Dykstra, & Lawrence, 1993; Ombudsman Victoria, 1993; Wolfensberger, 1992). Such a statement would specify (a) the objectives of the use of facilitated communication; (b) the theoretical bases of the practice of facilitated communication; and (c) the method of determining if the practice is achieving the objectives.

An examination of the major sources where such a comprehensive statement might be found is disappointing. Publications by the principal proponents of facilitated communication, such as Biklen and Crossley (and the DEAL Centre), tend to be essentially anecdotal and descriptive of case examples (e.g., Biklen, 1990, 1993; Crossley, 1991; DEAL Communication Centre,1992). When discussing what he calls the principles of facilitated communication, Biklen (1990) lists 7 "attitudinal dimensions" and 18 skills of facilitated communication. The list of attitudinal dimensions includes items such as being apologetic about the assessment process and assuming the subject's competence. The list of skills is a set of instructions about how to do it, rather than a rationale as to why it should be done.

4.1. Objectives of Facilitated Communication

A logical starting point in examining the theoretical basis of facilitated communication is to consider its objectives. Because of the absence of a comprehensive statement of theory, much needs to be inferred from the literature in regard to identifying the objectives of the procedure. However, several objectives can be identified.

1. A major objective is to teach selected individuals to point accurately. This is clear from the various definitions of facilitated communication offered, particularly by Crossley (e.g., 1992a). The need to be taught to point is predicated on the assumption that the individuals concerned have some form of motor impairment that prevents them from acquiring the skill to point in the way that most people do. A form of apraxia is often putated, particularly a global apraxia, which will also limit an individual's ability to voluntarily move the facial muscles necessary for speech.

2. A second objective of facilitated communication seems to be to provide access for the individual to an intact cognitive- and literacy system that previously had been inaccessible because of the motor problems. It is this function of facilitated communication that is considered to be the basis of the phenomenon of people previously thought to be severely intellectually disabled and noncommunicative suddenly being able to generate complex written language (Biklen, 1993).

3. A third objective of facilitated communication appears to be to provide emotional support for people with disabilities. This need for support is seen to exist in a context of a history of failure and general lack of acceptance. The close physical contact afforded by facilitated communication, combined with strong expectations of success on behalf of the facilitator, are considered to provide the emotional support necessary for the individual with the disability to try and to succeed in generating functional

communications. Furthermore, this element of emotional support is seen by proponents of facilitated communication as being crucial in validity assessments. It is argued that the lack of emotional support allegedly inherent in any quantitative validity testing will prevent the individual from being able to respond, and hence will invalidate the assessment (Crossley, 1992c; Kurtz, 1992).

4. A fourth objective of facilitated communication that can be inferred from the literature is to enable individuals to overcome forms of specific language disabilities. It appears to be accepted that people with disabilities are highly susceptible to aphasic-type conditions, particularly that of having "word-finding problems" (Crossley, 1992a; Kurtz, 1992). In facilitated communication, the facilitator is able to use contextual cues to prompt the person to find the appropriate words. The potential existence of word-finding problems has been argued as a reason for not using validation testing that screens the facilitator from the question and requires one-word or short-answer responses from the disabled person. It is argued that without knowledge of the context, the facilitator cannot effectively facilitate (Remington-Gurney, 1992).

Each of these objectives is reasonable as it stands. A critical point, however, is that the disability service system already has well-developed and empirically based methods for achieving each of these objectives. With regard to the first objective of teaching an individual to point, the developmental psychology, special education, occupational therapy, and physical therapy fields of study are replete with literature that explicates well-established procedures to assist an individual to develop fine motor skills such as pointing (Bernstein, Ziarnik, Rudrud, & Czajkowski, 1981; Cole & Chan, 1990; Crosby, 1980; Fredericks, 1980). A properly developed instructional program involving progressive reduction of physical prompts can be used to teach skills that are much more complex than the pointing response necessary to activate a key on a computer or a Canon Communicator. Facilitated communication is simply not needed to teach somebody to point.

The second objective of providing access for a disabled person to an intact cognitive and literacy system is important. There are many people who have high-level cognitive skills but because of physical impairments associated with conditions such as cerebral palsy are not able to communicate using speech. The technology associated with the field of alternative and augmentative communication is well-developed, and many options are available. In reality, a person only has to be able to reliably control one muscle and hence will have the ability to operate a switch. Reliable control of a switch indicates possession of the ability to communicate independently. Facilitated communication is simply not necessary to help a disabled person access an intact cognitive- and literacy system.

The third objective of providing emotional support for the disabled person is certainly laudable as it stands. Nobody would argue this point. The critical issue has to do with how this support is provided. There are two parts to the provision of emotional support. The first has to do with adopting a positive set of expectations about the capacity of the person with the disability, and all workers in the disability field should have such an attitude. It would also be expected that this attitude should be realistic for the disabled person concerned. The second part of the provision of emotional support has to do with the manner in which it is provided. With facilitated communication, the holding of the hand doing the pointing appears to be a generic component. Clearly this is not necessary. Equivalent emotional support can be provided by physical contact with any other part of the person (e.g., a hug), or simply by supportive and encouraging comments.

The final objective of overcoming the effects of specific language disabilities, such as word finding problems, could be important if it were thought that such conditions could be assessed as reliably existing for individuals using facilitated communication. The literature on word-finding problems (German, 1992; Nippold, 1992; Snyder & Godley, 1992) highlights the difficulties of assessment in this area. The empirical studies reviewed earlier suggest that, at least for the clients involved in those studies, the existence of word-finding problems could not be considered to be a source of invalidity for the findings. In some of these studies (Hudson et al., 1993; Moore, Donovan, Hudson, Dykstra, & Lawrence, 1993; Wheeler et al., 1993) the existence of this condition could be precluded because under at least some conditions the subjects appeared to answer the questions asked. If word finding was a genuine problem, the subjects could not have been able to answer questions in any of the conditions. Word-finding problems could also not have invalidated those studies using the message-passing methodology (Szempruch & Jacobson, 1992; Moore, Donovan, & Hudson, 1993). Under these conditions the facilitator was free to use standard facilitation procedures, including any cuing suggested by the context of the conversation, to elicit accurate answers from the disabled person.

4.2. Theoretical Bases of the Practice of Facilitated Communication

An important beginning point in addressing the theory underlying facilitated communication is to note that it is used with people with a wide variety of disabilities. It began in Australia at St. Nicholas Hospital and was used primarily with people who had cerebral palsy. During the 1980s, it came to be used with people who had chromosomal disorders such as Down's syndrome, people with autism, people with Rett syndrome, and people with acquired brain injury. The use of the procedure with such a variety of disabling conditions indicates that the origins of the theory are not disability-specific. The basis of a theory of facilitated communication cannot therefore be rooted in the etiology or symptomatology of a particular disability, but rather must be more general in nature.

In recent years, particularly in the United States, facilitated communication seems to have been used most extensively with people with autism. This use in the autism field has been associated with attempts to define autism as a movement disorder (Attwood, 1992). However, such attempts to relate autism to some form of general apraxia theory are discounted by Jacobson and Mulick (1992) and Jacobson et al. (1994) as not being consistent with data collected regarding the relationship between cognitive-, language-, and motor abilities. The search for the theoretical genesis of facilitated communication must begin somewhere other than a consideration of the etiology of the disability of the person using it.

Perhaps the most essential component of facilitated communication is the physical assistance provided to the disabled person by the facilitator. The physical assistance is considered to be different from the coactive physical prompting usually used in teaching a motor skill (Crossley, 1992a). With physical prompting the teacher begins by leading the student through the movement. In facilitated communication it is the student who does the leading. The facilitators are supposed to help disabled people execute their intentions of pointing to a particular letter or word. The assistance may take several forms, and will vary according to putated motor problems of the person. These problems include the following (Crossley, 1991, 1992a).

1. Poor eye-hand coordination
2. Low muscle tone
3. High muscle tone
4. Index finger isolation and extension problems
5. Perseveration
6. Using both hands for a task requiring one
7. Tremor
8. Radial/ulnar muscle instability
9. Initiation problems
10. Impulsivity
11. Proximal instability

The precise nature of the facilitation is dependent upon the presence of one or more of these problems. The facilitated communication literature is, however, totally silent on the reliable and valid assessment of these problems. They are usually discussed under the umbrella term of apraxia (Biklen, 1993). It is interesting to note that individuals placed on facilitated communication rarely, if ever, have apraxia diagnosed by an appropriately qualified professional such as a neurologist or neuropsychologist.

A stated intent of facilitated communication is that the physical assistance will be progressively faded until the person can communicate independently (Crossley, 1991, 1992b). The usual path to fading would be to move from assistance on the hand, to the wrist, to the forearm, and finally to the shoulder. When the assistance is to the shoulder it is usually seen only as providing emotional support. The total duration of withdrawal of all physical contact is seen as potentially several years. Crossley (1992c) cites Haney (1988) as saying that 6 years is the time suggested for basic competence to be achieved in communication-aid use. This may be the case for learning to master the use of complex aids. Demonstrable progress in skill acquisition should be observable in much shorter time frames than this. It is interesting to note that some of the subjects in the Moore, Donovan, Hudson, Dykstra, and Lawrence (1993) study had been on facilitated communication for 33 months but still required full physical assistance to be able to respond. There are anecdotal references in the facilitated communication literature to individuals who now type independently (Biklen, 1993; Crossley, 1992a), but there is an absence of detailed information about their initial skill levels and the steps involved in fading the assistance.

For some disabled people, facilitated communication is seen as a mechanism that enables them to assess an intact literacy system. People who have previously been thought to have been severely intellectually disabled and noncommunicative are suddenly able to generate sophisticated communications. This sudden ability to generate complex written language is seen to be particularly surprising for those individuals who have had minimal educational opportunities (Cummins & Prior, 1992). The unexpected literacy skills are explained in terms of incidental learning while watching television or viewing street signs (Biklen, 1993; Crossley, 1991). A major gap in the facilitated communication literature is the provision of convincing evidence that any persons, particularly those from an educationally impoverished background, can incidentally develop such literacy skills.

A final point in connection to the theory of facilitated communication has to do with the relationship between what is communicated via facilitated communication and what is communicated via other means. Several researchers have commented on a lack of congruence between these sources. For example, Hudson et al. (1993) and Moore, Donovan, and Hudson (1993) noted that facilitated communications about the subject feeling uncomfortable or tense were totally inconsistent with the nonverbal behaviour exhibited by the subjects. The subjects, in fact, looked to be quite relaxed, smiled often, and appeared to be very keen to cooperate with completion of the required tasks. Perhaps the most interesting contrast is between that which is spoken and that which is produced via facilitation. It is not uncommon for facilitators to suggest that an individual's verbal communication should be disregarded since the facilitated communication was the valid one (e.g., Szempruch & Jacobson, 1993). Several studies have found that subjects could verbally provide the answer to a question but were unable to do so through facilitation (Moore, Donovan, & Hudson, 1993; Szempruch & Jacobson, 1993). The issue of lack of congruence between communications which are facilitated and those which are not is one that the facilitated communication literature has not dealt with adequately. What is the theoretical rationale for accepting what a person types with facilitation ahead of what that person says? This question is particularly pertinent when it is considered that there is strong evidence that the facilitator can influence the typing.

4.3. Method of Determining Whether the Practice Is Achieving the Objectives

The lack of a comprehensive and cohesive statement about the objectives and underlying theory of facilitated communication does not provide a sound basis for specifying procedures to determine whether the objectives of facilitated communication are being achieved. In particular, there is an absence of a theoretically driven method of determining the ability to validly communicate using the procedure.

Proponents of facilitated communication typically object to the use of the various experimental procedures used in the studies discussed earlier. The objections are usually based on concerns such as the lack of trust and confidence inherent in any form of testing, or about the methodology being inappropriate for subjects with specific disabilities such as word-finding problems.

Despite the objections to experimental assessment articulated by proponents of facilitated communication, there is usually some reference in their articles to the issue of validation of the ability of individuals to communicate using the procedure. The preferred validation procedures are qualitative in nature and based on the observation of the subject while using facilitated communication in natural settings. Biklen and his colleagues (Biklen, 1990, 1992a, 1993; Biklen et al., 1992) encourage the use of seven unobtrusive indicators which, they argue, provide as much proof of ability to communicate as the experimental methods. These are as follows:

1. Some subjects make typographical errors that are unique to them, even with different facilitators.
2. Some subjects produce phonetic and inventive spelling errors that are unique to them.
3. For some subjects, the style, speed, and accuracy of fine motor control in pointing to letters is consistent across facilitators.
4. Some subjects type information that is unknown to the facilitator.
5. Some subjects type words, phrases, or sentences that are unusual and would not be expected from facilitators.
6. Some subjects are able to reveal their personalities through facilitation.
7. Some subjects achieve independence in typing.

The first three statements are general, for which no empirical supporting evidence is provided. In fact, the evidence available regarding consistencies across facilitator–subject pairs is that there is more likely to be consistency across facilitators working with the same client, suggesting facilitator influence (Beck et al., 1992; Ombudsman Victoria, 1993; Wheeler et al., 1993).

Statements 4 and 5 are assertions that are very difficult to empirically test. This issue of the production of information unknown to the facilitators is complicated by the fact that while most of the experimental studies have demonstrated quite clearly that facilitator influence can be substantial, it has to be assumed that the influence is totally unintentional. Von Tetzchner (1992) suggested that a phenomenon called automatic writing may be a plausible explanation for this unintentional influence. He argued that some sort of self-induced hypnotic trance may enable the facilitator to influence the communication of the subject without being consciously aware of it.

Statement 6 refers to the subjects' personalities. There is no doubt that all subjects have their own individual personalities. The critical question is whether the personality being exposed by the use of faciltated communication is in fact the subject's own, or is it one being imposed by the facilitator?

The final statement about moving from a need for the use of facilitated communication to being able to communicate independently is a very important one. The literature supporting facilitated communication (e.g., Biklen, 1993; Crossley, 1992c) makes occasional references to subjects who have become independent, but very little is actually documented about issues such as what skills they had to begin with and how long it took them to become totally independent.

The critical comments made regarding Biklen's seven unobtrusive indicators are not meant to suggest that qualitative information plays no part in the validation process. Indeed, Hudson (1992) argued that when assessing an individual's ability to communicate using facilitated communication both quantitative (experimental) and qualitative procedures ought to be used. He argued that the task is to look for convergence of the quantitative and qualitative evidence.

Returning to Biklen's seven indicators, the concern is that qualitative information by itself is simply not adequate to provide conclusive evidence about an individual's ability (Cummins & Prior, 1992). This situation has been brought about by the fact that facilitators do influence the communications of the subjects. What needs to be determined is what proportion, if any, of facilitated communication is actually emanating from the subject.

5. Facilitators and Influence in Facilitated Communication

The fact that facilitators influence the communications of their subjects does not seem to be an issue about which there is disagreement. The experimental studies discussed earlier clearly demonstrate the existence of such influence, and its existence is accepted by the proponents of facilitated communication. The literature is strangely silent in regard to the motivation for such influence, but those who do address it consider it to be unintentional (Eberlin et al., 1993; Wheeler et al., 1993).

Almost all of the experimental studies discussed earlier led to conclusions that the subjects could not validly communicate using facilitated communication. The only logical conclusion that can be drawn from this is that for the subject–facilitator pairs involved in these studies, all of the communication is actually emanating from the facilitator. It is difficult to explain how this could happen. Maybe the mode of training facilitators, with its emphasis on belief in the subject's ability (e.g., Kurtz, 1992), is a critical element. Perhaps the automatic writing phenomenon referred to by Von Tetzchner (1992) is relevant. Wolfensberger (1992), perhaps a little unkindly and certainly without any supporting evidence, stated that facilitated communication attracts or recruits hysteroid personalities into the facilitation role. The fact of the matter is, however, that a large number of facilitators are unwittingly influencing their subjects. Furthermore, if we accept the data that is in to date, very little facilitated communication involves communication that emanates from the disabled person.

6. Ethical Issues Associated with the Use of Facilitated Communication

On the face of it, facilitated communication offers hope to people with communication impairments. Individuals who previously were not able to indicate their needs and wishes could use the method to increase their own contribution to decision making about their lives. This would, in turn, greatly enhance their quality of life. It is not surprising, therefore, that those who have questioned the usefulness of facilitated communication have met with considerable resistance from its proponents. The usefulness of facilitated communication must, however, rest upon its demonstrated validity.

The reviewed results of the experimental evaluations of the ability of individuals to communicate using facilitated communication have not shown that the subjects can validly communicate while using the method. Furthermore, the studies show that facilitators are very likely to exert influence on a subject's attempt to communicate during its use. Although this influence appears to be totally unintentional, there must be serious ethical concerns about the use of facilitated communication. These concerns can be conceptualized at various levels.

First, there must be a fundamental concern about the notion of attributing a communication as originating from another person when this, in fact, is not the case. All human beings would see it as a right that others do not put words into their mouths. Most human beings have the cognitive and communication skills necessary to dispute what they are alleged to have said. People with intellectual disabilities do not usually have these skills, and hence the erroneous attribution of a communication is a particular problem in their case. It is encumbent upon service providers to provide maximum safeguards in regard to this issue.

A second ethical concern relates to the issue of providing the best possible service to people with disabilities. It is imperative that service providers make available to their clients those programs that have empirically been shown to be effective in meeting their needs. Facilitated communication is not well-supported empirically or theoretically, and as such, ought to be closely scrutinized by service providers before selection for adoption with a particular client.

The final ethical concern relates to the propensity for users of facilitated communication to become involved in disputes. These disputes may be about matters that are relatively minor, for example, which visitors the person will have, or they may be very serious and involve issues such as allegations of sexual abuse. All disputes generate stress and should be avoided if at all possible. If programs other than facilitated communication can be used to achieve a particular objective, ethical concerns would suggest that those programs ought to be used as a first preference.

7. Current Developments in Australia

Throughout the 1980s, the State Government of Victoria paid less attention to the uses and abuses of facilitated communication than perhaps it should have. In 1989 it did accept a recommendation of the Intellectual Disability Review Panel (1989) that validity testing ought to be conducted in dispute situations, and that the protocol developed by the IDRP should be used in such testing.

Following the much publicized Carla (Hudson et al., 1993) and Mr. W. (Ombudsman Victoria, 1993) cases, the government took two proactive steps to prevent further controversy developing in the use of facilitated communication. First, the government developed a set of policy guidelines for the selection of a communication program for any person who had a severe communication impairment (Health and Community Services Victoria, 1993a). The proper implementation of these guidelines will ensure that clients with a communication impairment will have the most appropriate communication program made available to them. In this context, "most appropriate" means a program which has empirically been demonstrated to be appropriate to that client's needs.

Second, the government has conducted a review into the management practices of the DEAL Communication Centre (Health and Community Services Victoria, 1993b). The review essentially concluded that the case management practices of DEAL were well-short of a desired standard. It specified that particular attention needed to be paid to the use of appropriately qualified staff in the assessment of clients with communication impairments. Government funding for DEAL was stopped in September 1993.

8. Conclusions

In a relatively short time period the phenomenon of facilitated communication has had a major impact on the field of disability. Much of this impact has unfortunately been associated with serious disputes about important issues in the lives of the disabled people. The use of facilitated communication has clearly been controversial.

This review has summarized the history of the development and spread of facilitated communication. It has also examined the research into the validity of its use. The extensive set of experimental studies have found little, if any, evidence of any individual's ability to validly communicate using facilitated communication, but did find evidence of pervasive influence exerted by the facilitators. It has been argued that the qualitative studies have not produced convincing evidence regarding the validity issue. A theoretical analysis of facilitated communication has been attempted, but this has been rendered difficult by an absence of a comprehensive and cohesive statement about its theoretical underpinnings. Finally, the ethical issues associated with the use of facilitated communication were discussed.

The general picture that has emerged is that facilitated communication does not have a sound theoretical base, and that the experimental data do not support the view that disabled persons can use it to validly communicate their wishes and opinions. There is no evidence that facilitated communication constitutes an advance in clinical child psychology.

References

Attwood, T. (1992). Movement disorders and autism: A rationale for the use of facilitated communication. *Communication Disorders, 26* (3), 27–29.

Attwood, T., & Remington-Gurney, J. (1992). Assessment of literacy skill using facilitated communication. In C. E. van Kraayenoord (Ed.), *A survey of adult literacy provision for people with intellectual disabilities* (pp. 169–196). Brisbane: Schonell Special Education Research Centre, The University of Queensland.

Autism Research Institute (1992a). Facilitated Communication: Courts say "no." *Autism Research Review International, 6* (3), 1 and 7.

Autism Research Institute (1992b). Facilitated Communication: What's going on? *Autism Research Review International, 6* (4), 1–2.

Autism Research Institute (1993). FC under siege. *Autism Research Review International, 7* (1), 2 and 7.

Beck, B., Warburg, M., Parving, A., Jansen, E., Arendt-Nielsen, L., Elbro, C., & Klewe, L. (1992) *The Copenhagen investigation of assisted communication between severely handicapped persons and their assistants.* Paper presented at the 9th World Congress of the International Association for the Scientific Study of Mental Deficiency, Broadbeach, Queensland.

Bernstein, G., Ziarnik, J., Rudrud, E., & Czajkowski, L. (1981). *Behavioral habilitation through proactive programming.* Baltimore, MD: Brookes.

Beukelman, D., & Mirenda, P. (1992). *Augmentative and alternative communication: Management of severe communication disorders in children and adults.* Baltimore, MD: Brookes.

Biklen, D. (1990). Communication unbound: Autism and praxis. *Harvard Educational Review, 60,* 291–314.

Biklen, D. (1992a). Autism orthodoxy versus free speech: A reply to Cummins and Prior. *Harvard Educational Review, 62,* 242–256.

Biklen, D. (1992b). Facilitated communication: Biklen responds. *American Journal of Speech-Language Pathology, 1,* 21–22.

Biklen, D. (1993). *Communication unbound: How facilitated communication is challenging traditional views of autism and ability/disability.* New York: Teachers College Press.

Biklen, D., Morton, M., Gold, D., Berrigan, C., & Swaminathan, S. (1992). Facilitated communication: Implications for individuals with autism. *Topics in Language Disorders,12* (4), 1–28.

Biklen, D., Morton, M., Saha, S., Duncan, J., Gold, D., Hardardottir, M., Karna, E., O'Conner, S., & Rao, S. (1991). "I AMN NOT A UTISTIVC ON THJE TYP" ("I'm not autistic on the typewriter") *Disability, Handicap, & Society,* 6, 161–180.

Biklen, D., & Schubert, A. (1991). New words: The communication of students with autism. *Remedial and Special Education,* 12 (6), 46–57.

Bligh, S., & Kupperman, P. (in press). Brief report: Facilitated communication evaluation procedure accepted in court case. *Journal of Autism and Developmental Disorders, 23,*

Calculator, S. (1992a). Perhaps the emperor has clothes after all: A response to Biklen. *American Journal of Speech-Language Pathology,* 1, 18–20.

Calculator, S. (1992b). Facilitated communication: Calculator responds. *American Journal of Speech-Language Pathology,* 1, 23–24.

Calculator, S., & Singer, K. (1992). Letter to the editor: Preliminary validation of facilitated communication. *Topics in Language Disorders,* 13 (1), ix–xvi.

Cole, P., & Chan, L. (1990). *Methods and strategies for special education.* Sydney: Prentice-Hall.

College of Speech Therapists. (1989). *Augmentative and Alternative Communication (AAC): Position paper.* London: Author.

Crosby, K. (1980). Implementing the developmental model. In J. Gardner, L. Long, R. Nichols, & D. Iagulli (Eds.), *Program issues in developmental disabilities* (pp. 63–85). Baltimore, MD: Brookes.

Crossley, R. (1991). Communication training involving facilitated communication. *Augmentative Communication,* 9, (2), 19–22.

Crossley, R. (1992a). Communication training involving facilitated communication. In DEAL Communication Centre, *Facilitated communication training* (pp. 1–9). Melbourne: DEAL Communication Centre.

Crossley, R. (1992b). Who said that? In Deal Communication Centre, *Facilitated communication training* (pp. 42–54). Melbourne: DEAL Communication Centre.

Crossley, R. (1992c). Reducing support: Increasing independence. In Deal Communication Centre, *Facilitated communication training* (pp. 28–35). Melbourne: DEAL Communication Centre.

Crossley, R. (1993). Facilitated Communication: Some further thoughts. *Communicating Together,* 11 (1), 14–16.

Crossley, R., & McDonald, A. (1980) *Annie's coming out.* Melbourne: Penguin.

Cummins, R., & Bancroft, H. (1981). *Supplementary report to the Report of the Committee of Inquiry to investigate claims about children at St. Nicholas Hospital.* Melbourne: Authors.

Cummins, B., & Prior, M. (1992). Autism and assisted communication: A reply to Biklen. *Harvard Educational Review,* 62, 228–241.

DEAL Communication Centre. (1992) *Facilitated communication training.* Melbourne: Author.

Dunn, L., & Dunn, L. (1981). *Manual for forms L and M for the Peabody Picture Vocabulary Test-Revised.* Circle Pines, MS: American Guidance Service.

Eberlin, M. McConnachie, G., Ibel, S., & Volpe, T. (1993). Facilitated Communication: A failure to replicate the phenomenon. *Journal of Autism and Developmental Disorders,* 23, 507–530.

Eisen, P. (1980). *Report of the Committee of Inquiry to investigate claims about children at St. Nicholas Hospital.* Melbourne: Government Printer.

Fredericks, H. (1980). *A data-based classroom for the moderately and severely handicapped* (4th ed.). Monmouth: Instructional Development Corporation.

German, D. (1992). Word-finding intervention for children and adolescents. *Topics in Language Disorders, 13* (1), 33–50.

Haney, C. (1988). Communication device today, competency tomorrow: Are we being realistic in our observations? *Assistive Device News, 2,* 5–6.

Health and Community Services. (1993a). *IDS policy and guidelines: Client's communication needs.* Melbourne: Author.

Health and Community Services. (1993b). *Review of the Dignity, Education and Language Program (DEAL).* Melbourne: Author.

Hudson, A. (1992). Assessing the validity of facilitated communication. *The Australian Educational and Developmental Psychologist, 9,* (2), 24–29.

Hudson, A. (1993). Assessing "Carla." *Communicating Together, 11* (4), 13–14.

Hudson, A., Melita, B., & Arnold, N. (1993). Brief report. A case study assessing the validity of facilitated communication. *Journal of Autism and Developmental Disorders, 23* (1), 165–173.

Intellectual Disability Review Panel (1989). *Report to the Director General on the reliability and validity of assisted communication.* Melbourne: Author.

Intellectually Disabled Persons' Services Act (1986). State of Victoria, Australia.

Interdisciplinary Working Party on Issues in Severe Communication Impairment. (1988). *DEAL Communication Centre operations: A statement of concern.* Melbourne: Author.

Jacobson, J., and Mulick, J. (1992). Speak for yourself, or . . . I can't quite put my finger on it! *Psychology in Mental Retardation and Developmental Disabilities, 17* (3), 3–7.

Jacobson, J., Eberlin, M., Mulick, J., Schwartz, A., Szempruch, J., & Wheeler, D. (1994). Autism, and facilitated communication: Future directions. In J. Matson (Ed.), *Autism: Etiology, assessment, and intervention* (pp. 59–83). Pacific Grove, CA: Brooks/Cole.

Kurtz, A. (1992). Testing for validity. *New England Newsletter of Facilitated Communication, 1* (1), 6–8.

Minnes, P. (1992). Facilitated communication: An overview and directions for research. *Journal on Developmental Disabilities, 1* (21), 57–67.

Moore, S., Donovan, B., Hudson, A., Dykstra, J., & Lawrence, J. (1993). Brief report: Evaluation of eight case studies of facilitated communication. *Journal of Autism and Developmental Disorders, 23,* 531–540.

Moore, S., Donovan, B., & Hudson, A. (1993). Brief report: Facilitator-suggested conversational evaluation of facilitated communication. *Journal of Autism and Developmental Disorders, 23,* 541–552.

Nippold, M. (1992). The nature of normal and disordered word finding in children and adolescents. *Topics in Language Disorders, 13* (1), 1–14.

Ombudsman Victoria. (1993). *Report on the investigation of a complaint of unjust dismissal because of allegations made by facilitated communication.* Melbourne: Author.

Pinto, P. (1984). Judge refuses plea for disable woman. *The Age,* 24 February, p. 3.

Prior, M., & Cummins, R. (1992). Questions about facilitated communication. *Journal of Autism and Developmental Disorders, 22,* 331–338.

Remington-Gurney, J. (1992). *Facilitated communication: A discussion of issues pertinent to validation of the technique.* Manuscript submitted for publication.

Rimland, B. (1992). Facilitated communication, now the bad news. *Autism Research Review International, 6* (1), 3.

Schubert, A. (1991) *Facilitated communication resource guide.* Brookline, MA: Adrianna Foundation.

Smith, M., & Belcher, R. (1993). Brief report: Facilitated communication with adults with autism. *Journal of Autism and Developmental Disorders, 23,* 175–183.

Snyder, L., & Godley, D. (1992). Assessment of word finding problems in children and adolescents. *Topics in Language Disorders, 13* (1), 15–32.

Szempruch, J., & Jacobson, J. (1993). *Evaluation process for facilitated communication with developmentally disabled individuals. Research in Developmental Disabilities, 14,* 253–264.

Thorndike, R., Hagen, E., & Sattler, J. (1986). *The Stanford–Binet Intelligence Scale Fourth Edition.* Chicago, IL: Riverside.

Wallace v. Health Commission of Victoria. (December, 1984). Supreme Court of Victoria. (No. 9859), ss. 13, 17.

Von Tetzchner, S. (1992). Facilitation and facilitators. *Communicating Together, 10* (4), 8–11.

Wheeler, D., Jacobson, J., Paglieri, R., & Schwartz, A. (1993). An experimental assessment of facilitated communication. *Mental Retardation, 31,* 49–60.

Wolfensberger, W. (1992). The facilitated communication craze: The cold fusion of human services. *Training Institute Publication Series, 12* (2–3), 39–46.

6

The Psychological Sequelae of Child Sexual Abuse

Vicky V. Wolfe and Jo-Ann Birt

1. Introduction

Traditionally, child psychopathology research has been focused on discrete symptomatology leading to diagnosable disorders or behavioral/emotional syndromes. For example, psychiatric nosologies for children and adolescents have typically focused on symptom constellations such as depression, anxiety, and conduct disorders. As research has progressed in these areas, etiological studies have contributed to a growing realization that many major childhood problems have their origins in dysfunctional environmental circumstances. For instance, research with conduct-problem children has identified numerous family processes that have functional relationships with externalizing forms of behavior problems (e.g., inconsistent consequences for positive and negative behaviors).

Recognizing the powerful influence of environmental circumstances, many researchers have turned their attention to pronounced and identifiable areas of environmental influence such as trauma and abuse. Cicchetti (1987) has suggested that childhood maltreatment be conceived of as *relational psychopathology*, resulting from dysfunction in the parent–child–environment transactional system. In fact, Cicchetti suggests the following:

> We believe that other than the pervasive developmental disorders and the organic forms of mental retardation, the vast majority of the disorders of the early years of life can best be characterized as transactional–relational pathologies and not as disorders arising solely within the child. (p. 840)

VICKY V. WOLFE AND JO-ANN BIRT • Department of Psychology, Children's Hospital of Western Ontario, London, Ontario N6A 2L2.

Advances in Clinical Child Psychology, Volume 17, edited by Thomas H. Ollendick and Ronald J. Prinz. Plenum Press, New York, 1995.

In recent years there has been a growing clinical and research emphasis on aspects of childhood that are seen as disruptive, such as sexual abuse, physical abuse, exposure to family violence, parental pathology, divorce, and acute and chronic illness. The new question is "What are the effects of these events during childhood and do these childhood events have long-term implications?" There is a growing realization that these events do not have uniform effects and numerous variables converge to determine the impact of stressful and traumatic childhood experiences. With this there is a growing body of literature on factors that relate to individual differences among children exposed to various stressful life events, such as developmental status, coping styles, premorbid adjustment, family functioning, and community support/stressor variables. This new line of thinking places less emphasis on childhood pathology and greater emphasis on viewing behavioral and emotional adjustment as a predictable outcome given certain child and environmental circumstances. Further, by emphasizing the causal aspects of child-adjustment difficulties, primary and secondary prevention strategies are better identified, with less reliance within the clinical world on tertiary interventions.

The purpose of this chapter is to examine individual differences in response to childhood sexual abuse, and compare commonalities of this population with other groups of children who have been known to experience other forms of stress and trauma. Current conceptual and diagnostic models for defining and understanding children's stress and trauma will be evaluated, with suggestions for improvements, particularly with regard to the stress and trauma experienced by sexually abused children.

2. Conceptual Model for Understanding Sexual Abuse Sequelae

V. Wolfe and D. Wolfe (1988) developed a conceptual model for predicting children's adjustment subsequent to the initiation of sexually abusive behavior. The premise behind the model was that children's responses to sexual abuse would be quite varied, reflecting individual differences in response to the abuse as well as numerous factors thought to attenuate or exacerbate sequelae. Using a grid format, mediators of impact (abuse variables, child characteristics, family functioning, and community stress/support factors) were seen as intertwined, and impact, evolving across the various phases the child encounters as a result of the abuse and disclosure (abuse, disclosure crisis, and recovery and readjustment phase). Thus, in order to predict and understand a child's response to the sexual abuse, one would need to consider the abuse; the child's current cognitive and social development and behavioral adjustment; family variables such as family composition, resources, marital relationships, and parent-child relations; and community variables such as reactions to disclosure, community attitudes towards victims and perpetrators, and the availability of resources to deal with the problems. The importance of each of these variables will differ depending upon the point at which the child presents: the time during which the abuse is occurring (e.g., child's response to the abuse, child's coping strategies for dealing with the abuse); the disclosure crisis (e.g., potential family disruption, family upset, stressful contacts with community agents, potential involvement with legal system); and the recovery and readjustment phase (e.g., ongoing contact with perpetrator, therapeutic involvement, family support, coping and attributional styles, and developing cognitive capacities such as cause–effect relationships, social cognition, moral reasoning).

At the time the model was first articulated, very little research was available to confirm its basic premises. However, over the past 5 years, the field has blossomed such that data are now available for many of the pieces of the grid. In the following section, literature is reviewed regarding the impact of child sexual abuse, particularly with regard to these mediating variables. A perusal of the literature on the impact of child sexual abuse reveals several extant themes: the effects of various abuse factors or conditions that contribute to different forms of sequelae; differential effects for preschool, latency-age, and adolescent victims; differential effects for girls and boys; and short-term and long-term effects.

Methodological variations among the studies limit the generalizability of some of the findings. Many of the studies rely on samples of clinic-referred sexually abused children, rather than more representative samples of sexually abused children, such as those presenting to child-protective service agencies. Comparison groups vary across studies, some relying on standardization samples, others community controls, and others using samples of children who have experienced other family problems, such as physical abuse. Finally, children are assessed at various points past disclosure, some relatively soon after disclosure, while others include children at any point postdisclosure.

3. Impact of Abuse: Global Adjustment Problems

In the following sections, literature on the impact of sexual abuse will be reviewed, beginning with the literature addressing global functioning followed by literature addressing symptoms thought to relate specifically to the abuse. Within each domain, comparisons to the population in general will be considered first, followed by comparisons to other groups, such as clinic samples and samples of children mistreated or traumatized in other ways (e.g., neglect, physical abuse).

3.1. Common Problem Areas for Sexually Abused Children

Several studies have used the Child Behavior Checklist (CBCL; Achenbach & Edelbrock, 1983) as a method of assessing children's post-sexual abuse adjustment. The CBCL is popular in this regard for several reasons. First, the measure is appropriate for all age groups and for boys and girls. Second, the items span most behavioral and emotional problems commonly identified for children and adolescents. Third, variations of the measure allow for parent-, teacher-, and youth-reports; however, the parent-report version is the most commonly used with this population. Fourth, well-established norms for both sexes and three age groups (preschool, school-age and adolescent) readily allow for appropriate age and sex comparisons.

Not surprisingly, the percentage of children who fall within the clinical range for the CBCL (t score > 70) varies according to the population from which the sample was recruited. V. Wolfe, Gentile, and D. Wolfe (1989) recruited a sample of sexually abused children, ages 7 to 16, from a child-protective service agency in an attempt to obtain a sample representative of sexually abused children as a whole (at least with regard to those who had disclosed their abuse): 23% fell in the clinical range for the Social Competence scale, 29% for the Internalizing scale, and 32% for the Externalizing scale. However, Friedrich, Urquiza, and Beilke (1986), drawing from a broad clinical sample, ages 4 to 12, found that 35% of males and 46% of females fell in the clinical range for the Internalizing scale, and 36% of males and 39% of females were in the clinical range for the Externalizing Scale. When the sample was broken down into 4- to 5-year-olds and 6- to 12-year-olds, the percentages of clinically elevated scores showed an interesting pattern. For the Internalizing scale, more preschool children fell in the clinical range (51%) as compared to school-age children (36%); for the Externalizing scale, more school-age children fell in the clinical range (44%) as compared to the preschool children (31%). Sirles and Smith (September, 1990) report similar percentages across age groups to those reported by Friedrich et al. (1986), with the exception that in their sample, younger children were consistently more symptomatic than older children for both internalizing and externalizing problems. Drawing from a clinic population of preschool, school-age, and adolescent sexual abuse victims, the following percentages fell within the clinical range: for the Internalizing scale, 45% of preschoolers, 39% of school-age children, and 21% of adolescents; for the Externalizing scale, 35% of preschoolers, 30% of school-age children, and 5.3% of adolescents.

Several studies have demonstrated significant differences between abused children and either the CBCL nonclinic, standardization sample (Cohen and Mannarino, 1988) or matched community controls (Einbender & Friedrich, 1989; Inderbitzen-Pisaruk, Shawchuck, & Hoier, 1992). However, when compared to CBCL clinical norms, Cohen and Mannarino (1988) found that their sexually abused sample (N = 24; referred from a rape crisis center) was less symptomatic on most scales, and was on no scale more symptomatic.

In their study with the CBCL, Tong, Oates, and McDowell (1987) contacted the parents of children who had been referred to a sexual-assault center on average 2½ years prior. Parents and teachers completed respective CBCL's and children completed the Youth Self Report (Achenbach, 1991). CBCL's and YSR's were completed for a matched sample. Parent- and teacher-completed CBCL's revealed significantly higher levels of internalizing and externalizing symptoms for the sexually abused children. From the YSR, sexually abused adolescents endorsed significantly higher levels of internalizing symptoms. Compared to the nonclinic CBCL standardization sample, 64% of the abused children fell in the clinical range for the parent-report version, 36% of the abused children fell in the clinical range for the teacher-report version, and 13% fell in the clinical range for the youth-report version.

Several other strategies have been used to assess global adjustment among sexually abused children and adolescents. Basta and Peterson (1990) reported the use of the Personality Inventory for Children (Porter & Cattell, 1975; parent-report questionnaire) and the Children's Personality Questionnaire (Lachar, Gdowski, & Snyder, 1984; child-report questionnaire) with a sample of sexually abused and nonabused children ages 6 to 10. Unlike the CBCL, which assesses behavior problems, these questionnaires were designed to assess normal personality variation. For the child-report measure, the CPQ, 11 of the 18 scales revealed significant differences in the negative direction. Sexually abused children scored lower on ego-strength, enthusiasm, social boldness, extroversion, and tough poise; they scored higher on anxiety, guilt proneness, loner tendencies, superego-strength, ideal self-concept, and individualism. From the parent-report questionnaire, the PIC, sexually abused children were rated as having poorer adjustment, social skills, and family relations, and as having more somatic concerns, depressive symptoms, social withdrawal, anxiety, psychotic symptoms, and delinquent forms of behavior problems.

Further evidence supports the position that sexually abused adolescents differ from their peers on personality dimensions. Using the High School Personality Questionnaire (R. Cattell, M. Cattell, & Johns, 1984), German, Habenicht, and Futcher (1990) found that sexually abused adolescents, as compared to the standardization group, tended to be cool and detached, shy, and withdrawn. They also tended to be more concrete in their thinking, expedient (i.e., low ego-strength, self-indulgent, frivolous), self-sufficient, and dominant.

Despite parental reports of behavioral and emotional problems, studies which have investigated self-reported negative affect (low self-esteem, depression, anxiety) among nonclinic-referred sexually abused children have tended to find no differences as compared to standardization samples (Cohen & Mannarino, 1988; Wolfe et al., 1989). However, among samples of clinic-referred sexually abused children, studies vary as to outcome. Two studies of clinic-referred sexually abused children that included matched control samples found significant differences between the samples on the Piers-Harris Children's Self Concept Scale (Piers, 1984), despite means which fell into the average range for the standardization sample (German et al., 1990; Tong et al., 1987). Einbender and Friedrich (1989) found no difference on the Children's Depression Inventory (CDI; Kovacs & Beck, 1977) when sexually abused, clinic-referred children were compared with a nonclinic, nonabused sample. On the other hand, Inderbitzen-Pisaruk et al. (1992) found clinically relevant, significant differences on the CDI between a clinic-referred population and a nonclinic-referred matched comparison group (raw score for sexual abuse group = 12.41; matched control group = 6.82). Wozencraft, Wagner, and Pellegrin (1991) also reported relatively high scores on the CDI from sexually abused children (28% had scores at the 90th percentile).

3.2. Unique Symptom Profiles for Sexually Abused Children

While it is clear that parents of sexually abused children tend to describe their children as more symptomatic than parents of nonabused children, it is not clear that sexually abused children differ from clinic-referred children with regard to global adjustment, as evidenced by the Cohen and Mannarino (1988) finding that CBCL scores for sexually abused children were not particularly elevated compared with the CBCL clinical norms. Gruber and Jones (1981) made a good point when commenting on the externalizing behavior of sexually abused children. They noted that the correlational nature of the findings might indicate that sexual abuse leads to externalizing behaviors, that externalizing behaviors place children at risk for sexual abuse, or that a third factor such as family disorganization and chaos is responsible for both the externalizing behavior and greater risk of sexual abuse. While this line of research does not lend itself to experimental designs that could answer such a question, use of appropriate control groups can help to determine whether the problems of sexually abused children relate to being sexually abused or to some other problem, such as family dysfunction. In the following section, studies that have compared sexually abused children to various control samples will be reviewed.

Two studies have investigated global adjustment problems by comparing sexually abused children with children who have experienced other forms of maltreatment. White, Halpin, Strom, and Santilli (1988) compared sexually abused preschoolers with neglected and nonreferred preschoolers using the Minnesota Child Development Inventory (MCDI; Ireton & Thwing, 1972), a measure of preschool development. Neglected children tended to score lower on this measure as compared with the nonreferred children; however, the sexually abused children did not differ significantly from either group. In another study targeting preschoolers, Gale, Thompson, Moran, and Sack (1988) compared sexually abused children with physically abused and nonabused children using a standard, comprehensive intake questionnaire used by the clinic where the research was conducted. The only behavior problem that differentiated the sexually abused children from the other two groups was inappropriate sexual behavior. Inappropriate sexual behavior was noted in 41% of the sexually abused group, but in less than 5% of the other two groups.

Several studies have made comparisons between clinic-referred sexually abused patients and clinic-referred, nonabused patients. Gomes-Schwartz, Horowitz, and Cardarelli (1990) made such a comparison using the Louisville Behavior Checklist (Miller, 1977) for preschoolers, school-age children, and adolescents. The only scale that discriminated the sexually abused children from the other clinic-referred children was the sexual behavior scale. Differences were found for this scale between both the preschool and school-age samples; however, the Louisville Behavior Checklist does not provide a sexual behavior scale for adolescents.

Recognizing that sexual abuse sequelae may relate to the dysfunctional nature of incestuous families rather than the abuse *per se*, Hotte and Rafman (1992) compared sexually abused and nonabused psychiatric inpatients, ages 8 to 14, who were matched with regard to indices of family dysfunction and family problems. Psychiatric staff completed CBCL's and the patients completed two measures designed to assess self-esteem, the Piers–Harris Children's Self Concept Scale (Piers, 1984) and the Harter and Pike Competence Scale (Harter & Pike, 1984). Although the groups did not differ with regard to the CBCL, the sexually abused patients showed evidence of lower self-esteem on both of the self-esteem measures.

Several studies have examined the effects of sexual abuse with adolescent inpatients. Sansonnet-Hayden, Haley, Marriage, and Fine (1987) examined differences in diagnostic classifications among sexually abused and nonabused psychiatric inpatients. Using the Diagnostic Interview Schedule for Children (Costello, Edelbrock, Dukan, & Kalas, 1984), patients were compared on the following scales: depression, separation anxiety, overanxiousness, conduct, mania, fears/phobias, schizoid/psychotic symptoms, somatic complaints, and sexual identity disturbance. The sexually abused patients reported more depressive symptoms and were more likely to report suicidal ideation and gestures. Furthermore, sexually abused patients were more likely to report schizoid/psychotic symptoms (i.e., hallucinations, but not more delusions). Edwall, Hoffman, and Harrison (1989) also found greater evidence of suicidal ideation and behavior when sexually abused and nonabused chemically dependent adolescents were compared. Cavaiola and Schiff (1988) examined differences between four groups of chemically dependent adolescents: sexually abused, physically abused, sexually and physically abused, and nonabused. While the three abused groups differed from the nonabused group on a number of variables (i.e., suicidal and homicidal ideation, legal problems, cruelty to animals, accidents, sexual acting out, and running away), the sexually abused group differed from the physically abused group only on the variable sexual acting out.

4. Impact of Abuse: Abuse-Specific Symptoms

Several researchers have approached the task of determining sexual abuse sequelae by assessing symptoms believed to be functionally related to the abuse. Several investigators have compiled lists of symptoms gleaned from clinical literature. Others have assessed specific symptoms thought to result from sexual abuse, such as problems with sexuality or post-traumatic stress symptoms. Still other investigators have assessed coping and adaptational styles felt to develop as a result of experiencing abuse. In the next section, each of these approaches will be reviewed, beginning with studies that documented the frequency of the symptoms among sexually abused children, followed by studies that have compared the frequency of those symptoms with various control groups.

4.1. Comprehensive Checklists

Conte and Schuerman (1987) developed a 38-item symptom checklist based upon the clinical literature, which was designed for completion by social workers familiar with the child. The scale was completed for 369 sexually abused children seen at a sexual assault center who had recently disclosed abuse. A factor analysis of the checklist yielded 12 scales: concentration problems (e.g., daydreaming), aggression (e.g., defiance), withdrawal (e.g., withdrawal from usual activities), somatic complaints (e.g., sleep disturbance), character/personality problems (e.g., overly compliant), antisocial behavior (e.g., hanging around a bad crowd), nervous/emotional symptoms (e.g., excessive activity), depression (e.g., very unhappy), regression (e.g., clinging to parents), body image problems (e.g., overly concerned about cleanliness), fear (e.g., afraid of the dark), and post-traumatic stress symptoms (e.g., panic attacks). A broad range of symptoms were reported across children, averaging 3.5, with 21% of the sample showing none of the symptoms and 27% of the sample showing four or more symptoms. The most commonly reported symptoms were: low self-esteem (33%), abuse-related fears (31%), emotional upset (23%), nightmares/sleep disorders (20%), repressed anger/hostility (19%), depression (19%), social withdrawal (15%) and academic problems (15%).

White et al. (1988) also developed a symptom checklist based upon "literature reports and clinical experience." The checklist included 116 "Sexual Abuse Sensitive" (SAS) items which were integrated into the Minnesota Child Development Inventory (Ireton & Thwing, 1972,), which is a parent-report measure intended for use with children under 7 years of age. Items were related to parent–child relationships, dependent behaviors, responses to unfamiliar adults, pseudosophistication, self-esteem, depression, regressions, safety concerns, somatic complaints, and interest in private parts and/or activities. In a comparison of clinic-referred sexually abused, neglected, and nonreferred boys and girls, White et al. (1988), who found no differences between sexually abused children and either neglected or nonabused non-neglected groups of children on global functioning, found that sexually abused boys showed more SAS behaviors than either neglected or nonreferred boys. These results highlight the importance of assessing abuse-specific symptoms as well as global adjustment. However, sexually abused and neglected girls showed more SAS behaviors than the nonreferred girls, but there were no differences between the sexually abused and neglected girls. Sexually abused boys scored higher on the SAS than the sexually abused girls. For the boys, the items that discriminated the groups fell into the following conceptually derived categories: intimate parts (e.g., masturbates in social situations), somatic complaints (e.g., headaches), safety problems (e.g., accident-prone), regressions (e.g., reverts back to old behaviors often), self-esteem (e.g., withdraws), parent relations (e.g., gets along with father), behavior problems (e.g., whines), and pseudosophistication (e.g., seems older than age). For girls, the items that discriminated the sexually abused and neglected girls from the nonreferred girls fell into the following categories: intimate parts, regressions, parent reactions, behavior problems, and relations with other adults (e.g., friendly to adult strangers, tries to win adults' favors).

Kolko, Moser, and Weldy (1988) developed two separate checklists for assessing abuse-related symptoms, one for parent report (26 items) and one for chart psychiatric reviews (19 items). Based upon a factor analysis of the parent-report checklist with 103 psychiatric inpatients aged 5 to 14, the following factors were derived: sexual activity, fear/mistrust, unhappiness/escape, conduct problems, school apathy/neglect, and withdrawal/poor appetite. The chart review checklist yielded 8 conceptually defined categories: aggression, adult roles, sexual behavior, isolation, fear/anxiety, sleep disturbance, fantasy/regression, and sadness/depression. Intercorrelations were significant between the checklists for sexual activities and sexual behaviors, withdrawal/poor appetite and fear/anxiety, and withdrawal/poor appetite and sadness/depression. Assessments were also made with two comparison groups of psychiatric inpatients: physically abused and nonabused. From the parent-report checklist, sexually abused children differed from the other groups on the following scales: sexual activity, fear/mistrust, and withdrawal/poor appetite. From the chart review, sexually abused patients demonstrated more sexual behavior, fear/anxiety, and sadness/depression. Females showed more signs of fear and anxiety and higher frequencies of sexually inappropriate behavior as compared to the males. Sexual activity discriminated the sexually and physically abused groups most dramatically, accounting for 9% of the variance.

Goldston, Turnquist, and Knutson (1989) also developed a checklist for chart review and compared sexually abused and nonabused inpatient and outpatient girls, ages 2 to 18. For girls ages 2 to 11, the 23-item checklist discriminated the two populations on the following dimensions: delinquent behaviors, surreptitious masturbation, public masturbation, sexual precocity, sexual experimentation with younger peers, seductiveness toward men, depression, and sleep disturbance; for girls ages 12 to 18: running away from home, sexual precocity, and seductive behavior toward men.

4.2. Sexuality Symptoms

As evident from the preceding literature surveys, problems with sexuality have been identified for sexually abused preschoolers, school-age children, and adolescents. In fact, in a recent literature review by Kendall-

Tackett, Williams, and Finkelhor (1993), sexuality problems, along with PTSD symptomatology, were the only sets of symptoms that consistently discriminated sexually abused children from other nonabused, clinic-referred children. From their review, it was estimated that 38% of sexually abused children exhibited sexualized behavior.

In order to assess sexuality problems for sexually abused children, several researchers have used the Sex Problems subscale of the CBCL, which is scored for female preschool and school-age children. This scale, which has since been altered (to be discussed) was derived via factor analytic research and contained the following items: feels too guilty, plays with own sex parts too much, prefers being with younger kids, sexual problems, talks too much, and thinks about sex too much. Several studies have reported clinical elevations for the 1983 version of the CBCL Sex Problems scale when compared to the nonclinical CBCL norms or when compared with nonclinical matched control samples (Cohen & Mannarino, 1988; Einbender & Friedrich, 1989; Mannarino, Cohen, & Gregor, 1989). However, when compared to clinical populations, the scale did not appear to discriminate sexually abused girls from nonabused girls reliably (Cohen & Mannarino, 1988; Mannarino et al., 1989).

Friedrich (1993) noted problems with the original CBCL Sex Problems scale, since it did not include all the CBCL items directly related to sex, yet included other items related to peer relations and verbal expression. As a result, Friedrich and his colleagues calculated an alternate sex problem subscale for the CBCL, utilizing the six sex-related items, for several investigations (Friedrich, Beilke, & Urquiza, 1987, 1988; Friedrich & Leucke, 1988). Results of these studies indicate that this revised sex problem scale discriminates sexually abused children from nonclinic children, nonabused children receiving outpatient therapy, abused boys and oppositional boys, and sexually aggressive and nonaggressive children. Interestingly, a recent standardization and scoring update for the CBCL (Achenbach, 1991), resulted in changes for the scoring of the Sex Problem subscale, such that it now includes the same six CBCL items that Friedrich and his colleagues identified for their scale. The CBCL Sex Problem subscale is scored only for children ages 4 to 11.

As a follow-up to consistent findings regarding sexual behavior among sexually abused children, Friedrich and his colleagues (Friedrich et al., 1992) developed the Child Sexual Behavior Inventory (CSBI) to assess the problem more thoroughly. The CSBI, a parent-report measure, contains 36 items, 25 of which discriminate between sexually abused and nonabused girls and boys, both preschool and school-aged. To date only one study has compared the CSBI with a nonabused clinic sample. Allen, Jones, and Nash (August, 1989) found no differences between sexually

abused and nonabused preschoolers; however, the sample size was relatively small for both groups (N's = 11 and 12).

In addition to parent-report and chart reviews, sexuality problems
have been documented via a number of assessment strategies, including
art, observation, and self report. With regard to drawings, Yates, Beutler,
and Crago (1985) noted considerable variations among incest victims with
regard to sexual features in their drawings. As compared to drawings by
nonabused children, incest victims tended to either exaggerate or mini-
mize sexual features. Hibbard, Roghmann, and Hoeckelman (1987) found
that sexually abused children were more likely to include genital features
in their drawings; however, even among sexual abuse victims the rates of
genital features is relatively low (Hibbard & Hartman, 1990). Regarding
play situations, it appears that sexually abused children are more likely to
demonstrate sexual behaviors with anatomically correct dolls (White,
Strom, Santilli, & Haplin, 1986). However, Everson and Boat (1990) found
that nonabused children are likely to show some level of sexual play with
anatomically correct dolls. While 2-year-olds showed no sexual play with
the dolls, 18% of 5-year-olds displayed intercourse positioning. Friedrich
and Lui (1985) reported that sexually abused children, as compared to
nonabused outpatient referrals, demonstrated more interpersonal boundary and sexual behavior problems during initial outpatient–therapist interviews.

Two recently developed self-report assessment instruments tap sexual
issues with children within the context of assessing children's traumatic
responses: The Children's Impact of Traumatic Events Scale-Revised
(CITES-R; Wolfe & Gentile, 1987) and the Trauma Symptom Checklist-
Children (TSC-C; Briere, 1989). The CITES-R, described more thoroughly
in the following section, contains two scales that pertain to sexuality:
Sexual Anxiety (a PTSD scale) and Eroticism. The Sexual Anxiety scale
contains five items, such as "Thinking about sex upsets me" and "I wish
there was no such thing as sex." The Eroticism scale contains four items,
such as "I think about sex even when I don't want to" and "I have sexual
feelings when I see people kiss on TV." The original CITES included both
types of items on one scale; however, a factor analysis suggested that the
two issues are relatively distinct (V. Wolfe, Gentile, Michienzi, Sas, & D.
Wolfe, 1991). A multibehavior-multimethod matrix analysis using the CIT-
ES-R scale revealed significant correlations between the CITES Sexual
Anxiety scale (then two items) and the Sexual Abuse Fear Evaluation-
Sexual Fears scale (Wolfe, Gentile, & Klink, 1988). However, the CITES
Eroticism scale (then two items) did not correlate significantly with either
the CBCL Sex Problem scale (original CBCL scale rather than the Friedrich
scale) or the CSBI total score. However, the CBCL Sex Problem scale and

the CSBI total score did not correlate significantly either. As the CITES-R has incorporated several new sexual anxiety and eroticism items, further psychometric analyses are needed to determine the current validity of the CITES-R sex-related subscales. For the original two Sexual Anxiety items, the average item mean (range: 1–3) was 1.75; for the original two Eroticism items, the average mean was 1.37. As compared to other self-reported symptoms associated with sexual abuse, children endorsed the sexuality items relatively infrequently. Because the CITES-R requires children to answer questions with regard to their victimization history, comparisons with nonabused children have not been conducted.

Unlike the CITES-R, the Trauma Symptom Checklist-Children (Briere, 1989) does not orient the respondent to victimization experiences, and thus allows for comparisons with nonabused populations. The 10-item Sexual Concerns scale (e.g., wanting to say dirty words, touching private parts too much, thinking about having sex) has been shown to discriminate between sexually abused and nonabused psychiatric inpatients. With a sample of 28 sexually abused children and adolescents, the Sexual Concerns subscale of the TSC-C had an alpha value of 0.62 (internal consistency).

Several theories have emerged in an attempt to understand the development of sexual problems following sexual abuse. Finkelhor and Browne (1985) described a process of traumatic sexualization that occurs as a result of the inherent stress of a precocious introduction to sexual behavior. The psychological consequences of traumatic sexualization included confusion of sex with love, increased salience of sexual issues, and several behavioral manifestations, including sexual preoccupation, sexual aggression, and the inappropriate sexualization of parenting.

Yates (1982) suggested that children who are exposed over time to intense genital and extragenital stimulation will become highly erotic. She suggested that eroticism may be viewed as learned behavior, as the behavior is self-reinforcing. As such, eroticized behavior may be difficult to modify.

Putnam and Trickett (1987) suggested a psychobiological model to account for the sexualized behavior often reported for sexual abuse victims. The model involves a stress-induced increase in delta-4 androstenedione (d4AD) and dehydroepiandrosterone (DHEA), both of which are hormones produced by the adrenal cortex in response to ACTH and other unknown stimuli. Both hormones are directly related to puberty and the development of libido in the female, as well as being strongly correlated with aggressive behavior in the male. Putnam and Trickett (1987) hypothesized that stress, related to repeated sexual abuse, causes increased in d4AD and DHEA, which then biochemically instigate the inappropriate sexual and aggressive behaviors reported in sexually abused children. An ongoing research project was underway investigating this hypothesis, using a control group of girls experiencing precocious puberty.

DeYoung (1984) attempted to explain some sexual behavior as "counterphobic" behavior, particularly among children who are revictimized after the initial set of sexually abusive behaviors. Counterphobic behavior refers to children's attempts to desensitize themselves to abuse-related stimuli, such as situations that the child may see as sexually provocative or where the child may feel sexually vulnerable. Children may "reenact" their abusive situation *in vivo* in hopes of gaining a sense of mastery over the situation; however, these counterphobic behaviors may lead to further victimizations, thus compounding their traumatic reactions and reinforcing their sense of vulnerability and helplessness.

4.3. Posttraumatic Stress Disorder Symptoms

Many researchers have considered sexual abuse to be potentially traumatizing to the child, thereby leading to post-traumatic stress disorder symptoms, such as reexperiencing the trauma, avoidance of trauma-related stimuli, and hyperarousal. Burgess, Hartman, McCausland, and Powers (1984) provided one of the first descriptive accounts of PTSD symptoms among sexual abuse victims. Parents of children who had been involved in child pornography or sex rings were interviewed about their children's symptoms. Parents were asked to recall their children's symptoms that were apparent when the abuse was occurring but not yet disclosed, as well as symptoms that occurred following disclosure. Their results suggested that children's trauma-related symptoms may be present while the abuse is ongoing and prior to disclosure; however, following disclosure, PTSD symptoms often become more obvious and severe. Prior to the disclosure, parents reported their children complained of genital soreness, anal irritations, and urinary tract infections. Many of their psychological complaints were somatic in nature: headaches, stomachaches, loss of appetite, nausea and vomiting, and sleep disturbance. Other symptoms included daydreaming, trouble concentrating on schoolwork, and poor academic performance. They began to withdraw from peer activities and were described as more irritable and edgy. More pathogenic responses included fire-setting, stealing, and sexually focused attitudes and behaviors. Following disclosure, parents reported the more salient PTSD symptoms of reexperiencing the event, avoidance of abuse-related stimuli, diminished responsiveness to the environment, and hyperarousal.

Other researchers have attempted to assess the prevalence of PTSD symptoms among child sexual abuse victims. Wolfe and her colleagues have developed a series of assessment strategies designed to assess PTSD symptoms among child victims. To assess PTSD symptoms via parent report, 20 PTSD-like behaviors from the CBCL were selected to comprise a CBCL–PTSD scale (Wolfe et al., 1989): difficulty concentrating, obsessive thoughts, feeling too guilty, feeling moody, difficulty sleeping, nightmares, irrational fears, feeling persecuted, irritable, arguing a lot, and somatic complaints (headaches, nausea, stomachaches, and vomiting). Based upon a sample size of 68, the PTSD scale had an alpha value of 0.89. Parents of both younger (ages 8 to 11) and older (ages 12 to 16) sexually abused girls showed five times more CBCL–PTSD symptoms than the standardization sample. Wolfe et al. (November, 1992) compared CBCL scales, subscales, and items among three samples: the CBCL standardization sample, a clinic-referred nonabused sample, and a sexually abused sample. For the scales and subscales a general pattern of significant group differences emerged, with the clinic-referred children scoring highest, followed by the sexually abused children, followed by the standardization sample. In contrast, however, for the majority of the CBCL–PTSD items, the sexually abused children scored higher than either the clinic-referred or the standardization samples.

In order to assess fears and phobias associated with the sexual abuse, V. Wolfe and D. Wolfe (1986) developed the Sexual Abuse Fear Evaluation (SAFE), which is a 27-item scale embedded into the 80-item Fear Survey Schedule for Children-Revised (Ollendick, 1983). The SAFE yields two factor-derived scales: Sex-Associated Fears (11 items; e.g., watching people kiss on TV; someone kissing or hugging me; having older boys or men look after me alone) and Interpersonal Discomfort (13 items; e.g., people not believing me, telling on someone for bothering me, being lied to by someone I trust). Alpha values for the two scales were 0.80 and 0.81, respectively. Comparisons with a school sample revealed that the Sex-associated Fears scale discriminated between the groups; however, significant differences were not found between the groups for the Interpersonal Discomfort scale (Wolfe et al., 1988). Interestingly, for both scales and for both groups, a fairly high number of girls reported fears along both dimensions.

The CITES-R (Wolfe & Gentile, 1987) is a 78-item questionnaire designed to assess children's perceptions and attributions concerning their own sexual abuse. The CITES-R contains 11 scales that fall along the following dimensions: PTSD (Intrusive Thoughts, Avoidance, Hyperarousal, and Sexual Anxiety), Social Reactions (Negative Reactions by Others, Social Support), Attributions about the Abuse (Self Blame/Guilt, Personal Vulnerability, Dangerous World, and Empowerment), and Eroticism. The CITES-R is based upon an earlier 54-item CITES version; scales were determined by factor analysis and conceptual advances in the literature, and new items were added to boost reliability of some of the relatively small scales defined by the factor analysis (Wolfe et al., 1992). To evaluate the convergent and discriminant validity of the CITES-R scales (using the previous 54-item version), a multibehavior-multimethod matrix analysis was conducted. As part of that analysis, the CITES-R–PTSD scales (Intrusive Thoughts, Avoidance, and Sexual Anxiety) were correlated with other methods of assessing PTSD, the CBCL–PTSD scale and the SAFE Sex-Associated Fears and Interpersonal Discomfort fears. Significant correlations were found between Intrusive Thoughts and Sexual Anxiety scales and the SAFE Sex-associated Fears scale (the Hyperarousal scale was added to the scale subsequent to the earlier version of the CITES, as were additional items for the Avoidance scale which had contained only two items for that analysis). Among a representative sample of sexually abused children, most presenting for assessment within two months of disclosure, Intrusive Thoughts and Sexual Anxiety items were endorsed relatively frequently, with average item means of 1.94 (s.d. = 0.67; possible range 1–3) and 1.75 (s.d. = 0.78), respectively. Avoidance items were endorsed relatively infrequently at the initial assessment following disclosure; however, at a 9-month follow-up, the item mean was 2.43 (s.d. = 0.66), suggesting that avoidance symptoms grow in frequency over time and are relatively common and strong one year after disclosure. A psychometric evaluation of the CITES-R is currently underway, with CITES-R data collected from a number of locations across North America.

McLeer, Deblinger, Atkins, Foa, and Ralphe (1988) developed a method for diagnosing sexually abused patients as having PTSD. Following structured interviews, a PTSD symptom checklist was completed. Items fell into one of three subcategories: (1) reexperiencing behaviors (e.g., repetitive conversations about the abuse, flashbacks, nightmares); (2) avoidant behaviors (e.g., avoidance of people, places, and things associated with the abuse), and (3) autonomic hyperarousal (e.g., difficulty falling asleep or staying asleep, irritability, anger). Scoring was dichotomous with symptoms judged as present or absent. To meet criteria for PTSD, the child had to demonstrate at least one symptom of reexperiencing behavior, three or more symptoms of avoidant behavior, and two or more symptoms of autonomic hyperarousal. Of the 31 clinic-referred sexually abused children interviewed, 48.4% met criteria for PTSD. In a separate analysis of 87 psychiatric inpatients, a similar checklist was developed for chart review. Sexually abused patients were compared with physically abused and nonabused patients using similar PTSD criteria; 20.7% of the sexually abused patients met PTSD criteria, whereas 6.9% of the physically abused patients and 10% of the nonabused patients met the criteria (Deblinger, McLeer, Atkins, Ralphe, & Foa, 1989). Despite the differences in percentages, the differences between the groups was not significant.

In a recent literature review, Kendall-Tackett et al. (1993) found that, based upon five studies of PTSD symptoms among sexually abused children, 53% exhibited PTSD symptomatology. However, one of the studies included a sample of children severely, ritualistically abused. When that study was excluded, 32% of the abused children showed symptoms of PTSD.

4.4. Maladaptive Attributional Styles and Coping Behaviors

Janoff-Bulman (1989) proposed a model to account for the reexperiencing aspect of PTSD, and suggested that the process of adjusting to traumatic experiences results in alterations in one's attributional style and worldview. He proposed that throughout childhood a conceptual system develops, which provides an individual with expectations about the world and the self. For the emotionally healthy individual, these assumptions include (a) the world is a benevolent place; (b) the world is meaningful; and (c) the self is worthy. According to the model, traumatic events present information contrary to these assumptions and require one to accommodate the new experiences into one's worldview. Recurrent, intrusive thoughts alternate with denial and avoidance until the process of accommodation is complete. In his study of 83 undergraduate trauma victims and 255 nonvictims, Janoff-Bulman (1989) found that victims differed significantly in terms of their attributional style and depression when compared to nonvictims, suggesting that trauma negatively affects one's worldview, which, in turn, leads to feelings of depression.

Several other researchers have suggested that attributional style plays a role as a mediator of sexual abuse sequelae (e.g., Gold, 1986; Seidner & Calhoun, July, 1984; Wolfe et al., 1989). Perhaps accommodation of one's worldview in response to trauma leads to differences in coping styles as well as attributions. Such alterations to one's cognitive schemas and coping styles may in turn increase the probability of developing long-term adjustment problems such as depression, generalized anxiety, and interpersonal relationship difficulties, as well as maladaptive coping strategies such as learned-helplessness response styles, avoidance reactions, and dissociative processes.

Terr (1987) has suggested that the sequelae associated with trauma vary according to the frequency and duration of the trauma. According to her model, two types of trauma can occur in children: Type I trauma usually results from exposure to a single traumatic event; whereas, Type II trauma results from multiple exposures to traumatic circumstances or a long-standing traumatic experience. Terr (1987) proposed that Type I and Type II traumas have similar symptoms; however, when children are exposed to frequent and/or long-term abuse (Type II trauma), they may develop abnormal coping strategies to deal with ongoing stressors such as denial, psychogenic numbing, rage, and unremitting sadness. As evidence of the effects of repeated abuse, Wachtel and Scott (1991) found that children who experienced more than one incident of child sexual abuse were more likely to show long-term effects.

Results from a study by Famularo, Kinscherff, and Fenton (1990) also support Terr's (1987) formulation of sexual abuse sequelae. Using DSM-III–PTSD diagnostic criteria, sexually abused children were diagnosed as either acute or chronic PTSD. Acute PTSD was diagnosed when symptoms developed within six months of the trauma and persisted for less than six months, whereas chronic PTSD was diagnosed if symptoms persisted for more than six months. Acute PTSD patients, as compared to the chronic PTSD patients, showed significantly more difficulties falling asleep, nightmares, hypervigilance, exaggerated startle response, and generalized anxiety. The chronic PTSD group exhibited a greater prevalence of detachment or estrangement from others, sadness, restricted effect, thinking that life would be difficult, and dissociative periods. Despite the different patterns of symptoms exhibited by each group of children, symptoms evident in the acute PTSD group were also evident in the chronic PTSD group. To further support Terr's conceptualization, children presenting with a mixture of acute and chronic PTSD symptoms tended to have histories of repeated traumatization.

Terr's conceptualization of Type I and Type II trauma is further supported by the findings of Gentile (1988), who factor analyzed the Sexual Abuse scale of the History of Victimization Form (Wolfe, Gentile, & Bourdeau, 1986). Six variables were entered into the analysis: severity of the sexual abuse act(s), severity of coercion or force employed, number of perpetrators, duration of sexual abuse, frequency of sexual abuse, and the relationship of the child to the perpetrators. Two factors emerged: "Severity of Sexual Abuse" (severity of sexual abuse acts, severity of coercion/force employed, and number of perpetrators) and "Course of Sexual Abuse" (frequency and duration of the sexual abuse, as well as the relationship of the child to the perpetrator). Wolfe and Gentile (1992) suggested that the "Severity of Abuse" factor reflects Type I trauma and the "Course of Abuse" factors reflect Type II trauma. In line with Terr's model, they propose that "Severity of Abuse" corresponds to core PTSD symptoms (reexperiencing, avoidance, and hyperarousal) and "Course of Abuse" relates to long-term global adjustment problems brought forth by alterations in attributional and coping styles. Wolfe (November, 1990) found that PTSD symptoms assessed fairly soon after disclosure of the abuse, such as intrusive thoughts and abuse-related fears, were primarily related to the Severity of Abuse factor. However, at a nine-month follow-up assessment, depression was primarily related to Course of Abuse. This research also revealed that the intensity of core PTSD symptoms among sexually abused children tended to decrease across time; however, those who continued to show depressive problems were those who experienced longer-term abuse. Kilpatrick, Veronen, and Resnick (1979) have also found that symptoms associated with PTSD decreased over time among a sample of rape victims. Together these findings give credence to the idea that PTSD symptoms tend to decrease as time passes; however, longer-term sequelae related to repeated victimization tend to persist.

Thus far, there has been little research into attributional style and coping behavior variations among sexual abuse victims. Although both attributional style (Wolfe et al., 1989) and coping strategies (Johnson & Kenkel, 1991) have been related to individual differences in adjustment among sexually abused children, no studies to date have demonstrated significant differences between abused and nonabused children for either general attributional style or general coping strategies. Wolfe et al. (1989) found that a self-deprecatory attributional style was related to both negative affect (i.e., symptoms of anxiety and depression) and symptoms specific to sexual abuse (i.e., guilt, feelings of betrayal). Furthermore, abuse-related attributions, such as a belief that similar negative events might happen again or that abuse is pervasive and adults in general are dangerous, were related to intrusive thoughts, guilt, and feelings of betrayal and stigmatization.

Johnson and Kenkel (1991) used a revised version of the Ways of Coping Scale-Revised (WCCL-R; Lazarus & Folkman, 1984) to assess coping styles among sexually abused adolescent females. Seven variables were derived from the original WCCL-R; problem-focused coping, wishful thinking, distancing/detachment, emphasizing the positive, tension reduction, self-isolation, and seeking social support. Additional coping items were added to the WCCL-R to reflect both characterological and behavioral self-blame. Multiple regression analyses were used to assess the degree to which coping strategies predicted self-reported distress. Two coping strategies were related to greater reports of distress: wishful thinking (i.e., fantasizing, daydreaming, wishing that things could be better than they are in reality) and tension reduction (i.e., eating, drinking, use of illicit drugs, or sex used to reduce abuse-related tensions). Therapist ratings of adjustment and distress were primarily related to the use of detachment or distancing behaviors (i.e., pretending nothing happened, trying to forget), although seeking social support (i.e., seeking out others for conversations, sympathy, or problem solving, asking for advice, praying) was also related to therapist ratings of distress. As with most studies of coping behaviors, it is difficult to determine whether higher levels of distress relate to the use of these coping strategies, or whether the distress is the result of past poor coping strategies, or whether both variables are related to a third variable, such as more severe abuse.

Although dissociation can be considered a disorder itself, dissociation is often considered a coping strategy used by individuals under extreme stress as a method of reducing unbearable anxiety. Because dissociation and the dissociative disorders have been closely associated with early childhood maltreatment and abuse, this "coping" strategy has been investigated more thoroughly than other adaptation processes. Malinosky-Rummell and Hoier (1990) used a behavioral framework to conceptualize dissociation as a breakdown in the correspondence between the three response modes: cognitive-, motor-, and physiological processes. Dissociation may include a number of symptoms that serve an escape function for sexual abuse victims: selective memory loss, alterations in consciousness or personality style, and/or alterations in emotional/physiological state. While dissociative strategies may be functional during the abusive episodes as a method of quelling overwhelming anxiety, dissociative strategies are typically dysfunctional in nontrauma-related situations, but are maintained outside the abusive situation in the same manner that many dysfunctional avoidance-types of behaviors are maintained; that is, the avoidance strategy results in a reduction in anxiety, thereby negatively reinforcing the dissociative strategy. Results from a study by Malinosky-Rummell and Hoier (1990) give further credence to Terr's notion of Type I and Type II PTSD. These authors found that both child- and caregiver-reported dissociative symptoms were higher for sexually abused children than for a community control sample. Furthermore, dissociative strategies were the most common among children who had experienced more frequent abuse.

5. Factors Mediating Adjustment Following Sexual Abuse

Several factors have generally been considered as potential influences on children's adjustment to sexual abuse disclosure: abuse variables (sexual acts involved, use of coercion or force, number of perpetrators, relationship with perpetrator, duration of abuse, frequency of abuse, age abuse began, time since abuse ended, and time since disclosure); child variables (age, IQ, general and abuse-specific attributional style, coping variables); family variables (family makeup, maternal adjustment, maternal reaction to the disclosure, mother–daughter relationships, family environment, continued contact with perpetrator); and, community variables (therapeutic involvement, courtroom testimony). Several methodological issues make interpretation of much of this research difficult. Most studies have included a subsample of mediating variables, thus not accounting for correlations among potential mediators. Among those studies that have examined multiple mediators, some have reported simple correlations while others have reported partial correlations or have used multiple regression strategies or group comparisons. While some studies have shown significant relationships among variables, others have not. Inconsistencies may be due to a number of factors: varying populations studies, varying numbers of subjects per study, and other variables partialing out the variance accounted for by particular variables.

Regarding abuse factors, it appears that more severe forms of abuse relate to higher levels of symptoms, both with regard to parental reports on the CBCL (Cohen & Mannarino, 1988; Friedrich, 1993), child reports on an anxiety measure (Wolfe et al., 1989), and social worker-completed checklists of abuse-specific symptoms (Conte & Schuerman, 1987). More frequent abuse has been related to both higher CBCL scores and to a greater likelihood of meeting diagnostic criteria for a DSM-III-R defined disorder (Sirles & Smith, September, 1990). Severity and frequency of abuse have been related to more sexual problems (Friedrich et al., 1986; Friedrich, 1993), more negative attitudes toward sex (Wolfe et al., 1989), and more sex-related fears (Wolfe et al., 1989).

Abuse perpetrated by a family member has been related to higher CBCL Externalizing Scale scores, higher child-reported symptoms of anxiety and tension, and higher numbers of abuse-specific symptoms reported by social workers (Conte & Schuerman, 1987). Additional family stress appears to have incremental effects (Conte & Schuerman, 1987; Sirles & Smith, September, 1990). Sirles and Smith (September, 1990) found higher behavior-problem scores when the sexually abused child had also witnessed family violence. Furthermore, sexually abused children who had also experienced physical abuse were incrementally more likely to show sufficient symptoms for diagnosis of a DSM-III-R psychiatric disorder. Maternal disbelief and poor maternal compliance to professional recommendations have also been shown to relate to greater suicidal ideation.

Kendall-Tackett et al. (1993) concluded from their literature review that sequelae from sexual abuse varied according to age. Like many common problems of childhood, there appears to be some continuity in the types of problems that present across the various age groups, but the manifestation of the problems may vary. In their summary of age effects, the most common problems reported for preschoolers were anxiety, nightmares, PTSD, internalizing and externalizing behavior problems, and inappropriate sexual behavior. For school-age children, the most common problems were fears, aggression, nightmares, and school problems including hyperactivity and regressive behavior. For adolescents, the most common symptoms were somatic complaints, delinquency, running away, and substance abuse. While the behavioral acts may differ across the age groups, the majority of symptoms identified fall within the domains of either PTSD or sexuality problems.

Sirles and Smith (September, 1990) reported more behavior problems on the CBCL for young children, and Wolfe et al. (1989) reported lower CBCL Social Competence scores. Wolfe et al. (1989) also reported relatively high self-reported anxiety scores among younger children. However, Wozencraft, Wagner, and Pellegrin (1991) reported that older children were more likely to show signs of depression. Unfortunately, none of the abuse studies included comparison groups of the children within the same age group to make cross-group and cross-age comparisons.

Children's attributional style, both general and abuse-specific (Stable and Global) have been related to children's social competence scores on the CBCL and to children's self-reported negative affect (CDI, CMAS-R, STAIC-T) (Wolfe et al., 1989). The PTSD symptoms of intrusive thoughts appear to relate to attributions that the factors leading to sexual abuse are Stable (i.e., likely to continue to affect the child's life) and Global (i.e., abuse is pervasive and many individuals sexually abuse children).

6. Long-Term Sequelae

Research results from studies of adult survivors of childhood sexual abuse have mirrored results of the research with child victims in terms of the types of problems experienced and factors that appear to influence sequelae. Overwhelmingly, studies have documented problems in global adjustment when adult survivors are compared to nonabused controls (Briere & Runtz, 1988; Feinauer, 1988; Fromuth, 1986; Gold, 1986; Greenwald, Leitenberg, Cado, & Tarran, 1990; Murphy et al., 1988; Pallotta & Hansen, 1990; Scott & Stone, 1986; Tsai, Feldman-Summers, & Edger, 1979). Studies have indicated that adults survivors, compared to nonabused adults, report more depressive symptoms (Gold, 1986; Lindberg & Distad, 1985; Peters, 1988; Ray, Jackson, & Long, 1990; Sedney & Brooks, 1984), more anxiety (Sedney & Brooks, 1984), poorer social adjustment (Ray et al., 1990; Seidner & Calhoun, July, 1986), more parenting difficulties (Cole & Woolger, March, 1989), more substance abuse (Briere & Runtz, 1988; Peters, 1988; Sedney & Brooks, 1984), more suicidal ideation and suicide attempts (Briere & Runtz, 1988; Lindberrg & Distad, 1985; Sedney & Brooks, 1984), and more revictimization (Alexander & Lupfer, 1987; Briere & Runtz, 1988; Sedney & Brooks, 1984).

The two most commonly reported abuse-specific symptom areas among child victims, PTSD and sexuality problems, are also the most commonly reported abuse-specific symptoms among adults. Several studies have documented that PTSD symptomatology often persists into adulthood (Elliot & Briere, 1992; Greenwald & Leitenberg, 1990; Lindberg & Distad, 1985). Other studies have reported a broad range of sexuality problems: fear of sex (Becker et al., 1982; Steele, 1986), low interest in sex (Becker et al., 1982; Gold, 1986; Steele, 1986), less sexual pleasure (Gold, 1986; Steele, 1986), more sexual partners (Tsai et al., 1979), and more compulsive sexual behavior (Anderson & Coleman, 1991). As well, Fromuth (1986), Gundlach (1977), and Meiselman (1978, 1980) found that a history of childhood sexual abuse was significantly associated with reports of homosexual experiences.

The mediators of long-term sequelae for adult survivors appear to be similar to the mediators of postsexual abuse childhood. Abuse-related variables that have been related to adult adjustment include: duration of abuse (Briere & Runtz, 1988; Peters, 1988; Tsai et al., 1979), frequency of abuse (Conte, Briere, & Sexton, August, 1989), relationship to perpetrator (Feinauer, 1988; Harter & Alexander, 1988; Ray et al., 1990), severity of the abusive acts (Peters, 1988; Tsai et al., 1979), use of force (Conte et al., 1989), feelings during the abuse (Tsai et al., 1979) and number of perpetrators (Briere & Runtz, 1988). Age at the time of the last abusive episode has also been related to sequelae during adulthood (Peters, 1988; Tsai et al., 1979), as well as the adult's recollection of maternal warmth (Peters, 1988) and parental caring (Greenwald et al., 1990) during childhood.

Attributional and coping styles among adult survivors have also been related to adult adjustment. Leitenberg, Greenwald, and Cado (1992), in their study of 54 adult female, childhood sexual abuse survivors, found that the most predominant modes of coping used among the victims were denial and emotional suppression. Despite the correlation between these coping strategies and distress, women who used these coping strategies perceived them as helpful. Several explanations may account for the relationships between these variables. First, higher levels of distress may require the need for the individual to use more powerful coping strategies. Second, due to the nature of the stressor (past "helplessness" situation, abuse survivors may select that strategy because other strategies would not be applicable (e.g., problem solution). Third, denial and suppression may temporarily reduce anxiety associated with the abuse; however, the distress may be negatively reinforced by these avoidance strategies so that the individual never faces his or her fears.

7. Conclusions

The past decade has witnessed a surge in research devoted to understanding the impact of child sexual abuse. Overall, the present review supports several general issues. First, despite considerable heterogeneity among sexual abuse victims, as a group, these children and adolescents tend to display significantly higher levels of symptomatology than their non-abused, nonclinic-referred peers. The percentages of children who fall within the clinical range on measures such as the CBCL vary according to the population (child-protective service populations vs. clinic referrals) and the age group sampled. For child-protective service populations, the percentage of children that fall within the clinical range appears to be around 30%. Among clinic-referred children, the percentage of children falling in the clinical range appears to be closer to 40%, with preschool children showing the highest rates of clinically significant problems.

Second, compared to other clinic-referred children, two problem areas appear to differentiate sexually abused children and adolescents: post-traumatic stress disorder symptomatology and sexuality problems. As a result many researchers have begun to assess both global adjustment (internalizing and externalizing problems) and abuse-specific adjustment (PTSD symptoms and sexuality problems). Research with adult survivors of child sexual abuse suggest that these abuse-related problems tend to persist into adulthood, and that histories of sexual abuse are common among several clinical populations, including patients initially diagnosed as depressed or as having borderline personality disorders.

Third, it appears that several variables mediate sexual abuse sequelae: severity and course of abuse; the child's age at the time of the abuse, at the time of disclosure, and at the time of psychological assessment; the child's attributional style, both regarding general sorts of events and the abusive situations; and, family variables, such as the perpetrator being a family member, additional family stressors, maternal reactions to the disclosure, and the child's experience of other forms of maltreatment such as physical abuse.

Altogether, these results suggest that clinicians working with sexually abused children need to conduct thorough multidimensional, multi-informant assessments that address issues of global and abuse-specific adjustment and consider aspects of the abuse, child premorbid adjustment, child development and child cognitive style, and family and community factors that may attenuate or exacerbate sexual abuse sequelae.

The study of sexual abuse sequelae has led to several theoretical advancements in the understanding of children's responses to stress and trauma, as well as the relationship between adult psychopathology to childhood events. Lenore Terr's notions of Type I and Type II trauma, as related to trauma severity and course, supplies theoretical foundations for understanding immediate PTSD symptoms, as well as other trauma-related symptoms such as dissociation, learned helplessness responses and depression, and problems with anger and rage. Regarding sexuality symptoms, several theoretical positions have been formulated; however, research around these lines is not well-developed, possibly due to the difficulty of accurately assessing the sexuality of children.

Perusal of the literature on sexually abused children suggests several areas where research should be extended. First, large-scale, longitudinal studies of child victims are needed that examine global functioning, abuse-specific functioning, and attributional and coping strategies, as well abuse-, child-, family-, and community factors. Such studies will provide information not only about the immediate effects of sexual abuse, but also about the factors that affect adjustment at later developmental stages and into adulthood.

Second, despite community efforts toward providing treatment services to sexually abused children, little treatment-outcome research is available to demonstrate the efficacy of the various treatment approaches currently being used (see O'Donohue and Elliot, 1993, for a review). Because of the heterogeneity of factors that can present for any one particular child, various "therapeutic modules" need to be developed to address specific child problems. For example, therapeutic modules could be developed to address PTSD symptoms such as intrusive thoughts, hyperarousal, or fears and avoidance. Furthermore, such models could be developed to help children cope with erotic feelings or sexual anxieties. Likewise, programs that emphasize identification of ineffectual attributional styles or coping strategies, and teach more adaptive strategies, may be particularly helpful for some children.

8. References

Achenbach, T. M. (1991). *A manual for the Child Behaviour Checklist/4-18 and 1991 profile.* Burlington, VT: University of Vermont, Department of Psychiatry.

Achenbach, T. M., & Edelbrock, C. (1983). *Manual for the Child Behaviour Checklist and Revised Child Behaviour Profile.* Burlington, VT: University of Vermont, Department of Psychiatry.

Alexander, P., & Lupfer, S. (1987). Family characteristics and long-term consequences associated with sexual abuse. *Archives of Sexual Behaviour, 16,* 235–245.

Allen, M., Jones, P., & Nash, M. (August, 1989). *Detection of sexual abuse among emotionally disturbed preschoolers: Unique effects of sexual abuse as observed on doll play and other standard assessment procedures.* Paper presented at the Annual Convention of the American Psychological Association, New Orleans, LA.

American Psychiatric Association (1987). *Diagnostic and Statistical Manual of Mental Disorders, Third Edition, Revised.* Washington, DC: American Psychiatric Association.

Anderson, A., & Coleman, E. (1991). Childhood abuse and family sexual attitudes in sexually compulsive males: A comparison of three clinical groups. *American Journal of Preventive Psychiatry & Neurology, 3,* 8–15.

Basta, S., & Peterson, R. (1990). Perpetrator status and the personality characteristics of molested children. *Child Abuse & Neglect, 14,* 555–566.

Becker, I., Skinner, L., Abel, G., & Treacy, E. (1982). Incidence and types of sexual dysfunctions in rape and incest survivors. *Journal of Sex & Marital Therapy, 8,* 65–74.

Briere, J. (1989). *The Trauma Symptom Checklist-Children.* Los Angeles: University of Southern California.

Briere, J., & Runtz, M. (1988). Symptomatology associated with childhood sexual victimization in a nonclinical adult sample. *Child Abuse & Neglect, 12,* 51–59.

Briere, J., & Runtz, M. (1990). Differential adult symptomatology associated with three types of child abuse histories. *Child Abuse & Neglect, 14,* 357–364.

Burgess, A. W., Hartman, C. R., McCausland, M. P., & Powers, P. (1984). Response patterns in children and adolescents exploited through sex rings and pornography. *American Journal of Psychiatry, 141,* 656–662.

Cattell, R., Cattell, M., & Johns, E. (1984). *Manual and norms for the High School Personality Questionnaire.* Champaign, IL: Institute of Personality and Ability Testing.

Cavaiola, A., & Schiff, M. (1988). Behavioral sequelae of physical and/or sexual abuse in adolescents. *Child Abuse & Neglect, 12,* 181–188.

Cicchetti, D. (1987). Developmental psychopathology in infancy: Illustration from the study of maltreated youngsters. *Journal of Consulting and Clinical Psychology, 55,* 837–845.

Cohen, J. A., & Mannarino, A. P. (1988). Psychological symptoms in sexually abused girls. *Child Abuse & Neglect, 12,* 571–577.

Cole, P., & Woolger, C. (March, 1989). *The role of emotion in the parenting difficulties of incest victims.* Paper presented at the Biannual Convention of the Society for Research in Child Development, in the symposium, "Social transmission of patterns of emotion regulation and dysregulation," Kansas City, Missouri.

Conte, J., Briere, J., & Sexton, D. (August, 1989). *Mediators of long term symptomatology in women molested as children.* Paper presented at the 97th Annual Convention of the American Psychological Association, New Orleans, LA.

Conte, J., & Scheurman, J. (1987). The effects of sexual abuse on children: A multidimensional view. *Journal of Interpersonal Violence, 2,* 380–390.

Costello, A., Edelbrock, C., Dukan, M., & Kalas, R. (1984). *Testing of the NIMH Diagnostic Interview Schedule for Children (DISC) in a clinical population.* Pittsburgh, PA: University of Pittsburgh.

Deblinger, E., McLeer, S., Atkins, M., Ralphe, D., & Foa, E. (1989). Post-traumatic stress in sexually abused, physically abused, and nonabused children. *Child Abuse & Neglect, 13,* 403–408.

DeYoung, M. (1984). Counterphobic behaviour in multiply molested children. *Child Welfare, 63,* 333–339.

Edwall, G., Hoffman, A., & Harrison, P. (1989). Psychological correlates of sexual abuse in adolescent girls in chemical dependency treatment. *Adolescence, 24,* 208–288.

Einbender, A. J., & Friedrich, W. N. (1989). Psychological functioning and behavior of sexually abused girls. *Journal of Consulting and Clinical Psychology, 57,* 155–157.

Elliot, D., & Briere, J. (1992). Sexual abuse trauma among professional women: Validating the Trauma Symptom Checklist-40 (TSC-40). *Child Abuse and Neglect, 16,* 391–398.

Everson, M., & Boat, B. (1990). Sexualized doll play among young children: Implications for the use of anatomical dolls in sexual abuse evaluations. *Journal of the American Academy of Child & Adolescent Psychiatry, 29,* 736–742.

Famularo, R., Kinscherff, R., & Fenton, T. (1990). Symptom differences in acute and chronic presentation of childhood post-traumatic stress disorder. *Child Abuse & Neglect, 14,* 439–444.

Feinauer, L. (1988). Relationship of long-term effects of childhood sexual abuse to identity of the offender: Family, friend, or stranger. *Women & Therapy, 4,* 89–107.

Finkelhor, D., & Browne, A. (1985). The traumatic impact of child sexual abuse: A conceptualization. *American Journal of Orthopsychiatry, 55,* 530–541.

Friedrich, W. N. (1993). Sexual victimization and sexual behaviour in children: A review of recent literature. *Child Abuse & Neglect, 17,* 59–66.

Friedrich, W., Beilke, R., & Urquiza, A. (1987). Children from sexually abusive families: A behavioural comparison. *Journal of Interpersonal Violence, 2,* 391–402.

Friedrich, W., Beilke, R., & Urquiza, A. (1988). Behaviour problems in young sexually abused boys. *Journal of Interpersonal Violence, 3,* 21–27.

Friedrich, W., Grambach, P., Damon, L., Hewitt, S., Koverola, C., Lang, R., Wolfe, V., & Broughton, D. (1992). The Child Sexual Behaviour Inventory: Normative and clinical findings. *Psychological Assessment, 4,* 303–311.

Friedrich, W., & Leucke, W. (1988). Young school-age sexually aggressive children. I. Assessment and comparison. *Professional Psychology, 19,* 155–164.

Friedrich, W., & Lui, B. (1985). *An observational rating scale for sexually abused children.* Unpublished manuscript. University of Washington, Seattle.

Friedrich, W. N., Urquiza, A. J., & Beilke, R. L. (1986). Behaviour problems in sexually abused young children. *Journal of Pediatric Psychology, 11,* 47–57.

Fromuth, M. (1986). The relationship of childhood sexual abuse with later psychological and sexual adjustment in a sample of college women. *Child Abuse and Neglect, 10,* 5–15.

Gale, J., Thompson, R., Moran, T., & Sack, W. (1988). Sexual abuse in young children: Its clinical presentation and characteristic patterns. *Child Abuse & Neglect, 12,* 163–170.

Gentile, C. (1988). *Factors mediating the impact of child sexual abuse: Learned helplessness and severity of abuse.* Unpublished master's thesis. University of Western Ontario, London, Ontario.

German, D. E., Habenicht, D. J., & Futcher, W. G. (1990). Psychological profile of the female adolescent incest victim. *Child Abuse & Neglect, 14,* 429–438.

Gold, E. (1986). Long-term effects of sexual victimization in childhood: An attributional approach. *Journal of Consulting and Clinical Psychology, 54,* 471–475.

Goldston, D. B., Turnquist, D. C., & Knutson, J. F. (1989). Presenting problems of sexually abused girls receiving psychiatric services. *Journal of Abnormal Psychology, 98,* 314–317.

Gomes-Schwartz, B., Horowitz, J., & Cardarelli, A. (1990). *Child sexual abuse: The initial effects.* Newbury Park, CA: Sage.

Greenwald, E., & Leitenberg, H. (1990). Post-traumatic stress disorder in a nonclinical and nonstudent sample of adult women sexually abused as children. *Journal of Interpersonal Violence, 5,* 217–228.

Greenwald, E., Leitenberg, H., Cado, S., & Tarran, M. (1990). Childhood sexual abuse: Long-term effects on psychological and sexual functioning in a nonclinical and nonstudent sample of adult women. *Child Abuse and Neglect, 14,* 503–513.

Gruber, K. J., & Jones, R. J. (1981). Does sexual abuse lead to delinquent behaviour? A critical look at the evidence. *Victimology: An International Journal, 6,* 85–91.

Gundlach, R. (1977). Sexual molestation and rape reported by homosexual and heterosexual women. *Journal of Homosexuality, 2,* 367–384.

Harter, S., & Alexander, P. (1988). Long-term effects of incestuous child abuse in college women: Social adjustment, social cognition, and family characteristics. *Journal of Consulting and Clinical Psychology, 56,* 5–8.

Harter, S., & Pike, R. (1984). The Pictorial Scale of Perceived Competence and Social Acceptance for Young Children. *Child Development, 55,* 1969–1982.

Hibbard, B., & Hartman, G. (1990). Emotional indicators in human figure drawings of sexually victimized and nonabused children. *Journal of Clinical Psychology, 46,* 211–219.

Hibbard, B., Roghmann, K., & Hoekelman, R. (1987). Genitalia in children's drawings: An association with sexual abuse. *Pediatrics, 79,* 129–137.

Hotte, J. P., and Rafman, S. (1992). The specific effects of incest on prepubertal girls from dysfunctional families. *Child Abuse and Neglect, 16,* 273–283.

Inderbitzen-Pisaruk, H., Shawchuck, C. R., & Hoier, T. S. (1992). Behavioural characteristics of child victims of sexual abuse: A comparison study. *Journal of Clinical Child Psychology, 21,* 14–19.

Ireton, H., & Thwing, E. (1977). *Minnesota Child Development Inventory.* Minneapolis, MN: Behavioral Systems.

Janoff-Bulman, R. (1989). Assumptive worlds and the stress of traumatic events: Applications of the schema construct. *Social Cognition, 7,* 113–136.

Johnson, B. K., & Kenkel, M. B. (1991). Stress, coping, and adjustment in female adolescent incest victims. *Child Abuse & Neglect, 15,* 293–305.

Kendall-Tackett, K. A., Williams, L. M., & Finkelhor, D. (1993). Impact of sexual abuse on children: A review and synthesis of recent empirical studies. *Psychological Bulletin, 13,* 164–180.

Kilpatrick, D. G., Veronen, L. J., & Resnick, P. A. (1979). Assessment of the aftermath of rape: Changing patterns of fear. *Journal of Behavioural Assessment, 1,* 133–148.

Kolko, D. J., Moser, J. T., & Weldy, S. R. (1988). Behavioural/emotional indicators of sexual abuse in child psychiatric inpatients: A controlled comparison with physical abuse. *Child Abuse & Neglect, 12,* 529–541.

Kovacs, M., and Beck, A. (1977). An empirical-clinical approach toward a definition of childhood depression. In J. G. Schulterbrandt & A. Raskin (Eds.). *Depression in childhood: Diagnosis, treatment and conceptual models* (pp. 1–25). New York: Raven.

Kreiger, M. J., & Robbins, J. (1985). The adolescent incest victim and the juvenile system. *American Journal of Orthopsychiatry, 55,* 419–425.

Lachar, D., Gdowski, C., & Snyder, D. (1984). External validation of the Personality Inventory for Children. *Journal of Consulting & Clinical Psychology, 54,* 155–164.

Lazarus, R. S., & Folkman, S. (1984). *Stress, appraisal, and coping.* New York: Springer.

Leitenberg, H., Greenwald, E., & Cado, S. (1992). A retrospective study of long-term methods of coping with having been sexually abused during childhood. *Child Abuse and Neglect, 16,* 399–407.

Lindberg, F., & Distad, L. (1985). Post-traumatic stress disorders in women who experienced childhood incest. *Child Abuse & Neglect, 9,* 329–334.

Malinosky-Rummell, R., & Hoier, T. S. (November, 1990). *Dissociation in sexually abused children: Behavioural assessment and treatment implications.* Paper presented at the annual meeting of the Association for the Advancement of Behavior Therapy, San Francisco, CA.

Mannarino, A., Cohen, J., & Gregor, M. (1989). Emotional and behavioural difficulties in sexually abused girls. *Journal of Interpersonal Violence, 4,* 437–451.

McLeer, S., Deblinger, E., Atkins, M., Foa, E., & Ralphe, D. (1988). Post-traumatic stress disorder in sexually abused children. *Journal of the American Academy of Child & Adolescent Psychiatry, 27,* 650–654.

Meiselman, K. (1978). *Incest: A psychological study of causes and effects with treatment recommendations.* San Francisco, CA: Jossey-Bass.

Meiselman, K. (1980). Personality characteristics of incest history psychotherapy patients: A research note. *Journal of Sexual Behaviour, 9,* 195–197.

Miller, L. (1977). *Louisville Behavior Checklist.* Los Angeles: Western Psychological Services.

Miller, L., Hampe, E., Barrett, C., & Nobel, H. (1971). Children's deviant behavior within the general population. *Journal of Consulting & Clinical Psychology, 37,* 16–22.

Murphy, S., Kilpatrick, D., Amick-McMullan, A., Veronen, L., Paduhovich, J., Best, C., Villeponteauz, L., & Saunders, B. (1988). Current psychological functioning of child sexual assault survivors. *Journal of Interpersonal Violence, 3,* 55–79.

O'Donohue, W., & Elliot, A. (1993). Treatment of the sexually abused child: A review. *Journal of Clinical Child Psychology, 3,* 218–228.

Ollendick, T. (1983). Reliability and validity of the Revised Fear Survey Schedule for Children. *Behaviour Research & Therapy, 21,* 685–692.

Pallotta, G., & Hansen, D. (November, 1990). *Long-term psychological adjustment in adult female survivors of intrafamilial and extrafamilial child sexual abuse.* Presented at the 24th Annual Convention of the Association for Advancement of Behaviour Therapy, San Francisco, CA.

Peters, S. (1988). Child sexual abuse and later psychological problems. In G. Wyatt & G. Powell (Eds.). *Lasting effects of child sexual abuse* (pp. 101–117). Newbury Park, CA: Sage.

Piers, E. (1984). *Piers-Harris Children's Self-Concept Scale* (Revised manual). Los Angeles: Western Psychological Services.

Porter, R. B., & Cattell, R. B. (1975). *Children's Personality Questionnaire.* Champaign, IL: Institute for Personality & Ability Testing.

Putnam, F., & Trickett, P. (1987). *The psychobiological effects of sexual abuse: Female growth and development during childhood and adolescence.* National Institute of Mental Health, Bethesda, MD.

Ray, K., Jackson, J., & Long, P. (1990, November). *History of sexual abuse and family environment: Understanding victims' later social and psychological adjustment.* Paper presented at the annual meeting of the Association for Advancement of Behavior Therapy, San Francisco, CA.

Reynolds, C., & Richmond, B. (1978). What I think and feel: A revised measure of children's manifest anxiety. *Journal of Abnormal Child Psychology, 6,* 271–280.

Sansonnet-Hayden, H., Haley, G., Marriage, K., & Fine, S. (1987). Sexual abuse and psychopathology in hospitalized adolescents. *Journal of the American Academy of Child & Adolescent Psychiatry, 26,* 753–757.

Scott, R., & Stone, D. (1986). MMPI Profile constellations in incest families. *Journal of Consulting and Clinical Psychology, 54,* 364–368.

Sedney, M., & Brooks, B. (1984). Factors associated with a history of childhood sexual experience in a nonclinical female population. *Journal of the American Academy of Child Psychiatry, 23,* 215–218.

Seidner, A., & Calhoun, K. (July, 1984). *Childhood sexual abuse: Factors related to differential adult adjustment.* Paper presented at the 2nd Annual National Family Violence Research Conference, Durham, New Hampshire.

Sirles, E. A., & Smith, J. A. (September, 1990). *Behavioural profiles of preschool, latency, and teenage female incest victims.* Paper presented at the annual meeting of the International Society for the Prevention of Child Abuse and Neglect, Hamburg, Germany.

Sirles, E. A., Smith, J. A., & Kusama, H. (1989). Psychiatric status of intrafamilial child sexual abuse victims. *Journal of the American Academy of Child and Adolescent Psychiatry, 28,* 225–229.

Spielberger, C. (1973). *Manual for the State-Trait Anxiety Inventory for Children.* Palo Alto, CA: Consulting Psychologist Press.

Steele, B. (1986). Notes on the lasting effects of early child abuse throughout the life cycle. *Child Abuse and Neglect, 10,* 283–291.

Terr, L. (1987). *Severe stress and sudden shock—the connection.* Sam Hibbs Award Lecture, American Psychiatric Association, Convention, Chicago, IL.

Tong, L., Oates, K., & McDowell, M. (1987). Personality development following sexual abuse. *Child Abuse & Neglect, 11,* 371–383.

Tsai, M., Feldman-Summers, & Edger, M. (1979). Childhood molestation: Variables related to differential impacts on psychosexual functioning in adult women. *Journal of Abnormal Psychology, 88,* 407–417.

Watchel, A., & Scott, B. (1991). The impact of child sexual abuse in developmental perspective. In C. Bagley & R. Thomlinson (Eds.), *Child sexual abuse: Critical perspectives on prevention, intervention, and treatment* (pp. 79–120). Toronto: Wall & Emerson.

White, S., Halpin, B. M., Strom, G. A., & Santilli, G. (1988). Behavioral comparisons of young sexually abused, neglected, and nonabused children. *Journal of Clinical Child Psychology, 17,* 53–61.

White, S., Strom, G., Santilli, G., & Halpin, B. (1986). Interviewing young sexual abuse victims with anatomically correct dolls. *Child Abuse & Neglect, 10,* 519–529.

Wolfe, V. V. (November, 1990). *Type I and Type II PTSD: A conceptual framework for sexual abuse sequelae.* In symposium "The Behavioral Assessment and Treatment of the Sexually Abused Child." Presented at the annual meeting of the Association for the Advancement of Behaviour Therapy, San Francisco, CA.

Wolfe, V. V., & Gentile, C. (1987). *Children's Impact of Traumatic Events Scale-Revised.* Unpublished assessment instrument. Children's Hospital of Western Ontario, London, Ontario.

Wolfe, V. V., & Gentile, C. (1992). Psychological assessment of sexually abused children. In W. O'Donahue and J. H. Geer (Eds.), *The sexual abuse of children: Clinical issues,* Vol. 2 (pp. 143–187). Hillsdale, NJ: Erlbaum.

Wolfe, V. V., Gentile, C., & Klinck, A. (1988). *Psychometric properties of the Sexual Abuse Fear Evaluation (SAFE).* Unpublished manuscript. Children's Hospital of Western Ontario, London, Ontario.

Wolfe, V., Gentile, C., Michienzi, T., Sas, L., & Wolfe, D. (1991). The Children's Impact of Traumatic Events Scale-Revised: A measure of postsexual abuse PTSD symptoms. *Behavioral Assessment, 14,* 359–383.

Wolfe, V., Gentile, C., & Wolfe, D. (1989). The impact of sexual abuse on children: A PTSD formulation. *Behavior Therapy, 20,* 215–228.

Wolfe, V. V., Sirles, E. A., Michienzi, T., & Evans, B. (November, 1992). *Child Behaviour Checklist item differences among sexually abused, nonabused/clinic-referred, and standardization samples.* Poster presented at the annual meeting of the Association for the Advancement of Behaviour Therapy, Boston, MA.

Wolfe, V., & Wolfe, D. (1986). *The Sexual Abuse Fear Evaluation (SAFE): A subscale for the Fear Survey Schedule for Children-Revised.* Unpublished questionnaire. Children's Hospital of Western Ontario, London, Ontario.

Wolfe, V., & Wolfe, D. (1988). The sexually abused child. In E. Mash & L. Terdal (Eds.), *Behavioural assessment of childhood disorders, 2nd ed.* (pp. 670–714). New York: Guildford Press.

Wolfe, V. V., Wolfe, D. A., Gentile, C., & Bourdeau, P. A. (August, 1981). *The Victimization History Form: Assessing type and severity of maltreatment.* Assessing type and severity of maltreatment. In symposium entitled, "Growing up with the violence: Victimization and maltreatment of children." Presented at the American Psychological Association, New York City.

Wozencraft, T., Wagner, W., & Pellegrin, A. (1991). Depression and suicidal ideation in sexually abused children. *Child Abuse & Neglect, 15,* 505–511.

Yates, A. (1982). Children eroticized by incest. *American Journal of Psychiatry, 139,* 482–485.

Yates, A., Beutler, L., & Crago, M. (1985). Drawings by child victims of incest. *Child Abuse & Neglect, 9,* 183–189.

7

Stimulant Medications and the Treatment of Children with ADHD

James M. Swanson, Keith McBurnett, Diane L. Christian, and Tim Wigal

1. Introduction to Stimulant Pharmacotherapy for Children with ADHD

Stimulant medications have been used for over 55 years to treat children affected by a condition once called *hyperactivity* and now termed *attention deficit disorder* (ADD) (DSM-III, 1980) or *attention-deficit hyperactivity disorder* (ADHD) (DSM-III-R, 1987; DSM-IV, 1994). In this chapter, we will use the term currently *en vogue* (ADHD) to refer to all of the conditions (e.g., minimal brain damage, minimal brain dysfunction, hyperactivity, hyperkinesis, attention deficit disorder) which over the years have shared some or all of the basic symptoms of this disorder (i.e., inattention, impulsivity, and hyperactivity).

Initially, d,l-amphetamine (Benzedrine) was used to treat children with ADHD (Bradley, 1937), but its clinical use was displaced by a refinement of the amphetamine compound, d-amphetamine (Dexedrine) (Bradley, 1950). Subsequently, amphetamine-like compounds, methylphenidate (Ritalin) and pemoline (Cylert), were tried as alternatives to Dexedrine (e.g., see Conners, 1971), and by the 1970s Ritalin became the primary stimulant used in the treatment of children with ADHD (see Millichap, 1973; Greenhill, 1991).

JAMES M. SWANSON, KEITH MCBURNETT, DIANE L. CHRISTIAN, AND TIM WIGAL • Department of Pediatrics, Child Development Center, University of California at Irvine, Irvine, California 92715.

Advances in Clinical Child Psychology, Volume 17, edited by Thomas H. Ollendick and Ronald J. Prinz. Plenum Press, New York, 1995.

Over the past half-century, a standard *stimulant pharmacotherapy* has emerged, which in the United States is now considered to be an essential part of treatment for children with ADHD. It has been estimated that between 60% and 90% of the diagnosed cases of ADHD are treated with stimulant medication (Whalen & Henker, 1991). Given the relatively high prevalence of ADHD diagnoses (e.g., 3% to 6%) and the size of the school-aged population, estimates of the absolute number of children being treated with stimulant medication are high (e.g., 0.75 to 1.5 million, see Safer & Krager, 1988; PGARD, 1990). In this chapter, we will use this new term (stimulant pharmacotherapy) to refer to the use of any of the three stimulant drugs (i.e., methylphenidate, amphetamine, and pemoline) for the treatment of children with ADHD.

The complexity and sheer size of the literature on stimulant pharmacotherapy for ADHD make it difficult to achieve a comprehensive perspective on what findings are widely accepted and how inconsistencies in conclusions have arisen (see Swanson et al., 1993). In this chapter, to achieve a perspective as comprehensive as possible, we briefly discuss the class of drugs labeled as *stimulants*, the neural and chemical basis of their psychoactive properties, and their pharmacologic characteristics. Next, we discuss the clinical use of the three primary stimulants, including the typical clinical titration methods, dose-related effects on behavior and cognition, and the time course of the available (approved and marketed) preparations of these drugs. Then, we present a summary of significant historical events that have affected the literature on stimulant pharmacotherapy. Finally, we present a synthesis of the vast literature, based on a "review of reviews" (see Swanson et al., 1993) that we conducted for the U.S. Department of Education, which defines the acknowledged benefits and limitations of stimulant pharmacotherapy and includes a discussion of controversies that exist in the literature. This chapter is intended to review some of the advances in research and clinical practice that have improved our understanding about basic pharmacological and behavioral effects of stimulant medications, to acquaint the readers with some of the consensus views that emerged in the literature, and to discuss some of the controversies that have persisted over time.

1.1. Stimulant Drugs: Methylphenidate, Amphetamine, and Pemoline

Methylphenidate (Ritalin), d-amphetamine (Dexedrine), and pemoline (Cylert), the drugs most often used to treat children with ADHD, are usually called *stimulants*, but they have also been called *sympathomimetics*, *central nervous system* (CNS) *stimulants*, and *catecholaminergic agonists*. These labels are based on the effects of these drugs on physiological and neural systems (Gittelman & Kanner, 1986; Gilman, Goodman, Rall, &

Murad, 1985). For example, these drugs are considered to be sympatho-mimetics because they act on the sympathetic nervous system and their peripheral effects are mediated by adrenaline (epinephrine) and the phys-iological systems involved in the "fight or flight" reaction. In contrast to some other stimulants, it is thought that these three drugs exert most of their effects on the central nervous system (e.g., see Gillman et al., 1985), and thus they are called CNS stimulants. The mechanisms of action of methylphenidate and amphetamine have been linked to effects on three neurotransmitters, dopamine (DA), norepinephrine (NE), and epinephrine (E), which are classified as catecholamines (Gillman et al., 1985). The common view is that when present at the synapse of a catecholaminergic neuron, these drugs increase the availability of neurotransmitters (i.e., DA, NE, or E) by a drug-induced release of stored neurotransmitter or inhibi-tion of presynaptic uptake of the released neurotransmitter (see Coyle & Snyder, 1969; Baldessarini, 1972; Snyder & Meyerhoff, 1973; Wender, 1971, 1973; Cohen & Young, 1977; Hauger, Angel, Janowsky, Berger, & Hulihan-Gilbin, 1990). Thus, these drugs are called catecholamine agonists.

1.2. Neural and Chemical Properties

The stimulants interact with catecholaminergic neurons and affect many areas of the CNS (see Baldessarni, 1972; Cohen & Young, 1977; Porrino, Lucignani, Dow-Edwards, & Sokoloff, 1984; Porrino & Lucignani, 1987; Zametkin & Rapoport, 1987). The neuroanatomy of brain systems dependent on catecholamine-mediated neurotransmission has been well-defined (see Coyle & Snyder, 1969; Cohen & Young, 1977; Cooper, Bloom, & Roth, 1986). Research on methylphenidate and amphetamine indicates that these drugs have effects on specific dopamine nuclei (including the substantia nigra, caudate nucleus, and the nucleus accumbens) and spe-cific norepinephrine nuclei and projections (including the locus coeruleus, the ventral bundle, and the dorsal bundle) (see Zametkin & Rapoport, 1987). Recently, brain imaging studies have improved our understanding of the sites of action of these two drugs: A PET (positron emission tomog-raphy) study on animals (Porrino & Lucignani, 1987) revealed that, in addition to a variety of unique effects, the common effect of low doses of d-amphetamine and methylphenidate was to increase glucose metabolism in the nucleus accumbens, and a SPECT (single photon emission computed tomography) study on children with ADHD (Lou, Henriksen, & Bruhn, 1990) revealed that the effect of a clinical dose of methylphenidate was to increase blood flow to striatal areas and to decrease blood flow to primary sensory areas of the brain.

The interactions of stimulants with catecholaminergic neurons are complex, and the mechanisms that account for the clinical effects of stimulant pharmacotherapy are not completely understood. For example, the clinical effects may be due to interactions with catecholaminergic neurons at presynaptic or postsynaptic receptor sites (see Solanto, 1986; McCracken, 1991). The presynaptic and postsynaptic sites are differentially sensitive to drug concentration (Carlsson, 1975), which may result in low doses of stimulants having an antagonist effect and high doses having an agonist effect on catecholaminergic neurons (see Solanto, 1986). Also, similar clinical effects may be dependent on different mechanisms. For example, even though methylphenidate and d-amphetamine have very similar effects on behavior, they may not have identical effects on dopaminergic neurons: both drugs may release DA, but d-amphetamine may release newly synthesized DA from the cytoplasm, whereas methylphenidate may release stored DA for vessicles (see McMillen, 1983; Haugher et al., 1990).

The DA and NE neurotransmitter systems and neural networks have been associated with possible etiologies of ADHD as well as the mechanisms of response to treatment with stimulant drugs (see Malone, Kershner, & Swanson, 1994; McCracken, 1991; Swanson et al., 1990; Zametkin & Rapoport, 1987; Shaywitz, Yager, & Klopper, 1976; Snyder & Meyerhoff, 1973; Wender, 1971). Some theories have emphasized the primary role of DA (e.g., Shaywitz et al., 1976), some the primary role of NE (e.g., Wender, 1971; Zametkin & Rapoport, 1987), and others the involvement of both (e.g., Swanson et al., 1990; McCracken, 1991). Recently, we (Swanson et al., 1990) suggested that the ADHD symptoms may reflect an underactive DA-mediated motor activation system and an overactive NE-mediated arousal system, but this hypothesis is speculative and has not been put to a rigorous empirical test.

1.2.1. Amphetamine

The catecholamines share a common chemical structure (see Gillman et al., 1985, Table 8-1, p. 149), a *catechol* group (a benzene ring with a hydroxyl (OH) groups substituted in the 3 and 4 positions), a 2-carbon (β and α) side chain, and a terminal amino group (NH_2). The basic chemical structure of amphetamine is similar (an unsubstituted benzene ring, a 2-carbon side chain, and a terminal amino group) (see Grinspoon & Hedblom, 1975), as shown in Figure 1.

The 2-carbon side chain provides the basis for stereoisomers. Stereochemistry deals with molecular structure in three dimensions, and basic chemistry textbooks (e.g., Morrison & Boyd, 1987) provide precise definitions of some terms used here (e.g., *isomers, optical isomers, stereoisomers, enantiomers, dextro, levo, erythro, threo, racemic, chiral centers, optical asymmetry*, etc.). Substitutions at different positions of the carbon atoms can give rise to stereoisomers (chemically identical compounds that are dis-

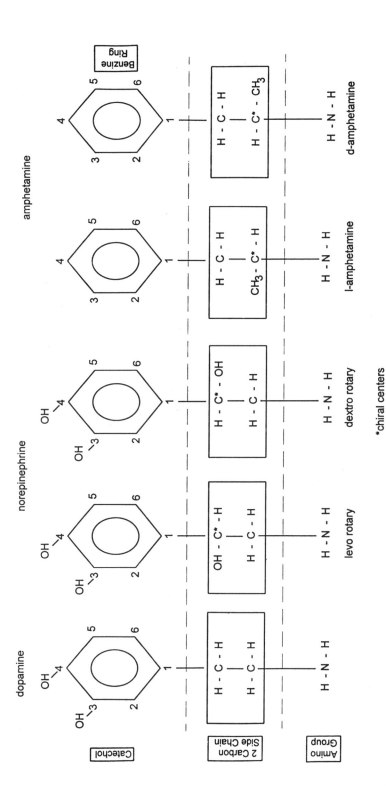

FIGURE 1. The basic chemical structure of catecholamines and amphetamines.

tinguished by how polarized light is rotated when passed through a solution of one of the stereoisomers).

As shown in Figure 1, for norepinephrine the β-carbon is a *chiral center* and substitution of an hydroxyl-group (OH) at different positions produces stereoisomers, while for amphetamine the α-carbon is a chiral center and substitution of a methyl-group (CH$_3$) at different positions produced stereoisomers. These stereoisomers are composed of the same atoms joined by bonds of the same length and set at the same angles, but they are mirror-image pairs and are called *enantiomers.*

The two stereoisomers of amphetamine (d-amphetamine and l-amphetamine) differ substantially in their effects on the catecholamine systems (see Coyle & Snyder, 1969) and on behavior (see Snyder & Meyerhoff, 1973; Arnold, Heustis, Scheib, Wemmer, & Colner, 1976). The initial clinical studies on stimulant pharmacotherapy were conducted before drugs based on the separate stereoisomers of amphetamine were available for clinical use, so Bradley (1937) used and reported on the effects of Benzedrine (d,l-amphetamine, a *racemic* mixture of equal amounts of the two stereoisomers). Later, he used Dexedrine (d-amphetamine, a pure stereoisomer). By combining data from these two experiences, Bradley (1950) was able to compare the clinically effective doses derived from large clinical samples of "maladjusted children" treated with Dexedrine (131 cases) and Benzedrine (275 cases). Statistics were not presented, but inspection of the tables from Bradley (1950) shows that the modal dose for Dexedrine (10 mg/day) was half the modal dose for Benzedrine (20 mg/day). This suggested that in stimulant pharmacotherapy for children with ADHD, one of the stereoisomers (l-amphetamine) was relatively inactive, and apparently this led to the general acceptance of the other stereoisomer, d-amphetamine (Dexedrine), as the preferred form of amphetamine for clinical use. However, the inactivity of the l-amphetamine isomer has been questioned (see Snyder & Meyerhoff, 1973; Arnold et al., 1976). Apparently, l-amphetamine has behavioral effects on some symptoms of ADHD (Arnold et al., 1976), and in other research areas l-amphetamine has been shown to be active for eliciting psychosis and stereotypies (see Snyder & Meyerhoff, 1973). This suggests that the l-amphetamine stereoisomer is not completely inactive. Instead it may be relatively inactive in terms of its effect on NE (and certain drug-induced behavioral effects), but active in terms of its effect on DA (and other drug-induced behavioral effects).

1.2.2. Methylphenidate

Methylphenidate (Ritalin) was developed in the 1940s, reformulated in the 1950s, and then tried as an alternative to the amphetamines (Benzedrine and Dexedrine) as a treatment for ADHD (e.g., see Greenhill & Osman, 1991). Apparently, when titrated to effective clinical doses, the two drugs are about equally effective, but some reports suggest that Ritalin has fewer side effects (see Conners, 1971; Millichap, 1973). Two brands of methylphenidate are available for clinical use: Ritalin which is manufactured by CIBA, but the patent expired in the 1980s, and a generic brand which is now manufactured by MD Pharmaceuticals. The Food and Drug Administration has evaluated these two products, and based on this and a review by the Therapeutic Inequivalency Action Coordinating Committee, the U.S. Department of Health and Human Services recently rated them as *AB* or *bioequivalent* drugs (see p. 47 of the HHS Approved Drug Products with Therapeutic Equivalence Evaluation, Supplement 12, 1991).

Methylphenidate is similar in chemical structure to amphetamine, with an unsubstituted benzine ring and a two-carbon side chain plus an ester group (see Fig. 2). For methylphenidate, both of the carbons are chiral centers, which produce optical asymmetries and stereoisomers (Patrick, Mueller, Gualtieri, & Breese, 1987). Two sets of terms (*dextro* and *levo; threo* and *erythro*) are used to describe the stereochemistry of methylphenidate. In order to unambiguously label the absolute configuration of the different substituents around the asymmetric carbons located in each half of the structure, these terms are used in a factorial combination to describe the four *diastereomers* of methylphenidate: d-threo-methylpheidate, l-threo-methylphenidate, d-erythro-methylpheidate, and l-erythro-methylphenidate. The threo isomers are *enantiomers* because both an ester group and an amine group change, forming a mirror-image pair (see Fig. 2). In the same way, the erythro isomers form a mirror-image pair. Both brands of methylphenidate (CIBA and MD) consist of an equal mixture of two of the four optical isomers (the threo pair, d-threo-methylphenidate and l-threo-methylphenidate).

Recent work in Canada (see Srinivas, Hubbard, Quinn, & Midha, 1992; Hubbard, Srinivas, Quinn, & Midha, 1989; Srinivas, Quinn, Hubbard, & Midha, 1987) suggests that only the d-isomer (d-threo-methylphenidate) portion of Ritalin has clinically significant effects. When l-isomer (l-threo-methylphenidate) was given alone, it had little or no effect on children with ADHD, and on an absolute-dose basis, the *racemic* mixture (d,l-threo-methylphenidate) was about half as potent as the same amount of the d-isomer optical isomer d-threo-methylphenidate. However, this perceived inactivity of l-threo-methylphenidate may be similar to the perceived inactivity of the l-amphetamine, which appears to be restricted to one of the catecholaminergic systems (i.e., NE) and does not extend to all behaviors (see Snyder & Meyerhoff, 1973; Arnold et al., 1976).

In summary, both amphetamine (see Fig. 1) and methylphenidate (see Fig. 2) have sets of stereoisomers that have different psychoactive qualities.

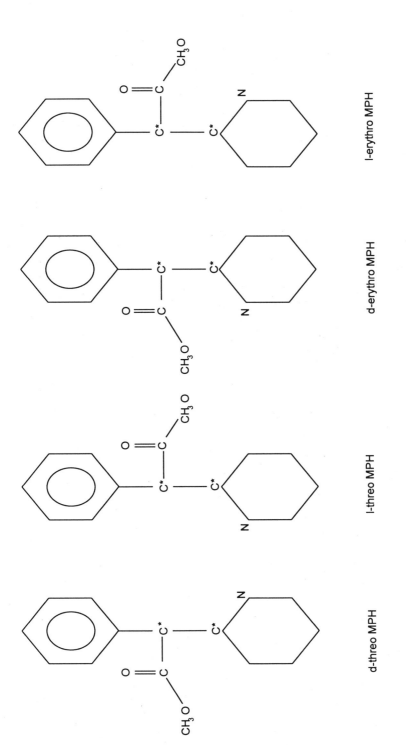

d-threo MPH   l-threo MPH   d-erythro MPH   l-erythro MPH

* chiral centers

FIGURE 2. The stereoisomer of methylphenidate.

Since Ritalin (d,l-threo-methylphenidate) consists of a racemic mixture of a psychoactive and a relatively inactive stereoisomer, it may be more like Benzedrine (d,l-amphetamine, also a racemic mixture) than Dexedrine (d-amphetamine, a pure stereoisomer). The clinical efficacy of each of these stimulant drugs is related to the amount of the psychoactive stereoisomer contained in the compound, and this offers a possible explanation of why the usual clinical dose of Ritalin (e.g., 10 mg per administration, which consists of 5 mg of d-threo-methylphenidate and 5 mg of l-threo-methylphenidate) is about twice the usual clinical dose of Dexedrine (e.g., 5 mg per administration, which consists of 5 mg of d-amphetamine and 0 mg of l-amphetamine).

In this chapter, we will use the generic term *methylphenidate* to refer to the combinations of stereoisomers of Ritalin (d-threo-methylphenidate and l-threo-methylphenidate), and the generic term *amphetamine* to refer to the stereoisomer of Dexedrine (d-amphetamine). The modifying prefixes (*d-* and *l-* and *erythro-*and *threo-*) will be used if the distinction is required for clarity.

1.3. Pharmacokinetic Properties

1.3.1. Relationship of Behavioral Effect to Serum Level

Methylphenidate and amphetamine are fast-acting drugs. After oral administration, both drugs are rapidly absorbed, and their clinical effects appear within 1 hour and last about 4 hours. However, even though the time course of behavioral effect is about the same for the two drugs, the relationship of behavioral effect to serum level over this short time course is different. The serum blood level and the primary behavioral effect of methylphenidate have a *similar* time course: both reach a maximum between 1 and 2 hours after oral administration and have a half-life of about 3 hours (see Swanson, Kinsbourne, Roberts, & Zucker, 1978; Chan et al., 1980; Chan et al., 1983; Shaywitz et al., 1982; Guaulteri et al., 1982; Srinivas et al., 1992). In contrast, the serum blood level and the primary behavioral effect of d-amphetamine have a *different* time course: the primary behavioral effect peaks at about 1 to 2 hours after administration but dissipates by the time of the serum level reaches its peak at about 4 hours after administration (see Brown, Hunt, Ebert, Bunney, & Kopin, 1979). The primary behavioral effect of amphetamine appears to be proportional to the slope of the rising serum-level curve; and based on this relationship, Brown, Ebert, Mikkelson, & Hunt (1980) suggested that the mechanism of action of amphetamine is related to the stimulation of release of catecholamines rather than inhibition of reuptake, and that this mechanism restricts its psychoactive properties to the absorption phase.

1.3.2. Individual Differences in Serum Level of Methylphenidate

Chan et al. (1980) contrasted serum levels of intravenous (IV) and oral administrations of methylphenidate (Ritalin), which provided an estimate of the bioavailability in 6 children with ADHD. Bioavailability (10.5% to 52.4%) varied by a factor of 5 across these individuals, which Shaywitz et al. (1982) pointed out was about the same as the variation in the clinical dose of methylphenidate (Ritalin) across individuals (i.e., from 5 mg to 20 mg per administration, on a twice per day (*bid*) or three times per day (*tid*) schedule). Gaultieri et al. (1982) have emphasized the variability of the absolute values of serum levels across individuals, and because of this they were not able to specify a narrow therapeutic range based on serum level that would be better than the range based on dose of medication. Even though both Shaywitz et al. (1982) and Gualteri et al. (1982) noted individual variability for absolute serum level, they both pointed out that the time course (peak time and half-life) of the serum level of methylphenidate was very similar across all individuals tested, and that this time course of serum level matched the time course of the behavioral effect on learning reported by Swanson et al. (1978) and replicated by others (e.g., Conners & Solanto, 1984; Rapport & Kelly, 1991; Kupietz, 1991) for cognitive measures of behavioral effect.

1.3.3. Long-Acting Forms of the Stimulants

One of the primary drawbacks of both amphetamine and methylphenidate is a short behavioral half-life. Long-acting forms of the stimulants have been developed (Cylert, Ritalin SR, and Dexedrine Spansules), but these forms of the stimulant drugs have not been widely adopted for clinical use. This may be due to problems of efficacy or tolerance (see Greenhill, 1991). For example, Brown et al. (1980) reported that a long-acting form of d-amphetamine designed to mimic the standard daily dose of 5 mg *bid* of Dexedrine (i.e., a 10-mg Dexedrine Spansule) did not produce a significantly longer effect than the single, morning administration of a short-acting form of d-amphetamine (i.e., a 5-mg Dexedrine tablet). They suggested that behavioral effect of the slow-release form of d-amphetamine may be limited by the mechanism of action (release of newly synthesized neurotransmitter) which restricts its psychoactive properties to the absorption phase. Similarly, Pelham et al. (1987) evaluated the slow-release form of methylphenidate and reported that a standard dose of methylphenidate (i.e., 10-mg *bid* Ritalin tablets) was more effective than the dose of the slow-release form designed to mimic this standard dose (i.e., 20-mg Ritalin SR). Pelham et al. (1987) speculated that this may be due to lower peak- and absolute serum levels associated with the gradual release of Ritalin SR compared to Ritalin tablets. Standard Ritalin tablets and Ritalin SR may be equated by adjusting the dose of the two forms of this drug. However, the individual titration of Ritalin SR is not an option in clinical practice at this time, since only a 20-mg Ritalin SR dose is available, and it should *not* be divided (e.g., by cutting it into pieces to make lower doses), due to the specific preparation (a wax matrix) used to achieve slow release.

Another stimulant, pemoline (Cylert), is considered to be a long-acting CNS stimulant for the treatment of children with ADHD. Based on the serum half-life in adults (about 12 hours), once-a-day dosing is recommended [see Physician's Desk Reference (PDR), 1990]. However, the serum and behavioral half-life of Cylert in children with ADHD is much less than in adults (Collier et al., 1985). The serum half-life values ($t_{1/2}$) reported by Collier et al. (1985, Table 3) are positively related to age (yr): under 6–7 yr: $t_{1/2}$ = 5.4 hr; 7–8 yr: $t_{1/2}$ = 7.2 hr; 8–9 yr: $t_{1/2}$ = 7.9 hr: 10–11 yr: $t_{1/2}$ = 8.4 hr. This suggests that in elementary school-aged children (i.e., 5 to 12 years), the recommended once-a-day dosing with Cylert may not be sufficient for clinical purposes. Swanson et al. (1978) recommended a sculpted *bid* dose regime of Cylert (an early morning 75-mg dose, followed by a noon 37.5-mg dose) to equate time and dose effects for comparison to a *tid* dose regime of Ritalin (a 10-mg dose at 7:30 AM, 11:30 AM, and 3:30 PM). Under these dosing conditions, the behavioral effect of these two stimulants appear to be about the same.

Cylert has been described as having a delayed onset of action, with clinical improvement emerging up to 2 weeks after treatment is initiated (see PDR, 1990). However, in research with children, Cylert has been shown to be a fast-acting drug, with maximum behavioral effect and peak serum level attained about 2 to 4 hours after the second administration (Swanson, et al., 1978; Pelham & Bender, 1982; Collier et al., 1985; Pelham et al., 1990). The manufacturer's initial recommendation was to start at 18.75 mg and to increase in weekly 18.75-mg increments (see Dykman, McGrew, Harris, Peters, & Ackerman, 1976), and when this is followed, the average effective morning dose (75 mg) is not prescribed until the fourth week of treatment. A change in the recommended starting dose to 37.5 mg (PDR, 1990) has reduced this delay to 3 weeks. Thus, the reported delayed onset of action may be due to a delay in prescribing the effective clinical dose, rather than to a delay associated with a pharmacologic process (e.g., the need to reach steady-state serum level) or a receptor process (e.g., the development of supersensitivity or subsensitivity).

The practice of using a slow increase in the initial dose of Cylert was probably developed because the initial dose tends to elicit motor side effects (e.g., tics, grimaces, etc.) in many drug-naive cases. Thus, the purpose of delayed prescribing may be to allow for adaptation to a side effect. However, in a systematic dose-response investigation of Cylert, we (Swanson et al., 1978; Pelham & Bender, 1982) observed that this tendency toward motor side effects can be avoided in most cases by using a titration schedule based on a slightly higher starting dose (e.g., 37.5 mg) and small *daily* increases (e.g., 18.75 mg). When this schedule is used, the average effective dose of Cylert may be reached in 3 to 4 *days* instead of 3 to 4 weeks.

2. Behavioral and Clinical Effects of Stimulant Pharmacotherapy

In clinical practice, stimulant pharmacotherapy typically involves two stages: titration and maintenance. The first stage, titration, is an experimental process of trying different doses or forms of stimulants (e.g., on a per-administration basis, 5 mg to 20 mg of methylphenidate, 2.5 mg to 10 mg of d-amphetamine, or 37.5 mg to 112.5 mg of pemoline) and evaluating therapeutic responses and side effects. The second stage, maintenance, involves periodic monitoring of the patient's functioning on the dose selected during the titration stage. Adjustments in the dose or form of stimulant medication may be made in response to changes in functioning, the observed time course of drug-induced changes, and side effects. Since methylphenidate is the stimulant used in most cases, our examples will focus on the titration of the dose of Ritalin. However, in general, the same procedures apply for titration of doses equivalent of Dexedrine (estimated by half the indicated doses of Ritalin) or doses of Cylert (estimated by six times the indicated dose of Ritalin).

2.1. Clinical Titration Methods

In typical clinical practice, the per-administration dose of methylphenidate (Ritalin) varies across individuals from 5 mg to 20 mg (given 1 to 3 times per day) (see Rapport, DuPaul, Stoner, & Jones, 1986; Swanson & Kinsbourne, 1979; Sprague & Sleator, 1977). This wide range requires titration to select the best therapeutic dose for each individual. Several different titration procedures have been described in the literature, so several general features of titration trials will be described here.

The first distinguishing feature is whether an open (nonblind) or a placebo-controlled (blind) procedure is used. In the typical open clinical trial, standard Ritalin tablets are used, and those involved (i.e., the child, the physician, and the parents) are aware of type and dose of medication administered. In the typical double-blind trial, active medication is contrasted with an inactive placebo substance, and both are packaged in capsules to disguise the contents. As the literature shows, the nonblind nature of the former procedure is problematic: "placebo effects" are common (see Ullman & Sleator, 1986), with favorable response attributed to nonpharmacological factors in up to 30% of the cases (see Ottenbacher & Cooper, 1983). In some cases, the placebo and drug conditions are disguised by a double-blind procedure, but the dose variations are made in a stepwise fashion and thus are not administered in a double-blind way (see Conners, 1971; Dykman et al., 1976; Elia, Borcherding, Rapoport, & Keysor, 1991).

The second feature is the method for scaling dose values. Two methods have support from practitioners and researchers: the mg/kg (or relative) procedure and the mg (or absolute) procedure. For example, the mg/kg method was used by Sprague & Sleator (1977) to investigate the effects of randomized morning doses of methylphenidate varying from 0.3 to 1.0 mg/kg, by Pelham et al. (1990) to investigate randomized *bid* doses of methylphenidate varying from 0.15 to 0.6 mg/kg per administration, and by Elia et al. (1991) to investigate a stepwise *bid* dose of methylphenidate up to 2.0 mg/kg per administration. The mg (absolute) method was recommended by Swanson & Kinsbourne (1979), and has been used by Swanson, Sandman, Deutsch, & Baren (1983) to investigate randomized *tid* regimes and by Rapport, Stoner, DuPaul, Birmingham, & Tucker (1985) to investigate randomized once-a-day regimes for doses of methylphenidate varying from 5 mg to 20 mg per administration.

In the elementary school-age range, the weight of older children is double that of younger children, but it is clear that the older, heavier children with ADHD do not require twice the dose of methylphenidate used to treat the younger, lighter children with ADHD. We (Swanson & Cantwell, 1989) encountered this problem when we attempted to use the mg/kg method of selecting doses for titration across a wide range of weights and doses in a research evaluation of the standard dose range recommended by the literature (i.e., randomized *tid* doses of 0.0, 0.3, 0.6, and 1.0 mg/kg). Of 75 referred children in the age range of 7 to 13 years, weight varied from 16 kg to 48 kg. In many cases, a 1.0 mg/kg dose exceeded the maximum recommended dose (20 mg per administration or 60 mg/day) (PDR, 1990). To avoid this, Swanson & Cantwell (1989) adopted a rule for modifying the maximum mg/kg dose: when the calculated mg/kg dose exceeded 20 mg, then the highest mg/kg dose was replaced by a new, lower mg/kg dose (equal to one-half the prior lowest mg/kg dose). In this study, for cases over 20 kg and less than 33 kg, the highest dose (1.0 mg/kg) was replaced by a new lowest dose (0.15 mg/kg), and the dose range of 0.0, 0.15, 0.3, and 0.6 mg/kg replaced the dose range of 0.0, 0.3, 0.6, and 1.0 mg/kg. This rule results in a mixture of the relative (mg/kg) and absolute (mg) dose procedures, by reducing the minimum dose for lighter children (rather than by increasing the maximum dose for heavier children) and by spacing the doses equally across the weight-related range. Functionally, it produces trial doses in the range of 5 to 20 mg for all children, which matches the range required in clinical settings (see Swanson, Cantwell, Lerner, McBurnett, & Hanna, 1991) and supported by research (see Rapport, DuPaul, & Kelly, 1989).

A third issue concerns the frequency of dosing. In clinical practice and in research studies, both once-a-day doses and multiple doses per day (*bid* or *tid*) have been used. For example, in clinical and research settings (e.g., Sleator & von Neumann, 1974; Sprague & Sleator, 1977; Rapport et al., 1985) have used once-a-day administration for making dose-response comparisons, while others (e.g., Swanson et al., 1983; Pelham, Bender, Cadell, Booth, & Moorer, 1985; Tannock, Schachar, Carr, Chajczyk, & Logan, 1989) have used multiple doses (*bid* or *tid*) per day. The use of a single dose regime may represent a strategy to avoid anorexia or insomnia (the most frequent side effects of stimulant medication) by allowing the pharmacologic effects of the short-acting medication to dissipate (see Sleator & von Neuman, 1974). However, in clinical practice, single daily doses of immediate-release Ritalin tablets are seldom used (Greenhill, 1991). In fact, after a single morning dose of methylphenidate, parent observations of after-school behavior fall outside the time period when this drug exerts its primary effect, and under double-blind conditions parents probably are not able to distinguish between drug and placebo conditions (Sleator & von Neumann, 1974). The use of *bid* or *tid* administrations counteracts the short behavioral half-life of the single-dose regime (3–4 hours) and extends the primary behavioral effect of methylphenidate to 6–8 hours (for a *bid* regime) or 9–12 hours (for a *tid* regime).

In some clinical and research settings (see Abikoff, 1991), a *sculpted* dosing procedure is used for a *bid-* or *tid-* methylphenidate regime, with the latter doses being smaller than the initial morning dose (e.g., 20 mg in the morning, 15 mg at noon, and 10 mg in the afternoon). This may be necessary when high morning doses are used, in order to avoid "carry-over" effects of large morning doses (see Swanson, 1989; Tannock, Schachar, Carr, & Logan, 1989) or when the drug's (e.g., Cylert) serum half-life is so long that the drug levels accumulate over the day (see Swanson et al., 1978).

A fourth issue is the choice of stimulant drugs. So far, we have used methylphenidate (Ritalin) in most of our examples, because in current clinical practice it is the drug of first choice (Greenhill, 1991). However, there is little empirical evidence to support this preference. For example, Arnold, Huetis, Smeltzer et al. (1976) has shown that d-amphetamine (Dexedrine) is at least as effective as methylphenidate (Ritalin), and several studies (e.g., Conners, 1971; Dykman et al., 1976; Swanson et al., 1978; Pelham et al., 1987) suggest that Cylert may be as effective as Ritalin when adjusted for time and dose characteristics. However, the literature (see Barkley, 1977; Swanson, 1989) indicates that in a short-term trial on any these stimulants, a majority of the children with ADHD (approximately 70%) will show a "favorable" clinical response and only a minority will not (in about 20% a "nonresponse" pattern and in about 10% an "adverse" response pattern) (see Bradley, 1950; Millichap, 1973; Barkley, Fisher, Newby, & Breen, 1988; Forness, Swanson, Cantwell, Youpa, & Hanna, 1992). A recent study at the National Institute of Mental Health (NIMH) (Elia et al., 1991) questioned the generally accepted percentage of the favorable response pattern, and suggested that if a sequential trial of two stimulants is provided, using wide dose ranges (e.g., up to 1.5 mg/kg/day of d-amphetamine or 3.0 mg/kd/day of methylphenidate), over 90% of the cases will show a "favorable" response. Even though this procedure suggest that there are few "true nonresponders" to stimulant pharmacotherapy, the "favorable response" reported by this group does not represent normalization of behavior, even when high doses are tried, and serious side effects (e.g., tics and stereotypies) are common (Elia & Rapoport, 1991). In addition, the use of multiple drugs and multiple doses complicates the identification of a favorable response (see Swanson et al., 1991), and the requirement of multiple measures of "favorable response" reduces the percentage of cases classified as favorable responders (Forness et al., 1992).

Thus, the percentage of nonresponders to a trial on multiple stimulants at multiple doses (e.g., 2.5 mg to 10 mg of d-amphetamine, *bid* or *tid*; 5 mg to 20 mg of methylphenidate, *bid* or *tid*; 37.5 mg to 112.5 mg of pemoline, once-a-day or *bid*) is not known. However, due to their rapid onset and short length of actions, trials on the stimulants can be accomplished quickly, so a trial on all three is practical. If a child with ADHD manifests a nonresponse pattern to all stimulants, then a trial is warranted on drugs from other classes of psychotropic medication, such as imipramine (see Werry, Aman, & Diamond, 1980), desipramine (see Biederman, 1988), or clonidine (see Hunt, 1987). The literature on these nonstimulant drugs will not be discussed in this chapter.

2.2. Examples of Clinical Titration

In the typical open trial utilizing the "office practice" model of stimulant pharmacotherapy, the preferred stimulant is prescribed (e.g., Ritalin) initially at a low starting dose (e.g., 5 to 10 mg), and the dose and frequency of administration are increased (e.g., in 5-mg increments, up to a maximum of 20 mg *tid*) on a daily or weekly basis as long as behavior improves and side effects are not prohibitive (see Greenhill, 1991). Even after a stable regime is established, the dose is likely to be increased if a crisis occurs. This procedure identifies most children who respond favorably, but this type of nonblind clinical titration, based solely on subjective reports of adults, may lead to unnecessary treatment (Ullman & Sleator, 1986) or inappropriately high doses for some children (see Gadow, 1989; Swanson et al., 1990; Barkley, Fischer, Edelbrock, & Smallish, 1990).

At the University of California, Irvine Child Development Center (UCI-CDC), a medication assessment protocol developed in the 1970s at the Hospital for Sick Children, Toronto (Swanson et al., 1978; Swanson & Kinsbourne, 1976) was adapted for clinical use, with a balance of rigor (through the use of double-blind controls and objective laboratory tests) and costs (imposed by repeated visits to the clinic and labor-intensive tests of the child). Since the early 1980s (see Swanson et al., 1983), we have used a 4-week assessment protocol for most children recommended for stimulant pharmacotherapy, which has been described in detail elsewhere (see Swanson, 1989; Swanson et al., 1991). A summary of these techniques and procedures will be presented here.

2.2.1. The UCI-CDC Clinical Procedure

At the UCI-CDC, following a careful diagnostic workup by a psychologist and a medical screening by a physician, a child with a diagnosis of ADHD is likely to be recommended for a trial on stimulant pharmacotherapy. As a clinical service, we offer a double-blind medication assessment that utilizes measures of performance on objective laboratory tests as well as subjective ratings of behavior. Specific procedures and materials are required for conducting a double-blind trial. The physician must write a special prescription to meet the requirements of a Schedule II drug, which in California requires a special prescription form (a *triplicate*). The typical prescription specifies two doses of methylphenidate (5 mg and 10 mg, *bid*) and two "doses" of placebo, each for 7 days (1 week), in the following manner: "Ritalin Double-Blind Evaluation, use 20-mg Ritalin Tablets and Lactose to prepare #84 Capsules: 5 mg *tid* × 7 days, 10 mg *tid* × 7 days, placebo *tid* for 14 days." The UCI-CDC consulting pharmacist pulverizes the 20-mg tablets, mixes this with lactose to prepare the capsules with the appropriate doses, packages each of the four conditions in a separate pill bottle, randomizes the four conditions, and keeps the *code* (i.e., the schedule of doses by week). Each week, the parent picks up a bottle of capsules and two sets of dated rating forms (one for the parent and one for the teacher). Three times per week (e.g., Monday, Wednesday, and Friday), parents and teachers complete the 15-item Conners, Loney and Milich (CLAM) rating scale (which includes a 3-item significant behavior log for narrative written responses) to measure severity of symptomatic behavior and a 7-item McBurnett Usual Behavior (MUB) scale to measure change in "usual" behavior. (These forms are presented in Appendix A). The parent makes the arrangements required for the afternoon dose to be given at school, and each week delivers and returns the teacher's rating forms.

Once per week, the parent brings the child to the clinic for cognitive testing. We administer a battery of laboratory tests (see Swanson, 1985), which includes a paired-associated learning (PAL) test and a memory/display scanning (MEM) test. For each case, the battery is first administered under baseline conditions, and by varying the number of items in the lists to be learned or scanned, we adjust the level of difficulty for each individual child, ensuring that during the double-blind drug-placebo trial good performance on the task will require intense effort. Also, since the bulk of the practice effect occurs between the first and second administration of these cognitive tests, baseline testing also allows us to shift most (but not all) of this potential confound away from the comparisons of dose conditions. On the subsequent four weekly clinic visits, the child is given similar versions of the PAL and MEM tests, administered and scored by a trained technician, who also collects and scores the multiple CLAM and MUB rating forms completed during the week by the parent and teacher. At the end of the 4-week trial, the ratings and test data are entered into a database program that generates summary graphs of the results for each week (see Figure 3).

2.2.2. Interpretation of the UCI-CDC Assessment

The physician who ordered the double-blind assessment can review the results presented graphically and select the "best week" without knowledge of the dose conditions. (Both *week* and *dose* are labeled on Figure 3, but the dose information can be withheld). Then, the contents of each weekly set of capsules can be revealed to "break the blind" and determine *responder status*. (In some cases, a community physician utilizing the UCI-CDC medication assessment service is unfamiliar with interpretation of the data from our protocol, and in those cases, a psychologist experienced with the protocol reviews the results and sends a written report with interpretations). In a follow-up consultation with the parent, based on the results of the 4-week double-blind trial in addition to all other

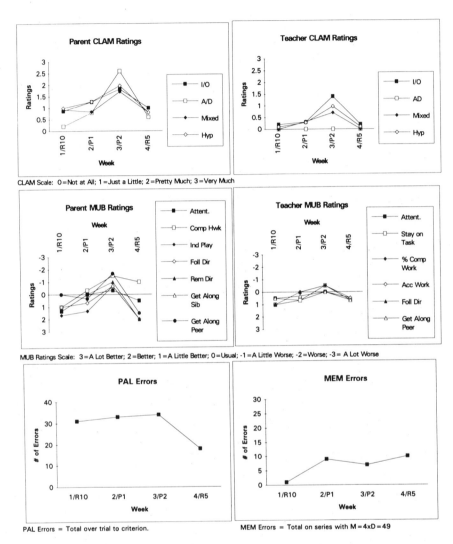

Figure 3. Results form the UCI-CDC Medication Assessment.

available information, the physician makes a recommendation for a maintenance dose.

The UCI-CDC responder status guidelines are based on research (Swanson et al., 1978; Swanson et al., 1983): relative to placebo, improving by 25% on a given measure indicates a favorable response; worsening by 10% indicates an adverse response; and staying within these limits indicates a nonresponse. Based on recent research described by Forness et al. (1992), our guideline for determining overall response is that a majority of the measures should indicate a favorable response. However, physicians base their decisions on all information available, including interview and narrative comments from the CLAM, and they weight certain measures over others as the individual case warrants.

The interpretation of the data from the UCI-CDC double-blind assessment is a complex decision-making process. Multiple sources of information about response and side effects must be considered, and the information sometimes involves inconsistencies or complicated interactions. The clinician must use the objective information and consider the behavioral and learning deficiencies, the seriousness of side effects, and the potential contribution of other treatment modalities for each individual case. Furthermore, an expert understanding of assessment data must take into account many theoretical and practical issues, such as whether the relationship of dose and response is linear, whether *cognitive toxicity* appears to be a potential risk, how to balance issues of practicality versus efficacy in choosing between long- and short-acting dosage forms, and a host of other issues. No simple algorithm exists for combining rating and test data to make a recommendation for a maintenance regime. In our clinical experience, the use of a graphical presentation of multiple measures (see Fig. 3) has proven to be the best way to present the data from our medication-assessment protocol. When multiple judges inspect the rating-scale data presented in the UCI graphical format, reliable judgments are made about *best condition.* In a review of 46 cases presented in this way, the consensus choices of *best condition* were 46% for 10 mg, 28% for 5 mg, 17% for placebo, and 9% uncertain.

2.3. Task Specificity of Response to Stimulants

Because stimulants do not have uniform effects on performance across different tasks, the choice of a measure of drug-induced change drastically affects how many cases are considered to have a favorable response. Some investigators rely on observer (e.g., teacher) ratings, while other investigators rely on cognitive tests (see Swanson, 1989 for a review). The rate of favorable response reported in the literature varies from 30% to 100%, but in general the consideration of cognitive measures reduces the percentage of favorable responders (see Swanson et al., 1983; Rapport et al., 1985; Forness, Swanson, Cantwell, Guthrie, & Sena, 1992). The specific cognitive tests included in the UCI-CDC battery, the PAL test and the MEM test, are used to achieve a conservative bias in our evaluations of response to stimulant pharmacotherapy.

Even when cognitive tests are used, there is considerable disagreement about the definition of a favorable response. Following an acute administration of typical clinical doses of stimulant medication, almost all subjects, including normal children free of ADHD, improve their performance on "low-level" attention and vigilance tasks such as the Continuous Performance test (CPT; Rapoport et al., 1978). Hence, there is no basis for claiming that a positive stimulant response to such tasks substantiates a diagnoses of ADHD, as implied by some for recently marketed commercial versions of the CPT (e.g., the TOVA by Greenberg, 1991; the GDS by Gordon, 1983). However, on certain laboratory measures, such as those requiring new learning and intense effort, impairment (or lack of improvement) is expected for normal cases (Weiss & Laties, 1963) and improvement is expected for clinical cases (e.g., see Conners & Eisenberg, 1963; Swanson et al., 1978; Swanson, 1989). Swanson (1989) asserted that a nonfavorable drug-response pattern based on performance on such laboratory tests may be used to *refute* a diagnosis of ADHD, even though a favorable response pattern should not be used to *confirm* a diagnosis of ADHD. This is the primary reason for including the PAL test in the UCI-CDC battery.

Douglas, Barr, Amin, O'Neill, and Britton (1988) used the PAL test and documented improved performance at a low dose (0.3 mg/kg) but relative impairment (compared to the low dose) at a high dose (0.6 mg/kg). They presented a thoughtful and detailed analysis of negative effects of high doses and made recommendations for the design of future studies: "In attempting to design more sensitive tasks, our most promising clues rest on the fact that the most consistent evidence of performance decrements at high dosages has been found on PAL tasks involving arbitrary associations." They reasoned that ". . . increasing demands for high-level processing, combined with high dosage levels, may over activate and over tax self-regulatory processes and thus lead to impaired performance" (pp. 471–472). Based on this literature and experience, Swanson (1989) recommended the PAL test as the primary test for assessing response to stimulant pharmacotherapy.

2.4. Dose-Response Characteristics of Stimulants

A dose-response curve is a plot of a dependent measure as a function of dose. In the typical dose-response curves, objective measures of performance (i.e., errors on the PAL and MEM tests) and subjective measures of behavior (i.e., parent or teacher ratings on the CLAM and MUB) are plotted on the ordinate, with increasing dose on the abscissa. [Note that if *correct responses* is the dependent variable or the scale of the ratings is reversed (see Sprague & Sleator, 1977), then the shape of the curve will be inverted]. Most subjective ratings and most measures of cognitive response to medication (e.g., number of math problems worked, CPT errors of omission or commission, Matching to Familiar Figures errors or time-to-response, etc.) yield *linear* dose-response functions; that is, improvements in performance are proportional to increase in dose (Pelham et al., 1985; Rapport et al., 1985; Barkley et al., 1988; Douglas et al., 1988). As discussed earlier, this is not always the case for tasks that place heavy demands on short-term memory (Sprague & Sleator, 1977) or new learning (Swanson et al., 1978). Under these conditions, the dose-response curve may be U-shaped, with optimal effects (identified by the asymptote) occurring at an intermediate dose of medication. Determining whether a function is linear or U-shaped can be accomplished either by visual inspection of the dose-response function, or by the statistical technique of trend analysis to test for a significant quadratic component in the dose-response function (see Swanson, 1989).

The influential study by Sprague and Sleator (1977) suggested that the shape of dose-response curves differs for measures of *learning* (U-shaped) or *behavior* (linear). These findings have been interpreted by Gadow (1989) and Sprague & Sleator (1977) to suggest that the usual clinical practice (dosage titration based on test *behavioral* response) may not be optimal for effects on *learning* or effortful cognitive processing. However, some investigators have failed to find a clear U-shaped dose-response curve for stimulant effects on most measures of cognitive performance. Recently, Rapport & Kelly (1991) reviewed the literature and challenged the Sprague & Sleator (1977) view. They concluded that high doses were the best for optimal performance on effortful tasks. We do not agree with that conclusion, and the reasons for our support of the Sprague & Sleator (1977) view will be summarized elsewhere.

We developed the MEM test for the UCI-CDC battery to match the information content of the difficult short-term memory task used by Sprague & Sleator (1977). They used a memory load (M) of 15 items and a display load (D) of 1, and we used a D of 4 and an M of 4, which has about the same *information load* ($M \times D = 16$). We also conducted a dose-response study that included the highest doses (1.0 mg/kg) used by Sprague & Sleator (1977). When we duplicated these critical features (i.e., high information load and high dose), we (Swanson & Cantwell, 1989) replicated Sprague & Sleator's (1977) dose-response patterns. This is the primary reason for including the MEM test in the UCI-CDC medication assessment battery.

3. Historical Events Influencing the Area

To understand the literature on stimulant pharmacotherapy that has accumulated over the past half-century, it is necessary to be aware of certain historical events that have been associated with trends in this area. Some of the trends in the literature have been shaped by political, social, legal, and public-policy issues that will be discussed here.

3.1. The 1950s and 1960s: Federal Policy to Facilitate Research

Lipman (1974) provides a historical account of the early research support provided by the Psychopharmacological Research Branch (PRB), which was created in 1956 by the NIMH. In 1958, the PRB sponsored a conference to ". . . formally enter the arena of pediatric psychopharmacology." The first research grant on child psychopharmacology, awarded in 1958 to Leon Eisenberg at Johns Hopkins University, addressed the use of tranquilizers on children and did not include plans for the investigation of stimulants. The second research grant was awarded in 1961 to Barbara Fish at New York University, who concentrated her research on severely impaired autistic and schizophrenic children who were unlikely to respond to stimulants. After these two initial grants, ". . . there was a hiatus of support provided for pediatric psychopharmacology. The few grants reviewed reflected the 'parlous' state of methodology in pediatric psychopharmacology and were not approved" (Lipman, 1974, p. 204). In 1965, concern about the indiscriminate use of phenothiazines in the treatment of the mentally retarded and documentation of a general lack of efficacy of these drugs on cognitive functioning, led the PRB to reevaluate the direction of research. In 1966, a PRB status report indicated that the NIMH-funded researchers had ". . . turned their attention toward the stimulants after negative experiences with the tranquilizers and with psychotherapy" and, on the basis of well-controlled studies, had shown that stimulants enhanced ". . . many aspects of cognitive functioning, as contrasted to the phenothiazines, while also providing a beneficial reduction in hyperactivity, distractibility, and impulsiveness" (Lipman, 1974, p. 204).

In 1967, the first grant specifically to study the effects of stimulants on children was awarded (to Keith Conners at Massachusetts General Hospital, to extend the work he initiated with Eisenberg at Johns Hopkins). According to Lipman, the year 1968 ". . . marked the beginning of a turning point" for research in pediatric psychopharmacology. That year, three grants were awarded (to Lawrence Greenberg at the University of California, Davis, Grace Steinberg at the District of Columbia Department of Mental Health, and Donald Klein at Hillside Hospital), and by 1972, another eight grants were awarded (renewals to Donald Klein and Lawrence Greenberg, and new awards to Robert Sprague at University of Illinois; David Engelhardt at State University of New York; Alberto DiMascio at Massachusetts Department of Mental Health; Judith Rapoport at Georgetown University; Patricia Cunningham at Our Lady of the Lake College; and Solomon Snyder at Johns Hopkins University). Some of these individuals are still working in this area 25 years later.

Thus, the public policy stated by NIMH (Fisher, 1959) was implemented by the PRB, which served ". . . as the node for the stimulation and support" for the development of pediatric psychopharmacology. It should be emphasized that before 1960, despite the early work of Bradley (1937; 1950), the interest in, and support of, research on stimulant pharmacotherapy ". . . was far from overwhelming" (Lipman, 1974, p. 202), and as noted earlier, the first grants in pediatric psychopharmacology did *not* address the use of stimulants. The literature suggests that this was because the early work with stimulants was based on outdated methods and uncontrolled clinical trials (see Cole, 1969). As a by-product of the initial grants and funded investigations which emerged in the 1960s and increased dramatically in the 1970s, many of the modern methods were developed (i.e., an "Early Clinical Drug Evaluation" package) that helped to set the stage for controlled research on the effects of stimulant pharmacotherapy on children with ADHD.

3.2. The 1970s: Negative Publicity in the Public Media

In 1970, a report in *The Washington Post* (Staff, June 29, 1970) questioned the widespread use of stimulant drugs in the schools of Omaha, Nebraska. This report was considered to be flawed (Medical Letter, August 10, 1970), but it generated considerable attention and even led to a congressional hearing (September 29, 1970) and a national conference (Office of Child Development and Department of Health, Education, and Welfare, January 11–12, 1971). This era was marked with controversy about drugs in general (e.g., see Brecher, 1972; Smith & Wesson, 1973), and some of the controversy has a philosophical (not pharmacological) basis, focusing on free will, personal responsibility, and a mechanistic view of human nature (Hentoff, 1972; Schrag & Divoky, 1975). Even though negative publicity about stimulant pharmacotherapy may have been based on unsubstantiated claims, it had important consequences for the clinical use of stimulant drugs. In the late 1960s and early 1970s, public concern about the abuse of all drugs (especially the stimulants) influenced the political process already in motion to change the laws and Federal departments involved in the control of drug abuse (e.g., the 1965 Drug Abuse

Control Amendments). In 1965, Congress adopted H.R. 2, which was designed to control ". . . the 'sievelike' distribution system of amphetamines in the United States" (Smith & Wesson, 1973, p. 17). The inconsistency in recommending use of stimulants for one purpose (treating children with ADHD) while trying to prevent use for other purposes (e.g., appetite suppression, performance enhancement in athletics, recreational use, etc.) was readily apparent. When the Federal law regulating drugs was revised (PL 91–513, the Comprehensive Drug Abuse Prevention and Control Act of 1970), amphetamine and methylphenidate were placed in Schedule III, which limited refills and the life of a prescription. In the atmosphere of the times, when large amounts of stimulant drugs were being manufactured and diverted for illicit use, this was considered to be insufficient control. By 1971 "administrative rescheduling" (Smith & Wesson, 1973, p. 18) was used to place amphetamine and methylphenidate on Schedule II, which tightened prescription regulations and imposed quotas on productions. These restrictions remain today. However, in 1993 the limited allocations of methylphenidate resulted in shortages for clinical use in the treatment of children with ADHD, and the need for the continuation of these severe restrictions has been questioned (Horn, 1994, Personal Communications, January 16, 1994).

3.3. The 1980s: National Groups

In this era, a number of national groups turned their attention toward issues associated with ADHD. These included groups of professionals, Federal commissions, parent groups, and special interest groups. Some of the activities of these national groups will be described here.

3.3.1. Professional Groups

In the early 1980s, Lewis Bloomingdale established an annual symposium for a group of physicians and psychologists engaged in research and treatment of the ADHD condition. Over the years, the proceedings of these meetings have been published, initially as the High Point Hospital Symposium Series (Bloomingdale, 1984, 1985, & 1988) and later as a book supplement to the *Journal of Child Psychology and Psychiatry* (Bloomingdale & Sergeant, 1988; Bloomingdale & Swanson, 1989). In 1988, the Bloomingdale group was renamed the Professional Group for Attention and Related Disorders (PGARD) and its membership was expanded to include almost equal numbers of psychologists, physicians, and educators (see Swanson, 1992).

Also in the 1980s, the Health Research Extension Act (P.L. 99–158) established the U.S. Interagency Committee of Learning Disabilities, which organized the National Conference on Learning Disabilities held in January, 1987. Educational issues relevant to ADHD were addressed (see S. Shaywitz & B. Shaywitz, 1988; Swanson, 1988), and the Interagency Committee recommended changes (denoted by the Committee's underlines) in the definition of LD, which included a reference to ADD (Kavanagh & Truss, 1988, p. 550).

> Learning disabilities is a generic term that refers to a heterogeneous group of disorders manifested by significant difficulties in the acquisition and use of listening, speaking, reading, writing, reasoning, mathematical abilities, *or of social skills.* These disorders are intrinsic to the individual and presumed to be due to central nervous *system* dysfunction. Even though a learning disability may occur concomitantly with other handicapping conditions (e.g., sensory impairment, mental retardation, social and emotional disturbance), *with socio-environmental influences* (e.g., cultural differences, insufficient or inappropriate instruction, psychogenic factors), *and especially attention deficit disorder, all of which may cause learning problems, a learning disability* is not the direct result of those conditions or influences."

As these recommended changes reflect, the Interagency Committee felt that the status of ADHD was separate from the handicapping conditions (e.g., learning disabilities, serious emotional disturbance, mental retardation, sensory impairment, etc.) that had been previously recognized in Federal law (P.L. 94–142).

3.3.2. Parent Groups

In the 1980s, several local groups were organized specifically by parents of children with ADHD who were dissatisfied with the Federal definitions of learning disabilities and the legal status of ADHD in educational law. These grass-roots groups eventually banded together to form two national groups, the Attention Deficit Disorder Associations (ADDA) and Children with Attention Deficit Disorder (CHADD), which now have large memberships (e.g., over 50,000) and widely distributed newsletters (i.e., ADDA's *Challenge* and CHADD's *Chadder*). In the mid-1980s, CHADD and ADDA started to hold annual meetings which have grown to be large events. These groups stimulated publications about ADHD, and many books by practitioners and researchers were written to meet this demand for consumer information. For example, this literature grew so large that even a catalogue (the *ADD Warehouse*) of ADHD literature now exists (see Parker, 1989). In the late 1980s, the existence of parent support groups was fortuitous, since they were called on in 1989 by the U.S. Congress to

provide testimony on the ADHD issues, and their involvement substantially contributed to the change in educational law about ADHD (see Parker, 1992; Swanson, 1992).

3.3.3. Opposition Groups

In the late 1980s, the Church of Scientology alleged widespread misuse of stimulant drugs in the treatment of children. (Apparently, this
group has a long history of acrimonious interactions and confrontations
with the psychiatry profession, dating from a court case which ruled that
Scientology was not a clinical discipline recognized to provide therapy).
Sponsored by the Church of Scientology, a group called Citizens Commission for Human Rights published a pamphlet in 1987 entitled "Ritalin: A
Warning for Parents." Apparently, this group and its president, Dennis
Clarke, worked with parents of children with ADHD to file lawsuits
against physicians who prescribed methylphenidate (Ritalin) and organized demonstrations at many meetings of professional societies to protest
the use of psychoactive drugs (see Cowart, 1988). This activity has been
summarized by Barkley, McMurray, Edelbrock, & Robbins (1990). The
negative publicity and controversies of the 1970s, although still unsubstantiated, were echoed in the 1980s. Eventually, these legal cases were
rejected or dropped, but as in the decade before, the consequences of the
publicity, demonstrations, and legal action were substantial (see Barkley et
al., 1990), including an increase in the literature on the topic of stimulant
pharmacotherapy for children with ADHD.

3.4. The 1990s: The Debate on the IDEA and the Notice of Inquiry

For most of the 55 years covered by the literature, ADHD has been
considered a condition that was treated primarily with medical rather than
educational interventions. This was partly due to the status of ADHD
under Public Law 94-142, the Education for the Handicapped Act (EHA),
which since 1975 has directed training, services, and research in special
education. In contrast to conditions such as Learning Disability (LD) or
Serious Emotional Disturbance (SED), ADHD was not considered to be
".... a handicapping condition as defined by the regulations implementing the EHA" (Bellamy, 1987). This regulation was questioned in 1990,
when the U.S. House of Representatives conducted hearings on its version
of a bill (H.R. 1013) to amend the EHA. Members of CHADD, ADDA, and
PGARD offered verbal testimony (see Swanson, 1992, Appendix B) in
favor of amending the EHA to recognize ADHD as a potentially "handicapping" (in the terminology of the EHA) or "disabling" (in the terminol-

ogy of the Individual Disability Education Act condition. Surprisingly, the House bill (H.R. 1013) recommended a modification of an EHA definition of one of the existing categories of handicapping conditions, Other Health Impaired (OHI), to include a specific reference to ADHD. A quotation from this bill shows how this recommendation was implemented.

> 1) The term "children with disabilities" means children—(A) with mental retardation, hearing impairments including deafness, speech and language impairments, visual impairments including blindness, serious emotional disturbance, orthopedic impairments, autism, traumatic brain injury, other health impairments including attention deficit disorder, or specific learning disabilities; and (B) who, by reason thereof, need special education and related services.

The four additional words recommended in H.R. 1013,"*including attention deficit disorder,*" created a heated debate. Most national organizations of educators opposed this change, including the National Association of State Directors of Special Education (NASDSE), the National School Board Association (NSBA), the American Association of School Administrators (AASA), the National Association of School Psychologists (NASP), and the Council for Exceptional Children (CEC). Various arguments were made against this change in educational law, including the assertion that children with ADHD were already being recognized and served in the public schools and the claim that ADHD did not exist separately as a *bona fide* condition. However, a primary reason for opposition was that a full review had not been conducted to evaluate the intended and unintended consequences of recognizing ADHD in Federal law. Also, it was clear that federal funds for training, service, and research were limited, and that the addition of another condition would dilute already severely limited resources for "handicapping" or "disabling" conditions for which the public school had legal responsibilities.

When the congressional committees met to finalize the form of the IDEA, the portion of Senate bill (S 1824) which did not recommend a change in the law about ADHD was adopted, instead of the portion of the House bill (H.R. 1013), which did recommend a change. However, the issue was not put to rest. The ADHD issue generated so much discussion that Congress issued a Notice of Inquiry on ADD (Federal Register, November 29, 1990). This represented an official fact-finding effort to obtain input from a wide variety of sources about the adequacy of educational law and educational practices concerning children with ADHD. Over 4,000 responses (a large number for a typical Notice) were received, including a lengthy response from PGARD (see Swanson, 1992, Appendix A). The Department of Education was charged by Congress to summarize this massive response, which expressed a consensus that the existing regulations governing ADHD (which denied the separate existence of the ADHD condition) were inadequate. Based on this, the Department acted to change the regulations implementing the IDEA with respect to ADHD, by issuing revised regulations, which stated that ADHD students could be considered disabled ". . . . solely on the basis of the disorder within the 'other health impaired' category" (Davila, Williams, & MacDonald, 1991, p. 3). This action accomplished the same change in legal status for ADHD as proposed in H.R. 1013 (discussed earlier). However, this was accomplished by an administrative decision to change the regulations that implement the Federal law (i.e., the IDEA), and did not require an official "Act of Congress."

3.5. Current Federal Policy on Research

Over the next decade, ADHD projects currently funded by two Federal agencies, the Department of Health and Human Services (HHS) through the National Institute of Mental Health (NIMH) and the U.S. Department of Education (DOE) through the Office of Special Education Projects (OSEP) are likely to influence the future trends in the literature on stimulant pharmacotherapy for children with ADHD. OSEP's ADHD initiative is likely to stimulate another surge in the literature on children with ADHD, with an emphasis on educational issues, and NIMH's support of multiple projects on ADHD is likely to expand the already considerable medical literature on stimulant pharmacotherapy for children with ADHD. Some of the policies and current projects of these Federal agencies will be reviewed here.

3.5.1. OSEP

In 1990, the Office of Special Education Programs (OSEP) recognized that the historical differences in the medical and educational approaches to disabilities or handicapping conditions had resulted in a large literature on ADHD contributed primarily by medical researchers. To correct this underrepresentation of educators, OSEP established three programs with an emphasis on ADHD: Centers, Promising Practices, and Training Projects. In 1991, the ADD Centers were established for 2 years to organize and synthesize the existing literature on children with ADHD. Two of the Centers, at Arkansas Children's Hospital (under the direction of Roscoe Dykman) and the University of Miami (under the direction of Don McKinney), were established to organize and synthesize the literature on *Assessments* for ADHD. The other two Centers, at Research Triangle Institute (under the direction of Tom Fiore) and at the University of California, Irvine (under the direction of James Swanson), were established to organize and synthesize the literature on *Interventions* for ADHD. The summary of the work of these centers was presented in January 1993 at the National ADD Forum, and the proceedings of the ADD Forum were published by the Chesapeake Institute (U.S. Department of Education, 1993).

In 1991, through its Division of Innovation and Development, OSEP funded the Kentucky Federal Resource Center to perform a survey of *promising practices*. Over 500 promising practices were nominated, and about 150 written descriptions were submitted for review. From this set, 26 promising practices were chosen and presented at the ADD Forum along with the other ADD Centers' reports. The 26 promising practices were classified into 4 groups: Identification (Anchorage, AL; San Diego, CA; Norwich, CT; Fort Lauderdale, FL; Louisville, KY; Salisbury, NC; Raleigh, NC; Sturgeon Bay, WI; Kenosha, WI); Behavioral Interventions (Irvine, CA; Suffield, CT; Jacksonville, FL; Bradenton, FL; Des Moines, IA; Omaha, NE; Lake Villa, IL; Baordman, OH; Drexel Hill, PA); Academic Interventions (Orlando, FL; Baton Rouge, LA; Sandy, UT); Training (Colorado Springs, CO; Towson, MD; Billings, MO; Reno, NV; North Canton, OH). As a follow-up, the Division of Innovation and Development will identify 8 of these promising practices and identify the contextual conditions that support their successful use in school settings (see the U.S. Department of Education, 1993).

In 1992, through its Division of Personnel Preparation, OSEP funded 13 projects in the area of teacher training. These projects involve well-established researchers in education, who have taken a new interest in the educational issues surrounding students with ADHD. The locations of these projects are the University of Alabama (teacher and administrator training), the University of Georgia (the ADDNET satellite-based broadcasts), the University of Arizona (the ADEPT preservice and inservice models), the University of Kentucky (graduate training in school psychology), Lehigh University (a regional consulting center for adolescents with ADHD), the University of Massachusetts (in-service training for regular and special education teachers), the University of North Carolina at Chapel Hill (curricula and material for preservice and in-service training), the Arkansas Children's Hospital Research center (in-service training), the University of Miami (in-service training), the Kansas State Board of Education (statewide model for personnel preparation), the Jewish Association for Attention Deficit Disorder (training for school-based support teams), the Council for Exceptional Children (continuing education projects), and Purdue University (development of in-service curricula materials and training modules).

3.5.2. NIMH

In 1992, the Department of Health and Human Services reorganized NIMH, assigning its research component to the National Institute of Health (NIH) and its training and service components to a new entity, the Center for Mental Health Services (CMHS). The Chief of the Child and Adolescent Research Branch of NIMH is Peter Jensen, an expert in the area of ADHD, and another well-known researcher in the area of ADHD, Gene Arnold, joined the Branch in 1992 and was made responsible for managing grants that addressed ADHD. In an article for a parent-group newsletter, Arnold (1993) described the NIMH funding for research on ADHD, which in 1993 totaled about $4.5 million for extramural grants.

In 1991, NIMH adopted a 5-year Child Mental Health Initiative that provided special funding for projects in the general area of child mental health. In 1992, a special project in this initiative was described in a Request for Applications (RFA) for a multimodality treatment project for children with ADHD. Based on responses to the RFA, six sites were selected to participate in this project: Columbia University (directed by Larry Greenhill), Duke University (directed by Keith Conners), Long Island Jewish Hospital/Montreal Children's Hospital (directed by Howard Abikoff and Lily Hetchmann), the University of California, Berkeley (directed by Steven Hinshaw), the University of California, Irvine (directed by James Swanson), and the University of Pittsburgh (directed by William Pelham). Stimulated by the ADHD initiative in the Department of Education, OSEP joined with NIMH to develop and fund a protocol that had an educational emphasis as well as a medical emphasis for treatment. This joint NIMH-OSEP project began in 1992, with the six sites collaborating to develop a common protocol for a prospective, long-term follow-up study of the effects of psychosocial and pharmacological interventions for children and parents affected by ADHD.

4. A Synthesis of the Literature: The UCI "Review of Reviews"

The literature on stimulant pharmacotherapy for children with ADHD includes many comprehensive reviews (e.g., see S. Shaywitz & B. Shaywitz, 1988; Barkley, 1990), books (e.g., see Bloomingdale & Swanson, 1989; Greenhill & Osman, 1991) and special issues of journals (e.g., the *Journal of Child Neurology*, 1990; the *Journal of Learning Disabilities*, 1991). Since these publications provide up-to-date reviews of this topic, Swanson et al. (1993) suggested that another traditional review of the literature would be redundant and unnecessary, and explained why the UCI-ADD Center performed a review of reviews instead. By using this method to organize and synthesize the literature, we gained some insights into the development of consensus and controversy that we will summarize here.

4.1. Trends in the Literature

Our work in the UCI-ADD Center allowed us to quantify the size of the literature. Initial computer searches of multiple databases (i.e., Medline, ERIC, PsychInfo, GPO) identified large nonoverlapping sets of original sources depending upon the profession of the expected reader. The size of these nonoverlapping sets led us to focus on reviews rather than original sources. Multiple *expert* and *computer* search procedures were utilized to locate 341 review articles. Figure 4 shows the number of reviews published in a 25-year period from 1966 to 1990, divided into five 5-year intervals, with additional intervals specified for pre-1966 publications and post-1990 publications.

Not all reviews referenced the same source articles. We used our operational definition of "the literature on stimulant pharmacotherapy," which we defined as the approximately 9,000 sources listed in the reference lists of the 341 reviews, to identify the most cited sources by the 341 reviews. We used the database of the sources from the review of reviews to generate lists of the most-often-referenced (by reviews) source articles published before 1950, in the next four decades (the 1950s, the 1960s, the 1970s, and the 1980s), and so far in this decade (the 1990s). These lists of

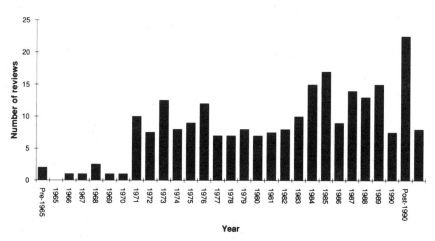

FIGURE 4. The UCI-ADD Center's Review of Reviews: Number of reviews located by year.

references are provided in Appendix B, Tables B.1 to B.6. The 25 most frequently cited sources over the entire time period covered by the review of reviews are marked by numbers representing their overall citation rank (based on the number of times each source was included in the reference lists of the 341 reviews). This information reveals that even the highest ranked source (Bradley, 1937) was cited by only 21% (72/341) of the reviews, which suggests to us that reading a limited number of reviews is unlikely to provide a comprehensive perspective of the massive literature that spans multiple disciplines (i.e., pediatrics, psychiatry, psychology, education, public policy, etc.) and many years (i.e., 1937 to 1994). To overcome the restricted perspective of a single review, we recommend the 25 highest ranked articles as a good introduction to the literature on the effects of stimulant pharmacotherapy for children with ADHD.

The lists provided in Tables B.1 to B.6 give information on the trends in the literature over the 55 years covered by the review of reviews. For example, the titles listed in Table B.1 indicate that the major topic addressed by reviews published before 1950 was the role of brain damage as a defining characteristic of affected children (12 of the most-cited articles), the effects of amphetamine (9 of the most-cited articles), and surprisingly, educational assessment or intervention (6 of the most-cited articles). The titles listed in Table B.2 indicate that in the 1950s the major focus shifted from brain damage to hyperactivity or hyperkinesis as a defining characteristic of affected children (7 of the most-cited articles) and consideration on nonstimulant drugs (3 of the most-cited articles), as well as amphetamines (3 of the most-cited articles) for the treatment of ADHD. The titles and authors listed in Table B.3 reflect the emergence of major laboratories in the 1960s that specialized in the assessment of children with ADHD and whose activity is represented in publications by Eisenberg and Conners (authors of 9 of the most-cited articles); Werry, Weiss, Douglas, and others (authors of 3 of the most-cited articles); Millichap and others (authors of 3 of the most-cited articles); Clements and others (authors of 2 of the most-cited articles). The titles and authors listed in Table B.4 indicate that in the 1970s, 19 of the 25 most-cited articles were published, representing the work of multiple new (and still active) laboratories and groups, and represented by the publications of the following authors: Sprague and colleagues (4 articles), Barkley and Cunningham (2 articles), Wender (1 article), Weiss and colleagues (3 articles), Rapoport and colleagues (3 articles), Douglas (1 article), Swanson and Kinsbourne (2 articles), Safer and Allen (2 articles), Cantwell and Carlson (1 article), Whalen and Henker (1 article), Stewart and colleagues (1 article), Rie and colleagues (1 article), Gittelman-Klein and Klein (1 article), and Werry and Aman (1 article). The titles in Table B.5 indicate that in the 1980s, the DSM Nosology of ADD and ADHD was the most referenced topic (2 articles, referenced by 94 of the reviews), and follow-up studies (6 articles), books on ADHD (3), neurochemistry (3 articles), side effects (2 articles), and other reviews (2) were also frequently cited in the reviews. The titles and authors listed in Table B.6 indicate that so far in the 1990s, the major topics have been comorbidity (11 of the most-cited articles) and biological factors such as neurochemistry, neuroanatomy, and neurology (5 of the most-cited articles).

We used a coding-sheet approach to analyze these reviews. Specific coding categories from traditional integrative review techniques (see Cooper, 1989) were adapted for the review of reviews (see Swanson et al., 1993). For each review, we recorded information on purpose and perspective, as well as information about the conclusions regarding the effects of stimulant pharmacotherapy in eight areas. We used these data to identify agreements in the literature that emerged over the last half-century, as well as to identify specific disagreements that have endured over time. This provided an empirical basis for defining *consensus* in the literature and for identifying issues of *controversy* about the use of stimulant medication.

4.2. Search and Source Overlap

In the process of performing this review of reviews, we identified *search overlap* and *source overlap* as important methodological issues that must be addressed when considering this massive literature and comparing the conclusions drawn by multiple reviews. The initial computer-search strategy revealed a very low overlap across four computerized databases, but our multiple-computer-search strategy did locate 183 reviews. We also polled multiple experts, and this search located 245 reviews. Only 87 of these reviews from the *expert search* were already identified by the *computer search*, so by using this dual search strategy we located a more comprehensive, or broader, set of 341 reviews than we would have located by using either single-search strategy. In this way, we made an effort to overcome the lack of search overlap.

We used our operational definition of the literature (the 9,000 references listed across all 341 reviews) to calculate the overlap of reference lists (source overlap) for selected sets of important reviews. For example, we compared selected sets of the 341 reviews from each 5-year era that addressed about the same topic, such as three influential reviews from the early 1970s (Sroufe & Stewart, 1973; Grinspoon & Hedblom, 1975; Fish, 1971), three often-cited reviews from the late 1970s (Whalen & Henker, 1976; Barkley, 1977; Adelman & Compas, 1977), three meta-analytic reviews from the early 1980s (Kavale, 1982; Ottenbacher & Cooper, 1983; Thurber & Walker, 1983), and three reviews of combined effects of stimulants and psychosocial interventions from the late 1980s (Abikoff, 1985; Gadow, 1985; Pelham & Murphy, 1986). When we started our review of reviews, we expected some differences in conclusions of reviews due to reliance on different sources, especially if we compared reviews from different eras (since the earlier reviews could not reference articles not yet published), or if we compared reviews that address different topics. We were surprised to find that reliance on different sources was a general occurrence we encountered even when we compared reviews from the same era that addressed similar topics. In our triadic comparisons of reviews by era, the pairwise source overlap (i.e., a source appearing in the reference list of 2 reviews) averaged about 20%, and the complete overlap (i.e., a source appearing in the reference list of all 3 reviews) was extremely low (less than 5%). In some cases, the low source overlap did not matter, and in our review of reviews this was the basis for identifying *robust* consensus (i.e., similar conclusions based on different samples of sources). In other cases, the low source overlap did matter and this was identified the reason for *controversy* (i.e., dissimilar conclusions based on different samples of sources). We will now discuss consensus and controversy in the literature with respect to benefits and limitations of stimulant pharmacotherapy for children with ADHD.

4.3. Acknowledged Benefits

One component of the favorable response to stimulant pharmacotherapy is the effect on the diagnostic symptoms of ADHD, which according to DSM-III-R (1987) is considered to be a disruptive behavior disorder described by symptoms representing "behavioral excesses." In the majority of children with ADHD who were tried on clinical doses of stimulants, the therapeutic response included temporary management of the diagnostic symptoms of ADHD (i.e., a decrease in inattention, impulsivity, and hyperactivity), accompanied by a time-limited increase in concentration and goal-directed effort. Across relevant reviews, 97% agreed with this description of short-term effects.

Another component of the favorable response to stimulant pharmacotherapy is the effect on "associated features" of the disorder, such as deviant deportment, high levels of aggression, and inappropriate social interaction. According to DSM-III-R (1987), these are symptoms of other disruptive behavior disorders (e.g., oppositional defiant disorder or conduct disorder) and represent a different and independent type of behavioral excesses, with a presumed different psychological basis (i.e., aggression not attention) (Loney & Milich, 1982). Even though these are not part of the diagnostic criteria for ADHD, it has been recognized since the early clinical studies of stimulants that this treatment reduces aggressive and defiant behavior as well as inattentive and overactive behavior (see Cole, 1969). In the survey of reviews, 94% agreed that a component of the therapeutic responses was a decrease in these associated features of ADHD.

Based on the review of reviews, the UCI-ADD Center's main conclusion was that on these broad domains of behavior (diagnostic symptoms and associated features), stimulants usually (but not in all cases) result in clear and immediate short-term benefits perceived by parents, teachers, and physicians in terms of the management of disruptive behaviors. Across reviews, there was a general consensus that of all ADHD children given trials on stimulant drugs, about 70% (the *favorable responders*) manifest clinical improvements on one or both of these broad domains of behavior that are sufficient to warrant continuation of treatment for an extended period of time.

We noted that the estimated response rate has changed only slightly across the 55 years of reviews, even though the diagnostic criteria were refined. For example, Bradley (1950) summarized the results of clinical evaluations of a heterogeneous group of children in a residential setting, and reported that about 65% of these subjects manifested a clinically significant response. Over 25 years later, Swanson et al. (1978) summarized the results of more refined evaluations of a more homogeneous group identified by the DSM-II (1968) criteria for Hyperkinetic Reaction to Childhood and reported a favorable response rate of about 70%. Over a decade later, Barkley et al. (1990) summarized the results of a systematic evaluation of a group of cases defined by rigorous DSM-III (1980) criteria and reported a favorable response rate of 80%. Forness et al. (1992) used the DSM-III-R (1987) criteria and, for traditional measures (i.e., parent and teacher ratings), reported a favorable response rate of about 70%. According to Cantwell's (1993) criteria for evaluating psychiatric diagnosis, this stable response rate is disappointing. In the future, other diagnostic criteria should be investigated, especially the ICD-10 criteria described by Taylor (1983), such as severity of symptoms (see Swanson et al., 1990) or pervasiveness of symptoms (see Swanson, 1989).

4.4. Acknowledged Limitations

In addition to the consensus on benefits of stimulant pharmacotherapy, our review of reviews identified important areas of consensus about *limitations* of stimulant pharmacotherapy including the following: the lack of a *diagnostic specific* or *paradoxical* response to stimulants; the lack of clear predictors of response to stimulants; the presence of side effects; the lack of significant effects on complex cognitive skills; and the lack of evidence in support of significant long-term effects.

We will provide one example of a surprising consensus about a limitation of stimulant pharmacotherapy. Some early influential articles (e.g., Wender, 1971; Laufer & Denhoff, 1957) asserted that stimulant medication has a paradoxical effects on children with ADHD (i.e., it "calmed or subdued" them), and a relatively recent study by Rapoport et al. (1978), which generated a considerable degree of publicity, led to a widespread acceptance that the clinical response of children with ADHD was not *paradoxical.* They reported that for the obvious behavioral measures of the effects of stimulants (mood, activity, concentration) the *direction* of response was the same for groups of children with ADHD and normal children (i.e., no mood evaluation, but decreased activity level and improved performance on some laboratory tasks). This undermined the views that a favorable drug response could confirm a diagnosis of ADHD (see Laufer & Denhoff, 1957), which had been based on the notion that children with the true form of the disorder would manifest a paradoxical response (sedation) to stimulant medication instead of the expected usual or normal response (stimulation). In our review of reviews, we were surprised to discover that the notion of *paradoxical response* was never accepted by many investigators. For example, one of the first reviews of the literature (Cole, 1969) recognized that the clinical response of children with ADHD was qualitatively the same as the response of nonpatients, and in reviews from different eras that addressed this topic, 78% concluded that in children with ADHD, the primary behavioral, physiological and psychological responses to clinical doses of stimulant medication (i.e., increased concentration and goal-directed effort) were not qualitatively different from the responses of normal children to equivalent doses.

4.5. *An Example of Synthesis Based on Analysis of Reviews*

In our review of reviews, we discovered that the comparison of reviews was very different than comparison of original sources. As an example of our analysis of consensus we will present synthesis of two important meta-analytic reviews, Kavale (1982) and Ottenbacher & Cooper (1983), which were published at about the same time (the early 1980s). They addressed approximately the same topic (i.e., the differential effects of stimulants on academic learning and behavior), but seemed to differ in their conclusions. To compare these two reviews, it was necessary to equate their definitions of *academics* and *behavior* by selecting equivalent subcategories of *outcome categories* from Kavale (1982) and *types of dependent measures* from Ottenbacher & Cooper (1983). Then we compared the equivalent effect sizes across the reviews to reveal the underlying consensus: stimulants improve both behavior and academics, but the size of the effect on our definition of *behavior* (mean effect size of 0.82) was about twice the size of the effect on our definition of *academics* (mean effect size of 0.43). We were surprised to note that Kavale (1982), who reported an effect size of 0.39 for academics, concluded that ".... academic learning and performance were improved by drug treatment" (p. 288), while Ottenbacher and Cooper (1983), who reported a large affect size of 0.47 for academics, concluded that stimulants has ".... relatively little direct effect on improving overt academic performance" (p. 362). This difference in emphasis is clearly not based on a difference in the empirical reports from the literature (despite a source overlap at only 7.5%), but instead represents a difference in interpretation of "importance" attached to a given magnitude of effect. This comparison of two reviews illustrates one type of problem we encountered in our review of reviews: a consensus (agreement) about the effects of stimulants existed in the literature, but despite this robust consensus, a controversy (disagreement) emerged from a comparison of some conclusions of reviews that agreed on the effects. In our synthesis (Swanson et al., 1993), we considered this to represent consensus rather than controversy.

Another analysis of these two reviews illustrates a different problem that we encountered in our review of reviews. In our analysis of *controversy* we noted a disagreement about the magnitude of placebo effect and the seriousness of this in clinical practice. Kavale (1982, p. 286) concluded that the placebo effect was negligible: ".... the present findings indicate that the placebo effect accounted for only 3% of the improvement shown by drug-treated subjects." Ottenbacher and Cooper (1983) concluded that the placebo effect was substantial: ".... approximately 30% of the effect found in the drug versus control conditions could be attributed to the placebo phenomenon" (p. 363). In our review of reviews, we discovered that this major disagreement about the magnitude of placebo effects was due to the lack of source overlap. Overall, Ottenbacher and Cooper (1983) referenced 86 articles, and Kavale (1982) referenced 74 articles, but only 6 of these were in common and referenced by both of these meta-analyses. We concluded that in the sample of references selected for review by Kavale (1982), the reported placebo effects were small, but in a different sample of references selected for review by Ottenbacher and Cooper (1983), the reported placebo effects were much larger. Viewed in a *statistical* fashion, the placebo effect appears not to be robust, since it does not emerge in the same way despite methodological differences or violations of assumptions of homogeneity in the samples (sets of sources) of the two reviews. We used the remainder of the literature to resolve this controversy. The magnitude of the placebo effect reported by Ottenbacher and Cooper (1983) was consistent with an earlier but important "literary summary" by Barkley (1977), who reported about a 30% placebo-response rate, so in the UCI-ADD Center's review of reviews, we (Swanson et al., 1993) accepted the conclusion that a significant and relatively large placebo effect should be expected when evaluating the short-term response to stimulant medication.

5. Summary: Controversy, Consensus, and Unresolved Issues

5.1. Controversy: Purpose of Stimulant Pharmacotherapy

Across the past half-century, most reviews were written by clinicians. The UCI-ADD Center's review of reviews indicated that most researchers (91%) supported some clinical use of stimulant medication to treat children with ADHD. However, in each era of the past half-century, some reviews have questioned this established clinical practice. In our synthesis of the literature in the review of reviews, we noted that even though reviews agreed about the *documented effects* of stimulants, they may differ in their *conclusions* about the clinical practice of using stimulant drugs to treat children with ADHD. Our analyses suggested that the conclusion of some reviews were dictated by a strongly stated *purpose* of the review, rather than documented effects of stimulants reported in the literature. This interesting observation deserves further comment in this chapter, because we believe that this is the basis of major controversies in the literature that have persisted over time.

For example, the stated purpose of a review by Adelman and Compas (1977) was not to simply summarize and organize the literature but to offer an alternative to the ".... pro-drug bias which permeates the massive body of literature in this area" (p. 377). Their approach was to emphasize the lack of long-term effects of stimulants on learning (a response domain with an acknowledged small or nonexistent effect), which led to the conclusion that ".... it remains unproven that the children taking stimulant drugs manifest important positive changes." While this may be consistent with their definition of "important," it is clearly inconsistent with the overall conclusions of most other literature reviews performed at the same point in time which focused on a broader definition of response (e.g., Barkley & Cunningham, 1978 or Whalen & Henker, 1976).

Cooper (1989) distinguished between reviews intended for scholarly audiences and reviews intended for the general public. In the UCI review of reviews, we encountered several reviews intended for the general public (e.g., Schrag & Divoky, 1975; McGuinness, 1989; Kohn, 1989) which were a major source of information for legislators during the debate on the status of ADHD in educational law (see Swanson, 1992). These reviews accepted the consensus about the benefits of stimulants drugs (i.e., short-term beneficial effects on behavior, concentration, and motivation as reported by parents and teachers), but they emphasized limitations of medication: that the literature does not support the notion of a paradoxical response of hyperactive children (normal children show increased attention and decreased undirected movement in response to stimulants); that no organic cause of the symptoms had been identified (such as brain damage, low arousal, or catecholamine deficiency); that prediction of response to medication had not been documented in the literature; that medication had no clear effect on academic performance or learning; and that there was no documented improvement in long-term adjustment associated with treatment with stimulants. As discussed above, these limitations were generally acknowledged, so the accounts of the limitations of stimulant pharmacotherapies were not the controversial part of these papers. Their *conclusions* about the use of stimulants were controversial, not their interpretation of the effects of stimulants.

The Schrag and Divoky (1975) review agreed that stimulants had clear effects, but the acknowledged effects were considered unacceptable for political and social reasons:

> In the final analysis, all the controversies about efficacy, safety and side effects, though highly significant, tend to be misleading. They turn attention from social and political considerations to individual medical questions and therefore conceal the most fundamental issue. From a political and social perspective, the most dangerous psychoactive drug is precisely the one that is medically the safest and psychologically the most effective. (p. 105)

The McGuinness (1989) review concluded that stimulant medications had clear effects which helped ".... teachers and parents, but they do nothing for children" (p. 229). A broad indictment of the clinical case of stimulant pharmacotherapy was advanced based on criticisms of the categorical diagnosis of ADHD and the lack of a paradoxical response to stimulant treatment, which led McGuinness to suggest that ".... drugs do not work" (p. 209). The Kohn (1989) review repeated many of the concerns of the other two general public reviews and concluded that stimulants had clear and reliable effects, but that this treatment was unacceptable because it did not offer a cure for ADHD children who do not suffer from a "disease."

As in the Adelman and Compas (1977) review, the purposes or goals of the general public reviews, rather than the acknowledged effects of stimulant drugs, seem to dictate their conclusions. The conclusions of these reviews for the general public suggest that the clinical practice of treating children with stimulants is unjustified. These conclusions conflict with the conclusions of most scholarly reviews (i.e., that the use of stimulants to achieve short-term reduction of symptoms is an effective and legitimate clinical treatment). Since the two types of reviews acknowledged similar effects of stimulants, in our review of reviews we suggested that different purposes of the reviews, rather than a different understanding of the drug effects, accounted for this controversy. Since these controversies have persisted over time, they are important topics to be acknowledged in any review of the effects of stimulant medication on children with ADHD.

5.2. Consensus

The UCI-ADD Center's review of reviews provided a list of consensus views about the effects of stimulant medication, which we have described as benefits (what should be expected) and limitations (what should not be expected) of stimulant pharmacotherapy for children with ADHD. It is appropriate to end this chapter with a summary of these points, which are shown in Table 1.

As outlined in Table 1, the literature, as interpreted by opponents and critics of stimulant pharmacotherapy, clearly supports the UCI-ADD Center's conclusion that this treatment decreases the diagnostic symptoms of ADHD and the associated features of ADHD. In both cases, this represents decreases in *behavioral excesses* or *disruptive behaviors* (DSM-IIIR, 1987). Also, as outlined in Table 1, stimulant pharmacotherapy does not typically correct social or academic deficits. These drugs do not improve learning, increase positive peer interactions, or enhance learning or achievement. Stimulants such as methylphenidate and d-amphetamine may act to decrease inappropriate behavior, but they are unlikely to act to increase appropriate behavior.

It was asserted by most reviews (75%) that the case of combinations of treatment modalities (e.g., psychosocial interventions such as behavioral interventions in the school and home, combined with psychopharmacological intervention such as pharmacotherapy) was superior in clinical benefits to either components used separately. Our review of reviews

TABLE 1.
What Should Be Expected

1. Temporary Management of Diagnostic Symptoms, due to decreased:
   a. hyperactivity (increased ability to modulate motor behavior)
   b. inattention (increased concentration or effort)
   c. impulsivity (improved self regulation)
2. Temporary Improvement of Associated Features, due to decreased:
   a. defiance (increased compliance)
   b. aggression (less physical and verbal hostility)
   c. negative social skills (improved peer interactions)

What Should Not Be Expected

1. Paradoxical Response does not characterize ADHD, because:
   a. most responses of normal children are in the same direction
   b. some responses of normal adults are in the same direction
   c. adults and children with ADHD have similar clinical responses
2. Prediction of Response has not been shown for nonsymptom variables such as:
   a. neurological signs
   b. physiological measures
   c. biochemical markers
3. Absence of Side Effects in clinical treatment is rare because:
   a. frequently there are problems with eating and sleeping
   b. sometimes negative effects on cognition and attribution occur
   c. infrequently motor or verbal tics appear or increase
4. Large Effects on most complex skills are considered unusual:
   a. no significant improvement of reading skills
   b. no significant improvement of basic athletic skills
   c. no significant improvement of positive social skills
5. Improvement in Long-Term Adjustment is considered unlikely:
   a. no improvement in academic outcome
   b. no reduction in antisocial behavior or arrest rate
   c. small effects on learning and achievement

noted that this laudatory recommendation had little empirical support in the literature (see Abikoff, 1985; Gadow, 1985; Pelham & Murphy, 1986). We believe that this issue is the most crucial one to be addressed in the literature over the next decade. We noted that this is a defining characteristic of the literature of the 1990s, and we expect this trend to continue throughout this decade.

Appendix A

The Conners, Loney, and Milich (CLAM) Questionnaire

Date _____ Age ___ Grade ___ Sex ___   Name of Child _____

Completed by _____

Mother ___ Father ___ Teacher ___ Other (specify)_____

Check the column that
best describes this child:

	Not at all	Just a little	Pretty much	Very much
1. Restless or overactive				
2. Disturbs other children				
3. Mood changes quickly and drastically				
4. Cries often and easily				
5. Demands must be met immediately (easily frustrated				
6. Teases other children and interferes with their activities				
7. Fidgeting				
8. Hums and makes other odd noises				
9. Excitable, impulsive				
10. Inattentive, easily distracted				
11. Fails to finish things he or she starts (short attention span)				
12. Quarrelsome				
13. Acts "smart"				
14. Temper outbursts (explosive and unpredictable behavior)				
15. Defiant				
16. Uncooperative				

Instructions:

In your own words, describe 3 noteworthy (favorable or unfavorable events which occurred during this rating period. (If there were no noteworthy events, describe 3 things which happened even if they were unremarkable.)

1. _____

2. _____

3. _____

PLEASE CONTINUE ON BACK IF NECESSARY

For office use only:	N	I/O	A/D	Mixed
	(1, 2, 3, 4, 5, 7, 9, 10, 11, 14)	(7, 8, 9, 10, 11)	(12, 13, 14, 15, 16)	(1, 2, 3, 5, 6)

Medication Assessment Additional Ratings—Teacher Form
(McBurnett Usual Behavior Scale)

Please circle the number that corresponds to this child's behavior today *compared to how the child typically behaves.* (For example, if the child never does any homework, but today did 10% of his/her homework, the child should get a positive rating even though the performance was below that of most children this child's age.)

Much worse than this child has ever been	Worse than usual for this child		About average for this child. No change in unusual behavior	Better than usual for this child		Much better than this child has ever been
-3	-2	-1	0	1	2	3

1. Attentiveness to teacher:

-3	-2	-1	0	1	2	3

2. Ability to stick with a task/activity:

-3	-2	-1	0	1	2	3

3. Percentage of completed seatwork:

-3	-2	-1	0	1	2	3

4. Accuracy of completed seatwork:

-3	-2	-1	0	1	2	3

5. Following directions:

-3	-2	-1	0	1	2	3

6. Getting along with classmates:

-3	-2	-1	0	1	2	3

Appendix B

Table B.1

1900–1949

1. Bradley, C. (1937). The behavior of children receiving benzedrine. *American Journal of Psychiatry, 94,* 577–585. . . . 72

20. Strauss, A. A., & Lehtinen, L. E. (1947). *Psychopathology and education of the brain-injured child.* New York: Grune & Stratton. . . . 29

Bradley, C., & Bowen, M. (1940). School performance of children receiving amphetamine (benzedrine) sulfate. *American Journal of Orthopsychiatry, 10,* 782–788. . . . 13

Kahn, E., & Cohen, L. H. (1934). Organic driveness: A brain stem syndrome and an experience. With case reports. *New England Journal of Medicine, 210,* 748–756. . . . 12

Bradley, C., & Bowen, M. (1941). Amphetamine (benzedrine) therapy of children's behavior disorders. *American Journal of Orthopsychiatry, 11,* 92–103. . . . 12

Still, G. G. (1902). The Coulstonian Lectures on some abnormal psychical conditions in children. *Lancet, 1,* 1008–1012, 1077–1082, 1163–1168. . . . 10

Hohman, L. B. (1922). Post-enciphalitic behavior disorders in children. *Johns Hopkins Hospital Bulletin, 380,* 372–375. . . . 10

Bender, L., & Cottington, F. (1943). The use of amphetamine sulfate (benzedrine) in child psychiatry. *American Journal of Psychiatry, 99,* 116–121. . . . 9

Molitch, M., & Eccles, A. (1937). Effects of benzedrine sulfate on the intelligence scores of children. *American Journal of Psychiatry, 94,* 587–590. . . . 8

Lindsley, D., & Henry, C. (1942). The effect of drugs on behavior and the electroencephalogram of children with behavior disorders. *Psychosomatic Medicine, 4,* 140–149. . . . 7

Molitch, M., & Sullivan, J. P. (1937). Effect of benzedrine sulfate on children taking new Stanford achievement test. *American Journal of Orthopsychiatry, 7,* 519. . . . 6

Bradley, C., & Green, E. (1940). Psychometric performances of children receiving amphetamine (benzedrine) sulfate. *American Journal of Psychiatry, 97,* 388–394. . . . 6

Cutler, M., Little, J. W., & Strauss, A. A. (1940). The effect of Benzedrine on mentally deficient children. *American Journal of Mental Deficiency, 45,* 59–65. . . . 5

Werner, H., & Strauss, A. A. (1941). Pathology of figure-background relation in the child. *Journal of Abnormal Social Psychology, 36,* 236–248. . . . 4

Orton, S. T. (1937). *Reading, writing and speech problems in children.* New York: Norton. . . . 4

Hollingworth, H. L. (1912). The influence of caffeine on mental and motor efficiency. *Archives of Psychology, 3,* 1–166. . . . 4

Ebaugh, F. G. (1923). Neuropsychiatric sequelae of acute epidemic encephalitis in children. *American Journal of Dis Child, 25,* 89–97. . . . 4

Bender, L. (1949). Psychological problems of children with organic brain disease. *American Journal of Orthopsychiatry, 19,* 404–441. . . . 4

Sherrington, C. (1906). *The integrative action of the nervous system.* New Haven, CT: Yale University Press. . . . 3

Kraepelin, E. (1921). *Manic-depressive insanity and paranoia.* Edinburgh: E. & S. Livingstone. . . . 3

Korey, S. (1944). The effects of benzedrine sulfate on the behavior of psychopathic and neurotic juvenile delinquents. *Psychiatry, 18,* 127–137. . . . 3

Gesell, A., & Amatruda, C. S. (1947). *Developmental diagnosis.* New York: Paul B. Hoeber. . . . 3

Dreisbach, R. H., & Pfeiffer, C. (1943). Caffeine-withdrawal headache. *Journal of Laboratory and Clinical Medicine, 28,* 1212. . . . 3

Bond, E. D., & Smith, L. H. (1935). Post-encephalitic behavior disorders. *American Journal of Psychiatry, 92,* 17. . . . 3

Bond, E. (1932). Postencephalitic, ordinary and extraordinary children. *Journal of Pediatrics, 1,* 310–314. . . . 3

Bender, L. (1942). Postencephalitic behavior disorders in children. In J. Neil (Ed.), *Encephalitis: A clinical study.* New York: Grune & Stratton. . . . 3

Table B.2

1950–1959

18. Laufer, M. W., Denhoff, E., & Solomons, G. (1957). Hyperkinetic impulse disorders in children's behavior problems. *Psychosomatic Medicine, 19,* 38–49. . . . 33

25T. Bradley, C. (1950). Benzedrine and dexedrine in the treatment of children's behavior disorders. *Pediatrics, 5,* 24–37. . . . 27

Laufer, M. W., & Denhoff, E. (1957). Hyperactive behavior syndrome in children. *Journal of Pediatrics, 50,* 463–474. . . . 25

Rosvold, E., Mirsky, R., Sarason, I., Bransome, E., & Beck, L. (1956). A continuous performance test of brain damage. *Journal of Counseling Psychology, 20,* 343–350. . . . 13

Strauss, A. A., & Kephart, N. C. (1955). *Psychopathology and education of the brain-injured child: Progress in theory and clinic.* New York: Grune & Stratton. . . . 10

Lytton, G., & Knobel, M. (1958). Diagnosis and treatment of behavior disorders in children. *Diseases of the Nervous System, 20,* 1–7 or 334–340. . . . 10

Ounsted, C. (1955). The hyperkinetic syndrome in epileptic children. *Lancet, 2,* 303–311. . . . 9

Pasamanick, B. (1951). Anticonvulsant drug therapy of behavior problem children with abnormal EEG. *Archives of Neurology and Psychiatry, 65,* 752–766. . . . 8

Knobel, M., Wolman, M. B., & Mason, E. (1959). Hyperkinesis and organicity in children. *Archives of General Psychiatry, 1,* 310–321. . . . 6

Bradley, C. (1957). Characteristics and management of children with behavior problems associated with organic brain damage. *Pediatric Clinics of North America, 4,* 1049–1060. . . . 6

Schulman, J. L., & Reisman, J. M. (1959). An objective measure of hyperactivity. *American Journal of Mental Deficiency, 64,* 455. . . . 5

Lapouse, R., & Monk, M. (1958). An epidemiologic study of behavior characteristics in children. *American Journal of Public Health, 48,* 1134–1144. . . . 5

Freedman, A. M., Effron, A. S., & Bender, L. (1955). Pharmacology in children with psychiatric illness. *Journal of Nervous and Mental Disease, 122,* 479–486. . . . 5

Davis, G. (1957). Effects of central exitant and depressant drugs on locomotor activity in the monkey. *American Journal of Physiology, 188,* 619–623. . . . 5

Oettinger, L. (1958). The use of deanol in the treatment of disorders of behavior in children. *Journal of Pediatrics, 53,* 671–675. . . . 4

Morris, J. V., MacGillivray, R. C., & Mathieson, C. M. (1955). The results of the experimental administration of amphetamine sulfate, in oligophrenia. *Journal of Mental Science/British Journal of Psychiatry, 101,* 131–140. . . . 4

Mackworth, N. H. (1950). *Researches on the measurement of human performance.* London: His Majesty's Stationary Office. . . . 4

Hunt, B. R., Frank, T., & Krush, T. P. (1956). Chlorpromazine in the treatment of severe emotional disorders of children. *American Journal of Diseases of Children, 86,* 268–277. . . . 4

Freed, H., & Peifer, C. (1956). Treatment of hyperkinetic emotionally disturbed children with prolonged administration of chloropromazine. *American Journal of Psychiatry, 113,* 22–26. . . . 4

Connell, P. H. (1958). *Amphetamine psychosis.* London: Chapman & Hall. . . . 4

Table B.3

1960–1969

6. Conners, C. K. (1969). A teacher rating scale for use in drug studies with children. *American Journal of Psychiatry, 126,* 884–888. . . . 50

17. Knights, R. M., & Hinton, G. G. (1969). The effects of methylphenidate (Ritalin) on the motor skills and behavior of children with learning problems. *Journal of Nervous and Mental Disease, 148,* 643–653. . . . 34

Eisenberg, L., Lachman, R., Molling, P. A., Lockner, A., Mizelle, J. D., & Conners, C. K. (1963). A psychopharmacologic experiment in a training school for delinquent boys: Methods, problems, findings. *American Journal of Orthopsychiatry, 33,* 431–446. . . . 25

Conners, C., Eisenberg, L., & Barcai, A. (1967). Effects of dextroamphetamine on children:

Studies on subjects with learning disabilities and school behavior problems. *Archives of General Psychiatry, 17*, 478–485. . . . 25

Werry, J. S., Weiss, G., Douglas, V. I., & Martin, J. (1966). Studies on the hyperactive child. III: The effect of chlorpromazine upon behavior and learning ability. *Journal of the American Academy of Child Psychiatry, 5*, 292–312. . . . 24

Conners, C. K., & Rothschild, G. H. (1968). Drugs and learning in children. In J. Hellmuth (Ed.), *Learning disorders* (pp. 191–223). Seattle: Special Child Publication. . . . 22

Conners, C. K., Rothschild, G., Eisenberg, L., Schwartz, L. S., & Robinson, E. (1969). Dextroamphetamine sulfate in children with learning disorders: Effects on perception, learning, and achievement. *Archives of General Psychiatry, 21*, 182–190. . . . 22

Stewart, M. A., Pitts, F. N., Craig, A. G., & Dierof, W. (1966). The hyperactive child syndrome. *American Journal of Orthopsychiatry, 36*, 861–867. . . . 21

Millichap, J., & Fowler, G. W. (1967). Treatment of minimal brain dysfunction syndromes. *Pediatric Clinics of North America, 14*, 767–778. . . . 21

Epstein, L. C., Lasagna, L., Conners, C., & Rodriguez, A. (1968). Correlation of dextroamphetamine excretion and drug response in hyperkinetic children. *Journal of Nervous and Mental Diseases, 146*, 136–146. . . . 21

Conners, C. K., & Eisenberg, L. (1963). The effects of methylphenidate on symptomatology and learning in disturbed children. *American Journal of Psychiatry, 120*, 458–464. . . . 21

Conners, C. K., Eisenberg, L., & Sharpe, L. (1964). Effects of methylphenidate (Ritalin) on paired associate learning and Porteus Maze performance in emotionally disturbed children. *Journal of Consulting Psychology, 28*, 14–22. . . . 21

Weiss, B., & Laties, V. G. (1962). Enhancement of human performance by caffeine and the amphetamines. *Psychological Review, 14*, 1–36. . . . 20

Weiss, G., Werry, J. S., Minde, K., Douglas, V. I., & Sykes, D. (1968). Studies on the hyperactive child V: The effects of dextroamphetamine and chlorpromazine on behavior and intellectual functioning. *Journal of Child Psychology and Psychiatry, 9*, 145–156. . . . 19

Menkes, M. M., Rowe, J.S., & Menkes, J. H. (1967). A 25-year follow-up study on the hyperkinetic child with minimal brain dysfunction. *Pediatrics, 39*, 393–399. . . . 19

Clements, S. E., & Peters, J. E. (1962). Minimal brain dysfunction in the school-age child: Diagnosis and treatment. *Archives of General Psychiatry, 6*, 185–197. . . . 19

Werry, J. (1968). Studies on the hyperactive child. IV. An empirical analysis of the minimal brain dysfunction syndrome. *Archives of General Psychiatry, 19*, 9–16. . . . 17

Knobel, M. (1962). Psychopharmacology for the hyperkinetic child-dynamic considerations. *Archives of General Psychiatry, 6*, 30–34. . . . 17

Millichap, J. G., & Boldery, E. E. (1967). Studies in hyperkinetic behavior. II: Laboratory and clinical evaluations of drug treatments. *Neurology, 17*, 467–471. . . . 16

Conrad, W., & Insel, J. (1967). Anticipating the response to amphetamine therapy in the treatment of hyperkinetic children. *Pediatrics, 40*, 96–98. . . . 13

Millichap, J. G., Aymot, F., Sturgis, L. H., Larsen, K. W., & Egan, R. A. (1968). Hyperkinetic behavior and learning disorders. III: Battery of neuropsychological test in controlled trial of methylphenidate. *American Journal of Diseases in Childhood, 116*, 235–244. . . . 12

Freeman, R. D. (1966). Drug effects on learning in children—A selective review of the past 30 years. *Journal of Special Education, 1*, 17–44. . . . 12

Eisenberg, L. (1966). The management of the hyperkinetic child. *Developmental Medicine and Child Neurology, 8*, 593–598. . . . 12

Clements, S. D. (1966). Minimal brain dysfunction in children: Terminology and identification. In U.S. Department of Health, Education, and Welfare, Public Health Service Publication. . . . 12

Table B.4

1970-1979

2. Sprague, R. L., & Sleator, E. K. (1977b). Methylphenidate in hyperkinetic children: Difference in dose effects on learning and social behavior. *Science, 198,* 1274–1276. . . . 65

4. Barkley, R. A. (1977). A review of stimulant drug research with hyperactive children. *Journal of Child Psychology and Psychiatry, 18,* 137–165. . . . 56

5. Wender, P. H. (1971). *Minimal brain dysfunction in children.* New York: Wiley-Interscience. . . . 54

7. Weiss, G., Kruger, E., Danielson, V., & Elman, M. (1975). Effect of long-term treatment of hyperactive children with methylphenidate. *Canadian Medical Association Journal, 112,* 159–165. . . . 41

8. Sprague, R. L., Barnes, K. R., & Werry, J. S. (1970). Methylphenidate and thioridazine: Learning, reaction time, activity, and classroom behavior in disturbed children. *American Journal of Orthopsychiatry, 40,* 615–628. . . . 40

9. Rapoport, J., Quinn, P., Bradbard, G., Riddle, D., & Brooks, F. (1974). Imipramine and methylphenidate: Treatments of hyperactive boys. *Archives of General Psychiatry, 30,* 789–793. . . . 40

11. Douglas, V. I. (1972). Stop, look, and listen: The problem of sustained attention and impulse control in hyperactive and normal children. *Canadian Journal of Behavioral Science, 4,* 259–282. . . . 37

12. Weiss, G., Minde, K., Werry, J. S., Douglas, V. I., & Nemeth, E. (1971). Studies on the hyperactive child. VIII: A five-year follow-up. *Archives of General Psychiatry, 24,* 409–414. . . . 36

14. Swanson, J., Kinsbourne, M., Roberts, W., & Zucker, K. (1978). A time-response analysis of the effect of stimulant medication on the learning ability of children referred for hyperactivity. *Pediatrics, 61,* 21–29. . . . 34

15. Safer, D. J., Allen, R. P., & Barr, E. (1972). Depression of growth in hyperactive children on stimulant drugs. *New England Journal of Medicine, 287* 217–220. . . . 34

16. Rapoport, J. L., Buchsbaum, M. S., Zahn, T. P., Wemgartner, H., Ludlow, C., & Mikkelsen, I. J. (1978). Dextroamphetamine: Cognitive and behavioral effects in normal prepubertal boys. *Science, 199,* 560–563. . . . 34

19. Safer, D. J., & Allen, R. P. (1976). *Hyperactive children: Diagnosis and management.* Baltimore, MD: University Park Press. . . . 30

21. Cantwell, D. P., & Carlson, G. A. (1978). Stimulants. In J. S. Werry (Ed.), *Pediatric psychopharmacology: The use of behavior modifying drugs in children* (pp. 171–217). New York: Brunner/Mazel. . . . 29

22. Barkley, R. A., & Cunningham, C. E. (1978). Do stimulant drugs improve the academic performance of hyperactive children? A review of outcome research. *Clinical Pediatrics, 17,* 85–92. . . . 29

23. Swanson, J. M., & Kinsbourne, M. (1976). Stimulant-related state-dependent learning in hyperactive children. *Science, 192,* 1354–1356. . . . 28

24. Riddle, K. D., & Rapoport, J. L. (1976). A 2-year follow-up of 72 hyperactive boys: Classroom behavior and peer acceptance. *Journal of Nervous and Mental Disease, 162,* 126–134. . . . 28

25T. Whalen, C., & Henker, B. (1976). Psychostimulants and children: A review and analysis of drug effectiveness. *Psychological Bulletin, 83,* 1113–1130. . . . 27

25T. Sprague, R. L., & Werry, J. (1971). Methodology of psychopharmacological studies with the retarded. In N. Ellis (Ed.), *International review of research in mental retardation.* New York: Academic Press. . . . 27

25T. Mendelson, W., Johnson, N., & Stewart, M. A. (1971). Hyperactive children as teenagers: A follow-up study. *Journal of Nervous and Mental Disease, 153,* 273–279. . . . 27

Rie, H. E., Rie, E. D., Stewart, S., & Ambuel, J. P. (1976). Effects of methylphenidate on underachieving children. *Journal of Consulting and Clinical Psychology, 44,* 250–260. . . . 26

Quinn, P., & Rapoport, J. (1975). One-year follow-up of hyperactive boys treated with imipramine and methylphenidate. *American Journal of Psychiatry, 132,* 241–245. . . . 25

Gittelman-Klein, R., & Klein, D. (1976). Methylphenidate effects in learning disabilities. *Archives of General Psychiatry, 33,* 655. . . . 25

Schleifer, M., Weiss, G., Cohen, N., Elman, M., Cvejic, H., & Kruger, E. (1975). Hyperactivity in preschoolers and the effect of methylphenidate. *American Journal of Orthopsychiatry, 45,* 38–50. . . . 24

Werry, J. S., & Sprague, R. L. (1974). Methylphenidate in children: Effect of dosage. *Australian and New Zealand Journal of Psychiatry, 8,* 9–19. . . . 23

Werry, J., & Aman, M. (1975). Methylphenidate and haloperidol in children: Effects on attention, memory, and activity. *Archives of General Psychiatry, 32,* 790–795. . . . 23

Table B.5

1980–1989

3. American Psychiatric Association (1980). *DSM-III.* Washington, DC: American Psychiatric Association. . . . 59

10. Rapoport, J. L., Buchsbaum, M. S., Weingartner, H., Zahn, T. P., Ludlow, C., & Mikkelsen, E. (1980). Dextroamphetamine: Its cognitive and behavioral effects in normal and hyperactive boys and normal men. *Archives of General Psychiatry, 37,* 933–943. . . . 38

13. American Psychiatric Association. (1987). *DSM-III-R.* Washington, DC: American Psychiatric Association. . . . 35

Douglas, V. I., Barr,R. G., O'Neill, M.E., & Britton, B. G. (1986). Short-term effects of methylphenidate on the cognitive, learning and academic performance of children with attention deficit disorder in the laboratory and the classroom. *Journal of Child Psychology and Psychiatry, 27,* 191–211. . . . 24

Lowe, T. L., Cohen, D. J., Detlor, J., Kremenitzer, M. W., & Shaywitz, B. A. (1982). Stimulant medications precipitate Tourette's syndrome. *Journal of the American Medical Association, 247,* 1729–1731. . . . 22

Weiss, G., & Hechtman, L. (1986). *Hyperactive children grown up: Empirical findings and theoretical considerations.* New York: Guilford. . . . 21

Ross, D. M., & Ross, S. A. (1982). *Hyperactivity: Current issues, research, and theory.* New York: Wiley. . . . 21

Mattes, J. A., & Gittleman, R. (1983). Growth of hyperactive children on maintenance regimen of methylphenidate. *Archives of General Psychiatry, 40,* 317–321. . . . 21

Barkley, R. A. (1981). *Hyperactive children: A handbook of diagnosis and treatment.* New York: Guilford Press. . . . 21

Pelham, W. E., Bender, M. E., Caddell, J., Booth, S., & Moorer, S. H. (1985). Methylphenidate and children with attention deficit disorder: Dose effects on classroom academic and social behavior. *Archives of General Psychiatry, 42,* 948–952. . . . 20

Gadow, K. D. (1983). Effects of stimulant drugs on academic performance in hyperactive and learning disabled children. *Journal of Learning Disabilities, 16,* 290–299. . . . 20

Satterfield, J. H., Satterfield, B. T., & Cantwell, D. P. (1981). Three-year multimodality treatment study of 100 hyperactive boys. *Pediatrics, 98*, 650–655. . . . 18

Satterfield, J., Hoppe, C., & Schell, A. (1982). A prospective study of delinquency in 110 adolescent boys with attention deficit disorder and 88 normal adolescent boys. *American Journal of Psychiatry, 139*, 797–798. . . . 18

Gittelman, R., Mannuzza, S., Shenker, R., & Bonagura, N. (1985). Hyperactive boys almost grown up. *Archives of General Psychiatry, 42*, 937–947. . . . 18

Abikoff, H., & Gittelman, R. (1985). Hyperactive children treated with stimulants. Is cognitive training a useful adjunct? *Archives of General Psychiatry, 42*, 953–961. . . . 18

Safer, D. J., & Krager, J. M. (1988). A survey of medication treatment for hyperactive/inattentive students. *Journal of the American Medical Association, 260*, 2256–2258. . . . 17

Loney, J., Kramer, H., & Milich, R. S. (1981). The hyperactive child grows up: Predictors of symptoms, delinquency, and achievement at follow-up. In K. D. Gadow & J. Loney (Eds.), *Psychosocial aspects of drug treatment for hyperactivity* (pp. 381–415). Boulder, CO: Westview Press. . . . 17

Hunt, R. D., Minderaa, R. B., & Cohen, D. J. (1985). Clonidine benefits children with attention deficit disorder and hyperactivity: Report of a double-blind placebo-crossover therapeutic trial. *Journal of the American Academy of Child Psychiatry, 24*, 617–629. . . . 17

Garfinkel, B. D., Wender, P. H., & Sloman, L. (1983). Tricyclic antidepressant and methylphenidate treatment of attention deficit disorder in children. *Journal of the American Academy of Child & Adolescent Psychiatry, 22*, 343–348. . . . 17

Charles, L., & Schain, R. (1981). A four-year follow-up study of the effects of methylphenidate on the behavior modification in the treatment of kindergarten-aged hyperactive children. *Journal of Abnormal Child Psychology, 9*, 495–505. . . . 17

Zametkin, A. J., & Rapoport, J. L. (1987). Neurobiology of attention deficit disorder with hyperactivity: Where have we come in 50 years? *Journal of the American Academy of Child & Adolescent Psychiatry, 26*, 676–686. . . . 16

Solanto, M. V. (1984). Neuropharmacological basis of stimulant drug action in attention deficit disorder with hyperactivity: A review and synthesis. *Psychological Bulletin, 95*, 387–409. . . . 16

Shaywitz, S. E., Hunt, R. D., Jatlow, P., Cohen, D. J., Young, J. G., Pierce, R. N., Anderson, G. M., & Shaywitz, B. A. (1982). Psychopharmacology of attention deficit disorder: Pharmacokinetic, neuroendocrine, and behavioral measures following acute and chronic treatment with methylphenidate. *Pediatrics, 69*, 688–694. . . . 16

Pelham, W., & Bender, M. E. (1982). Peer relationships in hyperactive children: Description and treatment. In K. Gadow & I. Bailer (Eds.), *Advances in learning and behavioral disabilities,* (pp. 365–436). Greenwich, CT: JAI Press. . . . 16

Kavale, K. (1982). The efficacy of stimulant drug treatment for hyperactivity: A meta-analysis. *Journal of Learning Disabilities, 15*, 280–289. . . . 16

Gualtieri, C. T., Wargin, W., Kanoy, R., Patrick, K., Shen, C. D., Youngblood, W., Mueller, R. A., & Breese, G. R. (1982). Clinical studies of methylphenidate serum levels in children and adults. *Journal of the American Academy of Child Psychiatry, 21*, 19–26. . . . 16

Table B.6

1990–1992

Pelham, W. E., Jr., Greenslade, K. E., Vodde-Hamilton, M., Murphy, D. A., & Greenstein (1990). Relative efficacy of long-acting stimulants on ADHD children: A comparison of

standard methylphenidate, Ritalin-SR, Dexedrene Spansule, and Pemoline. *Pediatrics,*
86, 226–237. . . . 9

Barkley, R. A. (1990). *Attention deficit hyperactivity disorder: A handbook for diagnosis and treat-*
ment. New York: Guilford. . . . 8

Zametkin, A. J., Nordahl, T. E., Gross, M., King, A. C., Semple, W. E., Rumsey, J., Hamburger,
S., & Cohen, R. M. (1990). Cerebral glucose metabolism in adults with hyperactivity of
childhood onset. *New England Journal of Medicine, 323,* 1361–1366. . . . 7

Barkley, R. A., Fischer, M., Edelbrock, C. S., & Smallish, L. (1990). The adolescent outcome of
hyperactive children diagnosed by research criteria I: An 8-year prospective follow-up
study. *Journal of the American Academy of Child & Adolescent Psychiatry, 29,* 546–557. . . . 6

Riddle, M. A., Nelson, J. C., Kleinman, C. S., Rasmusson, A., Leckman, J. F., King, R. A., &
Cohen, D. (1991). Sudden death in children receiving Norpramin: A review of three
reported cases and summary. *Journal of the American Academy of Child & Adolescent*
Psychiatry, 30, 104–108. . . . 5

McClellan, J. M., Rubert, M. P., Reichler, R. J., et al. (1990). Attention deficit disorder in
children at risk for anxiety and depression. *Journal of the Academy of Child and Adolescent*
Psychiatry, 29, 534–539. . . . 5

Jacobvitz, D., Sroufe, L. A., Stewart, M., & Leffert, N. (1990). Treatment of attentional and
hyperactivity problems in children with sympathomimetic drugs: A comprehensive
review. *Journal of the American Academy of Child & Adolescent Psychiatry, 29,* 677–688. . . . 5

Gadow, K. D., Nolan, E. E., Sverd, J., Sprafkin, J., & Paolicelli, L. (1990). Methylphenidate in
aggressive-hyperactive boys: I. Effects on peer aggression in public school settings.
Journal of the American Academy of Child & Adolescent Psychiatry, 29, 710–718. . . . 5

Whalen, C. K., Henker, B., & Granger, D. A. (1990). Social judgment processes in hyperactive
boys: Effects of methylphenidate and comparisons with normal peers. *Journal of Abnor-*
mal Child Psychology, 18, 297–316. . . . 4

Swanson, J. M., Cantwell, D., Lerner, M., McBurnett, K., & Hanna, G. (1991). Effects of
stimulant medication on learning in children with ADHD. *Journal of Learning Disabilities,*
24, 219–230. . . . 4

Rapport, M. D., & Kelly, K. L. (1991). Psychostimulant effects on learning and cognitive
function: Findings and implications. *Clinical Psychology Review, 11,* 61–92. . . . 4

Pelham, W., Jr., McBurnett, K., Harper, G. W., Milich, R., Murphy, D. A., Clinton, J., & Thiele,
C. (1990). Methylphenidate and baseball playing in ADHD children: Who's on first?
Journal of Consulting Clinical Psychology, 58, 130–133. . . . 4

Elia, J., Borcherding, B. G., Potter, W. Z., Mefford, I. N., Rapoport, J. L., & Keysor, C. S. (1990).
Stimulant drug treatment of hyperactivity: Biochemical correlates. *Clinical Pharmacology*
and Therapeutics, 48, 57–66. . . . 4

Denckla, M. B. (1991). Attention deficit hyperactivity disorder-residual type. *Journal of Child*
Neurology 6, 44–50. . . . 4

Biederman, J., Faraone, S. V., Feenan, K., et al. (1990). Family-genetic and psychosocial risk
factors in DSM-III attention deficit disorder. *Journal of the American Academy of Child &*
Adolescent Psychiatry, 29, 526–533. . . . 4

Barkley, R. A., McMurray, M. B., Edelbrock, C. S., & Robbins, K. (1990). Side effects of
methylphenidate in children with attention deficit hyperactivity disorder: A systemic,
placebo-controlled evaluation. *Pediatrics, 86,* 184–192. . . . 4

Strober, M., Morrell, W., Lampert, C., et al. (1990). Relapse following discontinuation of
lithium maintenance therapy in adolescents with bipolar I illness: A naturalistic study.
American Journal of Psychiatry, 147, 457–461. . . . 3

Shaywitz, B. A., & Shaywitz, S. E. (1991 supplement). Comorbidity: A critical issue in
attention deficit disorder. *The Journal of Child Neurology, 6,* S13–S22. . . . 3

McGee, R., Feehan, M., Williams, S., et al. (1990). DSM-III disorders in a large sample of adolescents. *Journal of the American Academy of Child & Adolescent Psychiatry, 29,* 611–619. . . . 3

Kendall, P. C. (1990). *Child and adolescent therapy: Cognitive-behavioral procedures.* New York: Guilford. . . . 3

Hynd, G. W., Semrud-Clikeman, M., Lorys, A., et al. (1990). Brain morphology in developmental dyslexia and attention deficit disorder/hyperactivity. *Archives of Neurology, 47,* 919–926. . . . 3

Hynd, G. W., Lorys, A. R., Semrud-Clikeman, M., et al. (1991). Attention deficit disorder without hyperactivity: A distinct behavioral and neurocognitive syndrome. *Journal of Child Neurology, 6,* 37–42. . . . 3

Dulcan, M. (1990). Using psychostimulants to treat behavior disorders of children and adolescents. *Journal of Child & Adolescent Psychopharmacology, 1,* 7–20. . . . 3

Brumback, R. A., & Weinberg, W. A. (1990). Pediatric behavioral neurology: An update on the neurologic aspects of depression, hyperactivity, and learning disabilities. *Neurologic Clinics, 8,* 677–703. . . . 3

Biederman, J., Newcorn, J., & Sprich, S. E. (1991). Comorbidity of attention deficit hyperactivity disorder with conduct, depressive, anxiety, and other disorders. *American Journal of Psychiatry, 148,* 564–577. . . . 3

Accardo, P. J., Blondis, T. A., & Whitman, B. Y. (1990). Disorders of attention and activity level in a referral population. *Pediatrics, 85,* 426–431. . . . 3

Abramowicz, M. (1990). Sudden death in children treated with a tricyclic antidepressant. *The Medical Letter on Drugs and Therapeutics, 32,* 53. . . . 3

References

Abikoff, H. (1985). Efficacy of cognitive training interventions in hyperactive children: A critical review. Special Issue: Attention deficit disorder: Issues in assessment and intervention. *Clinical Psychology Review, 5,* 479–512.

Abikoff, H. (1991). Cognitive training in ADHD children: Less to it than meets the eye. *Journal of Learning Disabilities, 24,* 205–209.

Adelman, H. S., & Compas, B. E. (1977). Stimulant drugs and learning problems. *Journal of Special Education, 11,* 377–416.

American Psychiatric Association. (1968). *Diagnostic and statistical manual for mental disorders (Second Edision).* Washington, DC: Author.

American Psychiatric Association. (1980). *Diagnostic and statistical manual for mental disorders (Third Edition).* Washington, DC: Author.

American Psychiatric Association. (1987). *Diagnostic and statistical manual for mental disorders (Third Edition-Revised).* Washington, DC: Author.

American Psychiatric Association (1994, work in progress). *Diagnostic and statistical manual for mental disorders option books (Fourth Edition).* Washington, DC: Author.

Arnold, L. E. (1993). *NIMH-funded research on ADHD.* Proceedings from the CHADD Conference, San Diego, CA.

Arnold, L. E., Huestis, R. D., Smeltzer, D. J., Scheib, J., Wemmer, D., & Colner, G. (1976). Levoamphetamine versus dextroamphetamine minimal brain dysfunction. *Archives of General Psychiatry, 23,* 292–301.

Baldessarini, R. J. (1972). Behavior modification by drugs: I. Pharmacology of the amphetamines. *Pediatrics, 49,* 694–701.

Barkley, R. A. (1977). A review of stimulant drug research with hyperactive children. *Journal of Child Psychology and Psychiatry, 18,* 137–165.

Barkley, R. A. (1990). *Attention-deficit hyperactivity disorder: A handbook for diagnosis and treatment.* New York: Guilford.

Barkley, R. A., & Cunningham, C. E. (1978). Do stimulant drugs improve academic performance of hyperactive children? A review of outcome research. *Clinical Pediatrics, 17,* 85–92.

Barkley, R. A., Fischer, M., Edelbrock, C. S., & Smallish, L. (1990). The adolescent outcome of hyperactive children diagnosed by research criteria, I: An 8-year prospective follow-up study. *Journal of the American Academy of Child and Adolescent Psychiatry, 29,* 546–557.

Barkley, R. A., Fischer, M., Newby, R. F., & Breen, M. (1988). Development of a multimethod clinical protocol for assessing stimulant medication drug response in children with attention deficit disorder. *Journal of Clinical Child Psychology, 17,* 14–24.

Barkley, R. A., McMurray, M. B., Edelbrock, C. S., & Robbins, K. (1990). Side effects of methylphenidate in children with attention deficit hyperactivity disorder: A systematic, placebo-controlled evaluation. *Pediatrics, 86,* 184–192.

Bellamy, G. T. (1987). Education for the Handicapped Law Report, 211:242. Alexandria, Virginia: CCR Publishing.

Biederman, J. (1988). Pharmacological treatment of adolescents with affective disorders and attention deficit disorders. *Psychopharmacology Bulletin, 24,* 81–87.

Bloomingdale, L. M. (Ed.). (1984). *Attention deficit disorder (Vol. 1): Diagnostic, cognitive, and therapeutic understanding.* Jamaica, NY: Spectrum.

Bloomingdale, L. M. (Ed.). (1985). *Attention deficit disorder (Vol. 2): Identification, course, and rationale.* Jamaica, NY: Spectrum.

Bloomingdale, L. M. (Ed.). (1988). *Attention deficit disorder (Vol. 3): New research in attention, treatment, and psychopharmacology.* New York: Pergamon Press.

Bloomingdale, L. M., & Sergeant, J. (Eds.). (1988). *Attention deficit disorder (Vol. 5): Criteria, cognitive, and intervention.* New York: Pergamon Press.

Bloomingdale, L. M., & Swanson, J. M. (Eds.). (1989). *Attention deficit disorder (Vol. 4): Current concepts and emerging trends in attentional and behavioral disorders of childhood.* New York: Pergamon Press.

Bradley, C. (1937). The behavior of children receiving benzedrine. *American Journal of Psychiatry, 94,* 577–585.

Bradley, C. (1950). Benzedrine and dexedrine in the treatment of children's behavior disorders. *Pediatrics, 5,* 24–37.

Brecher, E. M. (1972). *Licit and illicit drugs.* New York: Consumer's Union.

Brown, G. L., Ebert, M. H., Mikkelsen, E. J., & Hunt, R. D. (1980). Behavior and motor activity response in hyperactive children and plasma amphetamine levels following a sustained release preparation. *Journal of the American Academy of Child Psychiatry, 19,* 225–239.

Brown, G. L., Hunt, R. D., Ebert, M. H., Bunney, W. E., & Kopin, I. J. (1979). Plasma levels of d-amphetamine in hyperactive children. *Psychopharmacology, 62,* 133–140.

Cantwell, D. P. (in press). Psychopharmacological treatment of ADD and related disorders: Current issues. *Journal of Child and Adolescent Psychopharmacology.*

Carlsson, A. (1975). Receptor-mediated control of dopamine metabolism. In E. Usdin & J. W. Bunney (Eds.), *Pre- and post-synaptic receptors.* New York: Marcel Dekker.

Chan, Y. M., Soldin, S. J., Swanson, J. M., Deber, C. M., Thiessen, J. J., & MacLeod, S. (1980). Gas chromatographic/mass spectroscopic analysis of methylphenidate (Ritalin) in serum. *Clinical Biochemistry Journal, 13,* 266–272.

Chan, Y. M., Swanson, J. M., Soldin, S. S., Thiessen, J. J., Macleod, S. M., & Logan, W. (1983).

Methylphenidate hydrochloride given with or before breakfast: II. Effects on plasma concentration of methylphenidate and ritalinic acid. *Pediatrics, 72*, 56–59.

Chesapeake Institute, U.S. Department of Education. (1993). *Proceedings of the forum on the education of children with attention deficit disorder.* Washington, DC.

Cohen, D. J., & Young, J. G. (1977). Neurochemistry and child psychiatry. *Journal of the American Academy of Child Psychiatry, 16*, 353–411.

Cole, J. (1969). The amphetamines in child psychiatry: A review. *Seminars in Psychiatry, 1*, 174–178.

Collier, C. P., Soldin, S. J., Swanson, J. M., MacLeod, S. M., Weinberg, F., & Rochefort, J. G. (1985). Pemoline pharmacokinetics and long term therapy in children with attention deficit disorder and hyperactivity. *Clinical Pharmacokinetics, 10*, 269–278.

Conners, C. K. (1971). Recent drug studies. *Journal of Learning Disabilities, 4*, 476–483.

Conners, C. K., & Eisenberg, L. (1963). The effects of methylphenidate on symptomatology and learning in disturbed children. *American Journal of Psychiatry, 120*, 458–464.

Conners, C. K., & Solanto, B. A. (1984). The psychophysiology of stimulant drug response in hyperkinetic children. In L. M. Bloomingdale (Ed.), *Attention deficit disorder (Vol. 1): Diagnostic, cognitive, and therapeutic understanding* (pp. 191–204). Jamaica, NY: Spectrum.

Cooper, H. M. (1989). *Integrating research: A guide for literature reviews,* (Vol. 2). Newbury Park, CA: Sage.

Cooper, J. R., Bloom, F. E., & Roth, R. H. (1986). *The biochemical basis of neuropharmacology.* New York: Oxford University Press.

Cowart, V. S. (1988). The Ritalin controversy: What's made this drug's opponents hyperactive? *Journal of the American Medical Association, 259*, S–W.

Coyle, J. T., & Snyder, S. H. (1969). Catecholamine uptake by synaptosomes in homogenates of rat brain: Stereospecificity in different areas. *Journal of Pharmacology and Experimental Therapeutics, 170*, 221–231.

Davila, R. R., Williams, M. L., & MacDonald, J. T. (1991). *Clarification of policy to address the needs of children with attention deficit hyperactivity disorders within general and/or special education.* Memorandum from the U.S. Department of Education: Office of Special Education and Rehabilitative Services.

Douglas, V. I., Barr, R. G., Amin, K., O'Neill, M. E., & Britton, B. G. (1988). Dosage effects and individual responsivity to methylphenidate in attention deficit disorder. *Journal of Child Psychology and Psychiatry, 29*, 453–475.

Dykman, R. A., McGrew, J., Harris, T. S., Peters, J. E., & Ackerman, P. T. (1976). Two blinded studies of the effects of stimulant drugs on children: Pemoline, methylphenidate, and placebo. In R. P. Anderson & C. G. Halcomb (Eds.), *Learning Disability/Minimal Brain Dysfunction Syndrome.* Springfield, IL: Thomas.

Elia, J., Borcherding, B. G., Rapoport, J. L., & Keysor, C. S. (1991). Methylphenidate and dextroamphetamine treatments of hyperactivity: Are there true nonresponders? *Psychiatry Research, 36*, 141–155.

Elia, J., & Rapoport, J. L. (1991). Ritalin versus dextroamphetamine in ADHD: Both should be tried. In L. L. Greenhill & B. B. Osman (Eds.), *Ritalin: Theory and Patient Management* (pp. 79–74). New York: Mary Ann Liebert, Publishers.

Fish, B. (1971). The "one child, one drug" myth of stimulants in hyperkinesis. *Archives of General Psychology, 25*, 193–203.

Fisher, S. (1959). *Child research in psychopharmacology.* Springfield, IL: Thomas.

Forness, S.R., Swanson, J. M., Cantwell, D. P., Guthrie, D., & Sena, R. (1992). Response to stimulant medication across six measures of school-related performance in children with ADHD and disruptive behavior. *Behavioral Disorders, 18*, 42–53.

Forness, S. R., Swanson, J. M., Cantwell, D. P., Youpa, D., & Hanna, G. L. (1992). Stimulant medication and reading performance. *Journal of Learning Disabilities, 25,* 115–123.

Gadow, K. D. (1985). Relative efficacy of pharmacological, behavioral, and combination treatments for enhancing academic performance. *Clinical Psychology Reviews, 5,* 513–533.

Gadow, K. D. (1989). Dose response effects of stimulant drugs: A clarification of issues. In L. M. Bloomingdale & J. M. Swanson (Eds.), *Attention deficit disorder: Current concepts and emerging trends in attentional and behavioral disorders of childhood* (pp. 25–56). New York: Pergamon Press.

Gittelman, R., & Kanner, A. (1986). Psychopharmacotherapy. In H. Quay & J. Werry (Eds.), *Psychopathological disorders of childhood* (pp. 455–495). New York: Wiley.

Gilman, A., Goodman, L., Rall, T., & Murad, F. (Eds.). (1985). *Goodman and Gilman's The pharmacological basis of therapeutics* (7th Edition). New York: Macmillan.

Gordon, M. (1983). *The Gordon Diagnostic System.* DeWitt: Gordon Systems.

Greenhill, L. L., & Osman, B. B. (Eds.). (1991). Methylphenidate in the clinical office practice of child psychiatry. In *Ritalin: Theory and patient management* (pp. 97–117). New York: Mary Ann Liebert, Publishers.

Greenberg, L. L. (1991). *TOVA Interpretation Manual.* Minneapolis, MN: Author.

Greenhill, L. L., & Osman, B. B. (Eds.). (1991). *Ritalin: Theory and patient management.* New York: Mary Ann Liebert, Publishers.

Grinspoon, L., & Hedblom, P. (1975). The treatment of hyperkinetic children. In L. Grinspoon & P. Hedlom (Eds.), *The speed culture: Amphetamine use and abuse in America* (pp. 227–257). Cambridge, MA: Harvard University Press.

Gualtieri, C. T., Wargin, W., Kanoy, R., Patrick, K., Shen, C. D., Youngblood, W., Mueller, R. A., & Breese, G. R. (1982). Clinical studies of methylphenidate serum levels in children and adults. *Journal of the American Academy of Child Psychiatry, 21,* 19–26.

Hauger, R. L., Angel, L. I., Janowsky, A., Berger, P., & Hulihan-Gilbin, B. (1990). Brain recognition sites for methylphenidate and amphetamines. In S. Deutsch, A. Weizman, & R. Weizman (Eds.), *Application of basic neuroscience to child psychiatry* (pp. 77–100). New York: Plenum Medical Book Company.

Hentoff, N. (1972, May 25). Drug pushing in the schools: The professionals (1). *The Village Voice,* pp. 20–22, 25.

Hubbard, J. W., Srinivas, N. R., Quinn, D., & Midha, K. K. (1989). Enantioselective aspects of the disposition of d1-threo-methylphenidate after the administration of a sustained-release formulation to children with attention deficit-hyperactivity disorder. *Journal of Pharmaceutical Science, 78,* 944–947.

Hunt, R. D. (1987). Treatment effects of oral and transdermal clonidine in relation to methyl-phenidate: An open pilot study in ADD-H. *Psychopharmacology Bulletin, 23,* 111–114.

Journal of Child Neurology (1986–). Littleton, MA: PSG Publishing Co.

Journal of Learning Disabilities (1968–). Austin, TX: Donald D. Hammill Foundation.

Kavale, K. (1982). The efficacy of stimulant drug treatment for hyperactivity: A meta-analysis. *Journal of Learning Disabilities, 15,* 280–289.

Kavanagh, J. F., & Truss, T. J., Jr. (Eds.). (1988). *Learning disabilities: Proceedings of the national conference.* Parkton, MD: York Press.

Kohn, A. (1989). Suffer the restless children. *The Atlantic Monthly, 264,* 90–98.

Kupietz, S. S. (1991). Ritalin blood levels and their correlations with measures of learning. In L. L. Greenhill & B. B. Osman (Eds.), *Ritalin: Theory and patient management* (pp. 247–256). New York: Mary Ann Liebert, Publishers.

Laufer, M. W., & Denhoff, E. (1957). Hyperkinetic behavior syndrome in children. *Journal of Pediatrics, 50,* 463–474.

Lipman, R. S. (1974). NIMH-PRB support of research in minimal brain dysfunction in children. In C. K. Conners (Ed.), *Clinical use of stimulant drugs in children* (pp. 203–213). Amsterdam: Excerpta Medica.

Loney, J., & Milich, R. (1982). Hyperactivity, inattention, and aggression in clinical practice. *Advances in Developmental and Behavioral Pediatrics, 3*, 113–147.

Lou, H., Henriksen, L., & Bruhn, P. (1984). Focal hypoperfusion in children with dysphasia and/or attention deficit disorder. *Archives of Neurology, 41*, 825–829.

Malone, M. A., Kershner, J. R., & Swanson, J. M. (1994). Hemispheric processing and methylphenidate effects in attention-deficit hyperactivity disorder. *Journal of Child Neurology, 9*, 1–8.

McCracken, J. T. (1991). A two-part model of stimulant action on attention-deficit hyperactivity disorder in children. *Journal of Neuropsychiatry Clinical Neuroscience, 3*, 201–209.

McGuinness, D. (1989). Attention deficit disorder: The emperor's clothes, animal "pharm," and other fiction. In S. Fisher & R. P. Greenberg (Eds.), *The limits of biological treatments of psychological distress* (pp. 151–187). Hillsdale, NJ: Erlbaum.

McMillen, B. A. (1983). CNS stimulants: Two distinct mechanisms of action for amphetamine-like drugs. *Trends in Pharmacological Science, 19*, 429–432.

Millichap, J. G. (1973). Drugs in management of minimal brain dysfunction. *Annuals of the New York Academy of Sciences, 205*, 321–334.

Morrison, R. T., & Boyd, R. N. (1987). *Organic chemistry* (5th ed.). Boston: Allyn & Bacon.

Ottenbacher, K. J., & Cooper, M. M. (1983). Drug treatment of hyperactivity in children. *Developmental Medicine and Child Neurology, 25*, 358–366.

Parker, H. C. (1992). *The ADD Hyperactivity Handbook for School*. Plantation, FL: Impact Publications.

Patrick, K. S., Mueller, R. A., Gualtieri, C. T., & Breese, G. R. (1987). Pharmacokinetics and actions of methylphenidate. In H. Y. Meltzer (Ed.), *Psychopharmacology: The third generation of progress*. New York: Raven.

Pelham, W. E., & Bender, M. E. (1982). Peer relationships in hyperactive children: Description and treatment. *Advances in learning and behavioral disabilities*, (vol. 1, pp. 365–436). Greenwich, CT: JAI Press.

Pelham, W. E., Bender, M. E., Cadell, J., Booth, S., & Moorer, S. H. (1985). The dose-response effects of methylphenidate on classroom academic and social behavior in children with attention deficit disorder. *Archives of General Psychiatry, 42*, 948–952.

Pelham, W. E., Jr., Greenslade, K. E., Vodde-Hamilton, M., Murphy, D. A., Greenstein, J. J., Gnagy, E. M., Guthries, K. J., Hoover, M. D., & Dahl, R. E. (1990). The efficacy of long-acting stimulants on ADHD children: A comparison of standard methylphenidate, Ritalin-SR, Dexedrene Spansule, and Pemoline. *Pediatrics, 86*, 226–237.

Pelham, W. E., & Murphy, H. A. (1986). Attention deficit and conduct disorders. In M. Hersen (Ed.), *Pharmacological and behavioral treatments: An integrative approach* (pp. 108–148). New York: Wiley.

Pelham, W. E., Sturges, J., Hoza, J., Schmidt, C., Bijlsma, J. J., Milich, R., & Moorer, S. (1987). Sustained release and standard methylphenidate effects on cognitive and social behavior in children with attention deficit hyperactivity disorder. *Pediatrics, 80*, 491–501.

Professional Group for Attention and Related Disorders. (1990). Submission to the U.S. Department of Education. Notice of Inquiry on ADD.

Physician's Desk Reference (44th Ed.). (1990). Oradell, NJ: Barnhart.

Porrino, L. J., & Lucignani, G. (1987). Different patterns of local brain energy metabolism associated with high and low doses of methylphenidate: Relevance to its action in hyperactive children. *Biological Psychiatry, 22*, 126–138.

Porrino, L. J., Lucignani, G., Dow-Edwards, D., & Sokoloff, L. (1984). Correlation of dose-dependent effects of acute amphetamine administration on behavior and local cerebral metabolism in rats. *Brain Research, 307,* 311–320.

Rapoport, J. L., Buchsbaum, M., Zahn, T. P., Weingartner, H., Ludlow, C., & Mikkelson, E. J. (1978). Detroamphetamine: Cognitive and behavioral effects on normal prepubertal boys. *Science, 199,* 560–563.

Rapport, M. D., DuPaul, G. J., & Kelly, K. L. (1989). Attention deficit hyperactivity disorder and methylphenidate: The relationship between gross body weight and drug response in children. *Psychopharmacology Bulletin, 25,* 285–290.

Rapport, M. D., DuPaul, G. J., Stoner, G., & Jones, J. T. (1986). Comparing classroom and clinic measures of attention deficit disorder: Differential, idiosyncratic, and dose-response effects of methylphenidate. *Journal of Consulting and Clinical Psychology, 54,* 334–341.

Rapport, M. D., & Kelly, K. L. (1991). Psychostimulant effects on learning and cognitive function: Findings and implications for children with attention deficit hyperactivity disorder. *Clinical Psychology Review, 11,* 61–92.

Rapport, M. D., Stoner, G., DuPaul, G. J., Birmingham, B. K., & Tucker, S. (1985). Methylphenidate in hyperactive children: Differential effects of dose on academic, learning, and social behavior. *Journal of Abnormal Child Psychology, 13,* 227–244.

Safer, D. J., & Krager, J. M. (1988). A survey of medication treatment for hyperactive/inattentive students. *Journal of the American Medical Association, 260,* 2256–2258.

Schrag, P., & Divoky, D. (1975). *The myth of the hyperactive child and other means of child control.* New York: Pantheon.

Shaywitz, S. E., Hunt, R. D., Jatlow, P., Cohen, D. J., Young, J. G., Pierce, R. N., Anderson, G. M., & Shaywitz, B. A. (1982). Psychopharmacology of attention deficit disorder: Pharmacokinetic, neuroendocrine, and behavioral measures following acute and chronic treatment with methylphenidate. *Pediatrics, 69,* 688–694.

Shaywitz, S. E., & Shaywitz, B. A. (1988). Attention deficit disorder: Current perspectives. In J. F. Kavanaugh & T. J. Truss (Eds.), *Learning Disabilities: Proceedings of the national conference* (pp. 369–523). New York: Maple Press.

Shaywitz, B. A., Yager, R. D., & Klopper, J. H. (1976). Selective brain dopamine depletion in developing rats: An experimental model of minimal brain dysfunction. *Science, 191,* 305–308.

Sleator, E. K., & von Neuman, A. W. (1974). Methylphenidate in the treatment of hyperkinetic children: Recommendations on diagnosis, dosage, and monitoring. *Clinical Pediatrics, 13,* 19–24.

Smith, S. E., & Wesson, D. R. (Eds.). (1973). *Uppers and downers.* Englewood Cliffs, NJ: Prentice-Hall.

Snyder, S. H., & Meyerhoff, J. L. (1973). How amphetamine acts in minimal brain dysfunction. *Annals of the New York Academy of Sciences, 205,* 310–320.

Solanto, M. V. (1986). Behavioral effects of low-dose methylphenidate in childhood attention deficit disorder: Implications for a mechanism of stimulant drug action. *Journal of the American Academy of Child Psychiatry, 25,* 96–101.

Sprague, R. L., & Sleator, E. K. (1977). Methylphenidate in hyperkinetic children: Difference in dose effects on learning and social behavior. *Science, 198,* 1274–1276.

Srinivas, N. R., Hubbard, J. W., Quinn, D., & Midah, K. K. (1992). Enantioselective pharmokinetics and pharmacodynamics of dl-threo-methylphenidate in children with attention deficit hyperactivity disorder. *Clinical Pharmacological Therapy, 52,* 561–568.

Srinivas, N. R., Quinn, D., Hubbard, J. W., & Midha, K. K. (1987). Stereoselective disposition of methylphenidate in children with Attention Deficit Hyperactivity Disorder. *Journal of Pharmacology and Experimental Therapy, 241,* 300–306.

Sroufe, L. A., & Stewart, M. A. (1973). Treating problem children with stimulant drugs. *New England Journal of Medicine, 289,* 407–413.

Swanson, J. M. (1985). Measures of cognitive functioning appropriate for use in pediatric psychopharmacological research studies. *Psychopharmacological Bulletin, 21,* 887–890.

Swanson, J. M. (1988). What do psychopharmacological studies tell us about information processing deficits in ADDH? In L. M. Bloomingdale & J. Sergeant (Eds.), *Attention deficit disorder: Criteria, cognition, intervention* (pp. 97–116). New York: Pergamon Press.

Swanson, J. M. (1989). Paired-associate learning in the assessment of ADDH children. In L. M. Bloomingdale & J. M. Swanson (Eds.), *Attention Deficit Disorder: Volume IV: Emerging trends in attentional and behavioral disorders of childhood* (pp. 87–124). New York: Pergamon Press.

Swanson, J. M. (1992). *School-based assessments and interventions for ADD students.* Irvine, CA: K.C. Publishing.

Swanson, J. M., & Cantwell, D. (1989). *Dose-related effects of methylphenidate on stimulus encoding and memory comparison times in ADHD children.* Paper presented at The Meeting of the American Academy of Child and Adolescent Psychiatry, New York.

Swanson, J. M., Cantwell, D., Lerner, M., McBurnett, K., & Hanna, G. (1991). Effects of stimulant medication on learning in children with ADHD. *Journal of Learning Disabilities, 24,* 219–320.

Swanson, J. M., & Kinsbourne, M. (1976). Stimulant-related state-dependent learning in hyperactive children. *Science, 192,* 1354–1356.

Swanson, J. M., & Kinsbourne, M. (1979). The cognitive effects of stimulant drugs on hyperactive (inattentive) children. In G. Hale & M. Lewis (Eds.), *Attention and the development of cognitive skills* (pp. 249–274). New York: Plenum Press.

Swanson, J. M., Kinsbourne, M., Roberts, W., & Zucker, K. (1978). A time-response analysis of the effect of stimulant medication on the learning ability of children referred for hyperactivity. *Pediatrics, 61,* 21–29.

Swanson, J. M., Kurland, L., Weinberg, F., & Kinsbourne, M. (1978). Comparing the behavioral effectiveness of two drugs which have different half lives. *Pediatric Research, 12,* 376.

Swanson, J. M., McBurnett, K., Wigal, T., Pfiffner, L. J., Lerner, M. A., Williams, L., Christian, D. L., Tamm, L., Willcut, E., Crowley, K., Clevenger, W., Khouzam, N., Woo, C., Crinella, F. M., Fisher, T. D. (1993). Effect of stimulant medication on children with Attention Deficit Disorder: A "review of reviews." *Exceptional Children, 60,* 154–162.

Swanson, J. M., Sandman, C. A., Deutsch, C., & Baren, M. (1983). Methylphenidate hydrochloride given with or before breakfast: I. Behavioral, cognitive and electrophysiologic effects. *Pediatrics, 72,* 49–55.

Swanson, J. M., Shea, C., McBurnett, K., Potkin, S. G., Fiore, T., & Crinella, F. M. (1990). Attention and hyperactivity. In J. Enns (Ed.), *The development of attention: Research and theory.* New York: Elsevier.

Tannock, R., Schachar, R. J., Carr, R. P., Chajczyk, D., & Logan, G. D. (1989). Effects of methylphenidate on inhibitory control in hyperactive children. *Journal of Abnormal Child Psychology, 17,* 473–491.

Tannock, R., Schachar, R. J., Carr, R. P., & Logan, G. D. (1989). Dose-response effects of methylphenidate on academic performance and overt behavior in hyperactive children. *Pediatrics, 84,* 648–657.

Taylor, E. A. (1983). Drug response and diagnostic validation. In M. Rutter (Ed.), *Developmental neuropsychiatry* (pp. 348–368). New York; Guilford.

Thurber, S., & Walker, C. A. (1983). Medication and hyperactivity: A meta-analysis. *The Journal of General Psychology, 108,* 79–86.

Ullmann, R. K., & Sleator, E. K. (1986). Responders, nonresponders, and placebo responders among children with attention deficit disorder. Importance of a blinded placebo evaluation. *Clinical Pediatrics, 25,* 594–599.

Weiss, B., & Laties, V. G. (1963). Enhancement of human performance by caffeine and the amphetamines. *Psychological Review, 14,* 1–36.

Wender, P. H. (1971). *Minimal brain dysfunction in children.* New York: Wiley-Interscience.

Wender, P. H. (1973). Some speculations concerning a possible biochemical basis of minimal brain dysfunction. In F. F. De La Cruz, B. H. Fox, R. H. Roberts, & G. Tarjan (Eds.), *Minimal brain dysfunction in children* (pp. 18–28). New York: Wiley-Interscience.

Werry, J. S., Aman, M. G., & Diamond, E. (1980). Imipramine and methylphenidate in hyperactive children. *Journal of Child Psychology and Psychiatry, 21,* 27–35.

Whalen, C. K., & Henker, B. (1976). Psychostimulants and children: A review and analysis of drug effectiveness. *Psychological Bulletin, 83,* 1113–1130.

Whalen, C. K., & Henker, B. (1991). Therapies for hyperactive children: Comparisons, combinations, and compromises. *Journal of Consulting and Clinical Psychology, 59,* 126–137.

Zametkin, A. J., & Rapoport, J. L. (1987). Noradrenergic hypothesis of attention deficit disorder with hyperactivity: A critical review. In H. Y. Meltzer (Ed.), *Psychopharmacology: The third generation of progress* (pp. 837–842). New York: Raven.

8

Toward Construct Validity in the Childhood Disruptive Behavior Disorders

Classification and Diagnosis in DSM-IV and Beyond

Irwin D. Waldman, Scott O. Lilienfeld, and Benjamin B. Lahey

1. Introduction

The number and coverage of child psychopathological disorders have expanded greatly since their rather cursory representation as adjustment reactions in the first edition of the *Diagnostic and Statistical Manual of Mental Disorders* (DSM) (American Psychiatric Association, 1952). The division of childhood disorders into the multitude of diagnoses that appear in the DSM-III-R (American Psychiatric Association, 1987) and the forthcoming DSM-IV (American Psychiatric Association, 1993) justifiably raises questions regarding the validity of these diagnostic distinctions. In the case of the disruptive (i.e., externalizing) disorders—which include the Attention Deficit Disorders (most notably, Attention-Deficit Hyperactivity Disorder, or ADHD), Oppositional Defiant Disorder (ODD), and Conduct Disorder (CD)—research generally has supported the differentiation of these dis-

IRWIN D. WALDMAN • Department of Psychology, Emory University, Atlanta, Georgia 30322. SCOTT O. LILIENFELD • Department of Psychology, State University of New York at Albany, Albany, New York 12203. BENJAMIN B. LAHEY • Department of Psychiatry, University of Chicago Medical School, Chicago, Illinois 60628.

Advances in Clinical Child Psychology, Volume 17, edited by Thomas H. Ollendick and Ronald J. Prinz. Plenum Press, New York, 1995.

orders from internalizing disorders, such as anxiety and depressive disorders (Achenbach & Edelbrock, 1978) and, to a lesser extent, the finer distinction among dimensions of inattention, hyperactivity, and impulsivity on the one hand and aggression, oppositional behaviors, and more serious conduct problems on the other (Hinshaw, 1987; Loney & Milich, 1982). It should be noted, however, that both sets of distinctions have been challenged, and that despite a flurry of research activity concerning these disorders, many questions remain regarding their validity.

In this chapter, we intend to cover a number of topics regarding the construct validity of the childhood disruptive behavior disorders. First, we will elaborate a construct-validational approach to science in general and to childhood psychopathology in particular. Specifically, we will draw parallels between scientific hypothesis generation and testing on the one hand and the validation of psychopathological constructs on the other, emphasizing in particular the distinct contributions of internal and external validational approaches for understanding diagnostic entities. Second, we will describe the rationale and design of the DSM-IV disruptive-behavior-disorders field trials and will attempt to cast these field trials within a construct-validational framework. In addition to discussing the structure of the field trials in general, we will focus specifically on two diagnostic issues that we feel illustrate well the application of a construct-validational framework to the classification and diagnosis of childhood disorders. Specifically, we will describe the examination of the validity of Attention Deficit Disorder without Hyperactivity and the distinction between childhood- and adolescent-onset subtypes of Conduct Disorder.

Third, we will discuss several fundamental issues concerning the construct validity of the childhood disruptive behavior disorders that remain unresolved despite the proliferation of research on these disorders. We will present statistical methods useful for addressing these issues which heretofore have been underutilized in the child psychopathology literature. Fourth and finally, we will conclude with suggestions for further framing research on the classification and diagnosis of the childhood disruptive behavior disorders within a construct-validational framework, especially under the formal mechanism of future DSM revisions and field trials. In particular, we will discuss potential modifications to field trials and other large-scale studies that may aid in the further enhancement of the construct validity of the childhood disruptive behavior disorders.

2. A Construct Validational Approach to Psychopathology

In our view, Cronbach and Meehl's (1955) principle of *construct validity* provides an indispensable unifying framework for approaching most of the important questions concerning the development and revision of psychiatric classification systems. As we will argue shortly, virtually all questions concerning the validity of psychiatric classification systems reduce ultimately to questions of construct validity. With some notable exceptions (e.g., Blashfield & Livesly, 1991; Cloninger, 1989; Garber & Strassberg, 1991; Morey, 1991), however, the application of construct validation to psychiatric classification has rarely been discussed explicitly. Moreover, it has been our experience that construct validity, although frequently cited and mentioned in the psychological literature (Sternberg, 1992), is frequently misunderstood and misinterpreted. Many researchers appear to view construct validation as a nebulous or mysterious enterprise that involves highly vague or subjective inferences (e.g., Bechtoldt, 1959). In contrast, a central theme of this chapter is that construct validation is not fundamentally different from the testing of scientific theories (Cronbach & Meehl, 1955). We will delineate a set of procedures for the construct validation of psychopathological syndromes, and discuss the application of these procedures to the DSM-IV field trials for disruptive disorders.

2.1. Definition and Fundamental Principles

Although a number of definitions of construct validity have been proposed, most of these definitions differ more in emphasis than in substance. Cronbach and Meehl (1955) essentially defined *construct validity* as the extent to which a test assesses a *construct*, or hypothesized attribute that cannot be observed directly. Thus, construct validation is to be used whenever no single criterion fully captures the entity being measured. In somewhat different language, construct validation is appropriate for psychological entities that cannot be *operationally defined* (Bridgman, 1927), that is, defined strictly and exhaustively in terms of the procedures used to measure them. The dictum, often attributed to Boring (1923), that "intelligence is whatever IQ tests measure" is a paradigmatic example of an operational definition. As we will discuss shortly, this dictum underscores the shortcoming of operational definitions for most entities in psychology and psychiatry: by defining an entity solely in terms of the operations used to assess it, one may prematurely reach closure on a concept that is not fully understood.

It is important to underscore the difference between *operational definitions* and the *operationalization* of variables, because these terms are often mistaken for one another in psychological and psychiatric research. Operationalization refers to the need, acknowledged by even the staunchest advocates of construct validation, to carefully specify and choose measures of the latent constructs in one's theory and research. Indeed, as will be discussed shortly, it is only by the inclusion of explicit measures which possess established psychometric properties that one may test adequately the construct validity of a measure or a diagnostic entity. Although the measures of latent constructs should be explicit and reliable, in construct validation it is also acknowledged that such measures will only be *fallible indicators* of the latent constructs.

In contrast to operationally defined entities, psychological constructs are *implicitly* or *constituitively defined* (Cook & Campbell, 1979) in terms of their relations with other constructs. Extraversion, honesty, musical ability, and attention-deficit hyperactivity disorder (ADHD) are all constructs, because they are latent entities that are inferred rather than observed. Moreover, they are defined implicitly rather than explicitly by means of their links to other constructs: extraversion, for example, can be defined in terms of sociability, impulsivity, low autonomic arousal, and other latent entities. It should be noted that constructs differ from *intervening variables* in that the latter (e.g., electrical resistance, Hull's concept of habit strength) are reducible to the empirical laws specifying them (MacCorquodale & Meehl, 1948). In contrast, constructs possess surplus meaning beyond the descriptive features upon which they are based (Morey, 1991). This surplus meaning permits investigators to generate falsifiable predictions regarding the relation of the construct to other constructs. In addition, the relations between these latent constructs and their proposed manifest indicators also represent testable hypothesis. As we will see shortly, it is these falsifiable predictions that form the basis of construct validation.

2.2. Psychopathological Constructs as "Open Concepts"

Most constructs in psychology and psychiatry, including virtually all psychopathological syndromes, are best conceptualized as "open concepts" (Meehl, 1977; 1986). Such concepts are characterized by (a) an indicator list that is indefinitely extendable, (b) indicators that are imperfectly correlated with the underlying construct of interest, and (c) an unclear or unknown "inner nature" (Meehl, 1977; Meehl & Golden, 1982). By applying an operational definition to an open concept, one prematurely "closes" the concept and thereby risks oversimplification. Although methodological rigor and precision are desirable goals in the development of any scientific classification system, such rigor and precision may be purchased at a considerable price. Indeed, DSM-III (American Psychiatric Association, 1980) and DSM-III-R (American Psychiatric Association, 1987) often have been accused of prematurely reifying diagnostic entities and of sacrificing validity for reliability (e.g., Faust & Miner, 1986; Vaillant, 1984; Wakefield, 1992). We shall return to these criticisms in our discussion of the design of the DSM-IV field trials for childhood disruptive disorders.

An alternative though compatible definition of construct validity that we find especially useful is the correlation of a test with its intended construct (Jensen, 1980). This definition underscores the epistemic dilemma facing the investigator who intends to construct validate a test. The investigator *wants* to know the correlation of a test with the construct of interest because this correlation provides an index of how adequately the test measures this construct, but of course the investigator cannot know the true value of this correlation because the construct is by definition unobservable. Indeed, if the investigator could determine this value, the entity in question would no longer be a construct, and forms of validity other than construct validity, such as criterion validity (Anastasi, 1990), would become applicable. Consequently, the investigator must bring a variety of forms of *indirect* evidence to bear upon the validity of the measure. The progressive accumulation of such indirect evidence is the essence of construct validation.

Loevinger (1957) pointed out that construct validity is an overarching principle that subsumes all other forms of validity, including content, convergent, discriminant, and predictive validity (also see Anastasi, 1990, and Messick, 1988). Thus, any and all data consistent with the assertion that a measure assesses the relevant construct provides evidence for its construct validity. Conversely, any and all data inconsistent with the assertion that a measure assesses a relevant construct provides evidence against its construct validity. These points often have been misunderstood by investigators, many of whom partition the evidence for a test's validity into ostensibly mutually exclusive sources such as content validity, criterion validity, and construct validity. As Loevinger (1957) noted, however, "construct validity is the whole of validity from a scientific point of view" (p. 636).

A key element in construct validation is the often misunderstood principle of *bootstrapping* (Cronbach & Meehl, 1955). Not infrequently in the psychological and psychiatric literature, one encounters statements such as "There is no way that a test can be more valid than an interview if an interview is the validating criterion" (Goldstein & Hersen, 1984, p. 5). Nevertheless, such assertions neglect the fact that researchers can "bootstrap" from more to less fallible measures. Noguchi and Moore's isolation of the syphilis spirochete as the cause of general paresis is perhaps the best-known example of bootstrapping (Meehl & Golden, 1982). The initial diagnosis of general paresis was based upon physicians' fallible judgments concerning each patient's history and presenting symptomatology. Following the discovery of the syphilis spirochete, which relied upon these judgments for provisional diagnoses of general paresis, the diagnosis of general paresis became nearly infallible. Similarly, Binet and Simon empirically selected intelligence test items based upon highly fallible teacher ratings of "intelligent" versus "unintelligent" children. Eventually, the test composed of these items came to possess higher validity than the judgments upon which they were derived. Thus, bootstrapping enables researchers to utilize construct validation as a vehicle for progressively improving the validity of their measures.

2.3. Parallels between Construct Validation and Theory Testing

Construct validation is a deductive enterprise, and can be thought of as similar to the process of testing scientific theories (Cronbach & Meehl, 1955). Like theory testing in science, construct validation is an iterative, ongoing process that has no clearly defined endpoint. As philosophers of science (e.g., Carnap, 1936; Meehl, 1978; Popper, 1959) have pointed out, there is an inherent asymmetry between theory refutation and theory confirmation. Scientific theories can be falsified, but they cannot be proven. The reasons for this asymmetry are twofold: (1) a potentially infinite number of theories can account for a given set of observations and (2) a theory that has generated successful predictions may be falsified in the future. Consequently, a theory generating successful predictions is said to be *corroborated* but not proven.

How then do scientific theories achieve widespread acceptance? As Popper (1959) argued, theories become strongly corroborated by passing stringent hurdles or, in his terms, by making successful "risky" predictions (i.e., predictions that have a low *a priori* probability of being correct absent the theory). Popper's view of theory testing can be thought of as selectionist (Richards, 1981): "fit" theories have repeatedly survived strong (i.e., risky) tests, whereas "unfit" theories have been progressively slain by falsifying data. In the advanced sciences, one or perhaps only a small handful of theories remain to account for a given set of observations (see Meehl, 1978, for a discussion of why this situation differs in psychology and other "soft" sciences).

Construct validation shares a number of important features with scientific theory testing. Just as scientific theories can never be proven, measures of psychological constructs can never be fully "validated," because (a) alternative explanations may account for the observed findings (i.e., the test may measure a different construct than intended) and (b) data that disconfirm the test as a measure of the construct may come to light in the future. Thus, statements such as "Test X has been validated," which are common in the psychological assessment literature, are somewhat misleading because they imply that the construct validation process has reached a clear termination point. Nevertheless, just as some scientific theories (e.g., natural selection and the "Big Bang" theory) are sufficiently corroborated to be considered "true" for working purposes, some psychological measures are sufficiently validated to serve as "quasi-criteria" for the validation of other instruments. (Researchers should, however, avoid the practice of referring to such measures as "gold standards," because this practice neglects the ongoing and provisional nature of construct validation.) Like well-corroborated scientific theories, such measures have attained their privileged status by surviving repeated attempts at disconfirmation.

2.4. Components of Construct Validation

Researchers wishing to validate a measure must first "lay their cards on the table." In more technical terms, they must explicitly delineate a "nomological network" (Cronbach & Meehl, 1955), or interlocking system of laws, in which the construct is embedded. Laying out a nomological network requires investigators to make *a priori* predictions concerning the relation of the construct to other constructs and to observable variables (i.e., manifest indicators). Specifically, there are three types of interconnections in a nomological network: Type I Relations—connections between the construct and other constructs; Type 2 Relations—connections between the construct and manifest indicators; and Type 3 Relations—connections among manifest indicators (Garber & Strassberg, 1991). By incorporating manifest indicators into the nomological network, the investigator generates a set of falsifiable predictions derived from the theory in which the construct is embedded. This point should not be overlooked. A number of individuals have criticized the principle of construct validity on the grounds that it allows researchers to draw unverifiable or unsubstantiated inferences (e.g., Bechtoldt, 1959). Nevertheless, Cronbach and Meehl (1955) were careful to note that "The network defining the construct, and the derivation leading to the predicted observation, must be reasonably explicit so that validating evidence may be properly interpreted" (p. 30). Thus, construct validation, like scientific theory testing, must involve the explicit postulation of falsifiable predictions concerning observable variables.

How should the investigator proceed if the data do not support the construct validity of a measure? As Cronbach and Meehl (1955) pointed out, there are three (nonmutually exclusive) possible reasons for negative data regarding a test's construct validity: (1) the measure does not adequately assess the construct (i.e., the measure has poor construct validity); (2) the investigator's nomological network is in error (i.e., the investigator's theory of the construct is mistaken); and (3) the design of the study did not permit an adequate test of the measure's construct validity (i.e., the investigator's auxiliary hypotheses concerning the other manifest indicators, experimental manipulations, or both are in error) (also see Garber & Strassberg, 1991). In response to negative data, the investigator must make an educated judgment regarding which of these three possibilities is most likely, and then decide how to proceed accordingly. This judgment will in part be based upon the extent to which the investigator's nomological network (i.e., theory) has "money in the bank," i.e., a strong track record of previously confirmed risky predictions (Meehl, 1990). If investigators have compelling reasons to believe that their nomological network is correct, they should entertain the possibility that the fault lies either with the construct validity of the measure, the adequacy of the research design, or both.

Loevinger (1957) delineated three successive stages in the construct validational process. The first stage of her scheme, *substantive validity*, refers to the extent to which the items on a measure accurately reflect the psychological attribute of interest. According to Loevinger, construct validation thus begins with the initial selection of the item pool. Substantive validity overlaps with, but differs from content validity, in that it permits items to be both included and excluded on the basis of empirical, as well as rational/theoretical considerations.

The second stage, *structural* validity, refers to the extent to which the internal structure of a measure parallels the internal structure of the intended construct. For example, if one's theory predicts that the construct of extraversion consists of two intercorrelated dimensions, factor analysis of an extraversion measure should reveal two oblique factors. Also relevant to structural validity are indices of internal consistency. This relation is not necessarily straightforward, however; high internal consistency only speaks to good structural validity if theoretical considerations dictate the construct to be homogeneous (Bollen & Lennox, 1991; Loevinger, 1957).

The third and final stage of construct validity, *external validity*, refers to the extent to which a test correlates with external variables, such as self-report measures, peer ratings, and laboratory and biological indices that would be expected to relate to the construct on theoretical grounds. External validity subsumes convergent, discriminant, and predictive validity, and has been the major form of validity emphasized in psychiatric classification, as discussed in Section 2.5.

2.5. Application of Construct Validity to Psychiatric Classification

How is construct validation relevant to the development and revision of psychiatric classification systems? Morey (1991) has argued compellingly that a psychiatric classification system can be viewed as a collection of constructs. According to Morey, the DSM-III and DSM-III-R criteria sets for each disorder can be conceptualized as intervening variables in that these criteria sets provide necessary and sufficient rules for assigning individuals to diagnostic categories. In contrast, the entities underlying these intervening variables can be conceptualized as constructs that contain surplus meaning regarding variables such as family history, biological and laboratory indices, natural history, and treatment response. These underlying constructs are fallibly, but not exhaustively, indexed by their respective diagnostic criteria (Morey, 1991). Pursuing Morey's logic, one can see that the validation of psychiatric diagnoses is similar in many ways to the construct validation of psychological measures (but see Blashfield & Livesly, 1991, for a discussion of the structural and analytic differences between psychiatric diagnoses and psychometric indices).

Skinner (1981, 1986) has outlined a construct-validation approach to psychiatric syndromes that is similar in many ways to Loevinger's (1957) three-stage scheme for the construct validation of psychological tests. The first stage of Skinner's approach, *theory formulation,* essentially involves an explicit delineation of the nomological network surrounding each diagnostic entity. This delineation permits the derivation of falsifiable hypothesis concerning the entity's internal structure and external correlates. The second stage, *internal validation,* involves the testing of hypotheses regarding the internal structure of a diagnostic entity. Such hypotheses concern issues that include:

1. The homogeneity or heterogeneity of this entity
2. Whether it is categorical or dimensional in nature
3. The number of categories or dimensions underlying its diagnostic indicators
4. The boundaries and relations among its underlying dimensions or categories.

Techniques such as internal consistency analyses, factor analysis, cluster analysis, taxometric analysis (Meehl & Golden, 1982) and latent class analysis (Goodman, 1974) are particularly informative in internal validation. The third and final stage, *external validation,* involves the examination of a diagnostic syndrome's covariation with important "external" correlates, such as family history, natural history, and treatment response. External validation subsumes descriptive validity, which is the extent to which a diagnostic syndrome exhibits convergent and discriminant validity with other syndromes (Campbell & Fiske, 1959), and predictive validity, which is the extent to which a diagnostic syndrome predicts future real-world outcomes. Skinner's approach to validation is ideally iterative, in that each of the three stages should successively inform and refine the other until a better understanding of the diagnostic entity is achieved.

In a seminal paper, Robins and Guze (1970) outlined a comprehensive approach for establishing the validity of psychiatric diagnoses that can be viewed as a special example of the external stage of construct validation. According to Robins and Guze, a valid diagnosis must accomplish five things:

1. Describe the clinical syndrome
2. Predict diagnosed individuals' performances on laboratory and psychometric measures
3. Predict diagnosed individuals' natural histories (i.e., course and outcome)
4. Predict diagnosed individuals' family histories of psychiatric syndromes
5. Differentiate the diagnosis from other psychiatric diagnoses.

In addition, although not discussed by Robins and Guze, a valid psychiatric diagnosis also ideally predicts diagnosed individuals' responses to treatment. Thus, each of these sources of information can be viewed as evidence for the construct validity of a psychiatric diagnosis.

A simplified nomological network for ADHD appears in Figure 1. It can be seen that the ADHD diagnosis is hypothesized to overlap with CD, to predict a positive response to stimulant medication, and to relate to poor response inhibition and peer rejection. In addition, this diagnosis is hypothesized to relate to a family history of attention deficit disorders, as well as an increased risk for future academic underachievement. Because each of these links in the nomological network has been borne out by data, the diagnosis of ADHD satisfies most or all of the Robins and Guze criteria for external validity and can thus be said to possess at least some degree of construct validity.

3. Construct Validity Considerations in the Design of the DSM-IV Disruptive Behavior Disorders Field Trials

As noted earlier, the DSM-III and DSM-III-R, as well as their associated field trials, have been criticized for an exclusive focus on reliability at the expense of validity and for adopting an atheoretical "blind empiricist," rather than a theoretically motivated research strategy (Faust & Miner, 1986; Kirk & Kutchins, 1992; Vaillant, 1984). It was thus especially important to design the DSM-IV Disruptive Behavior Disorders field trials to emphasize issues of validity while continuing to address issues of relia-

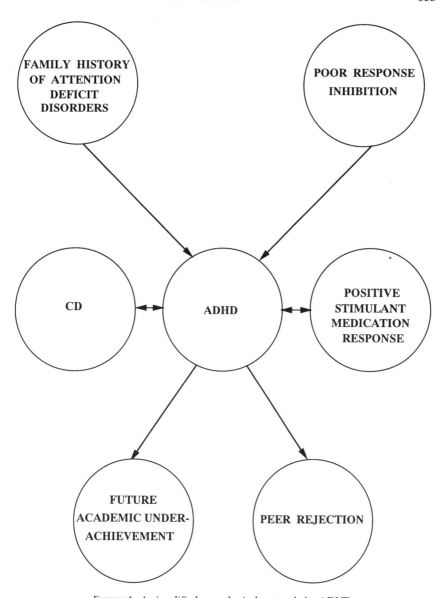

Figure 1. A simplified nomological network for ADHD

bility. In this section, we will describe some of the ways in which this increased emphasis on validity was implemented in the Disruptive Behavior Disorder field trials, as well as provide a brief description of the methods, analyses, and selected results (a more detailed description appears in Waldman & Lahey, 1994). In terms of the latter, we will focus on two classificatory issues—the validity of Attention Deficit Disorder without Hyperactivity (ADD w/o H) and the distinction between childhood- and adolescent-onset subtypes of Conduct Disorder—that highlight a construct validity approach to resolving issues in the classification of childhood psychopathology.

Although most of the construct validity considerations were reflected in *external validation* analyses and in the choice of relevant measures for these analyses, a number of *internal validation* analyses also were conducted. In particular, preliminary factor analyses (Applegate, Waldman, et al., 1994; Applegate, Lahey, et al., 1994) of the disruptive behavior disorder symptoms and signs were conducted prior to relating symptom scales and diagnoses to external criteria. Perhaps the most interesting finding to emerge from these factor analyses was the suggestion that the best fitting factor model for the ADHD symptoms consisted of an inattention factor and a combined hyperactivity–impulsivity factor. These two ADHD factors were treated as separate dimensions in the majority of analyses that followed.

An integral concept underlying the construct validity of psychopathological disorders is that of *impairment*. Despite the difficulties inherent in constructing a coherent and explicit definition of mental disorder (Gorenstein, 1992), the concept of impairment or "harm" appears in almost all of the varied conceptualizations of psychopathology (Wakefield, 1992). This concept of impairment was critical in the selection of both constructs and measures for the external validation of the disruptive disorders examined in the DSM-IV field trials. Further, most of the indices of impairment were selected on the basis of their conforming to theoretical notions regarding the types of impairment associated with each disruptive disorder. For example, the number of school suspensions and police contacts were chosen as impairment indices for Conduct Disorder, whereas unpopularity with classmates, parent ratings of difficulty in completing homework, and teacher ratings of academic performance were chosen as impairment indices for ADHD. In addition, a measure of global impairment, the Children's Global Adjustment Scale (C-GAS; Shaffer, Gould, Brasic, Ambrosini, Fisher, Bird, & Aluwhalla, 1983) was used for all disruptive behavior disorders, since it assesses functioning across a number of important domains.

Perhaps the strongest attempt at enhancing construct validity in the Disruptive Behavior Disorders field trials was in the overall analytic strategy adopted. This strategy was adopted in part to address a particular conundrum that arises often in classificatory research of this scope, which can be thought of as having more unknowns in the validational enterprise than pieces of information to resolve them. For example, we need to choose an optimal diagnostic threshold and an optimal list of symptoms for each disorder, but our ability to settle each issue depends on our already having settled the other! An important step in choosing the list of symptoms was assessing the utility of each symptom in predicting the diagnosis. One cannot do this without knowing the threshold number of symptoms for the diagnosis. One cannot choose the threshold, however, without already having chosen the constituent symptoms.

In the Disruptive Behavior Disorder field trials, this conundrum was resolved by employing an *iterative multiple bootstrapping strategy* for conducting analyses. In this analytic process, we bootstrapped toward enhanced construct validity for the disruptive disorders by making tentative decisions at each analytic step and conducting each of the major analyses multiple times, taking into account successive adjustments to the symptoms or other criteria suggested at each analytic pass. The analytic strategy used in these field trials thus is sequential and iterative, as preliminary decisions were made and implemented, but could be modified and revised at subsequent analytic stages. This analytic cycle in which symptoms were added or deleted, diagnostic thresholds were changed, and age of onset cutoffs were modified, was repeated for each disorder until no further changes appeared to enhance either reliability or validity.

3.1. A Construct Validity Approach to Two Issues in the Classification of the Disruptive Disorders

After its inclusion in DSM-III, ADD w/o H largely was omitted from DSM-III-R (cf. Undifferentiated Attention Deficit Disorder), just as research on its status as a unique diagnostic entity was beginning to accumulate. Studies of ADD w/o H have suggested differences from ADHD in a number of important respects, including overlap with other disorders and associated impairment (see review by Lahey & Carlson, 1991). This literature formed the basis for the decision to reexamine the diagnostic status of ADD w/o H vis-à-vis ADHD and the other disruptive behavior disorders in the DSM-IV field trials. Drawing on the results of this literature, a number of hypotheses were formulated. First, it was hypothesized that the age of onset for ADD w/o H would be a few years later, on average, than that of ADHD. Second, although ADD w/o H and ADHD are believed to share some of the same types of impairment—such as academic problems and peer relations difficulties—they were hypothesized to show quite different patterns of overlap with other disorders. Specifically, whereas ADHD was hypothesized to overlap primarily with ODD and CD, ADD w/o H was hypothesized to overlap primarily with anxiety disorders and depression. Third, it was hypothesized that the ratio of boys to girls would be lower in ADD w/o H than in ADHD. Preliminary results provided support for these hypotheses. Many of these analyses were conducted in parallel fashion to those above, except that impairment indices were plotted simultaneously against both the inattention and hyperactivity–impulsivity dimensions. In addition to affording a view of how the relations between the external variables and either of these symptom dimensions may differ depending on the level of symptoms on the other dimension, these plots aided in determining whether a different diagnostic threshold for the number of inattention symptoms was warranted for ADD w/o H and ADHD, which proved not to be the case.

The literature on CD has suggested a number of different methods of subtyping this disorder in the hopes of achieving greater homogeneity of outcome, treatment response, developmental trajectory, and etiology within subtypes. Recently, several authors (Loeber, 1990; Lahey, Loeber, Quay, Frick, & Grimm, 1992) have posited the existence of childhood- and adolescent-onset subtypes of CD that differ in meaningful ways. This literature has been sufficiently provocative to examine this issue in the field trials data. We hypothesized that these two subtypes of CD would differ in a number of important ways. First, and most obviously, we predicted that an age-of-onset distribution for CD would exhibit at least some evidence for bimodality. Second, the types of symptoms that characterize each of the subtypes were hypothesized to differ, with the adolescent-onset subtype thought to involve primarily serious *nonaggressive* symptoms, such as stealing, breaking and entering, and running away from home, whereas, the childhood-onset subtype would involve both these symptoms and serious *aggressive* symptoms. This prediction suggests that a nonlinear relation of aggressive symptoms with age of onset should be exhibited. Third, the ratio of boys to girls was hypothesized to differ by subtype, with a lower ratio occurring for the adolescent-onset than for the childhood-onset subtype. Fourth, the adolescent-onset subtype was hypothesized to show a lower degree of overlap with ODD and ADHD than the childhood-onset subtype. These analyses were carried out in a similar fashion to those described earlier, with the only addition being a split of CD by age of onset. Preliminary results furnished support for these hypotheses and thus for the existence of childhood- and adolescent-onset subtypes.

3.2. Methodology of the Disruptive Behavior Disorders Field Trials

3.2.1. Sample Characteristics and Diagnostic Information

The field trials sample included 440 clinic-referred children (336 boys and 104 girls) ranging in age from 4 to 17 years, with an average age of 9.5 years. The age distribution was actually somewhat bimodal, with greater representation in early childhood and adolescence than in middle childhood. The sample was ethnically diverse and was composed of 61% white, 20% African-American, 15.2% Hispanic, 1.6% Asian, and 2.1% other ethnic groups. A similar effort was made to enhance geographical diversity, as children were sampled from a broad range of clinics across the country. The sample consisted of 75 child psychiatry inpatients, 177 child psychiatry outpatients, 19 child psychology outpatients, 30 students referred for school psychology evaluations, 57 pediatric psychology outpatients, 26 inpatients of a forensic psychiatry unit for juvenile sex offenders, and 56 residents of a state juvenile detention facility, where they were undergoing routine psychological intake evaluations.

The primary measure used to establish the presence of symptoms and diagnoses for childhood disorders was the Diagnostic Interview for Children (DISC-2; Shaffer, Fisher, Piacentini, Schwab-Stone, & Wicks, 1992). A modified version of the DISC-2 was used in the field trials to cover a broader range of symptoms than those in the DSM-III-R and to assess information on the age of onset of the Attention Deficit Disorder symptoms in a slightly different fashion than in the original DISC. Both parent and child versions of the DISC (the DISC-P and DISC-C, respectively) were administered and a modification of the parent version was used to interview teachers (the DISC-T). The DISC-T was identical to the DISC-P except that it asked about CD symptoms occurring only during a 6-month period, did not inquire regarding age of onset, and did not assess some anxiety disorders symptoms that teachers would not have the opportunity to observe.

Drawing on the literature on the optimal informants for childhood psychiatric disorders (e.g., Loeber, Green, Lahey, & Stouthamer-Loeber, 1990), not all informants were interviewed for all children. Instead, the two informants were interviewed who were judged to be the best providers of information at a given age level. In most cases, the DISC-P and DISC-T were administered for children ages 4 to 8 and the DISC-P and DISC-C were administered for children ages 9 to 17. Nonetheless, parents were unavailable for the 56 children in juvenile detention and some informants declined to participate at all age levels.

3.2.2. Indices of Reliability and Validity

The intention in conducting the disruptive behavior disorders field trials was to provide a number of different indices for the examination of reliability and validity. A number of different procedures was used to enhance the examination of reliability in this study. First, for each of the disruptive behavior disorders more symptoms were proposed for testing than were eventually selected as diagnostic criteria in DSM-IV. This facilitated reliability in that different combinations and numbers of symptoms could be explored for their internal consistency (i.e., the extent to which symptoms of a disorder index a fairly homogenous diagnostic entity). Second, in order to estimate the test–retest reliability of alternative versions of the disruptive behavior disorder diagnoses, DISC's were readministered to 89 of the clinic-referred subjects approximately 2 weeks after the original assessment.

Third, clinician diagnoses were obtained and examined for their concordance with DISC-derived diagnoses. For this criterion, clinicians were asked either to administer the DISC's or to read them prior to assigning their diagnoses, but the clinicians' own opinions about the presence or absence of disorders in the children were sought, rather than their opinion as to whether children met formal diagnostic criteria for disorders. Although almost all of the clinicians were trained in the use of the DSM criteria, they were instructed to feel free to ignore these criteria in assigning diagnoses and to simply follow whatever criteria they felt were applicable. In addition, clinicians were free to interview the child, parent, and teacher and to use any other sources of information that they considered relevant.

Similarly, a number of impairment indices were used as validational criteria for the various disruptive behavior disorders. First, immediately following the DISC, global ratings of impairment were provided by both the parent and the interviewer using the C-GAS. Parents also rated their children on a checklist of problems in completing homework and provided information on both the number of school suspensions and police contacts. Teachers rated both the accuracy and quantity of children's academic work completed in the classroom and estimated the proportion of classmates that like and dislike the youth. Although not used explicitly as validational criteria, individually administered intelligence tests (usually the WISC-R) and achievement tests (usually the WRAT-R) were available for most of the sample. In addition, information was obtained on demographic variables and psychiatric service utilization.

3.2.3. Major Analyses Conducted for Each Disruptive Disorder

At each iterative step, a number of analyses were conducted in order to address the reliability and validity of each disruptive disorder. First, preliminary symptom lists were compiled and tentative age-of-onset cutoffs were set for each disorder based on the DSM-IV Options Book suggestions, as well as on reanalyses of large datasets from both clinic-referred and nonreferred samples. Attempts were made to be especially inclusive at this stage but to use DSM-III and DSM-III-R criteria as initial guides.

Second, impairment criteria for each disorder were selected based on their correspondence to previous conceptualizations of the disorders and their sequelae. These criteria were then analyzed for their utility as *specific* indices of impairment for each disorder. This process was accomplished through a series of multiple regression analyses in which each impairment measure was regressed simultaneously on the symptom scales for each disorder (viz., inattention, hyperactivity–impulsivity, ODD, CD, anxiety, and depression) in order to determine whether an impairment index was specifically associated with a particular disorder after controlling for its relation to the symptoms of other disorders. This ensured that the hypothesized indices of impairment were in fact associated predominantly with specific disorders, rather than with the symptoms of most disorders, which might indicate only general dysfunction or distress.

Third, provisional diagnostic thresholds were set by examining the relations of the symptoms of each disorder with relevant impairment indices, clinicians' diagnoses, and test–retest reliability. Through such analyses, an effort was made to determine the diagnostic threshold that most validly and reliably identifies cases that are impaired and viewed by clinicians as manifesting a clinically significant disorder. In these analyses, impairment indices were plotted against the number of symptoms for each disorder and the plots were examined for evidence of nonlinear relations. Nonlinear relations were thought to be most informative, as they might suggest a discrete point (*viz.*, a "natural" diagnostic threshold) above which individuals demonstrated maladjustment in important domains, although linear relations also were helpful in suggesting diagnostic cutoffs. Families of Kappa Statistics (Cohen, 1960) were generated to determine diagnostic thresholds that maximized the relation between clinician diagnoses and provisional DSM-IV symptom lists. In addition, kappas between original and retest diagnoses were compared for varying diagnostic thresholds to examine 2-week test–retest reliability in a sample of 89 children for whom diagnostic data were collected at both time points.

Fourth, symptom utility analyses were conducted (Frick et al., 1994) to identify optimal diagnostic criteria for each of the disruptive disorders.

In these analyses, symptoms were eliminated if they were associated weakly with their particular disorder, whereas symptoms not previously considered strongly for inclusion could be added if they were associated strongly with their particular disorder. Previous studies (Milich, Widiger, & Landau, 1987; Waldman & Lilienfeld, 1991) have shown that diagnostic efficiency indices such as Positive Predictive Power (PPP), Negative Predictive Power (NPP), sensitivity, and specificity can be helpful in selecting optimal criteria for diagnosing the disruptive disorders. In the field trials, all of these indices were used to judge the optimality of diagnostic criteria, though special emphasis was placed on PPP (corrected for base rates and maximum possible value) as the primary diagnostic efficiency index.

These four general analytic steps were repeated incorporating any changes in symptom composition, diagnostic threshold, and age-of-onset cutoff suggested by the previous round of analyses until further iterations failed to substantially enhance reliability or validity. A number of subsequent analyses were conducted following these iterative analytic cycles. These consisted primarily of comparisons of the DSM-IV instantiations of the disruptive behavior disorders to their DSM-III, DSM-III-R, and *International Classification of Diseases, 10th Edition* (viz, ICD-10, World Health Organization, 1990) counterparts. Comparisons with DSM-III and DSM-III-R were performed in order to see whether the DSM-IV versions of these disorders outperformed the prior versions, in line with the conservative philosophy guiding the approach to changing disorders from the DSM-III-R (Frances, Widiger, & Pincus, 1989). Comparisons with ICD-10 criteria were performed primarily in an effort to foster comparability across these diagnostic schemes.

3.3. Selected Results of Disruptive Behavior Disorder Field Trials Analyses

The findings from the field trials analyses will be published in a series of manuscripts over the next several years. As detailed presentations of the research findings will appear in these papers, we provide only a brief summary of some of the more interesting findings that have emerged thus far. Two papers (Lahey, Applegate, McBurnett, et al., in press; Lahey, Applegate, Barkley, et al., 1994) summarizing the results of the iterative analytic steps described previously for ADHD and ADD w/o H and for ODD and CD have already been completed and accepted for publication. The authors describe the establishment of optimal diagnostic thresholds for the symptom dimensions underlying these disorders based on the identification of impaired cases and on their agreement with clinicians' diagnoses. An additional paper on the diagnostic utility of disruptive behavior disorders symptoms (Frick et al., in press) has also been accepted for publication.

With regard to ADHD, several interesting findings emerged. First, as previously noted, factor analyses of an enriched set of attention-deficit/hyperactivity disorder symptoms (Applegate, Waldman, et al., 1994) supported the existence of two distinct symptom dimensions—inattention and hyperactivity–impulsivity—underlying these symptoms. This is in contrast to the DSM-III-R unidimensional framework and to the DSM-III tridimensional framework for ADHD. Second, following in part from these analyses, evidence for three subtypes of ADHD appeared to emerge from the field trials analyses. These included Predominantly Inattentive, Predominantly Hyperactive–Impulsive, and Combined Types. Third, the Predominantly Hyperactive–Impulsive subtype appeared to be especially useful for identifying preschool children who were impaired but below the threshold for inattention symptoms and thus might not receive a diagnosis in previous diagnostic symptoms. Further presentation of the construct validity of the DSM-IV attention-deficit disorder subtypes will appear in Waldman et al. (1994). Fourth, there was insufficient evidence to support either a clear choice of age of onset or the importance of situational pervasiveness for attention-deficit/hyperactivity disorder. Analyses examining age of onset and situational pervasiveness will be presented in Applegate, Lahey, et al. (1994).

A number of interesting findings also emerged for ODD and CD. First, the optimal time window for the occurrence of CD symptoms was refined with corresponding increases in reliability and validity. This disorder was found to be most reliably and validly diagnosed when symptoms were counted as present if they occurred in a 12-month rather than a 6-month window. Second, as mentioned earlier, evidence for the validity of childhood-onset and adolescent-onset subtypes of CD was found. The childhood-onset subtype, as compared with the adolescent-onset subtype, was characterized by a greater number of aggressive symptoms, a greater ratio of boys to girls, and greater overlap with other disruptive behavior disorders.

Third, two different conceptualizations of CD that have been suggested in the developmental psychopathology literature were examined in the field trials. A number of researchers (e.g., Loeber, Keenan, Lahey, Green, & Thomas, 1993) have suggested developmentally based diagnoses of ODD and CD that incorporate the common developmental pathway from ODD to CD and different levels of symptom severity. Mixed evidence for this developmentally based conceptualization of ODD and CD diagnoses was obtained in the field trials analyses. In addition, field trials analyses provided support for the ICD approach of counting CD symptoms toward the diagnosis of ODD in the absence of a CD diagnosis. Despite the results of these analyses, it was decided not to include this change to ODD and CD in DSM-IV due to the complexities that would result for clinicians in assigning these diagnoses. Despite their exclusion from DSM-IV, the importance of carefully considering both of these changes for the next revision of the DSM was highlighted.

4. Unresolved Issues in the Construct Validity of the Disruptive Behavior Disorders

4.1. The Importance of Internal Validation and the Role of Latent Variable Models

In this section, we present six unresolved issues regarding the construct validity of the childhood disruptive behavior disorders. One may wonder whether construct validation is not already the approach that is followed in much of child psychopathology research, as the majority of extant studies are concerned with establishing differences among diagnostic groups in treatment response, course and outcome, familial psychopathology, and putative etiological factors. Nonetheless, we contend that the construct validity approach we are outlining differs in a number of crucial respects from that followed in most child psychopathology research.

First, most studies in the child psychopathology literature have concentrated on the *external validity* of the childhood disorders (Skinner, 1981, 1986), in that they have investigated differences in treatment response, course and outcome, family history, and putative etiological factors among groups that are implicitly *presumed* to already possess a high degree of *internal validity*. It seems potentially premature to examine differences in such characteristics among groups that themselves have not been demonstrated to have some degree of internal validity. For example, suppose that in a comparison of ODD and CD that a researcher finds that children with CD have a worse prognosis, greater family history of antisocial personality disorder, and less treatment success than those with ODD. Should he or she then conclude that ODD and CD are distinct psychopathological entities? Although this conclusion would be tempting, these findings would not distinguish it from the competing hypothesis that ODD simply is a less severe form of CD. This is where internal validation studies are necessary in combination with external validation studies, ideally conducted in an iterative fashion as described by Skinner (1981, 1986).

Second, one also may wonder whether internal validation studies have not already been conducted on the childhood disruptive behavior disorders. For example, a large number of factor analytic studies have been performed in an effort to discriminate problems with inattention, impulsivity, and hyperactivity on the one hand from aggression and conduct problems on the other (see Hinshaw, 1987, for a review). Although the bulk of these studies suggest that inattention/impulsivity and aggression/conduct problems represent separate though highly related problem domains, *exploratory* factor analysis has been the statistical method of choice in this literature.

Exploratory factor analysis has certain disadvantages for internal validation research. In particular, the results of these analyses are often arbitrary and *post hoc* in the sense that prespecified models cannot be explicitly tested, alternative models cannot be formally compared, and no statistical criterion exists for ascertaining the adequacy of the fit of a given model to the data or for concluding that one model fits better than another. In contrast, the analytic techniques that we will be discussing are *confirmatory* in nature. These methods share certain advantages over exploratory techniques, including the ability to test *a priori* hypothesized models, compare alternative hypothesized models, and provide a statistical basis for choosing among alternative models and for assessing the goodness-of-fit of a model to the observed data. All of the techniques that we will be discussing use data from observed measures (e.g., symptom ratings) to make inferences regarding latent constructs that are thought to correspond to underlying diagnostic entities. In addition to the fit of the overall model, these techniques yield information on the relation between the observed measures and the latent constructs. Given our focus on conceptual rather than statistical issues, we will not describe each specific latent variable method in detail, although we provide references for each that contain further information.

Hence, in our presentation of unresolved issues in the construct validity of childhood disruptive behavior disorders we will be relying in large part on latent variable models that are confirmatory in nature. Although the advantages of applying such models have been discussed with reference to adult psychopathology (e.g., Grove & Andreasen, 1986, 1987) there has been little discussion of such models in the child psychopathology literature (cf. Fergusson & Horwood, 1989; Fergusson, Horwood, & Lloyd, 1991). We will begin by emphasizing the utility of latent variable models in examining internal validation issues and then illustrate their utility in addressing issues on the border of internal and external validation. Wherever possible, we will emphasize the use of a number of different latent variable methods, given that constructive replication (Lykken, 1968) of results derived from different latent variable models should make for more trustworthy conclusions regarding the construct validity of disruptive syndromes (Meehl, 1979).

Although we will be describing a number of latent-variable modeling techniques that differ in many arcane ways, one can obtain a preliminary understanding of these methods by considering the differences among them along two dimensions; namely, (a) whether they assume the *latent variables* (i.e., diagnostic dimensions or classes) are categorical or continuous and (b) whether they assume the *manifest indicators* (i.e., symptoms and signs) are categorical or continuous. A classification of latent variable models (adapted from Young & Tanner, 1983) along these dimensions is presented in Figure 2. For example, confirmatory factor analysis and structural equation modeling (e.g., *LISREL*, Joreskog & Sorbom, 1989) assume that both the latent and the manifest variables are continuous, whereas latent trait models—or item response theory (*IRT*, Hambleton, Swaminathan, & Rogers, 1991)—assume that the latent variable is continuous and the manifest indicators are categorical. In contrast, latent class analysis (Clogg, 1977) assumes that both the latent and the manifest variables are

Latent variables

Manifest variables	Categorical	Continuous
Categorical	Latent class analysis	Latent trait models/IRT
Continuous	Taxometric analysis and mixture model analysis	Confirmatory factor analysis

FIGURE 2. Classification of latent variable models (Adapted from Young & Tanner, 1983)

categorical, whereas taxometric analysis (Meehl & Golden, 1982) and mixture model analysis (Titterington, Smith & Makov, 1985) assume that the latent variables are categorical and the manifest indicators are either categorical or continuous. Naturally, it would be desirable to review the available research applying latent variable methods to issues in the classification of the disruptive behavior disorders. Given the virtual absence of such research, however, we will focus on the ways in which such methods could be applied to classification issues in future studies.

4.2. Are Childhood Disruptive Syndromes Continuous or Categorical in Nature?

One of the more persistent issues in childhood psychopathology is whether disorders such as ADHD, ODD, and CD are categorical or dimensional in nature. In a categorical taxonomic scheme, individuals within a diagnostic class are thought to differ qualitatively, i.e., "in kind," from individuals outside of this diagnostic class. In contrast, in a dimensional taxonomic scheme, individuals are thought to differ quantitatively, i.e., "in degree," from other individuals on one or more dimensions. In addition, within a dimensional scheme, "disorder" is thought simply to represent the extreme of normal functioning with no natural break point, whereas within a categorical scheme, "disorder" is thought to represent a qualitatively different state from normality with a corresponding natural break point. The fact that there continues to be disagreement in the child psychopathology literature about the categorical versus dimensional nature of childhood disorders is testament to the lack of resolution concerning this fundamental issue. A similar lack of resolution characterizes the stance taken by DSM-III-R, which provides diagnostic criteria for the assignment of individuals to discrete diagnosis classes, but explicitly states (in the introduction) that no assumption is made regarding the categorical versus dimensional nature of psychiatric disorders (American Psychiatric Association, 1987).

Fortunately, a number of latent variable models have recently been applied to this problem that may help to shed light on whether childhood disruptive syndromes are categorical or dimensional in nature. Although no statistical methods—including latent variable models—are panaceas, some of these models allow researchers to explicitly test whether the latent diagnostic entity is categorical or continuous. For example, by fitting a series of latent class models with a successively greater number of latent classes and comparing the relative fit of these and the relations among the latent classes and symptoms, one can discern whether a set of symptoms has a latent categorical or continuous structure (e.g., Eaves et al., 1993). In addition, both taxometric analysis and mixture model analysis provide statistical and consistency tests for distinguishing a latent category from a latent dimension. Finally, IRT can be used to distinguish a latent category from a latent dimension. Methods for accomplishing this distinction were provided by Gibbons and Young (1989), who showed how the fit of a latent continuous trait can be statistically compared with that of a two-class latent class model by imposing certain restrictions on the latent and manifest variables in the IRT analyses.

4.3. How Many Distinct Disruptive Dimensions or Categories Are There? What Are the Relations and Boundaries among These Dimensions or Categories?

Once one establishes whether the latent structure of a diagnostic entity (e.g., ADHD) is categorical or dimensional, a logical next step is to examine *how many* latent categories or dimensions are necessary for characterizing the syndrome. In reality, this step likely would go hand in hand with the preceding issue, such that in practice the two issues may be decided jointly or iteratively. Many of the methods for distinguishing a categorical from a dimensional latent structure also can be used to ascertain how many latent categories or dimensions provide a good fit to the data. For example, mixture model analyses can discern the presence of *multiple* latent classes in a seemingly continuous distribution (i.e., a mixture distribution). Similarly, latent-class analysis can discern the presence of *multiple* latent classes in a multisymptom contingency table, given a sufficiently large sample size.

Suppose, on the other hand, that the above analyses suggest that the latent structure of ADHD is dimensional. How could one go about discerning the number of latent dimensions necessary for an adequate characterization of ADHD? The ideal approach would be to use confirmatory factor analysis to contrast a set of competing models, each of which specifies a different hypothesized dimensional structure for ADHD. For example, in Figure 3 we present two alternative models for the underlying structure of ADHD, one of which represents the hypothesis that a single general factor best captures the underlying structure of ADHD symptoms (somewhat akin to the approach followed in DSM-III-R), and the second of which represents the alternative hypothesis that two specific factors—inattention and hyperactivity/impulsivity—best capture the underlying structure of ADHD symptoms (akin to the approach followed in DSM-IV).

Note that the key word in describing these analyses is *hypothesized*. Confirmatory factor analysis and structural equation modeling were de-

MODEL 1: TWO SPECIFIC DIMENSIONS   **MODEL 2: ONE GENERAL DIMENSION**

PROPOSED DSM-IV ADHD CRITERIA

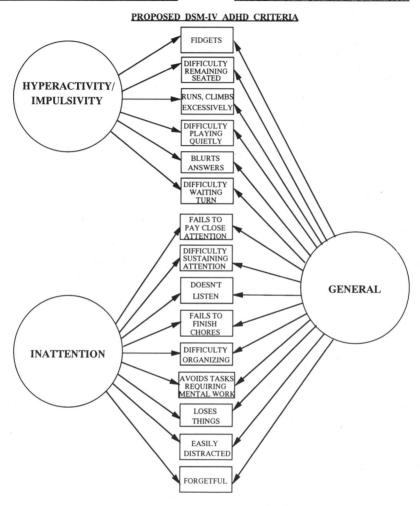

FIGURE 3. Two models for the underlying structure of ADHD

veloped primarily for research situations in which a relatively small number of alternative *a priori* hypotheses for the underlying structure of a measure or diagnostic entity could be statistically contrasted for their fit to the observed data (*viz.*, the variances of and covariances among items or symptoms and signs). This is in fact the chief advantage of such techniques compared with the more commonly used exploratory factor analytic techniques; confirmatory factor analysis allows the researcher to statistically compare the fit of a restricted number of alternative latent dimensional models that have been prespecified by the researcher. Note also that the presence of a general factor and of a number of specific factors underlying ADHD are not mutually exclusive, as both general and specific factors may be necessary for adequately characterizing the underlying structure of ADHD. The substantive meaning of a general factor in the presence of specific factors would likely differ from that of a general factor that is present on its own, since the general factor in the former case may often indicate something about the individuals rated (e.g., a general severity or impairment factor) or about the individuals completing the ratings (e.g., a rater bias or threshold factor, to be discussed subsequently) that is unique from the aspects of ADHD captured by the specific factors.

Once one finds evidence for a number of dimensions or classes, it makes sense to examine the relations among such dimensions or the boundaries among such classes. In confirmatory factor analysis, examining the relations among the latent symptom dimensions is straightforward, as it simply involves estimation of the correlations among the latent factors in the model. A test of the *orthogonality* of two latent symptom dimensions is accomplished by fixing the estimate of their correlation equal to zero and comparing the fit of this model to one in which the interfactor correlation is freely estimated. Likewise, a test of the *distinctiveness* of two latent symptom dimensions is accomplished by fixing the estimate of their correlation equal to unity and comparing the fit of this model to one in which the interfactor correlation is freely estimated. The higher the interfactor correlation, the greater is the relation between the two latent dimensions. Conversely, the lower the interfactor correlation, the more separable are the two latent dimensions. One additional advantage of estimating the relation among latent dimensions within a confirmatory factor analytic framework is that the correlation thus estimated represents the relation between the "true" latent symptom dimensions without the contaminating influences of measurement error (i.e., influences extraneous to the symptom dimensions of interest). This is in contrast to the usual practice of simply correlating symptom dimensions by summing symptoms and signs into scales and then correlating these scales, since such correlations reflect not only individuals' true standing on the latent symptom dimensions of interest but also any shared extraneous influences on the symptoms and signs.

The case of examining the boundaries among latent classes is a bit more complicated than that of the relations among latent dimensions. In mixture model analyses, one can estimate the distance among the latent component distributions that correspond to the different latent diagnostic classes, which would serve as an index of the boundary among these classes. In latent class analysis, one can estimate the probability of membership in each of the latent classes given the pattern of response (i.e., positive or negative) for each of the symptoms. It is easy to imagine that for certain research examples the distance among latent component distributions would be quite large or the assignment to latent diagnostic classes given different patterns of symptoms would be quite clear, whereas for other research examples the distance may be small and latent class assignment more murky. This latter situation would correspond to a relatively large number of diagnostic "gray cases," i.e., individuals who are not clearly assignable to one diagnostic condition versus another.

One final point regarding the presence of a number of latent classes, dimensions, or both, is that a number of psychopathology researchers have formulated classificatory models that combine latent classes and dimensions (e.g., Mezzich, 1979; Skinner, 1979). One example of such a "hybrid" model would be the case in which a diagnostic class is composed of individuals who are extreme on a number of latent symptom dimensions (Grove & Tellegen, 1991). To return to our ADHD example, ADHD may represent a latent diagnostic class composed of individuals who are extreme on a number of symptom dimensions (e.g., inattention, hyperactivity/impulsivity). Such hybrid models may represent useful alternatives for classificatory researchers to consider in future research.

4.4. How Useful Are the Symptoms of Disruptive Syndromes in the Diagnosis of These Syndromes? Are Some Symptoms Better Than Others as Indicators of the Presence or Absence of Syndromes? Which Symptoms Are Best for Discriminating among Disruptive Syndromes?

If the results of previous latent variable modeling analyses suggest that the latent diagnostic entity is categorical, it then makes sense to investigate which symptoms are most useful in the diagnosis of the disorder, i.e., are the most useful *inclusion* and *exclusion* criteria. Traditionally, the diagnostic efficiency indices most often used have been *Sensitivity*, the proportion of individuals with a disorder who are positive for a particular symptoms, and *Specificity*, the proportion of individuals without a disorder who are negative for a particular symptom. More recently, a number of researchers (e.g., Baldessarini, Finkelstein, & Arana, 1983) have suggested that two other diagnostic efficiency indices actually may be more useful in some cases, since they are better suited to the diagnostic task of the clinician. These indices are *Positive Predictive Power*, the proportion of individuals positive for a symptom, who have the disorder, and *Negative Predictive*

Power, the proportion of individuals negative for a particular symptom, who do not have the disorder.

Latent variable models, latent class analysis in particular, also could be used to investigate issues of diagnostic efficiency (Young, 1982/1983) and, in fact, have certain advantages over more traditional methods. First, researchers (e.g., Uebersax & Grove, 1990) have elaborated methods for deriving diagnostic efficiency indices from the parameter estimates yielded by latent class analyses. It would be desirable to estimate diagnostic efficiency in this fashion, as one would avoid difficulties in conceptualizing the diagnosis that are present in more traditional analyses. In traditional analyses of diagnostic efficiency, one typically compares a particular symptom to the presence or absence of the diagnosis by using all of the other symptoms in creating a symptom scale and then examining whether an individual is above the diagnostic threshold. This creates the difficulty that, if symptoms are differentially useful for making the diagnosis (indeed, this is what one is trying to determine), one is comparing each particular symptom to a different diagnosis and thus confounding cross-symptom comparisons of diagnostic efficiency. An additional difficulty concerns whether to use the same diagnostic threshold or a threshold based on fewer symptoms. The latent class analysis approach alleviates both of these difficulties, since each symptom is compared to the same diagnosis, which is conceptualized as a latent class, using the same threshold.

Second, in traditional analyses of diagnostic efficiency there are no formal statistical criteria (e.g., standard errors or confidence intervals) for comparing diagnostic efficiency indices across symptoms. For example, if positive predictive power is 0.87 for one ADHD symptom and 0.70 for another, one has no statistical basis for judging the magnitude or statistical significance of the difference in their diagnostic efficiency. Another advantage of the latent class analytic approach is that restrictions can be placed on the latent class analytic model and tested. This enables researchers to equate the diagnostic efficiency of two symptoms and test this restriction against the unconstrained model in which the two symptoms differ in their diagnostic efficiencies.

4.5. How Can Latent Variable Models Shed Light on Issues of Diagnostic Overlap and Situational Pervasiveness or Specificity? To What Extent Are the "Comorbidity" and Situational Specificity of Disruptive Syndromes Due to Factors Such as Rater Bias or Severity of Behavior Problems?

Two issues that have received considerable research attention in the recent child psychopathology literature are *comorbidity* (i.e., diagnostic overlap or covariation) among different disorders and the *situational pervasiveness* versus *specificity* of disruptive syndromes. In this section, we will show how latent variable models can shed light on these issues and perhaps even foster a resolution of them that would be difficult, if not impossible, using more traditional statistical techniques.

Comorbidity is a term that emerged from the medical epidemiology literature (Feinstein, 1970; Kaplan & Feinstein, 1974) to describe a number of important ways in which two or more diseases may relate to or interact with one another. Kaplan and Feinstein (1974; Feinstein, 1970) delineated several different types of comorbidity, including:

1. One disease modifying the course and outcome of another
2. One disease modifying the treatment response of another
3. The presence of symptoms or signs that could be due to either of two (or more) coexisting diseases
4. Two or more diseases co-occurring at rates greater than chance due to their sharing etiological factors.

Use of the term *comorbidity* in the child psychopathology literature appears to correspond most closely to meaning 3 (or, less commonly, 4), as it is most often used by researchers to refer to diagnostic overlap or covariation. Nonetheless, there is a major difference in the use of this term in the medical and psychopathological literatures, since in the former it typically is used to refer to the relation among *diseases,* whereas in the latter it is used to refer to the relation among *diagnoses* (Lilienfeld, Waldman, & Israel, 1994).

A disease entity in medicine is a pattern of signs and symptoms for which the underlying pathogenic and etiological processes are relatively well understood (Kazdin, 1983; Meehl & Golden, 1982). Although there is admittedly some ambiguity in this definition, few or no psychopathological entities currently appear to meet these criteria. Given this, *comorbidity* among psychopathological syndromes may be due to many factors other than the four cited by Kaplan and Feinstein, and a number of authors (e.g., Caron & Rutter, 1991; Frances, Widiger, & Fyer, 1990; Lilienfeld, Waldman, & Israel, 1994) have outlined various factors that may contribute to apparent or spurious comorbidity.

Latent variable models can contribute to better understanding the causes of overlap or covariation among diagnostic entities in child psychopathology. By addressing the issues raised previously, researchers can clarify the latent structure of the childhood disruptive syndromes, their categorical or dimensional structure, and their degree of overlap. In addition, latent variable models are well-equipped to discriminate latent dimensions or categories that correspond to the disorders of interest as opposed to latent dimensions or categories that correspond to factors that are potentially responsible for apparent or spurious comorbidity. These factors include general severity or impairment, and rater biases whereby ratings of symptoms and signs originating from a single source (e.g., one parent, teacher, or clinician per child being rated) reflect the raters' thresholds for rating symptom presence or their implicit theories regarding the covariation among symptoms. Traditional methods of assessing *comorbidity*, such as correlating symptom scales or tabulating diagnostic overlap, confound these spurious contributors to comorbidity with the true relations among latent diagnostic entities that investigators are interested in. It is only by separately assessing these latent factors that researchers can begin to disentangle the true degree of overlap and covariation among latent diagnostic entities from extraneous confounding influences.

A second area in the child psychopathology literature in which latent variable models could make a unique and valuable contribution is in understanding the situational specificity versus pervasiveness of childhood disruptive syndromes. Achenbach, McConaughy, and Howell (1987) reviewed numerous studies on childhood behavior problems rated across a number of settings (e.g., school, home, clinic) and concluded that the cross-situational consistency of such problems was quite low (although the consistency for disruptive or externalizing problems was higher than that of internalizing problems). Correlations between raters in different settings (e.g., teachers, parents, clinicians) of the same behavior problems in the same children averaged only about 0.2 to 0.3 and led Achenbach and his colleagues to conclude that childhood behavior problems are highly situationally specific, such that a child who shows considerable problems at home may not do so at school, and vice versa. The flip side of this coin is reflected in differences between the DSM and the ICD conceptualizations of certain childhood disorders, particularly ADHD. In contrast to DSM-III and DSM-III-R, ICD-10 mandates that the child must display behaviors indicative of inattention, impulsivity, and hyperactivity across a variety of different settings (*viz.*, home, school, and clinic) in order for the diagnosis of ADHD to be made.

Latent variable models can shed light on issues of situational specificity versus pervasiveness in a similar way to that discussed earlier. One factor that may contribute to low correlations across raters are rater biases, of the sort mentioned previously, that are consistent across a particular class of raters (e.g., teachers) but different across different classes of raters (e.g., teachers and parents). Failure to disentangle latent diagnostic entities from rater biases that may be present in ratings of symptoms may result in the low cross-setting correlations that are often observed (Achenbach et al., 1987). Such factors can be disentangled within latent variable models and may provide a more accurate picture of the cross-situational generality of childhood disruptive syndromes.

In a similar vein, in order for a child to be viewed as having certain symptoms (e.g., of ADHD) by teachers, parents, and clinicians—especially at a level that surpasses a diagnostic threshold within each setting—the child's "true" level of behavior problems would have to be sufficiently severe that each of these raters would view him or her as disordered, despite any unique rater biases that may also influence their ratings (Elder, 1993). Hence, traditional analyses of situational pervasiveness in ADHD confound situational pervasiveness *per se* with severity. Once again, latent variable modeling approaches to this issue could alleviate this confound and provide a more accurate view of the importance of situational pervasiveness to ADHD.

4.6. How Can Latent Variable Models Aid in Addressing Issues of External Validation?

It should be evident from the issues discussed thus far that clarification of the internal validity of diagnostic entities is ideally a prerequisite for examining their relations with external variables. Illuminating whether a diagnostic entity is categorical or dimensional, consists of one or more categories or dimensions, and is distinct from other diagnostic entities and from latent constructs representing other factors (e.g., rater bias, general severity) is critical for determining the relation of latent diagnostic entities to external variables, such as course and prognosis, treatment response, and family history. A few examples should suffice to illustrate the usefulness of latent variable modeling techniques for examining issues pertaining to the external validation of diagnostic syndromes.

First, consider again the models for the underlying structure of ADHD portrayed in Figure 3. If one general and two specific factors are necessary for adequately characterizing the underlying dimensional structure of ADHD, failure to specify such a model prior to conducting external validity analyses could have unfortunate consequences. For example, consider an investigator interested in examining the relation of familial psychopathology to ADHD. Further, suppose that hyperactivity/impulsivity and inattention are moderately to highly correlated (e.g., $r = .6-.8$). If these two dimensions are related to different disorders in the family members of children with ADHD, failure to distinguish them from each other could result in a misleading picture of the familial pattern of psychopathology associated with ADHD.

Second, consider another investigator interested in the relation between ADHD and treatment response. Failure to distinguish the specific ADHD dimensions from the general dimension may yield a cloudy picture of such a relation. For example, if the general dimension represents general

severity or impairment, this dimension may be related to treatment response independent of the specific dimensions underlying ADHD. Conversely, if this general dimension represents a rater bias (e.g., a threshold
effect), it may be largely or entirely unrelated to treatment response. Without separately examining the relation of treatment response to the specific
ADHD dimensions on the one hand and to general severity on the other,
one cannot obtain a clear understanding of how ADHD is related to
treatment response independent of general impairment.

Third and finally, consider another investigator who is interested in
studying the adolescent and adult outcome of children with ADHD,
specifically whether such children are at greater risk for antisocial personality disorder (ASPD) than children without ADHD. Extant research suggests that ADHD children with concomitant aggression and conduct problems, but not other ADHD children, are at heightened risk for later ASPD
(Lilienfeld & Waldman, 1990). Casting this research problem within a latent variable framework could facilitate disentangling the prognostic implications of each of these sets of childhood problems, because latent variable models are better than traditional statistical techniques at separating
different diagnostic entities (e.g., ADHD and CD), describing their overlap,
and providing estimates of their unique relation to future ASPD.

4.7. How Can We Understand the Relation between Normality and Maladjustment? What Is the Relation between Functioning within the Normal Range and at the Pathological Extreme (i.e., above the Diagnostic Threshold)?

One final (and, unfortunately, future) application of latent variable
modeling that includes external validity indicators is worth mentioning, as
it could allow researchers to better understand the relation between functioning within the normal range and at the pathological extreme. Both
child and adult psychopathology researchers have struggled with the
problem of determining where normal functioning ends and maladjustment begins. Despite numerous attempts at answering this question,
which is closely tied to the categorical–dimensional distinction discussed
previously, the issue remains largely unresolved.

An approach to this question using more traditional statistical techniques might be to examine both linear and nonlinear relations of the
number of symptoms of a disorder with an external validity indicator
using multiple regression analysis. A graphical example of this is shown
in Figure 4, in which two possible nonlinear relations between level of
impairment and the number of symptoms of a disorder are portrayed. If
the relation between a criterion variable and the number of symptoms of

a disorder changes throughout the range of symptoms (i.e., a nonlinear model better explains the disorder-criterion relation than does a linear model), this finding furnishes some support for distinguishing the pathological extreme of a diagnostic entity from functioning within the normal range and could aid in determining a diagnostic threshold.

It is our sense that latent-variable modeling techniques might be especially useful in addressing this issue, though we are not aware of any extant examples. Behavior genetic methods may hold special promise, in particular for examining whether functioning above a diagnostic threshold differs qualitatively from functioning below the threshold (i.e., in the "nonclinical" range) or whether it represents only the extreme of normal functioning. Multivariate behavior genetic analyses (Plomin, 1986) of a diagnosis and of the number of symptoms for a disorder, and of relevant laboratory measures of the constructs underlying the disorder, may be useful for testing these competing possibilities, as may tests of multiple-threshold models for disorder (Reich, James, & Morris, 1972).

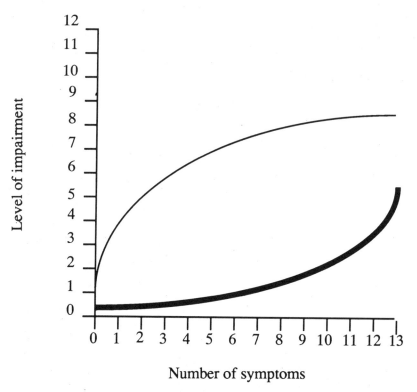

FIGURE 4. Two examples of a nonlinear relation

5. Suggestions for Future Research on the Classification of the Childhood Disruptive Behavior Disorders

In this final section we offer a number of suggestions for future research on the classification of the childhood disruptive behavior disorders. It is our hope that these suggestions will influence not only individual studies conducted as part of the ongoing child psychopathology research enterprise, but also large collaborative studies such as multisite projects and future DSM field trials.

A number of conclusions follow from the points raised in the first three sections of this chapter. One general conclusion is that researchers studying childhood disruptive disorders should be more attentive to construct validity considerations in the planning and implementation of studies. Such considerations include:

1. Formulating specific, *a priori* alternative hypotheses that can be contrasted in terms of their fit to the data
2. Including a larger number and broader scope of competing hypotheses than is currently the norm
3. Paying greater attention to issues of internal validity, given that comparing diagnostic groups of unknown internal validity on indices of course and outcome, treatment response, family history, and putative etiology can in some cases be more misleading than informative
4. Increasing the use of latent variable models.

As discussed earlier, latent variable models can aid in examining issues of internal validity, such as whether latent diagnostic entities are categorical or dimensional, the number of these entities and their boundaries and relations, and the diagnostic efficiency of signs and symptoms, as well as issues that border on internal and external validity, such as the sources of diagnostic overlap and covariation (i.e., *comorbidity*), the situational specificity versus pervasiveness of childhood behavior problems, and the relation between functioning within the normal range and at the pathological extreme.

A number of conclusions more germane to large-scale research projects, such as future DSM field trials, also follow from these points. First, investigators with a broad range of perspectives should be included in such studies to aid in formulating alternative hypotheses regarding both general and specific issues in the childhood disruptive disorders. Perhaps the best way to ensure that a broad range of alternative hypotheses are formulated and tested in such studies is to include investigators who hold competing perspectives on such issues. For example, a large, multisite study could include both researchers with dimensional and categorical views of child psychopathology in an effort to contrast these views. Second, one should ensure that a sufficient database is available for testing primary and alternative hypotheses and for replication and cross-validation. Even samples that would in most instances be considered large may not be large enough in such research projects. In the DSM-IV Disruptive Behavior Disorder field trials, for example, the sample was large enough to test the central hypotheses, but not large enough to adequately examine whether results of all analyses differed by sex and age. Ideally, a number of large samples, both clinically referred and nonreferred, should be available to examine the central hypotheses of interest and relevant alternative hypotheses, as well as to permit replication and cross-validation.

Third, a multimethod approach to measurement should be used both for the assessment of symptoms and signs, as well as for indices of impairment and other criterion measures. Although multiple informants were interviewed in the DSM-IV Disruptive Behavior Disorder field trials, only a single method of assessing psychopathology (the DISC; Shaffer et al., 1992) and single measures of relevant impairment constructs were used. Multimethod assessment entails at least two advantages over single-method assessment. Relations among constructs (e.g., a diagnostic entity and some relevant aspect of impairment) are generally stronger and clearer when they are operationalized using a number of different measures than when they are operationalized using only a single measure (Cole, Howard, & Maxwell, 1981). In addition, relations among constructs are more likely to generalize to other measures and studies when multimethod operationalization rather than single-method operationalization is used.

A fourth and final issue involves the structure of such large-scale research projects. Given our focus on the advantages of latent variable models for addressing unresolved issues in classification and diagnosis, the reader may be wondering why these analyses were not carried out as part of the DSM-IV disruptive behavior disorder field trials. Quite simply, such analyses require greater commitments of time, effort, and money than the more traditional analyses that are typically conducted in the child psychopathology literature. With their formidable time constraints, the current structure of the field trials does not promote the use of latent variable modeling analyses. In addition, relatively few child psychopathology researchers are conversant with latent variable modeling techniques—which creates difficulties for communicating and understanding the findings of such analyses—and a significant amount of time and effort must be invested in order to learn these statistical methods as well as apply them to classification problems.

Heretofore, most of the time, effort, and money in large-scale studies has been devoted to data collection. It may be more advantageous, however, to restructure such studies so that a much greater proportion of these resources are devoted to data analysis. One step in this direction might be to have data collected by an independent organization under a subcontractual arrangement. Another step would be to assemble a data analytic team made up of researchers with particular interests and expertise in issues pertaining to the classification and diagnosis of childhood disruptive disorders. These researchers would play a crucial role in the planning of such studies—e.g., to ensure that the right types and amount of data are being collected to permit testing of the hypotheses of interest—and in data analysis, but would be unencumbered by the day-to-day exigencies of data collection. An arrangement of this type would foster creativity in hypothesis generation and testing and would allow sufficient time for thoughtful interpretation of the results and their substantive and methodological implications.

6. References

Achenbach, T. M., & Edelbrock, C. (1978). The classification of child psychopathology: A review and analysis of empirical efforts. *Psychological Bulletin, 85,* 1275–1301.
Achenbach, T. M., McConaughy, S. H., & Howell, C. T. (1987). Child/adolescent behavioral and emotional problems: Implications of cross-informant correlations for situational specificity. *Psychological Bulletin, 101,* 213–232.
American Psychiatric Association. (1952). *Diagnostic and statistical manual of mental disorders* (1st Edition). Washington, DC: Author.
American Psychiatric Association. (1980). *Diagnostic and statistical manual of mental disorders* (3rd Edition). Washington, DC: Author.
American Psychiatric Association. (1987). *Diagnostic and statistical manual of mental disorders* (3rd Edition, Revised). Washington, DC: Author.
American Psychiatric Association. (1993). *DSM-IV draft criteria.* Washington, DC: Author.
Anastasi, A. (1990). *Psychological testing.* New York: Macmillan.
Angold, A., Cox, A., Prendergast, M., Rutter, M., & Simonoff, E. (1989). *The child and adolescent psychiatric assessment.* MRC Child Psychiatry Unit, University of London and Developmental Epidemiology Program, Duke University.
Applegate, B., Lahey, B. B., Hart, E. L., Waldman, I., Biederman, J., Hynd, G. W., Barkley, R. A., Ollendick, T., Frick, P. J., Greenhill, L., McBurnett, K., Newcorn, J., Kerdyk, L., & Garfinkel, B. (1994). Age of onset and pervasiveness criteria for DSM-IV attention deficit/hyperactivity disorder: Report of the DSM-IV field trials. Manuscript in preparation.
Applegate, B., Waldman, I., Lahey, B. B., Frick, P. J., Ollendick, T., Garfinkel, B., Biederman, J., Hynd, G. W., Barkley, R. A., Greenhill, L., McBurnett, K., Newcorn, J., Kerdyk, L., &

Hart, E. L. (1994). DSM-IV field trials for disruptive and attention deficit disorders: Factor analysis of potential symptoms. Manuscript in preparation.

Baldessarini, R. J., Finkelstein, S., & Arana, G. W. (1983). The predictive power of diagnostic tests and the effect of prevalence of illness. *Archives of General Psychiatry, 40,* 569–573.

Bechtoldt, H. P. (1959). Construct validity: A critique. *American Psychologist, 14,* 619–629.

Blashfield, R. K., & Livesley, W. J. (1991). Metaphorical analysis of psychiatric classification as a psychological test. *Journal of Abnormal Psychology, 100,* 262–270.

Bollen, K., & Lennox, R. (1991). Conventional wisdom on measurement: A structural equation perspective. *Psychological Bulletin, 110,* 305–314.

Boring, E. G. (1923). Intelligence as the tests test it. *The New Republic,* June 6, 35–37.

Bridgman, P. W. (1927). *The logic of modern physics.* New York: Macmillan.

Campbell, D. T., & Fiske, D. W. (1959). Convergent and discriminant validation by the multitrait-multimethod matrix. *Psychological Bulletin, 56,* 81–105.

Carnap, R. (1936). Testability and meaning. *Philosophy of Science, 3,* 420–471.

Caron, C., & Rutter, M. (1991). Comorbidity in child psychiatry: Concepts, issues, and research strategies. *Journal of Child Psychology and Psychiatry, 32,* 1063–1080.

Clogg, C. C. (1977). Unrestricted and restricted maximum likelihood latent structure analysis: A manual for users. Working paper 1977–09, Pennsylvania State University, Population Issues Research Center.

Cloninger, C. R. (1989). Establishment of diagnostic validity in psychiatric illness: Robins and Guze's method revisited. In L. N. Robins & J. E. Barrett (Eds.), *The validity of psychiatric diagnosis* (pp0. 9–16). New York: Raven.

Cohen, J. (1960). A coefficient of agreement for nominal scales. *Educational and Psychological Measurement, 20,* 37–46.

Cole, D. A., Howard, G. S., & Maxwell, S. E. (1981). Effects of mono- versus multiple-operationalization in construct validation efforts. *Journal of Consulting and Clinical Psychology, 49,* 395–405.

Cook, T. D., & Campbell, D. T. (1979). *Quasi-experimentation: Design and analysis for field settings.* Chicago, Rand McNally.

Costello, A. J., Edelbrock, C. S., Duncan, M. K., & Kalas, R. (1984). *Testing of the NIMH Diagnostic Interview Schedule for Children (DISC) in a clinical population* (Contract No. DB-81-0027). Final report to the Center for Epidemiological Studies, National Institute for Mental Health. Pittsburgh, PA: University of Pittsburgh.

Cronbach, L. J., & Meehl, P. E. (1955). Construct validity in psychological tests. *Psychological Bulletin, 52,* 281–302.

Eaves, L. J., Silberg, J. L., Hewitt, J. K., Rutter, M., Meyer, J. M., Neale, M. C., & Pickles, A. (1993). Analyzing twin resemblance in multisymptom data: Genetic applications of a latent class model for symptoms of conduct disorder in juvenile boys. *Behavior Genetics, 23,* 5–19.

Elder, R. W. (1993). *Group differences among situationally and pervasively hyperactive children reexamined: The influence of reliability.* Unpublished manuscript.

Faust, D., & Miner, R. A. (1986). The empiricist and his new clothes: DSM-III in perspective. *American Journal of Psychiatry, 143,* 962–967.

Feinstein, A. R. (1970). The pretherapeutic classification of comorbidity in chronic disease. *Journal of Chronic Disease, 23,* 455–468.

Fergusson, D. M., & Horwood, L. J. (1989). Estimation of method and trait variance in ratings of conduct disorder. *Journal of Child Psychology and Psychiatry, 30,* 365–378.

Fergusson, D. M., Horwood, L. J., & Lloyd, M. (1991). Confirmatory factor models of attention deficit and conduct disorder. *Journal of Child Psychology and Psychiatry, 32,* 257–274.

Frances, A. J., Widiger, T. A., & Fyer, M. R. (1990). The influence of classification methods on comorbidity. In J. D. Maser & C. R. Cloninger (Eds.), *Comorbidity of mood and anxiety disorders* (pp. 41–59). Washington, DC: American Psychiatric Press.

Frances, A. J., Widiger, T. A., & Pincus, H. A. (1989). The development of DSM-IV. *Archives of General Psychiatry, 46,* 373–375.

Frick, P. J., Lahey, B. B., Applegate, B., Kerdyk, L., Ollendick, T., Hynd, G. W., Garfinkel, B., Greenhill, L., Biederman, J., Barkley, R. A., McBurnett, K., Newcorn, J., & Waldman, I. (in press). DSM-IV field trials for the disruptive behavior disorders: Symptom utility estimates. *Journal of the American Academy of Child and Adolescent Psychiatry.*

Garber, J., & Strassberg, Z. (1991). Construct validity: History and application to developmental psychopathology. In D. Cicchetti & W. G. Grove (Eds.), *Thinking clearly about psychology: Essays in honor of Paul Everett Meehl* (pp. 219–358). Minneapolis: University of Minnesota Press.

Gibbons, R. D., & Young, M. A. (1989). *Comparison of discrete and continuous latent structures.* Unpublished manuscript.

Goldstein, G., & Hersen, M. (1984). Historical perspectives. In G. Goldstein & M. Hersen (Eds.), *Handbook of psychological assessment* (pp. 3–13). New York: Pergamon Press.

Goodman, L. A. (1974). The analysis of systems of qualitative variables when some of the variables are unobservable. *American Journal Sociology, 79,* 1179–1259.

Gorenstein, E. E. (1992). *The science of mental illness.* San Diego, CA: Academic Press.

Grove, W. M., & Andreasen, N. (1986). Multivariate statistical analysis in psychopathology. In T. Millon & G. L. Klerman (Eds.), *Contemporary directions in psychopathology* (pp. 347–362). New York: Guilford.

Grove, W. M., & Andreasen, N. (1987). Quantitative and qualitative distinctions between psychiatric disorders. In L. N. Robins & J. E. Barrett (Eds.), *The validity of psychiatric diagnosis* (pp. 127–139). New York: Raven.

Grove, W. M., & Tellegen, A. (1991). Problems in the classification of personality disorders. *Journal of Personality Disorders, 5,* 31–41.

Hambleton, R. K., Swaminathan, H., & Rogers, H. J. (1991). *Fundamentals of item response theory.* Newbury Park, CA: Sage.

Hinshaw, S. P. (1987). On the distinction between attention deficits/hyperactivity and conduct problems/aggression in child psychopathology. *Psychological Bulletin, 101,* 443–463.

Jensen, A. R. (1980). *Bias in mental testing.* New York: Free Press.

Joreskog, K. G., & Sorbom, D. (1989). *LISREL VII: User's guide.* Mooresville, IN: Scientific Software, Inc.

Kaplan, M. H., & Feinstein, A. R. (1974). The imporance of classifying initial comorbidity in evaluating the outcome of *diabetes mellitus. Journal of Chronic Disease, 27,* 387–404.

Kazdin, A. E. (1983). Psychiatric diagnosis, dimensions of dysfunction, and child behavior therapy. *Behavior Therapy, 14,* 73–99.

Kirk, S. A., & Kutchins, H. (1992). *The selling of DSM: The rhetoric of science in psychiatry.* New York: Aldine deGruyter.

Lahey, B. B., Applegate, B., Barkley, R. A., Garfinkel, B., McBurnett, K., Kerdyk, L., Greenhill, L., Hynd, G. W., Frick, P. J., Newcorn, J., Biederman, J., Ollendick, T., Hart, E. L., Perez, D., Waldman, I., & Shaffer, D. (1994). DSM-IV field trials for oppositional defiant disorder and conduct disorder in children and adolescents. *American Journal of Psychiatry, 151,* 1163–1171.

Lahey, B. B., Applegate, B., McBurnett, K., Biederman, J., Greenhill, L., Hynd, G. W., Barkley, R. A., Newcorn, J., Jensen, P., Richters, J., Garfinkel, B., Kerdyk, L., Frick, P. J., Ollendick, T., Perez, D., Hart, E. L., Waldman, I., & Shaffer, D. (in press). DSM-IV field trials for attention-deficit/hyperactivity disorder in children and adolescents. *American Journal of Psychiatry.*

Lahey, B. B., & Carlson, C. L. (1991). Evidence for a distinction between attention deficit disorder with and without hyperactivity. *Journal of Learning Disabilities, 24,* 110–120.

Lahey, B. B., Loeber, R., Quay, H. C., Frick, P. J., & Grimm, J. (1992). Oppositional defiant and conduct disorder: Issues to be resolved by DSM-IV. *Journal of the American Academy of Child and Adolescent Psychiatry.*

Lilienfeld, S. O., & Marino, L. A. (1993). *A critique of Wakefield's "harmful dysfunction" analysis of disorder.* Manuscript submitted for publication.

Lilienfeld, S. O., & Waldman, I. D. (1990). The relation between childhood attention-deficit hyperactivity disorder and adult antisocial behavior reexamined: The problem of heterogeneity. *Clinical Psychology Review, 10,* 699–725.

Lilienfeld, S. O., Waldman, I. D., & Israel, A. O. (1994). A critical note on the use of the term and concept of "comorbidity" in psychopathology research. *Clinical Psychology: Science and Practice, 1,* 71–83.

Loeber, R. (1990). Development and risk factors of juvenile antisocial behavior and delinquency. *Clinical Psychology Review, 10,* 1–41.

Loeber, R., Green, S. M., Lahey, B. B., & Stouthamer-Loeber, M. (1990). Optimal informants on childhood disruptive disorders. *Development and Psychopathology, 1,* 317–337.

Loeber, R., Keenan, K., Lahey, B. B., Green, S. M., & Thomas, C. (1993). Evidence for developmentally based diagnoses of oppositional defiant disorder and conduct disorder. *Journal of Abnormal Child Psychology, 21,* 377–410.

Loevinger, J. (1957). Objective tests as instruments of psychological theory. *Psychological Reports, 3,* 635–694.

Loney, J., & Milich, R. (1982). Hyperactivity, inattention, and aggression in clinical practice. In M. Wolraich & D. Routh (Eds.), *Advances in behavioral pediatrics* (Vol. 2), (pp. 113–147). Greenwich, CT: JAI Press.

Lykken, D. T. (1968). Statistical significance in psychological research. *Psychological Bulletin, 70,* 151–159.

MacCorquodale, K., & Meehl, P. E. (1948). On a distinction between hypothetical constructs and intervening variables. *Psychological Review, 55,* 95–107.

Meehl, P. E. (1977). Specific etiology and other forms of strong influence: Some quantitative meanings. *Journal of Medicine and Philosophy, 2,* 33–53.

Meehl, P. E. (1978). Theoretical risks and tabular asterisks: Sir Karl, Sir Ronald, and the slow progress of soft psychology. *Journal of Consulting and Clinical Psychology, 46,* 806–834.

Meehl, P. E. (1986). Diagnostic taxa as open concepts: Metatheoretical and statistical questions about reliability and construct validity in the grand strategy of nosological revision. In T. Millon & G. L. Klerman (Eds.), *Contemporary directions in psychopathology* (pp. 215–231). New York: Guilford.

Meehl, P. E. (1990). Appraising and amending theories: The strategy of Lakatosian defense and two principles that warrant it. *Psychological Inquiry, 1,* 108–141.

Meehl, P. E., & Golden, R. R. (1982). Taxometric methods. In P. C. Kendall & J. N. Butcher (Eds.), *Handbook of research methods in clinical psychology* (pp. 127–181). New York: Wiley.

Messick, S. (1988). Validity. In R. L. Linn (Ed.), *Educational measurement* (3rd ed., pp. 13–103). New York: Macmillan.

Mezzich, J. E. (1979). Patterns and issues in the multiaxial psychiatric diagnosis. *Psychological Medicine, 9,* 125–137.

Milich, R., Widiger, T. A., & Landau, S. (1987). Differential diagnosis of attention deficit and conduct disorders using conditional probabilities. *Journal of Consulting and Clinical Psychology, 55,* 762–767.

Morey, L. C. (1991). Classification of mental disorder as a collection of hypothetical constructs. *Journal of Abnormal Psychology, 100,* 289–293.

Pelham, W. E., & Bender, M. E. (1982). Peer interactions of hyperactive children: Assessment and treatment. In K. D. Gadow & I. Bialer (Eds.), *Advances in learning and behavior difficulties* (pp. 365–436). Greenwich, CT: JAI Press.

Popper, K. R. (1959). *The logic of scientific discovery.* New York: Basic Books.

Reich, T., James, J. W., & Morris, C. A. (1972). The use of multiple thresholds in determining the mode of transmission of semi-continuous traits. *Annals of Human Genetics, 36,* 163–184.

Reich, W., Herjanic, B., Welner, Z., & Gandhy, P. R. (1982). Development of a structured interview for children: Agreement on diagnosis comparing parent and child. *Journal of Abnormal Child Psychology, 10,* 325–336.

Richards, R. J. (1981). Natural selection and other models in the historiography of science. In M. B. Brewer & B. E. Collins (Eds.), *Scientific inquiry and the social sciences* (pp. 37–76). San Francisco, CA: Jossey-Bass.

Robins, E., & Guze, S. B. (1970). Establishment of diagnostic validity in psychiatric illness: Its application to schizophrenia. *American Journal of Psychiatry, 126,* 983–987.

Shaffer, D., Gould, M. S., Brasic, J., Ambrosini, P., Fisher, P., Bird, H., & Aluwhalla, S. (1983). A Children's Global Assessment Scale (CGAS). *Archives of General Psychiatry, 40,* 1228–1231.

Shaffer, D., Fisher, P., Piacentini, J., Schwab-Stone, M., & Wicks, J. (1992). *Diagnostic Interview for Children, Version 2.3.* New York: Columbia University.

Skinner, H. A. (1979). Dimensions and clusters: A hybrid approach to classification. *Applied Psychological Measurement, 3,* 327–341.

Skinner, H. A. (1981). Toward the integration of classification theory and methods. *Journal of Abnormal Psychology, 90,* 68–87.

Skinner, H. A. (1986). Construct validation approach to psychiatric classification. In T. Millon & G. L. Klerman (Eds.), *Contemporary directions in psychopathology* (pp. 307–330). New York: Guilford.

Sternberg, R. J. (1992). *Psychological Bulletin's* Top 10 "Hit Parade." *Psychological Bulletin, 112,* 387–388.

Titterington, D. M., Smith, A. F. M., & Makov, U. E. (1985). *Statistical analysis of finite mixture distributions.* New York: Wiley.

Uebersax, J. S., & Grove, W. M. (1990). Latent class analysis of diagnostic agreement. *Statistics in Medicine, 9,* 559–572.

Vaillant,G. (1984). The disadvantages of DSM-III outweigh its advantages. *American Journal of Psychiatry, 141,* 542–545.

Wakefield, J. C. (1992). The concept of mental disorder: On the boundary between biological facts and social values. *American Psychologist, 47,* 373–388.

Wakefield, J. C. (1992). Disorder as harmful dysfunction: A conceptual critique of DSM-III-R's definition of mental disorder. *Psychological Review, 99,* 232–247.

Waldman, I. D., & Lahey, B. B. (1994). Design of the DSM-IV Disruptive Behavior Disorder Field Trials. *Child and Adolescent Psychiatric Clinics of North America, 3,* 1–14.

Waldman, I. D., Lahey, B. B., Applegate, B., Biederman, J., Hynd, G. W., Barkley, R. A., Ollendick, T., Frick, P. J., Kerdyk, L., Garfinkel, B., Greenhill, L., McBurnett, K., Newcorn, J., & Hart, E. L. (1994). *The construct validity of DSM-IV attention-deficit/hyperactivity disorder subtypes: Report from the DSM-IV field trials.* Manuscript in preparation.

Waldman, I. D., & Lilienfeld, S. O. (1991). Diagnostic efficiency of symptoms for Oppositional Defiant Disorder and Attention-Deficit Hyperactivity Disorder. *Journal of Consulting and Clinical Psychology, 59,* 732–738.

World Health Organization. (1990). *International classification of diseases and related health problems* (10th ed.). Geneva: Author.

Young, M. A. (1982/1983). Evaluating diagnostic criteria: A latent class approach. *Journal of Psychiatric Research, 17,* 285–296.
Young, M. A., & Tanner, M. A. (1983). Recent advances in the analysis of qualitative data with application to diagnostic classification. In R. D. Gibbons & M. W. Dysken (Eds.), *Statistical and methodological advances in psychiatric research* (pp. 149–180). New York: Spectrum.

9   Play Psychotherapy Research

State of the Science

Sandra W. Russ

1. Introduction

I was sitting in the cafeteria at the San Diego airport, amidst the usual chaotic airport scene, when I noticed a little boy, about six or seven years old, sitting at the table next to mine. He was with an older brother or very young father who was reading. The boy had laid out in front of him four figures—a cowboy, an Indian, a large monster, and a larger rubber dinosaur. He was totally engrossed in fantasy play with these creatures and was making up dialogue and action. I could not hear all of it, but I could hear, "Do this," "No you won't," "Here's this." Some of the play was with an angry tone, some with a cooperative tone. There was a definite story line. His play went on for about 30 minutes. He was totally engaged and comfortable and was clearly having a good time. He was also doing work—expressing feelings, learning to modulate affect, mastering problems, and developing coping skills.

Finally, his older companion indicated it was time to leave. He helped the child carefully pack all of the creatures into his knapsack. The boy told one of them to "Have a good day," he kept the dinosaur out and put it under his arm. The older companion was handling the situation very well in that he was gentle, didn't rush the boy, respected his little creatures and did not intrude in the play. The boy was totally comfortable playing in front of him. I don't know what kind of family situation this boy comes from or what kind of stress he's going on to, but I do know that he has a terrific resource—he can use play and he likes to play. He is a good player, and that will help him in a variety of ways.

SANDRA W. RUSS • Department of Psychology, Case Western Reserve University, Cleveland, Ohio 44106.

Advances in Clinical Child Psychology, Volume 17, edited by Thomas H. Ollendick and Ronald J. Prinz. Plenum Press, New York, 1995.

While watching this boy, questions arose in my mind that the psychotherapeutic field has been wrestling with for a number of years. How does play help? What does it help with? Can we teach good play skills? How can the therapist use play most effectively to help the child? Can we really measure play?

This last question is a crucial one because we cannot study the dimensions of play if we cannot measure them. Can we truly capture the private, spontaneous fantasy play that most expresses the child's thoughts, feelings, fantasies, wishes, and fears? There is a growing number of instruments that attempt to measure play—my own included—that now have a growing empirical base that supports their reliability and validity. These measures are capturing important aspects of play, even though they may not capture fantasy play in "full force."

1.1. Overview

The ability to enjoy play and use play is a major resource for children and a tool which they can use for a variety of purposes. Play psychotherapy is based upon this principle.

What we have learned about play has come mainly from three separate lines of inquiry. The first line is drawn from the clinical literature on child psychotherapy. The clinical experiences of child psychotherapists have yielded principles of the role of play in child development and have resulted in theory building based on these clinical observations. A second line of inquiry is the play and child development research literature. This is a rather large empirically based body of knowledge about play. The third line of inquiry is what can be labeled play intervention research. This research focuses on the effects of play on specific problem areas, such as anxiety reduction in presurgery situations. Each of these lines of inquiry will be reviewed in this chapter.

Another area that will be reviewed briefly is the child psychotherapy outcome-research literature. The child psychotherapy literature is important to review because it provides an important context in which to think about *play* psychotherapy research. Also, the lessons learned from this research have implications for future play psychotherapy research.

The major purpose of this review is to show that the clinical play psychotherapy literature, play research literature, and play intervention-research literature need to be integrated into a theoretical framework that leads to the establishment of a systematic program of research and clinical practice. Also, play psychotherapy and intervention techniques must be adapted to current populations and to problems of the contemporary scene of child and family service delivery.

The first section of this chapter will review the play psychotherapy literature and theories of play as a mechanism of change in psychotherapy. Then, research on play, child psychotherapy outcome research, and play intervention research will be reviewed. The final section will discuss future directions in research, and implications for clinical practice.

2. Traditional Play Psychotherapy

The concept of play psychotherapy is a bit of a misnomer because most psychotherapy with children is a mix of play and talk. The mix depends upon the child's age, ability to verbalize, developmental level, and ability to play. Play is a tool that the therapist facilitates, relies on, and uses to help effect change in the child. Play is a vehicle for change, through which different mechanisms of change in psychotherapy can operate.

The use of play in psychotherapy comes from two basic therapeutic traditions—the psychoanalytic tradition and the nondirective client-centered tradition. In both traditions, play is both a form of communication with the therapist and a form of expression of inner thoughts, feelings, and wishes. As Tuma and Russ (1993) point out, today's predominant mode of play therapy is no longer psychoanalytic, but rather psychodynamic. The psychodynamic approach is a broader model that encompasses a variety of therapeutic concepts and techniques.

Historically, Melanie Klein (1955) and Anna Freud (1965) were early major theorists who saw the importance of play in therapy and developed play techniques in child therapy. For excellent reviews of the history of the use of play in psychotherapy see Chethik (1989), Kessler (1966, 1988), Koocher and D'Angelo (1992), and Tuma and Russ (1993).

Currently, play psychotherapy is a major intervention approach with children. As Koocher and D'Angelo (1992), state, "play-oriented therapy remains the dominant and most enduring approach to child treatment . . . practiced by clinicians" (p. 458). Traditionally, the basic ingredients of individual child psychotherapy include: regular, individual meetings between the child and the therapist; an understanding that the therapist is there to help the child understand and change feelings, thoughts, and behaviors; the development of a trusting relationship between the therapist and the child; and open communication between the therapist and the child. Play is a major way that the child communicates with the therapist (Chethik, 1989; Freedheim & Russ, 1992). Most contemporary therapists utilize child psychotherapy in conjunction with a variety of other interventions such as behavior therapy, family therapy, school consultation, parent guidance, and medication. For multiproblem families, a number of different types of interventions are necessary (Koocher & Broskowski, 1977).

2.1. Play and Change in Psychotherapy

Play serves two major functions in psychotherapy. First, it is a major form of communication between the child and the therapist, so it aids in the development of the therapist–child relationship. It is crucial that the therapist understand the "language of play" as Chethik (1989) puts it, so that the relationship can develop. Because empathy on the part of the therapist is so important in developing a relationship, understanding and empathizing with play content and process is crucial.

The second function of play is as a vehicle for change in psychotherapy. Change occurs in many different ways in psychotherapy and play aids the change process. Actually, play therapy uses a natural resource of the child—play—to effect change. Play is an arena in which children normally work out problems and develop cognitive and affective processes. In section 3.1 these cognitive and affective processes will be discussed in detail. In therapy, several elements are added to the normal play situation. First, an adult is present to help provide a safe place where play can occur. The therapist sets up a permissive environment. Second, the therapist uses the play by actively working with it. The therapist labels, empathizes, interprets, and as Chethik (1989) states, helps "the child work towards meaningful play" (p. 53).

Expanding on work by Applebaum (1978) and Garfield (1980) in the adult literature, Freedheim and Russ (1983, 1992) identified six major mechanisms of change that occur in individual child psychotherapy. Here, the role of play in each of these categories of change will be described.

1. *Catharsis and Labeling of Feelings.* Play is a major way in which children express feelings and release emotion. This catharsis, or release of emotion, is thought to be therapeutic (Axline, 1947; A. Freud, 1965; Moustakas, 1953). By labeling the affect, the therapist helps to make the feeling less overwhelming and more understandable. Much of the labeling of affect occurs during the child's pretend play. Because play is safe and in a pretend mode, many troubling feelings can be expressed in this fashion.

2. *Corrective Emotional Experience.* By accepting the feelings and thoughts of the child, the child's learned expectations are not met. For example, the automatic connection between angry thoughts and anxiety gradually decreases as the therapist accepts the feeling and helps the child understand the reasons for the anger. The therapist is not angry or punishing. Again, much of the work with feelings occurs throughout the play of the child. The therapist might discuss angry feelings of the girl puppet

towards the mother puppet, giving permission for feelings to occur and a context in which to understand them.

3. *Insight and Working Through.* The emotional resolution of conflict or trauma is a major mechanism of change in child therapy. Children reexperience major developmental conflicts or situational traumas in therapy. Frequently, play is the vehicle through which the feelings, thoughts, and conflicts, are expressed, mastered, and resolved. For some children, this working-through process also results in cognitive insight into behaviors and symptoms. Often in children cognitive insight does not occur, but emotional reexperiencing, working through and mastery do occur. In Erickson's (1963) concept of mastery, the child uses play to gain mastery over traumatic events and everyday conflicts. Play has long been thought of as a form of conflict resolution. Waelder (1933) describes the play process as one in which the child repeats an unpleasant experience over and over until it becomes manageable. Chethik (1989) describes central themes in the play that are played out. Freedheim and Russ (1992) describe the slow process of gaining access to conflict-laden material and playing it out until the conflict is resolved. Because issues have been genuinely resolved, the child can truly move on to other developmental tasks.

4. *Learning Alternative Problem-Solving Techniques and Coping Strategies.* The therapist, in a directive approach, helps the child think about alternative ways of viewing a situation and problem-solving strategies. This approach can be used through play as well. Knell (1994) discusses cognitive behavioral techniques in a play situation and D. Singer (1993) gives examples of modeling techniques during play therapy.

5. *Development of Internal Structure.* Many children have structural deficits that results in problems with self/object differentiation, object relations, self-esteem regulation, impulse control, object constancy, and separation of reality from fantasy. Based upon conceptualizations by Mahler (1968) and Kohut (1977), structure-building approaches view the therapist as serving as a stable, predictable, caring figure who helps the child develop the necessary cognitive and affective functions. Development of good object relations is a major goal of play therapy. Gilpin (1976) stressed the role of the therapist as becoming an internalized object. The relationship between the therapist and child is probably the most important aspect of therapy in helping this process to occur. Play is important here as a form of communication in that the therapist can empathize with the child's expressions. It is essential that the therapist understand the child's play and communicate this effectively so that the child feels the empathy from the therapist.

6. *A Variety of Nonspecific Variables.* Play is probably not critical for a number of nonspecific variables, including expectations of change, awareness of parental concern, or no longer feeling so alone; yet, because play

is so much a part of the therapist–child interaction, it does have a role in the manifestation of these variables.

Freedheim and Russ (1983, 1992) state that different types of child therapy with different populations of children emphasize different mechanisms of change and different techniques. For example, in insight-oriented psychodynamic therapy, where the goals are conflict resolution and mastering developmental crises, insight and working through are major mechanisms of change. Major techniques consist of verbal labeling of feelings, impulses, and conflicts, and interpretation of causes of behavior. Forbidden wishes and thoughts would be expressed in play and would be worked through in play. Major mechanisms of change in this type of therapy would be insight, working through, catharsis, and corrective emotional experiencing. Insight-oriented therapy would be most appropriate for the internalizing disorders such as anxiety and depression (Tuma & Russ, 1993). Tuma and Russ pointed out that this approach is also appropriate for children with good inner resources who have experienced a specific trauma. For example, Altschul (1988) described the use of insight-oriented approaches in helping children mourn the loss of a parent.

More supportive therapy approaches would focus on helping the child develop problem-solving skills and coping strategies. The externalizing disorders such as characterological problems and impulse control problems are more amenable to supportive approaches that focus on corrective emotional experiences and teaching or modeling problem-solving strategies. Gil (1991) and Knell (1994) give good examples of using modeling in a play therapy situation.

Structure-building therapy approaches focus on children with structural deficits and problems in developing good object relations, such as borderline psychotic children (Tuma & Russ, 1993). Empathy is a more important intervention technique than interpretation, as are supportive techniques that "shore up" defenses (Chethik, 1989). Empathy around the empathic failure of the parents is especially important (Kohut & Wolfe, 1978). Much of the change occurs through the relationship with the therapist, who becomes a stable internal object. Play with these children frequently is used to express raw, drive-laden impulses that need to be integrated. Play can also be used to help the child differentiate between fantasy and reality.

Freedheim and Russ (1992) point out that in psychodynamic and client-centered approaches, all six mechanisms of change occur in all types of individual therapy with children. However, different mechanisms and techniques should be emphasized with different types of children and problems for optimal change to result.

2.2. Contemporary Focused Play-Therapy Approaches

Freedheim and Russ (1992) have pointed out that as child psycho-therapy research is becoming more specific, so child psychotherapy practice is becoming more specific. This is true in the play area as well.

Chethik (1989) described "focal therapy" as therapy that focuses on a specific problem and is of short duration. Play is frequently used in this therapy. Focal stress events such as death in the family, divorce, hospitalization, or illness are examples of problems that would be dealt with. Chethik stated that focal therapy is effective when the child has accomplished normal developmental tasks before the stressful event occurs.

Mann and McDermott (1983) discussed play therapy with abused and neglected children. Often, these children must be taught how to play. Gil (1991) has a good review and discussion of post-traumatic play. An active approach in which she brings in outside material and events is often necessary.

D. Singer (1993) described the active use of modeling, imagery techniques, and teaching adaptive skills within the play therapy context. Along with traditional play therapy techniques, she utilizes imagery techniques that help the child visualize people, conflicts, and resolutions. She also incorporates behavior modification techniques that reinforce positive behavior and lead to self-reward.

Knell (1994) presents an overview and a variety of case examples of cognitive-behavioral approaches in play therapy. She states that cognitive-behavioral play therapy differs from traditional play therapy in that it is more goal oriented, the play is used to teach skills and alternative behaviors, the therapist is more active in making interpretations and connections, and there is more use of praise. The therapist makes active use of modeling and shaping techniques.

The road map for therapeutic change has come mainly from the clinical and theoretical literature. There is little *direct* empirical support for these intervention strategies and the use of play in psychotherapy. However, there is a strong empirical base in the children's play literature about the role of play in child development.

3. Play and the Developmental Process

Why is play thought to help in psychotherapy? We can get some clues if we ask a different question: What are the correlates of play in normal child development? There is a large body of research on this question. Children's play is related to a number of cognitive and affective processes and there is evidence that play facilitates cognitive and emotional development. Major reviews of these areas can be found in J. Singer and D. Singer (1990) and Russ (1993).

3.1. Play and Cognitive Processes

J. Singer and D. Singer (1990) suggested areas of cognitive development that are facilitated by pretend play activities. Play helps the child to (a) expand vocabulary and link objects with actions, (b) develop object constancy, (c) form event schemas and scripts, (d) learn strategies for problem solving, (e) develop divergent thinking ability, and (f) develop flexibility in shifting between different types of thoughts (narrative and logical). In a review of the literature in 1976, J. Singer and D. Singer concluded that the capacity for pretend play is positively related to verbal fluency, divergent thinking, and general cognitive functioning. Saltz, Dixon and Johnson (1977) found that fantasy play facilitated cognitive functioning on a variety of measures.

Smilanksy (1986) carried out a well-designed study with culturally disadvantaged kindergarten children and found that children who engage in sociodramatic play show significant cognitive improvement when compared to other children who do not. There were several experimental groups, each receiving the same amount of intervention time. Group A was taught how to better understand their observations and experiences. Group B was taught play skills. Group C combined techniques of Groups A and B. There were two matched control groups who received no intervention. All experimental groups received the intervention for 1½ hours a day, 5 days a week, for 9 weeks. In the play groups, the teachers were very active in that they commented on the children's play, worked on specific weak areas in the children's play, made suggestions, and gave demonstrations. After treatment, there was significant improvement in children who were taught to play—that is, in both groups B and C.

3.2. Play and Creativity

Play has been found to facilitate divergent thinking in preschool children (Dansky, 1980; Dansky & Silverman, 1973). Divergent thinking is thinking that "goes off in different directions" and has been found to be an important component of the creative process (Guilford, 1959). A typical question on a divergent thinking test would be "How many uses for a newspaper can you think of?" A good divergent thinker can generate a variety of solutions to a problem or associations to a word.

In the Dansky and Silverman (1973) study, children who had opportunities to play with a variety of objects gave significantly more uses for those objects than did control subjects. In a more refined study in 1980, Dansky found that make-believe play was the mediator of the relationship between play and divergent thinking. Free play enhanced divergent thinking, but only for children who engaged in make-believe play.

A number of correlational studies have found a relationship between play and divergent thinking. D. Singer and Rummo (1973) found a relationship between playfulness and creativity in kindergarten boys. Lieberman (1977) found a relationship between "playfulness" and divergent thinking. She was looking at affective dimensions of spontaneity and joy in play. Russ and Grossman-McKee (1990) found a significant relationship between the amount of affect in play and the quality of fantasy in play and divergent thinking in first- and second-grade children, independent of intelligence. This finding was replicated in a different sample of children by Russ and Peterson (1990; Russ, 1993).

The study of the relationship between play and creativity is a good example of how focused and specific the research needs to be to really learn about play and change in the child. As Russ (1993) pointed out, creativity, fantasy, and play areas are especially important because of the cognitive-affective links that can be investigated. Because both cognitive and affective process are involved in creativity and in play, both kinds of processes must be investigated in this research.

For the most part, the play and creativity research has focused on cognitive processes. Dansky's hypothesis that make-believe play will facilitate divergent thinking was based on the concept that the free combination of objects and symbolic transformations involved in make-believe play helped to loosen old associations. Sutton-Smith (1966) has also speculated that play provides an opportunity to develop new combinations of ideas and new associations for old objects. Kogan (1983) suggested that in play the child searches for alternate modes of relating to the object, a process similar to searching for alternate uses for objects in divergent thinking tasks. Kogan (1983) and Wallach (1970) have postulated the importance of breadth-of-attention deployment as an underlying variable in divergent thinking. Breadth-of-attention deployment involves a scanning of memory and the environment in an associational manner. Fantasy activity in play and divergent thinking both may share this variable. Thus, the two major cognitive processes proposed as mediating variables between play and creative problem solving have been breadth-of-attention deployment and the capacity to form new combinations of ideas.

There has been little attention given to affective processes that may account for the play–creativity link. One of the main reasons for this lack of attention has been the lack of valid, standardized measures of affective expression in children's play. To investigate the area of affect in play and creativity, the author developed the Affect in Play Scale (Russ, 1987, Russ, 1993), which measures various dimensions of affect in play in a standardized puppet-play situation. In two studies, children who expressed more affect in play and a greater variety of affect categories were more creative on divergent thinking tasks, independent of IQ (Russ & Grossman-McKee, 1990; Russ & Peterson, 1990; see Russ, 1993). These results are consistent with those of Lieberman (1977), who found that "playfulness" which included affective components of spontaneity and joy was related to divergent thinking in children. The theoretical basis for expecting a relationship between affect and creativity was that access to a wide range of affect and affect-laden thoughts would increase the associative network and broaden the range of associations. Experimental studies with adults by Isen, Daubman, and Nowicki (1987) found that inducing positive affect states in adults facilitated creative problem solving. Greene and Noice (1988) found similar results with eighth-grade children. Play may be one real-life example of self-induced affective states. Russ (1993) has proposed that the expression of affect states in play and the expression of affect-laden thoughts in play are the two major affective dimensions that account for the relationship between play and creativity. These affective dimensions facilitate breadth-of-attention deployment and the recombination of old ideas in new forms. Affective processes and cognitive processes interact in play and creativity.

Russ (1993, p. 59) reached the following conclusions from the play, affect, and creativity literature about how play aids in the development of creative thinking ability. Play helps the child to achieve the following:

1. Express affect and develop the ability to experience and express emotions as they arise.
2. Express and think about affect themes. Affect-laden content is permitted to surface and be expressed through play. Over time, the child develops access to a variety of memories, associations, and affective and nonaffective cognition. This broad repertoire of associations helps in creative problem solving.
3. Resolve conflicts and master the many traumas of daily life. The child is freer to have access to a variety of affect states. Affective content does not get repressed and become unavailable.
4. Develop cognitive structure that enables the child to contain and modulate affect. Future stressors can then be more easily handled.
5. Experience positive affect, which is part of the play experience. Positive affect is important in creativity.

6. Practice with the free flow of associations that is part of divergent thinking.

3.3. Play and Adjustment

Although there is much theory and clinical observation that play and adjustment are related, there is little empirical work to support this contention. There is some evidence that play is related to adjustment, however. Singer and Singer (1976), for example, found that children who are less imaginative in play are more aggressive. J. Singer and D. Singer (1990) concluded that imaginative play in children is related to academic adjustment and flexibility of thought. They also found that toddlers and preschoolers who engage in make-believe play are better adjusted across different situations. Burnstein and Meichenbaum (1979) found that children who voluntarily played with stress-related toys prior to surgery demonstrated less distress and anxiety following surgery than children who avoided the toys. One might speculate that those children were accustomed to using play to deal with stress and problems. In a study of 4- to 11-year-olds, Kenealy (1989) investigated strategies that children use when they are feeling depressed and found that 50% of the children's responses included play strategies. Also, indirectly, if play facilitates flexible problem solving, there is evidence that flexible problem solving, in turn, aids the coping process (Follick & Turk, 1978).

In a study of urban children from 4- to 5-years of age, Rosenberg (1984) found that the quality of fantasy play for children playing in dyads was positively related to measures of social competence and ego resilience (Block-Q sort). Frequency of positive themes and relationship themes in the play was also related to ego resilience and social competence. In general, children with behavior problems and attachment problems had fewer positive and negative themes in play, with the exception of diffuse hostility.

Grossman-McKee (1990) found, using the Affect in Play Scale with first- and second-grade boys, that boys who expressed more affect in play had fewer pain complaints than boys with less affect in play. Good players were also less anxious on the State-Trait Anxiety Inventory for Children (Spielberger, 1973). Peterson (1989) found that affect in play and quality of fantasy in play were predictive of self-esteem in children over a 1-year period.

In a study of 7- to 9-year-olds, Christiano (1994) found a positive relationship between play and coping, and a negative relationship between play and distress. Children who were "good" players on the Affect in Play Scale implemented a greater number and variety of cognitive coping strategies (correlations ranged from .52 to .55) during an invasive dental procedure. In addition, good players reported less distress during the procedure than children who expressed less affect and fantasy in their play.

The research programs on children's play and the development of cognitive and affective processes have not had a direct impact on the use of play in psychotherapy. Many of these play and cognitive-affective links are probably at work in child psychotherapy, although not in a systematic fashion. Before discussing implications for the future, we need to review psychotherapy-outcome and play-intervention research more specifically.

4. Psychotherapy Outcome Research

Global child psychotherapy outcome studies have not focused specifically on play. However, since play is so frequently a part of child therapy we can glean something from the results of these studies. Also, the directives from leaders in the field for future research programs are clear. What follows is a brief review of this literature. For complete reviews, see Hartmann, Roper, and Gelfand, 1977; Barrett, Hampe, and Miller, 1978; Kazdin, 1990; and Weisz and Weiss, 1993.

In general, the early reviews of child therapy outcome studies concluded that there was little or no support for child therapy. More recent work has concluded that there is support for the effectiveness of child psychotherapy if the research is well designed.

A classic early review by Levitt (1957) concluded that the mean improvement rate for children was not significantly better than the baseline improvement rate of 72.5% for untreated controls. In later work, in a review of 47 reports of outcome studies, Levitt (1963, 1971) concluded that approximately two-thirds of treated children in therapy were improved, but again treated children were no better off than untreated controls. Levitt's conclusions were taken seriously by the field of child psychotherapy.

A number of researchers responded to Levitt's conclusions (Halpern, 1968; Heinicke & Goldman, 1960; Hood-Williams, 1960). One of the major methodological issues was that so many of the untreated controls were defectors from treatment. Defectors were children who were evaluated and recommended for treatment but who had not entered treatment. Therefore, there may have been a number of confounding variables operating here, to account for the results.

Barrett et al. (1977) and Hartmann et al. (1978) took a closer look at Levitt's reviews and at the research literature in general. They concluded that there was still no solid empirical evidence for the effectiveness of psychotherapy. Barrett et al. (1978) stated that the global nature of the research was a major problem and concluded that most of the research studies were not specific enough or focused enough to enable research questions to be answered. There was too much of a mix of populations, therapeutic approaches, and interventions in these studies. Often, the outcome measures were unrefined or nonexistent. This led to their often quoted conclusion that the question in psychotherapy research should not be "Does psychotherapy work?" but rather "Which set of procedures is effective when applied to what kinds of patients with which sets of problems and practiced by which sorts of therapists?" (p. 428)

Heinicke and Strassman (1975) also called for specificity in child therapy research as well as for theoretical validity, and along with Bergin and Lambert (1978) stressed that the measures should be theoretically linked to the clinical problem and to the group being investigated.

A number of other methodological issues important for research in the child therapy area have been identified: the importance of classification according to developmental level (Heinicke & Strassman, 1975); controlling for maturational effects (Koocher & Broskowski, 1977); the need for homogeneous treatment groups (Achenbach, 1978; Hartmann et al., 1977); the need to control for sex and age variables (Cass & Thomas, 1979); and the need for adequate outcome measures given at appropriate intervals (Kazdin, 1990, 1993b).

The field of child therapy research has taken to heart these research guidelines and the research studies have become more focused and methodologically sophisticated. In addition, the technique of meta-analysis has enabled the field to do a more systematic evaluation of outcome studies. As Weisz and Weiss (1993) described it, meta-analysis is a technique that enables the pooling and statistical summarizing of the results of outcome studies. The effect size (ES) is the statistical summary of the treatment efficacy across studies. Use of this systematic procedure helps avoid reviewer subjectivity in coming to conclusions.

Weisz and Weiss (1993) reviewed the major meta-analytic studies in the field of child psychotherapy. Casey and Berman (1985) calculated the effect of psychotherapy across 64 studies and found a mean effect size of 0.71. A slightly higher effect size of 0.79 was found by Weisz, Weiss, Alicke, and Klotz (1987) in a review of 163 treatment-control comparisons. Both studies concluded that the average treated child functioned better after treatment than three-fourths of the untreated controls. In the Casey and Berman review, effect sizes did not differ as a function of whether play was used. In a recent meta-analyses by Kazdin, Bass, Ayers, and Rodgers (1990), for 64 studies involving treatment versus no-treatment comparisons, the mean effect size was 0.88. Weisz and Weiss (1993) concluded that "the mean effect sizes reported in child meta-analyses are quite comparable to those of adult meta-analyses and that findings in both categories point to quite positive effects of therapy" (p. 46).

As Kazdin (1990) has pointed out, the results of these meta-analyses have contributed to the field in that they offer evidence that psychotherapy is more effective than no treatment with children. This conclusion is, of course, more encouraging than the conclusions based on the reviews in the 1950s, 1960s and 1970s. Although these child therapy outcome studies did not focus on play *per se*, one might infer that play is an effective form of treatment since it is so frequently part of the therapy process. The Casey and Berman (1985) review found no difference in effectiveness between those studies stating that they used play and those that did not. These studies do not tell us anything about why and how play helps facilitate change, however.

Weisz and Weiss (1989, 1993) pointed out that most of the research studies in the meta-analyses involved controlled laboratory interventions. In many of these studies children were recruited for treatment and were not clinic-referred; samples were homogeneous; there was a focal problem; therapy focused on the target problem; therapists were trained in the specific treatment approaches to be used; and the therapy relied primarily on those techniques. In essence, this was good research that followed many of the methodological guidelines for adequate research design. On the other hand, Weisz and Weiss (1993) cautioned that the evidence for the effectiveness of psychotherapy is based on studies that are not typical of conventional clinical practice. Thus, the findings may not be generalizable to real clinical work. However, Weisz and Weiss (1989) made the important point that the control and precision of therapy for research purposes may be needed in clinical practice. Freedheim and Russ (1992) recommended that we need to begin to build bridges between research efforts and everyday treatment approaches.

4.1. The Need for Focus and Specificity

Kazdin (1993a,b) has called for systematic research on specific processes in child psychotherapy. This directive builds on the growing consensus in the literature that focus and specificity are essential if we are going to learn about how to effect change in different populations of children. Researchers in the child (Barrett et al., 1978; Hartmann et al., 1972; Heinicke and Straussman, 1975) and adult literature (Bergin & Strupp, 1972; Bergin & Lambert, 1978; Frank, 1979; Kiesler, 1966) have recognized the need to investigate specific mechanisms that effect specific variables in the individual. The results of the meta-analyses also point to the need for specificity. Weisz (1993) concluded that the studies showing positive results tend to be those that "zoom in" on a specific problem with careful planning of the intervention. Freedheim and Russ stated in 1983, and again in 1992, that we need to become very specific and ask: "Which specific interventions affect which specific cognitive, personality, and affective processes? How are these processes related to behavior and practical clinical criteria?" (1983, p. 988). It is only by asking these specific questions that we will be able to identify which interventions facilitate the development of specific cognitive and affective processes and which do not.

In a review of the play therapy research, Phillips (1985) also called for a systematic program of research with well-controlled studies. He concluded that the play therapy research that found positive results were those studies of a cognitive-behavioral nature that were carefully designed. Phillips speculated that the specificity of treatment goals and focused methods of the cognitive-behavioral studies partially account for the positive results. He recommended that all forms of play therapy be investigated with the precision of the cognitive-behavioral studies. In general, there are not many play therapy studies in the literature and little exploration of variables that leads to change (Faust & Burns, 1991).

It should be relatively easy to apply the principles of specificity and focus to the play area. Play interventions and the cognitive and affective processes that they effect can be broken down into discrete units in controlled conditions. The large body of research in the play and child development literature offers a wealth of ideas and research lines that could be followed. Recently, measures of play and play processes have been developed and are being validated (Schaeffer, Gitlin, & Sandgrund, 1991). The basis on which to build a systematic research program is available.

One small body of research that has begun to apply these principles is the play intervention research.

5. Play Intervention Research

Some studies exist that have investigated the effect of play on specific types of problems, or in specific populations. These studies are a good bridge between empirical laboratory studies of play and specific processes, like creativity, and more global clinical practice outcome studies. These studies are labeled play intervention rather than play therapy, because the focus is highly specific. Usually, they involve only a few sessions with no emphasis on forming a "relationship" with a therapist. On the other hand, these studies differ from specific process research in child development in that they are problem focused and are not as fine-tuned as they would be in laboratory research. These play intervention research studies seem to fit some of Weisz and Weiss's (1993) criteria by including children who were not clinic-referred, by having homogeneous samples, and by having a focal problem that the therapy focused on.

Phillips (1985) reviewed two studies that would fall into this play intervention research category. Both involved the use of puppet play to reduce anxiety in children facing surgery. Johnson and Stockdale (1975) measured Palmer Sweat Index level before and after surgery. Puppet play in this study involved playing out the surgery. Johnson and Stockdale found less anxiety for the puppet-play group before and after surgery. The one exception was immediately before surgery, when the increased information may have elevated their anxiety. Cassell (1965) used puppets with children undergoing cardiac catheterization and found that anxiety was reduced before surgery for the puppet-play group compared with the no treatment control. There were no differences after surgery. The treatment group was less disturbed during the cardiac catheterization and expressed more willingness to return to the hospital for further treatment. Although the results are encouraging, there are several methodological limitations in this study. First, the control group received no intervention or contact whatsoever, so that a number of variables, such as contact with a friendly adult, were not controlled. Second, the play intervention included a great deal of information-giving about the procedure. The play setting consisted of situation-appropriate puppets and equipment (doctors, parents, stethoscope) with an active therapist who played the cardiologist and demonstrated the procedure. Thus, it is impossible to tease out which aspect of the intervention—play, verbal support, or information-giving—accounted for the results.

In a study that did attempt to separate out play from verbal support, Rae, Worchel, Upchurch, Sanner and Dainiel (1989) investigated the effects of play on the adjustment of 46 children hospitalized for acute illness. Children were randomly assigned to 1 of 4 experimental groups:

- A therapeutic play condition in which the child was encouraged to play with medical and nonmedical materials. Verbal support, reflection, and interpretation of feelings were expressed by the research assistant.
- A diversionary play condition in which children were allowed to play with toys but fantasy play was discouraged. The toys provided did not facilitate fantasy, nor did the research assistant.
- A verbally oriented support condition in which children were en-

couraged to talk about feelings and anxieties. The research assistant was directive in bringing up related topics and would ask about procedures.

* A control condition in which the research assistant had no contact with the child.

All treatment conditions consisted of two 30-minute sessions. The main result of this study was that children in the therapeutic play group showed significantly more reduction in self-reported hospital-related fears than children in the other 3 groups. There were no differences among the groups for parent ratings.

Another specific problem area that lends itself to focused intervention research is that of separation anxiety. In an excellent example of a well-designed play intervention study, Milos and Reiss (1982) used play therapy for preschoolers who were dealing with separation anxiety. They identified 64 children who were rated as high-separation-anxiety children by their teachers. The children were randomly assigned to 1 of 4 groups. Three play groups were theme related: the free-play group had appropriate toys; the directed-play group had the scene set with a mother doll bringing the child to school; the modeling group had the experimenter playing out a separation scene. A control group also used play with toys irrelevant to separation themes (blocks, puzzles, crayons). All children received three individual 10-minute play sessions on different days. Quality of play was rated. The results showed that all three thematic play conditions were effective in reducing anxiety around separation themes when compared to the control group. An interesting finding was that, when the free-play and directed-play groups were combined, the quality of play ratings were significantly negatively related ($r = -.37$) to a posttest anxiety measure. High-quality play was defined as play that showed more separation themes and attempts to resolve conflicts. One might speculate that the children who were already good players used the intervention to master their separation anxiety. Milos and Reiss concluded that their results support the underlying assumption of play therapy, that play can reduce anxiety associated with psychological problems. The finding that quality of play was related to effectiveness of the intervention is consistent with the finding of Dansky (1980) that free play facilitated creativity only for those children who used make-believe well.

A well-designed study by Barnett (1984) also looked at separation anxiety and expanded upon work by Barnett and Storm (1981) in which free play was found to reduce distress in children following a conflict situation. In the 1984 study, a natural stressor, the first day of school, was used. Seventy-four preschool children were observed separating from their mothers and were rated anxious or nonanxious. These two groups were further divided into play or no-play conditions. The play condition was a free play condition. The no-play condition was a story-listening condition. For half of the play condition, play was solitary. For the other half, peers were present. The story condition was also split into solitary and peers present segments. Play was rated by observers and categorized in terms of types of play. Play significantly reduced anxiety in the high-anxious group. Anxiety was measured by the Palmer Sweat Index. There was no effect for low-anxious children. For the anxious children, solitary play was best in reducing anxiety. High-anxious children spent more time in fantasy play than did low-anxious children, who showed more functional and manipulative play. They engaged more in fantasy play when no other children were present. Barnett interprets these results to mean that play is used to cope with a distressing situation. The findings support the idea that it is not social play that is essential to conflict resolution, but rather imaginative play qualities that the child introduces into playful behavior. Actually, the presence of peers increased anxiety in the high-anxious group.

These play intervention studies are a few examples of the kind of studies that tell us about how play can be helpful in dealing with specific problems. The results of these studies suggest that play helps children deal with fears and reduce anxiety and that something about play itself is important and serves as a vehicle for change. The play experience is separate from the experience of a supportive and empathic adult. Results also suggest that children who are already good players are more able to use play opportunities to resolve problems when these opportunities arise. Teaching children good play skills would provide children with a resource for future coping.

6. Future Directions in Play Research

Based upon the work to date in the field of play psychotherapy, the following types of research programs emerge as most likely to advance the field:

1. *Specific-Processes Research on Play and Cognitive/Affective Processes.* Continuing the more traditional play in child development research is also essential. Concurrent, longitudinal, and experimental studies on specific dimensions of play and specific cognitive, affective, and personality processes need to be carried out in a systematic fashion. For example, in the play, affect, and creativity area, the most important research questions as articulated by Russ (1993), p. 106, are as follows:

- What are the different affective dimensions involved in the creative process? Russ (1993) proposed five affective dimensions important in the creative process: openness to affect states; access to affect-laden themes in fantasy; pleasure in challenge; pleasure in problem solving; and overall cognitive integration of affect. Do these different dimensions have different kinds of effects on cognitive creative processes?
- Do affective processes make a unique contribution to creativity or are they simply reflective of cognitive fantasy skills?
- Do different categories of affect content (sadness, happiness, aggression) have differential effects on creativity?
- Are there gender differences for the effect of different kinds of affect content and affect processes on creativity?
- Can we begin to break down divergent-thinking tasks and cognitive set-breaking tasks into more specific components so we can zero in on exactly where affective processes have their affect?
- When is a mood-induction approach the better research paradigm for investigating affect and creativity and when is affect in a play situation the better research paradigm?
- What are the developmental properties of affective processes important in creativity? Is there an element of heritability?
- What are the dimensions of play that are most related to and most facilitate creativity?
- Is play predictive of creativity over time?

Research at the "micro" level is necessary in investigating these processes.

2. *Focused-Play Intervention Research.* We need to develop a body of studies that focus on different aspects of play intervention. There could be different types of play-intervention research.

a. *Specific Play Interventions with Specific Populations and Specific Situations.* The Barnett (1984) study with children who were experiencing the first day of school is a good example of this type of study. We need more of this type of study. There are a variety of natural stressors that could be used to investigate play intervention. Divorce, natural disasters, dental visits, presurgery, and loss of a parent are all situations in which play therapy is used. We need to develop an empirical base for play intervention in these situations.

b. *Refining Specific Play Techniques.* The general question of what kinds of intervention by the therapist best facilitate play needs to be studied empirically. There are many guidelines in the clinical literature about how to facilitate play, but few are based on empirical work. How do we best encourage affect in play? When is modeling more effective than a less directive approach? When is it less effective? For example, Gil (1991) pointed out that it is frequently important with sexually abused children to be nondirective, so that the child does not feel intruded upon. What kinds of intervention most enhance the working-through process and conflict resolution? These kinds of research questions can be posed in well-controlled experimental studies and in psychotherapy-process research.

  c. *Research with Play Intervention Modules.* Kazdin (1993a) discussed the possibility of having different modules of intervention for different problems. Children with multiple problems might have different modules of intervention at different times. This concept is an intriguing one for the play area. We could develop 6- to 12-week play modules with different foci for different types of problems. Constricted children might benefit from play directed at increasing affective expression. Children who recently experienced trauma might benefit from the opportunity to play-out the issues in a focused approach. Impulse-ridden children might benefit from a play module focused on helping them to regulate affect. One of my students has suggested the idea of play profiles (D'Angelo, personal communication, September, 1993). If we could develop play profiles for children that are predictive of meaningful clinical criteria, then we could develop interventions for those children that would alter their profiles. D'Angelo is currently carrying out a study investigating play profiles of internalizers and externalizers, using Achenbach's Child Behavior Checklist (Achenbach & Edelbrock, 1983).

  3. *Quasi-Experimental Studies in Clinical Practice.* A recent article by Kazdin (1993b), "Evaluation in Clinical Practice: Clinically Sensitive and Systematic Methods of Treatment Delivery," outlines numerous research issues in carrying out systematic assessment and evaluation in clinical practice. Kazdin's main point here and elsewhere (1993a) is that we need to attempt to integrate assessment and evaluation and single-case design wherever possible in clinical practice, in spite of the fact that controlled laboratory conditions cannot be achieved. He states that the primary goal of clinical research is to isolate variables to test hypotheses, whereas the primary goal of clinical practice is to manage and treat the individual case. Systematic assessment and evaluation can be integrated into a single-case research design. Kazdin stresses the importance of ongoing assessment

and repeated measurement over time. Even though single-case designs have been used most frequently to evaluate behavioral interventions, Kazdin points out that this approach is appropriate for other intervention approaches. It would be quite applicable to play psychotherapy.

4. *Systematic Integration of All Types of Play Research and Clinical Practice.* On a policy level, we need to find ways to support the types of research programs outlined above and integrate them with clinical practice. These studies are "do-able," the concepts are measurable, and we need to find the policies and mechanisms that foster these research programs. Integrating these research programs is a long-term strategy. It is one that we will have to do, given the increasing need for "effectiveness and efficiency" demanded by third-party payers (Koocher & D'Angelo, 1992). This is consistent with Ross's (1981) call for the need to develop a programmatic series of "interrelated consecutive and simultaneous" studies that are both methodologically rigorous and clinically relevant. He stressed the importance of having a closer relationship between the clinic and the laboratory, with a reciprocal relationship between the clinical case study and the experiment.

5. *Research on the Measurement of Play.* To carry out assessment in the play therapy situation, or in any study investigating play, reliable, valid, and standardized measures of play are essential. More research programs that develop measures of different components of play are necessary. For a review of a number of play measures that are available, see Schaeffer et al. (1991). Until recently, there were very few instruments available.

Most researchers developed their own play observation instruments. J. Singer (1973) and J. Singer and D. Singer (1981, 1990) have developed a number of measures of children's play, especially focusing on the fantasy and imagination components. Howe and Silvern (1981) developed a Play Therapy Observation Instrument. Milos and Reiss (1982) developed a measure for rating separation themes in play. Most of the measures have not assessed affect in play. In fact, the lack of adequate measures of affective processes has been one of the reasons that cognitive processes, not affective processes, have been the focus of play research. Rubin, Fein, and Vandenberg (1983) described this phenomenon as the "cognification" of play.

In order to study affect in play and creativity, Russ (1987, 1993) and her students developed the Affect in Play Scale. This scale consists of a standardized puppet-play task and criteria for a rating scale. The play task utilizes two neutral-looking puppets, one boy and one girl, and three small blocks that are laid out on a table. It is administered individually to the child. The play task is appropriate for children from 5- to 10 years of age.

The instructions ask the child to play with the puppets any way they like for 5 minutes. The play is videotaped. The instructions can be altered to pull for specific affective themes such as aggression or happiness. An extensive manual has been developed for rating the play. The Affect in Play Scale measures the amount of affect, type of affect, variety of affect, intensity of affect, comfort, quality of fantasy, imagination, and affective integration in the play. There are 11 possible affective categories: Happiness/Pleasure, Anxiety/Fear, Sadness/Hurt, Frustration/Displeasure, Nurturance/Affection, Aggression, Orality, Oral Aggression, Anality, Sexuality, and Competition. Any verbal or physical expression between the puppets that reflects an affective category is rated as one affective unit. For example, if one puppet says to the other "I don't like you," it would be scored for one unit of aggressive content.

The Affect in Play Scale has good interrater reliability, internal consistency, and good stability of scores across different populations. It also has a growing body of validity studies. A review of the Affect in Play Scale and the manual can be found in Russ (1993). This scale could be used as a measure of change in play intervention research and in play psychotherapy.

7. Implications of Research for Current Clinical Practice

The gap between play research and implications for clinical practice is indeed wide. There are a few broad implications that emerge from this review.

1. Build in assessment and evaluation of the play process and the child as much as possible in therapy. This is a repeat of Kazdin's (1993b) recommendation for research, but the two go hand in hand. Even though at times it is inconvenient, we need to start carrying out single-case studies in our clinical work.

2. Decide how play will be used before beginning to work with the child. The use of play should be tied to the treatment goals. The mechanisms of change in the therapy should be conceptualized before therapy begins. Developing a kind of play profile during the assessment process should aid in this endeavor. This could be done with a play-assessment instrument or by the observation of an experienced child clinician during a play session.

3. Be focused and active. As the research has shown, those studies that have therapists targeting specific problems in a focused way have the highest likelihood of demonstrating the efficacy of treat-

ment. In order to be focused and active, the therapist must understand the child's play. Gaining experience in working with a variety of children in a variety of play situations is important.

8. Play and the Future

As we develop a more solid empirical base for the importance of play in child development, we need to think broadly and flexibly about how play interventions can be carried out. One needs to think about the integration of play into innovative service-delivery models. Culbertson (1993) outlined the changes in populations and the problems that must be addressed in intervention programs for the future. She stressed the need to prepare for culturally diverse populations that include ethnic minorities, an increase in children of poverty, and immigrant populations. She stated that "the field of clinical child psychology needs more models for alternative approaches to treatment that can be effective despite the presence of factors that makes treatment difficult" (p. 119). Clinical services must be more tailored to these underserved populations, must be community based, and must include a variety of coordinated and integrated services. What is the role of play therapy or more specific play interventions in this picture? Because play interventions have been found to be effective by clinicians and because there is a growing empirical base for the importance of play in child development, we need to develop innovative ways of using play in a variety of intervention approaches. We need to experiment with a variety of approaches and evaluate their effectiveness.

Play Centers in schools might be one way to reach large numbers of children (Russ, 1993). Adults who are able to teach play skills and guide the play would help facilitate play. Smilansky (1986) has demonstrated that play skills can effectively be taught to children by teachers in a relatively short time. More training groups for parents on how to help children play at home would also be worthwhile. Play preparation for procedures in hospital settings might become a regular occurrence. Teaching children to use play as a major coping resource might be a trend of the future.

In the present, at the recent Tenth Annual International Play Therapy Conference (October, 1993), it was evident from the presentations that play interventions are being used with a variety of populations having a variety of problems. There were presentations on play therapy with homeless children, children who experienced Hurricane Andrew, children of addicted families, foster children, and urban, disadvantaged ethnic-minority children. The field is experimenting with innovative approaches and it is our hope that the empirical base will come. There is a tremendous opportunity now to integrate research and practice so that we can learn how play helps children develop and how we can help children play.

9. References

Achenbach, T. (1978). Psychopathology of childhood: Research problems and issues. *Journal of Consulting and Clinical Psychology, 46*, 759–776.

Achenbach, T., & Edelbrock, L. S. (1983). *Manual for the Child Behavior Checklist and Revised Child Behavior Profile.* Burlington, VT: University of Vermont, Department of Psychiatry.

Altschul, S. (1988). *Childhood bereavement and its aftermath.* Madison, WI: International University Press.

Applebaum, S. (1978). Pathways to change in psychoanalytic therapy. *Bulletin of the Menninger Clinic, 42*, 239–251.

Axline, V. (1947). *Play therapy.* Boston: Houghton Mifflin.

Barnett, L. (1984). Research note: Young children's resolution of distress through play. *Journal of Child Psychology and Psychiatry, 25*, 477–483.

Barnett, L., & Storm, B. (1981). Play, pleasure and pain: The reduction of anxiety through play. *Leisure Science, 4*, 161–175.

Barrett, C., Hampe, T. E., & Miller, L. (1978). Research on child psychotherapy. In S. Garfield & A. Bergin (Eds.), *Handbook of psychotherapy and behavior change* (pp. 411–435). New York: Wiley.

Bergin, A., & Lambert, M. (1978). The evaluation of therapeutic outcome. In S. Garfield & A. Bergin (Eds.), *Handbook of psychotherapy and behavior change* (pp. 139–189). New York: Wiley.

Bergin, A., & Strupp, H. (1972). *Changing frontiers in science of psychotherapy.* Chicago: Aldine-Atherton.

Burstein, S., & Meichenbaum, D. (1979). The work of worrying in children undergoing surgery. *Journal of Abnormal Child Psychology, 7*, 121–132.

Casey, R. J., & Berman, J. S. (1985). The outcome of psychotherapy with children. *Psychological Bulletin, 98*, 388–400.

Cass, L., & Thomas, C. (1979). *Childhood pathology and later adjustment.* New York: Wiley.

Cassell, S. (1965). Effect of brief puppet therapy upon the emotional responses of children undergoing cardiac catheterization. *Journal of Consulting Psychology, 29*, 1–8.

Chethik, M. (1989). *Techniques of child therapy: Psychodynamic strategies.* New York: Guilford.

Christiano, B. (1994). Play as a predictor of coping and distress during an invasive dental procedure. Unpublished master's thesis, Case Western Reserve University, Cleveland, OH.

Culbertson, J. (1993). Clinical child psychology in the 1990s: Broadening our scope. *Journal of Clinical Child Psychology, 22*, 116–122.

Dansky, J. (1980). Make-believe: A mediator of the relationship between play and associative fluency. *Child Development, 51*, 576–579.

Dansky, J., & Silverman, F. (1973). Effects of play on associative fluency in preschool-aged children. *Developmental Psychology, 9*, 38–43.

Erikson, E. N. (1963). *Childhood and Society.* New York: Norton.

Faust, J., & Burns, W. (1991). Coding therapist and child interaction: Progress and outcome in play therapy. In C. Schaefer, K. Gitlin, & A. Sandgrund (Eds.), *Play diagnosis and assessment* (pp. 663–689). New York: Wiley.

Follick, M., & Turk, D. (1978). *Problem specification by ostomy patients.* Paper presented at the 12th Annual Convention for the Advancement of Behavior Therapy. Chicago, IL.

Frank, J. (1979). The present status of outcome studies. *Journal of Consulting and Clinical Psychology, 47,* 310–316.

Freedheim, D. K., & Russ, S. W. (1983). Psychotherapy with children. In C. E. Walker & M. C. Roberts (Eds.), *Handbook of clinical child psychology* (pp. 978–994). New York: Wiley.

Freedheim, D. K., & Russ, S. W. (1992). Psychotherapy with children. In C. E. Walker & M. C. Roberts (Eds.), *Handbook of clinical child psychology* (2nd ed.) (pp. 765–780). New York: Wiley.

Freud, A. (1965). *Normality and pathology in childhood: Assessments of development.* New York: International Universities Press.

Garfield, S. (1980). *Psychotherapy: An eclectic approach.* New York: Wiley.

Gil, E. (1991). *The healing power of play.* New York: Guilford Press.

Gilpin, D. (1976). Psychotherapy of borderline psychotic children. *American Journal of Psychotherapy, 30,* 483–496.

Greene, T., & Noice, H. (1988). Influence of positive affect upon creative thinking and problem solving in children. *Psychological Reports, 63,* 895–898.

Grossman-McKee, A. (1990). The relationship between affective expression in fantasy play and pain complaints in first and second grade children. *Dissertation Abstracts International, 50-09B,* 4219.

Guilford, J. P. (1959). *Personality.* New York: McGraw-Hill.

Halpern, W. I. (1968). Do children benefit from psychotherapy? A review of the literature on follow-up studies. *Bulletin of the Rochester Mental Health Center, 1,* 4–12.

Hartmann, D. P., Roper, B. L., & Gelfand, D. M. (1977). An evaluation of alternative modes of child psychotherapy. In B. Lahey & A. E. Kazdin (Eds.), *Advances in clinical child psychology* Vol. 1, (pp. 1–37). New York: Plenum Press.

Heinicke, C., & Goldman, A. (1960). Research on psychotherapy with children: A review and suggestions for further study. *American Journal of Orthopsychiatry, 30,* 483–494.

Heinicke, C., & Strassman, L. (1975). Toward more effective research on child psychotherapy. *Journal of Child Psychiatry, 14,* 561–588.

Hood-Williams, J. (1960). The results of psychotherapy with children. *Journal of Consulting Psychologist, 24,* 84–88.

Howe, P., & Silvern, L. (1981). Behavioral observation of children during play therapy: Preliminary development of research instrument. *Journal of Personality Assessment, 45,* 168–182.

Isen, A., Daubman, K., & Nowicki, G. (1987). Positive affect facilitates creative problem solving. *Journal of Personality and Social Psychology, 52,* 1122–1131.

Johnson, P. A., & Stockdale, D. E. (1975). Effects of puppet therapy on palmar sweating of hospitalized children. *Johns Hopkins Medical Journal, 137,* 1–5.

Kazdin, A. E. (1990). Psychotherapy for children and adolescents. In *Annual Review of Psychology,* M. R. Rosenzweig & L. W. Porter (Eds.), (Vol. 41, pp. 21–54). Palo Alto, CA: Annual Reviews, Inc.

Kazdin, A. (1993a, August). Child and adolescent psychotherapy: Models for identifying and developing effective treatments. In S. Eyberg (Chair), *Psychotherapy for children and adolescents.* Symposium conducted at the meeting of the American Psychological Association, Toronto.

Kazdin, A. (1993b). Evaluation in clinical practice: Clinically sensitive and systematic methods of treatment delivery. *Behavior Therapy, 24,* 11–45.

Kenealy, P. (1989). Children's strategies for coping with depression. *Behavior Research Therapy, 27,* 27–34.

Kessler, J. (1966). *Psychopathology of childhood.* New Jersey: Prentice-Hall.

Kessler, J. (1988). *Psychopathology of childhood.* New Jersey: Prentice-Hall.

Kiesler, D. (1966). Some myths of psychotherapy research and the search for a paradigm. *Psychological Bulletin, 65,* 110–136.

Klein, M. (1955). The psychoanalytic play technique. *American Journal of Orthopsychiatry, 25,* 223–237.

Knell, S. (1993). *Cognitive-behavioral play therapy.* Northvale, NJ: Aronson.

Kogan, N. (1983). Stylistic variation in childhood and adolescence: Creativity, metaphor, and cognitive styles. In P. Mussen (Ed.), *Handbook of child psychology,* (Vol. 3, pp. 631–706). New York: Wiley.

Kohut, H. (1977). *The restoration of the self.* New York: International Universities Press.

Kohut, H., & Wolfe, E. (1978). The disorders of the self and their treatment: An outline. *International Journal of Psychoanalysis, 59,* 413–424.

Koocher, G., & Broskowski, A. (1977). Issues in the evaluation of mental health services for children. *Professional Psychology, 8,* 583–592.

Koocher, G., & D'Angelo, E. J. (1992). Evolution of practice in child psychotherapy. In D. K. Freedheim (Ed.), *History of psychotherapy* (pp. 457–492). Washington, DC: American Psychological Association.

Lieberman, J. N. (1977). *Playfulness: Its relationship to imagination and creativity.* New York: Academic Press.

Levitt, E. E. (1957). The results of psychotherapy with children: An evaluation. *Journal of Consulting Psychology, 21,* 189–196.

Levitt, E. E. (1963). Psychotherapy with children: A further evaluation. *Behavior Research and Therapy, 1,* 45–51.

Levitt, E. E. (1971). Research in psychotherapy with children. In A. E. Bergin & S. L. Garfield (Eds.), *Handbook of psychotherapy and behavior change: An empirical analysis* (pp. 474–484). New York: Wiley.

Mahler, M. S. (1968). *On human symbiosis and the vicissitudes of individuation.* New York: International Universities Press.

Mann, E., & McDermott, J. (1983). Play therapy for victims of child abuse and neglect. In C. E. Schaefer & K. J. O'Connor (Eds.), *Handbook of play therapy* (pp. 283–307). New York: Wiley.

Milos, M., & Reiss, S. (1982). Effects of three play conditions on separation anxiety in young children. *Journal of Consulting and Clinical Psychology, 50,* 389–395.

Moustakas, C. (1953). *Children in play therapy.* New York: McGraw-Hill.

Peterson, N. (1989). *The relationship between affective expression in fantasy play and self-esteem in third-grade children.* Unpublished master's thesis, Case Western Reserve University, Cleveland, Ohio.

Phillips, R. (1985). Whistling in the dark?: A review of play therapy research. *Psychotherapy, 22,* 752–760.

Rae, W., Worchel, F., Upchurch, J., Sanner, J., & Daniel, C. (1989). The psychosocial impact of play on hospitalized children. *Journal of Pediatric Psychology, 14,* 617–627.

Rosenberg, D. (1984). *The quality and content of preschool fantasy play: Correlates in concurrent social-personality function and early mother–child attachment relationships.* Unpublished dissertation, University of Minnesota, Minneapolis.

Ross, A. O. (1981). On rigor and relevance. *Professional Psychology, 12,* 318–327.

Rubin, K., Fein, G., Vandenberg, B. (1983). Play. In P. Mussen (Ed.), *Handbook of child psychology* (Vol. 4, pp. 693–774). New York: Wiley.

Russ, S. W. (1987). Assessment of cognitive affective interaction in children: Creativity, fantasy and play research. In J. E. Butcher & C. Spielberger (Eds.), *Advances in personality assessment* (Vol. 6, p. 141–155). Hillsdale, NJ: Erlbaum.

Russ, S. W. (1993). *Affect and Creativity: The role of affect and play in the creative process.* A volume in The Personality Assessment Series. Hillsdale, NJ: Lawrence Erlbaum Associates.

Russ, S. W., & Grossman-McKee, A. (1990). Affective expression in children's fantasy play, primary process thinking on the Rorschach, and divergent thinking. *Journal of Personality Assessment, 54,* 756–771.

Russ, S. W., & Peterson, N. (1990). *The Affect in Play Scale: Predicting creativity and coping in children.* Manuscript submitted for publication.

Saltz, E., Dixon, D., & Johnson, J. (1977). Training disadvantaged preschoolers on various fantasy activities: Effects on cognitive functioning and impulse control. *Child Development, 48,* 367–380.

Schaefer, C., Gitlin, K., & Sandgrund, A. (1991). *Play diagnoses and assessment.* New York: Wiley.

Singer, D. (1993). *Playing for their lives.* New York: The Free Press.

Singer, D. L., & Rummo, J. (1973). Ideational creativity and behavioral style in kindergarten-age children. *Developmental Psychology, 8,* 154–161.

Singer, D. L., & Singer, J. (1990). *The house of make-believe.* Cambridge: Harvard University Press.

Singer, J. L. (1973). *Child's world of make-believe.* New York: Academic Press.

Singer, J. L. (1981). *Daydreaming and fantasy.* New York: Oxford University Press.

Singer, J. L., & Singer, D. (1976). Imaginative play and pretending in early childhood: Some experimental approaches. In A. Davids (Ed.), *Child personality and psychopathology,* (Vol. 3, pp. 69, 112). New York: Wiley.

Smilansky, S. (1986). *The effects of sociodramatic play on disadvantaged preschool children.* New York: Wiley.

Spielberger, C. D. (1973). *State-trait anxiety inventory for children.* Palo Alto, CA: Consulting Psychological Press.

Sutton-Smith, B. (1966). Piaget on play—a critique. *Psychological Review, 73,* 104–110.

Tuma, J., & Russ, S. W. (1993). Psychoanalytic psychotherapy with children. In T. Kratochwill & R. Morris (Eds.), *Handbook of psychotherapy with children and adolescents* (pp. 131–161). Boston: Allyn & Bacon.

Waelder, R. (1933). Psychoanalytic theory of play. *Psychoanalytic Quarterly, 2,* 208–224.

Wallach, M. (1970). Creativity. I. P. Mussen (Ed.), *Carmichael's manual of child psychology,* (Vol. 1, pp. 1211–1272). New York: Wiley.

Weisz, J. (1993, August). Psychotherapy efficacy with children and adolescents? Lab and clinic evidence. In S. Eyberg (Chair) *Psychotherapy for children and adolescents.* Symposium conducted at the meeting of the American Psychological Association, Toronto.

Weisz, J. R., & Weiss, B. (1989). Assessing the effects of clinical-based psychotherapy with children and adolescents. *Journal of Consulting and Clinical Psychology, 57,* 741–746.

Weisz, J., & Weiss, B. (1993). *Effects of psychotherapy with children and adolescents.* Newbury Park, CA: Sage.

Weisz, J. R., Weiss, B., Alicke, M. D., & Klotz, M. L. (1987). Effectiveness of psychotherapy with children and adolescents: A meta-analysis for clinicians. *Journal of Consulting and Clinical Psychology, 55,* 542–549.

Author Index

Subject Index